Corporate entrepreneurship

Corporate entrepreneurship

Innovation and strategy in large organizations

Third edition

PAUL BURNS

Professor of Entrepreneurship and former Dean,
University of Bedfordshire Business School, UK

First edition 2005
Second edition 2008
This edition 2013
published by
PALGRAVE MACMILLAN

Palgrave Macmillan in the UK is an imprint of Macmillan Publishers Limited,
registered in England, company number 785998, of Houndmills, Basingstoke,
Hampshire RG21 6XS.

Palgrave Macmillan in the US is a division of St Martin's Press LLC,
175 Fifth Avenue, New York, NY 10010.

Palgrave Macmillan is the global academic imprint of the above companies
and has companies and representatives throughout the world.

Palgrave® and Macmillan® are registered trademarks in the United States,
the United Kingdom, Europe and other countries

ISBN: 978-0-230-30403-1   paperback

This book is printed on paper suitable for recycling and made from fully
managed and sustained forest sources. Logging, pulping and manufacturing
processes are expected to conform to the environmental regulations of the
country of origin.

A catalogue record for this book is available from the British Library.
A catalog record for this book is available from the Library of Congress.

10   9   8   7   6   5   4   3   2   1
22   21   20   19   18   17   16   15   14   13

Printed in China

Contents overview

To my wife, Jean,
Who brings me happiness every day
And the boys: Oliver, Alex and Ben,
Who remind me not to take it for granted

Contents

Part 2   Organizational architecture   69

3   Entrepreneurial architecture   71

4   Becoming an entrepreneurial leader   97

List of figures

List of tables

Acknowledgements

The author and publishers would like to thank the following for permission to reproduce copyright material:

> **Harvard Business School Publishing** for Figure 2.6 from Greiner, L.E. (1972) 'Evolution and Revolution as Organizations Grow', *Harvard Business Review*, 50, July–August 55–67.
>
> **McGraw Hill** for Table 5.1 from Hofstede, G. (2010) *Cultures and Organizations: Software of the Mind*, London: McGraw Hill.
>
> **Emerald Group Publishing Ltd.** for Table 8.1 from Christensen, K. S. (1985) 'Enabling Intrapreneurship: The Case of a Knowledge-Intensive Industrial Company', *European Journal of Innovation Management*, 8(3).
>
> **Palgrave Macmillan** for Figure 12.5 from Lambin, J. (2000) *Market-Driven Management*, Basingstoke: Palgrave Macmillan and Figure 12.6 from Chaston, I. (2000) *Entrepreneurial Marketing: Competing by Challenging Convention*, Basingstoke: Palgrave Macmillan

I have quoted extensively from entrepreneurs throughout the book, with many of the contributions coming from Richard Branson's *Losing my Virginity* (1988, London: Virgin) and Michael Dell's *Direct from Dell, Strategies that Revolutionized an Industry* (1999, New York: Harper Business).

Every effort has been made to contact all copyright-holders, but if any have been inadvertently omitted the publishers will be pleased to make the necessary arrangements at the earliest opportunity.

I would particularly like to thank Durham University Business School for permission to reproduce an electronic version of their General Enterprise Tendency (GET) Test on the website accompanying this book. Their work on entrepreneurship over the years has inspired all of us.

I would like to thank my wife, Jean, who helped with inspiration, particularly at the time she was completing her own doctorate, and much-needed proof reading. Finally I would like to thank editor, Ann Edmondson, for her hard work, particularly on the revisions. Without her diligence this book would be littered with errors and omissions. Any that remain I claim as my own.

Preface to the third edition

Most entrepreneurship courses focus on start-ups. What a waste! Think what could be achieved if the entrepreneurial DNA could be retained as the business grows – even transplanted into large, more bureaucratic firms. *Corporate Entrepreneurship* is about doing just that by creating an organizational architecture – leadership, culture, structure and strategies – that encourages creativity, innovation and entrepreneurship. It synthesizes research from a number of business disciplines, focused on the business imperatives of the age – how to make the most of the opportunities created by the increasing pace of change in today's interconnected world.

A lot has happened since the first edition in 2005. The process of organizational transformation is now better understood. The need to change corporate practices has become so pressing that we can now point to more examples of good (and bad) practice. In many ways the need for entrepreneurship in larger organizations has been accepted and the concept has entered the mainstream. However, the holistic approach in this book, linking a number of disciplines, is still novel and challenging.

This third edition has been extensively updated and rewritten. Sections on organizational structure have been improved with an emphasis on multi-business operations. Strategies for growth and innovation have been framed within this context. Risk management is now better integrated into the frameworks developed in the book. There is a greater emphasis on improving shareholder value by generating strategic options rather than just improving profitability. There is a new section on corporate governance and the section on corporate social responsibility has been expanded. Sections on disruptive innovation and market paradigm change have also been expanded. The new edition has 78 cases. New cases feature some of the outstanding innovators of the last decade. They reflect a wider international perspective and the growing importance of Asian businesses. Corporate websites are now referenced so that students can update information through their own research. The website accompanying the book has been updated and strengthened particularly by the inclusion of video commentaries by the author and links to other related teaching videos.

The major strengths of the book have been retained:

▷ The informal style that makes the book accessible and easily understood by students.
▷ The breadth of coverage which allows a strategic and holistic approach to the issue of creating an entrepreneurial organization.
▷ The way it synthesizes theory and research with practical examples and quotes.
▷ The large number of short case insights that demonstrate how theory links to real corporate strategic decision-making.
▷ Longer cases with questions that can be used in class to reinforce learning and extend understanding.

I would like to thank all those academic colleagues who have contributed the research I have quoted in the book. Without their work I could not have written it. I hope I have reported your findings accurately. I would also like to thank those who continue to recommend the book and those who have suggested improvements. I hope I have met your expectations.

How to use the book and website

The book is written for postgraduate and undergraduate courses that wish to focus on entrepreneurship in large organizations. It complements my other market-leading book, *Small Business and Entrepreneurship: Start-up, Growth and Maturity*, which focuses on start-up and small business (also in its third edition). It is supported by a website (www.palgrave.com/business/burns) which contains additional teaching resources, including video commentaries by the author. It can be used as a specialist text for both postgraduate, particularly MBA, and advanced undergraduate courses. It is particularly valuable for Executive MBA courses where participants wish to apply the principles of entrepreneurship to their existing business. Included is a Corporate Entrepreneurship Audit tool that can be applied to existing organizations to assess their entrepreneurial orientation.

The book can also be used as supplementary or alternative text for courses on corporate strategy. In an interconnected world facing rapid and continual change many of the traditional approaches to the development of corporate strategy are looking increasingly inadequate. At the same time the idea that all organizations need to become more entrepreneurial is seen as increasingly relevant. Corporate entrepreneurship is becoming mainstream.

The book can also be used for courses on creativity and innovation. It emphasizes the strategies needed to encourage and sustain both individual and organizational creativity and innovation. These topics are integral to entrepreneurship and the entrepreneurial context facilitates a focus on market opportunities and commercial imperatives.

Entrepreneurship involves taking a holistic view of management and business and this textbook is no exception. The central thesis is that organizational transformation can be obtained by constructing an entrepreneurial architecture based on leadership, culture, structures and strategies.

Learning styles and the learning resources

Daniel Kim (1993) suggests that effective learning can be considered to be a revolving wheel (Figure A). During half of the cycle you test and experiment with concepts and observe what happens through concrete experience – learning 'know-how'. In the second half of the cycle you reflect on the observations and form concepts or theories – learning 'know-why'. This is often called 'double-loop learning' – the best sort of learning which links knowing how with knowing why, linking theory with practice. So effective learning involves forming concepts, testing concepts, experience and reflection. Traditionally education has focused too much on the second half of the cycle – forming concepts or theories and reflection – and it is difficult to break away from this in a textbook which, inevitably, focuses on the concepts and theories.

However, I have tried to do so by including a number of learning resources. Each learning resource is designed to influence a particular learning style. Taken together, they should complete the wheel of learning.

Cases with questions

Embedded in each chapter are cases with questions, designed to make students think about and apply the concepts being explained and discussed in that chapter. This is the testing stage of the wheel of learning. Additional cases are available on the supporting website. Case notes are available on the lecturers' website. Other recommended cases, which are typically longer and more complex, are provided in the Learning Resources section on the website.

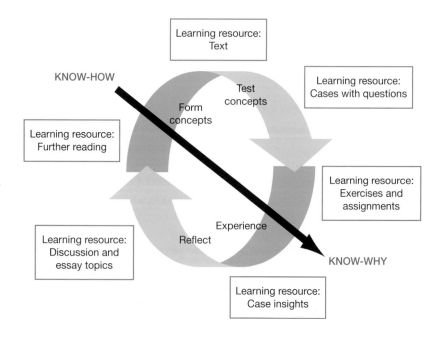

F A Wheel of learning

Exercises and assignments

In the testing and experimenting phase of the cycle are exercises and assignments, which involve doing something, in the main further research. This research is often desk-based – including visits to websites – but some of the most popular assignments, in my experience, involve students going out to do things – such as interviewing entrepreneurs. This is very much the 'test concepts' part of the wheel of learning.

Case insights and summaries

Spread throughout this book, there are case insights and quotes from entrepreneurs around the world. They are designed to illustrate and reinforce the theoretical points being made in the text with practical examples and opinions from the real world – there is nothing like an endorsement from an entrepreneur. The summary at the end of each chapter links cases to the main points being made in that chapter. This is the experience element of the wheel of learning, linked to the concepts and theories through the summaries and case questions.

Discussion and essay topics

Each chapter has topics for group discussion or essay writing. These can be used as a basis for tutorials. They are designed to make students think about the text material and develop their critical and reflective understanding of it and what it means in the real world. The summary and discussion topics help students discriminate between main and supporting points and provide mechanisms for self-teaching. The discussion and essay topics also form the reflective element of the wheel of learning, forcing students to think through the theories and concepts, often linking them to the real world.

Selected further reading and journals

Each chapter has full journal and book references. There are also selected further textbooks, organized by topic, and selected journals included at the end of the book.

Website (www.palgrave.com/business/burns)

All my books have accompanying websites that can be accessed by clicking on the appropriate cover. The student website accompanying this book provides further resources:

▷ Video commentaries by the author.
▷ Links to teaching videos and videos to support case studies.
▷ General Enterprise Tendency (GET) test – an interactive version of the entrepreneurship test produced by Durham University Business School that allows you to assess whether you are entrepreneurial.

▷ Corporate Entrepreneurship Audit tool – an interactive tool that matches the entrepreneurial orientation of an organization against the commercial environment that it faces.
▷ Leadership Style Questionnaire – a self-assessment questionnaire that allows you to assess your own leadership style.
▷ Download and print versions of the cases with questions, including additional cases not included in the book.
▷ Links to selected websites offering further learning resources.
▷ Any updates or revisions.

There is a password-protected lecturers' website which contains:

▷ Powerpoint slides for each chapter;
▷ Teaching notes for Cases with questions;

Learning outcomes

Each chapter has clear learning outcomes that identify the key concepts to be covered. These assume that students will undertake the essays and discussion topics as well as assignments and exercises, at the end of each chapter.

On completing the course based on this book a student should be able to:

1 Research, critically analyze and evaluate the entrepreneurial architecture of an organization.
2 Critically address how any deficiencies in this architecture might be addressed.
3 Describe the nature of entrepreneurship in individuals – character traits and approaches to business and management – and evaluate their own entrepreneurial qualities.
4 Describe the process of creativity and innovation, evaluate their own aptitude to be creative and innovative and explain how creativity might be encouraged in others and in themselves.
5 Critically analyze what is required to be an effective leader in different contexts.
6 Critically analyze the culture of an organization.
7 Critically analyze the appropriateness of different organizational structures for different contexts.
8 Be able to develop entrepreneurial strategies that encourage growth and innovation in different contexts.

Key and cognitive skills for the course

Having completed a course in corporate entrepreneurship using this book, with the seminar discussion topics, exercises and activities designed around it, a student should have developed a number of important skills:

▷ Information interpretation, critical analysis and evaluation skills;
▷ Data analysis and interpretation skills;
▷ Problem identification and solving skills;
▷ ICT skills, in particular the use of the internet;
▷ Independent and/or team-working skills;
▷ Writing and presentation skills.

Students should also have developed a range of applied business and management skills in a holistic way that can be applied to help a developing or existing organization become more entrepreneurial.

Guided tour of the book

Learning outcomes identify the key concepts to be covered within the chapter and the key knowledge and skills that students will obtain by reading it

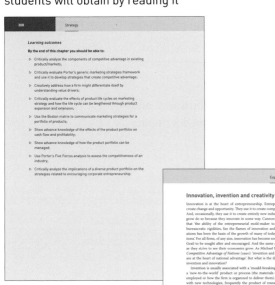

Case insights and **quotes** illustrate theoretical points with practical examples and opinions from the real world

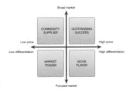

Executive insights present assessment resources that can be accessed by the student and practitioner implementation tips

Cases with questions encourage students to apply theory to real-world situations

Essays and discussion topics encourage students to critically reflect on the material within the text and to link theory to real-world scenarios. They can be used as a basis for tutorials

Summaries link the in-chapter case insights and quotes to the main points discussed in the chapter

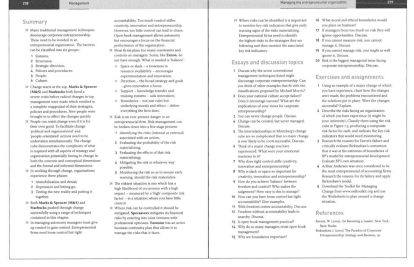

Exercises and assignments involve students in additional research activities in order to develop their knowledge and skills much further

Part 1

Entrepreneurship

Chapter 1

The entrepreneurial revolution

Learning outcomes

By the end of this chapter you should be able to:

▷ Critically analyze the changing commercial environment;

▷ Explain why entrepreneurs and small firms are so important to the economies of modern countries and the particular importance of a small number of rapidly growing firms called 'gazelles';

▷ Critically analyze the problems large firms have in coping with the new age of uncertainty and the advantages enjoyed by small, entrepreneurial firms;

▷ Define an entrepreneur, what they do and why they are so important;

▷ Critically analyze the link between innovation, entrepreneurship and economic growth;

▷ Define 'corporate entrepreneurship' and critically analyze the 'schools' of literature that have delineated the discipline;

▷ Explain what is meant by, and what the benefits are, of corporate entrepreneurship;

▷ Critically analyze the different schools of corporate entrepreneurship literature.

The new age of uncertainty

The old world order has changed and continues to change. Economic power is moving east from the USA and Europe to China and India. If the most startling evidence of this was the financial crisis of 2008/9, followed by the recession that engulfed the mature western economies, the seeds of the change were sown much earlier. The twenty-first century has seen enormous turbulence and disruption. There have been unpredictable shocks such as the terrorist attack on the twin towers in New York in 2001 followed by attacks in London, Bali, Madrid and Mumbai and the wars in Afghanistan and Iraq. The upheavals caused by the so-called 'Arab spring' of 2011 have continued to affect the Middle East. There have been natural disasters like the Icelandic volcano in 2010 and the earthquake and tsunami in Japan in 2011. There have been enormous shocks to the international monetary system precipitated by the financial crisis of 2008/9 which particularly affected Iceland in 2008 and then Portugal, Ireland, Greece and Italy in 2010/11 and subsequently the entire Eurozone. There have also been some spectacular corporate failures from Lehman Brothers in the USA to Royal Bank of Scotland (RBS) in the UK. Corporate integrity has come to be questioned. In the USA the unexpected failure of Enron, one of the most admired firms of the 1990s, in 2001 became a benchmark for management greed and lack of integrity. But such scandals were not confined to the USA. Parmalat in Italy became the largest bankruptcy in Europe in 2003. The Olympus scandal of 2012 in Japan led to prosecutions. Alongside this the twenty-first century has seen unprecedented volatility in just about every market from commodities to exchange rates, from stock markets to bond markets. And underpinning this volatility is the uncertainty surrounding climate change and whether we have reached a 'tipping point' in global warming.

The major themes running through this new age of uncertainty are complexity and change. We are living in an increasingly complex world, full of interconnections formed by a truly global market place linked by technology which allows instant communication. Small changes tend to be amplified in highly connected systems. Actions in one part of the market place can have unexpected and rapid consequences in another part of it. And nobody, not even sovereign states, seems able to control this. And the pace of change has accelerated. Change itself has changed to become a continuous process of often-discontinuous steps, abrupt but all-pervasive. The idea that change has become endemic, continuous and, above all, unpredictable, sometimes resulting in discontinuous or revolutionary shifts that can create chaos has powerful implications for us all, but it is not new. The ancient Chinese saw change as an endless and essential feature of our universe – a pattern of cyclical coming and going, growth and decay, winter and summer, the yin of night and yang of day. Somehow the west had forgotten this, believing instead that it could create stability and certainty, that change was a series of discrete events that moved societies from one stable state to another. Economists based theories on it. And economists, politicians and managers focused on the ways that change could be controlled in a systematic way. Managers turned to rational techniques of long-term planning and tight control systems. But this new age of uncertainty has powerful implications for all organizations. Planning becomes problematic if you cannot predict the future and strategic management faces completely new challenges as the linear models based on knowledge and information that have been used for decades seem increasingly unrealistic. Centralized control seems increasingly unable to cope and traditional views of leadership need to be reconsidered as people increasingly show they also have power.

'We now stand on the threshold of a new age – the age of revolution. In our minds, we know the new age has already arrived: in our bellies, we're not sure we like it. For we know it is going to be an age of upheaval, of tumult, of fortunes made and unmade at head-snapping speed. For change has changed. No longer is it additive. No longer does it move in a straight line. In the twenty first century, change is discontinuous, abrupt, seditious.'

Gary Hamel, author, 2000

'We need to nurture future business leaders … to shape the vision of the world to come. It is not possible to draw a picture of this universe, but we know it and how fast it is moving and developing. It is like describing the shape of a large cloud in the sky, blown off by a strong wind. Yet we know its shape and where it is because we see it and sense it. Although it is not entirely possible to describe it in a static way, a world-class entrepreneur can describe it and even capture a large chunk of it, converting it into raindrops or profit.'

Kenichi Ohmae, author, 2005

McMillan (2004) characterized what she called the 'traditional, classical, mechanistic' view of change as abnormal, potentially calamitous, an incremental linear event that is disruptive but that can be controlled. She contrasted this to what she called the 'new, modern dynamic' view that change is normal, continuous, turbulent, both revolutionary and incremental, uncontrollable and non-linear but full of opportunities. These two views are contrasted in Figure 1.1. McMillan went on to question traditional approaches to leadership and strategy development and to cast the net wide in searching for ideas about how to deal with change by saying that we need to look at quantum physics and complexity theory – to which we shall indeed return in Chapter 3.

From opportunity to austerity

The economic boom at the end of the twentieth century came to an end in the twenty-first. The banking crisis of 2008/9 led to recession and stagnation, particularly in western markets. The age of opportunity gave way to a new age of austerity to accompany the age of uncertainty. The shift simply made us realize our vulnerability in this new era. Commercial opportunities remain but competition is now as much about survival as growth. And, as global competition continues to increase, sources of competitive advantage are proving increasingly difficult to sustain over any period of time. Indeed, it is the ability to create new sources of competitive advantage quickly, again and again, that is proving to be the only sustainable source of real competitive advantage. At the same time as seeking new sources

Traditional, classical, mechanistic views of change

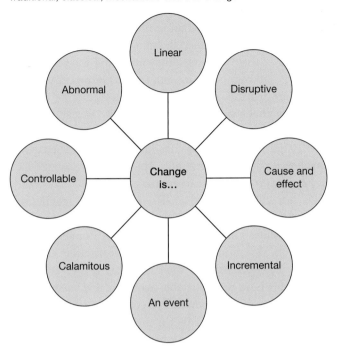

New, modern, dynamic views of change

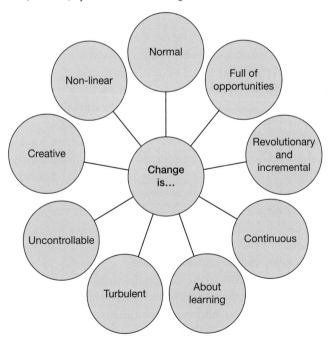

Adapted from E. McMillan (2004) *Complexity, Organisations and Change*,
London: Routledge.

F 1.1 Views of change

of competitive advantage companies must continue to manage existing businesses. They must find ways of managing to achieve cost efficiencies whilst at the same time differentiating themselves from the competition. They must find ways to innovate at the same time as managing products at the mature stage of their life cycle. They must find ways of understanding and reconciling customer needs in both India and the USA, of reconciling global integration with local differentiation. And, despite their size, they must respond to changes in these needs quickly just as they must react quickly to the actions of competitors. All these pressures and paradoxes have caused large firms to reconsider how they are structured and how they manage their diverse operations. They need to manage for survival today but plan for growth when an upturn comes.

This new imperative of survival has led to some reappraisal of how shareholder value is maximized. Certainly the previous focus on short-term profits has shifted to liquidity and cash flow. But also there is a focus on risk minimization and a realization that companies need to maximize their flexibility if they are to survive in this new, unpredictable age. And that means they need to maximize the number of commercial options they face at any time, even if that comes at the expense of short-term profits. Strategic options are valuable when you face either an unexpected downturn or upturn and are essential in the age of uncertainty. Flexibility increases shareholder value. This all has implications, not only for how strategy is developed, but also for deciding which sectors are attractive.

> 'Today's businesses, especially the large ones, simply will not survive in this period of rapid change and innovation unless they acquire entrepreneurial competence.'
>
> Peter Drucker, author, 1985

The age of austerity has coincided with a shift in sources of value being in physical assets to virtual assets – a shift from assets that are purchased and restrict flexibility to those that can be built up and can increase flexibility. We have moved from an industrial economy to a knowledge economy driven by new digital technologies. And with this new economy commercial opportunities continue to emerge both from technological and market innovation, sometimes breaking down established industry barriers and creating new and unexpected sources of competition. For example, the internet has caused many high street retailers to radically reappraise their customer offering and will probably lead to the high street looking very different in the future. It has caused the music, video and print industries to reappraise how their products are distributed. It has caused disruption, generating as many opportunities as threats.

The new age has also seen companies face new social pressures. Corporate scandals such as Enron and Parmalat have led to cries for improved corporate governance and board room accountability. Excessive executive salaries and bonuses that bore no relationship to the performance of the organization, exemplified in RBS and Merrill Lynch, have redoubled these cries. At the same time companies have been pressurized to take a more socially responsible role. This pressure comes from many sources.

Environmentalists want companies to reduce their 'carbon footprint', espouse 'green' issues and become more sustainable. Social reformers want them to change some of their behaviours, for example exploitation of child labour in developing economies. Social activists want them to espouse 'corporate citizenship' programmes and undertake charity work in the community. Finally ethical activists see companies such as Enron and Parmalat behaving in unacceptable ways and want business ethics to be re-established in the board room. All these issues have become bundled together under the umbrella of Corporate Social Responsibility (CSR). CSR is seen as increasingly important for large companies for both ethical and commercial reasons. CSR stock market indices have been developed and there is increasing pressure from customers and shareholders to implement CSR.

The entrepreneurial revolution

While we have moved from the age of opportunity to an age of austerity there has been a quiet revolution taking place. Entrepreneurs have emerged as the species most able to cope with the turbulence caused by both opportunity and austerity. Over the last three decades entrepreneurs establishing new firms have done more to create wealth than firms at any time before them – ever! Ninety-five per cent of the wealth of the USA has been created since 1980. Bill Gates started Microsoft in 1975, Steve Jobs started Apple in 1976, Michael Dell set up Dell Corporation in 1984, Pierre Omidyar launched eBay in 1995 and Larry Page and Sergy Brin set up Google in 1996. And this was not just happening in the USA. In the UK Alan Sugar launched Amstrad in 1968, Richard Branson started what has become his Virgin empire in 1972, James Dyson started selling his now ubiquitous Dyson vacuum cleaners in 1976, Anita Roddick opened the first Body Shop in 1976 and Julian Metcalfe and Sinclair Beecham opened their first Pret A Manger sandwich bar in 1986. In India Sunil Mittal started his first business, later to become Bhati Enterprises, in 1976 and Kiran Mazumdar-Shaw started Biocon in 1978. These are now gigantic corporations that made their founders into millionaires.

People have begun to appreciate the contribution all small firms make to the economies of their countries. It was David Birch (1979) who, arguably, started this process with his seminal research which showed that 82%of new jobs in the USA created between 1969 and 1976 were in small firms (under 500 employees). Although the detailed statistics have been disputed, this general pattern has been repeated every year.

> 'The Entrepreneurial Revolution is here to stay, having set the genetic code of the US and global economy for the 21st century, and having sounded the death knell for Brontosaurus Capitalism of yesteryear. Entrepreneurs are the creators, the innovators, and the leaders who give back to society, as philanthropists, directors and trustees, and who, more than any others, change the way people live, work, learn, play, and lead. Entrepreneurs create new technologies, products, processes, and services that become the next wave of new industries. Entrepreneurs create value with high potential, high growth companies which are the job creation engines of the US economy.'
>
> Jeffrey Timmons, author, 1999

Small, growing firms have outstripped large ones in terms of job generation, year after year. At times when larger companies retrenched, smaller
firms continued to offer job opportunities. It has been estimated that in the
USA small firms now generate 50% of GDP, and over 50% of exports now
come from firms employing fewer than 20 people.

Europe lags a little behind the USA, but the pattern is similar. Small
firms, virtually no matter how they are defined, now make up over 95%
of enterprises in the European Community. Overall, they generate 67% of
employment and 58% of value added (Eurostat, 2008). In Italy the proportion of value added is 79%, in France it is 63% and in Germany it is 60%.
In the UK they generate 62% of employment and over 25% of GDP. With
4.7 million small firms in 2007 (an increase of almost 96% in 28 years), the
UK has one of the highest business start-up rates in Europe. By just about
any measure the contribution small firms make to the economy of any
country is increasing and their importance is now fully recognized.

But the focus is not just on small firms. It is also on high-growth firms.
Despite being few in number, young, high-growth businesses – often
called 'gazelles' – are disproportionately important to national economies.
Definitions of gazelles vary. The OECD proposed definition is enterprises
with 10 or more employees, with an average employment growth of over
20% for three consecutive years (Ahmad, 2006). In the USA it has been
estimated that gazelles, although they comprise less than 1% of all companies, generate about 10% of new jobs in any given year. Indeed the top-
performing 1% of all firms generate about 40% of all new jobs (Strangler,
2010). The pattern is replicated in other countries. In the UK, a government
survey of the literature concluded that gazelles, although they represent
just 2 to 4% of all firms, were responsible for the majority of employment
growth (BERR, 2008). And, although medium-sized businesses (turnover
£20–£800 million) represent 1% of businesses they generate over 30% of
GDP and employ more than one-third of the workforce (GE Capital, 2012).
But again Europe lags somewhat behind the USA. An EU survey found US
SMEs were on average larger and expanded more rapidly than EU firms
(European Commission, 2008) and, whilst a higher percentage of UK firms
achieve high growth than European firms, the UK still lags behind the USA
(BERR, op. cit).

As the pace of change in just about every aspect of our life accelerates,
small firms seem more able to cope than large. Start-ups are on the increase
across the world. While the number of small firms is increasing, big firms
are struggling to survive. In the UK there are only around 7000 firms
employing over 250 employees. Many large firms are slimming down or
deconstructing – becoming many small firms – because this is the only way
they can cope with the pace of change and remain responsive to changes
in the market. The entrepreneur has been recognized as a vital part of the
process of economic wealth generation. But large organizations are desperate to learn from the entrepreneur and become more entrepreneurial

themselves. After all, increasing size is a natural consequence of businesses being successfully started by entrepreneurs. The trick is to learn the lessons of that success and not allow the organization to fossilize and die. However, according to Arie de Geus (1997) large organizations have proved amazingly inept at survival. He quoted a Dutch survey showing the average corporate life expectancy in Japan and Europe was 12.5 years. 'The average life expectancy of a multinational corporation – the Fortune 500 or equivalent – is between 40 and 50 years.' The reality is that large companies often die young or at least their ownership changes fairly quickly. But the other side of the coin is that most small firms remain very small and do not grow. In the UK 74% have no employees and 96% have fewer than 10 employees (www.statistics.gov.uk). What is more, almost 50% of businesses will cease trading within the first three years of their existence.

🗁 Case insight AirAsia

Entrepreneurial opportunity

Former Time Warner executive Tony Fernandes set up Asia's first low-cost airline, AirAsia, in 2001, buying the heavily indebted state-owned company from the Malaysian government for only 25p. He set about remodelling it as a short-haul, low-cost operator flying around Asia. Being first in the Asian market with an idea copied from the West from companies such as easyJet, the company expanded rapidly from a fleet of only two planes in 2002 to 86 planes flying 30 million people around the world by 2010. It created a new Asian market in low-cost air travel. By 2007, UBS research showed it to be the lowest-cost airline in the world. Now with hubs in Kuala Lumpur and Singapore, it has won the Skytrax World's best low-cost airline award in 2007, 2009, 2010 and 2011. It has also established associate airlines in Thailand and Indonesia.

Economic, technological and societal influences

A number of other influences have accelerated the trend towards smaller firms. Firstly there has been the shift in most economies away from manufacturing towards the service sectors where small firms often flourish because of their ability to deliver a personalized, flexible, tailor-made service at a local level. The move to a knowledge economy has meant that economies of scale become less important as a form of competitive advantage. For example, a high proportion of innovations in the pharmaceutical industry now come from small firms set up specifically to undertake R&D. A high proportion of our gazelles hold intellectual property and intangible assets such as trademarks and patents (BERR, op. cit.). SMEs can build value in the knowledge economy rather than having to buy it in the form of physical assets – and they often seem better at doing that than large firms.

Technology has played its part. It has influenced the trend in three ways. Firstly, the new technologies that swept the late twentieth century business world were pioneered by new, rapidly growing firms. Small firms pioneered innovation in computers, the internet and digital communications, creating new markets for these innovations. These markets are starting to consolidate and amalgamate into larger units now, as they mature. We look at the 'cyber-wars' this process has spawned in Chapter 11. Secondly, these technologies have actually facilitated the growth of self-employment and small business by easing communication, encouraging working from home and allowing smaller and smaller market segments to be serviced. Indeed information has become a product in its own right and one that can be generated anywhere around the world and transported at the touch of a button. Finally, many new technologies, for example digital printing, have reduced fixed costs so that production can be profitable in smaller, more flexible units. They have also simplified the routes to market so that small firms can sell to larger firms or direct to customers around the world, without the expense of putting in place a distribution network. And as large firms increasingly outsource non-core activities, the beneficiaries are often small firms.

Social and market trends have also accelerated the growth of small firms. Firstly, customers increasingly expect firms to address their particular needs. Market niches are becoming slimmer and markets more competitive – better served by smaller firms who can get close to their customers. Secondly, people want to control their own destiny more. After periods of high unemployment, they see self-employment as more attractive and more secure than employment. Redundancy has pushed many people into self-employment at the same time as the new 'enterprise culture' has given it political and social respectability. And, in an age of uncertainty people seek to control as many aspects of their economic security as possible. The growth of the 'new-age' culture and 'alternative' life styles, encouraged by worries about climate change, have also led to the development of a whole range of new self-employment and sustainable opportunities, albeit often at the periphery of the economy.

Big companies

Big companies are struggling with these challenges – and seem not to be winning. They cut budgets, close plants, downsize, rightsize, deconstruct – and go out of business. The 'deconstruction' of larger firms into smaller, more responsive units concentrating on their core activities, often sub-contracting many of their other activities to smaller firms has also contributed to the trend towards SMEs. Large firms and even the public sector became leaner and fitter in the 1980s in a bid to reduce fixed costs and reduce risks, a process that continues to the present day. Small firms have benefited, although they may be seen as dependent on large ones.

But the core of the problem is that traditional management practices focus on efficiency and effectiveness rather than creativity and innovation – control rather than empowerment. They look for cost savings through scale efficiencies rather than differentiation through economies of small scale. They look for uniformity rather than diversity and stress discipline rather than motivation. And they often discourage what they see as the risk-taking associated with a market opportunity without the information to evaluate it. By the time they get that the opportunity will have been seized by a small firm. Add all this to the danger that bureaucracy will swamp the organizations that practise this traditional form of management, that they will ossify, and you have the makings of disaster. No wonder big is no longer beautiful.

'The guiding principles in a traditional corporate culture are: follow the instructions given; do not make any mistakes; do not fail; do not take initiatives but wait for instructions; stay within your turf; and protect your backside. The restrictive environment is of course not conducive to creativity, flexibility, independence, and risk taking.'

Robert Hisrich and Michael Peters, authors, 1992

And yet big business comes with significant advantages – financial resources, credibility with stakeholders, established routes to market, trusted brands and, most valuable of all, large work-forces. Indeed up to the middle of the twentieth century big companies were thought of as the route to economic plenty. If only more organizations can continue to be entrepreneurial as they grow and, just perhaps, others can turn from being bureaucratic to become entrepreneurial. The Holy Grail they seek is sustainable competitive advantage through the ability to change and adapt to suit a constantly changing environment where continuous innovation yields substantial rewards – and increases longevity. But most big business remains typically risk averse. Whether this comes from size or age is difficult to discern. And this creates the culture of bureaucracy which in turn stifles entrepreneurship and all it represents – particularly innovation.

And with this, entrepreneurship has become something that society, governments and organizations of all sizes and forms wish to encourage and promote. Whether it be creating a new venture or breathing life into an old one, whether it is creating new products or finding new ways to market old ones, whether it is doing new things or finding new ways of doing old things, entrepreneurial management – whatever that is – has become a highly valued skill to be nurtured, developed and encouraged. Fostering entrepreneurship in all aspects of their teaching is probably one of the major challenges facing Business Schools in the twenty-first century.

However, whilst the boards of larger companies are often criticized for the marked absence of entrepreneurs, there is a pervading suspicion that, whilst entrepreneurs might be good at that 'vision thing' and launching new ventures, they can become a dangerous liability once a company is established. And too many entrepreneurs in one organization is bound to lead to conflict, disagreement and disaster as they move off, often at speed, in different directions. There is some truth in this and it is a real danger. But it is a predictable danger and one, therefore, that can be avoided with proper management. What is more, to be effective within an organization, entrepreneurial behaviour needs to be encouraged and focused at all levels within it, not just at the top. It needs to be institutionalized, ingrained in the culture of the organization. But equally it needs to be focused and directed. Finally it needs to be the appropriate response to the environment the organization faces. Not all industrial sectors or tasks face turbulence and change – these were broad generalizations. Not all firms need to encourage innovation. Outside of an appropriate context, entrepreneurial actions may be inappropriate and reckless. For example, in the early twenty-first century RBS was seen as one of the most entrepreneurial banks in the world, but its entrepreneurial risk-taking led to its nationalization and precipitated the UK financial crisis of 2008/9. However, at the risk of generalizing, entrepreneurial management has by and large proved more successful than traditional management at coping with the new age of uncertainty.

'In the years ahead all big companies will find it increasingly difficult to compete with – and in general will perform more poorly than – smaller, speedier, more innovative companies. The mindset that in a huge global economy the multinationals dominate world business couldn't have been more wrong. The bigger and more open the world economy becomes, the more small and middle-sized companies will dominate. In one of the major turnarounds of my lifetime, we have moved from economies of scale to "diseconomies of scale"; from bigger is better to bigger is inefficient, costly, wastefully bureaucratic, inflexible, and, now, disastrous. And the paradox is that that has occurred as we move to a global context: The smaller and speedier players will prevail on a much expanded field.'

John Naisbitt, entrepreneur and author, 1994

By looking at both successful and unsuccessful entrepreneurs and their businesses we can start to understand what it takes to build and sustain a truly entrepreneurial organization. And the lessons are valuable to organizations of any size that need to make the most of the opportunities and threats generated by rapid change. The challenge, then, is to isolate the very DNA of entrepreneurship and, through genetic engineering, replicate it within and throughout a larger organization using all the skills of systematic management. The challenge is to develop 'corporate entrepreneurship'.

Entrepreneurs

Most owner-managers of small firms are, in fact, not at all entrepreneurial. They prefer to manage businesses that will not grow but rather deliver a life style that they enjoy. The real driving force behind this entrepreneurial revolution are those 'super-heroes' called entrepreneurs who lead our gazelles. They have become the stuff of legends, increasingly held in high esteem and held up as role models to be emulated. They are often held out as embodying many ephemeral qualities – freedom of spirit, creativity, vision, zeal. They have the courage, self-belief and commitment to turn their dreams into realities. They are the catalysts for economic change.

They see an opportunity, commercialize it and in the process create jobs from which the rest of society benefits. Entrepreneurs can be described in terms of their character traits and by their actions. And we shall explore this in detail in the next chapter, where we attempt to isolate their very DNA.

Interestingly for something so popular, there is no universally accepted definition of the term 'entrepreneur'. The Oxford English Dictionary defines an entrepreneur as 'a person who attempts to profit by risk and initiative'. This definition emphasizes that entrepreneurs exercise a high degree of initiative and are willing to take a high degree of risk. But it covers a wide range of occupations, including that of a paid assassin. No wonder there is an old adage that if you scratch an entrepreneur you will find a 'spiv' or a 'con-man' – somebody who will try to get you to part with your money by deception. However, the difference is more than just one of legality. Therefore a question you might ask is 'How do they do these things?'

Back in 1800, Jean-Baptiste Say, the French economist usually credited with inventing the word, said: 'entrepreneurs shift economic resources from an area of lower productivity into an area of higher productivity and greater yield'. In other words entrepreneurs create value by exploiting some form of change, for example in technology, materials, prices or demographics. We call this process 'innovation' and this is an essential tool for entrepreneurs. Entrepreneurs, therefore, create new demand or find new ways of exploiting existing markets. They identify a commercial opportunity and then exploit it. Indeed, these two factors – the ability to spot opportunities and to innovate – are probably the major factors defining true entrepreneurs.

Central to all of this is change. Change causes disequilibrium in markets out of which come the commercial opportunities that entrepreneurs thrive upon. To them change creates opportunities that they can exploit. Sometimes they initiate the change themselves – they innovate in some disruptive way and do things differently from how they have been done in the past. They question the 'dominant logic' and create new market paradigms. At other times entrepreneurs exploit a change created by the external environment. Often, in doing so, they destroy the established order and complacency of existing social and economic systems. How entrepreneurs manage and deal with change is central to their character and essential if they are to be successful. Most 'ordinary people' find change threatening. Entrepreneurs welcome it because it creates opportunities that can be exploited and they often create it through innovation.

'I am often asked what it is to be an entrepreneur and there is no simple answer. It is clear that successful entrepreneurs are vital for a healthy, vibrant and competitive economy. If you look around you, most of the largest companies have their foundations in one or two individuals who have the determination to turn a vision into reality.'

Richard Branson, from Anderson, 1995

Another key feature of entrepreneurs is their willingness to accept risk and uncertainty. In part this is simply the consequence of their eagerness to exploit change. However, the scale of uncertainty they are willing to accept is altogether different from that of ordinary owner-managers. This high degree of uncertainty reflects itself in the risks they take for the business and for themselves. And for some this can become so addictive that they become 'serial entrepreneurs', best suited to continually starting up businesses and unwilling to face the tedium of day-to-day management. But just because entrepreneurs accept risk does not mean that they like it, because they have ways of mitigating its effects on them. All these character traits and approaches to business and management will be analyzed in the next chapter.

It is no wonder that entrepreneurship has been described as 'a slippery concept ... not easy to work into a formal analysis because it is so closely associated with the temperament or personal qualities of individuals' (Penrose, 1959). But notice in these definitions that there is no mention of small firms. The point is that *entrepreneurs are defined by their actions, not by the size of organization they happen to work within.* Any manager in any organization in the private or public sectors can be entrepreneurial. The manager of a small firm may not be an entrepreneur – an important distinction that is often missed in the literature. Equally entrepreneurs can exist within large organizations, even ones that they did not set up themselves, and how large organizations encourage and deal with this is an important issue for them.

☐ Case insight TutorVista

Entrepreneurial opportunity

Based in India, Krishnan Ganesh launched TutorVista in 2006. It offers a very twenty-first century service. The company uses the internet to connect students in high-wage cost countries like the USA and Britain with private tutors from low-wage cost countries like India. It is completely dependent on the internet and the widespread availability of home computers. TutorVista is an intermediary. The part-time tutors are mainly employed full-time as teachers in schools and work from home for TutorVista – a remote business model that allows the company to keep capital and running costs to a minimum and minimize risks. Teachers are vetted and quality is monitored. The company markets the service directly using Google search advertisements. When somebody searches for tutor support in any subject an advertisement for TutorVista comes up. When they click on the website they can talk to staff about the service. By 2011 the company had over 2000 students in the USA alone and Pearson had acquired a controlling stake in the business.

And yet Krishnan had no experience of the education sector. He got the idea when he was travelling around the USA and was shocked to hear a media debate about 'the crisis in the US school education system'. He investigated and realized that personal tutors in the USA were charging $40–$60 an hour and were regarded by most people as unaffordable. That got him thinking about how he could link teachers from his home country, India, to the market demand in the USA.

Innovation, entrepreneurship and economic growth

It was the work of Joseph Schumpeter, an Austrian economist, which most strongly linked entrepreneurship to innovation. He was the first economist to challenge classical economics and the way it sought to optimize existing resources within a stable environment and to treat disruptions as a 'god sent' external force. In his primary work, Schumpeter (1934) set out his overall theory of economic development – an endogenous process within capitalism of wrenching the economy out of its tendency towards one equilibrium position and directing it towards a different one – a process of 'creative destruction'. This fundamental phenomenon entailed carrying out new combinations of the means of production – which Schumpeter labelled 'enterprise' but we could equally call 'innovation' – by individuals called 'entrepreneurs'. These new combinations 'as a rule ... must draw the necessary means of production from some old combinations'.

Schumpeter was arguing against traditional economic theory which presumed that the economy was always tending towards equilibrium and that changes in that equilibrium could only occur through changes in underlying conditions of the economy, such as population growth or changes in savings ratios, or through external shocks such as wars or natural disasters. The former were thought to change only slowly and the latter only unpredictably. Schumpeter sought to explain the process of economic development as a process caused by enterprise – or innovation – and carried out by entrepreneurs.

For Schumpeter a normal healthy economy was one that was continually being 'disrupted' by technological innovation producing the 50-year cycles of economic activity noticed earlier by the Russian economist, Nikolai Kondratieff. Using data on prices, wages and interest rates in France, Britain and the USA, Kondratieff first noticed these 'long waves' of economic activity in 1925. Unfortunately he was executed by Stalin some ten years later because he predicted (accurately as it turned out) that Russian farm collectivization would lead to a decline in agricultural production. It was therefore left to Schumpeter to study these waves in depth.

Schumpeter said that each of these cycles was unique, driven by different clusters of industries. The upswing in a cycle started when new innovations came into general use:

▷ Water power, textiles and iron in the late eighteenth century.
▷ Steam, rail and steel in the mid nineteenth century.
▷ Electricity, chemicals and the internal combustion engine in the early twentieth century.

These booms eventually petered out as the technologies matured and the market opportunities were fully exploited, only to start again when a new set of innovations changed the way things were done. For the last twenty years of the cycle the growth industries of the last technological wave might be doing exceptionally well. However, they are in fact just repaying capital that is no longer needed for investment. This situation never lasts longer than twenty years and returns to investors then start to decline with the dwindling number of opportunities. Often this is precipitated by some form of crisis. After the twenty years of stagnation new technologies will emerge and the cycle will start again.

The other factor at work is that innovation – particularly technological innovation – also seems to generate growth that cannot be accounted for by changes in labour and capital. Although the return on investment may decline as more capital is introduced to an economy, any deceleration in growth is more than offset by the leverage effects of innovation. Because of this the rich western countries have seen their return on investment increasing, while the poorer countries have not caught up.

By the time Schumpeter died in 1950 the next cycle of boom was starting, based upon oil, electronics, aviation and mass production. Since then we have seen booms based upon software, digital networks and new media. The internet created e-commerce and made information and knowledge a commodity that can be traded. And we have seen frequent booms followed by the inevitable downturns across a wide range of these new industries. One reason for these shortening cycles may be the more systematic approach entrepreneurs now have towards exploiting innovation.

But innovation does not happen as a random event. Central to the process are the entrepreneurs. It is they who introduce and then exploit the new innovations. For Schumpeter, 'the entrepreneur initiates change and generates new opportunities. Until imitators force prices and costs into conformity, the innovator is able to reap profits and disturb equilibrium'. By way of contrast, early classical economists such as Adam Smith saw entrepreneurs as having a rather minor role in overall economic activity. He thought that they provided real capital, but did not play a leading or direct part in how the pattern of supply and demand was determined.

Aghion and Howitt (1992) have produced a formal restatement of Schumpeter's theories whereby new entrants replace existing inefficient firms. Other economists have emphasized the Schumpeterian assumption that innovation-based growth needs entrepreneurs and effective selection among entrepreneurs (Acemoglu et al., 2006; Michelacci, 2003). Building on Schumpeter's work, recent theories of 'industrial evolution' have linked entrepreneurship and economic growth directly (Audretsch, 1995; Ericson and Pakes, 1995; Hopenhayn, 1992; Jovanovic, 1982; Klepper, 1996; Lambson, 1991). These theories focus on change as the central phenomenon and emphasize the role knowledge plays in charting a way through this. Innovation is seen as the key to entry, growth and survival for an enterprise and the way entire industries change over time. But the information they need in order to innovate is crucial – being inherently uncertain, asymmetric (one party may have more than another) and associated with high transaction costs. As a result there are differences in the expected value of new ideas which encourages their exploitation. Acs et al. (2005) and Audretsch et al. (2006) expanded on this notion that the important feature of entrepreneurs – and entrepreneurial firms – is that they act as 'knowledge filters', facilitating 'knowledge spillovers' or 'knowledge transfers'.

However, underpinning all this is a realization that change has changed. Change is increasingly seen as a continuous flow. Rather than change taking us from one 'equilibrium state' to another, it is now seen as a continuous phenomenon, with occasional disruptive large-scale changes. And continuous innovation is driving this change. Large firms need to be able to innovate continuously, just to survive the tide of change.

Corporate entrepreneurship

Corporate entrepreneurship is a loose term used to describe entrepreneurial behaviour in established, larger organizations. The objective of this is simple – to gain competitive advantage by encouraging innovation at all levels in the organization – corporate, divisional, business unit, functional or project team levels. Even as late as the 1980s some academics still believed it was difficult, if not impossible, for entrepreneurial activity to take place in larger, bureaucratic organizations (Morse, 1986). Nevertheless there is a large literature on the general phenomenon stretching back over 30 years. Despite this there has been no real consensus on what the term means (Sharma and Chrisman, 1999). Vesper (1984) suggested it was characterized by three very broad sorts of activities:

▷ creation of new business units by an established firm;
▷ development and implementation of entrepreneurial strategic thrusts;
▷ emergence of new ideas from various levels in the organization.

Notwithstanding this, Zahra (1991) still defined corporate entrepreneurship narrowly as 'activities aimed at creating new businesses in established companies'. Guth and Ginsberg (1990) expanded the definition to include 'transformation of organizations through strategic renewal' – in effect turn-arounds of ailing companies. Zahra et al. (1999) added further dimensions suggesting that there are many facets to entrepreneurship at firm level which reflect different combinations of:

▷ content of entrepreneurship – corporate venturing, innovation, proactivity;
▷ sources of entrepreneurship – both internal and external;
▷ focus of entrepreneurship – formal or informal.

Views about what constitutes corporate entrepreneurship are diverse and cover a wide range. Trying to pull them together into some order, Birkinshaw (2003) identified four strands of the literature that he called 'basic schools of thought': corporate venturing, intrapreneurship, bringing the market inside, entrepreneurial transformation.

Corporate venturing

This is concerned with larger businesses needing to manage new, entrepreneurial businesses separately from the mainstream activity (internal corporate venturing) and how they might eventually be 'spun off'. It is also concerned with the organizational structures needed to encourage new businesses whilst aligning them to the company's existing activities (Burgelman, 1983; Drucker, 1985; Galbraith, 1982). It also deals with how companies can manage disruptive technologies (Christensen, 1997). These aspects are dealt with in Chapter 8. However, the term is also concerned with investment by larger firms in strategically important smaller firms (external corporate venturing) and the different forms of corporate venturing units needed to undertake both roles (Chesbrough, 2002). This is dealt with in Chapter 11.

Intrapreneurship

This is concerned with individual employees and how they might be encouraged to act in an entrepreneurial way within a larger organization. It is part of how internal corporate venturing can take place and is covered in Chapter 8. The literature is concerned with the systems, structures and cultures that inhibit this activity and how they might be circumvented or even challenged. It is concerned with the character and personality of this strange hybrid of entrepreneur and 'company-man'. The term was introduced and popularized by Gifford Pinchot (1985) building on the earlier work of Ross Kanter (1982). In many ways it was this school that launched the idea that large organizations could change and be something different from what, all too often, they had become.

Bringing the market inside

This focuses mainly on the structural changes needed to encourage entrepreneurial behaviour and argues for a market approach to resource allocation and people management systems using market-based techniques such as spin-offs and venture capital operations (Foster and Kaplan, 2001; Hamel, 1999). Structural issues are covered in Chapter 6 but other issues emerging from this school are covered throughout the book.

Entrepreneurial transformation

The premise behind this strand of literature is that large firms need to adapt to an ever-changing environment if they are to survive, and to do so they need to adapt their structures and cultures so as to encourage entrepreneurial activity in individual employees (Ghoshal and Bartlett, 1997; Kanter, 1989; Peters and Waterman, 1982; Tushman and O'Reilly, 1996). According to this school individual behaviour is fashioned by various elements in the organization – its leadership, strategies, systems, structures and culture. One aspect of this school – the identification and exploitation of opportunities by creating and sustaining competitive advantage – has also been called 'strategic entrepreneurship' (Ireland et al., 2003; Kuratko and Audretsch, 2009; Morris et al., 2008). Another term associated with this school is 'strategic renewal' (Sharma and Chrisman, op. cit.), and combinations of the words 'strategic', 'organizational' and 'corporate' with the words 'renewal', 'rejuvenation' and 'redefinition' are often used in the literature associated with corporate entrepreneurship. For example, Covin and Miles (1999) say that corporate entrepreneurship generates competitive superiority in four ways:

> *'There is a real need for corporate entrepreneurs at the moment. For too long the prevailing consensus has been if it ain't broke, don't fix it but entrepreneurs recognize that action and change are crucial for maximizing potential and taking advantage of opportunities. You have to be tough and outgoing and not afraid of leaving calm waters to ride the waves of a storm. I consider myself to be a corporate entrepreneur. I have not created the company I am in charge of, but I have changed the way it is run and have made a real difference. I think times have changed and entrepreneurs don't have to be totally out on a limb. There are plenty of opportunities for entrepreneurialism in large companies too.'*
>
> **Diane Thompson**, Chief Executive, **Camelot** (also founder of an advertising agency) *Sunday Times* 17 March 2002

▷ *Organizational regeneration* – by altering the organization itself, its internal processes, structures and capabilities – an aspect covered in Chapters 6 and 7.

▷ *Sustained regeneration* – by regularly entering new markets or introducing new products – an aspect covered in Chapters 10, 11 and 12.

▷ *Domain redefinition* – by developing a completely new product/market arena and, effectively, creating a new industry (disruptive innovation and paradigm shift) – an aspect covered in Chapters 11 and 12.

▷ *Strategic renewal* – by fundamentally altering how it competes and redefining its relationship with the market place and competitors. The most effective form of strategic renewal is entrepreneurial transformation because it creates the capacity for continuous renewal. It is also likely to lead to organizational regeneration, sustained redefinition and domain redefinition. How to go about creating this entrepreneurial transformation is outlined in the next section.

Entrepreneurial transformation

This book is about corporate entrepreneurship as transformation – a transformation that is continuous and sustainable. However, it is also about all the other schools mentioned in the previous section, regarding them simply as tools that help the transformation. The book is written from the viewpoint that, in order to be truly entrepreneurial, the whole organization must be transformed – but also that transformation must be sustainable. The very DNA of the entrepreneur must, somehow, be replicated in the larger corporate entity. As Drucker (op. cit.) says: 'Entrepreneurship is based upon the same principles, whether the entrepreneur is an existing large institution or an individual starting his or her new venture single-handed. It makes little or no difference whether the entrepreneur is a business or a non-business public-service organization, nor even whether the entrepreneur is a government or non-government institution. The rules are pretty much the same, and so are the kinds of innovation and where to look for them.' So we need to unpick the character traits and the approaches to business, management and strategy development of successful entrepreneurs. And when Mintzberg et al. (1998) said that the entrepreneurial school of strategy (yes, there is one) 'presents strategy formation as all wrapped up in the behavior of a single individual, yet never really says much about what the process is', the challenge is to start to delineate what those processes are and the principles on which they are based. We shall isolate the DNA of entrepreneurship in Chapter 2.

This process of entrepreneurial transformation can be achieved by building what I call 'entrepreneurial architecture'. This entrepreneurial architecture creates within the organization the knowledge and routines that allow it to respond flexibly to change and opportunity in the way the entrepreneur does. It is better suited to survive in the age of uncertainty. It is a very real and valuable asset. It creates competitive advantage in its own right and is sustainable. This architecture is based upon relationships, but it is built on the three pillars of leadership, culture and structure and underpinned by appropriate strategies, as shown in Figure 1.2. It can be constructed and this book provides a blueprint for that – a blueprint we outline in Chapter 3. One of the paradoxes of entrepreneurial architecture is that it cannot be too prescriptive as it must be able to evolve and develop as people in the organization direct it. However it needs some degree of prescription to ensure this can happen. And to build this architecture requires a holistic, multidisciplinary approach to managing an organization. It needs a renaissance leader who is able to use all the management levers and techniques at their disposal and is willing to take leadership by giving it away. It is not easy. But entrepreneurs like Bill Gates, Michael Dell, Richard Branson and Kiran Mazumdar-Shaw have managed it and in so doing transformed themselves from entrepreneurs into entrepreneurial leaders.

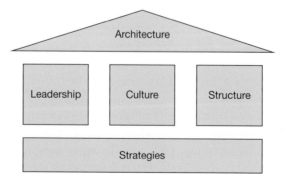

F 1.2 Pillars of entrepreneurial architecture

The entrepreneurial organization

So, if you are successful in constructing this entrepreneurial architecture what will the organization look like? What will it do that is different from other organizations? What is corporate entrepreneurship about?

Corporate entrepreneurship is about encouraging opportunity-seeking and innovation in a systematic manner throughout the organization, always questioning the established order, seeking ways to improve and create competitive advantage. It is about encouraging the qualities enjoyed by successful entrepreneurs such as vision and drive, empowering staff to do the right things for the organization on their own initiative. It is about learning new ways to manage organizations involving relationships and culture rather than discipline and control. It is about new ways of dealing with risk, uncertainty and ambiguity so as to maintain flexibility – and allowing failure but mitigating and learning from its consequences. It is about institutionalizing a process of continuous strategizing, learning from customers, competitors and the environment. It is about remaining flexible, encouraging change and managing rapid growth. And it is about doing these things throughout an organization so that it reflects the entrepreneurial characteristics of its managers – responding quickly and effectively to opportunities or changes in the market place. Successfully implemented, corporate entrepreneurship provides competitive superiority and is a blueprint for survival and even growth in the age of uncertainty.

🗁 Case insights Entrepreneurial leaders

Michael Dell

Born in 1965, Michael Dell is one of the richest men in the world with a fortune in excess of $17 billion. He started Dell Computers in 1984 with just $620. Today the company is worth billions and employs some 76,500 people, globally.

Michael's entrepreneurial career started early. At the age of 12 he made $1200 by selling his stamp collection. At the age of 14 he devised a marketing scheme to sell newspapers which earned him over $11,000. From the age of 15 his interest in calculators and then computers started to grow. He started buying microchips and other bits of computer hardware in order to build systems because he realized that he could buy, say, a disk drive for $500 which would sell in the shops for $1800. In 1983 he began a pre-med degree at the University of Texas but dropped out fairly quickly to set up his own business selling computers direct to end-users.

From the start Michael Dell knew the critical success factor for his business. He used an expert to build prototype computers whilst he concentrated on finding cheap components so he could keep prices low. The firm grew at an incredible pace, notching up sales of $3.7 million in the first nine months. The company went on to pioneer direct marketing in the industry and integrated supply chain management, linking customers' orders and suppliers through the internet – both strategies helping to keep prices low. At all times the focus on a low-cost/low-price marketing strategy has been maintained.

→

Michael Dell has moved from being an entrepreneur, wheeling and dealing, to become an entrepreneurial leader; understanding where his competitive advantage lies and then putting into place the systems and processes to keep his company two steps ahead of the competition.

Richard Branson

Richard Branson is probably the best known entrepreneur in Britain today and his name is closely associated with the many businesses that carry the Virgin brand name. He is outward-going and an excellent self-publicist. He has been called an 'adventurer', taking risks that few others would contemplate. This shows itself in his personal life, with his transatlantic power boating and round-the-world ballooning exploits, as well as in his business life where he has challenged established firms like British Airways and Coca-Cola. He is a multimillionaire with what has been described as a charismatic leadership style.

Born in 1950, Richard comes from a well-off background. His father was a barrister and he went to school at Stowe, a leading private school (called 'public' in Britain, just to confuse). However, he was never academic and suffered from dyslexia. He left school at the age of sixteen. Famously his head teacher commented; 'Congratulations, Branson. I predict that you will either go to prison or become a millionaire.' Needless to say, leaving school at sixteen did not dent his self-confidence. His mother encouraged this. She commented that 'bringing him up was like riding a thoroughbred horse. He needed guiding but you were afraid to pull the reins too hard in case you stamped out the adventure and wildness.'

Now in his sixties, Richard Branson's business life started as an 18-year-old schoolboy when he launched *Student* magazine, selling advertising space from a phone booth. He wrote to well-known personalities and celebrities – pop and film stars and politicians – and persuaded many to contribute articles or agree to interviews. He persuaded a designer to work for no fee, negotiated a printing contract for 50,000 copies and got Peter Blake, the designer of The Beatles' Sgt Pepper album cover, to draw the cover picture of a student. The magazine made money by selling advertising space. It was so successful that the BBC featured Richard in a documentary called 'The People of Tomorrow'. And that is probably how the Richard Branson legend started and how he realized the importance of self-publicity – a lesson he has never forgotten. Since then he has become known for his, often outrageous, publicity stunts, such as dressing up as a bride for the launch of Virgin Bride.

After *Student* magazine he started Virgin Records, originally selling discounted, mail-order records but soon decided he needed a retail site. In 1972 he got his first store, above a shoe shop on London's Oxford Street, rent-free on the grounds that it could not be let and would generate more customers for the shoe shop. It was a great success and Richard earned enough money from it to buy a country estate, in which he installed a recording studio. Mike Oldfield's enormous hit Tubular Bells was recorded in Virgin's first recording studio – an Oxfordshire barn – and released in 1973. Other star names signed by Virgin Records included The Rolling Stones, Genesis, Phil Collins, Peter Gabriel, Bryan Ferry, Janet Jackson, Culture Club, Simple Minds and The Sex Pistols.

Since those early days the Virgin brand has found its way onto aircraft, trains, cola, vodka, mobile phones, cinemas, a radio station, financial services, fitness studios and the internet. Virgin Atlantic Airways was launched in 1984. In 1986 Virgin was floated but later re-privatized because Richard did not like to be accountable for his actions to institutional shareholders. In 1992, to keep his airline company afloat, he sold the Virgin record label to EMI for $1 billion. In 1999 a 49% stake in the airline was sold to Singapore Airlines. In the same year Virgin Mobile was launched.

Virgin is now one of the best known brands in Britain with 96% recognition and is well-known worldwide. It is strongly associated with its founder, Sir Richard Branson – 95% can name him as the founder.

Bill Gates

Bill Gates and Microsoft is probably the outstanding business success story of a generation. Born in 1955 in Seattle, he and his friend Paul Allen, 'begged, borrowed and bootlegged' time on their school's computer to undertake software commissions. The two went to Harvard University together, using the University's computer to start their own business. Bill's big break came when he approached Altair, a computer company in Albuquerque, New Mexico, trying to sell it a customized version of the BASIC programming language for the PC it produced. The only problem was that, at the time, he and his partner, Paul Allen, had not finished writing it. He had a vision of what it would look like and how it would operate, but no software. That was not finished until some weeks later and with it Microsoft came about. The package was later licensed to Apple, Commodore and IBM. IBM later commissioned Microsoft to develop its own operating system and that was how Microsoft Disk Operating System (MS DOS) was born.

Founded in 1975, Microsoft's growth has been amazing. It is now the world's largest software company producing a range of products and services, including the Windows operating systems and Office software suite. And its ambitions are still anything but small. The company has expanded into markets such as video game consoles, interactive television and internet access. With its core markets maturing, it is targeting services for growth, looking to transform its software applications into web-based services and looking to establish itself in the fast growing digital communications market. In 2008 it entered the cloud computing market. Since 2010 it has also partnered with Nokia to secure market share for its Windows Phone OS smartphone operating system and other digital services, competing with the Google Android system and the Apple iPhone. In 2011 Microsoft founded the Open Networking Foundation which is meant to speed innovation through simple software changes in telecommunications and wireless networks, data centres and other networking areas.

Now a billionaire, Bill Gates stepped down as CEO of Microsoft in 2000 and retired as Chief Software Architect in 2008 while still retaining other positions in the company, including non-executive chairman. Although criticized for his anti-competitive business tactics at Microsoft, he has become a generous philanthropist and now works full time for the Bill and Melinda Gates Foundation.

Kiran Mazumdar-Shaw

Born in 1953 in Bangalore, India, Kiran Mazumdar-Shaw is one of the richest women in India. She is the founder of Biocon, a bio-tech company and India's largest producer of insulin. With a degree in zoology, she went on to take a postgraduate course and trained as a brewer in Australia, ahead of returning to India hoping to follow in her father's footsteps as a brew-master. Despite working in the brewing industry in India for a couple of years, she never achieved her ambition, finding her career blocked by sexism. Instead, in 1978, she was persuaded to set up a joint venture making enzymes in India.

Kiran Mazumdar-Shaw started Biocon India with Irishman Les Auchincloss in 1978 in the garage of her rented house in Bangalore with seed capital of only Rs 10,000. It was a joint venture with Biocon Biochemicals, Ireland. Eventually she found a banker prepared to loan the company $45,000 and, from a facility in Bangalore making enzymes for the brewing industry, started to diversify. It became the first Indian company to manufacture and export enzymes to the USA and Europe. This gave her a flow of cash that she used to fund research and to start producing pharmaceutical drugs. The early years were hard.

→

'I was young, I was twenty five years old ... banks were very nervous about lending to young entrepreneurs because they felt we didn't have the business experience ... and then I had ... this strange business called biotechnology which no one understood ... Banks were very fearful of lending to a woman because I was considered high risk.'

BBC News Business 11 April 2011

In 1989, Kiran met the chairman of ICICI Bank, which had just launched a venture fund. The fund took a 20% stake in the company and helped finance its move into bio-pharmaceuticals. Shortly after this Unilever took over Biocon Biochemicals, and bought ICICI's stake in Biocon India, at the same time increasing it to 50%. In 1996 it entered the bio-pharmaceuticals and statins markets. One year later Unilever sold its share in Biocon Biochemicals, and Mazumdar-Shaw bought out Unilever and was able to start preparing Biocon India to float on the stock market, which it did in 2004, with a market value of $1.1bn.

In 2003 it became the first company to develop human insulin on a Pichia expression system. Since then it has obtained a listing on the stock exchange and entered into thousands of R&D licensing agreements with other pharmaceutical companies around the world. Today Biocon has a turnover in excess of Rs 24,000 million. It has Asia's largest insulin and statin production facilities and its largest perfusion-based antibody production facility. It produces drugs for cancer, diabetes and auto-immune diseases and is developing the world's first oral insulin, currently undergoing Phase III clinical trials.

Kiran Mazumdar-Shaw has enjoyed many awards and honours. In 2010 *TIME* magazine included her in their 100 most powerful people in the world, in the same year the *Financial Times* had her in their list of the top 50 women in business and in 2009 Forbes included her in their list of the 100 most powerful women. Passionate about providing affordable health care in India, she has funded the 1400-bed Mazumdar-Shaw Cancer Centre, a free cancer hospital in Bangalore. Every year, she donates $2 million to support health insurance coverage for some 100,000 Indian villagers.

She remains involved in breaking gender barriers:

'We see many women entrepreneurs today when it comes to small businesses. But where we do not see many success stories is in large businesses. I think it stems from lack of self confidence. Most women feel that they have limitations and they are not cut out to hold such large businesses. That has to change. It is heartening to see family businesses are encouraging their daughters which was not so in the past. That is a good sign.'

Rediff Business, 10 August, 2011

Summary

▷ We are living in an age of uncertainty characterized by continuing, unpredictable and rapid change – change that is both incremental and discontinuous. It is an increasingly complex world full of interconnections formed by a global market place linked by technology allowing instant communication.

▷ Whilst large firms find this environment challenging, small, entrepreneurial firms have thrived and entrepreneurs like **Michael Dell**, **Richard Branson**, **Bill Gates** and **Kiran Mazumdar-Shaw** have become millionaires.

▷ Small, entrepreneurial firms are a vital part of the economies of most Western countries. 95% of the wealth of the USA was created since 1980. SMEs generate 50% of GDP in the USA, and over 25% in the UK. In the EU they generate 67% of employment. Fast growing 'gazelles' – like **AirAsia** – generate most of this employment growth.

- ▷ Entrepreneurs are defined primarily by their actions. As with **Krishnan Ganesh** and **TutorVista**, they identify and capitalize upon commercial opportunities in the market. They have certain identifiable character traits and approaches to business and management that set them apart – their DNA.

- ▷ Corporate entrepreneurship is the term used to describe entrepreneurial behaviour in an established, larger organization. The views on what constitutes corporate entrepreneurship are diverse, however there are four identifiable strands of literature or schools of thought:
  - ▷ Corporate venturing;
  - ▷ Intrapreneurship;
  - ▷ Bringing the market inside;
  - ▷ Entrepreneurial transformation.

- ▷ Entrepreneurial transformation is about adapting the whole organization so that it is better able to cope with the new age of uncertainty. Corporate venturing, intrapreneurship and bringing the market inside are simply techniques to help achieve this.

- ▷ This transformation is achieved by building an entrepreneurial architecture. Although based on relationships it can be constructed through leadership, culture and structures, and is underpinned by appropriate strategies.

- ▷ This entrepreneurial architecture creates within the organization the knowledge and routines that allow it to respond flexibly to change and opportunity in the same way as entrepreneurs.

Essays and discussion topics

1 What do you understand by the term 'age of uncertainty'? Does it accurately describe the environment of today?

2 How are the challenges posed by the age of opportunity different/the same as those posed by the age of austerity?

3 Why do you think small firms have prospered rather than large firms over the last 50 years?

4 In a turbulent, changing environment what advantages/disadvantages do small firms have?

5 In a turbulent, changing environment what advantages/disadvantages do large firms have?

6 Were Enron and RBS entrepreneurial organizations? If so, what are the dangers facing an entrepreneurial organizations? How might they be mitigated?

7 How important are CSR issues? How responsive to them are large firms? How might this be increased?

8 Why is there more entrepreneurial activity in the USA than anywhere else?

9 Why are owner-managers not all entrepreneurs?

10 Have you ever thought about setting up your own business? What attracts you to do so and what blocks you from doing so? In what circumstances might you actually do it?

11 Can large firms also be entrepreneurial? Is it in their interests to be so? What pressures are there for them not to be entrepreneurial?

12 If large firms were more entrepreneurial what would be the individual, economic and societal advantages?

13 What do you understand by the term corporate entrepreneurship? Do you agree that it is the same as entrepreneurial transformation?

14 How are the three other schools of thought related to entrepreneurial transformation?

15 Using the description of an entrepreneurial organization outlined in the final section, speculate how architecture – leadership, culture and structures underpinned by appropriate strategies – might build this.

Exercises and assignments

1 Identify two large organizations that you would describe as entrepreneurial and explain why you would describe them this way. Are they commercially successful? Can you identify any clues as to why they might be successful?

References

Acemoglu, D., Aghion, P. and Zilibotti, F. (2006) 'Distance to the Frontier, Selection and Economic Growth', *Journal of the European Economic Association*, 4.

Acs, Z., Audretsch, D., Branerhjelm, P. and Carlsson, B. (2005) 'The Knowledge Spillover Theory of Entrepreneurship', CEPR Discussion Paper No. 5326, London, CEPR.

Aghion, Ph. and Howitt, P. (1992) 'A Model of Growth through Creative Destruction', *Economica*, 60(2).

Ahmad, N. (2006) *A Proposed Framework for Business Demographic Statistics, OECD Statistics Working Paper Series*, Paris: STD/DOC(2006)3.

Anderson, J. (1995) *Local Heroes*, Scottish Enterprise, Glasgow.

Audretsch, D.B. (1995) *Innovation and Industry Evolution*, Cambridge: MIT Press.

Audretsch, D.B., Keilbach, M.C. and Lehmann, E.E. (2006) *Entrepreneurship and Economic Growth*, Oxford: Oxford University Press.

BERR (2008) *High Growth Firms in the UK: Lessons from an Analysis of Comparative UK Performance*, Business, Enterprise and Regulatory Reform (BERR) Economics Paper 3, November.

Birch, D.L. (1979) 'The Job Creation Process', unpublished report, *MIT Program on Neighborhood and Regional Change*, prepared for the Economic Development Administration, US Department of Commerce, Washington, DC.

Birkinshaw, J.M. (2003) 'The Paradox of Corporate Entrepreneurship', *Strategy and Business*, 30, Spring.

Branson, R. (1998) *Losing my Virginity*, London: Virgin.

Burgelman, R.A. (1983) 'A Process Model of Internal Corporate Venturing in the Diversified Major Firm', *Administrative Science Quarterly*, 28.

Chesbrough, H.W. (2002) 'Making Sense of Corporate Venture Capital', *Harvard Business Review*, March.

Christensen, C.M. (1997) *The Innovator's Dilemma: When New Technologies Cause Great Firms to Fail*, Boston: Harvard Business School Press.

Covin, J. and Miles, M. (1999) 'Corporate Entrepreneurship and the Pursuit of Competitive Advantage', *Entrepreneurship Theory and Practice*, 23(3).

de Geus, A. (1997) *The Living Company*, Boston: Harvard Business Press.

Drucker, P.F. (1985) *Innovation and Entrepreneurship: Practice and Principles*, London: Heinemann.

Ericson, R. and Pakes, A. (1995) 'Markov-Perfect Industry Dynamics: A Framework for Empirical Work', *Review of Economic Studies*, 62.

European Commission, (2008) *European Competitiveness Report 2008*, available free online at www.ec.europa.eu/enterprise.

Eurostat (2008) *Enterprises by Size Class – Overview of SMEs in the EU, Statistics in Focus, 31/2008*. Available on epp.eurostat.ec.europa.eu.

Foster, R.N. and Kaplan, S. (2001) *Creative Destruction: Why Companies that are Built to Last Underperform the Market – and How to Successfully Transform Them*, New York: Currency Doubleday.

Galbraith, J. (1982) 'Designing the Innovating Organization', *Organizational Dynamics*, Winter.

GE Capital (2012) *Leading from the Middle: The Untold Story of British Business*, London: GE Capital

Ghoshal, S. and Bartlett, C.A. (1997) *The Individualized Corporation: A Fundamentally New Approach to Management*, New York: Harper Business.

Guth, W.D. and Ginsberg, A. (1990) 'Corporate Entrepreneurship', *Strategic Management Journal* (Special Issue) 11.

Hamel, G. (1999) 'Bringing Silicon Valley Inside', *Harvard Business Review*, September.

Hamel, G. (2000) *Leading the Revolution*, Boston: Harvard Business School Press.

Hisrich, R.D. and Peters, M.P. (1992) *Entrepreneurship: Starting, Developing and Managing a New Enterprise*, Homewood, IL: Irwin.

Hopenhayn, H.A. (1992) 'Entry, Exit and Firm Dynamics in Long Run Equilibrium', *Econometrica*, 60.

Ireland, R.D. Hitt, M.A. and Sirmon, D.G. (2003) 'A Model of Strategic Entrepreneurship: The Construct and its Dimensions', *Journal of Management*, 29(6).

Jovanovic, B. (1982) 'Favorable Selection with Asymmetrical Information', *Quarterly Journal of Economics*, 97(3).

Kanter, R.M. (1982) 'The Middle Manager as Innovator', *Harvard Business Review*, July.

Kanter, R.M. (1989) *When Giants Learn to Dance: Mastering the Challenge of Strategy, Management and Careers in the 1990s*, New York: Simon & Schuster.

Klepper, S. (1996) 'Entry, Exit, Growth and Innovation over the Product Life Cycle', *American Economic Review*, 86(3).

Kuratko, D. and Audretsch, D. (2009) 'Strategic Entrepreneurship: Exploring Different Perspectives of an Emerging Concept', *Entrepreneurship Theory and Practice*, 33.

Lambson, V.E. (1991) 'Industry Evolution with Sunk Costs and Uncertain Market Conditions', *International Journal of Industrial Organisations*, 9.

McMillan, E. (2004) *Complexity, Organisations and Change*, London: Routledge

Michelacci, C. (2003), 'Low Returns in R&D due to Lack of Entrepreneurial Skills', *Economic Journal*, 113.

Mintzberg, H., Ahlstrand, B. and Lampel, J. (1998) *Strategy Safari*, New York: The Free Press.

Morris, M., Kuratko, D. and Covin, J. (2008) Corporate Entrepreneurship and Innovation, Mason, OH: Thomson/South-Western.

Morse, C.W. (1986) 'The Delusion of Intrapreneurship', *Long Range Planning*, 19(2).

Naisbitt, J. (1994) *Global Paradox: The Bigger the World Economy, the More Powerful its Smallest Players*, London: BCA.

Ohmae, K. (2005) *The Next Global Stage: Challenges and Opportunities in our Borderless World*, New Jersey: Pearson Education.

Penrose, E.T. (1959) *The Theory of the Growth of Firms*, Oxford: Basil Blackwell.

Peters, T. and Waterman, R. (1982) *In Search of Excellence: Lessons from America's Best-Run Companies*, New York: Harper Row.

Pinchot III, G. (1985) *Intrapreneuring: Why You Don't Have to Leave the Company to Become an Entrepreneur*, New York: Harper Row.

Sharma, P. and Chrisman, J.J. (1999) 'Toward a Reconsideration of the Definitional Issues in the Field of Corporate Entrepreneurship', *Entrepreneurship Theory and Practice*, 23(3).

Schumpeter, J.A. (1934) *The Theory of Economic Development: An Inquiry into Profits, Capital, Credit, Interest and the Business Cycle* (trans. by Redvers Opie), Oxford University Press.

Strangler, D. (2010) *High Growth Firms and the Future of the American Economy*, Kaffman Foundation Research Series: Firm Growth and Economic Growth.

Timmons, J.A. (1999) *New Venture Creation: Entrepreneurship for the 21st Century*, Boston: Irwin/McGraw-Hill.

Tushman, M.L. and O'Reilly, C.A. (1996) 'Ambidextrous Organizations: Managing Evolutionary and Revolutionary Change', *California Management Review*, 38(4).

Vesper, K.H. (1984) 'The Three Faces of Corporate Entrepreneurship: A Pilot Study', in J.A. Hornaday et al. (eds), *Frontiers of Entrepreneurial Research*, Wellesley, MA: Babson College.

Zahra, S.A. (1991) 'Predictors and Financial Outcomes of Corporate Entrepreneurship: An Exploratory Study', *Journal of Business Venturing*, 6(4), July.

Zahra, S.A., Jennings, D.F. and Kuratko, D.F. (1999) 'The Antecedents and Consequences of Firm Level Entrepreneurship: The State of the Field', *Entrepreneurship: Theory and Practice*, 24.

Chapter 2

Entrepreneurial DNA

Learning outcomes

By the end of this chapter you should be able to:

▷ Critically analyze how their character traits and antecedent influences affect owner-managers and entrepreneurs and their approach to management, whilst understanding the methodological problems associated with trying to measure their influence;

▷ Critically analyze how entrepreneurs approach management through forming personal relationships and networks with all the stakeholders in the business;

▷ Understand how entrepreneurs approach decision-making and the formulation of strategy and critically analyze how this affects their approach to management;

▷ Understand how entrepreneurs mitigate risk;

▷ Understand how entrepreneurs need to change as the business grows and critically assess the implications of this for the way the organization is structured and managed.

The DNA of entrepreneurship

In order to understand the nature of corporate entrepreneurship we need to understand entrepreneurs themselves. We need to analyze their very DNA and be able to replicate it in a larger organization. Entrepreneurs shape the organization they start up. They dominate it to the extent that it takes on many of their personal characteristics through its culture. Entrepreneurs have a particular and characteristic approach to doing business and managing the organization, and their management style also influences the organizational culture. They approach decision-making and strategy formulation differently.

In this chapter we shall analyze the DNA of the entrepreneur. We shall look at their character traits and how they are fashioned. We shall look at their approach to management and how – in contrast to large organizations that typically rely far more on formal, often contractual, relationships – entrepreneurs rely on informal relationships to manage staff. We shall look at how they develop close relationships and networks with all the stakeholders of the organization so as to obtain knowledge and information and mitigate the high risks that they face. We shall look at how they approach strategy development and decision-making, noting what works and what does not. In the next chapter, based upon these characteristics, we shall draw conclusions about how an organization that practises corporate entrepreneurship should look and how it might be created. These characteristics and approaches are shown in Figure 2.1. At the centre of this jigsaw puzzle are the personal character traits of the entrepreneur.

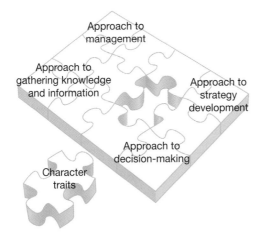

F 2.1 DNA of entrepreneurship

Personal character traits

It is generally believed that entrepreneurs have certain personal character traits. A few people believe that they are born with them, but most believe they are shaped by their background, history and experience of life – called antecedent influences – as well as the culture of the different groups of society in which they operate. Some cultures may encourage entrepreneurial activity, others may discourage it. In addition, situational factors, like unemployment or immigration may 'push' people into self-employment whilst other factors, like economic opportunity or opportunities arising from being employed, may 'pull' them into it. Research indicates that owner-managers have a certain identifiable set of character traits and entrepreneurs – who set up businesses that grow – have an additional set that we particularly might want to capture in an entrepreneurial organization. These influences on an entrepreneur's decision to start up a business are summarized in Figure 2.2.

However, before looking at these traits we need to sound a note of caution. Some academics dispute the link between traits and setting up and growing a business (Gartner, 1988). Cognitive theory, however, may explain this link by providing a basis for understanding how these characteristics influence entrepreneurial behaviour and, indeed, some strands of cognitive theory reinforce ideas about how particular traits may influence particular behaviour. We shall return to cognitive theory later in this chapter. Nevertheless, the problem of linking the personal character traits of any individual to the success of a business needs to be approached with caution and can be an academic minefield. Success or failure in business comes from a mix of many different things and the character of the entrepreneur is just one factor in the equation. We have no way of knowing how important the different ingredients are at any point of time. What is more, it takes time for the owner-manager entrepreneur to prove that the business he or she manages is in fact a successful growth business. So, do you measure aspirations or reality, and over what time scale? We have held

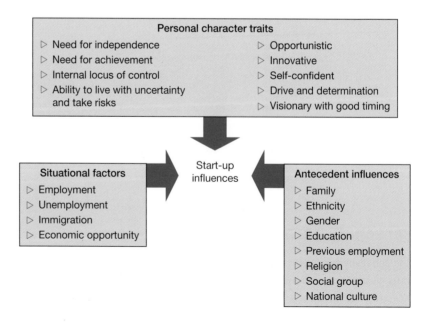

F 2.2 Start-up influences

up Michael Dell and Richard Branson as successful entrepreneurs, but will their companies eventually fail and their reputations become tarnished? And, if so, what part will their personalities play in this? Later in this chapter we look at Steve Jobs. Whilst he exhibited many entrepreneurial characteristics the resulting, albeit highly successful, Apple is very unusual for a successful entrepreneurial organization (as we shall see in Chapter 6). So how do these characteristics translate into actions?

Furthermore, many of the character traits that have been found to be significant in entrepreneurs are similar to those found in other success-ful people such as politicians or athletes (Chell et al., 1991). Perhaps, the argument goes, it just happens that the individual has chosen an entrepre-neurial activity as a means of self-satisfaction (Gartner, op. cit.). There are also a number of methodological problems associated with attempting to measure personality characteristics. For example, they can change over time and can require subjective judgements. What is more, measures tend to ignore the influence of antecedent, cultural and environmental factors (Deakins, 1996).

Notwithstanding these issues, many researchers believe that, collec-tively, owner-managers and entrepreneurs have certain typical character traits, although the mix and emphasis of these characteristics will differ between individuals. The character traits of the owner-manager might be characterized as an instinct for survival – most owner-managed busi-nesses never grow to any size. The entrepreneur has certain additional character traits. These might be characterized as an instinct for growth. Together these form the entrepreneurial DNA that we need to replicate in our organizational architecture. Figure 2.3 summarizes the character traits for owner-managers and entrepreneurs, accumulated from the numerous academic studies cited.

Sources: Aldrich and Martinez, 2003; Andersson et al., 2004; Baty, 1990; Bell et al., 1992; Blanchflower and Meyer, 1991; Brockhaus and Horwitz, 1986; Brush, 1992; Buttner and More, 1997; Caird, 1990; Chell et al., 1991; Cuba et al., 1983; de Bono, 1985; Doern, 2009; Hirsch and Brush, 1987; Kanter, 1983; Kirzner, 1973, 1979, 1997, 1999; Lumpkin and Lichtenstein, 2005; McClelland, 1961; Ozgen and Baron, 2007; Pinchot, 1985; Rosa et al., 1994; Schein et al., 1996; Schumpeter, 1996; Schwartz, 1997; Shapero, 1985; Shaver and Scott, 1992; Storey and Sykes, 1996.

F 2.3 Character traits of owner-managers and entrepreneurs

Character traits of owner-managers

Need for autonomy and independence

'Entrepreneurs don't like working for other people … I was once made redundant by the Manchester Evening News. I had a wife who had given up a promising career for me, and a baby. I stood on Deansgate with £5 in my pocket and I swore I would never work for anyone else again.'

Eddy Shah, founder of **Messenger Group**
The Times 16 March 2002

Owner-managers and entrepreneurs have a high need for autonomy and independence. This is most often seen as the need to 'be your own boss' and is the trait that is most often cited, and supported, by researchers and advisors alike. It has been said that once you run your own firm you cannot work for anybody else. However, independence means different things to different people, such as controlling your own destiny, doing things differently or being in a situation where you can fulfil your potential.

Need for achievement

'We don't feel like millionaires at all. Money doesn't come into it. It's not really why you do it, it really isn't.'

Brent Hoberman, co-founder of **Lastminute.com**
Sunday Times 17 September 1999

'You have to enjoy what you do and have a passion for it, otherwise you're bound to fail. But of course the financial rewards are important and apart from anything else reflect how successful your company is.'

Martyn Dawes, founder of **Coffee Nation**
Startups: www.startups.co.uk

'Money doesn't motivate me. But it's not to say I don't drive a Bentley Continental T2.'

Stephen Waring, founder of **Green Thumb**
Sunday Times 2 October 2005

'As a child I never felt that I was noticed. I never felt that I achieved anything or that there was any expectation of me achieving anything. So proving myself is something that is important to me and so is establishing respect for what I have achieved.'

Chey Garland, founder of **Garlands Call Centres**
Sunday Times 27 June 2004

'Most of the pleasure is not the cash. It is the sense of achievement at having taken something from nothing to where it is now.'

Charles Muirhead, founder of **Orchestream**
Sunday Times 17 September 1999

'I am motivated by my success not money. But success is partly measured by money.'

Wing Yip, founder of **W Wing Yip & Brothers**
Sunday Times 2 January 2000

Owner-managers and entrepreneurs typically have a high need for achievement, a driving force that is particularly strong for entrepreneurs. Achievement for individuals means different things depending on the type of person they are: for example, the satisfaction of producing a beautiful work of art, employing their hundredth person, or making the magic one million pounds. Often money is just a badge of achievement to the successful entrepreneur. It is not an end in itself. Public recognition of achievement can be important to some entrepreneurs. And this can lead to certain negative behaviours or unwise decisions: for example, overspending on the trappings of corporate life – the office, the company car and so on (often called the corporate flag-pole syndrome) – or the 'big project' that is very risky but the entrepreneur 'knows' is achievable. These can lead to cash-flow problems that put at risk the very existence of the business.

Internal locus of control

If you believe that you can exercise control over your environment and ultimately your destiny, you have an internal locus of control. If, however, you believe in fate, you have an external locus of control and you are less likely to take the risk of starting a business. Entrepreneurs typically have a strong internal locus of control, which is the same for many senior managers in large firms.

'I want to take control of my life and achieve something.'

Jonathan Elvidge, founder of **Gadget Shop**
Sunday Times 17 March 2002

In extreme cases this trait can also lead to certain negative behaviours. In particular, it can show itself as a desire to maintain personal control over every aspect of the business. That can lead to a preoccupation with detail, over-work and stress. It also leads to an inability or unwillingness to delegate as the business grows. Again, in extreme cases it might show itself as a mistrust of subordinates. Kets de Vries (1985) thinks these behaviours can lead to the danger of subordinates becoming 'infantilized'. They are expected to behave as incompetent idiots, and that is the way they behave. They tend to do very little, make no decisions and circulate very little information. The better ones do not stay long. This need for control can also show itself in the unwillingness of many owner-managers to part with shares in their company. They just do not want to lose control, at any price. This also needs to be avoided because, as we shall see later, sharing owner-ship can be a very positive motivation for staff and one that encourages an entrepreneurial culture.

Ability to live with uncertainty and take measured risks

Owner-managers are willing to take risks and live with uncertainty. Human beings, typically, do not like uncertainty and one of the biggest uncertain-ties of all is not having a regular salary coming in – particularly when you have a family to support. That is not to say owner-managers like this aspect of risk and uncertainty. Uncertainty about income can be a major cause of stress. The possibility of missing out on some piece of business that might affect their income is one reason why they are so loath to take holidays. There are other commercial aspects of uncertainty that owner-managers have to cope with. Often they cannot influence many aspects of the market in which they operate, for example, price. They must therefore react

'Taking a chance, a risk or a gamble is what unites entrepreneurs. Without risk there is no reward. You won't discover America if you never set sail ... You have to be prepared to lose everything and remember that the biggest risk is not taking any risk at all.'

Jonathan Elvidge, founder of **Gadget Shop**
The Times 6 July and 17 March 2002

'Don't worry about failure: if you lose because of market conditions then another time someone will say "Hey, this guy can make things happen. I'll back him".'

Gururaj Deshpande, serial entrepreneur and founder of **Sycamore Networks**
The Financial Times 21 February 2000

'You have to have nerves of steel and be prepared to take risks. You have to be able to put it all on the line knowing you could lose everything.'

Anne Notley, co-founder of **The Iron Bed Company**
Sunday Times 28 January 2001

to changes in the market that others might bring about. A business with a high level of borrowing must find a way of paying interest charges but has no direct influence over changes in interest rates. Many small firms also have a limited customer or product base and this can bring further uncertainty. If, for whatever reason, one large customer ceases buying, it can have an enormous impact on a small firm.

Hand in hand with the ability to live with uncertainty is the willingness to take measured risks. Most people are risk averse. They try to avoid risks and insure against them. Setting up your own business is risky and owner-managers are willing to take more risks with their own resources than most people. They might risk their reputation and personal standing if they fail. However, they do not like this risk and try always to minimize their exposure; hence their preference to risk other people's money and borrow, sometimes too heavily, from the bank. Another example of this is the way they often 'compartmentalize' various aspects of their business. For example, an entrepreneur might open a second and third restaurant but set each one up as a separate limited company just in case any should fail and endanger the others. In this way they sometimes develop a portfolio of individually small businesses and their growth and success is measured not just in the performance of a single one but rather by the growth of the portfolio.

Character traits of entrepreneurs

In addition to the character traits of owner-managers, those who grow their business – true entrepreneurs – also have the following traits that are particularly relevant to the entrepreneurial organization that also wants to grow.

Opportunistic

'I have always lived my life by thriving on opportunity and adventure. Some of the best ideas come out of the blue, and you have to keep an open mind to see their virtue.'

Richard Branson

'Running a company that is listed on the Stock Exchange is different from building up and running a private company. The history of the City is littered with entrepreneurs who hold onto their creations for too long, failing to recognize the changing needs of the company. I am a serial entrepreneur … It is all part of growing up. I've built something and now it is time to move on.'

Stellios Haji-Ioannou, founder of **easyJet**
The Times 19 April 2002

This is one of two prime distinguishing features of entrepreneurs. Indeed some academics believe it is at the very heart of entrepreneurship (Lumpkin and Lichtenstein, 2005). By definition, entrepreneurs exploit change for profit. In other words, they seek out opportunities to make money. Opportunities can be recognized, discovered or created. Often entrepreneurs see opportunities where others see problems. Whereas ordinary mortals dislike the uncertainty brought about by change, entrepreneurs love it because they see opportunity and they do not mind the uncertainty.

For many entrepreneurs the problem is focusing on just one opportunity, or at least one opportunity at a time, and then exploiting it systematically. They see opportunity everywhere and have problems following through on any one before becoming distracted by another. This is one reason why some entrepreneurs are not able to grow their business beyond a certain size. They get bored by the routines and controls; they see other market opportunities and yearn for the excitement of another start-up. Many would probably be well advised to sell up and do just that, but go on to try to manage a company they have really lost interest in. And the result can be disastrous. However, some entrepreneurs do appreciate this element of their character and play to it, becoming serial entrepreneurs, moving to set up and sell on one business after another. They make money by creating a business with capital value, not necessarily income for themselves.

'Hundreds of computer stores were popping up in Houston. And dealers would pay $2000 for an IBM PC and sell it for $3000, making $1000 profit. They also offered little or no support to the customer. Yet they were making lots of money because people really wanted computers. At this point, I was already buying the exact same components that were used in these machines, and I was upgrading my machines selling them to people I knew. I realized that if I could sell even more of them, I could actually compete with the computer stores – and not just on price but on quality. I could also earn a nice little profit and get all the things your typical high school kid would want. But beyond that, I thought, "Wow, there's a lot of opportunity here." '

Michael Dell

Innovative

The ability to innovate is the second of the most important distinguishing features of entrepreneurs. Innovation is the prime tool they use to create or exploit opportunity. Entrepreneurs link innovation to the market place so as to exploit an opportunity and make their business grow. Although innovation is difficult to define and can take many forms, entrepreneurs are always, in some way, innovative. Later in this book we shall explore how spotting opportunities and developing innovation can be institutionalized.

'True innovation is rarely about creating something new. It's pretty hard to recreate the wheel or discover gravity; innovation is more often about seeing new opportunities for old designs.'

Neil Kelly, owner and managing director of **PAV**
Sunday Times 9 December 2001

Self-confident

Facing uncertainty, you have to be confident in your own judgement and ability to start up your own business. Many training programmes for start-ups recognize this by trying to build personal self-confidence through developing a business plan that addresses the issue of future uncertainty. As well as being a useful management tool, the plan can become a symbol of certainty for the owner-manager in an otherwise uncertain world. Some keep it with them at all times, using it almost like a Bible, to reassure them of what the future will hold when the business eventually becomes successful.

'My mother gave me a massive self-belief. I will always try things – there is nothing to lose.'

Richard Thompson, founder and chairman of **EMS**
Rupert Steiner; *My First Break: How Entrepreneurs Get Started*, Sunday Times Books, 1999

'When people ask me if I ever imagined that my business would be as successful as it has turned out to be, I have to say yes… It helps to have a strong belief in your abilities and not to feel insecure.'

Stephen Waring, founder of **Green Thumb**
Sunday Times 2 October 2005

Entrepreneurs, therefore, need self-confidence aplenty to grow their business, given the extreme uncertainty they face. If they do not believe in the future of the business, how can they expect others to do so? However, self-confidence can be overdone and turn into an exaggerated opinion of their own competence and even arrogance. Some researchers believe entrepreneurs are actually 'delusional'. In an interesting piece of research, two American academics tested the decision-making process of 124 entrepreneurs (defined as people who started their own firm) and 95 managers of big companies in two ways (Busenitz and Barney, 1997). Firstly, they asked five factual questions each of which had two possible answers. They asked respondents to rate their confidence in their answer (50%, a guess; 100%, perfect confidence). Entrepreneurs turned out to be much more confident about their answers than managers, especially those who gave wrong answers. Secondly, they were given a business decision. They were told they must replace a broken foreign-made machine and they had two alternatives. The first was an American-made machine, which a friend had recently bought and had not yet broken down, and the second a foreign-built machine, which was statistically less likely to break down than the other. 50% of the entrepreneurs opted for the American machine whilst only 10% of the managers opted for it. The researchers concluded that the entrepreneurs were more prone to both delusion and opportunism than normal managers, who were seen as more rational. So the question is raised, is entrepreneurial self-confidence so strong as to make entrepreneurs delusional, blinding them to the reality of a situation?

Drive and determination

Entrepreneurs have drive and determination. They tend to be proactive rather than reactive and more decisive than other people. They are proactive in the sense that they seek out opportunities, they do not just rely on luck – this is part of their nature. They act quickly and decisively to make the most of the opportunity before somebody else does – this is the only way to achieve success. They are often seen as restless and easily bored. They can easily be diverted by the most recent market opportunity and often seem to do things at twice the pace of others, unwilling or unable to wait for others to complete tasks. Patience is certainly not a virtue many possess. They seem to work 24 hours a day and their work becomes their life with little separating the two. It is little wonder that this places family and personal relationships under strain. As a result they can be difficult to work for and can be intolerant of those who do not share their enthusiasm. For example, the late Steve Jobs, founder of Apple, was notoriously difficult to work for and was often accused of being rude and abusive and even bullying in order to get his own way.

Entrepreneurs' drive and determination comes from being highly self-motivated, amounting almost to a driving urge to succeed in their economic goals. This is driven by their exceptionally strong inner need for achievement, far stronger than with the average owner-manager. Running your own business is a lonely affair, without anyone to motivate and encourage you. You work long hours, sometimes for little reward. You therefore need to be self-motivated, committed and determined to succeed. This strong inner drive – what psychologists call type 'A' behaviour – is quite unique and can be seen as almost compulsive behaviour. This is not to say that entrepreneurs are not motivated by other things as well, such as money. But often money is just a badge of their success that allows them to measure their achievement. What drives them is their exceptionally high need to achieve. 'A' types tend to be goal-focused, wanting to get the job done quickly. However, they also tend to try to proactively affect events, focusing on the future when they are often not in control of the present.

An important aspect of this self-motivation is the enjoyment of doing it – enjoyment in the challenges of being entrepreneurial. Entrepreneurs do what they do because they enjoy doing it, not because they are forced to in any way. They actually enjoy their work – often to the exclusion of other things in more ordinary people's lives such as spouse and family. Ultimately entrepreneurs will always regard their business as 'fun', and this is one reason they can be so passionate about it. This provides for them an intrinsic motivation and generally people with an intrinsic motivation outperform those who undertake tasks because of extrinsic motivation – doing something because of an external influence or simply because they 'have to'.

Another important result of this characteristic is that entrepreneurs act first and then learn from the outcomes of the action. They tend to learn by doing. This is logical since time is important in pursuing opportunity. Extensive analysis of a market opportunity is likely to mean that the entrepreneur will not be the first to market. It is part of their incremental approach to decision-making, each small action and its outcomes take them closer to the market opportunity and contribute to the learning process which mitigates the risks they face.

> *'Never sit back and admire what you've achieved, never think you have a divine right to succeed. What you have already done is just the starting point – it's all about the future, about the ability to push the boundaries out as far as they will go and create concepts and answers that don't yet exist.'*
>
> **Derrick Collin**, founder of **Brulines Ltd**
> *The Times* 10 October 2002

> *'I have never had anything to do in my life that provides so many challenges – and there are so many things I still want to do.'*
>
> **Martha Lane Fox**, co-founder of **Lastminute.com**
> *Sunday Times* 17 September 1999

> *'Fun is at the core of the way I like to do business and has informed everything I've done from the outset. More than any other element fun is the secret of Virgin's success.'*
>
> **Richard Branson**

Visionary with good timing

In order to succeed, entrepreneurs need to have a clear vision of what they want to achieve – a vision that stays with them, giving them direction when all around is uncertainty. That is part of the fabric of their motivation. It helps bring others with them, both employees and customers. It is the cornerstone of their motivation and self-confidence. Entrepreneurs combine this vision with the ability to be in the right place at the right time. Timing is everything. Vision with flair links aspiration with a timing that makes attainment a realistic possibility. Innovation that is before its time can lead to business failure. Innovation that is late results in copycat products or services that are unlikely to be outstanding successes. A question constantly asked about successful entrepreneurs is whether their success was due to good luck or good judgement? The honest answer in most cases is probably a bit of both.

'My strength and my weakness is that I am very focused. Some people would describe me as obsessive … The secret is to have vision and then build a plan and follow it. I think you have to do that, otherwise you just flounder about … You change your game plan on the way, as long as you are going somewhere with a purpose …. I wouldn't say it was at the cost of everything else, but when I am at work, I work hard and do long hours – and when I am not at work my mind still tends to be there anyway.'

Mike Peters, founder of **Universal Laboratories**
Sunday Times 11 July 2004

'You must have a vision of what you want to achieve and be very single minded in achieving it. Do not be deflected. Never say die.'

Terry Saddler, founder of **Bioglan Pharma**
The Times 10 October 2001

Willingness to take greater risks and live with greater uncertainty

It is worth stressing that entrepreneurs are willing to take even greater risks and live with even greater uncertainty to grow their business than the ordinary owner-manager. True entrepreneurs thrive on uncertainty and risk. They love pitching their judgment against the odds, although they always believe they will win. This is one reason why so many grow tired of a business after a while and sell it on or bring in professional managers to free them from day-to-day involvement. And do not underestimate the uncertainty and risks they face. Most firms do not grow. It has been estimated that only 26% of new firms ever increase their employment after start-up (Liedholm, 2002).

Storey (2011) views growth almost as a game of chance – a casino environment – and argues that, 'while the operation of business is not solely a matter of chance, in relation to the probability of growth, two consecutive

'People ask me now, "Were you scared?" Sure. Nearly everyone's motivated by fear in some form. I was afraid that I wouldn't do a good enough job, that the business would be a complete failure. However, in my case the downside was limited.'

Michael Dell

'A can-do attitude is essential because obstacles and difficulties are inevitable. I've had many failures in terms of technology, business and even research failures. I really believe entrepreneurship is about being able to face failure, manage failure and succeed after failing. The key is to be able to tell the difference between total failure and setbacks which can be overcome.'

Kiran Mazumdar-Shaw, founder of **Biocon**
BBC News Business 11 April 2011

time periods can be viewed as close to independent events.' He argues that entrepreneurial optimism and self-confidence and chance or simple luck more accurately explain why some businesses grow, whilst others do not, rather than the often cited influences of networking, education, learning, attitudes and prior experience. So, growth businesses need luck. They face high levels of risk that can never be eliminated. Nevertheless most academics and business people do believe risk can be minimized through careful management. Whilst few things are certain, you can indeed play the odds.

🗀 Case with questions Duncan Bannatyne, Dragon

Entrepreneurial character traits

Duncan Bannatyne is probably the best known entrepreneur in the UK because of his appearances on the BBC TV series *Dragons' Den* rather than his achievements as a serial entrepreneur. His life has, however, been a colourful one. He was born in 1949 into a relatively poor family in the town of Clydebank, Scotland. The second of seven children, his father was a foundry-man at the local shipyard. When told that the family could not afford to buy him a bicycle he tried to get a job delivering newspapers for the local newsagents, only to be set the challenge of finding 100 people who wanted a newspaper delivered. By knocking on doors he collected the names, got his newspaper round and eventually was able to buy his bicycle.

Duncan left school at 15 to serve in the Royal Navy. He served for five years before receiving a dishonourable discharge – after 9 months detention – for threatening to throw an officer off a boat landing jetty. He spent his twenties moving from job to job around the UK, including taxi driving and selling ice creams, ending up in Stockton-on-Tees. It was here, in his early 30s, that Duncan's entrepreneurial career started when, using his personal savings, he bought an ice cream van for £450. He built this into a fleet of vans selling 'Duncan's Super Ices'. Even here he showed entrepreneurial flair. He was innovative – he started using a scoop that speeded up serving and made a shape like a smile in the ice cream, which the children loved. He was good at spotting opportunities – he bought one pitch in a local park for £2000 which gave him profits of £18,000 in one summer. He eventually sold the business for £28,000 but not before he had spotted another opportunity. In the 1980s the government started helping unemployed people by paying their rent. Duncan used his profits from the ice cream business to buy and convert houses into bedsits for rent. He rented to the unemployed, so the rents were guaranteed by the government.

Duncan used the proceeds from the sale of the ice cream business – and almost everything else he owned – to move into residential care homes with a business partner. He took out a bank loan, remortgaged his own home and started building up credit card debt. The building costs of the care home were to be financed by a 70% mortgage, but this would only be released when

→

building work was complete and the home was available for occupation. When building costs for the first home spiralled out of control and no more funds were available, he, his partner, friends and family decided to finish the work themselves. The total costs for the care home came to £360,000, and nearly bankrupted Duncan. But the bank then valued the finished home at £600,000, giving a mortgage of £420,000. This meant that Duncan could re-cover his costs, pay off his debts and still have equity to put into the next care home. Using a mix of retained profits and borrowings and by offering shares in the company, he expanded the number of homes.

'When I opened my first nursing home, I had considered newsagents and bed and breakfast establishments but then Margaret Thatcher started to revolutionize care for the elderly... I spotted an opportunity. I came to the conclusion that landlords who owned nursing homes could make a lot of money from the scheme. I took advantage and bought a plot of land with a bank loan and set up my first nursing home in Darlington as soon as I could. When that was full, I paid off all my debts, bought another plot and repeated the process until the portfolio included 45 homes.'

The company was called Quality Care Homes and it was eventually floated on the stock exchange. Duncan also went into children's nurseries with the Just Learning chain. In 1996 he sold Quality Care Homes for £26 million and Just Learning for £22 million. By now, however he had expanded into health clubs with the popular Bannatyne's chain.

'I remember while I was working in the nursing home industry, I injured my knee and used to travel 30 minutes to a local gym in the North East for exercise and physiotherapy. While working out my knee, I also tried to work out the gym's business plan. I knew the membership fees and the number of members and I calculated approximately how much the building cost because I sat and counted the number of tiles on the ceiling and equated them to square footage in my nursing homes. I did the necessary sums and worked out that, if I opened my own health club, I would make a 35%–40% return on capital. It was a no-brainer.'

Daily Telegraph, 30 July 2009

By buying plots of land next to the health club sites Duncan expanded into the hotel business. He worked out that by sharing staffing, reception and other facilities he could save costs and offer hotel residents use of the health club facilities during their stay. So Bannatyne Hotels was born. Duncan has since acquired 26 health clubs from Hilton Hotels, making it the largest independent chain of health clubs in the UK. He has also launched Bar Bannatyne and, in October 2008, opened Bannatyne Spa Hotel in Hastings.

Duncan's wealth is estimated by the *Sunday Times* 2010 Rich List at £320 million, which places him as the 167th richest person in the UK. He is also by far the wealthiest of the Dragons in the Den.

QUESTIONS

1 What character traits of an entrepreneur can you spot in Duncan?

2 How much of Duncan's success do you think is down to luck?

Antecedent influences

Trait theory remains hotly debated. However, whilst we may be born with certain character traits, we are certainly influenced by the social environment that we find ourselves in, for example, our family, ethnic group, education and so on. They influence our values, attitudes and even our behaviours. Research has started to distinguish certain 'antecedent influences' – the entrepreneur's history and experience of life – that impact on these traits (Carter and Cachon, 1988). In many ways the academic research in this area is even more confusing than with personal character traits, and is sometimes contradictory. There are a myriad of claimed influences that are difficult to prove, or indeed, disprove. There are simply too many variables to control. There is further confusion between owner-managers and entrepreneurs. Most of the research is about influences on start-ups. But start-ups comprise both owner-managers and entrepreneurs. However, there is a body of research on antecedent influences on managers of growth businesses which can apply, in the main, to entrepreneurs. The problem here is that some of the influences that seem to influence growth are not those that can be proved to influence start-ups. The only really safe conclusion is that, except for a handful of influences, the research is inconclusive.

'The fear of failure is extremely strong in India, and that's one of the reasons that deter entrepreneurial ideas coming. The society, the neighbors, the family – especially the in-laws – look at failure with a jaundiced eye, and it creates pressure on people either not to start, or to start slower, more conservative businesses. When I mentor young people, especially highly qualified people, I tell them you have nothing to lose. If you don't work after two years, you will get a job that pays you a good salary. Hopefully it will change over the next ten, twenty years.

Krishnan Ganesh, serial entrepreneur and founder of **TutorVista**
BBC News Business 20 May 2011

Education

One influence that comes through on many studies for both start-up and growth is educational attainment. Clearly there are problems measuring educational attainment consistently over studies. However, particularly in the USA, research consistently shows a positive association between the probability of starting up in business and higher educational attainment (Evans and Leighton, 1990). You might indeed question this given that Bill Gates, Steve Jobs and Michael Dell all dropped out of university, but similar research in other countries tends to support the result, albeit less strongly and not consistently. A review of the literature by van der Sluis et al. (2005) found 86 studies that linked education to some measure of entrepreneurial performance such as survival or growth. What is altogether stronger is the relationship between educational attainment and business growth. A review of 23 studies by Storey and Greene (2010) found that 11 linked education and growth and the other 12 were not significant, but none indicated a negative relationship. They pointed to 'education being clearly linked to higher earnings in entrepreneurship.' The numerous

Global Entrepreneurship Monitor (GEM) studies also consistently suggest that people with higher incomes and better education are more likely to be entrepreneurs.

Curiously this is not a widely acknowledged result. It is the stuff of folk lore that the entrepreneur comes from a poor, deprived background and has little formal education. In fact some writers have gone further and claimed that 'anecdotal evidence' suggests that too much education can discourage entrepreneurship (Bolton and Thompson, 2000). But times are changing and if you ask venture capitalists why they think certain firms will grow rather than others, they will tell you that they are looking for background and track record in the firm's management, and education counts. It is also particularly true of the new generation of entrepreneurs pursuing internet opportunities.

The rationale for the relationship might be two-fold. Firstly, educational attainment might provide the basis for better learning through life, enabling entrepreneurs to deal better with business problems and giving them a greater openness and more outward orientation. Secondly, it might give them higher earning expectations that can only be attained by growing the business. What is more, it might also give them greater confidence in dealing with customers and other business professionals. It is also worth observing that those firms accessing 'knowledge spillovers', such as University Science Parks, have been shown to exhibit superior performance (Audretsch et al., 2006). Ability to learn and knowledge are important.

Partnering and age

In a review of the research, Storey and Greene (op. cit.) concluded that there were two further factors that are positively correlated with growth businesses. Firstly, growth companies are more likely to be set up by groups rather than individuals and these groups share in the ownership and therefore the success (or failure) of the business. Secondly, middle-aged owners are more likely to be associated with growth companies than younger or older entrepreneurs. Age brings experience and knowledge. It also brings an invaluable network of relationships and contacts. Interestingly, partnering with groups of people to set up a business can bring the same advantages. Knowledge, experience, networks and relationships are important.

> 'Persevere and never see anything as failure. Look at what you can learn from something that does not go the way you want. It's all about attitude. I do not believe in failure. I have needed sheer determination – although my shareholders would probably describe it as stubbornness.'
>
> **Elizabeth Gooch**, founder of **EG Solutions**
> *Sunday Times* 23 November 2008

Emigration and ethnicity

Observation tells us that immigration to a foreign country is another influence on start-up (Harper, 1985). Saxenian (2000) observed that one-quarter of all high-tech start-ups in Silicon Valley had chief executives who were from India or China and came to the USA to study. Evidence about

🗂 Case insight Kenyan Asians

Entrepreneurial immigrants

It is an astonishing fact that six of the most successful wholesale companies supplying drugs and medicines to Britain's retail pharmacies and hospitals were founded by Kenyan Asians now in their fifties. All left poverty in Kenya to come to Britain in the late 1960s and early 1970s where they went to college to achieve pharmacy qualifications, generally supporting themselves with menial part-time jobs. Then they set up their own retail pharmacy before building their much bigger wholesale businesses. All are now multi-millionaires.

Bharat Shah has built up the family firm of **Sigma Pharmaceuticals**. It sells some 100 generic medicines and also deals in parallel imports – whereby drugs are bought in a country where wholesale prices are much lower and repackaged for a country where the price is higher. Two of his brothers work in the business – Manish, who is an accountant, and Kamal, who works in operations. His son Halul runs retail pharmacies.

Bharat and **Ketan Mehta** founded **Necessity Supplies** in 1986. It also sells generic drugs and deals in parallel imports. **Vijay** and **Bikhu Patel** have built up **Waymade Healthcare** into a business with 700 employees. They have ambitions to turn the company into a 'mini-Glaxo' and in 2003 launched Amdipham to develop medicines that are too small for the big pharmaceuticals.

Ravi Karia founded **Chemilines** in 1986. It claims to be one of Britain's fastest growing companies.

Naresh Shah founded **Jumbogate** with his wife Shweta in 1982. Whilst still involved in retailing, the business is predominantly wholesale.

Navin Engineer came to London with only £75 in his pocket in 1969 at the age of 16 to live with his aunt. He worked in a Wimpy burger restaurant in Oxford Street in the evenings to support himself through sixth form and then the London School of Pharmacy. On graduation he took a job with Boots, the retail chemist. Eventually he opened his own pharmacy in Chertsey, Surrey, working long hours to make money to buy other pharmacies. By 1999 he had 14 such shops and, when the German group GEHE offered him £12 million for the retail chain, he decided to take it. He invested most of the proceeds in his much smaller wholesale business. He bought a range of small-turnover branded pharmaceuticals from bigger companies, switched production to established factories in Eastern Europe and the Far East, and realized cost savings as profit. He then went into generic medicines – copies of branded drugs produced after the expiry of their patent. This involves checking patents and making certain the drug can be developed without infringing the patent. At the same time regulatory authorities have to be satisfied. His company, **Chemidex**, is now a wholesaler of both branded and generic medicines including treatments for gout, depression and an antibiotic for anthrax.

ethnicity, as opposed to immigration, however is mixed. Self-employment rates in the UK for ethnic minorities are not uniform. Those for Asians (Indian, Pakistani, Bangladeshi etc.) and Chinese are higher than those for white males, whilst those for black African and black Caribbean are lower, typically more comparable to white women (Annual Population Survey, 2004). There are some 200,000 Asian-owned businesses in the UK, collectively punching above their weight in their contribution to the economy. Asians are recognized as the most likely ethnic minority group in the UK to become entrepreneurs and are represented across all sectors of business. One reason for the high self-employment rate for Asians compared black African and black Caribbean appears to be family background and expectations. Traditionally Asian families have valued the independence of self-employment. This seems to be changing, with second generation Asians in the UK being encouraged to enter more traditional professions. However, one of the problems is that these ethnic groups are no longer homogeneous and there is a complex set of family, community and societal influences at play.

Other influences

There are other influences, most of which have few implications for the entrepreneurial organization. Self-employment normally needs a trigger. Unemployment is a strong push into self-employment but entrepreneurial growth businesses are more likely to set up for more positive motives such as the need for independence, achievement etc. (Abdesselam et al., 1999; Storey and Greene, op. cit.). It is possible that having a parent who was previously self-employed is more likely to lead a person to set up his or her own firm (Stanworth et al., 1989). Conversely, women are less likely to start a business than men and there is consistent research support that their businesses are likely to perform less well, however measured – turnover, profit or job creation (Cliff, 1998; Kalleberg and Leicht, 1991; Rosa et al., 1996). More recent data from the Global Entrepreneurship Monitor (GEM, 2009) showed that in most high income countries, men are about twice as likely to be entrepreneurially active as women.

Cognitive theory

Cognitive theory shifts the emphasis from the individual towards the situations that lead to entrepreneurial behaviour. In particular it seeks to understand how people think and react in different situations. It is looking at cognitive heuristics – mental models, shortcuts or 'rules of thumb' – that influence entrepreneurial behaviour. Some strands of cognitive theory reinforce ideas about how traits may influence behaviour.

One strand of cognitive theory reinforces at least three elements of trait theory. Chen et al. (1998) set out the idea that successful entrepreneurs possess high levels of *self-efficacy*. Self-efficacy is 'the strength of an individual's belief that he or she is capable of successfully performing the roles and tasks of an entrepreneur'. Clearly this is exhibited by the self-confidence of entrepreneurs referred to in the previous section, but it is also created by their internal locus of control and rooted firmly in their need for achievement. It is therefore more than just self-confidence. Chen et al. argue that it is self-efficacy that motivates entrepreneurs and gives them the dogged determination to persist in the face of adversity when others just give in. With this characteristic entrepreneurs become more objective and analytical and attribute any failure to outside factors such as insufficient effort or poor knowledge. They argue that self-efficacy is affected by a person's previous experiences – success breeds success, failure breeds failure. And people can therefore be trained to change their beliefs.

Delmar (2000) outlines two other cognitive concepts. *Intrinsic motivation* suggests that people who undertake tasks for their own sake perform better than those motivated by external factors. This strong inner drive – type 'A' behaviour – underpins the drive and determination entrepreneurs have. *Intentionality* suggests that people who intend to do things are more likely to do them than people who do not. This is the result of entrepreneurs' internal locus of control and is what underpins both their vision and their drive and determination. Other studies underline the importance of 'passion' and 'tenacity' in achieving outstanding performance (Baum et al., 2001; Baum and Locke, 2004).

Cognitive theory underlines the fact that an entrepreneurial organization *can* be created, with individuals within it shaped by the environment it creates and the experiences it faces – part culture, part structure. However, it also implies that the organization itself must deal with the environmental context in which it is placed – commercial, political and economic. It also underlines the complexity of the influences on individuals, many of which are outside the control of the organization – family, race, religion, nationality. Developing the entrepreneurial organization is an imprecise science.

Relationships and networks

Entrepreneurs have a particular and characteristic approach to doing business and managing an organization. At the core of this is the development of relationships – with customers, staff, suppliers and all the stakeholders in the business. It is this personal touch that distinguishes them from the faceless, grey-suited managers in large companies. Relationships are based on trust, self-interest and reciprocity (Dubini and Aldrich, 1991; Larson, 1992). They are strengthened by increased frequency and depth of interaction. These relationships build into an invaluable network of contacts and goodwill that can be used whenever the firm needs to change or do something just a little more risky than the average firm.

Entrepreneurs start to develop their relationship-building skills at the inception of the business. They need resources to start up but often have to work hard to gain the credibility to obtain money from a banker or venture capitalist. And there are other less obvious needs. They need customers, suppliers, perhaps employees and a landlord. The process of assembling these resources is a difficult one and is crucially dependent on one factor – credibility. So how does the entrepreneur establish this credibility? Education and track record are important. Demonstrating achievements, particularly in the same industry as the start-up, counts for a lot. But networks of strong personal relationship with friends and commercial contacts can be vitally important. They can deliver the first customer – someone who already trusts the entrepreneur to deliver. They might yield someone willing to provide low-cost or free office space. They might even provide the cash that the banker is so reluctant to provide. Networks can also provide professional advice and opinion, often without charge. Research indicates that strong networks influence not only new firms' start-up but also their growth prospects (Dubini and Aldrich, op. cit.).

> 'Contacts are important but you have to get out there and meet people. It can be difficult when you are absorbed in running a business. But there is always something to learn from meeting someone new and a lot to learn from meeting someone old. The right contacts can become an invaluable source of learning as well as an inspiration and support.'
>
> **Jonathan Elvidge**, founder of **Gadget Shop**
> *The Times* 6 July 2002

After start-up, the entrepreneur can use strong relationships to help sell their product or service. Again this is born out of necessity, because of problems of credibility and lack of cash to spend on the more conventional tools of the marketing mix such as advertising and promotion. This has been christened 'relationship marketing', which can be contrasted to the more traditional transaction marketing mainly practised by larger companies. Supporters of this approach, long used by small firms, believe that it can deliver sustainable customer loyalty (Webster, 1992). The two approaches are contrasted in Table 2.1.

Personal relationships become more important as the business grows. Entrepreneurs use external networks to obtain information and knowledge

T 2.1 Relationship vs. transactional marketing

Relationship marketing	Transactional marketing
▷ Encourages close, frequent customer contact	▷ Limited contact
▷ Encourages repeat sales	▷ Orientated towards single purchase
▷ Focus on customer service	▷ Limited customer service
▷ Focus on value to the customer	▷ Focus on product/service benefits
▷ Focus on quality of total offering	▷ Focus on quality of product
▷ Focus on long-term performance	▷ Focus on short-term performance

that feeds into their decision-making. Networks blur the boundaries of the firm, extending them to a community of interest rather than restricting them to a legal or economic entity, which is important for small firms. Strong extended networks mean not only resources but also knowledge and risks can be shared across economic units. It is an important way for successful entrepreneurs to seek out opportunities, pool the resources needed to exploit them and mitigate the associated risks.

'Dell is very much a relationship orientated company ... how we communicate and partner with our employees and customers. But our commitment doesn't stop there. Our willingness and ability to partner to achieve our common goals is perhaps seen in its purest form in how we forge strong alliances with our suppliers ... As a small start-up, we didn't have the money to build the components ourselves ... but we actually had an option: to buy components from the specialists, leveraging the investment they had made and allowing us to focus on what we did best – designing and delivering solutions and systems directly to customers. In forging these early alliances with suppliers, we created exactly the right strategy for a fast-growing company.'
Michael Dell

Organization structure

Entrepreneurs also tend to manage staff by developing strong personal relationships. It underpins their approach to management. Their reliance on informal relationships to manage their firm is reflected in the typical organization structure they adopt. Most clearly seen at start-up, this has been likened to the spider's web (Figure 2.4A). The entrepreneur sits at the centre of the web with each new member of staff reporting to him or her. Their management style tends to be informal, one of direct supervision. Just as entrepreneurs prefer informal marketing techniques, building on relationships, they prefer informal organization structures and influences rather than rigid rules and job definitions. They persuade and cajole employees, showing them how to do things on a one-to-one basis, rather than having prescribed tasks. They rely on building a personal relationship. After all, the business is growing rapidly and there are no precedents to go by. The future is uncertain, so flexibility is the key. The pace of change probably means that rigid structures would be out of date quickly. What is more, in a small firm everybody has to be prepared to do other people's jobs because there is no cover, no slack in

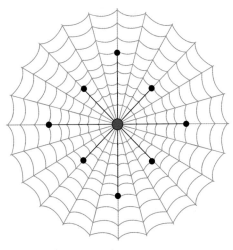

Formal reporting lines ————

F 2.4A An entrepreneur's organizational web

the system if, for example, someone goes off sick. It is also perfectly flat and therefore efficient – overheads are reduced – and it is responsive – communication times are minimized. This is the typical small, entrepreneurial structure with the entrepreneur leading by example and communicating directly. It is motivating and works – up to a certain size – with the right person as leader.

However, even as the entrepreneur tries to delegate, appointing new staff to report to existing managers, their strong internal locus of control makes them inclined to meddle. Consequently new employees often find an informal reporting line to the entrepreneur, short-circuiting the manager or supervisor they are supposed to report to (Figure 2.4B). The root cause of this problem lies in the entrepreneurial character and in particular the strong need for control that can exhibit itself in some entrepreneurs. Derek du Toit (1980), an entrepreneur himself, said that 'an entrepreneur who starts his own business generally does so because he is a difficult employee.' He probably finds it difficult to be in the alternating dominant and then submissive role so often asked of middle management. He hates being told what to do

A growing organizational web

Formal reporting lines   ———

Informal reporting lines   - - - - - -

and wants to tell everybody what to do. He also believes he can do the job better than others, which may be true, but he must find a way of working through others if the business is to grow successfully. Kets de Vries (op. cit.) was probably the first to argue that these traits can lead to entrepreneurs wanting to over-control their business – becoming 'control freaks'. This is not such a problem in micro businesses, where the owner-managers do everything themselves anyway, where their business is their life and their life is the business. Indeed it can be a virtue – making certain everything gets done properly. However, as the business grows this characteristic starts to be a problem. The danger is that this creates frustration, resentment and an unwillingness to accept responsibility in managers – sometimes called 'infantilization'. Why should they take responsibility when their decisions are likely to be questioned or reversed, or when staff supposedly reporting to them are constantly being supervised by the entrepreneur?

Postulated by Northcote Parkinson and now called 'Parkinson's Coefficient of Inefficiency', the optimum *inefficient* number of staff this informal structure will support can be calculated mathematically as 21. So, beyond a certain size, more formal organization structures are required. However, the spider's web remains very efficient for a small number of people. The entrepreneurial firm faces the challenge of maintaining close personal relationships with staff and flexible job structures – which are motivating and effective in an uncertain environment – whilst avoiding the dangers of over-control and 'infantilization'.

Decision-making and strategy development

Entrepreneurs approach decision-making and strategy development differently from most people. They are often seen as being intuitive, almost whimsical, in their decision-making. True, economists find it difficult to understand and to model their approach. It certainly does not fit well into 'logical' economic models such as discounted cash flow. The reason lies at the heart of any entrepreneurial venture – the greater degree of risk and uncertainty it faces. The result is a different approach to developing strategy and making decisions that is just as logical but little understood.

The first thing to realize is that entrepreneurs may not use the jargon or established frameworks of strategy. Many do not produce business plans. Indeed a study by Bhidé (2000) found that only 28% of a sample of Inc. 500 companies completed a formal business plan. Nevertheless, entrepreneurs instinctively arrive at the right decision. There is nothing wrong with this. The words and frameworks we might use in strategic analysis merely give meaning and logic to what they do. Many excellent musicians or athletes were not taught. They picked up the skills instinctively – although they developed them through training and exercise. The second point is that entrepreneurs often claim to have achieved their success through luck rather than strategy. Never underestimate luck. We all need it and it plays a part, but remember that entrepreneurs have a strong internal locus of control which means that, whilst they may believe in luck, they do not believe in fate. They believe they can, and will, shape their own destinies and that may mean working to create more opportunities than most people. By creating more strategic options and opportunities they improve their chances of successfully pursuing at least one. Make no mistake – entrepreneurs to a large extent create their own luck.

One well documented characteristic of owner-managers, particularly in Britain, is their apparent short-term approach to business decision-making, especially investment and financing (Burns and Whitehouse, 1995a, 1995b). This reflects their incremental approach to decision-making, despite a strong long-term vision, in an uncertain environment. It is also part of a wide-ranging approach to risk mitigation. For example, successful entrepreneurs tend to keep fixed costs as low as possible, for example by sub-contracting some activities. They tend to commit costs only after the opportunity has proved to be real, which may be prudent and reflect their resource limits but then they run the risk of losing first mover advantage in the market place – a difficult judgment call. Frequently, therefore, they will experiment with a 'limited' launch into the market and learn from this. They also view an asset as a liability rather than just an asset in the balance-sheet sense, meaning that it may limit the flexibility that they need and commit them to a course of action that may prove unsound. Successful entrepreneurs find ways of reconciling these issues – ways of developing strategy without over-committing to one course of action and ways of minimizing their investment in resources. They start with the resources they can afford to lose and then move forward.

The way entrepreneurs develop strategy is just as important as their approach to decision-making. It is one of their defining characteristics, more important than the actual strategies they adopt. For them strategies evolve on a step-by-step basis. If one step works then the next is taken. At the same time entrepreneurs will keep as many options open as possible, because they realize that the outcome of any action is very uncertain. Whilst strategy can be developed in a systematic, almost mechanistic, manner many entrepreneurs develop strategy instinctively and intuitively – often they call it 'gut feel'. The 'science of muddling through' (Lindblom, 1959) is, in fact, as old as strategy itself. The implications of this for strategy were developed by Mintzberg (1978) who contrasted what he called 'emergent' strategy development with the text-book approach which he called 'deliberate'. As he put it, with emergent strategy 'the strategy-making process is characterized by reactive solutions to existing problems ... The adaptive organization makes its decisions in incremental, serial steps.' In a later work Mintzberg et al. (1998) went on to characterize the 'entrepreneurial school' of strategy development, which focused 'exclusively on the single leader' – the entrepreneur.

> *'The ideal business has no fixed overheads, commission only sales, large volume and low overheads.'*
> **David Speakman**, founder of **Travel Counsellors**
> *Sunday Times* 6 December 1998

And here we recognize reflections of how the entrepreneur, in their spider's web of influence, approaches decision-making in a risky, uncertain and rapidly changing environment – through intuition, judgement, wisdom, experience and insight with holistic knowledge of operations and a strong vision of what they want to achieve. And there is nothing wrong with strategy that is emergent, incremental and adaptive. Indeed it is an approach that resonates in complexity theory. However, that does not mean that strategy cannot be analyzed, managed and controlled and strategic frameworks can be an aid in doing that. These frameworks can help entrepreneurs to strategize – to think about the future and analyze their options. Indeed, many businesspeople have gone so far as to suggest that formalized strategic planning is inappropriate in today's changing environment. What is needed instead is more

> *'In leadership, it's important to be intuitive, but not at the expense of facts. Without the right data to back it up, emotion-based decision making during difficult times will inevitably lead a company into greater danger.'*
> **Michael Dell**

> *'You just need to look at where Virgin is now to see that business is a fluid, changing substance. As far as I'm concerned, the company will never stand still. It has always been a mutating, indefinable thing and the past few years have demonstrated that.'*
> **Richard Branson**

strategizing and the development of strategic options – options that lead the firm in the general direction it wants to go – with decisions on which option to select depending upon market conditions and opportunities (Mathewson, 2000). The greater the number of strategic options open to the firm, the safer it is in an uncertain environment.

One interesting research study indicates that the strategy development process for growing firms actually changes from emergent to deliberate as they go through recurrent crises followed by periods of consolidation (McCarthy and Leavy, 2000). The study suggests that the strategy development process is *both* deliberate and emergent in nature. Over time, strategy formation follows a phase pattern, moving from an early fluid phase to a more defined phase, usually triggered by a crisis or defining episode, so that the degree of deliberateness is also a function of history, with firms oscillating between emergent strategy development, when learning is taking place, and deliberate planning modes over time. These crises force the entrepreneur to change their preconceptions and 'unlearn' bad habits or routines ahead of learning new ones (Cope, 2005). Rather than entrepreneurs having only one style, they would seem to adopt both, depending on circumstances. In this way the well-documented process of growth to crisis to consolidation parallels a process of emergent to deliberate and back to emergent strategy formulation, represented in Figure 2.5.

'If you set yourself goals that are really high and keep working to achieve them, then success should be possible. Just look back and say I gave it my best shot.'

David Darling, founder **Codemaster**
The Times 10 October 2002

F 2.5 Strategy formulation cycle

Successful entrepreneurs therefore have a strong *vision* and this helps them build a *strategic intent* for the organization that allows them to reconcile where they are with where they want to be, even when the path to achieve this vision is not clear. They continually *strategize* and that means that strategy will often be seen as *emergent*. However, there are always *strategic options* that they have thought through and developed. Decision-making is then incremental, based upon opportunistic circumstances at the time.

Effectual reasoning

Support for these conclusions about entrepreneurs' management methods comes from a research study of how 27 of the USA's most successful entrepreneurs approached business decisions (Sarasvathy, 2001). The subjects all had at least 15 years of entrepreneurial experience, including successes and failures, and had taken at least one company public. They were presented with a case study about a hypothetical start-up with the founder facing 10 decisions. The rationale for these decisions was then explored in more detail. Some years later the same research was conducted on a group of successful professional managers in large organizations, allowing contrasts to be made.

The conclusion was that the entrepreneurs relied upon something that was christened 'effectual reasoning' or 'effectuation' – quite in contrast to the causal or deductive reasoning used by the professional executives. Effectuation has gained popularity by contrasting itself with what might be called traditional principles of management (Read et al., 2011). Sarasvathy (op. cit.) came to five main conclusions about how successful entrepreneurs approach decision-making in their uncertain, rapidly changing environment.

1 Whilst the executives set goals and sought to achieve them sequentially and logically, the entrepreneurs' goals were broad and evolving, based on whatever personal strengths and resources they had, creatively reacting to contingencies as they occurred – reflecting the approach to strategy development outlined in the last section. They start with the resources they have and go to market quickly. They do not wait for perfect knowledge or the perfect opportunity. They learn by doing.

2 Whilst executives wanted to research opportunities and assess potential return before committing resources, entrepreneurs were far more inclined to go to market as quickly and cheaply as possible and assess market demand from that – an approach labelled 'affordable loss' – and reflecting their approach to learning and risk minimization outlined earlier. They set an 'affordable loss', evaluating opportunities based upon whether that loss was acceptable, rather than trying to evaluate the attractiveness of the predictable upside.

3 They did not like extensive, formal research and planning, particularly traditional market research. This was explained by entrepreneurs' lack of belief that the future was predictable (and that the upside could be evaluated), preferring instead to believe in their own ability to obtain the information needed to react quickly to changing circumstances. They believed that, while they could not predict the future, they could control it (internal locus of control) or, more precisely, 'recognize, respond to, and reshape opportunities as they develop'. Entrepreneurs use uncertainty to their advantage by developing contingencies and remaining flexible rather than slavishly sticking to existing goals. They do not worry about formal strategic planning. However, it was significant that they did adopt more formal structures as their businesses grew and, as the study put it, they became both 'causal as well as effectual thinkers', mirroring the cycle between deliberate and emergent strategy development.

4 Also prominent was the entrepreneurs' propensity to partner with stakeholders – customers, suppliers and advisors – to help them shape the business, reflecting the importance of building relationships. They use networks of partnerships to generate knowledge, leverage resources and make the future become the reality. By way of contrast, the executives tended to know exactly where they wanted to go and then follow that set path without seeking partnerships.

5 It was noticeable also that the entrepreneurs were less concerned about competitors than the executives. This might be explained in terms of their inherent self-confidence but the study explained it in terms of them seeing themselves as on the fringe of a market or creating an entirely new market through some sort of disruptive innovation. They believed they were different or better than competitors in a way that gave them a differential advantage.

'We had to learn the basic steps that most companies, which grow and mature more slowly, learn when they are much smaller in size. We were moving in the right direction with our emphasis on liquidity, profitability and growth. But we were also challenged by a cultural issue. We had created an atmosphere in which we focused on growth … We had to shift the focus away from an external orientation to one that strengthened our company internally. For us growing up meant figuring out a way to combine our signature informal, entrepreneurial style and want-to attitude with the can-do capabilities that would allow us to develop as a company. It meant incorporating into our everyday structures the valuable lessons we'd begun to learn using P&Ls [profit and loss accounts]. It meant focusing our employees to think in terms of shareholder value. It meant respecting the three golden rules at Dell:

1. Disdain inventory.

2. Always listen to the customer.

3. Never sell indirect.'

Michael Dell

The challenges of growth

As the business grows entrepreneurs face challenges and problems as the nature of the organization changes. As it changes, they too need to change and adapt. The more rapid the growth, the more difficult this is. Entrepreneurs need to metamorphosize into entrepreneurial leaders and we can learn from the problems they face. They need to change the way they operate – recruit reliable managers, delegate to them and control and monitor their performance. The organization must become more formal, but, if it wishes to retain its entrepreneurial character, without becoming more bureaucratic. And all of these changes need to be properly managed if the firm is to grow successfully. It is little wonder that so few firms grow to any size. Some entrepreneurs even decide not to grow their business because they realize they cannot manage these changes or because they do not want to change the way they do business.

Growth models seek to describe the changes that the entrepreneur faces and, by inference, how the changes need to be managed. They give us an insight into what a successful entrepreneurial firm might look like. One of the most widely used models was developed by Greiner (1972). This is shown in Figure 2.6. It offers a framework for considering the development of a business, but more particularly the managerial challenges facing the founder. Each phase of growth is followed by a crisis that necessitates a change in the way the founder manages the business if it is to move on and continue to grow. If the crisis cannot be overcome then it is possible that the business might fail – replicating the process of growth/crisis/ consolidation illustrated also in Figure 2.5. The length of time it takes to go through each phase depends on the industry in which the company operates. In fast-growing industries, growth periods are relatively short; in slower-growth industries they tend to be longer. Each evolutionary phase requires a particular management style or emphasis to achieve growth. Each revolutionary period presents a management problem to overcome.

Crisis of leadership Growth initially comes through entrepreneurial creativity. However, this constant seeking out of new opportunities and the development of innovative ways of doing things leads to a crisis of leadership. Staff, financiers and even customers increasingly fail to understand the focus of the business – where it is going, what it is selling – and resources become spread too thinly to follow through effectively on any single commercial opportunity. Growth then comes from the direction given by effective leadership. The entrepreneur becomes a leader, giving the direction the business needs.

Crisis of autonomy Entrepreneurs are short of cash and have a strong internal locus of control, which means there is a danger that, as the business grows, they will try to do everything themselves – the business is a one-man-band. The next crisis is therefore one of autonomy. It will only be addressed by putting an effective management team in place and delegating work to it.

Crisis of control Entrepreneurs are, typically, not interested in the detail of controlling a business. There is therefore a danger that delegation becomes an abdication of responsibility and, as the firm continues to grow, there is a loss of proper control. Growth then comes from effective coordination of management and its work force. Controls are in place and are working effectively.

Crisis of bureaucracy By this stage the firm will have ceased to have many of the characteristics of an owner-managed firm because there are set procedures and policies for doing things. The danger now is that it might lose its entrepreneurial drive and the next crisis it might face is one of red tape or bureaucracy. Greiner says this can only be overcome by collaboration – making people work together through a sense of mission or purpose rather than by reference to a rule book.

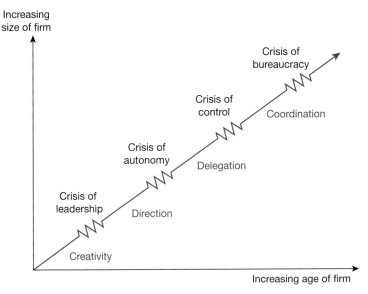

Increasing
size of firm

Crisis of
bureaucracy

Crisis of
control

Coordination

Crisis of
autonomy

Delegation

Crisis of
leadership

Direction

Creativity

Increasing age of firm

Source: Greiner, L.E. (1972) 'Evolution and Revolution as Organizations Grow', *Harvard Business Review*, 50, July–August: 55–67

F 2.6 Greiner's growth model

Griener's model suggests that the challenges the entrepreneur faces as the business grows are:

▷ To give direction through leadership;
▷ To delegate and encourage team-working;
▷ To coordinate decision-making through appropriate organizational structures and culture that encourage collaboration;
▷ To balance the need for autonomy and control, avoiding at all costs too much red-tape which would signal that the organization is becoming too bureaucratic.

These challenges must be addressed in the architecture of the entrepreneurial firm.

Other models emphasize the shift in the personal skills required of entrepreneurs as the business grows – away from their operational abilities towards their strategic and management abilities (Burns 1996; Churchill and Lewis, 1983). They also underline the changing management style needed as the organization grows, with the increasing importance of developing a management team and more conventional or formal structures. However, none of these models outlines what precisely these structures should be, and all too often 'conventional' structures are seen as hindering entrepreneurship in larger organizations. They also do not explain what constitutes effective leadership or how you achieve coordinated, collaborative delegation and how you balance the need for autonomy and control. These are the issues addressed in this book.

🛄 Case with questions Steve Jobs and Apple

Entrepreneurial character traits

Steve Jobs died on 5 October 2011, aged 56, of pancreatic cancer. He was the epitome of an entrepreneurial leader who revolutionized three industries. With Steve Wozniak, he co-founded Apple in 1976. Apple revolutionized the computer industry through its innovative designs; the Macintosh with its computer mouse, the iPod with its click wheel and the iPhone with its 'user-interface'. Apple also revolutionized the way that digital content, in particular music, could be sold rather than pirated. Through Jobs' animation studio, Pixar, films such as *Toy Story* (1995) completely changed our ideas about how films could use computer generated animations. And yet he was not an inventor. He was the bridge between the business idea and the market place – the entrepreneur. Not only did he start up Apple, he was also forced out of it in 1985 after an acrimonious board room battle. He returned in 1997 to turn it around from near bankruptcy and, by 2011, had created the second most valuable company in the world, measured by market capitalization, with a cash mountain of some $80 billion.

The story of Steve Jobs is the story of a Silicon Valley hero. Born to a Syrian father and an American mother in San Francisco, he was adopted by a blue-collar couple and grew up in Mountain View, a suburb of San Francisco close to what is now known as Silicon Valley. The fact that he was put up for adoption by his birth parents was said to have left a deep scar. Whilst at high school, he met Steve Wozniak working on a summer job with Hewlett-Packard in Palo Alto. He left high school, reluctantly going to Reed, an expensive liberal arts college in Portland, Oregon, but failed to attend his required classes and dropped out after one term. He grew his hair and did the sort of things that drop-outs at the time did, including visiting a guru in India. His engagement with Zen Buddhism was to become ingrained in his personality with a focus on stark, minimalist aesthetics and a belief in intuition. However, he never achieved the inner peace associated with Zen Buddhism, rather always being driven by the particular challenges facing him at the time.

It was his friend, Steve Wozniak, who had the talent for electronics and designing circuits with the minimum number of chips, and who built the first Apple computer. At the time Wozniak was working for Hewlett-Packard and Jobs for Atari. Apple I was a hobbyist machine, assembled by hand in Steve Jobs' parents' home and housed in a wooden box. The couple sold many of their personal possessions to get the start-up finance that was needed. Jobs' role was that of the businessman, the marketeer who persuaded the local store to order 50, and then persuaded the local electrical store to give him 30 days credit on the parts to build them. He also eventually persuaded Mike Markkula, a former Intel employee, to invest in the company and become its first chief executive. What followed was the beautifully designed, classic Apple II with its built-in color graphics, easily accessible expansion slots and ability to connect to a TV set. Its simple design, understandable instruction manual and consumer-friendly advertising guaranteed it success until the launch of the IBM PC. Apple went public in 1980 with a market valuation of $1.8 billion only four years after being launched.

Steve Wozniak retired from Apple one year later following a serious plane accident. Jobs took over the development of the Apple II's successor, the Apple Macintosh. The Mac was intended to be the first mass-market, closed-box computer based on the now ubiquitous mouse and a graphic user interface. These ideas were not new. They were developed by scientists at Xerox's Palo Alto Research Center (PARC) and had been tried out in high priced computers (Xerox Star and Apple Lisa), without commercial success. The launch of the Mac was the start of what became the signature Steve Jobs product launch. He appeared on stage with Bill Gates promising

Mac versions of Word, Excel and PowerPoint. There were 20-page advertisements in major US magazines. But it was the TV commercial that had the biggest impact. Shown in the USA during the 1984 Super Bowl, it associated IBM with George Orwell's *1984* Big Brother. Despite the dramatic launch, the Mac failed to sell in the expected volumes, signalling the start of Apple's decline. In 1985 it closed three of its six factories, laying off 1200 employees. In the same year Steve Jobs was forced to leave Apple and in 1987 the Mac II was launched as a conventional three-piece computer system.

Jobs resented being thrown out of Apple, particularly by someone he had recruited two years earlier to the job of Chief Executive Officer – John Sculley, formerly president of PepsiCo. He took several Apple employees with him and set up another company called NeXT, to produce a powerful Unix workstation targeted at business and universities. It was very expensive and flopped, so the company switched to selling the operating systems, again without much success.

Steve Jobs bought the company that became Pixar in 1986 from Lucasfilm. Initially, the company produced expensive computer hardware. The core product was the Pixar Image Computer, a system primarily marketed to government agencies and the medical market, but it never sold particularly well. The company struggled for years and, in an effort to demonstrate its capabilities, Pixar began producing computer-animated commercials. This lead to a deal in 1991 with the Walt Disney Corporation to produce three computer-animated films, the first of which was the ground-breaking *Toy Story*. Until this point Pixar had been in decline, having already sold off its hardware operations. Released in 1995, *Toy Story* was an outstanding box-office success, which was just as well because, as late as 1994, Jobs had considered selling off Pixar. After a series of highly successful, award-winning films such as *A Bug's Life* (1998), *Toy Story 2* (1999), *Monsters Inc.* (2001), *Finding Nemo* (2003) and *The Incredibles*

(2004), the Walt Disney Company eventually bought Pixar in 2006 at a valuation of $7.4 billion, making Jobs the largest shareholder in Disney.

Meanwhile the PC market was again transformed in 1995 by the launch of Microsoft Windows 95 which really popularized the mouse and the graphic user interface. Apple was struggling to survive and the new Mac OS software development was not working. It was managed by committees and had lost its innovative flair. Apple knew it needed to buy in a new operating system, and fast, so it turned to Steve Jobs and paid a much-inflated price to buy NeXT. In reality this turned out to be a reverse take-over and Jobs took over as 'interim CEO' in 1997.

Jobs killed off weak products and simplified the product lines. He adapted NeXT's NextStep operating system to become the Mac OS X operating system. He also started the process of creating the distinctive eye-catching Apple designs with the teardrop shaped iMac, followed by the portable iBook. Explaining himself to the 1997 meeting of the Apple Worldwide Developers Association, Jobs said:

> 'Focusing is about saying no ... and the result of that focus is going to be some really great products where the total is much greater than the sum of the parts ... One of the things I've always found is that you've got to start with the customer experience and work backwards to the technology and try to figure out where you are going to try to sell it. I've made this mistake probably more than anyone else in this room, and I've got the scar tissue to prove it, and I know that it's the case.'

But Apple's fortunes were really transformed when Jobs completely changed direction and launched the iPod in 2001, although it was the launch of the iTunes music store in 2003 that made the iPod popular. It transformed the music industry, which was facing a decline in CD sales as more and more

→

music was being pirated through online sites like Napster, by allowing music to be easily downloaded, but at a price. Apple started on its growth path, which was reinforced in 2007 by its launch of the iPhone – a clever but expensive combination of cell phone, iPod and internet device. This was followed in 2010 by the iPad – a tablet computer without a physical keyboard. By 2011 the iPad was selling more than Macintosh.

Of course, Jobs was at the right place at the right time to capitalize on developments in computing and the change from analogue to digital technologies. But he shaped these developments to appeal to customers. The distinctive feature about Apple products was never the innovation – that normally came from elsewhere – but rather the application of an innovation to make the product easier and simpler to use, whether it be the physical product design or applications such as iTunes. All Apple products also enjoy a distinctive, eye-catching design. And they are never cheap. They were also supported by massive marketing campaigns with Jobs, dressed in black turtle neck, jeans and trainers, launching products himself with carefully choreographed, pseudo-religious stage presentations (known as 'Stevenote') that attracted adoring fans and received massive world-wide press coverage. In many people's eyes Jobs enjoyed the status of a rock star. At the same time the Apple brand had become iconic.

And yet many of Jobs' personal character traits did not endear him to others. He was a perfectionist who was highly secretive and had, at the very least, what might be described as a hard-driving management style. In 1993 *Fortune* magazine placed him on the list of America's Toughest Bosses for his time at NeXT, quoting cofounder Daniel Lewin as saying: 'The highs were unbelievable ... but the lows were unimaginable' (18 October 1993). Fourteen years later it called him 'one of Silicon Valley's leading egomaniacs' (19 March 2007). Jobs was notorious for micromanaging things from the design of

new products to the chips they used. In his obituary, the *Daily Telegraph* (6 October 2011) claimed he was 'almost pathologically controlling' when it came to dealing with news reporters and the press, actively trying to stifle any reports that might seem critical of himself or Apple. It went on to reveal some elements of his dark side:

> 'He oozed arrogance, was vicious about business rivals, and in contrast to, say, Bill Gates, refused to have any truck with notions of corporate responsibility. He habitually parked his car in the disabled slot at Apple headquarters and one of the first acts on returning to the company in 1997 was to terminate all of its corporate philanthropy programmes ... He ruled Apple with a combination of foul-mouthed tantrums and charm, withering scorn and flattery ... and those in his regular orbit found he could flip with no warning from one category to the other ... Yet members of Jobs' inner circle, many of whom came with him from NeXT, found working for him an exhilarating experience. To keep them on the board, Jobs eliminated most cash bonuses from executive compensation and started handing out stock options instead.'

The *Sunday Times* (30 October 2011) was just as scathing about his personality, giving examples of his bad tempered, often rude, tantrums with staff and suppliers. He had a propensity for tears and the article cited the example of him throwing a tantrum and crying when he was assigned No. 2 on the Apple payroll after Wozniak who was No. 1. Jobs insisted on being 'number zero'. It cited examples of him often claiming the ideas of other Apple employees as his own and described him as 'selfish, rude, aggressive, lachrymose, unpredictable ... a good candidate for the boss from hell.' And yet it also observed that Jobs could inspire incredible loyalty, albeit in the people he had helped to make rich.

Jobs' personal life was equally murky. Before starting up Apple, he famously paid his partner Steve Wozniak only $300 for a job for which he was paid $5000 by Atari, when the agreement with Wozniak was for a 50:50 split. At a point in his life where he was already wealthy, he denied paternity of a daughter, leaving the mother on welfare, even swearing an affidavit that he was not the father because, in effect, he was 'sterile and infertile'. He eventually acknowledged paternity and went on to marry Laurene Powell and have three more children, living in an unassuming family home in Palo Alto, on the San Francisco Bay.

QUESTIONS

1 How many of the elements of the entrepreneurial DNA can you spot in Steve Jobs?

2 Was he a great entrepreneurial leader? If so why?

3 Do you have to be a likable character to be a great entrepreneurial leader? What elements of the entrepreneurial character might trigger this sort of behaviour?

General Enterprise Tendency (GET) test

The General Enterprising Tendency (GET) test has been developed by staff at Durham University Business School over a number of years as a measure of entrepreneurial personality. It is a 54-question instrument that measures personal character traits in five important dimensions of the entrepreneurial character highlighted by research. It has been proved to be good at identifying owner-managers. The five dimensions are:

Need for achievement
If you have a high score (over 9 or 75%) in this section you are likely to exhibit the following qualities:

▷ Forward looking
▷ Self sufficient
▷ Optimistic rather than pessimistic
▷ Task-orientated
▷ Results-orientated
▷ Restless and energetic
▷ Self-confident
▷ Persistent and determined
▷ Dedicated to competing a task

Need for autonomy/independence
If you have a high score (over 4 or 67%) in this section you are likely be a person who:

▷ Likes doing unconventional things
▷ Prefers working alone

▷ Needs to do their 'own thing'
▷ Needs to express what they think ·
▷ Dislikes taking orders
▷ Likes to make up their own minds
▷ Does not bow to group pressure
▷ Is stubborn and determined

Creative/innovative tendency
If you have a high score (over 8 or 67%) in this section it means that you:

▷ Are imaginative and innovative
▷ Have a tendency to daydream
▷ Are versatile and curious
▷ Have lots of ideas
▷ Are intuitive and guess well
▷ Enjoy new challenges
▷ Like novelty and change

Moderate/calculated risk taking
If you have a high score (over 8 or 67%) in this section you tend to:

▷ Act on incomplete information
▷ Judge when incomplete data is sufficient
▷ Accurately assess your own capabilities
▷ Be neither over- nor under-ambitious
▷ Evaluate likely benefits against likely costs
▷ Set challenging but attainable goals

➡

Drive and determination

If you have a high score (over 8 or 67%) in this section you tend to:

▷ Take advantage of opportunities
▷ Discount fate
▷ Make your own luck
▷ Be self-confident
▷ Believe in controlling your own destiny
▷ Equate results with effort
▷ Show considerable determination

The test is relatively quick and simple to administer – with either agree or disagree questions. The final composite score measures inherent entrepreneurial character traits on a scale of 0–54. If your score is above average it predicts you would be happy being, and make a good, owner-manager.

Stormer et al. (1999) applied the test to 128 owners of new (75) and successful (53) small firms. They concluded that the test was acceptable for research purposes, particularly for identifying owner-managers; it was poor at predicting small-business success. They concluded that either the test scales need to be refined for this purpose or that the test did not include sufficient indicators of success such as antecedent influences on the individual or other factors related to the business rather than the individual setting it up. It would seem that, while entrepreneurs are both born and made, success requires more than an ounce of commercial expertise ... oh yes ... and a little luck!

The GET test is available free online at the website accompanying this book: (www.studyskillsconnected.com/selfevalutions/). It only takes about 10 minutes to answer the questions and the results are automatically analyzed and can then be printed out. Why not try it and see if you are entrepreneurial?

I would like to thank Durham University Business School for permission to use this test.

Summary

▷ Owner-managers and entrepreneurs have certain personal character traits that they are born with, but that can also be developed over time. These character traits are summarized in Figure 2.3. Entrepreneurs like **Duncan Bannatyne** and **Steve Jobs** exhibit many of these traits. You can assess your character traits using the GET test. Cognitive theory provides some underpinning to these traits by showing how they might affect motivations and decision-making.

▷ Education is an important antecedent influence on start-ups but more particularly on entrepreneurial growth businesses. Growth companies are more likely to be set up by groups rather than individuals, often sharing ownership to attract experienced managers. They are also more likely to be set up by middle-aged owners. These factors underline the importance of knowledge and learning and the value of a network of personal contacts.

▷ Immigrants also seem to be associated with business start-ups and growth – as was the case with the **Kenyan Asians**. However, there is no obvious or uniform link with ethnicity.

▷ Entrepreneurs have a particular and characteristic approach to doing business and managing an organization. At the core of this is the development of relationships – with customers, staff, suppliers and all the stakeholders in the business.

▷ Entrepreneurs tend to manage staff by developing strong, informal personal relationships with them, rather than by having rigid job definitions and hierarchical business structures.

▷ These relationships can build into an invaluable network of contacts that can be used to obtain information and knowledge that feeds into their decision-making. Networks blur the boundaries of the firm, extending them to a community of interest rather than restricting them to a legal or economic entity. They mean that not only resources but also knowledge and risks can be shared across economic units.

▷ Successful entrepreneurs have a strong vision and this helps them to build a strategic intent for the organization through which they reconcile where they are with where they want to be, even when the path to achieve this vision is not clear. They continually strategize and that means that strategy will often be seen as emergent. However, there are always strategic options that they have thought through and developed. Decision-making is then incremental, based upon opportunistic circumstances at the time.

▷ Greiner's growth model (Figure 2.6) predicts the crises a business will face as it grows. The implications of the model are that, in order to retain its entrepreneurial edge, an organization needs to retain its creativity but with clear direction. It needs delegated but coordinated decision-making with effective collaboration. It needs to avoid potential crises through effective leadership, balancing the need for autonomy and control and avoiding at all costs too much red tape. This means putting in place an appropriate organizational structure and, most important of all, an appropriate organizational culture.

Essays and discussion topics

1 Are entrepreneurs born or made?

2 Do you think you have what it takes to be an owner-manager or entrepreneur?

3 How do you think a manager of an entrepreneurial organization might differ from an entrepreneur?

4 What are the defining characteristics of an entrepreneur?

5 What character traits do you think affect the success or otherwise of a business venture?

6 What are the possible negative consequences of the entrepreneur's strong internal locus of control?

7 Does previous business failure mean that you are more likely to succeed in the future?

8 Is entrepreneurship just a set of beliefs, a way of thinking and an approach to life?

9 How do entrepreneurs approach decision-making? Why?

10 Are entrepreneurs short-term in their decision-making? If so, is this a bad thing?

11 What does emergent strategy really mean? Is it just *ex post* rationalization?

12 Are strategic tools really useful or are they just the fabrication of academic theorists?

13 How do entrepreneurs approach the task of managing people? How is this different from the approach in larger organizations? Is it better?

14 Discuss how the typical entrepreneur's preference for physical intervention and informal, personal control shows itself. Is this a good thing?

15 What does it take to develop a lasting relationship – with anybody?

16 What are the advantages of forming personal relationships with customers?

17 Can a spider's web organization work? What are the limits and how might they be overcome?

18 How does the role of the entrepreneur change as the organization grows?

19 Is the Greiner growth model an accurate predictor or descriptor of the growth process and the problems it creates? What is the difference between a descriptive model and a predictive model?

20 How important is good luck in business? Can you make your own luck, or at least influence the odds of achieving a particular outcome?

21 Can training help develop entrepreneurship?

22 Has your education, so far, encouraged you to be entrepreneurial? If so, how? If not, how could it be changed?

23 Does this course encourage entrepreneurship?

Exercises and assignments

1 Write a mini case study on the motivations and other influences on an entrepreneur you know who set up their own business.

2 List the questions you would ask an owner-manager or entrepreneur in trying to assess their character traits and antecedent influences on them.

3 Use this list of questions to conduct an interview with an owner-manager of a local small firm. Once you have done this get them to complete the GET test. Summarize the most important observation and insights you have gained from the interview. Write a report describing their character. Ensure you justify your conclusions about their character with evidence from the interview and the GET test.

4 Find out all you can about a well-known entrepreneur and write an essay or report describing their character. Give examples of their actions that lead you to arrive at your conclusions.

5 Using the GET test and the questions developed in Exercise 2 as a basis, evaluate your own entrepreneurial character. Write a report describing your character. Give examples of actions or behaviours that support these conclusions.

References

Abdesselam, R., Bonnet, J. and Le Pape, N. (1999) 'An Explanation of the Life Span of New Firms: An Empirical Analysis of French Data', *Entrepreneurship: Building for the Future*, Euro PME 2nd International Conference, Rennes.

Aldrich, H.E. and Martinez, M. (2003) 'Entrepreneurship as a Social Construction: A Multi-Level Evolutionary Approach', in Z.J. Acs and D.B. Audretsch (eds) *Handbook of Entrepreneurship Research: A Multidisciplinary Survey and Introduction*, Boston, MA: Kluwer Academic Publishers.

Andersson, S., Gabrielsson, J. and Wictor, I. (2004) 'International Activities in Small Firms – Examining Factors Influencing the Internationalization and Export Growth of Small Firms', *Canadian Journal of Administrative Science*, 21(1).

Annual Population Survey (2004) *Annual Population Survey, January–December 2004*, London: Office for National Statistics.

Audretsch, D.B., Keilbach, M. and Lehmann, E. (2006) *Entrepreneurship and Economic Growth*, Oxford: Oxford University Press.

Baty, G. (1990) *Entrepreneurship for the Nineties*, New Jersey: Prentice Hall.

Baum, J.R. and Locke, E.A. (2004) 'The Relationship of Entrepreneurial Traits, Skills and Motivation to Subsequent Venture Growth', *Journal of Applied Psychology*, 89(4).

Baum, J.R. Locke, E.A. and Smith, K.G. (2001) 'A Multidimensional Model of Venture Growth', *Academy of Management Journal*, 44(2).

Bell, J., Murray, M. and Madden, K. (1992) 'Developing Expertise: An Irish Perspective', *International Small Business Journal*, 10(2).

Bhidé, A. (2000) *The Origin and Evolution of New Businesses*, New York: Oxford University Press.

Blanchflower, D.G. and Meyer, B.D. (1991) 'Longitudinal Analysis of Young Entrepreneurs in Australia and the United States', *National Bureau of Economic Research*, Working Paper 3746, Cambridge, MA.

Bolton, B. and Thompson, J. (2000) *Entrepreneurs: Talent, Temperament, Technique*, Oxford: Butterworth-Heinemann.

Brockhaus, R. and Horwitz, P. (1986) 'The Psychology of the Entrepreneur', in D. Sexton, and R. Smilor (eds) *The Art and Science of Entrepreneurship*, Cambridge: Ballinger Publishing Company.

Brush, C.G. (1992) 'Research on Women Business Owners: Past Trends, A New Perspective and Future Directions', *Entrepreneurship: Theory and Practice*, 16(4).

Burns, P. (1996) 'Growth', in P. Burns and J. Dewhurst (eds) *Small Business and Entrepreneurship*, Basingstoke: Macmillan – now Palgrave Macmillan.

Burns, P. and Whitehouse, O. (1995a) *Investment Criteria in Europe*, 3i European Enterprise Centre, Report no. 16, July.

Burns, P. and Whitehouse, O. (1995b) *Financing Enterprise in Europe 2*, 3i European Enterprise Centre, Report no. 17, October.

Busenitz, L. and Barney, J. (1997) 'Differences between Entrepreneurs and Managers in Large Organisations: Biases and Heuristics in Strategic Decision Making', *Journal of Business Venturing*, 12.

Buttner, E. and More, D. (1997) 'Women's Organizational Exodus to Entrepreneurship: Self-Reported Motivations and Correlates with Success', *Journal of Small Business Management*, 35(1).

Caird, S. (1990) 'What does it Mean to be Enterprising?', *British Journal of Management*, 1(3).

Carter, S. and Cachon, J. (1988) *The Sociology of Entrepreneurship*, Stirling: University of Stirling.

Chell, E., Haworth, J. and Brearley, S. (1991) *The Entrepreneurial Personality*, London: Routledge.

Chen, P.C., Greene, P.G. and Crick, A. (1998) 'Does Entrepreneurial Self Efficacy Distinguish Entrepreneurs from Managers?', *Journal of Business Venturing*, 13.

Churchill, N.C. and Lewis, V.L. (1983) 'The Five Stages of Small Business Growth', *Harvard Business Review*, May/June

Cliff, J. (1998) 'Does One Size Fit All? Exploring the Relationship Between Attitudes Towards Growth, Gender and Business Size', *Journal of Business Venturing*, 13(6).

Cope, J. (2005) 'Toward a Dynamic Learning Perspective of Entrepreneurship', *Entrepreneurship Theory and Practice*, 29(4).

Cuba, R., Decenzo, D. and Anish, A. (1983) 'Management Practices of Successful Female Business Owners', *American Journal of Small Business*, 8(2).

Deakins, D. (1996) *Entrepreneurs and Small Firms*, London: McGraw-Hill.

de Bono, E. (1985) *Six Thinking Hats*, Boston: Little Brown & Company.

Delmar, F. (2000) 'The Psychology of the Entrepreneur', in S. Carter and D. Jones-Evans (eds) *Enterprise and Small Business: Principles, Practice and Policy*, London: Prentice Hall.

Doern, R. (2009) 'Investigating Barriers to SME Growth and Development in Transition Environments: A Critique and Suggestions for Developing the Methodology', *International Small Business Journal*, 27(3).

Dubini, P. and Aldrich, H. (1991) 'Personal and Extended Networks are Central to the Entrepreneurial Process', *Journal of Business Venturing*, 8(3).

du Toit, D.E. (1980) 'Confessions of a Successful Entrepreneur', *Harvard Business Review*, November/December.

Evans, D.S. and Leighton, L.S. (1990) 'Small Business Formation by Unemployed and Employed Workers', *Small Business Economics*, 2(4).

Gartner, W.B. (1988) '"Who is the Entrepreneur?" is the Wrong Question', *American Journal of Small Business*, 12(4).

GEM (2009) *Global Entrepreneurship Monitor 2008*, reports by individual GEM national teams available free online at www.gemconsortium.org.

Greiner, L.E. (1972) 'Evolution and Revolution as Organizations Grow', *Harvard Business Review*, July/August.

Harper, M. (1985) 'Hardship, Discipline and Entrepreneurship', *Cranfield School of Management*, Working Paper 85(1).

Hirsch, R.D. and Brush, C.G. (1987) 'Women Entrepreneurs: A Longitudinal Study', *Frontiers in Entrepreneurship Research*, Wellesley, MA: Babson College.

Kalleberg, A.L. and Leicht, K.T. (1991) 'Gender and Organization Performance: Determinants of Small Business Survival and Success', *Academy of Management Journal*, 34(1).

Kanter, R.M. (1983) *The Change Masters*, New York: Simon & Schuster.

Kets de Vries, M.F.R. (1985) 'The Dark Side of Entrepreneurship', *Harvard Business Review*, November/December.

Kirzner, I.M. (1973) *Competition and Entrepreneurship*, Chicago: University of Chicago.

Kirzner, I.M. (1979) *Perception, Opportunity and Profit: Studies in the Theory of Entrepreneurship*, Chicago: University of Chicago.

Kirzner, I.M. (1997) 'Entrepreneurial Discovery and Competitive Market Processes: An Austrian Approach', *Journal of Economic Literature*, 35.

Kirzner, I.M. (1999) 'Creativity and/or Alertness: A Reconsideration of the Schumpeterian Entrepreneur', *Review of Austrian Economics*, 11.

Larson, A. (1992) 'Network Dyads in Entrepreneurial Settings: A Study of the Governance of Exchange Relationships', *Administrative Science Quarterly*, 37.

Liedholm, C. (2002) 'Small Firm Dynamics: Evidence from Africa and Latin America', *Small Business Economics*, 18 (1–3).

Lindblom, L.E. (1959) 'The Science of Muddling Through', *Public Administration Review*, 19, Spring.

Lumpkin, G.T. and Lichtenstein, B.B. (2005) 'The Role of Organizational Learning in the Opportunity-Recognition Process', *Entrepreneurship Theory and Practice*, 29(4).

Mathewson, Sir G. (2000) Keynote address, *British Academy of Management Annual Conference*, Edinburgh.

McCarthy, B. and Leavy, B. (2000) 'Strategy Formation in Irish SMEs: A Phase Model of Process', *British Academy of Management Annual Conference*, Edinburgh.

McClelland, D.C. (1961) *The Achieving Society*, Princeton, NJ: Van Nostrand.

Mintzberg, H. (1978) 'Patterns in Strategy Formation', *Management Science.*

Mintzberg, H., Ahlstrand, B. and Lampel, J. (1998) *Strategy Safari*, New York: The Free Press.

Ozgen, E. and Baron, R.A. (2007) 'Social Sources of Information in Opportunity Recognition: Effects of Mentors, Industry Networks and Professional Firms', *Journal of Business Venturing*, 22(2).

Pinchot, G. (1985) *Intrapreneuring*, New York: Harper & Row.

Read, S., Sarasvathy, S., Dew, N., Wiltbank, R. and Ohlsson, A. (2011) *Effectual Entrepreneurship*, Abingdon/New York: Routledge.

Rosa, P., Hamilton, S., Carter, S. and Burns, H. (1994) 'The Impact of Gender on Small Business Management: Preliminary Findings of a British Study', *International Small Business Journal*, 12(3).

Rosa, P., Carter, S. and Hamilton, D. (1996) 'Gender as a Determinant of Small Business Performance: Insights from a British Study', *Small Business Economics*, 8.

Sarasvathy, S.D. (2001) 'Causation and Effectuation: Toward a Theoretical Shift from Economic Inevitability to Entrepreneurial Contingency', *The Academy of Management Review*, 26(2).

Saxenian, A. (2000) *Silicon Valley's New Immigrant Entrepreneurs*, Working Paper 15 San Diego: Center for Comparative Immigration Studies, University of California.

Schein, V., Mueller, R., Lituchy, T. and Liu, J. (1996) 'Thinking Manager – Think Male: A Global Phenomenon?', *Journal of Organisational Behaviour*, 17.

Schumpeter, J.A. ([1983] 1996) *The Theory of Economic Development*, New Jersey: Transaction Publishers.

Schwartz, E.B. (1997) 'Entrepreneurship: A New Female Frontier', *Journal of Contemporary Business*, Winter.

Shapero, A. (1985) *Managing Professional People – Understanding Creative Performance*, New York: Free Press.

Shaver, K. and Scott, L. (1992) 'Person, Processes and Choice: The Psychology of New Venture Creation', *Entrepreneurship Theory and Practice*, 16(2).

Stanworth, J., Blythe, S., Granger, B. and Stanworth, C. (1989) 'Who Becomes an Entrepreneur?', *International Small Business Journal*, 8(1).

Storey, D. (2011) 'Optimism and Chance: The Elephants in the Entrepreneurship Room', *International Small Business Journal*, 29: 303, originally published online 26 April.

Storey, D.J. and Greene, F.J. (2010) *Small Business and Entrepreneurship*, Harlow: Prentice Hall.

Storey, D. and Sykes, N. (1996) 'Uncertainty, Innovation and Management', in P. Burns and J. Dewhurst (eds) *Small Business and Entrepreneurship*, Basingstoke: Macmillan – now Palgrave Macmillan.

Stormer, R., Kline, T. and Goldberg, S. (1999) 'Measuring Entrepreneurship with the General Enterprise Tendency (GET) Test: Criterion-related Validity and Reliability', *Human Systems Management*, 18(1).

van der Sluis, J., van Praag, M. and Vijverberg, W. (2005) 'Entrepreneurship Selection and Performance: A Meta-Analysis of the Impact of Education in Developing Economies', *World Bank Economic Review*, 19(2).

Webster, J.E. (1992) 'The Changing Role of Marketing in the Corporation', *Journal of Marketing*, 56, October.

Part 2

Organizational architecture

Chapter **3**
Entrepreneurial architecture

Learning outcomes

By the end of this chapter you should be able to:

▷ Understand the meaning of the term organizational architecture and critically analyze how it might be constructed so as to replicate the character traits and approaches to management and business of an entrepreneur;

▷ Understand how architecture affects the dominant logic of an organization;

▷ Understand the meaning and organizational implications of the term 'learning organization' and critically analyze its relevance to entrepreneurial architecture;

▷ Understand how real knowledge is created and critically analyze how this might be replicated in an organization;

▷ Measure entrepreneurial intensity and critically evaluate the implications of this information;

▷ Understand how environment affects organizational architecture and how different architectures might be needed in different environments.

Architecture

The challenge for corporate entrepreneurship is to transplant the entrepreneurial DNA outlined in the previous chapter into a large, established organization, using frameworks appropriate to large organizations. Individuals within the organization need to be infused with this DNA. As we have already noted, the 'entrepreneurial transformation' school of thought believes this can be done through appropriate leadership, strategies, systems, structures and cultures. In this chapter we start building this framework into what we call an entrepreneurial architecture.

Architecture is a term used by John Kay (1993) to describe the relational contracts within and around the organization – with customers, suppliers and staff. These are long-term relationships, although not necessarily just legal contracts, which are only partly specified and only really enforced by the needs of the parties to work together. Like all relationships, architecture is based upon mutual trust, although underpinned by mutual self-interest. This self-interest discourages one party from acting in some way at the expense of the other because it is important that they continue to work together. We have already stressed the importance of relationships and partnerships in the way entrepreneurs do business.

Just as entrepreneurs use networks of relationships to help them operate in a way that allows them to seize opportunities quickly, architecture allows the entrepreneurial firm to respond quickly and effectively to change and opportunity. Developing organizational architecture is the systematic exploitation of one of the main distinctive capabilities of entrepreneurs. It builds in dynamic capabilities that are difficult to copy. It does so by creating within the organization the knowledge and routines that enable this to happen smoothly and unhindered. Staff are motivated in themselves to make this happen, knowing it is good for the organization – what has been called 'empowerment'. Architecture can create barriers to entry and competitive advantage by institutionalizing these relationships. It is difficult to copy because it is not a legal contract and not written down anywhere, relying instead on the complex network of personal relationships throughout the organization. Architecture is created partly through appropriate strategies, partly through appropriate structures, but mainly through developing the appropriate culture in the organization.

Kay (op. cit.) emphasizes the advantages of architecture:

> 'The value of architecture lies in the capacity of organizations which establish it to create organizational knowledge and routines, to respond flexibly to changing circumstances, and to achieve easy and open exchanges of information. Each is capable of creating an asset for the firm – organizational knowledge which is more than the sum of individual knowledge, flexibility, and responsiveness which extends to the institution as well as to its members.'

Using examples of small and large organizations, Kay emphasizes that architecture comprises patterns of long-term relationships which are 'complex, subtle and hard to define precisely or to replicate' and he observes that it is easier to sustain than to create and even more difficult to create in an organization that does not have it in the first place. Individuals participate in these relationships voluntarily out of a strong personal feeling that it is in their interests because they are participating in a 'repeated game' in which they share the rewards of collective achievement. These strong relationships solve problems of cooperation, coordination and commitment. They set the rules of the game. If you cheat you would find it difficult to play the game again with the same players. These relationships are characterized as having a high but structured degree of informality, something that can be mistaken to be haphazard, chaotic or just lucky. In this way the architecture is distinctive and difficult to copy because individuals only know or understand a small part of the overall structure.

Kay (op. cit.) continues:

> 'There is an expectation of long-term relationships both within the firm and between its members, a commitment to a sharing of the rewards of collective achievement, and a high but structured degree of informality. This informality is sometimes mistaken for disorganization – in popular discussion of chaos, entrepreneurship, or adhocracy as conditions of innovation – but truly chaotic organizations rarely perform well, and a system of relational contracts substitutes an extensive set of unwritten rules and expectations of behavior for the formal obligations of the classical contract.'

With this description we glimpse reflections of the start-up entrepreneur in the middle of the spider's web of informal, personal relationships, recognizing opportunity everywhere, trying to innovate and trying to replicate success, using networks, relying on personal relationships with customers, staff and suppliers. Entrepreneurs prefer influence and informal relationships to formal contracts. They use these to secure repeat sales at the expense of competitors and to secure resources or competitive advantage that they might not otherwise have. Close partnerships with suppliers where information and knowledge is shared can lead to significant advantages in lowering costs, lead times and inventories. All these relationships are based on trust – 'my word is my bond' – and most involve a degree of self-interest. The challenge is to replicate these relationships across the organization and develop that entrepreneurial architecture.

Kay (op. cit.) sees no conflict between the need for stability and continuity in relationships and the equal need for change and flexibility in an entrepreneurial firm:

> 'If there is a single central lesson from the success ... of cases developed in this book, it is that the stability of relationships and the

capacity to respond to change are mutually supportive, not mutually exclusive, requirements. It is within the context of long-term relationships, and often only within that context that the development of organizational knowledge, the free exchange of information, and a readiness to respond quickly and flexibly can be sustained.'

And here lies an important by-product of this architecture – it creates organizational learning and knowledge that can be used to create additional competitive advantage.

Entrepreneurs learn by doing, and they learn quickly not to repeat mistakes but to capitalize on success. Because they are one person, knowledge and learning is transferred continuously, quickly and without barriers. As the organization grows the challenge is for knowledge and learning to continue to be transferred in this way. But how do you translate what happens in the brain of one person into the operations of an entire organization? And what does learning really mean? The answer to this lies in the literature surrounding the concept of the 'learning organization'.

The learning organization

The person most associated with the concept of the learning organization is Peter Senge. His book, *The Fifth Discipline: The Art and Science of the Learning Organization*, published in 1990, was a loose collection of ideas about change, learning and communication drawn from an eclectic variety of sources. However the central concept was inherently attractive:

> 'As the world becomes more interconnected and business becomes more complex and dynamic, work must become more "learningful" ... It is no longer sufficient to have one person learning for the organization ... It's just not possible any longer to "figure it out" from the top, and have everyone else following the orders of the "grand strategist". The organizations that will truly excel in the future will be the organizations that discover how to tap people's commitment and capacity to learn at all levels in the organization.'

If the grand strategist is the entrepreneur, then you can see that the challenge laid down is one of making the whole organization entrepreneurial.

A learning organization has been defined as one that 'facilitates the learning of all its members and continuously transforms itself ... adapting, changing, developing and transforming themselves in response to the needs, wishes and aspirations of people, inside and outside' (Pedler et al., 1991).

'There are countless successful companies that are thriving now despite the fact that they started with little more than passion and a good idea. There are also many that have failed, for the very same reason. The difference is that the thriving companies gathered the knowledge that gave them the substantial edge over their competition, which they then used to improve their execution, whatever their product or service ... The key is not so much one great idea or patent as it is the execution and implementation of a great strategy.'
Michael Dell

Writings on the learning organization stress how it is flexible, adaptable and better equipped to thrive in a turbulent environment – the very environment that entrepreneurs and entrepreneurial firms inhabit. A learning organization facilitates learning for all its members and continually transforms itself:

▷ Encouraging systematic problem-solving;
▷ Encouraging experimentation and new approaches;
▷ Learning from past experience and history;
▷ Learning from best practice and outside experience;
▷ Being skilled at transferring knowledge in the organization.

Peter Senge (1992) observes that learning organizations need leaders with fire and passion: 'Learning organizations can be built only by individuals who put their life spirit into the task.' The similarity to the entrepreneur is striking. Indeed the similarities can also be seen from the literature about entrepreneurs. Timmons (1999) says that successful entrepreneurs are: 'patient leaders, capable of instilling tangible visions and managing for the long haul. *The entrepreneur is at once a learner and a teacher,* a doer and a visionary.' Being a learner and a teacher are two of the prime tasks for a leader in a learning organization. Stata (1992) even predicts that the rate at which individuals or organizations learn may become the only sustainable competitive advantage, and this perspective sees learning as a capability that can be nurtured and developed by organizations (e.g., Leonard-Barton, 1992; Teece et al., 1997).

Truly entrepreneurial organizations, therefore, are also learning organizations. This goes to the heart of the architecture that needs to be put in place to develop them and, as we shall explore in the next chapter, it also goes to the heart of the qualities demanded of a successful entrepreneurial leader.

A learning organization thrives in turbulent and changing environments. It is fast and responsive. It requires unitarism – a belief that the interests of the organization and the individual are the same. Shared values are at the core of this, as is being part of a team or an 'in-group' - the terminology used by Hofstede in his analysis of culture, to which we shall return in Chapter 5. Unitarism results in staff feeling empowered to influence the direction of the organization and believing that continually developing, learning and acquiring new knowledge is the way to do this.

Continually developing, learning and acquiring new knowledge is therefore at the heart of a learning organization. But knowledge is about more than just information-sharing. It is about learning from each other and from outside the organization. It is about a better understanding of interrelationships, complexities and causalities. Daniel Kim (1993) suggests effective learning can be considered to be a revolving wheel (Figure 3.1). During half the cycle, you test concepts and observe what happens through experience

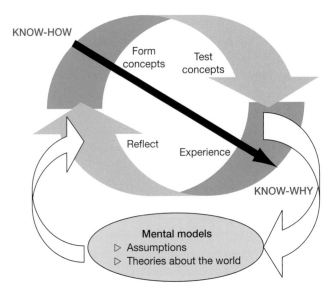

KNOW-HOW

Form concepts

Test concepts

Reflect

Experience

KNOW-WHY

Mental models
▷ Assumptions
▷ Theories about the world

F 3.1 Wheel of learning

– learning 'know-how'. In the second half of the cycle, you are reflecting on the observations and forming concepts – learning 'know-why'. This is often called 'double-loop learning'. It is the second sort of learning that is of particular value to the organization because it is at this point that root causes of problems are diagnosed and systems-based solutions put in place.

So real learning is about application, continuous problem-solving, understanding the root cause of problems rather than being distracted by the symptoms. It is about continually challenging the mental models we hold – deeply-held beliefs about how the world works that are shaped by our experiences and, in turn, shape our experiences. It occurs when people within organizations share, explore and question those embedded ideas of the world. When this happens the wheel of learning both affects and is affected by our mental models, as shown in Figure 3.1.

Once we start to share our knowledge of know-why and/or know-how with others, organizational learning takes place. The constantly increasing amount of know-how and know-why, accumulated through years of turning the wheel of learning and sharing mental models becomes part of the collective memory of the organization. Although this accumulated knowledge is tacit, shadowy and fragile it is unique and can be part of the organizational architecture that underpins competitive advantage. However, the difficulty in developing organizational learning increases as an organization grows. Table 3.1 summarizes some of the major concepts about learning organizations.

The similarities with the way entrepreneurs operate are pronounced. The learning organization literature stresses the importance of tacit knowledge – intuition, judgment and expertise – the importance of incrementalism and learning by doing on the job, rather than in the classroom.

T 3.1 Major concepts of the learning organization

▷ True learning requires the acquisition of both know-how and know-why through the wheel of learning so that chains of causality can be identified

▷ Mental models are shaped by experience and help shape experience

▷ Learning occurs when individuals share, examine and challenge their mental models

▷ The most important learning occurs on the job

▷ The most effective learning is social and active, not individual and passive

▷ The most important things to learn are tacit things – intuition, judgement, expertise

It stresses the accumulation of knowledge and information, the questioning of the status quo. What is more, it explains why entrepreneurs are more comfortable continuously strategizing and why strategy tends frequently to emerge, based on the learning that is continuously taking place. The ability to adapt is what makes the difference between survival and growth in an uncertain, turbulent environment, and an organization's ability to adapt is the direct result of its ability to learn collectively about the factors that influence it. Constant learning by organizations requires the acquisition of new knowledge and skills and the willingness to apply them to decision-making (Miller, 1996). It includes the unlearning of old routines (Markóczy, 1994) so that the range of potential behaviour is altered (Wilpert, 1995).

Some academics however, are cynical about the concept of a learning organization, arguing that the literature relies on 'metaphor, exaggeration and justification' (Symon, 2002). Certainly Senge's 1990 book was a loose collection of ideas couched in mystical terminology and was light on practicality. But others have built on this in a more structured manner. Theoretical and empirical research does, however, show that there are many barriers to implementing the concept of a learning organization and many academics would say that, in its extreme form, the learning organization is indeed a utopian ideal and that it is a journey rather than a destination ever to be arrived at.

Dominant logic and mental models

Entrepreneurship is primarily a frame of mind, a set of beliefs, a way of thinking and approaching life. It is what we have termed a mental model. And from school onwards, all too often, conformity is rewarded, mistakes punished and too much questioning discouraged. How can we possibly make the leap of faith required to convince us that things could be different? And how robust are our learning processes? In this modern world do we have the skill, let alone the time, to reflect? Can these learning processes ever be sufficiently robust to get us to see how information, action and results form a chain of causality – the key to understanding the root cause of a problem? And how can an organization encourage all this to take place?

The mechanism by which architecture affects these things in a large organization is called the 'dominant logic' of the organization – a sort of accumulation of similar mental models. 'Dominant logic' is the phrase coined by Prahalad and Bettis (1986) to describe the way managers in an organization conceptualize the business and make important resource allocation decisions. It is the mindset with which managers see the organization, the world it inhabits and its position with customers, competitors and other stakeholders. It filters the information they receive, subconsciously interpreting environmental data in a certain way. In fact, managers may only consider information that they believe relevant to the prevailing dominant logic in the organization. Dominant logic influences behaviour, routines, strategies, structures, culture and systems – virtually everything the organization does and is. But equally, dominant logic can be influenced by these factors. Architecture therefore affects dominant logic and dominant logic is the mechanism that makes the organization entrepreneurial.

Dominant logic is a social construct. It can be changed in the same way that mental models can change. However it takes time to change and therefore a change of architecture takes time to have an effect. What is more, the dominant logic that may be appropriate for today's environment may not be appropriate for tomorrow's. Dominant logic must therefore constantly be learned and unlearned through the wheel of learning. This can be a

Service-dominant logic in marketing

In their award winning paper 'Evolving to a New Dominant Logic for Marketing', Vargo and Lusch (2004) seem to have changed the dominant logic of marketing academia. They argued that customers valued and purchased services rather than goods, and goods should therefore be viewed as a medium for delivering or 'transmitting' the firm's services. They defined service as 'the application of specialized competences (knowledge and skills) through deeds, processes, and performances for the benefit of another entity or the entity itself'. In this way companies manufacturing cars are not in the business of selling cars but in the business of providing 'mobility services' through the cars that they manufacture – a concept adopted by Andrew Valentine and his company called Zipcar (Streetcar). Thus all industries are service industries and it therefore becomes vital for firms to understand the service that consumers are seeking from them. This logic requires firms to shift their focus from the product to the consumer and become continuous learning organizations that understand consumers' needs and translate these into the services they value. These, in turn, need to be translated into comprehensive customer value propositions that are regularly reviewed and renewed.

Vargo, S.L. and Lusch, R.F. (2004) 'Evolving to a New Dominant Logic for Marketing', *Journal of Marketing*, 68(1).

difficult thing to do because the dominant logic of the old way may inhibit the learning related to the new way. And the longer the logic has been in place the more difficult it is likely to be to unlearn. However, entrepreneurs are famous for ignoring the dominant logic and challenging the status quo when they set up their business. Michael Dell famously asked, 'Why should a computer cost five times as much as the sum of its parts?' His pursuit of an answer to this question led him to create Dell Computers. Most people resist change and it often takes a crisis to push an organization into changing its ways and changing its dominant logic. In that sense, today's environment with its fierce competition, rapid changes in markets and technologies, uncertainties about the future and ever-increasing complexity is likely to throw up crises aplenty and act as a catalyst for change.

The business model adopted by an organization – what business it is in and how it creates value – is part of this dominant logic. But this is not an absolute construct. Entrepreneurs spot opportunities and create multiple strategic options by being able to challenge their own dominant logic – challenging their own business model or that adopted by other organizations. Similarly an entrepreneurial organization must be able to continuously challenge its dominant logic and be able to change it quickly. Sometimes this involves changing the business model so completely that whole new industries can be created – a paradigm shift in how a market is perceived. This is part of what a learning organization does all the time through its wheel of learning (Figure 3.1). And it is important that the lessons from this are built into the architecture. An entrepreneurial organization is also a learning organization.

The challenge, therefore, is to make entrepreneurship the dominant logic pervading the organization by embedding double-loop learning within the organizational architecture. Entrepreneurship embraces and welcomes change as creating new commercial opportunities. It promotes flexibility, creativity and innovation in pursuing those opportunities. And the implications for how the organization functions are enormous.

📂 Case insight Zipcar (Streetcar)

Paradigm shifts: changing dominant logic

Entrepreneurial start-ups are often not hindered by the dominant logic of an industry. Andrew Valentine studied modern languages and anthropology at Durham University. Whilst there, he and a friend set up a student radio station, Purple FM. After graduating he joined the shipping company P&O and worked for them for six years, doing a part-time MBA. But in 2002 Andrew got itchy feet and decided he wanted to set up his own business, rather than work for other people. The problem was that he did not have a business idea. So he and a friend, Brett Akker, became partners and set about searching systematically for the right business. They spent 18 months researching many ideas from organic food to training courses, meeting twice a week, before coming up with the final idea.

> 'We looked at hundreds of ideas. We were basically trying to identify gaps, so we were looking at how society was changing and what was missing. Our business had to have potential, be capable of being scaled up and play to our strengths. We kept looking until we found something that matched our criteria.'

The final idea came from something Andrew read about in another country – a car sharing club. The idea is that people in towns and cities can rent a car for as little as half an hour, replacing the need to buy. Cars are parked in residential streets and are ready to drive away using an electronic card to open the door and start up.

> 'I read about a similar business overseas and immediately thought, what an amazing idea. There were a couple of other companies already running this kind of service in Britain but they weren't doing it the way we imagined we would be able to do it. We thought we could be more effective.'

Once Andrew and Brett had the idea, they spent four months holding market research focus groups to test out the business model and developing financial projections to estimate the resources they would need. This decided them to launch Streetcar.

> 'We were satisfying ourselves that not only would it work but that there was enough demand for it.'

The business model has changed slightly now. There is no deposit, just an annual membership fee, and cars are rented by the hour, which includes 30 miles of petrol.

> 'Brett and I share a healthy level of permanent dissatisfaction with the service. This means that we are constantly working at making it better and improving everything. I really enjoy the creativity of growing a business.'

Although the business model has been modified, at its heart is a fundamental paradigm shift about how we might use and 'own' cars in the future, particularly in cities and very much in line with service-dominant thinking in marketing.

In 2007 Andrew and Brett gave up 43% of the business to Smedvig, a venture capital company, who invested £6.4 million in Streetcar. In 2010, the US company Zipcar bought Streetcar for £32 million, giving the founders £11 million.

Source: *Sunday Times*, 15 November 2009

☐ Up to date information on Zipcar can be found on their website: www.zipcar.co.uk

Complexity theory

Complexity theory also has something to say about organizational archi-tecture. Complex adaptive systems – the result of multiple independent actions – are unpredictable. Small actions at one level can have large-scale unexpected consequences elsewhere. Here we think of the increasingly interconnected global market place of today and the turbulent environment it generates. Complexity theory hints that there is no stable equilibrium in these situations. But we also realize that small actions within an organiza-tion can have a big effect, particularly if they can be marshalled. At the same time, complex social systems have a capacity to self-organize, changing and creating new structures and systems without being directed to do so. It is the capacity to self-organize that can give direction to the changes. The three main requirements for self-organization are: '*identity* that permits a common sense-making process within the organization, *information* that provides the possibility of synchronized behavior and *relationships* that are the pathways through which the information is transformed into intel-ligent, coordinated action' (Grant, 2010, emphasis in original). And here we start to see the organizational architecture that we are trying to build; based on relationships, knowledge and information, with a strong domi-nant logic that aids understanding and provides direction.

Complexity theory also gives us an intellectual basis for the apparent dilemma of whether to encourage incremental or radical change. The two are not mutually exclusive and systems that have the capability of making *both* small-scale adaptations as well as large-scale revolution are most likely to thrive in a turbulent environment. They exist at the 'edge of chaos', adapting all the time but able to make the occasional radical leap. The theory also provides intellectual support to the 'emergent' school of strategy development in contrast to the 'deliberate' school with its linearity of approach, since it would support the view that the complex, intercon-nected world of today is inherently unpredictable. As Grant (op. cit.) says:

> 'Not only is it impossible to forecast the business environment but managers cannot predict with any certainty what the outcome of their actions will be. The concept of the CEO as the peak decision maker and strategy architect is not only unrealistic – it is undesir-able. Managers must rely on the self-organizing properties of their companies. The critical issues are how can they select *structures, systems and management styles* that will allow these self-organizing properties to generate the best outcomes.' (emphasis added)

To this I would add the pervasive organizational culture. And this brings us to how we build these things through organizational architecture.

Creating architecture

As already noted, architecture is based upon mutually supportive, long-term relationships which in turn are based on trust, self-interest and reciprocity (Dubini and Aldrich, 1991; Larson, 1992). They are strengthened by increased frequency and depth of interaction. They take a long time to build but can be lost very quickly. They are therefore based on knowledge and information. They are informal rather than formal but can be planned and engineered. Relationships need cultivating and managing, and their roots lie deep in the interpersonal relationships within the organization. Strong architecture can be both internal and external:

Internal architecture focuses on the employees, generating a strong sense of collectivism rather than individuality and implying strong job security. This collectivism comes from shared objectives and commonly accepted strategies. And this brings with it potential weaknesses: 'Firms with strong internal architecture tend to restrict individuality and recruit employees of characteristic, and familiar type, inflexibility is a potential weakness' (Kay, op. cit.). This we also recognize as a familiar potential weakness for entrepreneurs in growing firms. As we saw in the last chapter, an entrepreneur must change and adapt as the organization grows, moving towards a more managerial style (Miner, 1990). They must adopt certain administrative traits (Cooper, 1993), but at the same time they must also remain essentially entrepreneurial. Retaining a balance is crucial, building on the distinctive traits, skills, capabilities and approach to business of the entrepreneur and institutionalizing elements of this approach – replicating their DNA within the organization's culture.

> *'The best way I know to establish and maintain a healthy, competitive culture is to partner with your people – through shared objectives and common strategies.'*
> **Michael Dell**

External architecture is found where firms share knowledge with outsiders, which encourages flexibility and fast response times. It is based on deep relationships and is often found in networks or clusters of small firms in particular geographic areas where they depend on each other for various aspects of their commercial activity. For example, in the UK there is a cluster of small firms in South Wales which manufacture sofas and beds. Around them is a skilled workforce and the infrastructure needed to support them. Italy has developed these clusters in numerous industries from knitwear and ties to tiles, all based in different geographic clusters. Some larger firms, such as Dell, have developed competitive advantage based upon the development of distinctive global, virtual supply networks – which are also based on effective external architecture.

> *'Early in Dell's history we had more than 140 different suppliers providing us with component parts … Today our rule is to keep it simple and have as few partners as possible. Fewer than 40 suppliers provide us with about 90 percent of our material needs. Closer partnerships with fewer suppliers is a great way to cut cost and further speed products to market.'*
> **Michael Dell**

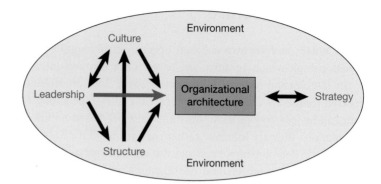

F 3.2 Influences on
organizational architecture

So how can architecture be shaped? The tools available are highlighted in Figure 3.2. The main tools, discussed in greater detail in subsequent chapters, are:

▷ Leadership;
▷ Culture;
▷ Structure.

Many elements are interrelated – each affecting the other – hence the direction of arrows in Figure 3.2. The leader has responsibility for shaping structure and culture and in this way architecture. The environment affects culture directly and strategy should always be responsive to it. Leaders are influenced by the organizational culture and hence their environment. Part of this environment is the nature and intensity of entrepreneurship the organization is seeking to encourage. We shall explore these factors later in this chapter. Strategies that lead to coping with change and delivering continuous innovation are the product of this organizational architecture. But how the organization approaches strategy development will also influence, and be influenced by, this architecture. Indeed, part of the strategy of the organization is to create this architecture. The interplay of these factors helps determine strategy and strategy development becomes part of the organization's architecture – something difficult to copy because it is constantly evolving and adapting to the changing market place.

The leader's role in creating organizational architecture is clearly crucial since they are responsible for the culture and structure of the organization and the strategies it develops. Indeed, I would suggest that taking a holistic, integrated approach to creating architecture is their prime responsibility and the major challenge they face.

Building entrepreneurial DNA into architecture

The last chapter highlighted the personal character traits of entrepreneurs and their particular approach to management and doing business. These need to be incorporated into the architecture of the organization through the three building blocks of leadership, culture and structure.

The personal character traits of the entrepreneur particularly need to be reflected in the culture and embedded in the dominant logic of the organization. The most important personal characteristics of the entrepreneur are, of course, the ability to spot opportunities and innovate. These are at the core of entrepreneurship. However, all the traits and characteristics must be reflected in the architecture, which should therefore facilitate the following 16 characteristics:

▷ Encourage opportunity spotting;
▷ Value creativity and innovation;
▷ Embed a strong vision of what the organization can become;
▷ Motivate people to achieve, setting goals and encouraging achievement through public recognition and reward;
▷ Encourage people to belong to and 'own' the organization, ensuring that they share in the success of the organization, so that staff are motivated to see it grow;
▷ Encourage a 'can-do' and 'work-is-fun' culture;
▷ Encourage delegation and decentralization, pushing decision-making down the organizational hierarchy;
▷ Empower staff to make the right decisions for the organization;
▷ Ensure there is a 'light touch' with management so that staff can exercise their sense of empowerment;
▷ Encourage organizational self-confidence and self-efficacy by celebrating achievement and success, but not at the expense of recognizing reality;
▷ Encourage open communication and the sharing of information and knowledge, so the organization can react quickly to environmental changes and capitalize on opportunities;
▷ Encourage continual learning (and unlearning) from this information and knowledge;
▷ Recognize change as the norm and something to be welcomed rather than avoided;
▷ Ensure success is celebrated;
▷ Recognize the importance of experimentation and balanced risk-taking;
▷ Not unnecessarily penalizing failure, but always learning from it.

The entrepreneur's approach to management also has implications for architecture. The two most important characteristics are their strong reliance on relationships rather than formal structures and procedures and their approach to developing strategy. The architecture should therefore facilitate the following seven characteristics:

▷ Encourage the building of deep relationships with all stakeholders throughout the organization – staff, customers and suppliers;

▷ Facilitate management through these relationships rather than relying on formal structures and hierarchies;
▷ Encourage collaboration, for example through team-working;
▷ Encourage continuous strategizing at all levels of the organization;
▷ Encourage the sharing of information, knowledge and learning, so that strategizing can take place;
▷ Encourage the development of strategic options;
▷ Adopt an incremental, adaptive approach to decision-making. When it comes to pursuing opportunities timing is crucial, but difficult to manage.

The lesson from growth models is that, to retain its entrepreneurial edge, an organization needs to retain its creativity and ability to spot opportunities but with clear direction. It needs to be able to continue to develop strategic options based upon real information and knowledge that adds shareholder value. It needs delegated but coordinated decision-making with effective collaboration. It needs to avoid potential crises through effective leadership, balancing the need for autonomy and control and avoiding at all costs too much red tape.

The challenge is to build all these characteristics into the organizational architecture through its leadership, culture and structure. This entrepreneurial architecture should provide the dynamic capabilities that allows the firm to 'achieve new resource combinations as markets emerge, collide, split, evolve, and die' (Eisenhardt and Martin, 2000) and in so doing create real shareholder value. Subsequent chapters will outline how this can be achieved.

Internal environment: entrepreneurial intensity

Entrepreneurship is an imprecise term and entrepreneurial activity can take many different forms. The nature of this entrepreneurial activity has implications for the entrepreneurial architecture adopted. Morris and Kuratko (2002) make a useful distinction between the *frequency* of entrepreneurial acts and the *degree* of each entrepreneurial act (a similar distinction is drawn for innovation – see Chapter 12). Entrepreneurial intensity is therefore a combination of degree and frequency of entrepreneurial activity. These factors, together with example companies, are shown in Figure 3.3. One firm might produce a small number of breakthrough developments (high on degree, low on frequency) whilst another might produce many small developments, none of which are breakthrough (low on degree, high on frequency). Morris and Kuratko argue that truly revolutionary firms combine high levels of degree with high levels of frequency – they exhibit a high degree of entrepreneurial *intensity*. These firms are forever pushing out the entrepreneurial frontier.

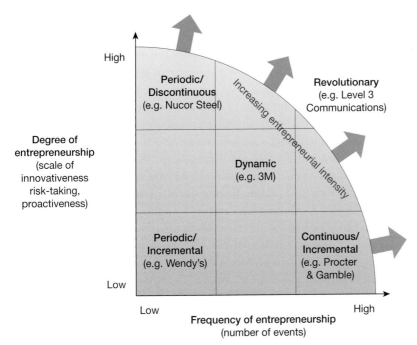

High

Periodic/
Discontinuous
(e.g. Nucor Steel)

Revolutionary
(e.g. Level 3
Communications)

Increasing entrepreneurial intensity

Degree of
entrepreneurship
(scale of
innovativeness
risk-taking,
proactiveness)

Dynamic
(e.g. 3M)

Periodic/
Incremental
(e.g. Wendy's)

Continuous/
Incremental
(e.g. Procter
& Gamble)

Low

Low   High

Frequency of entrepreneurship
(number of events)

Source: Adapted from Morris, M.H. and Kuratko, D.F. (2002) *Corporate Entrepreneurship*,
Fort Worth, Harcourt College Publishing.

F 3.3 Entrepreneurial
intensity

The grid is more a conceptual than a precise tool and locating firms on it requires a degree of judgement. However, by identifying where a firm falls on the grid, you are effectively describing the nature of its entrepreneurial strategy – entrepreneurial degree vs entrepreneurial frequency. The five examples used by the authors are all successful companies in their own right – the degree of entrepreneurial intensity does not necessarily guarantee success. Other factors, in particular an appropriate environment, need to be present. Wendy's, the US-based fast-food chain, rapidly captured third place in the industry by developing an innovative product delivery system and by targeting young adults who want higher-quality fast-food. Since then their innovations have been neither frequent nor dramatic (e.g. drive-by windows, new menus). Procter & Gamble remain at the top of the highly competitive consumer packaged goods industry by releasing a continuous stream of product improvements and the occasional new product. Nucor introduced a radically new technical process for producing sheet metal in small arc furnaces – mini-mills – transforming the competitive and economic structure of the steel industry. Level 3 Communications was the first company to build an end-to-end, internet-protocol, international communications network for internet service providers and telecom carriers and is aggressively expanding its network in the USA and Europe where it is continuously offering more and more services. However, frequent large-scale entrepreneurial events bring with them a high degree of risk. Whilst commercially successful, Level 3's high level of gearing adds to the perception of a high-risk business. 3M (see Case with questions) has for many years seemed to be able to continuously develop new commercial uses for new technologies. It is the most frequently cited example of successful corporate entrepreneurship, with a culture, structure and systems that encourage it.

Infrequent major innovation is risky and requires a certain culture and structure that is different from that required for what might be described as continuous, incremental improvement, which is less risky. It requires a different dominant logic in the organization. If Nucor's mini-steel mills had not been successful the company would have been in deep trouble. The way this was managed and then subsequently rolled out into the market is very different from the way Procter & Gamble manage their product innovations. However, entrepreneurial firms often have to combine the management of *both* continuous/incremental and periodic/discontinuous innovations. And this may mean that the organization has to be split into different organizational entities, each with its own delegated leadership, structure and culture. We shall explore the implications of this in later chapters.

Despite the success of all these companies, some researchers claim a statistically significant linkage exists between entrepreneurial intensity and a number of measures of firm performance such as profitability, income/sales ratio, revenue growth, asset growth, employment growth (Covin and Slevin, 1989; Davis et al., 1991; Miller and Friesen, 1983; Morris and Sexton, 1996; Peters and Waterman, 1982). This is particularly the case in changing, turbulent environments. Hence they would argue that the most successful firms are those that exhibit the greatest entrepreneurial intensity. However, one factor to be borne in mind is risk. All entrepreneurial activity is inherently risky. However, it can be argued that a strategy involving *both* large scale *and* high frequency is extremely risky. And any finance expert will tell you that risk and return go hand in hand so lower returns would be expected from lower risk strategies. This articulates a core strategic dilemma facing entrepreneurial firms – whether to focus on the size or scale of change or the frequency of the changes undertaken. Either way, risk management plays an important role in an entrepreneurial firm and one that we shall return to later.

External environment

Entrepreneurial organizations thrive within certain external environments – ones that are changing, unstable, disruptive even chaotic. They thrive where there is complexity and fierce competition. Using the framework of Porter's Five Forces, we could describe these environments as having a low concentration of firms, a high degree of product or market heterogeneity and where technology is constantly changing. They thrive in environments where change is the norm and opportunities (and threats) are constantly presenting themselves. These environments are characterized by high degrees of uncertainty, even contradiction, which make planning difficult. That means they can thrive in times of recession as well as growth, although 'thrive' is a relative concept when other firms might be failing. Entrepreneurial organizations are also likely to be most effective early in a product's life cycle, with its emphasis on growth and innovation. Perhaps unsurprisingly therefore, research supports the view that the external environment is an important influence on the success, or otherwise, of corporate entrepreneurship (Ferreira, 2002).

When the environment is stable or hospitable, entrepreneurship is less likely to flourish. There is simply no need to change. Using Porter's framework again, this is most likely when industries are highly concentrated and firms have little direct competition, when customers are locked into their supplier, margins are high and technologies rarely change. In these cases radical action is inappropriate, fine tuning the order of the day – that is until an entrepreneurial firm comes along with a different dominant logic and new business model. Similarly products at the mature stage of their life cycle need to be managed to generate cash and there is little scope for entrepreneurial flair. In these circumstances a more conservative or bureaucratic approach to management is likely to be more effective. If we accept that the firm follows the same path as a product life cycle, it may face maturity and stability at some stage. By this point the entrepreneurial organization would probably have re-invented itself by going into different product/market offerings. And this creates the problem of accommodating the need for different managerial approaches within one organizational structure.

However, the effect of the environment is altogether more complex than these broad generalizations imply. It can affect the very architecture of the organization. The complex interplay of different market conditions, different countries with different laws, cultures and customs and practices, even different local cultures, make it very difficult to be prescriptive about how the successful entrepreneurial organization might look in different parts of the world – what leadership style is appropriate, what the culture might be and how the organization might be structured. Entrepreneurial architectures that might succeed in one geographic environment might fail in another without significant local variation. And this book is written very much from a western perspective, underpinned by research based mainly in western organizations.

So within these broad generalizations it is quite possible that the same company may have different degrees of entrepreneurship in different subsidiaries, divisions, units, departments and geographical areas depending on both the internal and external environments they face. Structuring the organization so that each operating unit – whatever its basis – can be organized in such a way as to best deal with the internal and external environment it faces is quite a challenge, one to which we shall return in Chapter 6. However, broadly speaking, the answer is structures within structures, sub-cultures within cultures and different approaches to leadership within an overall approach – a real portfolio approach to management. This is particularly complex when the core business faces a stable internal and external environment and the core is large and needs to be maintained. In that case the overarching structures, culture and leadership will struggle to accommodate entrepreneurship, even at the peripheries of the organization, seeing it as destabilizing and disruptive. At this point separate organizational structures need to be considered which is where spin-outs or corporate venturing may be relevant, a topic to which we return in Chapter 7.

The point is that there cannot be a prescriptive blueprint for entrepreneurial architecture. And there will always be exceptions to the general rule. The principles outlined in subsequent chapters must be adapted and modified to suit specific environments. But then we always knew that management was an art rather than a science.

🗂 Case with questions 3M

Corporate entrepreneurship

3M has been known for decades as an entrepreneurial company that pursues growth through innovation. It generates a quarter of its annual revenues from products that are less than five years old. 3M started life as the Minnesota Mining and Manufacturing Company back in 1902. Its most successful product – flexible sandpaper – still forms an important part of its product line but this now comprises over 60,000 products that range from adhesive tapes to office supplies, from medical supplies to traffic signs, from magnetic tapes and CDs to electrical equipment. Originally innovation was encouraged informally by the founders, but over more than a century some of these rules have been formalized. Most important of all, however, there has built up a culture which encourages innovation. For example, there is a 'hall of fame' of staff elected on the basis of their innovative achievements. And because this culture has built up a history of success, it perpetuates itself as well as helping the company to recruit people with innovative characteristics.

3M started life selling a somewhat inferior quality of sandpaper. The only way the company could promote this was by getting close to the customer – demonstrating it to the workmen that used it and persuading them to specify their product – an early form of relationship selling. This was the first strategic thrust of the fledgling business – get close to customers and understand their needs. For example, when it developed its overhead projector business it got technical staff to contact users to find out how the product could be improved. To this day it encourages close links with users.

However, the company was desperate to move away from selling a commodity product and competing primarily on price, and its closeness to the customer led it to discover market opportunities that it had the expertise to capitalize on. The first such product was Three-M-Ite Abrasive – an abrasive cloth using aluminium oxide for durability in place of a natural abrasive. This was followed by waterproof sandpaper – an idea bought from an inventor who subsequently came to work for 3M. This was followed shortly by Wetordry – a product designed for use by the car industry in finishing bodywork. And with this the second strategic thrust of the company was developed – to seek out niche markets, no matter how small, which would allow it to charge a premium price for its products. The company began to realize that many small niche markets could prove to be more profitable than a few large ones.

In the 1990s this began to change somewhat, to the extent that some technologies became more sophisticated and the investment needed to develop new products increased. Therefore the required return became larger and markets needed to be correspondingly bigger. Luckily the world was increasingly becoming a global market place. At the same time, competition was becoming tougher and the rapidity of technological change and shortening of product life cycles made 3M recognize the need to dominate any market niche quickly – so refining its second strategic thrust. Speed of response was vital. By the 1990s, many of the market niches 3M was pioneering were turning out to be not that small at all, particularly in the global market place. So, the approach remained the same, but the speed of response and size of market niche, world-wide, increased.

The company really started to diversify when it entered the tape market in the 1920s, but even this built on its expertise in coatings, backings and adhesives. What is more, the way the first product evolved demonstrates perfectly how an entrepreneurial architecture works. By being close to its customers 3M saw a problem that it was able to solve for them through its technical expertise. In selling Wetordry to car-body finishers, an employee realized how difficult it was for the painters to produce the latest fad in car painting – two tone paintwork. The result was the development of masking tape – imperfect at first, but developed over the years 'out-of-hours' by an employee to what we know it to be today, and from that technology developed the Scotch range of branded tapes. So, the third strategic thrust was developed – diversify into the related areas identified as market opportunities by customers. Once 3M found a niche product to offer in a new market, it soon developed other related products and developed a dominant position in the new

market. In the 1990s 3M came to recognize that it did best when it introduced radically innovative products into a niche market in which it already had a toe hold.

This experience not only taught 3M the value of research but also to appreciate maverick inventors who were so attached to their ideas that they would push them through despite the bureaucracy of the company. In the late 1920s it developed the policy of allowing researchers to spend up to 15% of their time working on their own projects. To this day, it tries to make innovation part of the corporate culture by encouraging staff to spend 15% of their time working on pet ideas that may one day become new products for the company. The company accepts that this can take time. Although staff are encouraged to 'bootleg' resources early in the development, they can also get money to buy equipment and hire extra help once an idea is accepted. To get an idea accepted, they must first get the personal backing of a member of the main board. Then an inter-disciplinary team of engineers, marketing specialists and accountants is set up to take the idea further. Membership of these teams is encouraged and often voluntary. Failure is not punished, but success is well rewarded.

Perhaps the best known contemporary example of the success of this policy is the development of the Post-It Note by Art Frye in the 1980s. He was looking for a way to mark places in a hymn book – a paper marker that would stick, but not permanently. At the same time the company had developed a new glue which, unfortunately as it seemed at the time, would not dry. Art spotted a use for the product but what was different was the way he went about persuading his bosses to back the project. He produced the product, complete with its distinctive yellow colour, and distributed it to secretaries who started using it throughout 3M. Art then cut their supplies, insisting that there would be no more unless the company officially backed the product. The rest is history.

→

So the fourth strategic thrust of the company was developed – to pursue product development and innovation at every level in the organization through research. This was formalized when the Central Research Laboratory was set up in 1937, but maverick research continued to be encouraged. In 1940, a New Product Department was developed to explore the viability of new products or technologies unrelated to existing ones. In 1943, a Product Fabrications Laboratory was set up to develop manufacturing processes. In the 1980s four Sector Labs were created with a view to being more responsive to the market place and undertaking medium-term research (5–10 years): Industrial and Consumer, Life Sciences, Electronic and Information Technologies and Graphic Technologies. The Central Lab, renamed the Corporate Lab, was maintained to undertake more long-term research (over 10 years). In addition most of the Divisions had their own Labs undertaking short-term, developmental research (1–5 years).

3M has always been admired for its ability to share knowledge across the organization and link technologies to produce numerous products that could be sold in different markets. It has a Technology Forum which seeks to encourage 'free and active interchange of information and cross-fertilization of ideas'. One product of this interchange is Scotchlite Reflective Sheeting used for road signs, developed in the 1940s – in fact as a result of failed research to develop reflective road markings. This combined research from three different laboratories to produce signs with a waterproof base onto which a covering of an opaque, light-reflecting pigment was added followed by microscopic beads. This was all sealed with a thin coat of plastic to ensure weather durability. The fifth strategy had emerged – get different parts of the organization to communicate and work together and, most important of all, share knowledge.

This became formalized in the 1950s with the establishment of the Technical Forum, set up with the aim of sharing knowledge across the company. It held annual shows. Out of this came the Technical Council, made up of technical directors and technical personnel, which met several times a year to review research and address common problems. Alongside this the Manufacturing Council and then the Marketing Council were established. At the same time Technical Directors and researchers regularly moved around the different divisions. The fifth strategy was in place – to share knowledge across the company.

The culture in 3M evolved out of its place of origin and has been called 'Minnesota nice'. It has been described as non-political, low ego, egalitarian and non-hierarchical as well as hardworking and self-critical. It has also, at least in its earlier days, been described as paternalistic in its approach to employees. Above all, 3M is achievement-orientated and achievement, particularly in research, is rewarded, often through promotion. For example successful new product teams were spun off to form new divisions. The leader of the team often became general manager of the new division and this was seen as a great motivator. Lesser achievements were also acknowledged. Researchers who consistently achieved 'high standards of originality, dedication and integrity in the technical field' – as judged by their peers, not management – were invited to join the exclusive 'Calton Society'. The 'Golden Step' and 'Pathfinder' awards were also given to those helping develop successful new products. Achievement was lauded at all levels. Strategy six was emerging – to encourage achievement through reward.

Today 3M faces many challenges to maintaining its reputation for innovation. As it becomes larger and more complex, involved in different markets with different products and technologies, at different stages of their life cycle, it recognizes that different managerial approaches may be necessary. The 'maverick', high-risk approach to research and development may not be appropriate in certain sectors. The 25% rule – the proportion of new product sales – may not be achievable by all Divisions. 3M also faces stiffer competition which means that cost economies have had to be made to maintain profitability. As a result the 15% rule – slack time to research new products – is under severe pressure, to the point where it is described as more of an attitude than a reality. Nevertheless, 3M has for over a century successfully practised corporate entrepreneurship.

☐ Up-to-date information on 3M can be found on their website: www.3M.com

A series of case studies on 3M, tracking its history and development since its inception in 1902, have been written by Research Associate Mary Ackenhusen, Professor Neil Churchill and Associate Professor Daniel Muzyka from INSEAD. They can be obtained from the Case Clearing House, England and USA.

QUESTIONS

1 List the six strategic thrusts of 3M. Are they appropriate for any company, even today?

2 Describe the organizational structures and devices 3M uses to encourage entrepreneurial activity. Why do they work?

3 How does 3M distinguish between incremental and fundamental innovations?

4 Describe, as best you can from the case, the culture of the organization. What does this depend upon?

5 Why has 3M been such a successful innovator for so long?

6 Can other companies just copy 3M's structures and culture and become successful innovators?

Summary

▷ Architecture is the term used to describe the long-term relational contracts within and around the organization – with customers, suppliers and staff. They are based upon trust and mutual self-interest. They are not necessarily legal contracts and often only partly specified, therefore not easy to copy. Because of this it can be a major source of sustainable competitive advantage.

▷ An entrepreneurial organization is a learning organization, one that facilitates learning for all its members and continuously transforms itself, thriving in a changing environment:

  ▷ Encouraging systematic problem-solving;
  ▷ Encouraging experimentation and new approaches;
  ▷ Learning from past experience and history;
  ▷ Learning from best practice and outside experience;
  ▷ Being skilled at transferring knowledge in the organization.

▷ Real knowledge is generated through the wheel of learning (F 3.1) so as to understand the root cause of problems and put in place systematic solutions – 'knowing-how', 'knowing-why' and doing something about it. It means linking this to our mental models – the dominant logic in an organization so as to challenge how things are.

▷ The most important learning occurs on the job. It is social and active. It is about learning tacit knowledge – intuition, judgement and expertise. Learning should therefore be a continuous process. Organizational learning and knowledge is an important by-product of architecture.

▷ Dominant logic is the mind set of managers that influences how they see the organization in its environment and how they interpret information. It influences everything they do and is the mechanism through which architecture operates. Changing dominant logic can cause a paradigm shift in business models, as we saw in the case of **Zipcar** (**Streetcar**).

▷ Complexity theory adds credence to the need for the three main elements of architecture – identity, information and relationships. These elements facilitate self-organization which gives direction to change.

▷ The tools available to construct architecture are culture, structure and leadership. Creating an appropriate architecture is the prime responsibility of a leader. Their role in taking a holistic, integrated approach to creating architecture is crucial.

▷ What the organization does with architecture depends on its strategies, but how it goes about developing strategies influences that architecture, and actively constructing architecture is a major strategic decision.

▷ To develop corporate entrepreneurship the organizational architecture must reflect the DNA of the entrepreneur – their character traits and approach to management and doing business. One of the most enduring examples of corporate entrepreneurship is **3M**.

▷ Entrepreneurial intensity can be measured in two dimensions: frequency (number of events) and degree (scale of innovativeness, risk-taking or proactiveness). These can be combined to develop an entrepreneurial grid that describes the nature of the organization's entrepreneurial strategy which in turn influences the appropriate architecture.

▷ Researchers claim a link between entrepreneurial intensity and firm performance but, equally, high entrepreneurial intensity is likely to mean high risk. Risk therefore needs to be carefully managed.

▷ Entrepreneurial firms thrive in environments of change, chaos, complexity, competition, uncertainty and even contradiction.

▷ The exact form of an effective entrepreneurial architecture depends on the internal and external environment the organization faces. It can be sectorally and geographically dependent. It can vary with the nature of the entrepreneurial intensity. The point is that there can be no prescriptive blueprint. This means structuring the organization so that each operating unit can be organized in such a way as to best deal with the environment it faces, possibly with structures within structures, sub-cultures within cultures and different approaches to leadership within an overall approach.

Essays and discussion topics

1 What is organizational architecture and how can it be created?

2 Why can the architecture of a firm give it sustainable competitive advantage?

3 Is it easier for an entrepreneur to build architecture as their business grows compared to reshaping it in a large organization? Explain.

4 What is needed to build long-term relationships?

5 Is the learning organization a romantic dream? Explain.

6 How can you spot a learning organization?

7 How does an entrepreneur learn?

8 Is the entrepreneurial organization really a learning organization? Explain.

9 How do you learn? Explain how the wheel of learning helps you to understand how you really learn?

10 How do you spread learning and knowledge in an organization?

11 Do you have mental models? How do these ever change? Give some examples.

12 Is there such a thing as an organizational mental model? Is it the same as dominant logic? Explain.

13 How can a leader change the dominant logic of an organization? What external factors might change the dominant logic? Explain.

14 Is Dell's competitive advantage based solely on its external architecture?

15 Why is the leader's role crucial in developing an entrepreneurial organization?

16 Which is riskier, frequent small-scale entrepreneurial activity or infrequent large-scale entrepreneurial activity? What are the implications of your conclusion? If you replace the phrase 'entrepreneurial activity' with the word 'innovation', would your conclusion change? Explain.

17 Why are organizations with a high degree of entrepreneurial intensity likely to show above-average performance? What are the negative implications?

18 Will an entrepreneurial organization succeed in all circumstances? Explain and give examples.

19 In what environment might a bureaucratic organization be more successful than an entrepreneurial organization? Explain and give examples.

20 How might geographic environment affect architecture? Give examples.

Exercises and assignments

1 List the type of organizations and market sectors or environments that face high degrees of change or turbulence. Select a particularly turbulent sector and research how the bodies within it are organized and the success, or otherwise, they have in dealing with it.

References

Bettis, R. A. and Prahalad, C. K. (1995) 'The Dominant Logic: Retrospective and Extension', *Strategic Management Journal*, 16.

Cooper, A.C. (1993) 'Challenges in Predicting New Firm Performance', *Journal of Business Venturing*, May.

Covin, J.G. and Slevin, D.P. (1989) 'Strategic Management of Small Firms in Hostile and Benign Environments', *Strategic Management Journal*, 10.

Davis, D., Morris, M. and Allen, J. (1991) 'Perceived Environmental Turbulence and Its Effect on Selected Entrepreneurship, Marketing and Organizational Characteristics in Industrial Firms', *Journal of Academy of Marketing Science*, 19.

Dubini, P. and Aldrich, H. (1991) 'Personal and Extended Networks are Central to the Entrepreneurial Process', *Journal of Business Venturing*, 8(3).

Eisenhardt, K.M. and Martin, J.A. (2000) 'Dynamic Capabilities: What are They?', *Strategic Management Journal*, 21.

Ferreira, J. (2002) 'Corporate Entrepreneurship: A Strategic and Structural Perspective', *47th International Council for Small Business World Conference*, Puerto Rico, June.

Grant, R.M. (2010) *Contemporary Strategic Analysis*, 7th edn, Chichester: Wiley.

Kay, J. (1993) *Foundations of Corporate Success*, Oxford: Oxford University Press.

Kim, D.H. (1993) 'The Link between Individual and Organizational Learning', *Sloan Management Review*, Fall.

Larson, A. (1992) 'Network Dyads in Entrepreneurial Settings: A Study of the Governance of Exchange Relationships', *Administrative Science Quarterly*, 37.

Leonard-Barton, D. (1992) 'Core Capabilities and Core Rigidities: A Paradox in Managing New Product Development', *Strategic Management Journal*, 13 (special issue).

Markóczy, L. (1994) 'Modes of Organizational Learning: Institutional Change and Hungarian Joint Ventures', *International Studies of Management and Organizations*, 24, December.

Miller, A. (1996) *Strategic Management*, Maidenhead: Irwin/McGraw-Hill.

Miller, D. and Friesen, P.H. (1983) 'Innovation in Conservative and Entrepreneurial Firms: Two Models of Strategic Momentum', *Strategic Management Journal*, 3(1).

Miner, J.B. (1990) 'Entrepreneurs, High Growth Entrepreneurs, and Managers: Contrasting and Overlapping Motivational Patterns', *Journal of Business Venturing*, July.

Morris, M.H. and Kuratko, D.F. (2002) *Corporate Entrepreneurship*, Fort Worth: Harcourt College Publishing.

Morris, M.H. and Sexton, D.L. (1996) 'The Concept of Entrepreneurial Intensity', *Journal of Business Research*, 36(1).

Pedler, M., Burgoyne, J.G. and Boydell, T. (1991) *The Learning Company: A Strategy for Sustainable Development*, London: McGraw-Hill.

Peters, T. and Waterman, R. (1982) *In Search of Excellence*, New York: Harper & Row.

Prahalad, C.K. and Bettis, R.A. (1986) 'The Dominant Logic: A New Linkage between Diversity and Performance', *Strategic Management Journal*, 7(6).

Senge, P. (1990) *The Fifth Discipline: The Art and Science of the Learning Organization*, New York: Currency Doubleday.

Senge, P. (1992) 'Mental Models', *Planning Review*, March–April.

Stata, R. (1992) 'Management Innovation', *Executive Excellence*, 9, June.

Symon, G. (2002) 'The "Reality" of Rhetoric and the Learning Organization in the UK', *Human Resource Development International*, 5(2).

Teece, D.J., Pisano, G. and Schuen, A. (1997) 'Dynamic Capabilities and Strategic Management', *Strategic Management Journal*, 18(7).

Timmons, J.A. (1999) *New Venture Creation: Entrepreneurship for the 21st Century*, Singapore: Irwin/McGraw-Hill.

Wilpert, B. (1995) 'Organizational Behavior', *Annual Review of Psychology*, 46, January.

Chapter **4**

Becoming an entrepreneurial leader

▷ **Leadership and management**
▷ **Defining the role of leader**
▷ **Building a shared vision**
▷ **Strategic intent**
▷ **Personal attributes of leaders**
▷ **Leadership style and contingency theory**
▷ **Leaders in a learning organization**
▷ **Leadership paradigms**
▷ **Leadership in the context of our time**
▷ **Entrepreneurial leaders**
▷ **Building the management team**
▷ **Summary**

Case insights
▷ Gary Redman and Now Recruitment – Leadership style

Case with questions
▷ Michael Dell – Entrepreneurial leaders

Executive insights
▷ Seven principles to successfully communicating a vision
▷ Leadership style questionnaire
▷ How do you behave in situations involving conflict?
▷ Are you a visionary leader?
▷ What sort of team player are you?

Learning outcomes

By the end of this chapter you should be able to:

▷ Describe the difference between management and leadership;

▷ Explain what the job of leader involves;

▷ Explain what is meant by vision and how it can be communicated effectively;

▷ Critically analyze the theories of leadership that have been proposed and their contribution to an understanding of how to lead an entrepreneurial organization;

▷ Understand and explain how leadership style can be tailored to different circumstances, and evaluate your preferred leadership style;

▷ Understand how conflict can be handled and evaluate how you handle it;

▷ Understand how effective management teams are put together, the process they go through before working effectively, and evaluate your preferred team role.

Leadership and management

Leading and managing an entrepreneurial organization is a challenge that requires some distinctive skills and capabilities. Leadership and management are different and distinct terms, although the skills and competencies associated with each are complimentary. Management is concerned with handling complexity in organizational processes and the execution of work. It is linked to the authority required to manage, somehow given to managers, within a hierarchy. Back in the nineteenth century Max Fayol defined the five functions of management as planning, organizing, commanding, coordinating and controlling. Today, these sound very much like the skills needed to lead a communist-style command economy. Fayol's work outlined how these functions required certain skills which could be taught and developed systematically in people. Management is therefore about detail and logic. It is about efficiency and effectiveness.

Leadership on the other hand is concerned with setting direction, communicating and motivating. It is about broad principles and emotion and less detail. It is a process of social influence that is particularly concerned with change. It is therefore quite possible for an organization to be over-managed but under-led, or vice versa. In a start-up good leadership is essential while effective management quickly becomes increasingly important to get things done. A larger organization, therefore, needs to be both effectively led and managed.

> 'A well-managed organization must produce the results for which it exists. It must be administered, that is, its decisions must be made in the right sequence and with the right timing and right intensity, In the long run, a well-managed organization must adapt to its external environment. The entrepreneurial role focuses on the adaptive changes, which requires creativity and risk taking. And to ensure that the organization can have a life span longer than that of any of its key managers, the fourth role – integration – is necessary to build a team effort. Effective and efficient management over the short and long term requires the use of all four roles.'
>
> **I. Adizes**, author, 1978

As with a manager, the role of leader is normally also based on some sort of authority. Authority can derive from role or status, tradition, legal position, expert skills or charismatic personality. Timmons (1999) believes that in successful entrepreneurial ventures leadership is based on expertise rather than authority and many of the best known, successful entrepreneurs, like Richard Branson or the late Steve Jobs, clearly also have charisma.

As with entrepreneurs, the idea that they may have enduring traits or characteristics which typify them has a long history, although by the latter half of the twentieth century any idea that these were somehow set in stone seemed to have been largely discredited as researchers realized that some leaders were good in one situation but not others. Nevertheless, like entrepreneurs, successful leaders do seem to behave in certain ways and this may well be influenced by character traits that are shaped by their history and experience. The one certain characteristic that separates them from others is the obvious one that they have willing followers. Leadership is situation-specific and it is therefore often argued that the characteristics and personality traits of good leaders tell us only a limited amount about good leadership. Leadership is about what you do with who you are and your relationships with followers rather than just who you are.

Blank (1995) argues that leadership is an 'event' – a 'discrete interaction each time a leader and a follower join ... Leadership can appear continuous if a leader manifests multiple leadership events.' One consequence of this is that, like entrepreneurs, leaders can have roller-coaster careers as they exhibit leadership characteristics at certain discrete times and with different people, in different circumstances, but not at others. Winston Churchill was widely acknowledged as a great war-time leader but a poor peace-time leader. Therefore entrepreneurs can be good leaders for the business at start-up but no good for either the growth or the maturity phase unless they adapt and change their style.

Trait theory, however, re-emerged as researchers showed that the same individuals can and do emerge as leaders across a variety of situations and tasks (Kenny and Zaccaro, 1983), although it is probably too simplistic just to say that their traits or characteristics define them as leaders. What it does is to give us some indications of the leadership characteristics and *behaviours* needed to lead an entrepreneurial organization. However, effective leadership is not just about leading an organization, it is also group-, task- and situation- or context-specific. And, as we see later in this chapter, leadership style can be crafted to meet these changing circumstances. In addition, the leader's personal cognitive abilities, motives, social skills, expertise and problem-solving skills may also be relevant to how effective they are as a leader (Zaccaro, 2007). What emerges is a complex interaction of many factors that underlines that effective leadership is an art rather than a science – and it is very dependent upon the context. Whilst we can isolate the main factors that influence it and point to good practice in particular contexts, there is no magic formula. However, at the heart of leadership is a relationship and leadership can be improved by improving the quality of the relationship – a theme amplified by Kouzes and Posner (2007).

Defining the role of leader

Our traditional view of leaders is that they are special people – charismatic 'heroes' like Churchill – who set direction, make key decisions and motivate staff, often prevailing against the odds at times of crisis. They have vision – something entrepreneurs certainly have aplenty. They are strategic thinkers and are effective communicators whilst still being able to monitor and control performance. Above all, they create the appropriate culture within the organization to reflect their priorities. Indeed leadership is more about guiding vision, culture and identity than it is about decision-making.

If there were ever a job description for a leader, therefore, it would probably include five elements:

1 *Having a vision for the organization*   This gives people a clear focus on the direction of the organization, the values it stands for and the key issues and concerns it faces in achieving its goals. Visions are underpinned by the values of the organization and the values are reflected in the culture of the organization. We shall return to this important element of leadership in Chapter 9.

2 *Being able to develop strategy*   It is one thing to know where you want to go, it is quite another to know how to get there. The heart of leadership is about being able to chart a course for future development that steers the organization towards the leader's vision. Whilst most text books talk about strategies being deliberate, consciously intended courses of action, we have noted that strategies often 'emerge' for entrepreneurs as they observe successful patterns, capitalize upon them and use them in the future. And to do this an understanding of strategic frameworks can help both in recognizing these patterns and then developing strategies based upon them. We shall return to this in Part 4.

3 *Being able to communicate effectively – particularly the vision*   There is no point in having a vision for the organization unless you can communicate it effectively and it inspires and motivates staff. Staff need to understand how the vision will be achieved, and believe that they can achieve it, particularly in an uncertain world. They need to understand where the organization is going and the strategies that are being adopted to take it there.

4 *Creating an appropriate culture in the organization*   The culture of an organization is the cement that binds it together. It influences how people think and how they act. Creating an appropriate culture for an entrepreneurial organization is probably the single most important thing a leader has to do – but it is not an easy task. We shall return to this in Chapter 5.

5 *Managing and monitoring performance*   Leaders still have to manage. This may be a routine task, but in an entrepreneurial organization there are special challenges such as dealing with rapid change, the balance between freedom and control and managing risk. We shall return to this in Part 3.

'Management is about communication and listening to people. I believe the people on the ground have the answer. If you can find what the answer is you'll get a much better solution for the business … Leadership to me is picking good teams and putting them together. And also putting yourself out for those people in terms of helping them when they're stuck, finding out what their concerns are, navigating them through problems. That, to me, is what leadership is about – not doing it yourself, but putting in place people who can do it for you.'

David Arculus, former MD, Emap group, Chief Operating Officer, United News and Media and chairman, IPC
The Times 3 May 2004

'Communicating is one of the most important tools in recovering from mistakes. When you tell someone, be it a designer, a customer, or the CEO of the company, "Look, we've got a problem. Here's how we're going to fix it," you diffuse the fear of the unknown and focus on the solution.'

Michael Dell

Building a shared vision

So, the first task of leadership is to have vision and building that shared vision is vital for an organization striving to succeed in a changing, uncertain world. It gives a sense of direction and helps develop organizational confidence. A vision is a shared mental image of a desired future state – an ideal of what the enterprise can become – a new and better world. It must be a realistic, credible and attractive future and one that engages and energizes people (Nanus, 1992). It is usually *qualitative* rather than quantitative (that is the role of the objectives). Vision is seen as inspiring and motivating, transcending logic and contractual relationships. It is more emotional than analytic, something that touches the heart. It gives existence within an organization to that most fundamental of human cravings – a sense of meaning and purpose. As Bartlett and Ghoshal (1994) explain: 'Traditionally top-level managers have tried to engage employees intellectually through the persuasive logic of strategic analysis. But clinically framed and contractually based relationships do not inspire the extraordinary effort and sustained commitment required to deliver consistently superior performance ... Senior managers must convert the contractual employees of an economic entity into committed members of a purposeful organization.' In other words, vision is the cornerstone of the entrepreneurial architecture we want to create.

Good visions motivate. Two strong motivations for people are fear and aspiration. Fear is probably the strongest motivation, galvanizing action and forcing people to change, but it tends to have a limited life. It worked well for Winston Churchill in the Second World War, but not thereafter. However, aspiration – what we might become – has greater longevity and is altogether a more positive motivator. It is the one that underpins most entrepreneurial organizations. It emphasizes striving – a continuous journey of improvement.

Visions are living things that evolve over time. Developing the vision is a continuous process. It involves continually checking with staff to ensure that the vision has a resonance with them – modifying it little by little, if appropriate. Some entrepreneurial leaders can find this difficult and frustrating as they are more used to setting goals and seeking compliance. But to succeed in a larger organization leaders need to develop their listening as well as influencing skills.

Successful entrepreneurs have a strong vision for their start-up. However, having your own individual vision is relatively easy. Building that shared vision with staff as the organization grows is altogether more difficult. It is not simply about going off and writing a vision statement that you circulate to staff. As Senge (1992) says: 'Building a shared vision is important early on because it fosters a long-term orientation and an imperative for learning ... Crafting a larger story is one of the oldest domains of leadership ... In a learning organization, leaders may start by pursuing their own vision, but as they learn to listen carefully to others' visions they begin to see that their own personal vision is part of something larger. This does not diminish any leader's sense of responsibility for the vision – if anything it deepens it.'

One important way a leader can build a shared vision is by becoming a storyteller. Gardner (1995) maintains this is the key leadership skill. This storytelling skill can be either verbal or written, however, leaders must 'walk the talk' – model the behaviour they expect from others (Kouzes and Posner, op. cit.) – otherwise they have no credibility and are not believed. Gardner maintains that the most successful stories are simple ones that hit an emotional resonance with the audience, addressing questions of identity and providing answers to questions concerning personal, social and moral choices. Is it any wonder that entrepreneurs skilled at developing personal relationships can also become powerful leaders?

Senge (op. cit.) highlights the creative tension this storytelling must engender by contrasting the shared vision with a constantly updated view of current reality: 'The leader's story, sense of purpose, values and vision, establish the direction and target. His relentless commitment to the truth, and to inquiry into the forces underlying current reality continually high-light the gaps between reality and the vision. Leaders generate and manage this creative tension – not just themselves but in an entire organization. This is how they energize an organization. That is their basic job. That is why they exist.' This creative tension therefore acts as a motivator. Too little tension produces inertia but too much can create chaos.

Senge goes on to underline how this tension can create within an entire organization the sense of internal locus of control that is part of the char-acter traits of an entrepreneur – emphasizing the belief in control over destiny: 'Mastering creative tension throughout an organization leads to a profoundly different view of reality. People literally start to see more and more aspects of reality as something that they, collectively, can influ-ence.' And this is one important psychological way that individuals within the entrepreneurial organization deal with the uncertainty they face. You might also recognize it as one aspect of 'empowerment' – a motivation for people to do 'the right thing' (whatever that might be) to resolve a problem or secure an opportunity for the good of the organization, even if it is not in their job description. *An entrepreneurial organization is an empowered learning organization.*

Bennis and Nanus (1985) talk about a 'spark of genius' in the act of leadership which 'operates on the emotional and spiritual resources of the organization.' For them the genius of the leader lies in 'this transcending ability, a kind of magic, to assemble – out of a variety of images, signals, forecasts and alternatives – a clearly articulated vision of the future that is at once simple, easily understood, clearly desirable, and ener-gizing ... leaders often inspire their followers to high levels of achievement by showing them how their work contributes to

'If there is a spark of genius in the leadership function at all, it must lie in the transcending ability, a kind of magic, to assemble ... out of a variety of images, signals, forecasts and alternatives ... a clearly articulated vision of the future that is at once simple, easily understood, clearly desirable, and energizing.'

Warren Bennis and **Burt Nanus**, authors, 1985

worthwhile ends. It is an emotional appeal to some of the most fundamental of human needs – the need to be important, to make a difference, to feel useful, to be part of a successful and worthwhile enterprise'. But entrepreneurial leadership that is to perpetuate itself is more than just charismatic leadership. Charismatic leaders deal in visions and crises, but little in between. Entrepreneurial leadership is about systematic and purposeful development of leadership skills and techniques within an organization – which can take a long time. It is about developing relationships. It is about creating long-term sustainable competitive advantage. And most of all it is about making the organization systematically entrepreneurial. We shall return to the issue of vision and how it can be developed in Chapter 9.

Seven principles for successfully communicating a vision

1 *Keep it simple*: Focused and jargon-free.
2 *Use metaphors, analogies and examples*: Engage the imagination.
3 *Use many different forums*: The same message should come from as many different directions as possible.
4 *Repeat the message*: The same message should be repeated again, and again, and again.
5 *Lead by example*: Walk the talk.
6 *Address small inconsistencies*: Small changes can have big effects if their symbolism is important to staff.
7 *Listen and be listened to*: Work hard to listen, it pays dividends.

Adapted from Kotter, J. P. (1996) *Leading Change*, Boston: Harvard Business School Press.

Strategic intent

Sometimes leaders know what they want to achieve but not how they might achieve it. Ambitious goals might exceed the obvious resources available to achieve them. In other words, there is no obvious, logical way of achieving the vision and creative tension is stretched to breaking point. And yet so many successful start-up businesses have succeeded, despite all the odds, in some cases creating new industries that could be only dreamed of.

Hamel and Prahalad (1994) give us an insight into how this comes about. Based upon a study of firms that have challenged established big companies in a range of industries, they observe that, in reconciling the misfit, successful firms use something they call 'strategic intent', which is about developing a common vision about the future, aligning staff behaviour with a common purpose and delegating and decentralizing decision-making.

They argued that 'the challengers had succeeded in creating entirely new forms of competitive advantage and dramatically rewriting the rules of engagement'. Managers in these firms could imagine new products, services and even entire industries that did not exist and then went on to create them. They were not just benchmarking and analyzing competition, they were creating new market places that they could dominate because it was a market place of their own making. But whilst these managers may be revolutionaries, they have their feet firmly on the ground because they understand very clearly the firm's core competences – that is, the skills and technologies that enable the company to provide benefits to customers.

Strategic intent is, therefore, used as a framework for achieving ambitious goals by energizing the organization into learning how to reach them. Entrepreneurial leaders using this approach need to set targets in the form of strategic intents that stretch the organization to perform significantly better or differently from the present. The 'intent' is the glue that binds the organization together and gets it to focus on achieving its goals. Staff need to be motivated to achieve these intents but also empowered to achieve them using knowledge from the market place. This approach is essential in an entrepreneurial organization that is looking to launch disruptive innovations or challenge the dominant logic of existing market conventions or paradigms and create new markets or even industries. We shall return to this in Chapter 12.

Personal attributes of leaders

A key mind-shift for a leader is the move away from operational detail to a broad, strategic, organizational perspective. It involves taking a longer-term, holistic view of the organization. Strategy sets a framework within which short-term actions can be judged and an important part of this is an understanding of the key strategic frameworks outlined in Part 4. Davies and Davies (2010) believe that strategic leaders exhibit or can develop a number of personal attributes or cognitive abilities that facilitate this mind-shift. In particular they become strategic thinkers. By this they mean that they have the ability to rise above day-to-day crises and see the bigger picture. They understand where they, or the organization, have come from and where they are going to. They also have an ability to ensure that strategy is turned into action. Mintzberg (2003) calls this 'seeing' – 'behind', 'ahead' and 'through' – a knowledge of the past, how it affects the current situation, where an organization wants to get to and how to get there. Strategic thinkers are also engaged in perpetually 'scanning' the environment, both for opportunities and risks, envisioning a new and desirable future based on this information and reframing this new future in the context of the organization. During the process they engage in synthesis as well as analysis. A key skill for this whole process is reflection and that requires time. Only if the leader is able to do this themselves can they hope to replicate it in the organization. Companies like Google and 3M build 'slack' into the workloads of managers so as to encourage this.

Davies and Davies (op. cit.) also believe that strategic leaders are strategic learners. Adapting the work of Hughes and Beatty (2005), they say learning for strategic leaders may involve looking at the big picture, trying to find patterns over time and looking for complex interactions so as to understand the underlying causes. Once more, this involves reflection and takes time. And if all of this seems familiar, it is. Refer back to Chapter 3 and you will see reflections of the learning organization. It seems that the strategic leader is a one-person learning organization, but the job of constructing an organizational architecture to replicate this remains a challenge. And, just as strategic leaders set up mechanisms and frameworks for ensuring learning takes place for themselves, they also need to ensure it happens for others in the organization using the organization's culture, structure and systems to support strategic learning.

According to Warren Bennis (quoted in George and Sims, 2007): 'As the world becomes more dangerous and our problems more complex and dire, we long for truly distinguished leaders, men and women who deserve our respect and loyalty.' Trust and respect underpin the relationship that a leader needs to establish with those they wish to lead. Trust is far more easily established with someone who has high moral characteristics or ethical values, particularly if the leaders are to command our respect and loyalty. And ethical leaders seem to generate more commitment and loyalty from staff. Trust and respect come from the actions of the leader. When asked what values they looked for in ethical leaders in a survey (Brubaker, 2005), respondents listed:

Regarding David Barclay, founder of Barclays Bank:

'We cannot form to ourselves, even in our imagination, the idea of a character more perfect than David Barclay, distinguished by his talent, his integrity, his philanthropy, his munificence. No man was ever more active than David Barclay in promoting whatever might ameliorate the condition of man.'

Morning Chronicle, London, 1809

▷   Truth and honesty;
▷   Integrity and alignment of words and actions;
▷   The keeping of promises;
▷   Loyalty to the organization and the people in it;
▷   Fairness between staff;
▷   Concern and respect for others;
▷   Law abiding;
▷   Pursuit of excellence;
▷   Personal accountability, taking responsibility, admitting mistakes and sharing success.

It is not easy to adopt personal attributes that do not represent the person you really are. Reflecting on interviews with 125 of today's top leaders, George and Sims (op. cit.) talk about 'authentic leadership' coming from these individuals who follow their real values and beliefs – their internal compass. George (2003) outlines the skills and personal attributes needed by authentic leaders. They have high levels of emotional intelligence incorporating:

▷ *Self-awareness* – the ability to understand yourself and your emotions;
▷ *Self-management* – control, integrity, initiative and conscientiousness;
▷ *Social awareness* – empathy, sensing other people's emotions;
▷ *Social skills* – communication, collaboration and, above all, relationship-building.

Authentic leaders build a support team of people with whom they have a close relationship (spouses, family members, mentors etc.) – people with whom they can reflect honestly on the issues they face – and they have a network of professional contacts to provide counsel and guidance. They have strong values and beliefs that they practise at work and at home – 'pursuing purpose with passion'. They have ethical foundations and boundaries and lead with their hearts as well as their heads. They establish enduring relations with staff because they listen to them and demonstrate that they care. George and Sims argue that, in this way, authentic leaders not only inspire those around them but also empower people to lead. But they only do this by always being true to their own principles, values and beliefs. They are authentic. And that cannot be faked.

'Even though I'm often asked to define my business philosophy, I generally won't do so because I don't believe it can be taught as a recipe. There aren't ingredients and techniques that will guarantee success. Parameters exist that, if followed, will ensure a business can continue, but you cannot clearly define business or business success and then bottle it as a perfume. It's not that simple: to be successful you have to be out there, you have to hit the ground running, and if you have a good team around you and more than your fair share of luck you might make something happen.'

Richard Branson

Leadership style and contingency theory

As we have noted, effective leadership is not just about the leader's characteristics or traits. It is a complex thing, also dependent upon the interactions and interconnections between the leader, the task, the group being led and the situation or context (Figure 4.1), and the appropriate leadership style depends upon how these factors interact. This is called situational or contingency theory. Three broad styles of leadership have been popularized. The authoritarian style – with decision-making powers focused in the leader – is thought appropriate in times of crisis but fails to win 'hearts and minds'. The democratic style – which favours group decision-making – seems more appropriate in other circumstances and involves consensus-building. Finally the 'laissez faire' style allows a high degree of freedom but the leader adopting this style is often perceived as weak. In reality there are many permutations of these three extremes.

'Once you have a business up and running the best way to keep in touch is to employ great people and empower them. This brings with it trust, communication and team spirit. When you work as a team you are in touch. My business style is non-aggressive, non-confrontational – it's who I am. It's important to be yourself. It comes from a background where you have to get on with people to get on. I believe that if you treat people like dirt on the way up it will come to haunt you as you find yourself on the way down.'

Jonathan Elvidge, founder of **Gadget Shop**
The Times 6 July 2002

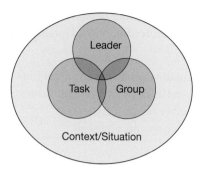

F 4.1 Leadership style

Contingency theory actually emphasizes that there is no one 'best' way of managing or leading. It depends on the interaction of all the factors in Figure 4.1 – leader, group, task and situation or context. A leader may personally prefer an informal, non-directional style, but faced with a young apprentice working a dangerous lathe they might be forgiven for reverting to a fairly formal, directive style with heavy supervision. In that situation the change in style is appropriate. Try the same style with a group of senior creative marketing consultants and there would be problems. Many different styles may be effective, with different tasks, different groups and in different contexts. Remember there is no evidence of any single leadership style characterizing successful businesses. What is more, the ability of leaders to change and adapt their styles may vary enormously.

Nevertheless, by picking off the individual elements of these four factors we can understand what style is best suited to different circumstances.

Leader and task

Leaders have to work through others to complete tasks. The degree of concern for the people they are leading, compared to the task in hand, will, in part, determine the style they adopt. The leadership grid shown in Figure 4.2 was developed by Blake and Mouton (1978). It shows style as dependent upon the leader's concern for task compared to the concern for people. Entrepreneurs are usually more concerned with completing the task but, as the firm grows, must become more concerned with people if the tasks are to be accomplished. Task leadership may be appropriate in certain situations, for example emergencies. However, concern for people must surface at some point if effective, trusting relationships are to develop. Low concern for both people and task is hardly leadership at all. High concern for people – the country club style – is rare in business but can

	Concern for task	
	Low	High
High	Country club	Team leadership
Concern for people		Firm but fair leadership
Low	Poor leadership	Task leadership

F 4.2 Leader and task

be appropriate in community groups, small charities or social clubs where good relationships and high morale might be the dominant objectives. You can find your preferred style on this grid by answering the leadership questionnaire overleaf and mapping your results on the grid (scoring is on the last page of this chapter). The questionnaire is also available on the website accompanying this book.

Timmons (op. cit.) believes that successful entrepreneurial ventures are more task-orientated although 'someone inevitably provides for maintenance and group cohesion by good humour and wit'. If this is the case then it is even more important to ensure that there is an appropriate and effective management team in place. Entrepreneurs must realize that, as the number of people they employ increases they must increase their 'concern for people' and move more towards a 'team leadership' style.

Leader and group

Leaders are likely to adopt different styles with different groups approaching the same task. Leadership style also depends on the relationship of the leader with the group they are leading. Figure 4.3 shows this in relation to the leader's degree of authority and the group's autonomy in decision-making. If a leader has high authority but the group has low autonomy, they will tend to adopt an autocratic style, simply instructing people what to do. If they have low authority, for whatever reason, they will tend to adopt a paternalistic style, cajoling the group into doing things, picking off individuals and offering grace and favour in exchange for performance. If the leader has low authority and the group has high autonomy, then they will tend to adopt a participative style, involving the whole group in decision-making and moving forward with consensus. If the leader has high authority then they will seek opinions but make the decision themselves using a consultative style.

A survey of small business managers in Britain, France, Germany, Spain and Italy showed that most used a consultative style (Burns and Whitehouse, 1996). However, 20–30% of managers in all countries other than Germany used an autocratic style. It has been said that growth-orientated companies are initially characterized by an autocratic or dictatorial style but as the company grows a more consultative style develops as the entrepreneur recruits managers and gives them more autonomy (Burns

		Leader's authority	
		Low	High
	High	Participative	Consultative
Group autonomy in decision-making			
	Low	Paternalistic	Autocratic

F 4.3 Leader and group

Leadership Style Questionnaire

For each of the following statements, tick the 'Yes' box if you tend to agree or the 'No' box if you disagree. Try to relate the answers to your actual recent behaviour as a manager. There are no right and wrong answers.

		Yes	No
1	I encourage overtime work	☐	☐
2	I allow staff complete freedom in their work	☐	☐
3	I encourage the use of standard procedures	☐	☐
4	I allow staff to use their own judgement in solving problems	☐	☐
5	I stress being better than other firms	☐	☐
6	I urge staff to greater effort	☐	☐
7	I try out my ideas with others in the firm	☐	☐
8	I let my staff work in the way they think best	☐	☐
9	I keep work moving at a rapid pace	☐	☐
10	I turn staff loose on a job and let them get on with it	☐	☐
11	I settle conflicts when they happen	☐	☐
12	I get swamped by detail	☐	☐
13	I always represent the 'firm view' at meetings with outsiders	☐	☐
14	I am reluctant to allow staff freedom of action	☐	☐
15	I decide what should be done and who should do it	☐	☐
16	I push for improved quality	☐	☐
17	I let some staff have authority I could keep	☐	☐
18	Things usually turn out as I predict	☐	☐
19	I allow staff a high degree of initiative	☐	☐
20	I assign staff to particular tasks	☐	☐
21	I am willing to make changes	☐	☐
22	I ask staff to work harder	☐	☐
23	I trust staff to exercise good judgement	☐	☐
24	I schedule the work to be done	☐	☐
25	I refuse to explain my actions	☐	☐
26	I persuade others that my ideas are to their advantage	☐	☐
27	I permit the staff to set their own pace for change	☐	☐
28	I urge staff to beat previous targets	☐	☐
29	I act without consulting staff	☐	☐
30	I ask staff to follow standard rules and procedures	☐	☐

Adapted from Pfeiffer, J. and Jones, J. (eds) (1974), *A Handbook of Structured Experiences from Human Relations Training*, vol. 1 (rev.), University Associates, San Diego, California.

Scoring for this test can be found on p. 132.

and Whitehouse, op. cit.; Ray and Hutchinson, 1983). Leadership styles also seem to be influenced by national culture. The survey revealed that a significant proportion (35%) of German managers use a participative style, despite the fact that none of them thought their subordinates liked it. This probably reflects cultural differences at a national level, where consultative or participative decision-making is the norm, particularly when unions are involved. However, this mismatch between actual style, dictated by cultural norms, and desired style must create tensions for German entrepreneurs.

Leader and context/situation

John Adair (1984) put forward the view that the weight the leader should put on these different influences depends on the situation or context. In an entrepreneurial firm that situation can be characterized as one of uncertainty, ambiguity and rapid change. What does that tell us about the context? Timmons (op. cit.) observed that: 'There is among successful entrepreneurs a well developed capacity to exert influence without formal power. These people are adept at conflict resolution. They know when to use logic and when to persuade, when to make a concession, and when to exact one. To run a successful venture, an entrepreneur learns to get along with different constituencies, often with conflicting aims – the customer, the supplier, the financial backer, the creditor, as well as the partners and others on the inside. Success comes when the entrepreneur is a mediator, a negotiator, rather than a dictator.'

How a good entrepreneurial leader approaches any task, with any group, therefore depends on the situation they face – the context. But entrepreneurial firms face an environment that is constantly changing, which can often lead to conflict as they try to get people to do different things or things differently. The Thomas-Kilmann Conflict Modes instrument gives us an insight into how conflict might be handled. Whilst each style has its advantages in certain situations, compromise, or better still collaboration, is generally thought to be the best way for a team to work.

Entrepreneurial leaders face uncertainty and ambiguity, trying to manage people who often have unclear job definitions because they have to cope with change. This can create conflict that has to be resolved on an everyday basis. The implications of the entrepreneurial situation are:

▷ As the business grows, entrepreneurs should move away from using an autocratic or dictatorial leadership style, especially with their senior management team, if they want staff to take more control over their actions and develop an entrepreneurial organization as it grows. However, many find it difficult to change their leadership style and in these circumstances it is essential that there is an effective management team in place that can demonstrate differences in style to suit differing circumstances.

How do you behave in situations involving conflict?

Often in business you find yourself at odds with others who hold seemingly incompatible views. For a leader to be effective they need to understand how they handle these conflict situations and be able to modify their behaviour to obtain the best results from others. Based on research by Kenneth Thomas and Ralph Kilmann, the Thomas-Kilmann Conflict Modes Instrument shows how a person's behaviour can be classified under two dimensions:

▷ Assertiveness – the extent to which individuals attempt to satisfy their own needs.

▷ Cooperativeness – the extent to which they attempt to satisfy the needs of others.

These two dimensions lead the authors to identify five behavioural classifications which the questionnaire can identify in individuals:

1 **Competing** is assertive and uncooperative. Individuals are concerned for themselves and pursue their own agenda forcefully, using power, rank or ability to argue in order to win the conflict. This can be seen as bullying with less forceful individuals or, when others use the same mode, it can lead to heated, possibly unresolved, arguments.

2 **Accommodating** is unassertive and cooperative, the opposite of competing. Individuals want to see the concerns of others satisfied. They might do so as an act of 'selfless generosity' or just because they are 'obeying orders', either way they run the risk of not making their own views heard.

3 **Avoiding** is both unassertive and uncooperative. It may involve side-stepping an issue or withdrawing from the conflict altogether. In this mode any conflict may not be even addressed.

4 **Collaborating** is both assertive and cooperative, the opposite of avoiding. Issues get addressed but individuals are willing to work with others to resolve the conflict, perhaps finding alternatives that meet everybody's concerns. This is the most constructive approach to conflict for a group as a whole.

5 **Compromising** is the 'in between' route, the diplomatic, expedient solution to conflict which partially satisfies everyone. It may involve making concessions.

Each style of handling conflict has its advantages and disadvantages and can be effective in certain situations. However, management teams or boards of directors, if they are to get the most from each member over a longer period of time, work best when all members adopt the collaborating or compromising modes. A team made up of just competitors would find it difficult to get on and, indeed, to survive. A team made up of just accommodators would lack assertiveness and drive.

☐ The Thomas-Kilmann Conflict Modes Instrument is available on www.kilmann.com/conflict.html

▷ Entrepreneurial leaders should be adept at using informal influence. Their powers of persuasion and motivation are important. They should meet and influence people. Relationships and organizational culture are important. The literature on emotional leadership (Goleman, 1996; 1998) gives us some insights into how leaders might be more sensitive to differences in groups and situations.

▷ Entrepreneurial leaders must be adept at conflict resolution. In these situations Timmons (op. cit.) observes: 'Successful entrepreneurs are interpersonally supporting and nurturing – not interpersonally competitive.' In terms of the Thomas-Kilmann Conflict Modes this is the 'collaborating' or 'compromising' mode.

Leaders in a learning organization

Our image of a leader tends to propagate the myth of the individual focusing on short-term results, often overcoming some sort of crisis, rather than the systematic pursuit of long-term excellence. The image is often based on implicit assumptions of the general powerlessness, lack of personal vision and inability or unwillingness to change of other people. But in reality successful entrepreneurial leaders are different. We have already noted Timmons' (op. cit.) description of successful entrepreneurs as 'patient leaders, capable of instilling tangible visions and managing for the long haul. The entrepreneur is at once a learner and a teacher, a doer and a visionary.' And we have already observed that this is almost identical to the definition of the leader of a learning organization – all very different from the charismatic hero much loved by folklore.

So what does the literature of the learning organization have to contribute to our understanding of leadership? We have observed that the learning organization must encourage systematic problem-solving, encourage experimentation and new approaches, learning from past experience and history, learning from best practice and outside experience and, finally, being skilled at transferring knowledge in the organization. Senge (op. cit.) explains that this is done by designing the organization and its architecture so as to encourage the learning process. This involves 'integrating vision, values, and purpose, systems thinking, and mental models.' It also involves designing an organizational architecture that is continually able to learn, adapt and change – encouraging people to focus activity where change, with the minimum of effort, will lead to significant and lasting improvement for the organization.

Leaders should put in place structures to encourage these things but they also should adopt a leadership style that is compatible with the architecture. The first thing they should do is to ensure there is an openness in their leadership style that encourages speedy and accurate transfer of information and learning. Information should not be used as a political tool to secure power. As we shall see in Chapter 13, opportunities for gaining information and learning should be built into the routine of an organization seeking to encourage creativity. Cases on HFL Sport Science (Chapter 5), Google (Chapter 12), LG and Hallmark (Chapter 13) show how this can be done routinely and systematically. Leaders should encourage experimentation and therefore tolerate mistakes.

'One thing is certain in business; you and everyone around you will make mistakes. When you are pushing the boundaries this is inevitable ... A person who makes no mistakes, makes nothing.'

Richard Branson
www.hrmagazine.co.uk 13 July 2010

Senge (op. cit.) talks about teaching learning and developing a systematic understanding of how to approach and exploit change through leadership style. 'Many visionary strategists have rich intuitions about the causes of change, intuitions that they cannot explain. They end up being authoritarian leaders, imposing their strategies and policies or continually intervening in decisions. They fall into this fate even if their values are contrary to authoritarian leadership – because they feel that they alone can see the decisions that need to be made. Leaders in learning organizations have the ability to conceptualize their strategic insights so that they become public knowledge, open to challenge and further improvement.'

So the leader should not be authoritarian. They need to manage with a 'light touch' and empower staff to use the information and learning that they have. At the heart of this is their ability to teach the organization how to restructure views of reality in such a way as to understand the root causes of a problem and address them in order to produce an enduring solution rather than simply addressing the short-term symptoms. This involves seeing interrelationships, not static images. It involves moving beyond blame to understanding the causes of problems. It involves understanding 'dynamic complexity' – cause and effect over time – rather than detail complexity. Ultimately it involves putting in place systematic structures that address the generic problem or opportunity. The leader's role is to provide that clear focus on the key issues and concerns for the organization and making sure that staff are empowered to address those issues and concerns, to do 'the right thing' for the organization – whatever that might be – without needing to be instructed to do so.

Leadership paradigms

We have seen that context is everything in leadership and the entrepreneurial context of leadership is one characterized by uncertainty, rapid change and risk-taking. It is part of the entrepreneurial DNA outlined in Chapter 3. One branch of the leadership literature gives us some further insights into how larger organizations are best led through periods of change. Bass (1985, 1998) contrasts what he calls 'transactional' leadership with 'transformational' leadership. The former is about setting goals, putting in place systems and controls to achieve them and rewarding individuals when they meet the goals. It is about efficiency and incremental change, reinforcing rather than challenging organizational learning. By way of contrast, transformational leadership is more emotional and is about inspiration, excitement and intellectual stimulation. It is a style best suited to highly turbulent and uncertain environments where crises, anxiety and high risk are prevalent (Vera and Crossan, 2004). It is a style that often challenges organizational learning. It has a number of similarities with what is called visionary leadership (see below).

Are you a visionary leader?

In *Becoming a Visionary Leader* (HRD Press, Amherst, MA, 1996) Marshall Sashkin defines a visionary leader as one who:

▷ Provides *clear* leadership which focuses people on goals that are part of a vision and on key issues and concerns;
▷ Has good *interpersonal communication skills* that gets everyone to understand the focus and to work together towards common goals;
▷ Acts *consistently* over time to develop trust;
▷ *Cares* and respects others, making them self-confident, whilst having an inner self-confidence themselves;
▷ Provides *creative* opportunities that others can buy into and 'own' – empowering opportunities that involve people in making the right things their own priorities.

The booklet contains a series of questions designed to see whether you might be a visionary leader. These start with an 'Impact Focus Scale' which looks at your motivations for wanting to be a leader. These are measured in three dimensions or scores. Effective leaders score high in each area:

1 *Impact belief score* – which measures your belief that you can make a difference within the organization.
2 *Social power need* – which measures the value you place on power and influence for the good that you can do with it within the organization.
3 *Dominance avoidance* – which measures your need for dominance or vice versa. Effective leaders do not need to dominate.

The second part involves a 'Cultural Functions Inventory' which is designed to help decide whether an organization's culture is effective at facilitating certain crucial functions. The resulting scores measure the ability to adapt to change, attain goals, coordinate teamwork and systems stability.

Finally, Sashkin has produced the *Leader Behavior Questionnaire* (available on www.hrdpress.com/visionary-leader-questionnaire-set-5-pack-VLQS), which is a 360-degree assessment instrument that measures visionary leadership behaviours, characteristics and contextual effects (filled out by 3–6 colleagues). The behaviours measured are:

▷ How well you manage to focus people's attention on key issues;
▷ How effective you are at communication, including 'active listening';
▷ How consistent your views and actions are and how you develop trust;
▷ Whether you demonstrate respect and regard for others;
▷ Whether you come up with ideas and opportunities that others find attractive and wish to take part in.

Both styles are appropriate in different circumstances (contingency theory) and leaders may switch as an organization cycles through periods of rapid change (transformational leadership) followed by consolidation (transactional leadership). However, there are clear similarities between what we have called entrepreneurial leadership and transformational leadership, reflecting the environmental context. Vera and Crossan (op. cit.) observe that 'highly transformational leaders tend to encourage open cultures, organic structures, adaptable systems, and flexible procedures – attributes that facilitate the implementation of change and challenge institutionalized learning. This type of internal context is characteristic of firms with aggressive strategies and a high potential for growth and innovation.' By way of contrast: 'Highly transactional leaders tend to encourage closed cultures, mechanistic structures, rigid systems, and procedures that facilitate the reinforcement and refinement of institutional learning. Organizations with this type of internal environment usually select conservative strategies.'

Transformational leaders are often seen as being charismatic, inspirational, intellectually stimulating and individually considerate (Avolio et al., 1999) and having empathy and self-confidence (Egri and Herman, 2000). They inspire and motivate people with a vision, create excitement with their enthusiasm and get people to question the tried-and-tested ways of doing things and 'reframe' the future (Bass and Avolio, 1990).

An entrepreneur may already have many of these leadership attributes. However, to be a leader of an entrepreneurial organization they will need to transform not only themselves but also the organization so that the organization itself demonstrates these qualities. So, being an entrepreneurial leader is subtly different from being an entrepreneur, as Collins and Porras (1994) eloquently explain: 'Imagine you met a remarkable person who could look at the sun or stars at any time of day or night and state the exact time and date ... This person would be an amazing time teller, and we'd probably revere that person for the ability to tell the time. But wouldn't that person be even more amazing if, instead of telling the time, he or she built a clock that could tell time forever, even after he or she was dead and gone.'

Being just a transformational, charismatic or visionary leader is 'time telling'. Being an entrepreneurial leader is about building an organization that can prosper far beyond the single leader, through multiple product life cycles – it is 'clock building'. So, entrepreneurial leaders are *builders of organizations that are both visionary and transformational.* They are clock builders not the time tellers. And instead of concentrating just on acquiring the individual attributes of leadership, they take an architectural approach and concentrate on building these leadership attributes within the organization and spreading them throughout it (Burns, 2005). More recently, Gary Hamel (2009) acknowledged this changing role of leadership: 'The notion of the leader as a heroic decision maker is untenable. Leaders must be recast as social-systems architects who enable innovation ... Leaders will no longer be seen as grand visionaries, all-wise decision makers, and ironfisted disciplinarians. Instead they will need to become social architects, constitution writers, and entrepreneurs of meaning. In this new world, the leader's job is to create an environment where every employee has the chance to collaborate, innovate, and excel.' The entrepreneurial leader realizes that organizations are networks of individuals, all exercising some form of leadership and with no one person in total control, but with everyone open to influence through patterns of relationship (Raelin, 2003; Rost, 1991).

The entrepreneurial leader, therefore, also draws on models of dispersed or distributed leadership which focus on leadership across all levels and in different forms (Bradford and Cohen, 1998; Chaleff, 1995; Mintzberg, 2009). This literature emphasizes the importance of 'emotional intelligence' in the leader and their ability to listen, empathize and communicate with those they lead (Goleman, 1996) – social skills essential to building effective relationships. As already mentioned, it emphasizes 'authenticity' (George, op. cit.; George and Sims, op. cit.) – leaders being true to their own beliefs (having an ethical underpinning) so that trust and respect can be built. The literature also emphasizes leaders as 'servants' of their workforce, acknowledging that self-interest is part of any relationship (Greenleaf, 1970) as well as 'educators' that develop organizational learning (Heifetz, 1994). These are all characteristics that we have already identified and themes we have explored. So, the entrepreneurial leader is subtly different from other leadership typologies. They are both visionary and transformational but, importantly, they set out to build and embed leadership into the organization.

Kirby (2003) likens the entrepreneurial leader to the leader of a jazz band. He decides on the musicians to play in the band and the music to be played but then allows the band to improvise and use their creativity to create the required sounds. In the process they have fun as the leader brings out the best in them. The leader's authority comes from his expertise and values rather than his position. Leaders of jazz bands lead by example – playing an instrument themselves. They empower their teams and nurture leaders at all levels – encouraging solo performances.

> 'Our view at Virgin is that collective responsibility bonds the team, and having pride in your work is a far better driver than a hierarchical culture where the boss calls the shots.'
>
> **Richard Branson**
> www.hrmagazine.co.uk 13 July 2010

Leadership in the context of our time

Leadership must also be based in the context of the time. The markets of the world now seem increasingly global, interconnected and complex. At the time of writing, investor capitalism is being criticized for causing a major global recession and being too focused on creating individual shareholder wealth at the expense of the well-being of employees, society and the ecology of the planet. Giltsham et al. (2011) summarize the challenges currently facing organizations as those of context, complexity and connectedness. Commenting upon these challenges, Turnbull (2011) says: 'Leadership can no longer be conceived as an activity to be undertaken by a single heroic individual at the top of an organization alone, but that as the business context becomes increasingly complex, interconnected and fast-changing, organizations that focus on building cultures that engage the leadership capacity of employees, and the connectivity with the communities in which they operate are more likely to be successful in today's world.' These are all familiar themes that underline the importance for the entrepreneurial leader of building sustainable organizational capacity – 'clock building'. However, it is a notable fact that, in response to the ongoing economic crisis and the need to cut costs and conserve cash, many organizations in 2012 were doing precisely the reverse of this: recentralizing management and making their leadership more interventionist and directive. Notwithstanding the academic literature, time will tell whether this was the appropriate response.

In transforming themselves into the leader of an entrepreneurial organization the entrepreneur must also reconcile the conflict between their natural impatience and the constraints imposed by an organization in its desire to control events. That is where different structures can be important as well as the role of change agents such as intrapreneurs. The leader's role, however, is more than that of the change agent, championing individual initiatives. Pursuing innovative ideas may be exciting but the leader needs to give the firm a sense of direction and purpose by aligning these developments to the vision and direction of the organization. That means standing back from the developments and providing a measure of impartial and objective evaluation. They must take an overview; reconciling differing perspectives – which may involve conflict resolution, creating a climate of cooperation – which will also involve coordination, but also exercising authority when needed to bring forward some initiative whilst pushing back others.

Entrepreneurial leaders

This chapter has highlighted many attributes, skills and behaviours needed to lead an entrepreneurial organization – one that is characterized by uncertainty, rapid change and risk-taking and tries to replicate many of the elements of the DNA of entrepreneurs (refer back to Chapter 3). We have supplemented this by drawing on the literature about 'strategic' and 'authentic' leaders. We have also drawn on a number of leadership paradigms – learning organization, transformational/transactional leadership, visionary leadership and dispersed leadership. Combining these elements, we have started to define the entrepreneurial leader using contingency/situational theory to describe the influence of the environment in which they find themselves. However, in doing this we must remember

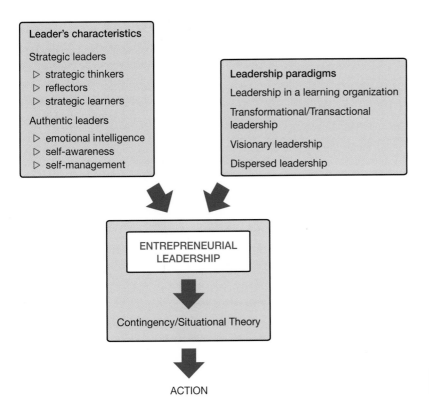

F 4.4 The entrepreneurial leader

that contingency theory tells us that the entrepreneurial leader should also modify their actions to fit the specific local circumstances – groups, tasks and situations – at any point of time. This is shown in Figure 4.4.

This chapter has underlined the need for the leader to be a good strategic thinker and learner – and all that entails from vision to execution. It has emphasized the need for the leader to have strong emotional intelligence – good interpersonal and team-working skills, alongside good conflict resolution skills – but, more than anything, they need strong influencing skills. These skills are all focused towards taking the organization with them by consensus and agreement rather than by dictating, and making the organization self-sustainingly entrepreneurial. These attributes, skills and behaviours are summarized in Table 4.1. However, they will need to be 'fine-tuned' for specific audiences undertaking specific tasks and they will shift over time. They can be developed and improved over time and some can be shared with the rest of the management team, who might be more at ease leading certain groups in certain situations. However, the main aim of the entrepreneurial leader is always to build an entrepreneurial architecture for the organization so that it can operate effectively on its own, without them. There is an ancient Chinese proverb that still rings true:

> The wicked leader is he who the people despise. The good leader is the one who the people revere. But the great leader is he who the people say 'we did it ourselves'.

T 4.1 Entrepreneurial leadership attributes, skills and behaviours

1   **Visionary** – the essential bedrock of leadership. The vision should give clear direction and be underpinned with values. It should, however, be grounded in reality.

2   **Good communicator/motivator** – the vision should be shared by all the staff in the organization and motivate them to achieve it. Motivation should be underpinned by loyalty to both the leader and the organization.

3   **Strategic thinker and learner** – the vision should be supplemented with an understanding of how to achieve it and what the strategic options for direction might be.

4   **Emotionally intelligent with strong interpersonal skills** – able to listen, to influence rather than direct, to resolve conflict and to manage 'with a light touch'. They should 'walk the talk'; model the behaviour they expect from others.

5   **Relationship builder** – able to build a cohesive, open and trusting management team. This comes about by acting consistently over time based upon a dominant set of values so as to generate trust (firm but fair) and is underpinned by care and respect for staff.

6   **Team player** – willing to share information and delegate to the team. This is based upon an understanding of how teams work.

7   **Builder of confidence** – encouraging organizational self-confidence and self-efficacy in the face of uncertainty and risk-taking. They should inspire others to share their visions and dreams.

8   **Builder of an open organization that shares information** – fostering the sharing of knowledge, information and ideas, and the willingness to question the status quo and to experiment and take measured risks.

9   **Clarifier of ambiguity and uncertainty** – so as to give a clear focus on the key issues and concerns facing the organization in the face of rapid change. This focus should be effectively communicated.

10 **Builder of empowering opportunities** – so that staff make 'the right thing' for the organization their own enthusiastic priority; in other words, spreading entrepreneurship and leadership throughout the organization.

Building the management team

As we have observed, leaders need followers and an entrepreneurial organization will only succeed if it has a good management team. And in an entrepreneurial organization all the management team needs to exhibit leadership characteristics in certain contexts. What is more, as we shall see, team-working is an effective way of pushing through change and innovation. Tappin and Cave (2008) have argued that team leadership is the most appropriate approach to dealing with turbulent times if there is strong cohesion between this top team. They argue that this top team, ideally, comprises just three or four individuals who share knowledge and, although having specialized roles, are able to cover for one another.

🗐 Case insight   Gary Redman and Now Recruitment

Leadership style

Now Recruitment, founded in 1991, is an industry award-winning global recruitment agency with offices across the UK and international offices in Australia and the United Arab Emirates. It is 90% owned by Gary Redman, who readily admits that his management style has had to change dramatically to accommodate the growth. The company stalled when turnover reached £6 million and staff turnover shot through the roof. Gary brought in a management consultant:

'He told me that the biggest problem in the business was me. He explained that staff were saying they were not clear where the business was going, they didn't know what I wanted and they didn't get a chance to voice their opinions ... The way I operated was to shout at people ... I thought you got results out of people by putting them under pressure. It was a ruthless kind of culture where if you performed well you were in, and if you didn't perform well you were out.'

Sunday Times 8 August 2004

Addressing another personal problem, Gary also went on a management development course which taught him how to delegate responsibility rather than try to control everything himself. Changing his style of leadership worked. Staff retention improved and the business started to grow again.

Attracting good managers may be difficult for a small, growing business, even one with ambitious plans. An entrepreneurial organization faces an uncertain future and because of this there may be a perceived lack of job security and uncertainty about promotion. Cash may not always be readily available to fund higher salaries, hence the need, often, to offer shares in the company. If the ambitions turn into reality, managers will share the rewards. Nevertheless a leader needs to attract a good management team with their vision of the future of the organization and the style of leadership they adopt. Leaders with clear values and characteristics can often attract like-minded managers.

Selecting an effective team will depend upon the mix of functional skills and market or industry experience required in the firm, as well as the personal chemistry between its members. For a team to be effective individuals need to have the right mix of a certain set of personal characteristics. Meredith Belbin (1981) identified nine

'The ability to find and hire the right people can make or break your business. It is as plain as that. No matter where you are in the life cycle of your business, bringing in great talent should always be a top priority ... The right people in the right jobs are instrumental to a company's success ... If you assume that people can grow at the same rate as your company – and still maintain the sharp focus that is critical to success – you will be sadly disappointed. When a business is growing quickly, many jobs grow laterally in responsibility, becoming too big and complex for even the most ambitious, hard-working person to handle without sacrificing personal career development or becoming burned out.'

Michael Dell

'Know what you are good at and, importantly, know your weaknesses, and get in good people to support you in these areas.'

Geoff Barrell, founder of **BlueArc Ltd**
The Times 16 March 2002

'Our guiding principle is this: give individuals the tools they need, outline some parameters to work within, and then just let them get on and do their stuff.'

Richard Branson
www.hrmagazine.co.uk 13 July 2010

clusters of personal characteristics or attributes which translate into 'team roles', each with positive qualities and allowable weaknesses; shaper, plant, coordinator, resource investigator, monitor-evaluator, team-worker, implementer, completer-finisher and specialist (see opposite). Individuals are unlikely to have more than two or three of these clusters of characteristics, yet all nine need to be present in a team for it to work effectively. It has been suggested that the 'prototypical entrepreneur' might be a plant (creative, ideas person), shaper (dynamism, full of drive and energy) and a resource investigator (enthusiastically explores opportunities) (Chell, 2001). In this case the first team member should not be strong in any of these categories, but ideally should be an implementer (reliable, efficient and able to turn ideas into practical action). The implementer will want a completer-finisher (conscientious, delivers on time), a team-worker (cooperative and unchallenging) and possibly a specialist (with particular knowledge or skills) working under them.

The leader's role is to select the team and then to build cohesion and motivation. In most cases this involves building consensus towards the goals of the firm, balancing multiple viewpoints and demands. However, too great a reliance on achieving consensus can lead to slow decision-making, so a balance is needed that will strain the interpersonal skills of the leader. In the best entrepreneurial firms leadership seems to work almost by infection. The management team are infected by the philosophies and attitudes of the leader and readily buy into the goals set for the firm, something that is helped if they share in its success.

All personal relationships are based upon trust. Trust is the cornerstone of a good team and the cornerstone of an effective organizational culture. It is imperative that the management team trusts their entrepreneurial leader. For leaders this involves having transparent vision and values, being firm but fair, flexible but consistent. It involves being straightforward – doing what they say and meaning what they say – 'walking the talk'. It involves

'The best teams stand out because they are teams, because the individual members have been so truly integrated that the team functions with a single spirit. There is a constant flow of mutual support among the players, enabling them to feed off strengths and compensate for weaknesses. They depend on one another, trust one another. A manager should engender that sense of unity. He should create a bond among his players and between him and them that raises performance to heights that were unimaginable when they started out as disparate individuals.'

Alex Ferguson, Manager, Manchester United Football Club
Managing My Life, London: Hodder and Stoughton, 1999

being open and spontaneous, honest and direct – being an authentic leader. Whilst always placing the interests of the firm first, it also involves being supportive of individuals and having their interests at heart. Trust also needs to be built up between individual members of the management team. Trust takes time to build and needs to be demonstrated with real outcomes, but can be lost very quickly by careless actions and then takes even longer to rebuild.

Effective teams, therefore, do not just happen, they have to be developed, and that can take time. Teams go through a development process, shown in Figure 4.5.

What sort of team player are you?

Developing a successful team depends not just on the range of professional skills it has, but also on the range of personal characteristics – the chemistry of the team. Based upon research into how teams work, Meredith Belbin identified nine clusters of personal characteristics or attributes which translate into 'team roles'. Most individuals are naturally suited to two or three roles. However, to work effectively a team must comprise elements of all nine roles. If a team lacks certain team roles it tends to exhibit weaknesses in these areas. The roles are:

The Shaper: This is usually the self-elected task leader with lots of nervous energy. Shapers are extrovert, dynamic, outgoing, highly strung, argumentative, pressurizers seeking ways around obstacles. They do have a tendency to bully and are not always liked. However, they generate action and thrive under pressure.

The Plant: This is the team's vital spark and chief source of new ideas. Plants are creative, imaginative and often unorthodox. However, they can be distant and uncommunicative and sometimes their ideas can seem a little impractical.

The Coordinator: This is the team's natural chairman. Coordinators are mature, confident and trusting. They clarify goals and promote decision-making. They are calm with strong interpersonal skills. However, they can be perceived as a little manipulative.

The Resource Investigator: This is 'the fixer' – extrovert, amiable, six phones on the go, with a wealth of contacts. Resource investigators pick other people's brains and explore opportunities. However, they can be a bit undisciplined and can lose interest quickly once initial enthusiasm has passed.

The Monitor-Evaluator: This is the team's rock. Monitor-Evaluators are introvert, sober, strategic and discerning. They explore all options and are capable of deep analysis of huge amounts of data. They are rarely wrong. However, they can lack drive and are unlikely to inspire or excite others.

The Team-worker: This is the team's counsellor or conciliator. Team-workers are mild mannered and social, perceptive and aware of problems or undercurrents, accommodating and good listeners. They promote harmony and are particularly valuable at times of crisis. However, they can be indecisive.

The Implementer: This is the team's workhorse. Implementers turn ideas into practical actions and get on with the job logically and loyally. They are disciplined, reliable and conservative. However, they can be inflexible and slow to change.

The Completer-Finisher: This is the team's worry-guts, making sure things get finished. Completer-Finishers are sticklers for detail, deadlines and schedules and have relentless follow-through, picking up any errors or omissions as they go. However, they sometimes just cannot let go and are reluctant to delegate.

The Specialist: This is the team's chief source of technical knowledge or skill. Specialists are single-minded, self-starting and dedicated. However, they tend to contribute on a narrow front.

☐ The Belbin Team Roles questionnaire can be obtained from: www.belbin.com

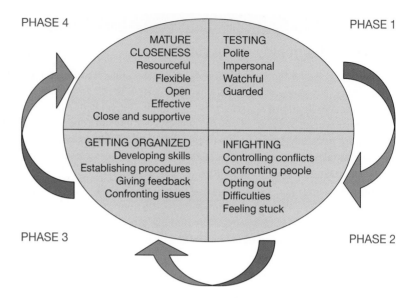

MATURE
CLOSENESS
Resourceful
Flexible
Open
Effective
Close and supportive

TESTING
Polite
Impersonal
Watchful
Guarded

GETTING ORGANIZED
Developing skills
Establishing procedures
Giving feedback
Confronting issues

INFIGHTING
Controlling conflicts
Confronting people
Opting out
Difficulties
Feeling stuck

F 4.5 Team development wheel

Phase 1   The group tests relationships. Individuals are polite, impersonal, watchful and guarded.

Phase 2   Infighting starts in the group and controlling the conflict is important. However, whilst some individuals might be confrontational others might opt out and avoid the conflict altogether. Neither approach is good. Collaboration is best. This is a dangerous phase from which some groups never emerge.

Phase 3   The group starts to get organized; developing skills, establishing procedures, giving feedback, confronting issues.

Phase 4   The group becomes mature and effective, working flexibly and closely, making the most of resources and being close-knit and supportive.

The whole process of team formation and development has been likened to courtship and marriage, involving decisions based partly on emotion rather than logic. For that reason it is important that the team shares the same values and is committed to the same goals – and that brings us back to issues of leadership. They may disagree on tactics but they all agree on the destination and how they are going to get there. It is also important that team roles are clearly defined, although given the uncertainty involved with rapid growth, it is also important that flexibility is maintained – which then brings us back to the way conflict is handled. An effective team will generate team norms of behaviour and that can be a powerful force for conformity and suggests skilful handling.

'Employees come number one, customers come number two. If you have a happy workforce they'll look after your customers anyway … You can have all the money you want in the world, and you can have all the brilliant ideas but if you don't have the people forget it … I look for people who have drive, who have ambition, who are humble.'

Tony Fernandes, founder **AirAsia**,
BBC News Business 1 November 2010

🗀 Case with questions Michael Dell

Entrepreneurial leaders

Michael Dell is now one of the richest men in the world with a fortune in excess of $17 billion. The background and early history of the company he founded, Dell Corporation, were outlined in the case insight in Chapter 1. From the start Michael Dell knew the critical success factor for his business. He used an expert to build prototype computers while he concentrated on finding cheap components so he could keep prices low. The company went on to pioneer direct marketing in the industry and integrated supply-chain management, linking customers' orders and suppliers through the internet – both strategies helping to keep prices low. At all times the focus on a low-cost/low-price marketing strategy has been maintained. The business model has been consistent and followed relentlessly:

▷ Sell directly to consumers;
▷ Keep prices low and quality high;
▷ Offer solid technological support to customers.

'We built the company around a systematic process: give customers the high-quality computers they want at a competitive price as quickly as possible, backed by great service.'

A custom-built Dell computer is shipped within 36 hours of being ordered through the company's website or by phone. The company maintains an extremely low inventory of computer parts, sufficient at any time to meet only a few days of orders. This strategy not only reduces costs but also the need for warehouse space as well as ensuring only the most up-to-date parts are in stock. The company's steady growth rate has been achieved by expanding its customer base in the USA and overseas – selling not just to individual consumers but also to large and small companies, educational institutions

and government agencies. The company has also expanded its product portfolio to include network servers, storage systems, laptops, tablets, HDTVs, cameras, MP3 players and printers, all built by other manufacturers.

'We were moving in the right direction with our emphasis on liquidity, profitability and growth. But we were also challenged by a cultural issue. We had created an atmosphere in which we focused on growth ... We had to shift the focus away from an external orientation to one that strengthened our company internally.

For us growing up meant figuring out a way to combine our signature informal, entrepreneurial style and want-to attitude with the can-do capabilities that would allow us to develop as a company. It meant incorporating into our everyday structures the valuable lessons we'd begun to learn using P&Ls [profit and loss accounts]. It meant focusing our employees to think in terms of shareholder value. It meant respecting the three golden rules at Dell:

▷ Disdain inventory.
▷ Always listen to the customer.
▷ Never sell indirect.'

Dell's mission is to be the most successful computer company in the world at delivering the best computer experience in markets it serves. In doing so, Dell sets out to meet customer expectations of:

▷ Highest quality;
▷ Leading technology;
▷ Competitive pricing;
▷ Individual and company accountability;
▷ Best-in-class service and support;
▷ Flexible customization capability;
▷ Superior corporate citizenship;
▷ Financial stability.

→

Dell calls its corporate philosophy the 'Soul of Dell'. It sees its core elements as:

▷ *Customers* – 'We believe in creating loyal customers by providing a superior experience at a greater value. We are committed to direct relationships, providing the best products and services based on standards-based technology, and outperforming the competition with value and a superior customer experience.'

▷ *The Dell team* – 'We believe our continued success lies in teamwork and the opportunity each team member has to learn, develop and grow. We are committed to being a meritocracy, and to developing, retaining and attracting the best people, reflective of our worldwide market place.'

▷ *Direct relationships* – 'We believe in being direct in all we do. We are committed to behaving ethically: responding to customer needs in a timely and reasonable manner; fostering open communications and building effective relationships with customers, partners, suppliers and each other; and operating without inefficient hierarchy and bureaucracy.'

▷ *Global citizenship* – 'We believe in participating responsibly in the global market place. We are committed to understanding and respecting laws, values and cultures wherever we do business; profitably growing in all markets; promoting a healthy business climate globally; and contributing positively in every community we call home, both personally and organizationally.'

▷ *Winning* – 'We have a passion for winning in everything we do. We are committed to operational excellence, superior customer experience, leading in the global markets we serve, being known as a great place to work and providing superior shareholder value over time.'

Michael Dell has always been keen on developing relationships – with customers, employees and suppliers. This underpins his direct selling strategy and his integrated supply chain network. Dell has been a pioneer of e-business. What makes Dell special today is its 'fully integrated value chain' – B2B2C. Suppliers, including many small firms, have real-time access to information about customer orders and deliveries via the company's extranet. They organize supplies of hard drives, motherboards, modems and so on, on a 'just-in-time' basis so as to keep the production line moving smoothly. From the parts being delivered to the orders being shipped out takes just a few hours. Inventories are minimized and, what is more, the cash is received from the customer before Dell pays its suppliers. Dell has created a three-way 'information partnership' between itself and its customers and suppliers by treating them as collaborators who together find ways of improving efficiency.

'The best way I know to establish and maintain a healthy, competitive culture is to partner with your people – through shared objectives and common strategies … Dell is very much a relationship orientated company … how we communicate and partner with our employees and customers. But our commitment doesn't stop there. Our willingness and ability to partner to achieve our common goals is perhaps seen in its purest form in how we forge strong alliances with our suppliers.'

Michael Dell has moved from being an entrepreneur, wheeling and dealing in cheap components, then innovating in direct marketing techniques, to being a visionary leader, understanding where his competitive advantage lies and then putting into place the systems and processes to keep his company two steps ahead of the competition. However, it has not always been like this. Michael's managerial experience was extremely limited. In the early days he was said to be most comfortable with the company's engineers. Although those who worked with him closely described him as likable, he was so shy that some employees thought he was aloof because he never talked to them. It was probably Lee Walker, a mature venture capitalist brought in during the company's organization-building years, who gave Michael the insight into management and leadership that he needed and developed his instinct for motivating people and winning their loyalty and respect. He can now delegate effectively and believes in team working.

'The right people in the right jobs are instrumental to a company's success ... If you assume that people can grow at the same rate as your company – and still maintain the sharp focus that is critical to success – you will be sadly disappointed. When a business is growing quickly, many jobs grow laterally in responsibility, becoming too big and complex for even the most ambitious, hard-working person to handle without sacrificing personal career development or becoming burned out ... The ability to find and hire the right people can make or break your business. It is as plain as that. No matter where you are in the life cycle of your business, bringing in great talent should always be a top priority.'

Michael is an accomplished speaker and his quiet, reflective manner now gives him an air of maturity. However, this probably disguises the competitive personality who has taken risks to make his business grow.

'Communicating is one of the most important tools in recovering from mistakes. When you tell someone, be it a designer, a customer, or the CEO of the company, "Look, we've got a problem. Here's how we're going to fix it," you diffuse the fear of the unknown and focus on the solution.'

In 2004 Michael Dell stepped aside as CEO of Dell while retaining his position as Chairman of the Board, Kevin Rollins became the new CEO. But under Kevin Rollins the company struggled – revenue targets were missed, the share price suffered and Dell lost its coveted number one position in the PC market to Hewlett-Packard. In 2007 the board decided it wanted Michael Dell back as CEO.

According to *Director* magazine (April 2009) Kevin Rollins had kept 'an emotional distance' from staff and Michael Dell's team-building track record made him ideal to 'glue the company back together again'. However, it reported that John Enck, managing vice-president of research analysts Gartner, thought Michael Dell had changed his management style to become more inclusive:

'I've seen a big difference in the two reigns ... The leadership of Dell isn't as autocratic as it used to be. When Michael was originally CEO he was the decision-maker. Coming back, he created a leadership board and did a very good job of delegating decisions and responsibility to his executive team. That will theoretically allow Dell to be more nimble.'

However, *Director* magazine reported that Michael Dell did not agree:

'That question assumes that during the entire 20-year period I only used one approach, which would be wrong. I constantly adjust my approach and way of doing things based on all the inputs and opportunities that I see.'

Michael has reverted to his tried and tested strategies: cutting costs, improving customer service (which had slipped very noticeably), introducing new products and investing in innovation. By 2009 he had made ten acquisitions, cut more than 10,000 jobs, outsourced 40% of production and entered the smart phone market in China. Product inspiration now also comes from a Dell

→

community website – www.ideastorm.com – that allows customers to identify and vote on new lines, while also rating current ones. The goal is to diversify beyond the mature PC market, which still accounts for more than half of revenues, into new markets such as computer storage and services. At the same time Dell is trying to enter new market sectors – for example by the purchase of Perot Systems in 2009 which enabled it to enter the health care sector.

Will Michael Dell pull his company around? Time will tell.

☐ Up-to-date information on Dell can be found on their website: www.dell.com

QUESTIONS

1 Re-read the case insight about Michael Dell in Chapter 1. What entrepreneurial character traits does he exhibit?

2 What leadership characteristics does he exhibit? Where would you place him on Blake and Mouton's leadership grid?

3 Why was Dell successful, at least until Michael Dell stepped down as CEO?

4 What do you think about Michael Dell's final comments about varying his management style?

5 What are the lessons for corporate entrepreneurship from Michael Dell and the Dell Corporation?

Summary

▷ Management and leadership are different and distinct terms, although the skills and competences associated with each are complementary. Management is concerned with handling complexity in organizational processes and the execution of work. It is about detail and logic, efficiency and effectiveness. Fayol defined the five functions of management as planning, organizing, commanding, coordinating and controlling.

▷ Leadership, on the other hand, is concerned with setting direction, communicating and motivating. It is about broad principles and emotion. It is particularly concerned with change.

▷ Leadership stems from authority. Entrepreneurial authority, in the main, stems from expertise. It can be seen as an 'event', a series of which may be joined up, one to another. It involves influencing others and therefore builds heavily on relationships.

▷ The ability to influence and build relationships requires certain characteristics in leaders – emotional intelligence, self-awareness and self-management. Leaders also need to be able to be strategic thinkers and learners and be able to reflect. As **Gary Redman** found, these skills can be developed.

▷ Contingency theory tells us that the leadership style appropriate for one 'event' may be inappropriate for another. The appropriate leadership style depends on the leader, the group, the task and situation or context facing the leader.

▷ The entrepreneurial context of leadership is one characterized by uncertainty, rapid change and risk-taking. There are various other leadership paradigms that inform us about leadership in this context – leadership in learning organizations, transformational leadership, visionary leadership and distributed leadership.

▷ Based upon the DNA of the entrepreneur (Chapter 3) and the characteristics needed for effective leadership, and building upon leadership paradigms, the attributes, skills and behaviours needed for effective leadership of an entrepreneurial organization are summarized in Table 4.1. In line with contingency theory, however, these may need to be 'fine-tuned' for specific contexts.

▷ The main aim of the entrepreneurial leader, like **Michael Dell**, is always to build an entrepreneurial architecture for the organization so that it can operate effectively on its own, without them. They are 'clock builders' not 'time tellers', building organizational sustainability.

▷ A vision is a desired future state. It must be attractive but credible – acknowledging the tension created by a realistic appraisal of the current situation. Developing vision is a continuous process, checking with staff that it resonates with them, modifying it to suit changing circumstances. Vision is best communicated as a 'story' that, in some way, appeals to emotions and motivates staff to achieve. It is formally communicated through a vision or mission statement.

▷ Picking a good team is not just about selecting people with appropriate functional skills. It is also about assembling a mix of different personalities. Belbin identified nine characteristics that need to be present to form an effective team: shaper, plant, coordinator, resource investigator, monitor-evaluator, team-worker, implementer, completer-finisher and specialist.

▷ A team takes time to become effective. It is likely to go through a four-stage development process before it reaches this point: testing, infighting, getting organized and mature effectiveness.

Essays and discussion topics

1 How does the role of leader differ from that of entrepreneur?

2 How does the role of leader differ from that of manager?

3 Leaders are born not made. Discuss.

4 Leadership is an event. Discuss.

5 Leaders must be charismatic. Discuss.

6 What do you think are the prime tasks of a leader in an entrepreneurial organization? Why?

7 Have Michael Dell and Richard Branson made the transition from entrepreneur to leader? Explain.

8 What is vision? How can it be developed? How can it be communicated?

9 Why is 'walking the talk' important in an entrepreneurial organization?

10 Is there such a thing as one 'best' leadership style for an entrepreneurial business?

11 How is entrepreneurial leadership different from transformational and distributed leadership?

12 How should contingency theory affect entrepreneurial leadership style?

13 Why is trust in the leadership of an organization important?

14 How do you build a relationship? Give examples.

15 How do you clarify ambiguity and uncertainty? Give examples.

16 Why is a 'light touch' important in an entrepreneurial organization? How is it achieved?

17 How do you build 'empowering opportunities'? Give examples.

18 Why is an ability to handle conflict important in the entrepreneurial firm?

19 Are there any additional contextual issues that currently affect the entrepreneurial leadership attributes, skills and behaviours outlined in Table 4.1? How might they affect them?

20 How do you build an effective team?

21 Give examples of the behaviours that result from a team going through the four development phases outlined in Figure 4.5. How might a break-up of the team be prevented?

22 There are many examples of businesses deteriorating after the retirement of their founder. Famously, Steve Jobs (Apple), Michael Dell (Dell) and Howard Schultz (Starbucks) all had to return to their companies and effect a 'turnaround'. How important is the founder to an entrepreneurial business? Can that person be replicated? What are the lessons for corporate entrepreneurship?

Exercises and assignments

1 Answer the Leadership Styles Questionnaire and plot your score on the Leadership Grid. Do you agree that this is your preferred style?

2 Obtain the Thomas-Kilmann Conflict Mode questionnaire and evaluate how you handle conflict.

3 Use the Belbin Team Roles questionnaire to evaluate your preferred team roles.

4 Using detailed examples, show how the appropriate leadership style might differ for:

   ▷ three different tasks, given the same group and situation;

   ▷ three different groups, undertaking the same task in the same situation;

   ▷ three different situations, where the same group is undertaking the same task.

5 Research and write a profile of a successful entrepreneurial leader, emphasizing their leadership style.

References

Adair, J. (1984) *The Skills of Leadership*, London: Gower.

Adizes, I. (1978) 'Organizational Passages: Diagnosing and Treating Life Cycle Problems of Organizations', *Organizational Dynamics*, Summer.

Avolio, B.J., Bass, B.M. and Jung, D.I. (1999) 'Re-examining the Components of Transformational and Transactional Leadership using the Multifactor Leadership Questionnaire', *Journal of Occupational and Organisational Psychology*, 72.

Bartlett, C. A. and Ghoshal, S. (1994) 'Changing the Role of Top Management: Beyond Strategy to Purpose', *Harvard Business Review*, November/December.

Bass, B.M. (1985) *Leadership and Performance Beyond Expectations*, New York: Free Press.

Bass, B.M. (1998) *Transformational Leadership: Industry, Military and Educational Impact*, Mahwah, NJ: Lawrence Erlbaum Associates.

Bass, B.M and Avolio, B.J. (1990) 'The Implications of Transactional and Transformational Leadership for Individual, Team and Organizational Development', *Research in Organizational Change and Development*, 4.

Belbin, R.M. (1981) *Management Teams – Why They Succeed and Fail*, London: Heinemann Professional Publishing.

Bennis, W. and Nanus, B. (1985) *Leaders: The Strategies for Taking Charge*, New York: Harper & Row.

Blake, R. and Mouton, J. (1978) *The New Managerial Grid*, London: Gulf.

Blank, W. (1995) *The Nine Laws of Leadership*, New York: AMACOM.

Bradford, D.L. and Cohen, A.R. (1998) *Power Up: Transforming Organizations Through Shared Leadership*, New York: John Wiley.

Brubaker, D.L. (2005) 'The Power of Vision', in D.L. Brubaker and L.D. Colbe (eds) *The Hidden Leader*, Thousand Oaks, CA: Corwin Press.

Burns, P. (2005) *Corporate Entrepreneurship: Building the Entrepreneurial Organization*, 1st edn, Basingstoke: Palgrave Macmillan.

Burns, P. and Whitehouse, O. (1996) 'Managers in Europe', *European Venture Capital Journal*, 45, April/May.

Chaleff, I. (1995) *The Courageous Follower: Standing Up, To and For Our Leaders*, San Francisco: Bennet-Koehler.

Chell, E. (2001) *Entrepreneurship: Globalization, Innovation and Development*, London: Thomson Learning.

Collins, J.C. and Porras, J.I. (1994) *Built to Last: Successful Habits of Visionary Companies*, New York: Harper Business.

Davies, B. and Davies, B.J. (2010) 'The Nature and Dimensions of Strategic Leadership', *International Studies in Educational Administration*, 38(1).

Egri, C.P. and Herman, S. (2000) 'Leadership in the North American Environmental Sector: Values, Leadership Styles and Contexts of Environmental Leaders and their Organizations', *Academy of Management Journal*, 43.

Gardner, H. (1995) *Leading Minds: An Anatomy of Leadership*, New York: John Wiley & Sons.

George, B. (2003) *Authentic Leadership: Rediscovering the Secrets to Creating Lasting Value*, San Francisco: Jossey-Bass.

George, B. with Sims, P.E. (2007) *True North: Discover your Authentic Leadership*, San Francisco: Jossey-Bass.

Giltsham, M., Pegg, M. and Culpin, V. (2011) 'The Shifting Landscape of Global Challenges in the 21st Century: What This Means for What Businesses Want from Tomorrow's Leaders, and the Implications for Management Learning', *Business Leadership Review*, 8(2).

Goleman, D. (1996) *Emotional Intelligence: Why It Can Matter More Than IQ*, London: Bloomsbury.

Goleman, D. (1998) 'What makes a Leader?', *Harvard Business Review*, 76 (1).

Greenleaf, R.F. (1970) *The Servant as Leader*, Mahwah, NJ: Paulist.

Hamel, G. (2009) 'Moon Shots for Management', *Harvard Business Review*, February.

Hamel, G. and Prahalad, C.K. (1994) *Competing For the Future: Breakthrough Strategies for Seizing Control of your Industry and Creating the Markets of Tomorrow*, Boston, MA: Harvard Business School Press.

Heifetz, R.A. (1994) *Leadership Without Easy Answers*, Cambridge, MA: Harvard University Press.

Hughes, R.L. and Beatty, K.C. (2005) *Becoming a Strategic Leader*, San Francisco: John Wiley.

Kenny, D.A. and Zaccaro, S.J. (1983) 'An Estimate of Variance due to Traits in Leadership', *Journal of Applied Psychology*, 68.

Kirby, D. (2003) *Entrepreneurship*, London: McGraw-Hill.

Kouzes, J.M. and Posner, B.Z. (2007) *The Leadership Challenge*, San Francisco: Jossey-Bass.

Mintzberg, H. (2003) 'Strategic Thinking as Seeing', in B. Garratt (ed.) *Developing Strategic Thought*, London: McGraw-Hill.

Mintzberg, H. (2009) *Managing*, London: FT Prentice Hall.

Nanus, B. (1992) *Visionary Leadership: Creating a Compelling Sense of Direction for your Organization*, San Francisco: Jossey-Bass.

Raelin, J.A. (2003) *Leading Organizations: How to Bring Out Leadership in Everyone*, San Francisco: Berrett-Koehler.

Ray, G.H. and Hutchinson, P.J. (1983) *The Financing and Financial Control of Small Enterprise Development*, London: Gower.

Rost, J.C. (1991) *Leadership for the Twentieth-first Century*, Westport, CT: Praeger.

Senge, P.M. (1992) *The Fifth Discipline*, London: Century Business.

Tappin, S. and Cave, A. (2008) *The Secrets of CEOs: 150 Global Chief Executives Lift the Lid on Business, Life and Leadership*, London: Nicholas Brealey.

Timmons, J.A. (1999) *New Venture Creation: Entrepreneurship for the 21st Century*, Singapore: Irwin/McGraw-Hill.

Turnbull, J. (2011) Editorial, *Business Leadership Review*, 8(2).

Vera, D. and Crossan, M. (2004) 'Strategic Leadership and Organizational Learning', *Academy of Management Review*, 29(2).

Zaccaro, S.J. (2007) 'Trait-based Perspectives of Leadership', *American Psychologist*, 62.

Leadership Style Questionnaire: Scoring

To obtain your leadership orientation rating, score 1 point for the appropriate response under each heading, then total your scores. If your response is inappropriate you do not score. As a guide, a score of 5 or less is low and 12 or more is high.

PEOPLE SCORE (maximum score 15)
'Yes' for questions 2, 4, 8, 10, 17, 19, 21, 23, 27.
'No' for questions 6, 13, 14, 25, 29, 30.

TASK SCORE (maximum score 15)
'Yes' for questions 1, 3, 5, 7, 9, 11, 15, 16, 18, 20, 22, 24, 26, 28.
No' for questions 12.

Next plot your position on the Leadership Grid below.

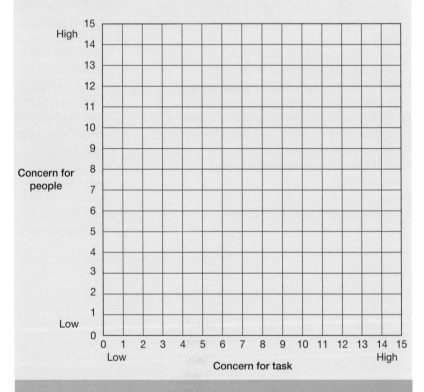

Chapter 5

Constructing the entrepreneurial culture

Learning outcomes

By the end of this chapter you should be able to:

▷ Critically analyze what is meant by culture, giving examples of the dimensions along which it can be measured, and evaluate the appropriateness of Hofstede's dimensions;

▷ Critically analyze what is meant by entrepreneurial culture, recognizing which 'high-level' elements are most important, and describing how it can be mapped onto Hofstede's dimensions of culture;

▷ Critically evaluate the influences on organizational culture, including the importance of national culture;

▷ Describe the managerial tools available to help construct or reconstruct the culture of an organization;

▷ Critically evaluate an organization in terms of the 'high-level' attributes of entrepreneurial culture;

▷ Explain what is required to develop an entrepreneurial culture in a larger organization and which leadership and management styles encourage it.

Culture

Culture is an illusive concept. Any group, family, organization, even a nation, has its own culture – all interacting and influencing each other. Culture is about the prevalent norms, basic beliefs and assumptions about behaviour that underpin that group. Culture is important because it manifests itself in the way people are inclined to behave. Hofstede (1980) defines it as the 'collective programming of the mind which distinguishes one group of people from another'. Culture is therefore based upon hidden and unspoken assumptions about the 'right' way to behave. It is a pattern of taken-for-granted assumptions and beliefs shared by individuals collectively about who they are.

Culture is the personality of the group. Schein (1990) says that it is 'invented, discovered, or developed by a given group'. It therefore underpins the mental models of individuals and the dominant logic of the group. Culture evolves over time under a multitude of influences. Therefore it can change and can also be shaped and influenced. Individuals 'learn' the culture of the group and it is passed down or taught to new members through the norms and conventions of the group.

Any one individual may be associated with a number of different groups, each with its own different and sometimes conflicting cultures. One group culture might be strong – where people have a strong sense of the 'right' thing to do – another weak. Culture affects how different groups communicate and interact internally and externally. Unless recognized, it can cause misunderstandings. For example, Graham and Lam (2003) noted the following basic cultural differences between Chinese and US negotiators affected the way they approached those negotiations:

Chinese		US
Collectivist	⬌	Individualist
Hierarchical	⬌	Egalitarian
Relationship orientation	⬌	Information orientation
Holistic	⬌	Reductionist
Circular	⬌	Sequential
Seeks the way	⬌	Seeks the truth
The haggling culture	⬌	The argument culture

The collectivist approach of the Chinese stems from their agrarian background. The US individualistic approach stems from their pioneering and industrial backgrounds. The Chinese preference for hierarchy has a long tradition, reinforced through the Communist Party, whereas the individualistic, egalitarian approach of the USA has its roots in the Founding Fathers.

Language is an essential element of culture because it transmits the view that the group has of itself and the world, and also because the words themselves help shape people's beliefs. For example, Graham and Lam (op. cit.)

suggested that it was the use of pictograms in the Chinese language that caused Chinese negotiators to take a holistic and circular approach to negotiations – returning to issues – even when facing a number of tradable negotiating points. This compares to Americans' preference for dealing with one point at a time – a reductionist and sequential approach. Without the words to describe situations, values or beliefs, they cannot be communicated. In the same way some groups start to carve out their own vocabulary with a view to influencing culture. In some companies, like Gortex, employees may be referred to as 'associates'. In John Lewis they are 'partners' (and really do own the business). The words are value-laden and convey the organization's view of their relationships with these people.

Central to any culture are the values that it holds. Some values are core, some are peripheral. Core values are stabilizing mechanisms that change only slowly over time, whilst peripheral values are less important and can change more quickly. Different nations have different cultures based upon underlying core values. Guirdham (1999) gives some examples: 'The status of women is a core value in Argentina, Chile, India and Israel, but less so in China, where the Confucian hierarchical concept of relations between individuals is more core ... Similarly, to a third generation American, the value of the democratic right of free speech might be core, but to her Singaporean cousin it might be peripheral, something to be traded off against the value of having a low-crime, drug-free society to live in.'

Cultures might be visible on a fairly superficial level – the costumes or uniforms people wear distinguish them as belonging to a particular group that might be associated with deeper things – the values and beliefs that the group holds and their view of themselves and the world. And often we make initial judgments about people based upon these superficial externalities. However, simply the fact that costumes or uniforms are worn does not necessarily guarantee a strong culture. The strength of a culture is rarely visible at the superficial level. Cultures become strong when they are reinforced in a consistent way by the different elements that influence them.

Dimensions of culture

Measuring the dimensions of culture in a scientific way is extremely difficult. The most widely used dimensions are those developed by Hofstede (1981) who undertook an extensive cross-cultural study, using questionnaire data from some 80,000 IBM employees in 66 countries across seven occupations. From his research he established the four dimensions shown in Figure 5.1. This figure also shows the dominant culture he found in employees in particular countries. This is instructive because you might expect the national culture of the USA to be highly entrepreneurial – one that fosters social attitudes that encourage entrepreneurship. Welsch (1998) described individual entrepreneurship as 'ingrained' in North American culture. It is an achievement-orientated society that values individualism

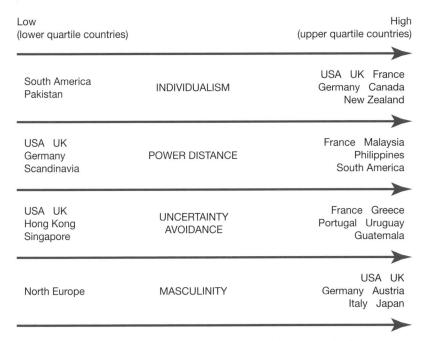

Low (lower quartile countries)		High (upper quartile countries)
South America Pakistan	INDIVIDUALISM	USA UK France Germany Canada New Zealand
USA UK Germany Scandinavia	POWER DISTANCE	France Malaysia Philippines South America
USA UK Hong Kong Singapore	UNCERTAINTY AVOIDANCE	France Greece Portugal Uruguay Guatemala
North Europe	MASCULINITY	USA UK Germany Austria Italy Japan

Adapted from Hofstede, G. (1981) *Cultures and Organizations: Software of the Mind*, London: HarperCollins.

F 5.1 Hofstede's dimensions of culture

and material wealth. We might therefore use the national culture of the USA as a benchmark for one that encourages individual entrepreneurship (but not necessarily corporate entrepreneurship).

Individualism versus collectivism

This is the degree to which people prefer to act as individuals rather than groups. Individualistic cultures are loosely knit social frameworks in which people primarily operate as individuals or in immediate families or groups. Collectivist cultures are composed of tight networks in which people operate as members of 'in-groups' and 'out-groups', expecting to look after, and be looked after by, other members of their 'in-group'. In the individualist culture the task prevails over personal relationships. The atmosphere is competitive. In collectivism it is cooperative within the 'in-group' although it may well be uncharacteristically competitive with 'out-groups'.

Hofstede found the 'Anglo' countries (USA, Britain, Australia, Canada and New Zealand) were the highest scoring individualist cultures, together with the Netherlands. France and Germany just made it into the upper quartile of individualist cultures. South American countries were the most collectivist cultures, together with Pakistan.

Power distance

This is the degree of inequality among people that the community is willing to accept. Low power distance cultures endorse egalitarianism, relations are open and informal, information flows are functional and unrestricted and organizations tend to have flat structures. High power distance cultures endorse hierarchies, relations are more formal, information flows are formalized and restricted and organizations tend to be rigid and hierarchical. Individuals in high power distance cultures have difficulty working in unsupervised groups whereas those in low power distance cultures might be thought to exhibit a lack of 'respect' for authority.

Hofstede found low power distance countries were Austria, Ireland, Israel, New Zealand and the four Scandinavian countries. The USA, Britain and Germany also made it into the lower quartile. High power distance countries were Malaysia, the Philippines and four South American countries, with France also making it into the upper quartile.

Uncertainty avoidance

This is the degree to which people would like to avoid ambiguity and resolve uncertainty, and prefer structured rather than unstructured situations. Low uncertainty avoidance cultures tolerate greater ambiguity, prefer flexibility, stress personal choice and decision-making, reward initiative, experimentation, risk-taking and team-play and stress the development of analytical skills. High uncertainty avoidance cultures prefer rules and procedures, stress compliance, punish error and reward compliance, loyalty and attention to detail.

The lowest uncertainty avoidance countries were Hong Kong, Ireland, Jamaica, Singapore and two Scandinavian countries, with the USA and Britain also in the lowest quartile. The highest uncertainty avoidance countries were Greece, Portugal, Guatemala and Uruguay, with France also in the highest quartile group. Germany was about halfway.

Masculinity versus femininity

This defines quality of life issues. Hofstede defined masculine virtues as those of achievement, assertiveness, competition and success. Masculine cultures reward financial and material achievement with social prestige and status. Feminine virtues include modesty, compromise and cooperation. Feminine cultures value relationships. Issues such as quality of life, warmth in personal relationships, service and so on are important, and in some societies having a high standard of living is thought to be a matter of birth, luck or destiny, rather than personal achievement (external locus of control).

Hofstede found the most masculine countries were Japan, Austria, Venezuela, Italy and Switzerland, with the USA, Britain and Germany all falling into the highest quartile. Four North European countries were the highest scoring feminine countries. France was about halfway.

At a later date Hofstede and Bond (1991) added a fifth dimension – short/long-term orientation. A short-term orientation focuses on past and present and therefore values respect for the status quo. For example, they include an unqualified respect for tradition and for social and status obligations. A long-term orientation focuses on the future and therefore the values associated with this are more dynamic. For example, they include the adaptation of traditions to contemporary conditions and have only qualified respect for social and status obligations. Entrepreneurial organizations look forward to and embrace change. They therefore have a 'long-term' orientation on this dimension.

Notice one more thing from Figure 5.1. Alongside the USA – our benchmark for a national culture that encourages individual entrepreneurship – at the extreme ends of these dimensions is the UK. In the 1970s, when these studies were conducted, the UK could hardly have been held up as the epitome of an enterprising nation. The explanation of this result may lie in the timing of the study. In the 1970s, in both the UK and USA, political interest focused on enterprise as a means of rescuing their stagnant economies (O'Connor, 1973). It was argued that structural change was needed to achieve an 'enterprise culture' (Carr, 2000; Morris, 1991) and this would have to be accompanied by cultural change at the level of the individual, so much so that it would bring about a revolution that was moral, economic and enduring. And in the UK it was, arguably, the Thatcher government that brought about that change at the end of the 1970s. Hence, attitudes were changing in advance of behaviour. The UK may not have been an enterprising nation, but its cultural attitudes were becoming entrepreneurial.

However, there is another possible explanation, and that is that Hofstede's dimensions of *organizational* culture were not designed specifically to measure *entrepreneurial* culture. Indeed his work was based on IBM employees and they could hardly be described as the most entrepreneurial in the world at the time the study took place – just as Microsoft was being launched. It is essentially constructed as a macro-measurement tool that reflects differences in *national* culture rather than *organizational* culture. So it is quite probable that there are other dimensions to consider – and we shall return to this later. In that sense it may not completely describe what we want to achieve at an organizational level and may not reflect the differences between an entrepreneurial and an administrative organization with sufficient discrimination. Nevertheless, although it may be a 'blunt instrument', it is a widely used and well respected framework. It also allows us to contrast individual and organizational entrepreneurial cultures and further explore the influence of national culture.

International influences on culture

The USA shows us the anatomy of a national enterprise culture: one that encourages individual enterprise and entrepreneurship, one where the probability of an entrepreneur being made, rather than just born, is highest.

This is the sort of culture that many other countries have been trying to promote and develop because it seems to encourage the characteristics that are needed to develop the largest number of entrepreneurs. As we have already noted, the UK also shares this profile. The USA emerges as a highly individualistic, masculine culture, with low power distance and uncertainty avoidance. It is a culture that tolerates risk and ambiguity, has a preference for flexibility and an empowered culture that rewards personal initiative. It is a highly individualistic and egalitarian culture, one that is fiercely competitive and the home of the 'free-market economy'. Assertiveness and competition are central to the 'American dream'. If there is a key virtue in the USA it is achievement, and achievement receives its monetary reward. It is an informal culture. All men are created equal, however, they also have the freedom to accumulate sufficient wealth to become very unequal. The USA is the original 'frontier culture'. It actually seems to like change and uncertainty and certainly rewards initiative and risk-taking. Interestingly again, as we shall see in Chapter 13, another study shows the USA as having the second highest level of national creativity.

Hofstede's study reminds us that there are many influences on culture and the many organizations or groups to which an individual might belong – such as race, sect, religion, gender, family and peer group, each with different cultures – also influence the culture within an organization. An entrepreneurial culture does not exist within an organization in isolation. It must somehow reconcile the behavioural norms generated by these other cultures. National culture remains a major influence. An empirical investigation by Morris et al. (1994), which covered the USA, South Africa and Portugal, supported this. Powerful national cultures can overpower weaker organizational cultures. For this reason Hofstede argued that is often very difficult for organizational cultures to cross national boundaries. The fact he was able to identify national influences within IBM tends to support this. What is more, cultural comparisons and analysis are inextricably bound to a particular time and a particular place. Over time they change.

In this context it is worth remembering that most management theory and research was developed in the West in the second half of the twentieth century and is both culture and gender bound. It is written in English. It was developed for and about men. It reflects the 'scientific method' – independence, lack of emotion, objectivity, rationality, logic. Hofstede (1991) himself stated that 'not only organizations are culturally bound; theories about organizations are equally culture bound. The Professors who wrote the theories are children of a culture: they grew up in families, went to schools, worked for employers. Their experiences represent the material on which their thinking and writing have been based. Scholars are as human and culturally biased as other mortals.' There is no guarantee therefore that theories developed around the cultural context of one country at any particular time can be applicable to another country or another time.

So, for example, many of the early motivational theories were developed by American academics (e.g. Herzberg, Maslow, McClelland) and were based around self-interest and the satisfaction of personal needs such as money, status and 'self-actualization'. These theories are based very firmly in the Anglo-Saxon capitalist culture which values individualism and masculinity (using Hofstede's dimensions) with low uncertainty avoidance. Hofstede (1991) suggests that in German and Austrian cultures the motivation to work derives instead from 'the need to relieve tension and stress' in their highly formal societies which are performance-orientated and value masculinity and low power distance with high uncertainty avoidance. Their desire for high uncertainty avoidance leads to high levels of personal stress. By way of contrast, the French, within their 'communitarian' society, deal with personal tension by having high power distance, which allows them to have 'father-figure' roles to absorb the stress of uncertainty. Similarly, Morden (1995) observed that, whilst strongly individualistic, the Scandinavian and Dutch interest in the 'quality of work, individual rights, farming co-operatives, etc. stem from a feminine characteristic which stresses interpersonal co-operation and de-emphasizes interpersonal competition.' He went on to make the point that combining this with low power distance meant that personalized merit or bonus systems of payment may be inappropriate or counterproductive in these countries.

Hofstede (1980) suggested that these characteristics themselves may confer competitive advantage on certain countries. For example, highly feminine countries such as The Netherlands or Denmark tend to be successful in consultancy, the service sector, helping relationships, horticulture and agriculture. He also observed that cultures can work in a complementary manner, citing the Anglo-Dutch multinationals Shell and Unilever where the national values on power distance, uncertainty avoidance and individualism are similar but where the people orientation of the Dutch complements the masculine, achievement orientation of the British.

Organizational culture

An organizational culture is therefore just one of the cultures that any individual may contribute to or be affected by. Even if a leader does not try to 'impose' an organizational culture, one will emerge. Ignoring culture can therefore be dangerous because the one that might emerge, if the process is not managed, may not help the organization to meet its objectives. At the same time, since culture influences behaviour, it is important as an alternative to rules and regulations. Chapter 2 highlighted the character traits and approaches to business and management that characterize the entrepreneur and drew from these some implications for the culture of an entrepreneurial organization. However, before we look at these, we need to understand more about organizational culture and how it can be constructed and shaped.

Schein (1983) defined organizational culture as 'the pattern of basic assumptions which a given group invented, discovered or developed in learning to cope with its problems of external adaptation and internal integration, which has worked well enough to be considered valid, and therefore to be taught to new members as the correct way to perceive, think and feel in relation to those problems.' Cornwall and Perlman (1990) echoed this, but added the dimension of behaviour. They saw it as 'an organization's basic beliefs and assumptions about what the company is about, how its members behave, and how it defines itself in relation to its external environment.'

Johnson (1992) talked about the cultural paradigm – how it is around here – as comprising stories, symbols, control systems, rituals and routines, power and organizational structures, that together both help to describe and contribute to the culture. This underlines the fact that culture is self-reinforcing. And taken together these factors make an interlinking cultural web for an organization, which is shown in Figure 5.2.

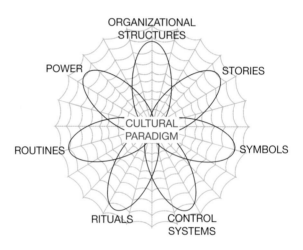

F 5.2 The cultural web

Handy (1985) popularized four organizational typologies:

Power culture – where power is concentrated in a single source, with communication and authority radiating out from the centre;

Role culture – where delegated power is exercised through clearly defined roles and strict procedures and individuals are judged by how well they adhere to these;

Task culture – where power is delegated to individuals and teams to perform given tasks and they are judged by how well they perform them;

Person culture – where the organization serves the individual and the individual thrives through their personal expertise.

These typologies should be capable of being described using the cultural web in Figure 5.2. Handy's work was in fact based upon that of Harrison

(1972) and you might observe echoes of Blake and Mouton's (1978) work on leadership styles that we explored in the previous chapter. In a later work Handy (1995) linked these typologies to leadership style and organizational structures. We shall explore this in the next chapter. The problem is that these may be cultures that we can describe and recognize, but these studies do not seem to measure culture in any scientific way. Nevertheless they do give us a language with which to discuss the illusive concept of organizational culture and an insight into how organizational culture can be shaped and constructed.

Culture in the entrepreneurial organization

We have already observed that Hofstede's dimensions were not specifically designed to capture differences in organizational culture. Rather they were constructed to reflect differences in national culture within one organization (IBM). Trying to map the dimensions of entrepreneurial culture within an organization tends to be far more subjective, lacking the sample base and scientific measurement involved in the original Hofstede study. Hofstede et al. (1990) looked at different dimensions of organizational culture in an attempt to discriminate between entrepreneurial and administrative organizations. Actually these were not so much dimensions as descriptors of what an entrepreneurial culture might look like compared to an administrative one. The entrepreneurial culture has:

▷ A results, in contrast to a process, orientation;
▷ A job, in contrast to an employee, orientation;
▷ A pragmatic, in contrast to a normative, orientation;
▷ An open, in contrast to a closed, system;
▷ Parochial, in contrast to professional, interest;
▷ Loose, in contrast to tight, control.

Morris and Kuratko (2002) have a slightly different view of what an entrepreneurial culture might look like within an organization. Based on synthesis of the work of Timmons (1999), Peters (1997) and Cornwall and Perlman (op. cit.), they say it would have the following elements:

▷ A people and empowerment focus;
▷ Commitment and personal responsibility;
▷ 'Doing the right thing';
▷ Value creation through innovation and change;
▷ Hands-on management;
▷ Freedom to grow and to fail;
▷ Attention to basics;
▷ Emphasis on the future and a sense of urgency.

In looking at the issue of freedom to grow and to fail, the authors distinguish between three types of failure: moral failure which occurs when there is a breach of ethics or moral standards; personal failure which relates to inadequate skills, knowledge or understanding; and uncontrollable failure which happens because of events or conditions out of the control of the individual. Whilst moral failure should not be tolerated, personal failure can be addressed through training, development and counselling. Uncontrollable failure is bound to happen in an entrepreneurial organization and valuable learning can take place as a result of it. Whilst you might be able to manage the risk, the danger of failure is always present. Indeed success and failure are constant bedfellows in an entrepreneurial firm where commercial decisions involving risk are continually being made. Rather than being viewed as the opposite ends of a spectrum, success and failure in the entrepreneurial firm can be seen within the continuum shown in Figure 5.3. The difference between overall success and failure requires the organization to make certain the volume (or value) of successes outweighs the volume (or value) of failures. And that means that the lessons from every failure must be learned. It has been said that the only way to avoid ever making a wrong decision is never to make a decision in the first place – not an option for the entrepreneurial organization.

Entrepreneurial organizations are also learning organizations. Schein (1994) listed some of the features of a learning culture and compared them to a culture that inhibits learning. These are shown in Table 5.1. If you are starting from scratch you might be able to establish these features from the outset but to change an established organizational culture is altogether more difficult. Most established organizations inhibit learning. Schein concluded that to nurture these qualities you need to establish a 'psychologically safe haven' or 'parallel system' within the organization where learning – as we have defined it – can occur. And as we shall see in the next chapter, large organizations have responded to this organizational challenge with some success.

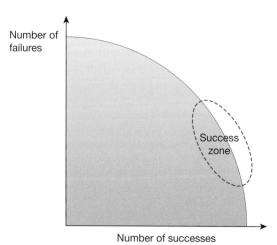

F 5.3 Success and failure in the entrepreneurial organization

T 5.1 Cultures that enhance vs cultures that inhibit learning

A culture that enhances learning	A culture that inhibits learning
Balances interests of all stakeholders	Believes tasks more important than people
Focuses on people rather than systems	Focuses on systems rather than people
Empowers people and makes them believe they can change things	Allows change only when absolutely necessary
Makes time for learning	Is preoccupied with short-term coping and adapting
Takes a holistic approach to problems	Compartmentalizes problem-solving
Encourages open communication	Restricts the flow of information
Believes in teamwork	Believes in competition between individuals
Has approachable leaders	Has controlling leaders

Source: Derived from Schein (1994).

The constant theme coming through both the entrepreneurship litera-ture and the learning organization literature is the need to empower and motivate employees to do 'the right thing' without having to be ordered to do so. This implies more of a consensus form of decision-making that takes time and can reduce the speed of action. However, in some circumstances this might just not be possible if an opportunity is to be seized quickly. This is when the organization should move back from collectivism to individual-ism, with the entrepreneur and leader asserting themselves. On the other hand, the different scenarios presented by an oppor-tunity might have already been considered as the organization strategizes and evaluates the options open to it. However, ultimately there may be a problem here that only considerations of size and structure can address. If the decision-making group is too large, the organization may well not be able to react with sufficient speed to changing circumstances. We have already observed that size is a significant factor in constructing the management team to support the leader and project groups are also typically small.

'Empower your staff. "People, people, people" is the mantra. If you do not have the right staff, fire them, quickly. Be nimble and act on your convictions'

Gururaj Deshpande, serial entrepreneur and founder of **Sycamore Networks**
Financial Times 21 February 2000

An entrepreneurial culture needs to motivate people to do the 'right things' in the right way, for the organization as well as for themselves. It needs to help them cope with an uncertain future by giving them a vision and a belief that they can achieve it. Entrepreneurs are naturally good at motivating staff by the example they set – 'walking the talk' – but as the firm grows the leader needs to find different ways of communicating with more people, infecting them with the entrepreneurial virus. The culture of a firm comes from the leader, it reflects their personal values and their vision, but it is made up of a lot of small items of detail. Cultures can come about by chance, but if leaders want to plan for success, they need to plan to achieve the culture they want.

🛄 Case insight AirAsia

Management style and culture

Tony Fernandes set up Asia's first low cost airline, Air Asia, in 2001. As we saw in Chapter 1, it has proved an outstanding success and now carries over 30 million passengers per year. An article in *The Economist* ('Cheap, but Not Nasty', March 2009) made a number of observations about Tony's management style and its effect on the company's culture.

> 'Mr. Fernandes says that he came to the industry with no preconceptions but found it rigidly compartmentalized and dysfunctional. He wanted AirAsia to reflect his own unstuffy, open, and cheerful personality. He is rarely seen without a baseball cap, open-neck shirt and jeans, and he is proud that the firm's lack of hierarchy (very unusual in Asia) means anyone can rise to do anyone else's job. AirAsia employs pilots who started out as baggage handlers and stewards; for his part, Mr. Fernandes also practises what he preaches. Every month he spends a day as a baggage handler, every two months as cabin crew, every three months as a check-in clerk. He even established a "culture department" to "pass the message and hold parties".'

Mapping the dimensions of entrepreneurial culture

Entrepreneurial culture is far harder to describe than it is to recognize – as might be expected given the lack of scientific measures available. Many of the detailed elements described aid recognition and are important in contributing to the overall culture. However, many elements are just detail and can get in the way of the big picture. These descriptors can be mapped onto Hofstede's four cultural dimensions (Figure 5.5). Notice that many descriptors apply to more than one of Hofstede's dimensions. Figure 5.4 also attempts to disentangle these descriptors and summarize or classify them as either important high-level attributes – shown in the middle of the web in green – or detail elements of culture. At the core is the value of creativity and innovation, linked to commercial opportunity. This is achieved through the entrepreneurial characteristics of strong relationships at all levels of the organization, continual learning through using and sharing information and knowledge and an acceptance of experimentation and measured risk-taking. The aim is to give staff a strong sense of empowerment consistent with the strategy of the organization. Finally, the culture must also have the future orientation of Hofstede's fifth dimension – a focus on the future, aligned with the vision for the organization.

Low uncertainty avoidance

Tolerance of risk and ambiguity, preference for flexibility, emphasis on personal choice and decision-making.

Implications: An empowered, 'can-do' attitude. Work is fun. A culture that recognizes change as endemic, the norm, not something to be avoided. A culture that values creativity and innovation and recognizes the importance of balanced risk-taking and does not penalize failure. Organizational self-confidence and self-efficacy.

Lower power distance

Open relationships, information flows and flat organizational structures.

Implications: Egalitarian, open culture, encouraging relationships not based on hierarchies. One that shares information and encourages learning.

High collectivism

A move from high individualism to collectivism as an organization grows. Encouragement of 'in-group' feeling, with strong sense of identity, strong relationships and competition with 'out-groups'.

Implications: A culture that builds relationships and networks with all stakeholders and sees these as more important than formal structures. Staff feel they belong and own the organization – motivated not to leave. An achievement-orientated culture that motivates people.

Balance between masculinity and femininity

Balance between an 'out-group', achievement orientation and an 'in-group' relationship orientation

Implications: A culture that builds relationships and networks with all stakeholders and sees these as more important than formal structures but also an achievement-orientated culture that motivates people to achieve collectively.

F 5.4 The cultural web in an entrepreneurial organization

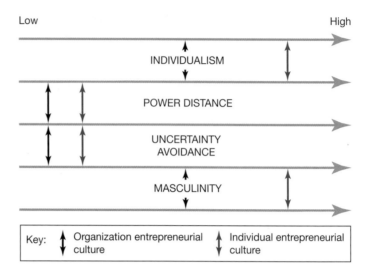

Low   High

INDIVIDUALISM

POWER DISTANCE

UNCERTAINTY AVOIDANCE

MASCULINITY

Key: Organization entrepreneurial culture   Individual entrepreneurial culture

F 5.5 Mapping the dimensions of entrepreneurial culture

This mapping onto Hofstede's four dimensions is summarized in Figure 5.5 and compared to the mapping for national cultures that encourage entrepreneurship. This mapping allows us to describe our entrepreneurial culture in a more structured way. By contrasting it to the position of the USA – our benchmark for a national culture that encourages individual entrepreneurship – we can explain the changes that are needed to encourage corporate entrepreneurship. An entrepreneurial organizational culture involves:

▷ *A move from individualism to collectivism as the organization grows and the entrepreneur must depend more upon a team* – Whilst the entrepreneur is initially very individualistic, to create the 'team leadership' style required as the organization grows they need to strike a careful balance between concern for people and concern for task and to become more of a team player. Rather than being an individual entrepreneur, they need to encourage group entrepreneurship. This implies cooperation and the development of relationships and networks with a strong sense of 'in-group', with a clear identity and a feeling of competition against 'out-groups' (us against competitors). This identity may come from the vision, values, norms and beliefs of the organization and, as in the case of Apple, can be reinforced by distinctive product design and the brand identity. However, there is a careful balance to be achieved between the need for individual initiative and cooperation and group-working. A cross-cultural, empirical investigation (Morris et al., op. cit.) supports this, observing that entrepreneurship appears to decline the more collectivism is emphasized, but, equally, dysfunctionally high levels of individualism can have the same effect.

▷ *Low power distance* – As we have observed, the architecture of an entrepreneurial organization requires low power distance, which is more in line with a consultative or participative leadership style. This implies an egalitarian organization with flat structures and open and informal relationships and unrestricted information flows. To reinforce this point Hall (2005) found in his study of organizational culture that innovation cannot occur in a power culture.

▷ *Low uncertainty avoidance* – Clearly our entrepreneurial culture involves low uncertainty avoidance. This implies a tolerance of risk and ambiguity, a preference for flexibility and an empowered culture that rewards personal initiative. It implies that failure may occasionally occur.

▷ *A balance between 'masculine' and 'feminine' dimensions* – Whilst individual entrepreneurs have a high need for achievement (masculine), we saw that they must temper this as the organization grows with a greater concern for others in the organization and relationships remain important (feminine). This need for achievement must become 'achievement through cooperation and relationships'. This is consistent with the balance required in Hofstede's first dimension. The aim here is to build a culture of achievement against 'out-groups' (other organizations) through cooperation, networks and relationships with the 'in-group'.

In terms of Hofstede's fifth dimension, an entrepreneurial organization, just like nations/individuals, will have a 'long-term' orientation; focused on the future and egalitarian with open communication and a lack of hierarchy.

Comparing Figure 5.5 to the countries shown in Figure 5.1 it is apparent that no single country, not even the USA, has the 'ideal' cultural profile for an entrepreneurial organization. If entrepreneurs in the USA (or UK) are to grow their businesses, whilst maintaining the business's entrepreneurial flair, they must move the organizational culture away from the national culture and more towards collectivism and femininity – developing a culture of achievement against 'out-groups' through cooperative team-working and network relationships with 'in-groups'. Cases such as 3M (Chapter 3), HFL Sport Science (Chapter 5) and Google (Chapters 5 and 12) show us how companies do this.

Sometimes the dominant national culture in which the company is based tends to discourage entrepreneurship. The dimensions of culture needed in an entrepreneurial organization (Figure 5.5) tend to suggest that it would be difficult to establish the appropriate culture in countries with both a high power distance and high uncertainty avoidance. If you look back at Figure 5.1 you will see France (in the 1970s) falls firmly into both categories. Figure 5.5 also suggests that balance is required between individualism vs collectivism and masculinity vs femininity, suggesting that a country with extreme results in either would pose problems for the entrepreneurial firm. Again it is noticeable that France has a high score in individualism. However, it is firmly in the middle ground on masculinity vs femininity. These observations imply that France would not be an easy place to establish an entrepreneurial organization. Interestingly, as we shall see in Chapter 13, another study shows that France has low and worsening levels of creativity, which begs the question as to whether these two factors could be linked.

Multinationals based in a number of different countries, each with different cultural profiles, will probably need to emphasize different things in different countries in order to combat the prevailing national culture. Often the prevailing national culture is such that the possibility of getting a homogenous organizational culture in a multinational is virtually impossible. Indeed, it might be argued that it is undesirable. Nevertheless management is the art of the possible and Morden's (op. cit.) work showed how national cultural issues might be addressed at a local level. What is more, Hofstede's (1980) work, cited earlier, indicates that intelligent use of different national cultures may confer competitive advantage by concentrating certain types of activities in particular countries.

We must always remember that, unlike most small firms, large organizations are complex. They contain many different environments, each with competing cultures based on the different tasks, individuals and environment, departments or operating units, even time horizons, they face. Often these cultures compete, resulting in different value choices. The role of management, therefore, is not just about selecting the culture to be emphasized, it is also about resolving these conflicts – emphasizing one or another and striking an appropriate balance between others. This is not an easy task and one that involves judgement rather than any sound scientific basis. Furthermore, as we shall observe in the next chapter, different departments or operating units within the same organization can have quite different cultures. Indeed these may be engineered deliberately to suit the roles they have within the larger organization. It is therefore quite possible that a complex organization may contain many different cultures, even if, overall, you might describe it as entrepreneurial.

One point to note is that one of the characteristics of a low uncertainty avoidance culture is that norms are less rigid and more open to different interpretation. Similarly, more feminine cultures are less rigid in the enforcement of norms. The conclusion is therefore that norms are likely to be less prevalent and less important in shaping culture in an entrepreneurial firm. They may also be more difficult to establish.

Constructing culture

Edgar Schein (1990) said that the only important thing that leaders do may be constructing their organization's culture. So, how do you go about creating an entrepreneurial culture in an organization – one that makes people feel empowered and emphasizes strong relationships, creativity and innovation, using and sharing information and knowledge and experimentation and measured risk-taking? Schein says that culture is grounded in the leader's basic beliefs, values and assumptions. As we saw in the last chapter,

🛍 Case insight Google

Corporate culture

The ubiquitous Google, a US multinational, runs over one million servers in data centres around the world and processes over one billion data requests every day. With a turnover in excess of $30 billion, it employs over 25,000 people worldwide and has its headquarters in Mountain View, California, on a campus called Googleplex. It is known for its informal corporate culture and regularly features in *Fortune* magazine's list of best companies to work for. It likes to think of itself as still 'small' despite the fact it is anything but. Phrases used to illustrate the culture include 'you can be serious without a suit', 'work should be challenging and challenge should be fun' and 'you can make money without being evil'. It has a tradition of creating April Fools' Day jokes. This started in 2000 when it 'launched' MentalPlex – Google's ability to read your mind and visualize the search result you want. It tries to add humour to its services. For example, if you ask the search engine for 'the answer to the ultimate question of life the universe and everything' it will actually give you the answer of '42' (Douglas Adams, *The Hitchhiker's Guide to the Galaxy*).

Google supports philanthropy. The not-for-profit Google.org creates awareness about climate change, global public health and poverty. After a two-year search, in 2010 Google gave some $10 million to various community projects. In 2011 it gave €1 million to the International Mathematics Olympiad. Google is also a noted supporter of network neutrality.

Google has a flat, decentralized organizational structure. It is highly democratic and tightly interconnected. All of the staff involved in product development work in teams of three or four people. Larger teams are broken down into smaller sub-teams, each working on specific aspects of the bigger project. Each team has a leader that rotates depending on the changing project requirements. Most staff work in more than one team. The Googleplex headquarters are noted for being a 'playful environment' with many social facilities that encourage employee interaction. There are free restaurants and numerous social events. Staff are encouraged to share information and ideas through a number of institutionalized initiatives and facilities. Idea generation is actively encouraged and staff have free time allocated to work on projects. Google has a low-cost, try-it-out, experimental approach to new product development and mistakes are tolerated and learned from.

More information on Google is given in the Case with questions in Chapter 12.

☐ You can find out more about the company and its culture from its website:
www.google.co.uk/about/corporate/company/culture.html

Organizational processes
- ▷ Leadership styles
- ▷ Structures
- ▷ Controls and rewards
- ▷ Empowerment
- ▷ Routines, rituals, rites and taboos
- ▷ Stories, symbols and myths

Cognitive processes
- ▷ Ethics, beliefs, assumptions and attitudes
- ▷ Norms and rules of conduct

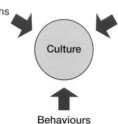

Culture

Behaviours
- ▷ How things actually get done – rational vs politicking, rule-following vs bending
- ▷ Vocabulary – job titles, slogans, metaphors, signals, gossip

F 5.6   Influences on culture

these basic beliefs underpin the approach of the authentic leader towards dispersed or distributed leadership. It is at the core of their emotional intelligence. It also underpins the vision for the organization. This is the first step – a necessary but not a sufficient condition. It underpins everything else. Building on the work of Johnson (op. cit.), Bowman and Faulkner (1997) talk about organizational culture being formed or embedded in an organization from three influences: organizational processes, cognitive processes and behaviours. All these influences are represented in Figure 5.6.

Organizational processes

These can be deliberate or emergent, evolving organically from within the organization and may not be intended. There are many influences on this:

- ▷ *Management and leadership styles*, as we have seen, are an important influence. They send signals about appropriate behaviour. How managers treat people, react to situations, even allocate their time, sends powerful signals about priorities to which employees react.
- ▷ *Organizational structure* influences culture. Hierarchical organizations can discourage initiative. Functional specialization can create parochial attitudes and sends signals about which skills might be valued. Flat, organic structures with broader spans of control encourage creativity, innovation and entrepreneurship – a factor to which we shall return in the next chapter.
- ▷ *Controls and rewards* send important signals about what the firm values. People take notice of what behaviour gets rewarded – as well as what gets punished – and behave accordingly. If salaries are based mainly on sales bonuses and there is a monthly league table of the best sales people, what does this tell you about the firm, its values and

its goals? Criteria used for recruitment, selection, promotion and retirement are all important. Status, praise and public recognition are powerful motivators.

▷ *The power to make decisions* is an important dimension for entrepreneurial organizations. Real empowerment sends the defining signal. Flat, decentralized structures with delegated decision-making send signals about encouraging local decision-making, although sometimes informal power can lie outside formal hierarchies. The reaction to failure is an important message in this.

▷ *Routines, rituals, rites and taboos* can have a strong subconscious influence. They form the unquestioned fabric of everyday life, but they say a lot about the organization. 'Guarded' or 'open' management offices, reserved or unreserved parking spaces, dress codes, normal methods of communication all influence the culture of the organization. What impression does a firm with reserved parking spaces and managers in offices 'guarded' by secretaries give you? An entrepreneurial organization should send out messages of egalitarianism with open relationships not based on status.

▷ *Stories and symbols* have a part to play in preserving and perpetuating culture. Who are the heroes, villains and mavericks in the firm? What do staff talk about at lunch? Are there symbols of status that are important such as car or office size? How do staff talk about customers? How do staff talk about the leader and other senior managers?

'Creating a culture in which every person in your organization, at every level, thinks and acts like an owner means that you need to aim to connect individual performance with your company's most important objectives … A company composed of individual owners is less focused on hierarchy and who has a nice office, and more intent on achieving their goals.'

Michael Dell

Cognitive processes

These are the beliefs, assumptions and attitudes that staff hold in common and take for granted. They are embedded and emanate from the organization's philosophy, values, morality and creed. They are likely to be strongest in firms that have a long history and where staff join young and stay in the firm for most of their careers. Many successful old family firms such as Wilkin & Sons and Cadbury were built around strong religious ethics whereby the success of the firm was shared with the workforce.

Norms – rules or authoritative standards – in an organization exist to enforce values and ensure conformity with the culture. An entrepreneurial firm may struggle with norms because one natural norm might well be to always ask the question 'why?', and to question the norms themselves. If norms are to be questioned, it is all the more important to have some deep values and beliefs that underpin them. Morris and Kuratko (op. cit.) talk about entrepreneurial organizations having a culture of 'healthy discontent' – one where there is a constant questioning, critiquing and changing of the way things are done. However, they do point out that this requires a balancing act, since too much discontent can easily become negative and destructive and lead to political gamesmanship.

💼 Case insights Wilkin & Sons and J. Cadbury & Sons

Ethics and culture

Wilkin & Sons

Wilkin & Sons is a family-owned business founded in 1885 and best known for its luxury Tiptree jams which sell to over 50 countries. The more esoteric jams such as 'Little Scarlet Strawberry' have attained almost a cult status among jam lovers. The company is committed to sharing success with its workforce. At the company's 450-hectare estate at Tiptree in Essex, managers and directors still test products as well as man the production lines when required. More than 100 of the 180 work force live in houses owned by the firm. The firm has operated a non-contributory pension scheme for over a century. It has also created a trust which will eventually leave employees with a 51% shareholding in the firm. There is another ethical dimension to the firm. It has never borrowed and does not intend to – a value that has proved its worth over the last few years.

J. Cadbury & Sons

J. Cadbury & Sons was a chocolate maker that was founded in 1824, based on Quaker values and ideals. It later became known simply as 'Cadbury' and lost its independence with the take-over by the US food giant Kraft in 2010. Originally the company promoted chocolate as a drink, providing a virtuous alternative to alcohol. In 1834, it started manufacturing drinking chocolate and cocoa, building the legendary Bournville factory and picturesque 'model village' for its workers. Workers were given a fair day's pay, good working conditions and homes and education for their children. The village offered red-brick terrace houses, cottages, schools, duck ponds and wide open park lands – a far cry from the conditions prevailing elsewhere at the time.

In a new entrepreneurial firm these beliefs can be moulded and developed by the enthusiasm and personality of the founding entrepreneur. In larger firms this can be developed through more formal training and communication processes. They are strongly influenced by what the leaders in the organization really pay attention to – not just what they say. But the important point is that they take time to frame. They do not happen overnight.

Behaviour

This is what actually happens in an organization. It decides whether outcomes are rational, transparent or the result of politicking. It influences whether the organization does actually follow rules, or is about bending them in the appropriate circumstances. Behaviour is also about vocabulary – job titles, slogans, metaphors, signals, even gossip. As we have seen, language is laden with value judgements that we do not realize most of the time – but they subconsciously influence the culture of the organization. Take an extreme example – a 'private' in the army 'salutes' an 'officer'. What messages do the words and actions convey and what culture do they reinforce? So, what should be the behaviours that reinforce the message that this is an entrepreneurial organization? To cement an organizational culture, behaviours should be congruent with the other influences.

Although behaviours in organizations normally reflect and reinforce culture, they can also be influenced by a wide variety of external influences, within society as a whole, within a profession or within a sector or industry. Schneider and Barsoux (1997) observe that the culture in Nordic and Anglo-Saxon countries dictates that they frequently adopt 'controlling' strategies – rational-analytic with a desire to control the external environment – whereas the Latin Europeans and Asians tend to adopt 'adapting' strategies – with a belief in a less certain and less controllable environment. We have already observed the deference to hierarchy in China. Behaviour that becomes routine can be difficult to change. However, attitudes can be influenced over time by getting people to behave in certain ways. Change behaviour first and attitudes will, eventually, follow.

🖿 Case with questions Apple

Organizational culture

The boss of any organization has an enormous influence on its culture, whether they intend it or not. In Chapter 1 we looked at Steve Jobs and his character traits. Adam Lashinsky's book (*Inside Apple: The Secrets Behind the Past and Future Success of Steve Jobs's Iconic Brand*, London: John Murray, 2012) gives us a rare insight into the effects this must have had in generating an organizational culture at Apple. As he says: 'you're expected to check your ego at the door' because there really is only room for one – that of Jobs, who he says exhibits 'narcissism, whimsy and disregard for the feelings of others'. Jobs emerges as a short-tempered, authoritarian dictator ruthlessly pushing, even bullying, staff to complete assigned tasks. On a (slightly) more positive note he is described as 'a visionary risk taker with a burning desire to change the world ... [representative of] charismatic leaders willing to do whatever it takes to win and who couldn't give a fig about being liked.'

Apple emerges as a cultish, paranoid, secretive and joyless organization, built on fear and mistrust, where competition and aggressive in-fighting between staff was encouraged and public humiliation was regular. For example:

> 'Apple is secretive ... Far from being empowered, its people operate within narrow bands of responsibility ... employees are expected to follow orders, not offer opinions ... Apple's CEO was a micromanager ... and to an amazingly low level ... Apple isn't even a nice place to work ... Jobs' brutality in dealing with subordinates legitimized a frighteningly harsh, bullying, and demanding culture ... a culture of fear and intimidation found roots.'

Words from the book that describe the culture are shown in the cultural web in Figure 5.7. Steve Jobs was very much at the centre of the web. It's a culture that seems quite the opposite of that in other successful Silicon Valley companies.

➞

Paranoia
Secretive   Control   Cultish
No fun   Product   Bullying
excellence
Discipline   Competitive
Follow orders
Relationship   Narrow bands of
of fear   STEVE   responsibility
JOBS
Task-orientated   Closed
Micromanage
Mistrust   Perfectionist
Attention
Serious   to detail   Focus
Top-down
management

F 5.7 Cultural web of Apple

Apple is characterized as a design-driven organization in which decisions were arbitrated by Jobs with his sense of simple aesthetic and design. Apple makes products simple – simple to use and simple to understand. Unlike many other firms of comparable size, it has a very limited product range that simplifies customer choice. And simplicity was a theme that came directly from Jobs. Ideas came from the top. Jobs notoriously despised focus groups. The iPhone and the iPad were both devices 'built for Steve'. As one former employee commented: 'Apple designed for Steve ... It is not an exaggeration. Steve was the user that everything orbited around and was designed for.'

Central to Apple's culture is product excellence – a cult of product – where employees do not want to let the company down by being the weakest link. And if they do, they can become collateral damage because of the aggressive, competitive environment. It is organized on a functional rather than product-line basis and functional expertise is highly valued. It is task- and work-orientated and definitely not play-orientated (Lashinsky frequently contrasts it with Google) and long hours, missed holidays and tight deadlines

were expected and encouraged. However, Lashinsky admits that 'by and large, Apple is a collaborative and cooperative environment, devoid of overt politicking ... but it isn't usually nice, and it's almost never relaxed.' In his view unquestioning collaboration and cooperation were necessary to ensure instructions were communicated and followed in this command-and-control structure. He believes that employee happiness was never a top priority for Steve Jobs. But on the other hand, employees derived pride from Apple's products and in working for Jobs' vision. Jobs appeared omnipresent, or at least visible, around the campus, despite the fact that very few people had access to his office suite.

Everything at Apple was elaborately planned and Jobs' notorious attention to detail – particularly marketing detail – is a theme emerging from the book. For example, there is the story of the iPod 'unboxing room' where there were experiments on hundreds of different types of boxes, packaging and signage so that customers got the maximum enjoyment out of the 'unboxing experience'. There is also the story of the launch of iMovie HD in 2005 when Apple produced an expensive one-minute film, shot at an Apple employee's wedding, to demonstrate its capabilities. Just weeks before the product launch Jobs decided it did not present the right image, and demanded a new one was shot – which it was on a Hawaiian beach. No detail seemed too small to avoid Jobs' scrutiny, and woe betide you if you got it wrong.

Secrecy, mistrust and paranoia seemed to underpin the Apple culture. Staff only knew about the elements of new product development that they needed to know about. Identity badges allowed only selective entry into parts of the Apple Infinite Loop campus. Staff could only enter rooms that directly related to something they were working on. It was not uncommon for an employee to have access to a room to which his boss did not to have access. The same applied to meetings.

Information was strictly on a 'need to know' basis and if you did not have the necessary clearance, you did not need to know. Staff used to eagerly await new product announcements, usually from Jobs, to find out about latest developments:

> 'Apple employees know something big is afoot when the carpenters appear in their office building. New walls are quickly erected. Doors are added and new security protocols put into place ... your badge, which got you into particular areas before the new construction, no longer works in those places ... Windows that once were transparent are now frosted. Other rooms have no windows at all. They are called lockdown rooms: No information goes in or out without a reason. All you can surmise is that a new, highly secretive project is under way, and you are not in the know. End of story.'

Of course there are some good reasons for product secrecy since designs can be copied and sales of old models suffer as soon as the launch of a new model is made public. But staff were encouraged not to talk about Apple outside of the organization, particularly to journalists, and when they did it had to be about product, not about the organization. And those making inappropriate disclosures were threatened with prosecution, not just termination. Journalists could be treated shabbily.

Secrecy started with new recruits, many of whom were recruited to 'dummy positions' – roles that may not have existed or were not explained in detail until months after they joined the company and had proved their trustworthiness. New employees were given an iMac but no help in assembling it – they were assumed to know enough about the computer to do that for themselves. Unlike other organizations, joining Apple was often a leap of faith and one that involved knowing

and believing in the product – a sort of self-selection process.

Apple still does not have organization charts, and that limits the people you know about outside your immediate environment – a cell-like structure. It had a small executive team – advisors to Steve Jobs – assisted by less than 100 vice presidents. Apple is still dominated by engineers but rank doesn't always confer status. As Lashinsky observes:

> 'Everyone is aware of an unwritten caste system. The industrial designers are untouchable, as were, until his death, the cadre of engineers who had worked with Steve Jobs for years, some dating to his first stint at Apple. A small group of engineers carries the title of DEST, distinguished engineer/scientist, technologist. These are individual contributors with clout in the organization but no management responsibilities. Otherwise, status fluctuates with the prominence of the products on which one works.'

But without an organization chart, the hierarchy is constantly changing. Every year there was a gathering of the 'Top 100' engineers and executives personally chosen by Jobs as 'those he would choose to start the company over again.' And as Lashinsky observes: 'Hurt feelings over exclusion were the norm, which is what Jobs expected and even relished.' With such an overarching influence of one person the inevitable question is 'Can Apple last without him?' Only time will tell.

QUESTIONS

1 Compare and contrast this culture to that of Google (see Case insight).

2 This is not the culture of the typical entrepreneurial organization. Why has it worked?

3 Will this culture work without Steve Jobs? How might it change?

Reconstructing culture

Constructing culture is like baking a cake. It takes the right ingredients and time for the mixture to bake. However the ingredients are far more volatile and unpredictable than a cake mix, particularly the relationships between individuals. Constructing the appropriate culture in a start-up is difficult enough, but that culture needs to shift and change as the organization grows. Most small firms start life with a 'task culture' – getting the job done. If the entrepreneur finds it difficult to delegate that may turn into a 'power culture' – where people vie to have power and influence over the entrepreneur. As this sort of firm grows, especially if the delegated authority is not genuine, there is a danger of developing a 'role culture' whereby job titles become too important – a culture that is quite different from the entrepreneurial culture outlined earlier.

But, whilst constructing and developing culture in a start-up is difficult enough, changing the culture in a large organization from one thing to another is altogether more difficult. It normally involves change at the top. Not just the MD or CEO but frequently the entire top team have to change – which is exactly what Stuart Rose did when he replaced Luc Vandevelde as Chief Executive of M&S in 2004 prior to turning the giant retailer around (see Case with questions in Chapter 7). This is partly about bringing in new core values but also about sending the strongest possible signals to the workforce that things are changing. When companies merge or acquire other companies their inability to reconcile conflicting corporate cultures is a major reason why the merger might fail – which is what happened after the disastrous merger of AOL and Time Warner in 2001 and the take-over of NCR by AT&T in 1991. Normally one top team will come to dominate the other and many in the dominated team will leave. Louis Gerstner is credited with turning around the ailing IBM in the 1990s. He claims management cannot change culture, it merely 'invites the workforce itself to change the culture'. His observations on the process (reproduced opposite) are insightful.

Reconstructing an existing culture is part of the skill involved in managing change – a topic addressed in Chapter 7. But reconstructing culture can also be a painfully slow process. It involves many detailed changes that, on their own, might not be considered significant, but, taken together, add up to the definition of 'how it is around here'. Consistent changes reinforce each other. Fundamentally, reconstruction involves a process of redefinition of values and priorities which then have to be effectively communicated. Many people will be unable to 'buy into' the changes in culture and will leave. Organizations with a strong culture, like Apple, tend to attract like-minded staff. In this way strong cultures become self-reinforcing. However, strong cultures are also the most difficult to change.

The difficulty in changing culture is one reason why larger organizations create new, smaller organizational units to push through new initiatives, leaving the core business and the prevalent culture unchanged in the larger parent. Size and structure can be important influences on culture as well as a useful tool to facilitate change.

🗂 Case insight Louis Gerstner and IBM

Changing culture

Louis Gerstner is credited with turning around the ailing giant IBM in the 1990s. He was brought in when the company lost $800 million plus write-offs, eventually totalling $8.1 billion, in the first four months of 1993 and was facing planned break-up. Today IBM is the world's number three brand measured by equity value. His comments about changing culture are insightful.

'Frankly, if I could have chosen not to tackle the IBM culture head-on, I probably wouldn't have ... Changing the attitudes and culture of hundreds of thousands of people is very, very hard to accomplish. Business Schools don't teach how to do it. You can't lead the revolution from the splendid isolation of corporate headquarters. You can't simply give a couple of speeches or write a credo for the company and declare that the new culture has taken hold. You can't mandate it, engineer it.

What you can do is create conditions. You can provide incentives. You can define the market place realities and goals. But then you have to trust. In fact, in the end, management doesn't change culture. Management invites the workforce itself to change the culture.

In the end, my deepest culture-change was to induce IBMers to believe in themselves again – to believe they had the ability to determine their own fate, and that they already knew what they needed to know ... In other words, at the same time I was working to get employees to listen to me, to understand where we needed to go, to follow me there – I needed to get them to stop being followers. It wasn't a logical, linear challenge. It was counter-intuitive, centered around emotion, rather than reason.

Change is hard work. It calls for commitment from employees way beyond the normal company–employee relationship. It is what I call a high performance culture ... The best leaders create high performance cultures. They set demanding goals, measure results and hold people accountable. They are change agents, constantly driving their institutions to adapt and advance faster than their competitors do.

Personal leadership is about visibility – with members of the institution. Great CEOs roll up their sleeves and tackle problems personally. They don't hide behind staff. They never simply preside over the work of others. They are visible every day with customers, suppliers and business partners. Most of all, personal leadership is about passion. They want to win every day, every hour. They urge their colleagues to win. They loathe losing. It's not a cold intellectual exercise. It's personal.'

Source: Gerstner Jnr, L.V. (2002) *Who Says Elephants Can't Dance?*, New York: HarperCollins.

Five ways to destroy a rich culture

1 Manage the bottom line (as if you make money by managing money).
2 Make a plan for every action: no spontaneity please, no learning.
3 Move managers around to be certain they never get to know anything but management well (and kick the boss upstairs – better to manage a portfolio than a real business).
4 Always be objective, which means treating people as objects (in particular hire and fire employees the way you buy and sell machines – everything is a 'portfolio').
5 Do everything in five easy steps.

Adapted from Mintzberg, H., Ahlstrand, B. and Lampel, J. (1998) *Strategy Safari*, New York: The Free Press.

Culture and leadership style

Many studies have shown significant national and gender differences in management style. For example, using Hofstede's dimensions, Torrington (1994) highlighted some of the differences in manager–subordinate relationships in six countries – Britain, USA, France, Germany, Japan and in a number of Arab countries. For example:

▷ British managers are willing to 'listen' to subordinates (low uncertainty avoidance) and like 'old boy networks' (high masculinity);
▷ US managers have a 'tough', results-orientated style in dealing with subordinates (high individualism and high masculinity);
▷ French managers like formality (high power distance) and 'intellectualism' (high individualism);
▷ German managers like routines and procedures and close control of apprentices (high uncertainty avoidance);
▷ The Japanese are high on both masculinity and collectivism producing a 'nurturing father' style of management;
▷ Arab countries value loyalty and the avoidance of interpersonal conflict (high power distance).

The dimensions of an entrepreneurial culture have resonance in motivation theory, in particular in 'Theory Z' (Ouchi, 1981). 'Theory Z' is a development of 'Theory Y', popularized by the American academic David McGregor in 1960. McGregor contrasted his 'Theory X' – which assumes that employees have an inherent dislike of their work, taking an instrumental view of it, so that managers must exercise strong control over their activities because they cannot be trusted – with 'Theory Y' – which assumes that employees can like their work and can be motivated and then trusted to exercise discretion within a framework of rules. 'Theory Z' develops the participative nature of 'Theory Y' further by assuming that consensus and trust can be established within an organization, particularly through participative, team-based, decision-making. These teams are responsible for achieving consensus and making decisions while the team's supervisor is still personally held responsible for the decision and its implementation. Relationships within the organization are based on trust and are long-term. Career development depends on total commitment and a willingness to do whatever is needed to further the organization – flexibility. The organization builds upon the experience of individuals, internalizing it and using it in a way that parallels the learning organization. Management is based upon walk-about – 'walking the talk'. All these characteristics have resonance in the entrepreneurial organization.

The interesting thing about 'Theory Z' is the cultures in which it will or will not flourish. As Morden (op. cit.) points out, 'Theory Z' would be difficult to establish 'in cultures characterized by large power distance, strong individualism, aggressive masculinity, strong uncertainty avoidance and a strong attachment to hierarchies'. Such cultures are clearly not entrepreneurial (refer back to Figure 5.1). Morden observes that these cultures exist in southern Europe and South America. He goes on to make the point that 'Theory Z' contains a tension between group power and individualism. This is exactly the problem facing the growing entrepreneurial organization as it develops from being very dependent on the entrepreneur. 'Theory Z' also ideally requires low individualism – or high collectivism – and low power distance. He observes that, whilst there are no such cultures recorded on Hofstede's culture maps, the nearest cultures shown are those of Austria, Israel and Finland.

So what sort of leadership style do you adopt in order to help achieve an entrepreneurial culture? Do you simply adopt a style, such as 'Theory Z', that reflects the values contained in the cultural web, even if the national culture in which the organization is placed finds this alien? Morden (op. cit.) supports the view that it is unrealistic to take a 'one style suits all' approach to the principles and practice of management as they are applied from one country to another: 'What works well in one country may be entirely inappropriate in another'. He advocates adapting to suit local circumstances and that means remembering two things:

1 Management is the art of the achievable and it may be impossible to achieve the 'ideal' entrepreneurial culture within some national cultures. That means a suboptimal solution – 'not quite an entrepreneurial culture' – may be appropriate. On the other hand, however, there is no theoretical guarantee that this solution will be effective in delivering entrepreneurial activity.

2 It is one thing knowing where you want to get to but quite another thing getting there. Leadership style can be adapted and changed

gradually over time to suit circumstances so that it moves towards a more entrepreneurial style. There is a lot of evidence that it takes quite some time to change inherent cultures, whether we are talking about the impact of national cultures or changing the cultures of existing organizations.

Even in the context of a multinational organization, Morden does not advocate the development of 'geocentricity' – an international culture within the multinational. He sees this as only an option when the multinational has clearly understood values and common technologies; 'the resources to create such a body of international managers, and the desire to maintain a high level of integration and control over diversity through its international management team.' The problem of reconciling the different leadership styles and cultures needed in different contexts – not just related to geography – is one reason pushing companies to fundamentally rethink many of their organization structures.

🗂 Case with questions David Hall and HFL Sport Science

Changing culture

Based in Newmarket at the heart of the UK's best-known horse racing and breeding area, HFL Sport Science started life in 1963 owned by the UK Horserace Betting Levy Board (HBLB – a quasi-governmental body, or quango). It enjoyed a steady stream of guaranteed income from the monitoring of racehorses and greyhounds to ensure that their performance was not artificially influenced by illegal substances. As a public sector organization, it had a bureaucratic, government-style organization structure and was not driven by profitability. This, therefore, seems an unlikely organization to consider as an exercise in change management and corporate entrepreneurship. But change it did, and by 2007 it had diversified into drug testing on humans and had been sold for £20.25 million. The buyer was Quotient Bioresearch Ltd which is owned by a consortium of investors, including a minority holding by HFL's Chief Executive David Hall and other senior managers.

Prior to privatization, HFL became the world's largest independent sports drug surveillance company, and a major competitor within the contract research market (testing for pharmaceuticals and biotechnology companies). It was the only laboratory in the world engaged in both sport drug surveillance and contract research. It has undertaken funded research for the World Anti-doping Agency as well as working extensively for British Horseracing. HFL has pioneered sports doping control research and surveillance in the UK, testing athletes and racing animals as part of forensic doping control processes and providing research and bio-analysis testing services to pharmaceutical, food, consumer products and health care clients.

The change catalyst was the appointment of David Hall as Chief Executive in 2001. His brief was to broaden the business base away from racehorses and greyhounds, and he effectively paved the way for the 'privatization' of the company. David is a scientist – Chartered Engineer with a PhD – but he also has an MBA, which is the source of his theoretical knowledge of how to change the culture of an organization. The challenge was to put it into practice at HFL. David would say that his passion for creativity and innovation and the pursuit of a 'perfect culture' provided a common thread throughout his career before joining HFL. For example, he set up a technology transfer organization in London – Thames Gateway Technology Centre. The challenge, as David sees it, is to get the very best from your staff and to truly differentiate your company on the basis of its people. The HFL culture demanded involvement across all levels and functions. It was a culture where knowledge was shared and communication was a vital element in this process. David wanted it to run downwards, upwards and sideways through all feasible routes, so there was no excuse for 'not knowing'.

David's preferred leadership style is to 'animate and facilitate' rather than 'command and control'. His preferred communication style at HFL, therefore, involved limiting group sizes to 20, which he saw as far more conducive to participation. He gave 'state of the union' addresses to these groups every six months. He also instituted informal 'coffee and cakes' sessions on Monday mornings to help communication and get people to mix across boundaries and functions. There were also more formal mechanisms like team briefs and a mythical 'Uncle Bernard' who answered e-mail questions from staff. The elected Staff Association also conducted regular surveys and played an important part in promoting and monitoring change, even chasing the introduction of new ideas. HFL also used cross-functional teams for project work and senior managers had spells of doing other people's jobs, staff working closely together in a culture that encouraged team-working.

HFL's scientific work depends critically on new ideas, which is why David was keen to encourage creativity. However, to start with he saw it also as an invaluable way to encourage culture change within the organization. To do this he set up a Creativity Club and an Innovation Club. Each provided an environment for the free exchange of ideas, to push boundaries, and to harness the creative energies of staff. David drove the Creativity Club, which had volunteers from all areas of the company. It met monthly, in groups of 6 to 8.

He adopted a 'softly, softly' approach with this receptive group, introducing creativity tools and focusing on techniques, not outcomes. He believed fun and playfulness were important in encouraging creativity. He introduced the groups to creativity exercises such as finger painting (a 'right-brain' activity) and asked staff to paint what they thought of the organization, then asked them to explain what they had painted (a 'left-brain' activity), thus linking the left and right brain. Creativity Club meetings were limited to one hour and operated under the terms of a 'Creativity Charter'. The ideas or problems brought to the Club – both business and non-business – used a wide range of creativity techniques to take the ideas or problems forward, often questioning the definition of the problem so as not to jump to conclusions. Every idea generated by the Club was posted on the company's intranet and staff were invited to comment. The best ideas might be taken forward by project teams. The senior managers also used the Club as a forum to take forward strategic issues that required a 'different way of thinking'. The Innovation Club focused more on issues of strategic importance and on implementation – corporate innovation. The Club met quarterly at lunch time and all staff were automatically members. David made the distinction that creativity is the generation of novel and useful ideas, whereas innovation is about making money out of creativity.

HFL also hosted an Ideas Centre comprising a group of like-minded organizations that had their own Creativity Clubs. It met for half a day each month. The Centre hosted outside speakers who challenged conventions and tried out new creativity techniques. Members were connected to university-based resources to help them push forward initiatives. The objective was to energize change agents in these organizations.

The company also had a Book Club that encouraged the reading of business books, which also can lead to the introduction of new ideas. In addition, there was the Business ➡

Intelligence Group, established to trawl the outside world for new ideas and to establish benchmarks for its activities. Everyone who saw or heard interesting things outside the company was debriefed and the ideas were passed on or project teams set up to take the idea further.

David is a great believer in the power of positive thinking – another attitude he liked to encourage in staff. He believes it can raise the proportion of time people spend working at maximum output. He arranged in-house training sessions on the topic which resulted in individuals producing 'affirmations' to complete challenging personal tasks. David participated in the training and his 'affirmation' led to him cycling coast-to-coast and back to raise money for charity.

HFL has performance reviews and a bonus scheme based upon four performance classifications: outstanding, achieving, aspiring and unacceptable. Staff are not paid any bonuses if their performance is unacceptable. HFL achieved 'Investors in People' status and was voted by its staff into the 2005 list of the *Times* '100 Best Companies to Work For'. But David will also admit that there have been casualties along the way, with less willing staff being replaced. In this respect new managers had a crucial part to play in changing the culture by signalling what behaviour was required and what behaviour was unacceptable in the 'new' HFL.

David has used creativity to change the culture of HFL. He wanted to achieve a 'target culture' in the organization and used a 'cultural survey' regularly to measure the progress towards this.

'Creativity and innovation are at the heart of HFL Sport Science's people-based culture. New ideas and ways of thinking all help provide energy that creates an environment and culture that maximizes performance. Our culture provides an environment for the free exchange of ideas, to push the boundaries, and to harness the collective energies of the people that make up HFL.'

HFL also used what it calls a 'strategy map' divided into four interconnecting areas: customer, reputation, people and finance. The aim in the 'customer' area was to become, or remain, 'first choice for analytical chemistry by improving loyalty, building relationships and innovating'. HFL aimed to be the best customer choice, but not necessarily the cheapest. To achieve this it had to remain at the leading edge of its science and at the forefront of innovation. But innovation need not always be scientific. It does however require creativity. Creativity was, therefore, not only a tool for pushing through change, it was also a core element in trying to differentiate HFL from its competitors. Staff involvement and enthusiasm at HFL is no accident. It is carefully nurtured with formal and informal techniques.

2010 saw big changes in HFL. Protracted negotiations for a management buy-out from Quotient came to an unsuccessful end. Despite this, in December it opened new $4 million laboratories in Kentucky, USA, after being awarded a contract to provide drug testing for the Kentucky Horse Racing Commission. In the same month came its surprise acquisition by UK-based LGC – an international leader in the laboratory services, measurement standards, reference materials and proficiency testing market places. LGC itself was the result of the privatization of the Laboratory of the Government Chemist in 1996. It is owned by the management and staff and has grown through a combination of organic growth and multiple acquisitions from 270 employees to 1400 in 2010.

In July 2011 David Hall left HFL to set up two new ventures of his own. He felt he had learnt valuable lessons but that the 'cycle was now complete' and he did not want to be part of a larger organization.

☐ Up-to-date information on HFL Sport Science, an HFL Creativity Presentation and some of the creativity exercises they use can be found on their website: www.ideascentregroup.com

Organizational Culture Assessment Instrument (OCAI)

Measuring the dimensions of organizational culture is extremely difficult and there are alternatives to Hofstede's model. The Organizational Culture Assessment Instrument (OCAI) is a simple validated instrument developed by Professors Robert Quinn and Kim Cameron and free to use. Consequently it is claimed to be used by over 10,000 companies worldwide. You are asked to distribute 100 points between statements that typify six dimensions of organizational culture: dominant organizational characteristics, organizational leadership style, management of employees, organization glue, strategic emphases and the criteria for success. The points can be distributed to represent how the organization is now and how you would prefer it to be. The dimensions are designed to measure an organization's position on the Competing Values Framework (Quinn and Rohrbaugh, 1983) which measures the conflict between the internal and external focus of the organization and its preference for stability and control or flexibility and discretion. The resulting analysis consists of four typologies:

▷ *Hierarchy culture* – the traditional organizational structure with hierarchical controls that respect position and power, emphasizing efficiency and stability;

▷ *Market culture* – controls through trying to minimize costs and moving towards market efficiency by looking outward at the cost of transactions, achievement- and results-orientated;

▷ *Clan culture* – less focused on structure and control through rules and regulations, with greater emphasis on flexibility, driving direction through vision, shared goals, a sense of family (Hofstede's 'in-group'), loyalty, mentoring and nurturing, often with flat structures using team-working;

▷ *Adhocracy culture* – even more independence and flexibility with greatest speed of response to change, more entrepreneurial with greater risk-taking, using ad-hoc teams to address new challenges.

→

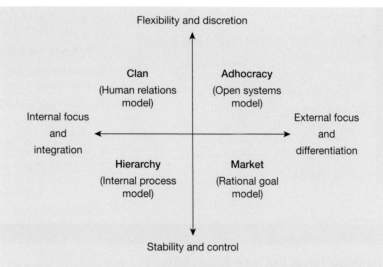

The OCAI analysis gives you a map showing where you are now and where you might want to be on these typologies.

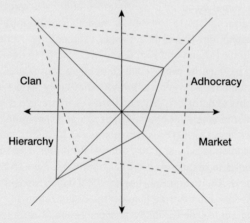

The instrument can be downloaded free from: www.tiplady.org.uk/pdfs/ocai.doc.
An on-line version is available at www.ocai-online.com. Individuals can use the test free and the analysis includes a brief explanation.

Summary

▷ Culture is an organization's basic beliefs and assumptions about what it is about, how its members behave, and how it defines itself in relation to its external environment. It is the collective programming of the mind, a pattern of taken-for-granted assumptions that influence how people in an organization perceive, think and feel in relation to situations. As in the cases of **J Cadbury & Sons** and **Wilkin & Sons**, it is grounded in the founder's basic beliefs, values and assumptions. Particularly when based on religious or ethical beliefs, these can produce strong cultures.

- Establishing an appropriate corporate culture is vital if you want to develop an entrepreneurial organization. However, the culture of an organization does not exist in isolation. An individual may participate in many different groups, each with its own dominant culture. Each group influences and is influenced by the other – and cultures can change over time. The dominant culture of the country in which the organization operates will be a major influence on individuals and may be a barrier to establishing an entrepreneurial culture.

- Culture within an organization is based on a firm set of enduring values. It can be constructed through organizational and cognitive processes and behaviours. It can be transmitted individually by the entrepreneur or through PR activities, induction, training and good communications generally.

- Whether you try to manage it or not, every organization will evolve a culture, be it strong or weak. Strong cultures attract like-minded people (see **Apple** and **Google**). They self-reinforce.

- Reconstructing the culture of an organization is very difficult, as **Louis Gerstner** of **IBM** discovered. It requires good change-management skills. However, as we saw in the case of **HFL Sport Science**, with a good change agent at the top it can be done. The difficulty is one reason why larger organizations often attempt to separate or spin out new initiatives so that they can create their own culture, leaving that of the core business unchanged. Size and structure matter.

- Hofstede measures culture in four dimensions. Figure 5.5 maps the descriptors of an entrepreneurial culture onto Hofstede's dimensions. It distinguishes between 'high-level' attributes – strong relationships, creativity and innovation, empowerment, continual learning and experimentation and measured risk-taking – and the detailed elements of culture.

- Hofstede's dimensions can be used to describe the culture in an entrepreneurial organization:

  - *Individuality vs collectivism.* An entrepreneurial culture would involve a move from individualism to collectivism as the organization grows. This implies cooperation and the development of relationships and networks with a strong sense of 'in-group', with a clear identity and a feeling of competition against 'out-groups';
  - *Power distance.* An entrepreneurial culture has low power distance. This implies an egalitarian organization with flat structures and open and informal relationships and open, unrestricted information flows;
  - *Uncertainty avoidance.* An entrepreneurial organization has low uncertainty avoidance. This implies a tolerance of risk and ambiguity, a preference for flexibility and an empowered culture that rewards personal initiative;
  - *Masculinity vs femininity.* An entrepreneurial organization has balance between the masculine and feminine dimensions to build a culture of achievement against 'out-groups' through cooperation, networks and relationships with the 'in-group'.

- The entrepreneurial culture described above is one that has worked in the majority of successful western organizations. **Google,** in common with most Silicon Valley companies, exhibits many of the characteristics of this culture. However, by way of contrast, **Apple** exhibits few. This underlines the fact that success is complex and there are few absolutes in management. It comes from the interaction of many different factors in different ways – including product/market characteristics – and can depend heavily on individuals, particularly founders. **Apple** attracts people who like its culture.

It also depends upon the local and national environment in which it is placed.

▷ The leadership style appropriate to 'Theory Z' reflects many of the dimensions of entrepreneurial culture. However, it is unrealistic to take a 'one style suits all' approach to the principles and practice of management as they are applied from one country to another. The style needs to be adapted to suit local circumstances and national cultures.

Essays and discussion topics

1 How do you describe culture? Can it be measured?
2 How does language affect culture? How does culture affect language?
3 Is strong culture good or bad? Give examples.
4 What are your core values? What are the core values of your national culture? What are the core values of entrepreneurship? What are the differences and can they be reconciled?
5 How do cognitive processes influence the culture of an organization? Give examples.
6 What organizational processes would reinforce the message that an organization is entrepreneurial?
7 What cognitive processes would reinforce the message that an organization is entrepreneurial?
8 What managerial behaviours would reinforce the message that an organization is entrepreneurial?
9 Do you notice any patterns in the national results of Hofstede's research?
10 The USA is normally seen as having an entrepreneurial national culture. If this is the case, how would you describe an entrepreneurial culture? How would you describe the culture in your country?
11 What methodological problems might emerge when using a study that sets out to discriminate national cultures as a basis for discriminating organizational cultures?

12 What methodological problems might emerge when organizing a study which tries to discriminate entrepreneurial from other organizations?
13 Why is the balance between individualism and collectivism so important? Why might it vary?
14 How would you describe an entrepreneurial organizational culture?
15 In what circumstances might an organization wish to see no mistakes or failures?
16 What particular problems face your country in developing an entrepreneurial organizational culture?
17 Why might it be better to separate or spin out new initiatives so that they can create their own culture, leaving that of the core business unchanged?
18 What additional elements of the cultural web of entrepreneurship do the works of Hofstede et al. (1990), Morris and Kuratko (2002) and Schein (1994) bring to the elements highlighted in Figure 5.5? Do you think they are important?
19 Do you agree that the most important elements of an entrepreneurial culture are creativity and innovation, empowerment, strong relationships, continual learning and measured risk-taking?
20 Could you recognize an entrepreneurial organization without understanding its culture? If so, how?

Exercises and assignments

1 Find an organization that is willing to learn about its culture (this could be your university department). Get a selected group of senior managers to complete the Organizational Culture Assessment Instrument (OCAI). Present your findings to the group.
2 Select two organizations, one that you would describe as entrepreneurial, the other that you would describe as administrative or

bureaucratic. Describe their cultures in a brief report and evaluate on the five dimensions of creativity and innovation, empowerment, strong relationships, continual learning and measured risk-taking.

References

Blake, R. and Mouton, J. (1978) *The New Managerial Grid*, London: Gulf.

Bowman, C. and Faulkner, D.O. (1997) *Competitive and Corporate Strategy*, London: Irwin.

Carr, P. (2000) *The Age of Enterprise: The Emergence and Evolution of Entrepreneurial Management*, Dublin: Blackwell.

Cornwall, J. and Perlman, B. (1990) *Organizational Entrepreneurship*, Homewood, IL: Irwin.

Graham, J.L. and Lam, M. (2003) 'HBR Spotlight: The Chinese Negotiation', Boston: *Harvard Business Review*, October.

Guirdham, M. (1999) *Communicating across Cultures*, Basingstoke: Macmillan – now Palgrave Macmillan.

Hall, D. (2005) 'Insight from Facilitating Entrepreneurial Business Development within Established Organisations', presented at *Institute for Small Business and Entrepreneurship conference*, Blackpool, UK.

Handy, C. (1985) *Understanding Organizations*, London: Penguin.

Handy, C. (1995) *Gods of Management*, London: Souvenir Press.

Harrison R. (1972) 'Understanding your Organization's Character', *Harvard Business Review*, May/June.

Hofstede, G. (1980) *Culture's Consequences: International Differences in Work-related Values*, Beverly Hills: Sage.

Hofstede, G. (1981) *Cultures and Organizations: Software of the Mind*, London: HarperCollins.

Hofstede, G. (1991) *Cultures and Organizations*, London: McGraw-Hill.

Hofstede, G. and Bond, M.H. (1991) 'The Confucian Connection: From Cultural Roots to Economic Performance', *Organizational Dynamics*, Spring.

Hofstede, G., Neuijen B., Ohayv, D.D. and Sanders, G. (1990) 'Measuring Organizational Cultures: A Qualitative and Quantitative Study across Twenty Cases', *Administrative Sciences Quarterly*, 35.

Johnson, G. (1992) 'Managing Strategic Change: Strategy, Culture and Action', *Long Range Planning*, 25(1).

McGregor, D. (1960) *The Human Side of Enterprise*, London: McGraw-Hill.

Morden, T. (1995) 'International Culture and Management', *Management Decision*, 33(2).

Morris, M.H. and Kuratko, D.F. (2002) *Corporate Entrepreneurship*, Orlando: Harcourt College Publishers.

Morris, M.H., Davies, D.L. and Allen, J.W. (1994) 'Fostering Corporate Entrepreneurship: Cross Cultural Comparisons of the Importance of Individualism versus Collectivism', *Journal of International Business Studies*, 25(1).

Morris, P. (1991) 'Freeing the Spirit of Enterprise: The Genesis and Development of the Concept of Enterprise Culture', in R. Keat and N. Abercrombie (eds) *Enterprise Culture*, London: Routledge.

O'Connor, J. (1973) *The Fiscal Crisis of the State*, New York: St. Martin's Press.

Ouchi, W. (1981) *Theory Z*, Reading, MA: Addison-Wesley.

Peters, T. (1997) *The Circle of Innovation*, New York: Alfred A. Knopf.

Quinn, R.E. and Rohrbaugh, J. (1983) 'A Spatial Model of Effectiveness Criteria: Towards a Competing Values Approach to Organizational Analysis', *Management Science*, 29.

Schein, E.H. (1983)'The Role of the Founder in Creating Organizational Culture', *Organizational Dynamics*, Summer.

Schein, E.H. (1990) 'Organizational Culture', *American Psychologist*, February.

Schein, E.H. (1994) 'Organizational and Managerial Culture as a Facilitator or Inhibitor of Organizational Learning', *MIT Organizational Learning Network Working Paper 10.004*, May.

Schneider, S.C. and Barsoux, J.-L. (1997) *Managing across Cultures*, London: Prentice Hall.

Timmons, J.A. (1999) *New Venture Creation: Entrepreneurship for the 21st Century*, Singapore: Irwin/McGraw Hill.

Torrington, D. (1994) *International Human Resource Management*, Hemel Hempstead: Prentice Hall.

Welsch, H. (1998) 'America: North', in A. Morrison (ed.) *Entrepreneurship: An International Perspective*, Oxford: Butterworth Heinemann.

Chapter **6**

Building the organization structure

- ▷ **Size**
- ▷ **Hierarchy**
- ▷ **Change and complexity**
- ▷ **Organic structures**
- ▷ **New forms of organizing**
- ▷ **Networks and the socially embedded firm**
- ▷ **The knowledge firm in the knowledge economy**
- ▷ **The globalizing firm and its changing boundaries**
- ▷ **Strategic alliances/partnerships and joint ventures**
- ▷ **Developing partnerships**
- ▷ **Leadership, culture and structures**
- ▷ **Hybrid organic structures and the multi-business organization**
- ▷ **Summary**

Case insights
- ▷ Jaguar/Williams, BBC/IBM and Sun Microsystems/Intel – Strategic alliances
- ▷ Lovefilm – Strategic partnerships

Cases with questions
- ▷ Apple – Organizational structures
- ▷ Tata Consultancy Services – Structures to encourage innovation
- ▷ Richard Branson and Virgin – Brand, culture and structure

Learning outcomes

By the end of this chapter you should be able to:

▷ Explain and give examples of how size, structure and different organizational forms interact and how they are related to the tasks being undertaken and the environment in which an organization finds itself;

▷ Critically analyze why organizations are increasingly exploring new forms of organizing and be able to give examples of what forms these might take;

▷ Analyze and evaluate the advantages of networks and strategic alliances;

▷ Critically analyze the relationship between leadership styles, organizational cultures and different structures;

▷ Creatively address how an organization can be structured to encourage corporate entrepreneurship including how a hybrid organic structure can be constructed;

▷ Critically evaluate the structure of an organization.

Size

Chapter 2 highlighted the limitations as well as the advantages of the spider's web organizational structure, so beloved by entrepreneurs. As an organization grows greater structure becomes vital. It creates order and allows coordination of complex tasks. There is no one 'best' structure and with too much structure comes the danger of bureaucracy. As we shall see in this chapter, the most appropriate structure depends on many factors including:

▷ The nature of the organization;
▷ The strategies it is employing;
▷ The tasks to be undertaken;
▷ The technology it uses;
▷ The cultures it wishes to encourage;
▷ The environment in which it operates;
▷ The size of the organization.

Size does seem to matter. Large organizations are more complex than small and complexity impedes information flows, lengthens decision-making and can kill initiative. To be entrepreneurial, a large organization needs to find ways of breaking itself down into a number of sub-organizations with varying degrees of autonomy. The span of control for management does seem to matter – 'walking the talk', a management approach advocated earlier, only seems possible up to a certain size. But large organizations can structure themselves so that they comprise smaller 'units'. Again there are no prescriptive 'correct' approaches. However, for some time large companies have been seeking to replicate the flexibility of the small firm and encourage entrepreneurial management by 'deconstructing' themselves – that is, breaking themselves down into smaller units. A number of trends have been apparent over the last few decades. These have been encouraged by global competitive pressures to cut costs and improve responsiveness to market changes.

Delayering and decentralizing

Delayering is reducing the number of layers of a management hierarchy. Decentralizing is pushing down decision-making in the organization. The trend towards flattening organizational structures started in the USA in the 1980s and then came to Europe. Since those early days the rapid pace of change has continued so that reorganizations are now just one of the natural things that managers do regularly, often in times of recession, simply to keep costs down. This is not just about deconstructing, it is about changing the attitudes of the remaining managers about the security of their jobs as well as putting many middle-aged managers in the position of having few alternatives other than self-employment. No wonder self-employment has blossomed. Charles Handy (1994) predicted that many larger firms would become increasingly 'shamrock organizations' – the three leaves being core staff, temporary staff to ease them over peaks and troughs in work and small organizations supplying sub-contracted specialist services, deeply embedded in, and dependent upon, the larger firm. He predicted that many people would mix five kinds of work: wage work, fee work, home work, gift work and study work. It is interesting to observe how many of his predictions have come true.

Downscoping and outsourcing

Downscoping occurs when an organization restructures so as to focus on its core activities. Outsourcing occurs when non-core activities are sub-contracted. Large firms are increasingly concentrating on their core activities, where they have competitive advantage, and sub-contracting non-core activities. This enables them to reduce fixed costs and therefore risk. It allows them to flatten organizational structures and improve their response time to changes in the market place. 'Partnership sourcing', whereby a close relationship is built between the bigger company and the smaller subcontractor that supplies it, is growing. As we saw in the case study in Chapter 4, Dell is a prime example of this, with internet-based systems facilitating the rapid exchange of information between customers and suppliers, creating one element of Dell's competitive advantage. Large firms are increasingly experimenting with different structures, organizational forms and processes and we shall explore some of these later in this chapter.

Amar Bhidé (2000) takes downscoping further. He believes that, rather than trying to re-invent themselves, large firms should concentrate on projects with high costs and low uncertainty, leaving innovative projects with low costs and high uncertainty to small entrepreneurial firms, at least in the early stages of development. As ideas mature and risks and rewards become more quantifiable, large firms can adopt them – effectively outsourcing innovation. Even in capital-intensive businesses such as pharmaceuticals, smaller entrepreneurial organizations can conduct early-stage research, selling out to large firms when they reach the expensive, clinical trial stage. About one-third of drug firms' revenue now comes from licensed-in technology. Outside of the pharmaceutical industry, many large companies, like General Electric and Cisco, have adopted the policy of buying up small firms who have developed new technology – external corporate venturing (see Chapter 8).

As an alternative, particularly at the development stage, many organizations are forming strategic alliances, pooling skills and resources and minimizing risk – an option we shall explore later in this chapter. Even where research and development is kept in-house, many companies believe that the initial stages of innovation require such a different culture that different forms of organizing and even separate premises need to be found, leading them to set up separate 'research' establishments. But research is not the same as development and, once developed, the new product has to be exploited commercially. Having separate organizational forms and even locations for many of these activities allows firms to maintain different cultures as well as different structures, leadership styles, staffing and remuneration strategies. Within these structures smaller, often cross-functional, teams are frequently set up to take projects forward. Team organization is a sub-structure often associated with innovative developments and frequently used in technology-based firms like Apple and Google. As Grant (2010) observes: 'Non-hierarchical, team-based organizations can achieve high levels of innovation, flexibility and employee motivation.'

Taking this idea further, big companies often 'spin off' new ventures, creating completely new, small companies that are lean and flexible and focused on getting their product to market. However, often the big companies have to put in place mechanisms to make this happen, mini-organizations within the big company with the task of spotting innovative opportunities and facilitating their development. This can be the corporate venture capital firm – an autonomous company that underwrites and assists new product/service developments that meet formal venture capital criteria. We shall investigate how new venture developments can be organized in Chapter 8.

Large organizations are increasingly aware that size tends to be the enemy of creativity and innovation. Peter Chemin, CEO of the Fox TV empire, broke down his studios into small units, even at the risk of incurring higher costs, because 'in the management of creativity, size is your enemy' (*Economist*, 4 December 1999). John Naisbitt (1994) also feels that the future lies with small independent firms, whether owner-managed or spun out from large firms. He sees much of the growing importance of smaller entrepreneurial firms coming from larger firms which are restyling themselves into networks of entrepreneurs: 'Economies of scale are giving way to economies of scope, finding the right size for synergy, market flexibility, and above all, speed: To survive, big companies today are all deconstructing themselves and creating new structures, many as networks of autonomous units. Deconstruction is now a fashion, because it is the best way to search for survival.'

One implication from all this experimentation is clear – size matters and small is, indeed, beautiful. But how do you organize large numbers of people and maintain an entrepreneurial culture? The greater the number of people in the unit of organization, the more likely it is that the required structure will involve hierarchies. And hierarchies tend to rely on power to make decisions, and the exercise of power tends to be slow and inflexible – what we call bureaucratic. Part of the answer to this dilemma is the use of smaller sub-structures, which form part of a larger whole. These, as we shall see, can take many different forms. Each sub-structure may have its own sub-culture depending on the nature of the workforce and the tasks they undertake. The smaller the units, the easier it is for them to remain entrepreneurial.

Hierarchy

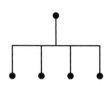

F 6.1A Hierarchy

F 6.1B Self-organizing team

Hierarchy is the fundamental feature of organizational structure, not only for humans, but for all complex systems (Simon, 1962). It gives managers confidence that they have the authority to manage (called 'the hierarchy of authority') and allows coordination, cooperation and specialization. Figure 6.1A shows a simple hierarchical structure with four interactions. This can be compared to the self-organizing structure in Figure 6.1B where there are ten interactions. Simple hierarchy offers fewer interactions and relationships to manage. However, whilst this may be efficient it says nothing about the quality of the interactions and the hierarchy structure discourages collaboration and sharing of knowledge.

Chapter 2 looked at the classic work of Larry Greiner (1972) on organizational life cycles. He observed that organizational structures evolve as the organization grows through a process of continuous change and development, moving from the spider's web that is so typical of a newly formed entrepreneurial organization. Early on, this can be a real advantage to the organization but, as the number of people reporting either formally or informally directly to the entrepreneur increases, it can become dysfunctional. As the organization grows, more structure is put in place, often with a functional hierarchy and centralized control. Departmentalization – forming people into functional groups such as marketing, production and accounting – tends to occur. Figure 6.2 shows a classic hierarchical structure. Each level of hierarchy might represent a particular grouping or sub-grouping within the organization. When the organization grows beyond a certain size there is a tendency for it to adopt a divisional structure – representing different product or market groupings – with each division then having its own departmental structure within it. This can be taken further by setting up each division as a subsidiary of the parent company implying an even greater degree of freedom. There are no rules but four of the principal bases for grouping employees into departments and divisions are: common tasks, common products, geographic proximity and processes (sales, manufacturing, R&D etc.).

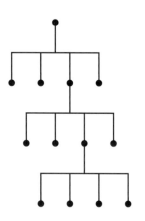

F 6.2 Hierarchical structure

Within departments a similar diagram could be drawn representing the hierarchy of individuals, with the head of department having managers reporting to them and each manager, in turn, having a hierarchy of individuals reporting to them. Individuals within these departmental groupings will require a similar degree and intensity of coordination. The functional departmental structure encourages centralized control. It fosters stability and encourages efficient, rule-driven operation. It shows individuals that there is a career path.

An issue with any hierarchy is the span of control within them. Some hierarchies have 'tall' structures with more managers each having a narrower span of control (fewer people reporting to them). Others have 'flat' structures, with fewer layers of management each having a wider span of control (more people reporting to them). The taller the structure and narrower the span of control, the more managers are required. And as we have already noted, the tendency over the recent past has been to delayer, decrease the number of managers and increase their span of control. Technology, in particular the internet, has made this easier. Google, for example, has a flat structure with lean hierarchies. Each manager has about twenty people reporting to them. Some Japanese manufacturing companies have only four layers of management: top, plant, departmental and section management.

Whatever the basis for groupings, an organization that has multiple products, functions or locations still needs to coordinate activities across all three of these dimensions. The organizational structure used to aid this is the matrix structure, shown in Figure 6.3. This was popular among large organizations in the 1960s and 1970s but became far less popular in the 1980s and 1990s and many companies dismantled their matrix structures as their excessive complexity and slow responsiveness to change became apparent. Nevertheless, the matrix blueprint is often the basis for establishing informal project teams, frequently used to explore new areas of knowledge and develop new products or services. It fosters communication and interaction and can be highly flexible. It is also used to allow informal coordination within the formal structures, for example, within multinational companies that need to maintain functional consistency between geographic locations. Starbucks uses a matrix structure, combining functional and product-based divisions, with employees reporting to two managers.

'It doesn't make sense to stay true to a structure that makes it more difficult for your people to succeed. Your organizational structure must be flexible enough to evolve along with your people, rather than work against them. This is one of the biggest and most challenging cultural issues we face as a fast growing company.'

Michael Dell

F 6.3 Matrix structure

Hierarchy, then, remains the basic structural form used by all companies. It marks the earliest influential theory of organizational design. Based on the work of Weber (1947), it stresses rationality and functional efficiency but says nothing about the quality of interactions. The literature was broadened by Chandler (1962), as technical and organizational complexity increased, by the inclusion of divisions – a development that was seen as a rational solution to increasing scale and complexity. However, much of the later literature focuses on the dysfunctional consequences of this structure where people got in the way of rational efficiency (Pugh and Hickson, 1976).

It was the contingency theorists of the late 1950s and 1960s that concluded there was no single best way of organizing a business (see Chapter 4). They reasoned that the best choice of organization depended on the extent to which the structure furthered the objectives of the firm and also on other factors such as:

▷ The environment the organization faces (Burns and Stalker, 1961; Emery and Trist, 1965; Haige and Aiken, 1967; Lawrence and Lorsch, 1967; Stinchcombe, 1959);
▷ The technology it uses (Perrow, 1967; Woodward, 1965);
▷ Its scale of operation (Blau, 1970; Pugh et al., 1969).

In all cases, variations in structure can be rationalized in terms of task predictability and diversity. However, these approaches tend not to explain the underlying processes – how things actually happen. The matrix structure came out of the contingency school. First posited by Galbraith (1973), it is based on the work of Lawrence and Lorsch (op. cit.) and is essentially an overlay on what is still a bureaucratic structure with hierarchical distributed power and decision-making. It spawned the development of teams and task-forces.

Change and complexity

In its simplest form, the traditional hierarchical structure is mechanistic, bureaucratic and rigid. It has been called a 'machine bureaucracy' because it is most appropriate where the organization (or sub-organization) is tackling simple tasks with extensive standardization, in stable environments, and/or where security is important and where plans and programmes need to be followed carefully. Well developed information systems reporting on production/processing activity need to exist for it to be effective. Power is concentrated in the top executives. It is more concerned with production than marketing and is good at producing high volumes and achieving efficiency in production and distribution. As such, it is particularly appropriate when a product is at the mature phase of its life cycle and is being 'milked' as a 'cash cow' (see Chapter 10). For example, at the restaurant level, McDonald's is highly bureaucratized with high levels of job specialization and formal systems emphasizing rules and procedures. This structure is the antithesis of an entrepreneurial structure and is designed to stifle individual initiative and promote standardization and efficiency. However, how McDonald's management operates at a higher level across restaurant sites is very different.

Galbraith (op. cit.) observed how task complexity increased with task uncertainty and the amount of information that needs to be processed by the decision-maker. Complex tasks in stable environments mean that it becomes worthwhile to develop standard skills to tackle the complexities. Matrix sub-structures can help to achieve this. Teams can work on their complex tasks within set protocols – as they do, for example, in a surgical operation. On the other hand, as the environment becomes more liable to change, standardization of the simple task may become less viable and responsibility for coping with unexpected changes needs to be pushed down the hierarchy. Once more, matrix sub-structures, within a more hierarchical structure, can help to achieve this. In these circumstances the team needs a high degree of discretion because established protocols may be inappropriate to the changing circumstances, even if the team faces simple tasks.

The implications of task complexity and environmental stability on organization structure are summarized in Figure 6.4. This can be applied

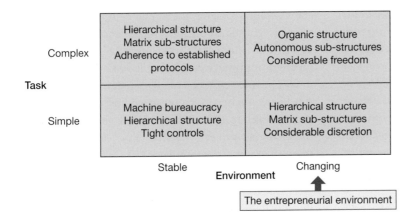

F 6.4 Organization structure, change and complexity

to different levels or organizational units within an organization. Therefore, the simple tasks in the stable environment of a McDonald's restaurant require a machine bureaucracy. How the higher level management of McDonald's should be organized depends on whether the tasks they face are relatively straightforward or complex and whether the environment is stable or complex. The main characteristic of the entrepreneurial environment is that it is one of rapid change. Entrepreneurial organizations therefore operate in the two quadrants on the right-hand side of Figure 6.4. Where there is low task complexity in a changing environment there is scope for centralization but the structure still needs to be responsive to change, albeit through a degree of central direction and supervision. Matrix-based team structures should be able to cope with the changes if they are given specific objectives and specified completion dates. The overall structure, although hierarchical, should be relatively flat with few middle-management positions. Whatever the structure, culture is still important because the work force still need to be motivated to make these frequent changes to their work practices. A business is a little like a house. If the organization structure is the plan and people are the bricks then culture is the cement that holds the whole thing together. Ignore any one element at your peril.

In a changing environment where there is high task complexity an innovative, flexible, decentralized structure is needed, often involving structures within structures. Authority for decision-making needs to be delegated and team-working is likely to be the norm with matrix-type structures somehow permanently built into the organization. Clear job definitions should never lead to a narrowing of responsibilities so that people ignore the new tasks that emerge. In many ways, far more important than the formal organization structure for a firm of this sort is the culture that tells people what needs to be done and motivates them to do it. This is often called an 'organic structure'. For example, Google operates in a fast-moving commercial environment that values innovation and swift action. It therefore has an informal culture with low job specialization, emphasizing principles rather than

'Hyper-growth companies are quintessentially learn-by-doing organizations. Their survival depends on swift adaptation. Because resources and people are stretched, they most likely don't have excessive formal or overly structured systems in place. The key is to have enough structure in place that growth is not out of control – but not so much that the structure impedes your ability to adapt quickly ... Balancing the need for supporting infrastructure without building infrastructure too far ahead of growth is one of the more difficult and ongoing challenges any hyper-growth company will face.'

Michael Dell

rules and encouraging horizontal communication. It has a flat, decentralized organizational structure and is highly democratic and tightly interconnected. All of the staff involved in product development work in teams of three or four people. Larger teams get broken down into smaller sub-teams, each working on specific aspects of the bigger project. Each team has a leader that rotates depending on the changing project requirements. Most staff work in more than one team. Similarly W.L. Gore, manufacturer of the famous hi-tech Gore-Tex fabric, makes extensive use of project-based-team structures with a minimum of top-down direction. Employees (called 'associates') apply to or are asked by other team members to join particular teams. They elect team leaders, decide upon their own goals and manage themselves.

Organic structures

Covin and Slevin (1990) argue that entrepreneurial behaviour within an organization is positively correlated with performance when structures are more organic, rather than mechanistic. In reality the dimension of structure from organic to mechanistic is a continuum and ought to correspond to the managerial dimension from entrepreneurial to administrative. A mechanistic structure is appropriate for a bureaucratic or administrative style of management because it will result in an efficient, albeit bureaucratic, organization. However, it will stifle, if not kill, an entrepreneurial style. On the other hand, an organic structure facilitates an effective entrepreneurial management style. Organizations are much more problematic when there is an incongruity between structure and style. Some authors (e.g. Morris and Kuratko, 2002) implicitly assume that all entrepreneurial organizations face complex tasks, based on the observation that the innovative process is complex. They then make the assertion that: 'major innovations are most likely under structures that most closely mimic the organic structure.'

Miller (1986) defines an organic structure as having 'limited hierarchy and highly flexible structure. Groups of trained specialists from different work areas collaborate to design and produce complex and rapidly changing products. Emphasis is on extensive personal interaction and face-to-face communication, frequent meetings, use of committees and other liaison devices to ensure collaboration. Power is decentralized and authority is linked to expertise. Few bureaucratic rules or standard procedures exist. Sensitive information-gathering systems are in place for anticipating and monitoring the external environment.'

Even if we accept that entrepreneurial firms innovate, the complexity of that innovation varies by its very nature. Technological innovation is not the same as market innovation. Innovation in the pharmaceutical industry is of a different nature to that in the furniture industry. Innovation can be radical or it can be incremental, and not all parts of the organization will be involved in the same degree of innovation. Innovation can be continuous or it can be discontinuous. For all these reasons, innovation of different sorts can come from structures that are not organic.

So, what does a simple organic structure look like? Unfortunately that is difficult to answer because, by its very definition, it is constantly forming and reforming to meet the changes it faces as it undertakes those complex tasks. According to complexity theory, this forming and reforming whereby business units are continually being created, merged and redefined is typical of a complex system coping with unpredictability. In its simplest form, an organic structure might be thought of as a partnership of individual professionals. They are each highly autonomous and the organization exists simply to provide them with support rather than direction. Figure 6.5 is an example of multiple organic structures which comprises a series of spider's-web organizations within one large spider's web. There is no hierarchy. The organization is flat. In this organization the reporting lines between the smaller spider's webs are informal. Each operates almost autonomously and, in that sense, this may be seen more as a loose coalition of entrepreneurial teams, perhaps forming and reforming as opportunities appear. The danger is that each might operate with too much autonomy and too little direction, resulting in anarchy. In many organizations, particularly larger ones, more structure and hierarchy may be needed. For example, Oticon, a manufacturer of hearing aids based in Denmark, famously reorganized into over 100 self-directed project teams, getting rid of most formal controls. Within six years it was forced to dismantle what it called its 'spaghetti organization' and reintroduce more conventional hierarchical control.

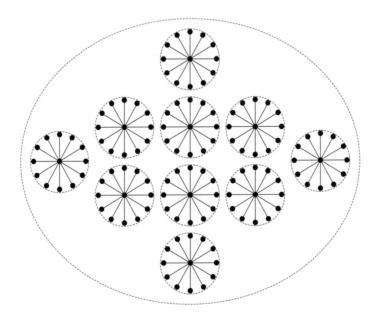

F 6.5 Organic structure

Remember that it is unlikely that one organizational structure – particularly an organic one – will suit all situations. Greiner (op. cit.) emphasized how organizations naturally change and adapt and Galbraith (1995) underlines the importance of change and variety rather than rigidity and conformity: 'Organizational designs that facilitate variety, change, and speed are sources of competitive advantage. These designs are difficult to execute and copy because they are intricate blends of many different policies.' So flexibility and ability to change quickly are key. Like the chameleon, the entrepreneurial organizational structure will adapt to best suit the environment it finds itself in.

The common themes are that an organic structure must be flexible, decentralized with a minimum of levels within the structures. It will be more horizontal than vertical. Authority will be based on expertise not on role and authority for decision-making will be delegated and individuals empowered to make decisions. It will be informal rather than formal, with loose control but an emphasis on getting things done. Spans of control are likely to be broader. Team-working is likely to be the norm. There will be structures within structures that encourage smaller units to develop, each with considerable autonomy, but there will be structures in place that encourage rapid, open, effective communication between and across these units and through any hierarchy. The success of these units will depend on the degree of fit with the mainstream organization, requiring a high degree of awareness, commitment and connection between the two (Thornhill and Amit, 2001). What is more, with such a loose structure, strong entrepreneurial leadership and culture will be needed to keep the organization together and moving in the right direction. At the end of this chapter we shall see how the organic structure can be combined with the other structures we have looked at to design something that meets the needs of different segments of the organization.

🗂 Case with questions Apple

Organizational structures

When Steve Jobs returned to Apple in 1997 it had become bureaucratic. He changed the culture and the structure. It is one company, organized on functional rather than product lines, with senior managers expected to have specialist as well as general managerial skills. Most senior managers are based at its main campus, the Infinite Loop at Cupertino in the USA. Jobs wanted Apple to be more like a start-up than a giant organization. New product development is broken down into elements so that only very senior managers have any detailed knowledge of the final product. Staff are frequently organized around small project teams with teams isolated from each other and operating under strict secrecy rules – 'siloes within siloes'. Apple still does not have organization charts, and that also limits the people staff know about outside their immediate environment – effectively a cell-like structure. For his book, *Inside Apple*, Adam Lashinsky constructed an organization chart based upon his interviews at Apple (Figure 6.6). He describes it as 'unconventional', with 15 senior vice presidents and vice presidents reporting directly to the CEO 'at the center'. Jobs had a small executive team of advisors assisted by less than 100 vice presidents. But status within the organization was not always reflected by rank. There was also an 'unwritten caste system' that fluctuated regularly. Industrial designers and a small group of engineers working with Jobs were 'untouchable' and there was a small group who carried the title of DEST (Distinguished Engineer/Scientist, Technologist) who had status but no management responsibility.

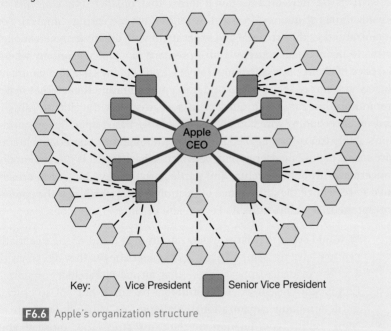

Key: ⬡ Vice President   ◼ Senior Vice President

F6.6 Apple's organization structure

Source: Adapted from Adam Lashinsky, *Inside Apple: The Secrets Behind the Past and Future Success of Steve Jobs' Iconic Brand*, London: Alan Murray (2012).

QUESTIONS

1 What organizational form does the structure at Apple remind you of?

2 Why is Apple structured this way? What advantages and disadvantages does it have?

3 Is Apple's structure consistent with its organizational culture? What do you think of this combination? What does it say about Apple?

New forms of organizing

Since the 1960s, firms have continued to organize based upon the enduring principles of Weber and Chandler. Whittington et al. (1999) noted that out of the top 500 companies in the three leading European economies the overwhelming majority used a multidivisional form of structure – 89% in the UK, 79% in Germany and 70% in France. However, Whittington et al. concede that their structural categories refer mainly to formal organizational characteristics and say little about the processes that go on under the surface – *how managers actually behave*. And informal team- and project-based organizations are used alongside these formal structures. Whittington et al. also observed that the character of the divisional organization of the 1960s was not the same as in the 1990s. New technologies had emerged and continue to be a strong driver of organizational change, particularly in multinational companies, improving communication and allowing the span of control to lengthen. Management styles had altered – and continue to do so – and internal processes were different.

So what is going on under the surface? Since the 1990s, there has been focus on coordination rather than control and on control by mutual agreement rather than command. There has also been recognition that individuals perform multiple roles. Over the time there has been a proliferation of writings on new organizational forms that broaden our concepts of organizational structures. In part this reflects the increasing complexity of organizations as they struggle and experiment with different organizational forms to maintain an effective global presence in a global economy where the pace of change is accelerating. In part it reflects the changing nature of society in terms of social norms and how computers and the internet make communication easier and quicker. In part it reflects the shift towards a knowledge economy with competitive advantage based upon the organization's ability to exploit knowledge quickly. Although this burgeoning literature seems to have no overarching perspective or theory it is fundamentally concerned with both structure and particularly process, but it has broadened to recognize the importance of relationships – which is at the core of entrepreneurial architecture. As Fenton and Pettigrew (2000) observe:

> 'It would seem that large organizations at the end of the twentieth century have the same structural characteristics as they did 50 years ago The evidence appears to be that formal hierarchical organization is still present as an institutional backdrop but not so crucial in determining organizational activities or capabilities. Instead "new" subtle coordination mechanisms stress the informal and social processes of the organization. There is also a move away from defining organizations purely in distributional terms toward more relational notions As firms add value via relationships and require ever greater internal and external interdependence to create, share and transfer knowledge, so the basis for organizational activity and configuration is centred on relationships and the wider social context within which firms are embedded.'

So the traditional hierarchical reporting structures mask important informal lateral relationships that add value to the firm through knowledge transfer. In looking at these new forms of organization Fenton and Pettigrew (op. cit.) identify three themes in the literature that we shall explore in greater detail:

▷ Networks and socially embedded firms;
▷ The knowledge firm in the knowledge economy;
▷ The globalizing firm and its changing boundaries.

Networks and socially embedded firms

It is not always necessary to 'own' resources to be able to use them. Professional jobs can be contracted out. Functions can be outsourced. Networks and other new forms of organizing allow different forms of expertise to be brought to bear in an organization. All these different ways of using resources without owning them allow firms to become smaller and more focused on their core activities and thereby simplify their structures. It is an example of how entrepreneurs and entrepreneurial organizations can partner with others.

The network structure comprises either an internal or external network of independent members (individuals or organizations), unified by a common purpose and sharing in the benefits that stem from collaboration. An example of an internal network would be a large company organized around strategic business units (SBUs). An external network could take the form of a strategic alliances or joint ventures.

Networks are based on personal relationships and reciprocity, and, therefore, on trust, self-interest and reputation (Dubini and Aldrich, 1991; Larson, 1992). Organizational networks develop based upon multiple networks of individuals. Each member of the network may have a different organization structure so relationships may be multi-level rather than flat, formed by clusters of coalitions at different hierarchical levels. The many links in these networks are strengthened by increased interaction and can be further strengthened by an entrepreneurial leader pulling the network together and giving it stability. These complex networks can facilitate many forms of organizational relationship. A network structure can be complex and difficult to chart – it could look very similar to Figure 6.5 – and it faces the same challenge of coordination as its size and complexity increases.

Networks create distinctive capabilities. It has been shown that international networks are an important stimulant for international start-ups (Johnson, 2004; McDougall et al., 1994; Oviatt and McDougall, 1995;). And, as we shall explore in Chapter 13, there is growing evidence of the benefits of networking as a way of stimulating creativity and knowledge transfer. At a macro-economic level strategic alliances and supplier networks are said to be crucial for the future success of US manufacturing (Goldhar and Lei, 1991).

A virtual network is one that uses information technology – computers and the internet – to link many individuals or independent organizations, based in many different locations. It is frequently used to build supplier networks, as in the case of Dell. Virtual networks come together to exploit specific opportunities, forming and reforming in different groupings to exploit different opportunities. It is a structure that is best used to undertake specific tasks that do not need contact or the building of relationships. It is likely to have a shorter life than a real network structure because no personal relationships are established. With this exception, it shares many

Dell partners on a global basis through its 'fully integrated value chain' – B2B2C. Suppliers, including many small firms, have real-time access to information about customer orders and deliveries via the company's extranet: 'The best way I know to establish and maintain a healthy, competitive culture is to partner with your people ... Our willingness and ability to partner to achieve our common goals is perhaps seen in its purest form in how we forge strong alliances with our suppliers.'

Michael Dell

of the advantages of the network structure. Handy (1996) described it as a 'box of contracts' and because of its lack of tangibility it has profound consequences for how we think of organizational forms.

Networks blur the boundaries of the firm, extending them to a community of interest rather than restricting them to a legal or economic unit. They mean that resources and risks can be shared across economic units so that networks of small firms can compete more effectively against large firms. They mean that organizational relationships are not necessarily dictated by hierarchies and power structures, rather by trust, respect and mutual self-interest. And ultimately it is quite conceivable that these networks are more important than formal organizational structures. It is therefore not unexpected that network structures are embedded into the daily working life of the entrepreneurial organization. They allow organizational units to be small, encourage knowledge-sharing and an outward-facing culture and reduce risk.

The knowledge firm in the knowledge economy

Entrepreneurial organizations are learning organizations – they add value in highly competitive, often technology-based, industries by sharing knowledge and learning throughout their structure. Indeed 'sharing information and knowledge' is one of the high-level attributes in the cultural web of an entrepreneurial organization (Figure 5.4) whereby it becomes both a vehicle for knowledge access and knowledge creation. This is important in the context of stimulating innovation. And it is the ability to innovate, again and again, that creates sustainable competitive advantage.

The literature on knowledge management sees organizations as complex, without clear structure but with a high degree of integration brought about partly by a strong culture. It explores how to achieve coordination and integration of individuals' knowledge within an organization as greater complexity and hence knowledge specialization occurs. The literature stresses the importance of tacit knowledge (embedded in minds and activities), which is difficult to share, rather than explicit knowledge (stated in verbal communications or documents), which can be easily copied. For example, Grant (1996) assumes that knowledge creation is primarily an individual activity and the primary role of the organization is harnessing it for the production of goods or services. It is therefore logical that the primary focus of the organization is to stimulate individual creativity and learning and translate that into products and services that the market values – a theme to which we return in Chapter 13. In this context Grant proposes that: 'Once firms are viewed as institutions for integrating knowledge, a major part of which is tacit and can be exercised only by those who possess it, then hierarchical coordination fails.' This means that structures need to be flat and non-hierarchical where knowledge must be shared, but the boundaries of the organization can extend beyond formal lines where knowledge sharing takes place. For knowledge firms new forms of organizing revolve around social and relational dimensions (Nahapiet and Ghoshal, 1998) and networks play an important role. Much of the literature in this area points to what must now be a familiar theme for this book.

The globalizing firm and its changing boundaries

Fenton and Pettigrew's final literature theme stresses the need to focus an organization on its core competences to add value in an increasingly global market place, whilst outsourcing other activities. It focuses on technology as a way of integrating the firm by making knowledge transparent and developing global IT networks (Konstadt, 1990). There is also a focus on managing business processes rather than departments which has emphasized horizontal structures and fed into the literature on teams and team-working (Stewart, 1992). However, as we have seen, when vertical structures are de-emphasized it inevitably emphasizes cooperation and relationship-building as a basis for coordination, an approach supported by empirical work on the relationships between headquarters and their subsidiaries conducted by Roth and Nigh (1992). This emphasis on informal relationships also presents us with some familiar themes. The global firm literature challenges the efficacy of the divisional structure with its emphasis on the integration of sub-units and the sharing of their resources (Ghoshal and Bartlett, 1995).

What so much of this literature reveals is that the traditional organization chart is a poor representation of how many organizations really function. Informal structures are important, based on strong relationships – the word that appears again and again. Networks are important – in one context and then in another – flexing and changing over time. As soon as we identify one structure (and name it), another appears, perhaps reflecting the rapidly changing environment in which organizations of today operate. And processes are just as important as structure, processes that are 'continually shaped and reshaped by the actions of actors who are in turn constrained by the structural positions they find themselves' (Nohria, 1992). What this literature does not give us is any clear agreement on how to think about these new structures. As with many things in management, firms are continually experimenting, both intentionally and unintentionally, both formally and informally, trying to face up to the organizational

🖿 Case with questions Tata Consultancy Services

Structures to encourage innovation

The 120-year-old Tata Group is India's largest business with a turnover of over $60 billion and employing some 350,000 staff. It is controlled by the Tata family through Tata Sons Ltd, parent company to the group. The group is a conglomerate. It consists of several hundred subsidiaries, in many different industry sectors around the world, each with its own structure, culture and leadership and management style. These include Tata Steel, Tata Motors (owner of Jaguar and Land Rover), Tata Tata (owner of Tetley Tea) and Tata Consultancy Services (TCS).

TCS was set up in 1968, based in Mumbai, India. It is now a public company with profits of over $2 billion and turnover of $8 billion in 2011. It is one of the largest private-sector employers in India with over 200,000 staff, and is now the largest provider of information technology in Asia and second largest provider of business process outsourcing in India, with offices in 47 countries worldwide. TCS prides itself on building innovation into its culture and believes that, whether innovation is incremental or disruptive, there need to be organizational structures and processes for moving the innovation forward and managers need to be able to direct employees down the appropriate route.

▷ Incremental innovations are handled and funded by the organizational unit originating them.

▷ Platform-level innovations that can be extended beyond the present product/service offering are directed to 19 Innovation Labs focusing on specific technologies or business sectors based in India, the USA and UK. One service that came out of these Labs provides cheap agricultural data and information to India's farmers. It won the *Wall Street Journal* Technology Innovation Award in the wireless category in 2008.

▷ Disruptive innovations (see Chapter 12) usually come from these Labs, but those coming from business units are redirected to a Lab or funded through a centrally administered incubator fund, which can also be used to fund innovations from the Labs.

In order to encourage the importing of ideas from outside TCS, the Co-Innovation Network was established in 2007. This comprises the Innovation Labs, university research units, research-based start-ups and venture capitalists. TCS also has a software and process engineering and systems research centre called the Tata Research Development and Design Centre. To help capture new ideas TCS has 'IdeaMax', a crowdsourcing social network that encourages staff to submit, comment and vote on new ideas.

TCS tries to stimulate original creative and innovative thinking in staff in a number of ways. It has training programmes such as the four-day 'Technovator' workshop and employees have five hours of their 45-hour working week free for their own projects that can include either personal or idea development. Employees have annual reviews based upon nine areas, one of which is creativity and ideas generation. There is also a Young Innovator Award which rewards staff with a salary rise and gives a boost to their career.

QUESTIONS

1 Why has TCS separated out these different organizational structures.

2 How might the organization and culture within the Labs differ from the operating units? Why is this important?

3 Compare and contrast the approach of the much larger TCS to that of HFL Sport Science, reviewed in the last chapter.

challenges they face. And organizational innovation often involves moving between extremes, yet maintaining business continuity, as firms battle with the contradictions between hierarchies and networks, vertical and horizontal integration and sharing knowledge across units that both compete and collaborate and the dilemmas then posed in making decisions (Pettigrew, 1999). We see this in how two successful companies like Google and Apple can emerge from very different structures and cultures. We have seen it since the global recession of 2008/9 as some firms centralize their decision-making in response. Management is an art, not a science. It involves judgement more than rule-following.

Strategic alliances/partnerships and joint ventures

One form of organizing that has featured quite prominently in the literature on corporate entrepreneurship is strategic alliances and partnerships. These often arise out of network contacts and are often based on supply chains. However they can develop based upon multiple motives – technological, market or organizational – where there is mutual advantage to be gained from some form of collaboration. A recent government survey in the UK concluded that: 'in both the UK and the USA we observe that the highest growth firms rely *heavily* on building relationship with other firms either through supply chains or strategic alliances' (Department of Business, Enterprise and Regulatory Reform, 2008, emphasis added).

Strategic alliances are relationships between independent organizations to achieve specific goals. Parkhe (1993) defines them as 'relatively enduring interfirm cooperative arrangements, involving flows and linkages that use resources and/or governance structures from autonomous organizations, for the joint accomplishment of individual goals linked to the corporate mission of each sponsoring firm.' A strategic partnership, where the alliance becomes closer and more formal, is usually designed to create value through synergy as partners achieve mutual gains that neither could gain individually (Teece, 1992). For example, since assets are owned or contributed by the constituent individuals or organizations, the financial resources needed and the associated risk are spread and flexibility increased. A more formal strategic partnership would be called a joint venture. This usually has a degree of direct market involvement and therefore needs to be underpinned by some form of legal agreement that determines the split of resource inputs and rewards. Often the joint venture takes the form of separate legal entity to either of the parties involved.

Strategic alliances can take a number of different forms. A strategic alliance can be internal – between departments or other structures of the same organization – or external – between different organizations. It can encompass all of the functional areas of an organization or just a single

🗀 Case insights Jaguar/Williams, BBC/IBM, Sun Microsystems/Intel

Strategic alliances

Jaguar/Williams

Jaguar and the Williams Formula 1 team announced a strategic alliance in 2011 to produce and sell a new supercar, the C-X75. It will be a hybrid electric/petrol car that can reach 60 miles per hour in three seconds and will have a top speed of over 200 mph. At over £700,000, only 250 are planned to be produced. Williams brings its exceptional engineering expertise to the project whilst Jaguar brings it brand positioning and distributor network. The car was unveiled at the 2010 Paris Motor Show and received widespread admiring reviews.

BBC/IBM

The BBC and IBM forged a strategic alliance in 2007 following an agreement for a framework outlining several joint projects. One of the first was applying IBM image/video search technology to CBeebies and CBBC programmes. The IBM research system, called 'Marvel', has the ability to visually analyze images so as to categorize content based upon appearance. This allows images/videos to be more easily searched online for specific content. The project is the first of a number that will allow the BBC to unlock the commercial value of its massive TV and radio archive.

Sun Microsystems/Intel

Sun Microsystems and Intel announced a broad strategic alliance in 2007 that centred on Intel's endorsement of Sun's Solaris operating system and Sun's commitment to deliver a comprehensive family of enterprise servers and workstations based on Intel's Xeon processors. The alliance also included joint engineering, design and marketing efforts as well as other Intel and Sun enterprise-class technologies. The alliance was expected to help with the widespread adoption of Sun's Solaris system. Perhaps more importantly, it was expected to move Intel's Xeon-based systems up the server value chain to data centres and other high-performance facilities into environments that were dominated by HP, with its range of servers powered by an Itanium chip, which itself was co-developed with Intel and IBM.

function, such as R&D. It can straddle countries, markets and hierarchies, providing a structure for cooperation. It might take the form of an informal collaborative arrangement, a joint venture through a newly formed organization or with one party (or both) taking an equity stake in the other. Virgin has been particularly adept at using strategic alliances and joint ventures as a basis for establishing new businesses. For example, Deutsche Telecom partnered with Richard Branson to create Virgin Mobile and Singapore Airlines owns 49% of Virgin Atlantic.

Developing partnerships

Karthik (2002) posited four distinct phases in the evolution of the relationship, based on the work of Dwyer et al. (1987) and Wilson (1995):

1 *Awareness and partner selection*: In this phase the need for an alliance is recognized and the search for a suitable partner begins. Learning starts but it is largely unilateral as each organization finds out about the other and decides whether they can work with the other and also seeks to better understand the external market environment in which the alliance will work.

2 *Exploration*: In this phase partners begin interacting and set the ground rules for future interaction. Partners start to build trust and establish a common culture in order to build the social bonding process. Learning is still largely unilateral but there are elements of experimentation and mutual learning as a way of bridging the compatibility gap between partners.

3 *Expansion*: As trust builds, greater interaction takes place and partners grow closer. They stop probing each other and start working as a partnership. Learning is partly mutual as partners share common perceptions and goals and bridge expectation gaps with a view to sustaining the relationship. Unilateral learning also takes place as partners attempt to internalize the other's embedded knowledge and skills.

4 *Commitment to the relationship*: This is the stage where 'significant economic, communication, and/or emotional resources may be exchanged' (Dwyer et al., op. cit.) and boundaries between the partners have little significance. There is commonality of purpose, multiple levels of relationships and mutual learning processes. Learning at this stage is one of mutual capacity-building (Hamel, 1991) and both parties seek to maintain the relationship, building psychological contracts instead of legal ones.

Strategic alliances can be an effective way of sustaining competitive advantage. They can be particularly important in relation to innovation. There are often explicit strategic and operational motives for alliances such as gaining access to new markets. Some firms have based their international expansion strategy almost entirely on foreign alliances. Similarly, acquiring new technologies, enhancing new product development capabilities or leveraging on economies of scale or scope may all be reasons for strategic alliances. Alliances can create economic advantage by leveraging market presence (Lewis, 1990; Lorange and Roos, 1992; Ohmae, 1989). An example is Oneworld, a strategic alliance of a dozen airlines including British Airways and American Airlines whose primary purpose is to encourage passengers to use partner airlines. Alliances can also provide vertical integration and scale economies at a greatly reduced cost (Anderson and

⌂ Case insight Lovefilm

Strategic partnerships

Lovefilm.com started life as a DVD rental firm and is therefore an unlikely success story. However, in 2011 Amazon bought the UK company for an undisclosed sum, thought to value the company at some £200 million. Lovefilm offers over 70,000 movies to its 1.5 million members in Britain, Sweden, Norway, Denmark and Germany. Founded by Simon Calver in 2002, as Online Rentals, it rebranded and expanded, acquiring smaller rivals, including Video Island and Amazon's European DVD rental business, which was when it first took a minority stake in the business.

Lovefilm's business model is copied from the much larger Netflix, a US listed company. Subscribers pay a monthly subscription to rent a number of physical and, now, digital movies or video games each month. DVDs, Blu-rays and video games are mailed out from a central warehouse and returned in postage-paid envelopes. There are no late-return fees. More recently it has started offering online films and an on-demand streaming video service – and this is where the future lies, despite the fact that even by 2011 some 90% of its revenues still came from physical rental. Partnering is the key to its success here. It joined with Sony and Samsung to offer a movie subscription service on their internet-connected TVs – 'Lovefilm players'. Similarly, an exclusive deal with Sony allows British owners of PlayStation 3 to stream some 2500 films. At the same time, by partnering with the leading independent film distributor Momentum Pictures, it offers members the opportunity to watch films ahead of widespread physical distribution. It has also signed exclusive agreements with Icon Film Distribution to offer online streaming of its films.

Weitz, 1992). In its simplest form this is the arrangement a distributor has with a manufacturer when they have sole distribution rights.

Alliances evolve and change in nature over time. Firms involved in an alliance often have a mix of motivations, involving competition and collaboration in varying proportions, as the partnership evolves. Over time the partners build trust and mutual respect – essential in any relationship. Mutual learning can also be an important element in many alliances. Alliances facilitate organizational learning (Parkhe, op. cit.). Karthik (op. cit.) observes that 'alliances are pooling mechanisms commingling diverse unique skills and capabilities, and thus are able to create potentially powerful learning opportunities for firms. In fact, learning opportunities create "learning organizations" that are able to increase their absorptive capacities and to assimilate new ideas easily to remain competitive.' So, strategic alliances increase the learning community and the potential knowledge base of the organization. The risks involved in this are minimal but there are costs in finding a partner and maintaining the relationship.

Leadership, culture and structures

Leadership styles, organizational cultures and structures are linked – one reinforcing the other. If any one is inappropriate for the other two then the organization will not function as well as it should. And, as we saw with leadership styles on their own, certain combinations are appropriate for different tasks, different groups of people and different situations or environments. In his book, *Gods of Management*, Charles Handy (1995) popularized four leadership typologies – based upon Greek mythology – and the cultures and structures for which they are most appropriate. These are summarized in Table 6.1. Zeus is characterized as the charismatic and visionary entrepreneur, managing through interpersonal relationships and sitting in the middle of the spider's web. This contrasts with Apollo's traditional hierarchical bureaucracy and its rules and regulations. Athena is the team-working leader in a matrix organization, continually solving problems or addressing new tasks. Finally there is Dionysus, the partner rather than leader in an organic organization that supports people's independence without threatening it.

T 6.1 Handy's Gods of Management

Leadership style	Organizational culture	Organizational structures
Zeus The patriarch of all gods. Charismatic/visionary leader: visionary, independent, instinctive, persuasive, builder of relationships, power and networks; excited by the challenge of uncertainty.	**Club culture**: Individuals are independent but responsible, trusted (not controlled) to make right decisions, understanding the consequences of wrong decisions. Power relationships influence behaviour.	**Spider's web structures**: Built upon relationships with the leader in the middle. Managers are professionals, free to follow instincts. They are also leaders.
Apollo The god of rules and order. Leader by appointment: authoritarian, logical, sequential, analytical, scientific, with everything in its place. Enjoys repetition.	**Role culture**: Individuals are assigned tasks and organized and controlled through rules, regulations, job descriptions and direct supervision. People are cogs in the wheel, predictable, inflexible, and unresponsive to change.	**Traditional hierarchical bureaucracies**: Strong management control. Managers are administrators.
Athena The warrior goddess and problem-solver of craftsmen and pioneering sea captain. Leader by expertise and experience: credible, convincing, focused, but unadventurous.	**Task culture**: The problem is the task. Individuals are judged on how well they undertake the task/problem. Talent, creativity, initiative and intuition are all valued.	**Matrix structures**: Project-based team-work. Managers define and solve problems by assigning staff and resources. They are valued for their expertise and experience. Teams form and reform to undertake different tasks/problems.
Dionysus The god of wine and song, individual and independent. Partner rather than leader. Professionally competent.	**Culture of individualism and independence**: The organization is the servant of the individual. No boss. Individual talent is valued. Decision-making by consent and consensus.	**Organic structures**: Supporting structures with loose coordination of independent individuals with talent. No boss.

Source: Handy, C. (1995) *Gods of Management*, London: Souvenir Press.

Of course no organization is exclusively dedicated to one god, they balance the gods. The task of leadership is getting that balance right. Handy sees this as influenced by four factors:

1 *Size*: The larger the group of people (or organizations) that need to work together, the more likely Apollo is to rule. Small groups or teams prefer Athena.
2 *Work patterns*: Where work is repetitive and routine, Apollo rules. Where work is continually changing, Zeus and Dionysus rule but if it is undertaken in groups, Athena rules.
3 *Life cycle*: If the life cycle is short and new product development is important, Athena rules. If the life cycle is long Apollo re-exerts his influence.
4 *People*: Professionals, the young and better educated people prefer Dionysus. Countries with conformist cultures are more comfortable with Apollo, whereas countries that value individualism prefer Zeus or Dionysus.

Hybrid organic structures and the multi-business organization

What this all means is that large organizations that want to remain entrepreneurial need to structure themselves very carefully because it is unlikely that the entrepreneurial leadership and culture described in previous chapters is appropriate for all segments of the organization. Different segments may require different structures, cultures and leadership styles and the organization may have to break itself up into different companies or divisions to facilitate this. A unitary structure is unlikely to work in a multi-business company. The overarching architecture of these companies or divisions should, however, remain firmly entrepreneurial. The structure of this sort of organization is likely to be a hybrid of the simple organic structure. An example is shown in Figure 6.7. In this structure individual businesses are structured in ways that reflect their operating characteristics. Each is relatively autonomous but linked in a flat structure to a head office in a divisional structure or to a legally separate holding company, in each case adopting a highly organic structure itself so as to ensure its flexibility and speed of response to the changing environment.

The multi-divisional structure is the dominant form for multi-business companies. Divisions can be organized in many ways, for example around products (3M), geographic regions (SAB-Miller) or vertically separate markets (oil companies such as ExxonMobil). As an alternative, the holding company structure is found particularly in multi-business private companies, especially those in global markets, with companies such as Tata, Samsung, Hyundai, Jardine Matteson, Mitsui and Mitsubishi. One very real advantage of a holding company structure is that it can help to

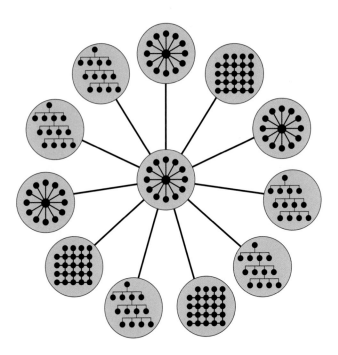

F 6.7 Hybrid organic structure

compartmentalize risk. If a legally separate part of a group of companies fails it does not endanger the survival of the others.

One example of this hybrid organization is the Virgin Group of companies. The Virgin Group is made up of more than 20 separate umbrella companies, operating over 370 separate businesses, employing approximately 50,000 people in 30 countries, with global brand revenue in excess of £11.5 billion. Virgin describes itself as a 'branded venture capital company' – a big brand made up of lots of smaller, legally separate companies each with different structures and with variations on the basic organizational culture.

🗂 Case with questions Richard Branson and Virgin

Brand, culture and structure

Richard Branson is probably the best known entrepreneur in Britain today. His background and the early history of Virgin, the company he founded, were outlined in the case insight in Chapter 1. Virgin is now one of the best known brands in Britain with 96% recognition and is well known worldwide. It has found its way onto aircraft, trains, cola, vodka, mobile phones, cinemas, a radio station, financial services, fitness studios and the internet. If there is any theme linking Virgin's reasons for setting up in these sectors it is simply commercial opportunity. Many have been bought from governments around the world as businesses were privatized (e.g. Virgin Money). Many were set up because of customer dissatisfaction with existing monopolistic suppliers (e.g. Virgin Atlantic), more recently bypassing the supplier to offer products/ services direct to customers (e.g. Virgin Direct). Also recently there has been a rash of businesses based upon the technology, media

→

and telecommunication boom at the turn of the twenty-first century (e.g. Virgin Media).

The Virgin brand is strongly associated with its founder, Sir Richard Branson – 95% can name him as the founder. Virgin believes their brand stands for value for money, quality, innovation, fun and a sense of competitive challenge. They believe they deliver a quality service by empowering employees and, whilst continuously monitoring customer feedback, striving to improve the customer's experience through innovation. According to Will Whitehorn, director of corporate affairs at Virgin Management and widely viewed as Branson's second in command and key strategist:

> 'At Virgin, we know what the brand name means, and when we put our brand name on something, we're making a promise. It's a promise we've always kept and always will. It's harder work keeping promises than making them, but there is no secret formula. Virgin sticks to its principles and keeps its promises.' (1)

The brand has been largely built through the personal PR efforts of its founder. According to Branson:

> 'Brands must be built around reputation, quality and price ... People should not be asking 'is this one product too far?' but rather, 'what are the qualities of my company's name? How can I develop them?' (2)

As to what these qualities are for Virgin, Branson gives us a candid insight into at least one of them:

> 'Fun is at the core of the way I like to do business and has informed everything I've done from the outset. More than any other element fun is the secret of Virgin's success.' (3)

Virgin describes itself as a 'branded venture capital company' – a big brand made up of lots of small companies. This structure mirrors a Japanese management structure called 'keiretsu', in which different businesses act as a family under one brand. The Virgin Group is made up of more than 20 separate umbrella companies, operating over 370 separate businesses, employing approximately 50,000 people in 30 countries, with global brand revenue in excess of £11.5 billion. The structure of the Virgin Group is complex and difficult to disentangle, involving offshore private companies and the existence of (unidentified) bearer shares. Equity interest in the umbrella organizations is owned by Virgin Group Investments. The Virgin trademark and logos are owned by Virgin Enterprises and these are licensed to companies both inside and outside the Virgin Group. Virgin Management is the management arm of the organization which appoints board members, senior executives and coordinates activities. Wikipedia states: 'Although Branson retains complete ownership and control of the Virgin Brand, the commercial set-up of companies using it is varied and complex. Each of the companies operating under the Virgin brand is a separate entity, with Branson completely owning some and holding minority or majority stakes in others. Occasionally, he simply licenses the brand to a company that has purchased a division from him, such as Virgin Mobile USA, Virgin Mobile Australia, Virgin Radio and Virgin Music (now part of EMI).'

> 'Virgin is not a big company – it's a big brand made up of lots of small companies. Our priorities are the opposite of our large competitors ... For us our employees matter most. It just seems common sense that if you have a happy, well motivated workforce, you're much more likely to have happy customers. And in due course the resulting profits will make your shareholders happy. Convention dictates that big is beautiful, but every time one of our ventures gets too big we divide it up into smaller units ... Each time we do this, the people involved haven't had much more work to do, but necessarily they have a greater incentive to perform and a greater zest for their work.' (2)

Virgin uses its brand as a capital asset in joint ventures. Virgin contributes the brand and Richard Branson's PR profile, whilst the partner provides the capital input – in some ways like a franchise operation – and often the operational expertise. Branson runs the Virgin empire from a large house in London's Holland Park. Although there does not appear to be a traditional head office structure, Virgin employs a large number of professional managers. The Virgin Group is characterized as being informal and information-driven – one that is bottom-heavy rather than strangled by top-heavy management. It sees itself as having minimal management layers, no bureaucracy, a tiny board and a small headquarters:

'Our companies are part of a family rather than a hierarchy ... They are empowered to run their own affairs, yet the companies help one another, and solutions to problems often come from within the Group somewhere. In a sense we are commonwealth, with shared ideas, values, interests and goals.' (4)

Companies in the Virgin group are diverse and independent. In 1986 Virgin was floated on the stock market but later re-privatized because Richard did not like to be accountable for his actions to institutional shareholders. Companies in the group have different organizational structures, reflecting the different nature of their core business. At the centre is Virgin Management Ltd., which provides advisory and managerial support to the group companies. It has offices in London, New York and Sydney each with Sector teams, run by a Managing Partner. The working environment is informal almost casual but there is a belief in hard work and individual responsibility. Generally, despite the informal structures, performance expectations are high. Managers at all levels in Virgin are set goals. Managers at headquarters are set overall goals such as improving brand loyalty or expanding the business. Managers in group companies are set more specific goals associated with their own business. The further down the hierarchy you go the more specific and short-term the goals.

Virgin has a devolved structure and an informal but complex culture based upon the Virgin brand. It is the brand that unifies the different companies in the group. Branson believes that finding the right people to work with is the key to success and the Virgin brand is so strong that it helps attract like-minded staff. He believes that it is not qualifications that matter in people, rather their attitude. He calls them 'Virgin-type' people – staff who will enjoy their work and are customer focused. And their enthusiasm for the brand rubs off on the customers. He believes in delegation and is good at it, encouraging senior managers to be entrepreneurial. He sets direction and then steps back to allow them to get on with things, giving them the freedom and initiative to be creative. This willingness to delegate helps develop trust between Branson and his management team.

'Our brand values are very important, and we tend to select people to work for us who share these values ... For as much as you need a strong personality to build a business from scratch, you must also understand the art of delegation. I have to be willing to step back now. I have to be good at helping people run the individual businesses – it can't just be me that sets the culture when we recruit people ... Our guiding principle is this: give individuals the tools they need, outline some parameters to work within, and then just let them get on and do their stuff ... Our view at Virgin is that collective responsibility bonds the teams, and having pride in your work is a far better driver than a hierarchical culture where the boss calls the shots ... I started Virgin with a philosophy that if staff are happy, customers will follow. It can't just be me that sets the culture when we recruit people. I have a really great set of CEOs across our businesses who live and breathe the Virgin brand and who are entrepreneurs themselves.' (4) →

Branson's main skills are said to be networking, finding opportunities and securing the resources necessary for their exploitation. His network of personal influence and contacts is legendary. He hates formal meetings and prefers to make decisions on a face-to-face basis, albeit sometimes over the phone, but always developing and testing his personal relationships. Another of Branson's skills seems to be inspiring staff and bringing out the best in them. He can do this on a very personal basis and still regularly invites groups of employees to his house. Most people who meet him find him extremely likeable – charismatic – with boundless enthusiasm and an inquisitive mind. He can be a good listener but says he never listens to critics. He encourages communication at all levels, using many different media. He seems to have an ability to 'connect' with people and loves challenges, whether related to the business or his own personal life.

'If people are properly and regularly recognized for their initiative, then the business has to flourish. Why? Because it's their business, an extension of their personality. Everyone feels Virgin is theirs to keep and look after. And it runs deeper. I am a firm believer in listening to your staff at all times. The moment you stop doing this, you are in danger of losing your best people.' (4)

Employees are encouraged to come up with new ideas and development capital is available. Once a new venture reaches a certain size it is launched as an independent company within the Virgin Group and the intrapreneur takes an equity stake. Branson's personal approach is to listen to all ideas and offer feedback.

'Many of our businesses run innovation schemes where employees can submit new business ideas to be considered by the strategic leaders. We also facilitate peer-to-peer nominations to recognize top performers around the four Virgin values of innovation, customer service, community and environment. One lucky person even gets to spend a week on [my] Necker Island.' (4)

Branson's view on risk is interesting. In many ways he has been expert at minimizing his personal exposure. His first record shop was 'given' to him rent-free. His Virgin Atlantic planes were all leased. He uses partners to contribute both capital and expertise to his new business ventures. At the same time he is not afraid to commit his own (or borrowed) money when needed, for example when Virgin Atlantic was re-privatized. He is also tolerant of risk-taking within the organization.

'One thing is certain in business; you and everyone around you will make mistakes. When you are pushing the boundaries this is inevitable – but it's important to recognize this. We need to look for new ways to shape up to the competition. So we trust people to learn from mistakes; blame and recriminations are pointless. A person who makes no mistakes, makes nothing.' (4)

In many ways Branson has not changed over the years. He is still an entrepreneur. Only the scale of his entrepreneurial activities has changed. He is the archetypal entrepreneurial leader and proponent of corporate entrepreneurship. Will Whitehorn, Branson's right-hand man since 1996, said of Richard some years ago:

'He doesn't believe that huge companies are the right way to go. He thinks small is beautiful ... He's a one-person venture capital company, raising money from selling businesses and investing in new ones, and that's the way it will be in the future.' (1)

Virgin is inexorably linked to Richard Branson. Now he is over 60, the question is how long will he continue? When he retires what will the future hold for Virgin? Is it just a loose confederation of diverse, independent businesses or is there something else unifying these business that will last beyond Branson? And, when he retires, what will happen to his shareholding?

References

1 *The Guardian*, 30 April 2002.
2 *Losing my Virginity*, 1998, R. Branson, Virgin, London.
3 *Local Heroes*, 1995, J. Andersen, Scottish Enterprise, Glasgow.
4 www.hrmagazine.co.uk, 13 July 2010.

☐ Up-to-date information on the Virgin Group can be found on their website: www.virgin.com

QUESTIONS

1 Re-read the case insight about Richard Branson in Chapter 1. What entrepreneurial character traits does he exhibit? Where would you place him on Blake and Mouton's leadership grid?

2 How would you describe the structure and culture of Virgin?

3 Why has Virgin been successful?

4 What is the essence of the Virgin brand? What role does it play in influencing both customers and employees?

5 What do you think might happen when Richard Branson retires?

6 What are the lessons for corporate entrepreneurship from Richard Branson and the Virgin Group?

Summary

▷ Structures create order in an organization but there is no single 'best' solution. The most appropriate structure depends on the nature of the organization, the strategies it employs, the tasks it undertakes, the culture it wishes to encourage, the environment it operates in and its size.

▷ Structures evolve as organizations grow. For larger firms, both hierarchical and matrix structures, or a combination, can be appropriate in different circumstances, depending on the complexity of tasks and the degree of change. However the traditional hierarchical structure can be mechanistic, bureaucratic and rigid. It is most appropriate for simple tasks in stable environments.

▷ Small organizational units are more responsive to change and large firms have responded to the entrepreneurial challenge by downsizing and deconstructing themselves. They are outsourcing non-core activities and downscoping, including the use of smaller firms to 'outsource innovation'. Internally they are making more use of

project teams, delayering and flattening their organizational structures and investing in information technology to improve communications.

▷ What much of this literature on new forms of organizing reveals is that the traditional organization chart is a poor representation of how many organizations really function. Because of the increasing pace of change and increasing complexity in a global environment where knowledge is possibly the most important resource, formal structures struggle to cope. Informal structures are becoming increasingly important, based on strong relationships and networks.

▷ Networks, virtual or real, encourage the sharing and transferring of knowledge. They encourage resource-sharing and therefore can mitigate risk.

▷ Strategic alliances and partnerships are important, particularly in the context of innovation and market penetration. As we saw in the case of **Lovefilm,** a company can partner with a number of other firms to enhance its business model. Similarly two firms might come together in pursuit of a market that neither has the capabilities to pursue on its own, as in the cases of **Jaguar/Williams**, **BBC/IBM** and **Sun Microsystems/Intel**. This allows them to pool resources and knowledge to tackle market opportunities but there must be a degree of synergy that can be realized between the two.

▷ Entrepreneurial organizations typically face a high degree of environmental turbulence. If the tasks they need to undertake are complex, they are best served by an organic organizational structure. However, whatever structure may be appropriate for a particular segment of an organization, it is important that the leadership and culture of that segment are appropriate. Hybrid organic structures can be constructed where different segments of the organization, each with different structures, culture and leadership styles, face different environments.

▷ An organic structure is difficult to describe because it can adapt and change. However, it has limited hierarchy and is highly flexible, decentralized with a minimum of levels within the structures. It is more horizontal than vertical. Authority is based on expertise not on role, and authority for decision-making is delegated so that individuals are empowered to make decisions. It is informal rather than formal, with loose control but an emphasis on getting things done. Spans of control are likely to be broader. Team-working is likely to be the norm. There are structures within structures that encourage smaller units to develop, each with considerable autonomy, but there are also structures in place that encourage rapid, open, effective communication between and across these units and through any hierarchy.

▷ In a hybrid organic structure individual businesses are structured in ways that reflect their operating characteristics. Each is relatively autonomous but linked in a flat structure to a head office, which adopts a highly organic structure itself so as to ensure its flexibility and speed of response to the changing environment.

▷ **Richard Branson** understands these organizational principles and his **Virgin** empire comprises some 370 separate, semi-independent companies with different structures. Often these were set up in strategic partnership with other organizations.

Essays and discussion topics

1 Why does size matter for an organization?
2 Should large firms concentrate on projects with high cost and low uncertainty and leave those with low cost and high uncertainty to small firms? Will this happen?
3 Will small firms become more important as time goes on?
4 Why do large firms deconstruct and downsize?
5 Consider Handy's 'shamrock organization'. What is in it for the company? What is in it for staff? What is in it for subcontractors?
6 How realistic are Handy's Gods of Management typologies? Give some examples of how leadership style, culture and structure may not be congruent and the results that might ensue.
7 What are the implications for an appropriate organizational structure of a turbulent environment?
8 What is an organic structure? Can it be defined? Is it a useful construct?
9 Do you agree that Virgin is just a 'branded venture capital company'? Why?
10 What are the advantages and disadvantages of the network structure – both real and virtual?
11 Explain why and how globalization, the increasing importance of knowledge and technology have encouraged the growth of networks.

12 Why has the increasing importance of knowledge encouraged the growth of networks?

13 How can networking encourage innovation? How can strategic partnerships encourage development of the innovation?

14 Why are relationships important in networks?

15 What is meant by process being just as important as structure?

16 What are the prerequisites for an effective strategic partnership?

17 Is an organic structure just another way of describing a large network of small operating units such as strategic business units?

18 Is there such a thing as an ideal organization structure for an entrepreneurial firm? If so, outline what its elements should be.

19 Why should the entrepreneurial firm find developing the 'new forms of organizing' easy?

20 If you do not have to own an asset to use it, under what circumstances would the owner let you use it?

21 The ultimate entrepreneurial organic structure consists of one person – the entrepreneur. Despite networks and strategic alliances, what are the limits to its effectiveness?

Exercises and assignments

1 Give some specific examples of an industry where a hierarchical, bureaucratic structure should be the best way to organize. Select three companies in this industry and use their websites to investigate their organizational structures. Explain why each structure conforms or does not conform to your expectations, taking into account the success of the business in that industry.

2 List the type of organizations and market sectors or environments that face high degrees of turbulence. Select a particularly turbulent sector and research how the organizations within it are organized and the success, or otherwise, they have in dealing with it.

3 List and describe the different ways in which large organizations break themselves down into smaller sub-organizations. Under what circumstances are each of these approaches appropriate?

4 Select a large company that has deconstructed itself (e.g. Asea Brown Boveri, ABB). Research and write up its history and describe its success or failure. What lessons are to be learnt from this?

5 Provide three examples of strategic alliances and indicate why they are important.

6 Provide three examples of business networks and explain what use they serve.

References

Anderson, E. and Weitz, B. (1992) 'The Use of Pledges to Build and Sustain Commitment in Distribution Channels', *Journal of Marketing Research*, 29 (February).

Bhidé, A. (2000) *The Origin and Evolution of New Businesses*, Oxford: Oxford University Press.

Blau, P.M. (1970) 'A Formal Theory of Differentiation in Organizations', *American Sociological Review*, 35(2).

Burns, T. and Stalker, G.M. (1961) *The Management of Innovation*, London: Tavistock.

Chandler, A.D. (1962) *Strategy and Structure: Chapters in the History of the American Industrial Enterprise*, Cambridge, MA: MIT Press.

Covin, D. and Slevin, J. (1990) 'Judging Entrepreneurial Style and Organizational Structure: How to Get Your Act Together', *Sloan Management Review*, 31 (Winter).

Department of Business, Enterprise and Regulatory Reform (2008) 'High Growth Firms in the UK: Lessons from an Analysis of Comparative UK Performance', *BERR Economic Paper 3*, November.

Dubini, P. and Aldrich, H. (1991) 'Personal and Extended Networks are Central to the Entrepreneurial Process', *Journal of Business Venturing*, 6.

Dwyer, R.F., Schurr, P.H. and Oh, S. (1987) 'Developing Buyer–Seller Relationships', *Journal of Marketing*, 51(2).

Emery, F.E. and Trist, E.L. (1965) 'The Causal Texture of Organisational Environments', *Human Relations*, 18.

Fenton, E. and Pettigrew, A. (2000) 'Theoretical Perspectives', in A. Pettigrew and E. Fenton (eds) *The Innovating Organisation*, London: Sage.

Galbraith, J.R. (1973) *Designing Complex Organizations*, Reading, MA: Addison-Wesley.

Galbraith J.R. (1995) *Designing Organizations: An Executive Briefing on Strategy Structure and Process*, San Francisco: Jossey-Bass.

Ghoshal, S. and Bartlett, C.A. (1995) 'Building the Entrepreneurial Corporation: New Organisation Processes, New Managerial Tasks', *European Management Journal*, 13(2), June.

Goldhar, J.D. and Lei, D. (1991) 'The Shape of Twenty-first Century Global Manufacturing', *Journal of Business Strategy*, 12(2).

Grant, R.M. (1996) 'Towards a Knowledge-based Theory of the Firm', *Strategic Management Journal*, 17 (Winter Special Issue).

Grant, R.M. (2010) *Contemporary Strategic Analysis*, 7th edn, Chichester: Wiley.

Greiner, L. (1972) 'Revolution and Evolution as Organizations Grow', *Harvard Business Review*, 50 (July/August).

Haige, J. and Aiken, M. (1967) 'Relationship of Centralization to other Structural Properties', *Administrative Science Quarterly*, 12.

Hamel, G. (1991) 'Competition for Competence and Inter-Partner Learning within International Strategic Alliances', *Strategic Management Journal*, 12 (Summer).

Handy, C. (1994), *The Empty Raincoat*, London: Hutchinson.

Handy, C. (1995) *Gods of Management*, London: Souvenir Press.

Handy, C. (1996) 'Rethinking Organisations', in T. Clark (ed.) *Advancement in Organisation Behaviour: Essays in Honour of Derek S. Pugh*, Aldershot: Ashgate.

Johnson, J.E. (2004) 'Factors Influencing the Early Internationalisation of High Technology Start-ups: US and UK Evidence', *Journal of International Entrepreneurship*, 2.

Karthik, N.S. (2002) 'Learning in Strategic alliances: An Evolutionary Perspective', *Academy of Marketing Science Review*, 10.

Konstadt, P. (1990) 'Into the Breach', *CIU*, 11 August.

Larson, A. (1992) 'Network Dyads in Entrepreneurial Settings: A Study of the Governance of Exchange Relationships', *Administrative Science Quarterly*, 37.

Lawrence, P.R. and Lorsch, J.W. (1967) *Organization and Environment: Managing Differentiation and Integration*, Boston, MA: Division of Research, Graduate School of Business, Harvard University.

Lewis, J.D. (1990) *Partnerships for Profit: Structuring and Managing Strategic Alliances*, New York: Free Press.

Lorange, P. and Roos, J. (1992) *Strategic Alliances: Formation, Implementation and Evolution*, Oxford: Blackwell.

McDougall, P.P., Shane, S. and Oviatt, B.M. (1994) 'Explaining the Formation of International New Ventures: The Limits of Theories from International Business Research', *Journal of Business Venturing*, 9.

Miller, D. (1986) 'Configurations of Strategy and Structure: Towards a Synthesis', *Strategic Management Journal*, 7.

Morris, H.M. and Kuratko, D.F. (2002) *Corporate Entrepreneurship*, Fort Worth, TX: Harcourt College Publishers.

Naisbitt, J. (1994) *Global Paradox*, London: Books Club Association.

Nahapiet, J. and Ghoshal, S. (1998) 'Social Capital, Intellectual Capital and the Creation of Value in Firms', *Academy of Management Best Paper Proceedings*.

Nohria, N. (1992) 'Introduction: Is a Networking Perspective a Useful Way of Studying Organizations?', in N. Nohria and R.G. Eccles (eds) *Networks and Organizations: Structure, Form and Action*, Boston, MA: Harvard Business School Press.

Ohmae, K. (1989) 'The Global Logic of Strategic Alliances', *Harvard Business Review*, March/April.

Oviatt, B.M. and McDougall, P.P. (1995) 'Global Start-ups: Entrepreneurs on a Worldwide Stage', *Academy of Management Executive*, 9(2).

Parkhe, A. (1993) 'Strategic Alliance Structuring: A Game Theoretic and Transaction Cost Examination of Interfirm Cooperation', *Academy of Management Journal*, 36 (August).

Perrow, C. (1967) 'A Framework for the Comparative Analysis of Organizations', *American Sociological Review*, 32.

Pettigrew, A.M. (1999) 'Organising to Improve Company Performance', *Hot Topics, Warwick Business School*, 1(5).

Pugh, D.S. and Hickson, D.J. (1976) *Organisational Structure in its Context: The Aston Programme* 1, Farnborough: Saxon House.

Pugh, D.S., Hickson, D.J. and Hinings, C.R. (1969) 'The Context of Organisation Structures', *Administrative Science Quarterly*, 13.

Roth, K. and Nigh, D. (1992) 'The Effectiveness of HQ–Subsidiary Relationships: The Role of Coordination, Control and Conflict', *Journal of Business Research*, 25.

Simon, H.A. (1962) 'The Architecture of Complexity', *Proceedings of the American Philosophical Society*, 106.

Stewart, T.A. (1992) 'The Search for the Organization of Tomorrow', *Fortune*, 125(10), 18 May.

Stinchcombe, A.L. (1959) 'Social Structure and Organization', in J.G. March (ed.) *Handbook of Organizations*, Chicago: Rand McNally.

Teece, D.J. (1992) 'Competition, Cooperation and Innovation: Organisational Arrangements for Regimes of Rapid Technological Progress', *Journal of Economic Behaviour and Organisation*, 18.

Thornhill, S. and Amit, R. (2001), 'A Dynamic Perspective of Internal Fit in Corporate Venturing', *Journal of Business Venturing*, 16(1).

Weber, M. (1947) *The Theory of Social and Economic Organisation*, Glencoe, IL: The Free Press.

Whittington, R., Mayer, M. and Curto, F. (1999) 'Chandlerism in post-war Europe: Strategic and Structural change in France, Germany and the United Kingdom, 1950–1993', *Industrial and Corporate Change*, 8(3).

Wilson, D.T. (1995) 'An Integrated Model of Buyer-Seller Relationships', *Journal of the Academy of Marketing Science*, 23(4).

Woodward, J. (1965) *Industrial Organisation: Behaviour and Control*, Oxford: Oxford University Press.

Part 3
Management

Chapter 7

Managing the entrepreneurial organization

Learning outcomes

By the end of this chapter you should be able to:

▷ Critically analyze the barriers to corporate entrepreneurship and explain how they can be overcome;

▷ Critically analyze how change can be facilitated, resistance reduced and blocks removed in an organization;

▷ Critically analyze the balance between managerial control and staff autonomy and understand how to manage staff that need greater autonomy;

▷ Understand the principles of open book management and how it is part of the loose control but tight accountability needed in an entrepreneurial organization;

▷ Understand how risk can be managed and use basic risk management techniques, such as risk classification and the development of key risk indicators, so that risks can be mitigated.

Barriers to corporate entrepreneurship

Warren Bennis (2009) once said 'Managers are people who do things right whilst leaders are those people who do the right thing'. The reality is that effective leadership is of little use without effective management to complement it and make things happen. Managers have to implement the policies and procedures to make an organization entrepreneurial. In doing that, they will face a number of predictable challenges that characterize the entrepreneurial environment; managing change and managing risk. They will also have to deal with the tension between freedom and control that is inherent in giving staff the autonomy they need in this sort of organization.

Many traditional management techniques unintentionally discourage corporate entrepreneurship. They dissuade individuals within the organization from behaving entrepreneurially. Examples of this include the way in which some organizations:

▷ *Focus on efficiency or return on investment*: An entrepreneurial organization is one that is going places, fast. It is probably first into a new market and needs to grow quickly in order to penetrate the market, persuading customers to buy the product or service before competitors have time to react. It needs to focus on the critical issues that it faces to achieve this, rather than being managed like a mature company – a 'cash cow' – with the simple objective of generating maximum short-term profit through greater efficiency.

▷ *Plan for the long term and then control against plan*: In a turbulent, changing environment the future is not certain. Five-year plans are of little use. They inhibit freedom of action and become increasingly unrealistic. The entrepreneurial organization needs to have goals and a vision but it also needs to learn from the changing reality as it moves towards its goals, changing plans as appropriate. Interim milestones need to be set, but progress needs to be re-assessed after each one is reached and benchmarked against reality.

▷ *Enforce standard procedures, rules and regulations*: This tends to block innovation and lead to missed opportunities. The entrepreneurial organization needs to be flexible, creating rules for specific situations but then being prepared to ditch them when circumstances change. But too much freedom can lead to chaos. That means having a culture where rules are challenged and only accepted when proved to be for the good of the organization. It also means there needs to be a balance between freedom and control.

▷ *Avoid risk*: Avoiding risk means missing opportunities. By way of contrast, an entrepreneurial organization will be willing to take measured risks. However, rather than launching headlong into the unknown, it progresses toward its goal in small, spider-like steps, building an understanding of the risks it faces as it progresses. Risks need to be identified, even if they cannot be avoided. Once identified, early warning mechanisms can be put in place so that appropriate action can be taken in good time.

▷ *Make decisions based on past experience*: In a changing environment the past is not always a good predictor of the future. The entrepreneurial organization takes small steps, testing its assumptions as it goes, learning from the changing reality.

▷ *Manage functionally with rigid job descriptions*: For many firms, this can be a barrier to creativity, which often relies on a holistic approach to problem-solving. Entrepreneurial organizations often create multidisciplinary teams to investigate and develop entrepreneurial opportunities (venture teams). Team-working is an invaluable approach to breaking down barriers, encouraging information flows and innovation. However, some firms, like Apple, have managed to organize successfully on functional lines with a design/technological focus, although they avoid rigid job descriptions.

▷ *Promote individuals who conform*: This is a certain way to lose innovators. An entrepreneurial organization must be able to accommodate, indeed encourage, those who do not conform. Ideas people and 'doers' need to be encouraged and rewarded.

There is nothing wrong with these management techniques, in the right environmental context. However they will not encourage the development of an entrepreneurial organization. Morris (1998) believes that structural barriers to corporate entrepreneurship can be classified into six groups – all of which we would recognize as the opposite of the entrepreneurial architecture we are trying to build. These conclusions were based upon an extensive review of the literature on corporate innovation and entrepreneurship, surveys of medium-sized and large companies and in-depth assessments of three Fortune 500 companies. These structural barriers were:

> '*To encourage people to innovate more, you have to make it safe for them to fail ... Communicating is one of the most important tools in recovering from mistakes. When you tell someone, be it a designer, a customer, or the CEO of the company, "Look, we've got a problem. Here's how we're going to fix it," you diffuse the fear of the unknown and focus on the solution.*'
>
> **Michael Dell**

1 *Systems* – inappropriate evaluation and reward systems, excessive and rigid control systems, inflexible budgeting systems, overly rigid and formal planning systems and arbitrary cost allocation systems. Formal systems evolve over a period of time and in most organizations are in place to generate order and conformity in a large complex organization. By way of contrast small, entrepreneurial companies rarely have strong systems. Their strategies evolve and planning becomes contingent, based upon different scenarios. The lesson is clear, if systems are too strong they can act as a disincentive for entrepreneurship.

2 *Structures* – too many hierarchical levels, top-down management, overly narrow span of control, responsibility without authority,

restricted communications and lack of accountability. Hierarchy is anathema to an entrepreneurial organization, instead authority and responsibility are pushed down to the point where they are most effective.

3 *Strategic direction* – no formal strategy for entrepreneurship, no vision from the top, no entrepreneurial role models at the top, no innovation goals, lack of senior management commitment. Visionary leaders with a commitment to make the entire organization entrepreneurial are essential. Equally tangible but achievable goals for product, process and marketing innovation are vital.

4 *Policies and procedures* – long, complex approval procedures, excessive documentation requirements, unrealistic performance criteria and over-reliance on established rules of thumb. As with systems, small, entrepreneurial firms rarely have sophisticated policies and procedures – and this gives them greater flexibility – but they are needed as the firm grows. The problem is that, as policies and procedures grow in complexity, the lead time to make things happen increases and the temptation 'not to bother' grows. The entrepreneurial organization needs to build some slack and leeway into its procedures so that innovation is encouraged.

5 *People* – fear of failure, resistance to change, parochial bias, complacency, protection of own sphere of activity, short-term orientation, inappropriate skills and talents. People can be the greatest barrier of all. Changing people – their attitudes and the way they do things – is the biggest challenge facing management. It is never easy. There is a natural tendency to resist change and preserve the status quo – but nobody said generating an entrepreneurial culture was easy.

6 *Culture* – ill-defined values, lack of consensus over priorities, lack of congruence, values that conflict with those of an entrepreneurial culture. As we have noted, culture is the cement that binds the entrepreneurial organization together. The stronger it is, the stronger the entrepreneurial architecture. Culture comes from the top but it rests on a set of commonly held values and beliefs. If they are not commonly held, or not seen to be held by top management, there is little chance of success.

If confronted with these barriers you can choose to do one of three things. You can ignore them – but this only works with the less important barriers, otherwise nothing changes. You can work around them – intrapreneurs are particularly good at this, but it may result in the organization not changing. Finally, you can attempt to have them removed. An entrepreneurial organization is one that embraces change but often change is resisted by individuals within it. Unblocking barriers to change can be particularly difficult when it comes down to dealing with individuals – and that comes down to the interpersonal skills of the organization's leader and its managers.

📋 Case with questions Starbucks

Turnaround

With a turnover of $10.7 billion from over 17,000 outlets in 50 countries, Starbucks is the largest coffeehouse company in the world, selling coffee and other hot drinks as well as sandwiches, panini, pastries and other snacks. It was originally set up as a coffee bean roaster selling from a single store in Seattle, USA, in 1971. Howard Schultz joined the company in 1982 as Director of Retail Operations and Marketing when there were three stores. After a trip to Milan, Italy, where he was enthused by the coffeehouse culture he tried to persuade the founders to sell coffee and espresso drinks as well as beans. They refused and, in 1986, he left to start *Il Giornale* coffee bar chain, only to purchase Starbucks from the founders the following year. Schultz rebranded his chain as Starbucks and that heralded the rapid expansion through both organic growth and acquisition that led to its dominant market position in 2012 as the largest 'coffeehouse' company in the world.

Schultz spearheaded that expansion and was lauded as the epitome of a successful entrepreneur. Starbucks' mission statement summarizes its business model and growth strategy: 'To Inspire and Nurture the Human Spirit – one person, one cup and one neighborhood at a time!' It offers good quality coffee in fashionable surroundings. There are comfortable chairs with newspapers to read to encourage customers to spend more time in the coffeehouse. There are cakes and pastries to encourage them to spend more money. The atmosphere is relaxed. The counter staff – called baristas – are central to creating this atmosphere and they receive extensive training in things ranging from customer service to the coffee beans used by Starbucks. There is no pressure for the customer to move on quickly, but service at the counter is swift and efficient so there is minimal waiting for service. Indeed, behind the scenes the Starbucks systems and procedures ensure that everything happens almost by clockwork from the mixing of sweeteners into different drinks to cleaning the toilets. Like McDonald's, it aims to ensure customers receive a consistent quality of product and service at every store. However, in contrast to McDonald's it charges a high price for its beverages. The relaxed atmosphere of the store is important and in the early days it certainly attracted a younger clientele who would spend some time (and money) in the stores. It became a fashionable place to be seen and benefited from word-of-mouth recommendations from its patrons. And Starbucks certainly offered these customers many opportunities to try them out. It would blanket whole areas with stores so that no one would be too far from one, recognizing that convenience of location was critical to driving sales. Starbucks was also innovative. It introduced music and wifi. It had its own loyalty card and introduced different snacks. Expansion was swift and relentless and the distinctive corporate branding of Starbucks came to dominate many towns and cities.

However, founding entrepreneurs retire and the question is often whether the business can survive without them. In 2001 Orin C. Smith took over as Chairman and CEO and, in 2005, Jim Donald took over the posts. After years of solid growth, sales started to decline as rivals copied the Starbucks formula and gained market share. There was price competition. The distinctive corporate branding came to be resented in some countries – too 'American' and unsympathetic to local surroundings. The coffeehouse market was saturated and Starbucks had over-expanded. Sales were dwindling and its outlets were looking tired and overpriced. The financial crisis of 2008 brought things to a head. As the *Guardian* newspaper commented (22 June 2008): 'It is no longer a coffee house offering a "coffee experience" with its novel culture and distinct language but a cumbersome global corporation selling a lifestyle brand in need of new energy and direction.' It quoted Schultz as saying that the innovation that once gave the company its edge was being suffocated by corporate thinking: 'We somehow evolved from a culture of entrepreneurship, creativity and innovation to a culture of, in a way, mediocrity and bureaucracy.' Schultz took control again in 2008.

Schultz took immediate and dramatic action. He cut costs by $600 million, closing 1000 outlets, mainly in the USA, most of which had been opened within the last two years. He refocused Starbucks' expansion plans on the growing market in China. He also retrained the baristas making the coffee in the Starbucks outlets so as to inject a little more theatre and romance into the process – but also to improve the quality of the coffee they produced. And by closing all its US outlets on the same afternoon to begin the process it gained some good PR and made a symbolic point.

'Pouring espresso is an art, one that requires the barista to care about the quality of the beverage. If the barista only goes through the motions, if he or she does not care and produces an inferior espresso that is too weak or too bitter, then Starbucks has lost the essence of what we set out to do 40 years ago: inspire the human spirit ... Starbucks has always been about so much more than coffee. But without great coffee, we have no reason to exist ... Ultimately, closing our stores was most powerful in its symbolism. It was a galvanizing event for Starbucks' partners – the term we use for our employees – a stake in the ground that helped reestablish some of the emotional attachment and trust we had squandered during our years of focusing on hypergrowth.' (H. Schultz and J. Gordon (2011) *Onward: How Starbucks Fought for its Life without Losing its Soul*, Rodale Books)

Schultz thought that some of the food items detracted from the Starbucks atmosphere and even masked the aroma of coffee

which was so important to creating it. He dropped these and introduced healthier food options. Responding to the negative feelings about its distinctive corporate branding, Schultz also started a process of designing new stores so as to better fit in with their local environment. He wanted them to have more individuality, rather than always having the same homogenous corporate look. Starbucks started advertising for the first time, stressing its ethical strengths such as its use of fair trade beans. It also entered the instant coffee business with a supermarket brand called Via.

Commenting on the remarkable turnaround, newspapers worried about the 'cult of Schultz' and what might happen if he leaves again. In response he said:

'The next CEO of Starbucks should come from within, and it is my intent to ensure that happens because it is very difficult to teach the imprint, the values and the culture and the complexity of what we do to an outsider. But I am not the only one who is capable of running Starbucks. I do think – as self-serving as it sounds – that I was the right person, given the very, very strong headwind we had from the economy and our own issues, to come back and rewrite the future of the company.' (*Guardian*, 21 January 2010)

☐ Up-to-date information on Starbucks can be found on their website: www.starbucks.com

QUESTIONS

1 What went wrong with Starbucks after Schultz left?

2 Was the turnaround of Starbucks anything to do with corporate entrepreneurship, or was it just good strategic management?

3 Does Starbucks still need to be entrepreneurial? If so, what does this mean?

4 What role do baristas and other staff at the retail outlets have? Do they have to be entrepreneurial?

Reactions to change

Many people do not like change. They may find it unsettling or threatening and can become emotional over it. To some extent this depends on their personalities. Individuals who are seen as reliable, steady or dependable often find change difficult, as do process-orientated people. And certain industries and disciplines can attract individuals with these character-istics. Would you want a nurse who was not reliable, steady and depend-able? Individual's priorities and motivations are also different at different stages in their lives and this can be reflected in their approach to change. Resistance to change can also be deeply rooted in historical experiences. People may have good reason to fear change if they have always suffered as a result of it in the past. And fear of change can lead to stress – the single most frequent cause of absenteeism in most Western organizations.

Employees do not have the responsibility to manage change, just to do their best. That responsibility rests with the managers of the organization. The skill of managing change is crucial. Any entrepreneurial organization will face change aplenty, often seeming like a succession of crises. As the organization passes through each change, individuals can encounter a roller coaster of emotion as they find themselves facing different roles with new demands, and we need to explore these emotions before understanding how to tackle change as a manager. The classic change/denial curve used by Kakabadse (1983) is shown in Figure 7.1. This illustrates these changes very well and can offer insights into the attitude of staff at each stage.

▷ **Phase 1: Immobilization and denial** The unfamiliarity of individuals with their new roles makes them feel anxious about their contribution and so their effectiveness drops slightly. They need to get used to the new circumstances. Within a short time, having become used to the role using previously successful skills, and finding support to help them, their effectiveness improves and they start to believe that they do not have to change. This is the denial phase.

▷ **Phase 2: Depression and letting go** Hard demands are now being made and individuals experience real stress as they realize that they do have to develop new skills to keep up with the job. They need to relearn their role. Although they may eventually learn how to do their new job, a period of anxiety makes them less effective because they can no longer rely on their old skills and they may believe that they can no longer cope. In fact this 'low' indicates that the person is realizing that they have to change and then, at some point, they abandon the past and accept the future. However, this is the most dangerous point in the change cycle as they feel really stressed and may be tempted to give up.

▷ **Phase 3: Testing the new reality and putting it together** This testing period can be as frustrating as it can be rewarding. Mistakes

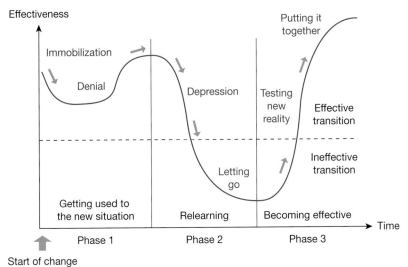

F 7.1 Work effectiveness through change

can recreate the 'low', but, as the newly learnt skills are brought into play effectively, performances should improve and a higher level of effectiveness than at the beginning of the stage should be achieved. They now have a set of new skills alongside their old ones.

However, this transition into a new effectiveness is not inevitable and some people fail to acquire new skills or cannot pull themselves out of the 'low'. The risk is that they may give up. The challenge for the entrepreneurial leader and their managers is to lead staff successfully through the three phases again and again and again. And there are some keys to managing change successfully.

Implementing change

An entrepreneurial architecture should embrace and encourage change. As we have seen, the key to a culture of continuous improvement and change is the acquisition of new knowledge – the development of a learning organization. Learning organizations 'combine an ability to manage knowledge with an ability to change continuously so as to prove their effectiveness' (Jackson and Schuler, 2001). As Hamel (2000) observed, 'organizational learning and knowledge management are first cousins to continuous improvement'. In an entrepreneurial organization change should be seen as the norm and individuals should continuously question the status quo. In other words, change should be easy to implement. But, as Machiavelli said: 'There is nothing more difficult to handle, more doubtful of success and more dangerous to carry through than initiating change.' And the bigger the change, the more difficult it is likely to be to implement. Luckily there are some tips about how this can be achieved.

Staff need to 'buy into' change and be clear about what they have to do to achieve it. They need to be encouraged and rewarded if they act appropriately and trained to make the necessary changes. Staff should be reprimanded and penalized if they do not act appropriately. It is easier to change behaviour than beliefs. Any potential barriers to the changes need to be tackled in advance. There needs to be a compelling reason for change and it needs to have the full and unequivocal commitment of all managers in the organization. And that compelling reason for change, together with a vision for how the organization will look after the change is made, must be communicated effectively – a narrative needs to be constructed around it. This is best done on a face-to-face basis rather than through emails or notices. Staff should be consulted, not so much on the need for change but on the process of change and in this respect project teams or task-forces are invaluable. Change should not be piecemeal; as much as possible it should be undertaken as quickly as possible so that a clean break can be made with the past. The change should aim to achieve clear, tangible results quickly so that success can be readily demonstrated. Information about the changes and the change effort should be made freely available. Good communication is, arguably, the key to success but all these tactical measures can help managers to push through change,

Based on the work of Kotter (1996; Kotter and Cohen, 2002), Yukl (2002) gives us a framework for successfully implementing change that involves engaging in two overlapping sets of actions – 'political and organizational actions' and 'people orientated actions'. These are shown in Figure 7.2. The political and organizational actions involve eight steps:

1 *Deciding who might oppose change and doing something about them.* You can try to convince sceptics and remove obvious barriers. As we've already noted, some individuals inevitably resist change – even if it is ultimately in their own interest. They may even resist it to the point of trying to sabotage it. The organizational reasons for this could be because:

   ▷ They think it will have a negative impact on them;
   ▷ It affects their social relationships within the organization;
   ▷ It means long-standing habits have to be changed;
   ▷ The needs for and benefits of change have not been properly communicated;
   ▷ Structures, systems, rewards are not aligned with the changes and inhibit them;
   ▷ They feel coerced, not in control.

   If any, or all, of these reasons for resisting change can be removed the likelihood of resistance will be reduced. However, understanding the reasons for resistance in one individual can be difficult and certainly requires a lot of emotional intelligence. The alternative is that you isolate the individuals or remove them from the change process.

CHANGE

Political and organizational actions

1 Remove blockers
2 Put in change agents
3 Build political support
4 Use task forces for implementation
5 Make symbolic changes
6 Demonstrate success quickly
7 Change structures as necessary
8 Monitor changes and ensure change
   is embedded

People-orientated actions

1 Create sense of urgency
2 Communicate with briefings about
   effects of change
3 Communicate with briefings about
   progress of change – celebrate
   success
4 Help with training and counselling
5 Break up change into small parts
6 Empower staff to make changes
7 Demonstrate commitment

 F 7.2 Framework for implementing change

2 *Putting change agents into key positions in the organization.* Often new people need to be brought into an existing organization if you are going to bring about major change, particularly when it involves shifts in culture. Change agents can employ any or all of the persuasive, political skills at their disposal. These sorts of changes need to start near the top and with the full approval of the Board of Directors, otherwise they are likely to be frustrated by the prevailing inertia. The big advantage of 'parachuting in' change agents at a senior level is that they are likely to get results – one way or another – quickly. And time is important in business. Either they will change the status quo or those opposing them will leave. This sounds rather like using force instead of persuasion and that threat can be important – 'change behaviour or leave' is the ultimate threat to those blocking change. You only have to look to see how often a new Managing Director replaces the top management team to realize that this has almost become a standard procedure when major change is to be pushed through in a limited time span.

3 *Building political support for the changes with stakeholders.* Board members, shareholders, employees, suppliers and so on, whether inside or outside the organization, need to be persuaded of the need for the changes so as to ensure that there is a coalition of support for them.

4 *Using task-forces to push through implementation.* The composition of the team depends on the nature of the task it faces and the resulting skills required. Team members need to be committed to the change and selection should have an eye to the personal characteristics for effective team-working (see Belbin's team roles in Chapter 4). Using multidisciplinary staff from different departments or units ensures a holistic approach to problems and helps subsequently to embed the changes within the organization.

5 *Making dramatic, symbolic changes early on.* Changing key staff helps to emphasize the importance placed on implementing the changes – and what might happen to blockers. When Starbucks closed for an

afternoon to implement its changes it signalled their importance to everyone.

6 *If possible, beginning with small projects and demonstrating success quickly.* This helps to convince doubters. It also allows you to learn from mistakes, if you make them, without necessarily jeopardizing the larger project.

7 *Remembering to change relevant parts of the organizational structure as you go along.* This is covered in greater detail later in this chapter.

8 *Monitoring the process of change so as to learn from it and ensure that the changes are successfully embedded.* Resistant people can reverse change all too easily if left to their own devices. On the other hand some of the changes may actually prove to be inappropriate – so always learn from mistakes.

People-orientated actions focus on getting staff motivated to undertake the changes. This involves seven steps:

1 *Creating a sense of urgency about the need for change.* You find that organizations often embark on change as a result of a crisis that threatens its survival. Frequently the crisis is needed to jolt managers out of their lethargy. It is a very real threat and the fear of the result of not changing outweighs the fear of change.

2 *Preparing people for the effects of change by proper briefings.* People want to know how big changes will affect them personally – only this makes it real for them.

3 *Keeping people informed about the changes being made as they progress and the successes being achieved.* Celebrate success so as to build confidence and help convince the septics.

4 *Helping people deal with change through proper training, counselling and so on.* If you are asking people to undertake new or different jobs they will need to be trained. Putting this in place in advance gives them assurance that they will be able to cope.

5 *Breaking up the change process into small parts or stages.* These provide opportunities to celebrate success as well as evaluate effectiveness.

6 *Empowering staff to make the necessary changes themselves.* Task-forces should have the necessary authority to undertake the tasks asked of them. There is nothing worse than being held accountable for something over which you have no authority.

7 *Demonstrating continued commitment to the changes from the highest levels in the organization right until the project is complete.* 'Walking the talk' is important, unblocking where necessary – all demonstrate that pushing through the changes is high on the agenda of senior management. Often a project is unsuccessful because management is diverted from it when the changes are only three-quarters complete and there is no final follow-through. The value of successful change should be reinforced through recruitment and promotion and change woven into the culture of the organization.

Jim Clemmer (1995) does, however, sound a note of caution. He believes that, whilst change can be created, it cannot be managed. 'Change can be ignored, resisted, responded to, capitalized upon, *and created*. But it cannot be managed and made to march to some orderly step-by-step process ... Whether we become change victims or victors depends on our readiness for change' (emphasis added). Which means that to some extent you must realize you cannot always predict its course but rather need to 'go with the flow'. One thing for certain is that the course change takes is rarely smooth and continuous.

Managing change in a successful, growing organization is easier than in one that is contracting because change brings tangible results that reward everyone. And an entrepreneurial organization will be looking to grow. If it does not succeed at first it will readjust and try again. But whilst fear of failure and redundancy may be a strong short-term motivator, an organization can only experience downsizing for just so long. Indeed an entrepreneurial architecture is not appropriate to an organization in decline.

Toolkit for managing change

Exercises to help initiate and manage change can be downloaded free from the US website www.esdtoolkit.org. Written by Rosalyn McKeown with Charles Hopkins, Regina Rizzi and Marianne Chrystalbridge, they comprise seven exercises with related worksheets:

1 Examining assumptions.
2 Steering around barriers.
3 Inventory of support and resistance.
4 Commitment charting.
5 Creating an action plan.
6 Identifying communication strategies.
7 Recognizing values in action

Cementing change

A final perspective on the scale of the task involved in managing change is given to us by Henry Mintzberg (1998). He developed the concept of a 'change cube', shown in Figure 7.3. The cube is three-dimensional: strategy/ organization, concrete/conceptual and formal/informal. The face of the cube shows strategy/organization. As we have explained, both have to be addressed in making change happen. However strategy can be highly conceptual (abstract) or concrete (tangible). The most conceptual element of strategy is vision, followed by strategic positioning (repositioning, reconfiguring) then programmes (reprogramming, re-engineering), whilst the

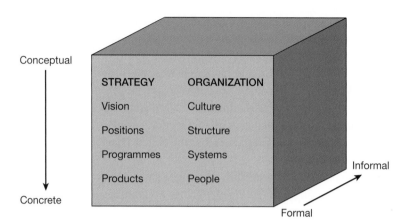

Conceptual

STRATEGY	ORGANIZATION
Vision	Culture
Positions	Structure
Programmes	Systems
Products	People

Concrete

Informal

Formal

F 7.3 The change cube

most concrete are products (redesigned, replaced). Similarly for the organization, culture is the most conceptual, followed by structures (reorganization), then systems (reworking, re-engineering), whilst the most concrete are people (retrained, replaced).

Put another way, vision and culture are highly abstract. Products and people are highly concrete and can be changed or replaced relatively easily – without affecting any element above them. However if you change vision or culture you will end up having to change everything below. The point is that, wherever on the face of the cube you intervene, you have to change everything below. For example, if you change structures, you must change systems and people.

The third dimension is formal/informal. For example, strategic positioning can be a formal process (deliberate) or an informal process (emergent). Similarly, people can change formally (training) or informally (coaching, mentoring). Mintzberg's point is that, to be effective, change in an organization must include the entire cube: strategy and organization, from the most conceptual to the most concrete, informally as well as formally. It is a three-dimensional move, down the face of the cube, dealing with formal and informal aspects of strategy and organization.

📁 Case with questions Marks & Spencer (M&S)

Turnaround

Marks & Spencer (now known as M&S) is a famous British retail chain selling clothes, food, household goods and furniture. It has over 1000 shops in the UK and more than 40 in other countries. M&S originated as a chain of 'penny bazaars' (market stalls selling everything for one penny) set up in 1884 by a Russian-born Polish-Jewish immigrant, Michael Marks, in Leeds with a £5 loan from

Isaac Dewhirst, a wholesaler. Interestingly, Dewhirst went into manufacturing and remains the biggest supplier of M&S to this day. Marks opened his first store below his home in Manchester in 1894. He went into partnership with Thomas Spencer (then a Dewhirst cashier) and the first Marks & Spencer store was opened in the prestigious Cross Arcade in Leeds in 1904. After the death of the founders, Simon Marks (son of Michael) took over as Chairman and started to work with his friend Israel Sieff. Together they turned M&S into the iconic British retailer it is today.

The original success of the M&S store was based upon a number of ideas that meant M&S, although never cheapest in the market place, offered high quality but most important of all very good value for money. They did this by adopting the then revolutionary idea of buying directly from manufacturers and placing their own label on goods – originally the St Michael brand (registered in 1928). By the 1950s all goods were sold under this label. By then it was known for selling only British-made goods, entering into long-term partnerships with British manufacturers which required them to commit solely to manufacturing M&S products. It was also known for its policy of accepting the return of unwanted goods, giving a full cash refund if the receipt was shown. M&S' first overseas store was opened in 1975 and it resisted the lure of television advertising until the mid-1990s.

But in the 1990s M&S started to lose direction. With the benefit of hindsight, Sir Richard Greenbury's tenure as Chairman (1991–99) saw profit margins pushed to unsustainable levels and the loyalty of customers seriously eroded as the costs of using British suppliers increased and M&S responded by offering reduced quality goods. Meanwhile competitors were sourcing overseas and beating M&S on value for money. M&S's reaction was to switch to overseas suppliers, but this undermined a core part of the company's philosophy and appeal. At the same time the company was losing touch with potential, younger customers who increasingly saw M&S designs as frumpy and old-fashioned. Alongside this the company steadfastly refused to accept credit cards except for their own store card. M&S simply failed to see that the high street had changed and competitors were now offering better products at lower prices in more attractive surroundings. However, the iconic M&S brand was so synonymous with success that the inevitable slump took the company, investors and analysts by surprise. Profits

dropped from more than £1 billion in 1997 and 1998 to £546 million in 1999. The share price plummeted and there was serious board-room instability. In the financial press M&S now came to be seen as an aging, lethargic and bureaucratic company.

1999–2004

How do you encourage a firm with over 100 years of history to re-invent itself and become more entrepreneurial? How do you drive through the necessary changes? Answer – you bring in new people .... and you start at the top. In 1999 Sir Richard Greenbury retired and Luc Vandevelde, a Belgian, took over as both Chairman and Chief Executive. He had previously been Chairman and Chief Executive of Promodès, the French hypermarket chain, where he oversaw a merger with Carrefour, its rival. Roger Holmes was brought in at about the same time and he became Chief Executive later in the year. Drastic action was needed simply to survive. Stores were closed on the Continent and in the USA, and jobs were cut as the company also closed down its Direct catalogue so as to enable it to focus on its core UK retail business. Sourcing was moved overseas, cutting back on UK suppliers, in order to increase margins and make prices more competitive. At the same time the supply chain was modernized, allowing clothes to be brought to market more quickly, bureaucracy was reduced and new talent brought in to drive innovation. Shops opened on Sundays and accepted credit cards.

Clothing fashions were improved by bringing in new people. George Davies, founder of Next, was brought in to produce a young, fashionable collection called Per Una. In the same year Yasmin Yusuf, the brains behind the Warehouse clothing chain, was appointed as creative director. The fashion strategy became one of targeted sub-brands, such as the Limited Collection label, Blue Harbour men's casual wear, the Perfect range of classic pieces and the more expensive Autograph label which has designers such

→

as Betty Jackson, Sonja Nuttall and Anthony Symonds. Fashion sales started to increase. By 2002 the company was gaining market share in areas like lingerie and men's casual wear. New ways of presenting clothes meant the average spend increased as shoppers were encouraged to buy entire outfits rather than just single items. M&S started innovating again with products ranging from seam-free underwear to 'steam cuisine' microwave meals. It opened new convenience food outlets called Simply Food, targeting new markets. Some, within railway stations and motorway service areas, are run by Compass Group, the specialist catering company, under franchise. Vittorio Radice, the brains behind the regeneration of the department store Selfridges was brought in to experiment with stand-alone homeware stores, the first of which was opened in Gateshead in 2004 with the name Lifestore.

But not all the initiatives worked and many of the underlying management problems remained. 2001 saw static sales and profits down to £146 million. Although sales remained static, by 2004 profits were up to £782 million. Nevertheless, amid rumours of a possible take-over bid, M&S announced that Chairman Luc Vandevelde would be leaving with immediate effect and that the Chief Executive, Roger Holmes would be replaced by Stuart Rose. At the same time Paul Myers, chairman of Guardian Media Group, took over as Chairman. Timing is crucial in business because shortly after this Philip Green, boss of the fashion retailers Arcadia Group, which includes Bhs stores, announced a take-over bid for M&S.

2004–2010

Stuart Rose came to M&S in 2004 with a track record of turning around struggling retailers. Indeed he is credited with turning around Arcadia Group, which is quite a coincidence. He was also a friend of Philip Green. Stuart quickly put together a recovery plan which included selling off the financial services business to HSBC Bank, buying control of the Per Una range, closing the Gateshead Lifestore (Vittorio Radice along with many senior managers subsequently left M&S) and stopping the expansion of the Simply Food outlets (there were only about 20 at the time). Philip Green eventually withdrew his bid after failing to get sufficient backing from shareholders.

Son of a civil servant, Stuart Rose was educated at a Quaker boarding school and started his career in retailing in 1972 after joining M&S as a management trainee. He remained with the company for 17 years, holding a variety of jobs in the textiles and food divisions before being appointed commercial director for M&S's European operation in Paris. In 1989 he joined Burton Group, which included Debenhams, Top Shop and Dorothy Perkins stores. The group later demerged into Arcadia and Debenhams. In 1998 he was appointed chief executive of the Argos catalogue/shop chain. Later, as boss of Booker, the cash-and-carry business, he arranged a merger with the frozen food retailer Iceland and became the new group's chief executive. He joined Arcadia in 2000, a company with £250 million of debt, which he turned around and then sold two years later to Philip Green for £855 million – making £25 million for himself. He took over as Chief Executive of M&S in 2004 at the age of 55.

Although always smartly dressed, Stuart Rose was known for his informal management style that circumvented formal structures. If he wanted to know something he was quite likely to go directly to the person who should have the answer rather than ask for a management report. He was seen as: 'very good at motivating people and giving them clear instructions. He brings the best out in people ... a dedicated networker, always lunching with someone from the City or the media ... He maintains a helicopter position ... [but nevertheless] ... sits in on merchandising reviews, knows how many of which style is sold where, and can reel off financial data about each of his many retail chains at will' (Times Online, 25 January 2007).

He was also known for bringing in his own trusted managers to focus on the minutiae – which is precisely what he did, reshuffling and firing many of M&S's top managers. For example, Steve Sharp was brought in as the new Marketing Director. He met Stuart Rose at Debenhams where he was Marketing Director. At M&S he introduced the new 'Your M&S' brand, together with the new clothing advertising campaign featuring the celebrated model Twiggy and younger models associated with the Bohemian styles of 2005–6. He was also responsible for the TV advertising campaign for their food range featuring Dervla Kirwan with the tag line, 'This is not just food, this is M&S food'. Managerial and directorial changes followed, including the appointment in 2007 of Martha Lane Fox, co-founder of Lastminute.com, as non-executive director to advise on the company's Direct business.

> 'We took out the whole board [when Stuart Rose joined in 2004] – we got rid of the stores chief, the personnel director and others. We had an exciting battle with Philip Green but, after it, we reduced the board to 12 non-executive directors and three executive directors … We sit here and take decisions very fast. Compared to the old M&S, we've cut out the jaw-jaw. Everything goes straight down the line. We're supported by a strong team of divisional heads, but it's very different from the old M&S … It's not about one person, it's about teams of people. We've got 85,000 in the organization. They're responsible for our success.' (Stuart Rose, *Management Today*, December 2006.)

Stuart Rose's strategy focused on three fundamentals: product, environment and service. He was returning to the core M&S value propositions:

▷ M&S's vision is 'to be the standard against which all others are measured'.

▷ M&S's mission is 'to make aspirational quality accessible to all'.

▷ M&S's values are 'quality, value, service, innovation and trust'.

'M&S is about three things – the product, the shops, the delivery of our service – and five words that describe what we do: quality, value, service, innovation and trust. Nothing else. There is no strategy. We're shopkeepers whose job is to satisfy customers … We don't just trade on price alone but price times quality times styling. We don't want fleeces at knockdown prices – that's not what our customers want from us. We're about eight to 80 (age), Christian and Jew, fat and thin. We want to deliver to all of them.' (Stuart Rose, *Management Today*, December 2006.)

Getting the product right was also top of the agenda. Many slow-moving, expensive suppliers were replaced by quick-turnaround specialists, often overseas. Prices were frequently cut whilst quality was maintained. Improving value, style and the amount of new product was important. In clothing the company initially focused on the classic designs it had historically always excelled at – the Classic Collection – but other lines were also expanded, particularly the Per Una range. It rationalized its menswear. For both menswear and womenswear it introduced innovative products such as machine washable suits. In food M&S focused on offering high-quality, innovative products such as the additive-free 'Marks and Spencer Cook!' range. After a pause the Simply Food stores continued to be rolled out across the UK in petrol stations, airports, railway stations and motorway services areas, many under franchise arrangements.

Getting the environment right meant that the store format was completely redesigned by Urban Salon Architects. The much-praised design was brighter, lighter and more ⟶

contemporary. It featured white tiles (black in Foods) replacing carpets and laminate flooring, brighter lighting, new product stands, display styles, mannequins, till points and staff uniforms. Most stores were completely refurbished by 2008 and many others temporarily updated as part of a massive investment programme.

The company also moved to improve its service levels by investing in its biggest ever customer service training programme based around the Mary Gober Method – called 'Your M&S – Our Service Style'. Our Service Style is defined as: 'We are friendly, helpful, courteous people, who are knowledgeable and enthusiastic about taking care of our customers'. The company also overhauled its pay rates and improved career planning for its 'customer assistants', reducing the number of grades to just four with clear progression. As well as attractive salaries, staff were paid a performance bonus based on company profits. There is also a saving scheme that allows staff to buy M&S shares at a 20% discount. As the turnaround gathered pace in 2007 sizable bonuses were triggered – a total of £56 million or an average of £4700 per member – based upon a share price that had tripled in less than three years. By 2008 sales were at the highest level ever at over £9 billion and profits again exceeded £1 billion for the first time since 1998.

However, the banking crisis of 2008 saw all retailers struggling to cope with more value-conscious, conservative shoppers and M&S had to introduce a restructuring plan which involved discontinuing some sub-brands and closing some stores. It also started to offer money-off promotions in an increasingly competitive market. 2009 saw sales static once more and profit fall to £706 million. In 2010 Stuart Rose stood down as Chief Executive, to be replaced by Marc Bolland, former Chief Executive of the successful supermarket chain Morrisons. Stuart Rose remained as non-Executive Chairman until 2011.

2010 and after

Marc Bolland took over in difficult trading conditions for all retailers and started to cut costs almost immediately. He carried on with many of Stuart Rose's strategies. He continued to cull lines that were not selling well; to offer money-off promotions; to feature well known stars in expensive television advertisements; to close poorly performing stores whilst opening new ones, particularly overseas in growing economies like China and India. However he was critical of M&S store designs which he thought were difficult to navigate around and he embarked on another major £600 million UK store revamp, to be completed by mid-2013. Signage is to be improved. The food stores are to get delicatessens and feature more specialist foods from around the world. 'Upstairs' the revamp is to focus on creating distinct identities for twelve key clothing brands. At the same time furniture and homeware will be expanded. Although profits before tax increased to £781 million in 2011, they dropped back to £658 million in 2012 as M&S encountered severe competition in clothing.

This case continues by looking at the environmental policies of M&S in Chapter 9.

☐ Up-to-date information on M&S can be found on their website: www.marksandspencer.com.

QUESTIONS

1 What are the lessons you learn from M&S about how to turn around an ailing, bureaucratic firm?

2 What lessons do you learn from Stuart Rose about the role of leader in this situation?

3 How important was it to change senior management at M&S in 2004?

4 Why did this not happen in 2010?

5 Compare and contrast this turnaround to that of Starbucks. Was the turnaround of M&S anything to do with corporate entrepreneurship?

Management style

An obstructive manager can block the transmission of the entrepreneurial ethos to staff working for them. So, it is important that there is complete congruence between the leader's style and that of the manager, in the same way as this style needs to be congruent with the overall organizational culture and the structures within it. The management style within the organization needs to reflect the ethos of the entrepreneurial organization. In particular:

▷ Authority for decisions should be based upon expertise, not position;
▷ Operating styles should be allowed to vary freely;
▷ Channels of communication should be open, free-flowing;
▷ Staff should feel they are free to adapt to changing circumstances rather than sticking rigorously to their job description;
▷ The emphasis should be on getting the job done, unconstrained by procedures;
▷ On-the-job behaviour should be shaped by the situation and the personality of the individual;
▷ Decision-making should frequently be achieved by participation and consensus;
▷ Control should be loose and informal with an emphasis on cooperation.

Most organizational control systems are aimed at minimizing risk/ uncertainty and promoting efficiency and effectiveness. We will deal with risk later in this chapter, but efficiency and effectiveness can be the enemy of entrepreneurship and innovation. By definition, a highly efficient organization has no slack. Everything is tightly controlled, every penny accounted for, all jobs are defined and individuals made to conform. This environment might lead to high degrees of efficiency but it does not encourage entrepreneurship and innovation. However, as we have observed, people are more likely to be entrepreneurial and innovative when they have a certain degree of autonomy in their activities. Foster and Kaplan (2001) echo the concern about over-control. They advocate a minimalist approach to control: 'Control what you must, not what you can: control when you must, not when you can. If a control procedure is not essential, eliminate it.' They promote the need for 'divergent thinking' to encourage creativity which they say 'requires control through selection and motivation of employees rather than through control of people's actions; ample resources, including time, to achieve results; knowing what to measure and when to measure it; and genuine respect for others' capabilities and potential.'

We have also observed that autonomy works best when there is a certain amount of organizational 'slack' or 'space' – a looseness in resource availability which allows employees to 'borrow' time, expertise, research, materials, equipment and other resources as they develop new concepts. 3M have slack built into their organization by allowing researchers to spend 15% of their time on their own projects. In Google staff have 20% of their time to spend on new projects. Garud and Van de Ven (1992) confirm that entrepreneurial activity in a large organization is more likely to continue, despite negative outcomes, when there is slack in resource availability and a high degree of ambiguity about the outcomes.

Managing autonomy

The crucial dilemma in an entrepreneurial firm is therefore the amount of freedom given to staff. Too much, and anarchy or worse might result. Too little, and creativity, initiative and entrepreneurship will be stifled. It is all well and good talking about empowerment, but at what stage does it become licence? The answer is a question of 'balance'. Birkinshaw (2003) outlined the model used by BP to help guide and control entrepreneurial action. BP's philosophy is that 'successful business performance comes from a dispersed and high level of ownership of, and a commitment to, an agreed-upon objective'. Within BP there are a number of business units. Heads of units have a 'contract' agreed between them and the top executives in the organization. Once agreed they have 'free rein to deliver on their contract in whatever way they see fit, within a set of identified constraints'. BP's model uses four components to help guide and control entrepreneurial action: direction, space or slack, boundaries and support. All four need to be in balance. If they are too tight they constrain the business unit, but if too slack they might result in chaos. This is shown in Figure 7.4.

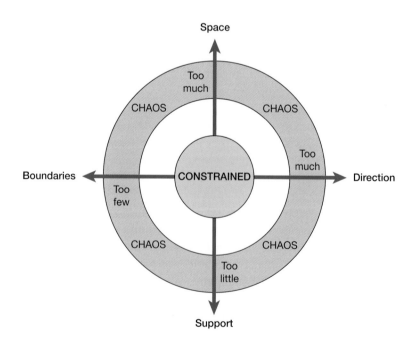

F 7.4 The balance between freedom and control

Direction This is the company's broad strategy and goals. Heads of units should have considerable scope to develop the strategy for their own unit, in line with BP's general direction, developing new products and markets within these constraints. However, without an overarching sense of values, mission and direction, entrepreneurship becomes a 'random set of initiatives … Although each initiative has its own rationale, when you put them together, the result is a mélange that stakeholders are likely to denounce as incoherent, vague, or chaotic.' Birkinshaw gives two pieces of advice on getting this balance right:

▷ Set broad direction and re-evaluate periodically as markets and the environment change;
▷ Let the company's strategy inform that of the unit and the unit's inform that of the company. A central role for senior executives is to magnify and reinforce those initiatives that most clearly fit the company's goals.

Space or slack As already explained, space or slack is to do with the degree of looseness in resource availability – monetary budgets, physical space and supervision of time. Companies have a responsibility to their shareholders to see that resources are put to their best use and are being used efficiently. However, in a tightly-run, highly-efficient organization there is no time or other resources to think, experiment and innovate. People do not have the time to work outside their job descriptions. All creative organizations require a degree of space or slack to allow experimentation. New ideas almost always require initial work to refine and adapt them. To circumvent this problem, employees' roles need to be defined by outcome rather than behaviour. As in the cases of 3M and Google, slack is built into the system, so that employees can do things that are not formally part of their job. However, if employees are given too much space they run the risk of losing focus on the day-to-day detail of the job and that can be wasteful. Birkinshaw also gives two pieces of advice on getting this balance right:

▷ Goal-setting should be carefully managed and clear and specific, but individuals should be given freedom in how the goals are to be achieved;
▷ Individuals should be allowed to learn from their own mistakes.

Boundaries These are the legal, regulatory and moral limits within which the company operates. They should be tightly defined but adherence should come from the creation of a set of shared values rather than through conforming to a set of rigid rules. Rigid rules without a shared agreement to adhere to them begs for the rules to be circumvented. Not having boundaries courts extreme danger, particularly if breaking them might lead to the failure of the organization. Birkinshaw again gives two pieces of advice on getting this balance right:

▷ Identify critical boundaries that, if crossed, threaten the survival of the organization and control them rigorously;
▷ Manage other boundaries in a non-invasive way through training, induction, codes of conduct and so on.

Support This refers to the information and knowledge transfer systems and training and development programmes provided by the company to help business unit managers do their job. Systems should encourage knowledge-sharing and collaboration. Training and career planning should be top-down. Both should, however, be discretionary. The danger here is that knowledge will not be shared and there will be little collaboration, encouraging the business unit to go its own way and raising the danger of duplication of effort. On the other hand if there is too much support the unit will always be oppressive or 'spoon-fed' and initiative will be stifled. Birkinshaw gives these final two pieces of advice on getting this balance right:

▷ Put in place enough support systems to help individuals and ensure they know where to go for help;
▷ Systems should encourage collaboration.

These elements need to be considered in the whole rather than individually. And balance is the key. Birkinshaw observes that most companies operate in the 'constrained' area in Figure 7.4 – direction defined too tightly, too little space, too tight boundaries and overly complex support structures – rather than the 'chaos' area, so most central management probably needs to 'let go' a little. The point is that management is an art, not a science, and it involves some fine judgements about the individuals you work with – their strengths and weaknesses – as well as their personal characteristics.

One final ingredient is needed to encourage entrepreneurship in this sort of organization – financial and resource support to get the ideas off the ground. The financial support might take the form of internal seed or venture capital that is separate from normal budgets. Different funds might be set up for different purposes, reflecting the stage of development of the idea. They might be administered by a committee or board with well-laid-down procedures for applying for resources – for example the presentation of a brief business plan. 3M support their '15% policy' with funding for equipment and extra help. To get an idea accepted in 3M the researcher must get the personal backing of a member of the main board. At that point an interdisciplinary team is set up to take the idea further.

🗁 Case insight Enron

Autonomy vs control

In his article in 2003, Birkinshaw (op. cit.) questioned whether the failure of Enron might signal a rethink about the value of corporate entrepreneurship. The company had been held up as a model of entrepreneurship, attracting aggressive and creative managers and encouraging internal entrepreneurship to achieve its growth. Whilst hindsight is a wonderful thing that gives everybody 20:20 vision, he concludes that Enron does not merit such a rethink because the company was at the outer boundaries of all four dimensions of BP's model.

Too little direction: In the 1990s the company moved out of the natural gas sector into electricity trading, online trading, weather derivatives and broadband networks. It started out with the goal of being the 'best gas distribution company', this became 'the world's best energy company' and finally 'the world's best company'. Enron's lack of direction became a strength as managers were encouraged to pursue any opportunity that might help in its headlong rush for growth.

Too much space: Enron gave managers enormous freedom to pursue these opportunities. Top management practised a philosophy of 'laissez-faire'. For example one gas trader started an online trading business (EnronOnline) while still working at her original job. It had some 250 people working for it before the President of Enron became aware of its existence.

Too few boundaries: Enron had explicit rules about capital allocation and risk and had a Risk Assessment Control Unit. However, Enron managers regularly broke the rules, for example by setting up new subsidiary companies and financing activities off the balance sheet. Instead of being dismissed for these things, managers were often rewarded. The culture within the organization was one of rule-breaking and there was no moral or ethical underpinning.

Too little support: Management at Enron were recruited from top US business schools. After a six-month induction working with different business units, they were largely left to their own devices. The reward system encouraged 'pushy', aggressive people and development start-ups or high-growth opportunities. Support was not a function that was rewarded and 'steady performers' did not stay long in the company.

The case of Enron, and indeed BP itself, underlines the fact that being entrepreneurial is risky. The line between too much and too little risk is never clear and forever moving and the concept of 'balance' is a subjective one. It also underlines that an entrepreneurial approach to management is not appropriate for every organization or department/division within it.

📖 Case with questions BP and Deepwater Horizon

Autonomy vs control

You might think that BP has proved an unfortunate example for Birkinshaw (op. cit.) to use, given the explosion on the Deepwater Horizon offshore oil rig that cost 11 lives and caused a vast oil spillage across in the Gulf of Mexico in 2010. Although financially very successful, at least until 2010, BP clearly got the balance wrong and took too many risks. In fact that had already been demonstrated with the explosion in the Texas City oil refinery in 2005 that cost 15 lives with 170 injuries and the Prudhoe Bay pipeline burst in 2006 for which it was fined $20 million. So what went wrong and why?

In the 1980s BP was seen as a cumbersome, bureaucratic organization spread across too many lines of business. In the late 1990s BP slimmed down its range of activities and changed direction to focus its exploration activities on riskier, 'new frontiers' of oil and gas exploration that would also yield higher returns. It also flattened its organization and decentralized in the way Birkinshaw described, reducing the size of its headquarters and establishing a number of business units, so as to encourage entrepreneurship and risk-taking. BP encouraged the use of self-managed teams as a way of organizing the different layers of management and engineering, encouraging the horizontal rather than vertical flow of information. Heads of business units, which included managers of oil fields, were given more authority to run things the way they wanted to so long as they met performance targets, which in turn were linked to bonuses and rewards – loose control with tight accountability. As already observed, once targets were agreed they had 'free rein to deliver on their contract in whatever way they see fit, within a set of identified constraints'.

Birkinshaw's article was published in 2003, but this highly decentralized, entrepreneurial approach was reinforced when a new CEO, Tony Hayward, took over in 2007. He reorganized roles, reducing the number of senior executives from 650 to 500 (mainly in head office)

and replacing almost one-third. Despite the incidents in 2005 and 2007, he emphasized the need for operational efficiency and cost-cutting in what was, essentially, a commodity supplier. The continued slimming down of BP's layers of management and specialist expertise was accompanied by increasing sub-contracting of operational activities. In this model the self-managed teams, including subcontractors, were responsible for all aspects of project management from costs to safety, with the inevitable tensions and conflict of interests that creates. However, this model continued to deliver good profits. Although BP regularly said safety was its primary consideration, the team responsible for Deepwater Horizon (which included the subcontractor Halliburton who installed the cement casings and caps that ruptured) clearly got the balance wrong. But why?

QUESTIONS

1 Given the reputational importance of safety at the corporate level, was there sufficient direction from head office at project level?

2 Was too much direction given regarding the importance of cost efficiency? Was there any mechanism for resolving the conflict between safety and cost, within BP and with its subcontractors such as Halliburton?

3 Was there sufficient management and technical support at project level in what was generally regarded as a complex and challenging drilling environment?

4 How do you make judgements about the degree of direction, support, space and boundaries?

5 With such enormous risks to life and the environment, was it appropriate to adopt entrepreneurial management structures at the project level in BP? If so, what safeguards would you want to prevent the Deepwater Horizon disaster happening again?

Open book management

Morris and Kuratko (2002) observe that the core principle in developing entrepreneurial control requires that managers need to 'give up control to gain control', Rather than tight budgetary controls, they advocate a 'no-surprises' approach – one that 'generates adequate information on a timely basis for all who need to know'. The authors believe that 'open book' management, where there is transparency of information, is important. Control mechanisms should produce indicators or early-warning signals of problems before they occur. A by-product of such a system is that it also conveys a sense of trust. Employees are trusted to get on with the job but the outcomes, rather than the processes, are monitored. They envisage the control system becoming 'a vehicle for managing uncertainty, promoting risk tolerance, encouraging focused experimentation, and empowering employees'. For them giving up control is also about greater accountability and a greater sense of responsibility:

> 'Where there is an elaborate system of control measures, the employee can be secure in the knowledge that, if the control system has been complied with, then his or her accountability is absolved, that his or her responsibility has been fulfilled. He or she need not take any further responsibility for outcomes or the implications of personal behavior for company performance. However, by giving up control to the employee, there is a much deeper sense of responsibility not only for accomplishing a task or behaving in a certain manner but also for the quality of task performance and the impact it has on the organization ... to give up control is to empower.'

Open book management focuses on the outcomes – the bottom line – rather than the processes. It gives people autonomy but focuses on the outcomes of their autonomy. It is built around free flows of information and seeks to motivate employees to improve the performance of the organization by thinking outside their narrow job definition and focusing on the consequences of their action. It encourages them to take ownership of and responsibility for their actions. In many ways it is the logical extension of the principles of the learning organization to financial information. But equally it encourages employees to think the way owner-managers would think about their own business. Case (1997) says it is built around six principles:

1 Free access to all financial information that is critical to tracking the firm's performance.
2 A continuous and overt attempt to present this information to employees.
3 Training processes that encourage understanding of this information.
4 Employees learning that part of their job is to improve the financial result in whatever way they can.

5 Empowering people to make decisions in their jobs based on what they know.

6 Giving employees a stake in the organization's success or failure.

Open book management is entirely consistent with corporate entrepreneurship. Indeed it would be difficult to achieve without it. This brings us back to the idea that entrepreneurial firms need *loose control but tight accountability.*

Managing risk

Risk is inherent in business and it is at its highest in an entrepreneurial business. Whilst it cannot be avoided, it can be managed – or, more accurately, identified and even quantified so that it can be managed down to acceptable levels. This might improve decision–making, not least because it encourages discussion about a factor that is inherent in the entrepreneurial organization. It might also help avoid the risks materializing or, by putting in place appropriate controls, at least provide an early warning of potential problems materializing. If risks can be avoided then less time is spent 'fire-fighting' when they materialize.

Risks are events that, when they happen, cause problems for the organization. Risk management can be broken down into a five stage process:

1 Identifying the risks (internal or external) associated with an action;
2 Evaluating the probability of the risk materializing;
3 Evaluating the effects of that risk materializing;
4 Mitigating the risk in whatever way possible;
5 Monitoring the risk to ensure early warning should it materialize.

Risk management is also about prioritization. Ideally the risks with the highest probability of occurrence and the greatest loss to the organization are handled first and those with the lowest probability of occurrence and the smallest loss are dealt with last. However, superimposed on this is the issue of whether the risks are controllable or not and whether they can be mitigated in some way. Figure 7.5 shows a useful way of classifying risks along these three dimensions. Any risks that have a major impact on the organization are undesirable, but those which are very likely to happen pose the greatest danger (quadrant D). By way of contrast risks with a low impact and a low likelihood of occurrence (quadrant A) pose the least risk. The third dimension is controllability. Some risks may be under your control or influence, others might be completely out of your control. Generally, the less you control or influence the risk, the greater the danger it poses. In this way the risk matrix becomes a Rubik cube, with the greatest danger being in the cube with the highest impact, highest likelihood and least controllability (quadrant G). These risks cannot be mitigated but must be closely monitored. The risks that are very likely to happen and have a

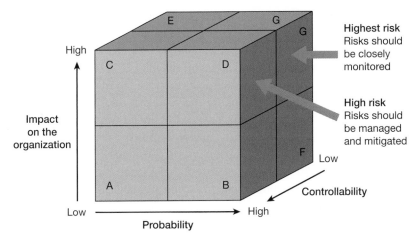

High

C   D

Impact
on the
organization

E   G
              G   **Highest risk**
                   Risks should
                   be closely
                   monitored

                   High risk
                   Risks should
                   be managed
                   and mitigated

F   Low

A   B   Controllability

Low ———————————→ High

Probability

F 7.5 Risk classification

major impact on the organization but can be controlled (quadrant D) will be the focus of managerial action to mitigate them.

Accurate identification of risks is at the core of the process. This can take a number of forms. The risks associated with a particular course of action or achieving particular objectives might be identified. The corporate risks an organization faces might be identified. One approach that can be useful in identifying these risks is called scenario planning and is explained in the next chapter. Based on the threats an organization faces, scenarios can be explored about the results of these threats materializing. The generic risks facing an industry might be relatively easy to identify (e.g. an oil well blowout). However, no matter how thorough the analysis, we can never expect to identify every possible risk.

It is often very difficult to quantify the probability of a risk materializing beyond a simple low (1), medium (2) or high (3). The monetary impact of the risk materializing might be just as difficult to establish beyond a similar low (1), medium (2) or high (3). The *composite risk factor* is defined as the probability of occurrence multiplied by the impact of the risk event. Using the simple classifications above, the highest composite risk factor is therefore 9 (3 x 3) and the lowest is 1 (1 x 1). The resulting index is then reclassified as low (1–3), medium (4–6) and high (7–9). Sometimes a scale of 1 to 5 is used resulting in a risk range of 25 (high) to 1 (low). The resulting reclassified index would then be low (1–8), medium (9–16) and high (17–25).

We can then decide what to do with the risk. Having identified a risk, its probability of occurrence and the impact it would have, there are four possible reactions:

1 *Attempt to eliminate the risk.* You might withdraw completely from the area of activity that generates the risk – an unlikely course of action initially for an entrepreneurial business, although if the risks continue

to be monitored, at some point in the future they may become unacceptable and this may be the best course of action. Generally these will be the risks that pose the greatest danger to the organization – high impact, high probability and least controllable.

2 *Attempt to reduce the risk.* You might increase internal controls, training or supervision depending on the nature of the risk. Alternatively you might select strategic alternatives that are less risky. Many of these strategies might involve transferring or sharing the risk with others.

3 *Transfer the risk.* There are many useful techniques that can be used to transfer both internal and external risks; for example insurance, outsourcing, sub-contracting, franchising and foreign-exchange or interest-rate hedging. So, companies constantly 'insure' against currency fluctuations – a risk they neither control nor influence – by buying forward in the currency market. When entering a new market or developing a new product, an organization might look for ways of spreading the risk by finding strategic partners or forming strategic alliances. This might also diminish the resources needed to exploit the opportunity but it will almost certainly also reduce the return that the organization achieves.

4 *Accept the risk.* You might simply accept all the risks, for example those with a 'low' composite risk factor. If you accept the risk completely, all you can attempt to do is plan to manage the risk and put in place early-warning indicators of it materializing, although this might be uneconomic if the impact on the organization is small. Many industries have inherent risks that need to be accepted if they decide to operate in that sector.

The riskiest situation in the risk cube is where you have a high likelihood of occurrence, with a high impact ('high' composite risk factor) in a situation where you have little control. In this situation you might consider any of options 1 to 3, but even if you end up accepting the risk it is vital that you monitor it and then take corrective action if it materializes.

🗂 Case with questions Specsavers

Mitigating financial risk

Specsavers was founded in 1984 by Doug and Mary Perkins. They started the business in their spare bedroom in Guernsey where they had moved after selling a small chain of West Country opticians. In the early 1980s the UK Government deregulated professional services, including opticians, allowing them to advertise for the first time. Doug and Mary seized the opportunity to try to launch a national chain of opticians. They opened their first stores in Guernsey and Bristol, followed rapidly by stores in Plymouth, Swansea and

Bath. They wanted the company to establish its brand so that it would be seen as offering a wide range of stylish, fashionable glasses at affordable prices. They wanted Specsavers to be seen as trustworthy, locally-based but with the huge buying power of a national company that meant savings could be passed on to the customer. Now with over 1600 outlets worldwide and a turnover of £1.5 billion, Specsavers is the largest privately-owned optician in the world and the Perkins family are believed to be billionaires.

Specsavers has used an interesting joint venture approach to grow its business, a stragegy which minimizes its capital requirements and the risks it faces. It enters into joint ventures with individual opticians, meaning that each joint venture is a separate legal entity. When the new company is formed, an equal number of 'A' shares and 'B' shares are issued. All the 'A' shares in the company are issued to the practice partners. All the 'B' shares are issued to Specsavers Optical Group. If there is more than one director in the business, for example an optometrist and a dispensing optician or retailer, then the 'A' shares are divided between the two parties. 'A' shareholders are delegated responsibility for the day-to-day running of the store. As 'B' shareholder, Specsavers provides supporting services, expertise, experience and information. As the number of practices has grown, so has the range of support services provided to practices, so that partners receive full support in all aspects of their business, tailored to their requirements. These can include property services, practice design, practice start-up, buying and distribution, retail training, professional recruitment as well as support in producing accounts, audits and tax returns. Individual opticians can sell on their 'A' shares, subject to certain conditions.

A typical joint venture start-up may cost in excess of £150,000, depending on location and practice size. In an equal partnership between two optician partners, each would be expected to provide the business with a loan of at least £20,000. Specsavers will match this loan. Specsavers Finance will provide a further 5-year loan for the remainder of the capital. Personal collateral is not required by Specsavers Finance to secure this loan. Specsavers and the partners sign a specific finance agreement. Loans are repaid from practice profits, sometimes within three years.

Specsavers claim the following advantages for opticians from this joint venture approach:

▷ A lower level of financial commitment from the opticians compared to a franchise;
▷ If targets are met the initial loan can be repaid from operating surpluses;
▷ Unlike a brand partnership, a joint venture partnership gives the partner the possibility of selling their shares in the future;
▷ The partner can end the relationship when they want.

☐ Up-to-date information on Specsavers can be found on their website: www.specsavers.co.uk

QUESTIONS

1 What are the advantages to both Specsavers and partners of this form of joint venture?

2 How is this different from a franchise?

Monitoring and mitigating risk

Early-warning mechanisms are indicators that alert you before a risk materializes, so that you can take remedial action. For major risks – those with a 'high' composite risk factor – it is important to identify parameters or events that indicate an increased propensity for the risk to materialize and to ensure that they are being monitored on a regular basis. A simple example would be bad debts which, in a low-margin business, can have an enormous impact on profitability. If that business is teetering on the edge of bankruptcy it is vital to monitor a *key risk indicator* for this on a regular and frequent basis. Key risk indicators for this might be the ratio of the number of days sales in debtors and the aged listing of debtors. To be effective key risk indicators must be easy to monitor as part of the regular activity of the organization, highlight when corrective action is needed and provide guidance on what action is needed. Entrepreneurial firms need to highlight the highest risks they face and monitor the associated key risk indicators for the strategy they are following. Only by doing this can they mitigate the high risks inherent in what they do.

All organizations have to accept some residual risk associated with their operations. Often they put in place contingency plans for dealing with serious risks, should they materialize. One example of this is business continuity planning through which an organization plans to stay in business after a major incident such as flood, fire and pandemic illness – external incidents – or the loss of sources of supply, malfunction of a major machine and product contamination – internal incidents. Often business continuity planning also involves actions to safeguard corporate or brand reputation, probably the most valuable asset for any organization.

Inherent in an entrepreneurial organization are certain characteristics that mitigate risk. Its external orientation, particularly towards the market, should make it sensitive to changes in the environment that might trigger danger. If information needs to be passed on within the organization knowledge transfer should be a strength. The way the organization approaches strategy and decision-making should mean that it is able to change its plans quickly and effortlessly. The fact that decision-making is delegated and staff feel empowered should mean that problems can be dealt with quickly by that person or people nearest to them. This improves speed of response but also minimizes information loss. In other words the architecture of the organization is sensitive to changes that signal danger and means that it can respond quickly once the risk materializes. Finally, if parts of the business are inherently more risky than others then it is sensible to compartmentalize the legal risk of failure by adopting a head office and group structure with legally separate subsidiaries (see Chapter 6). However, often with this structure loans may go through head office and subsidiaries may have cross guarantees.

⌂ Case insight Eurostar

Risk management

Eurostar started its high-speed rail services under the English Channel in 1994. These now run daily from London St Pancras to Paris, Lille, and Brussels with services also to the French Alps and Disneyland Resort, Paris. As you might expect with a major transport provider, Eurostar takes risk management very seriously. It has identified the risks it faces and has a business continuity plan for use when disruption occurs. Every Eurostar department has helped to establish the risk register. Examples of risks on the register range from losing the main offices because of fire, bomb scares, train derailment, computer systems failure and even financial catastrophe. Using the techniques outlined in the text, it has developed a risk matrix showing the impact of a risk and its likelihood of occurrence that allows the company to calculate a composite risk factor and consider what actions might mitigate those risks with a high impact.

For example, Eurostar has a telephone contact centre at Ashford in England that handles sales, ticketing and customer service. In the event of a serious fire, the company would lose much of its booking capacity with a resulting impact on revenue and reputation. Risk is mitigated through fire alarms, trip switches on electrical circuits, fire procedures and, ultimately back-up locations that can be activated so that operations can be continued if the fire happens despite the other precautions. The company has even carried out exercises using different locations in its own offices to simulate these actions. Eurostar rescores the composite risk factor after considering the mitigations that have been implemented until an acceptable level is reached. It revisits the risk matrix every six months just to check that the risks have not changed and that the mitigating activities are working as planned.

Eurostar has a Business Continuity department, but implementing the continuity plan is firmly the responsibility of line management. Every line department has a business continuity champion. They are responsible for: assessing business impact, assessing the risk of the events, identifying who is responsible for ensuring that mitigating actions are carried out, considering what further mitigations might be possible, coordinating business continuity within the department, investigating failures and departmental risk training. Eurostar has a full training programme of exercises that simulate various 'disasters'. These might involve simple round-table discussions or practical simulations. For example, it has carried out major evacuation exercises in the Channel Tunnel with Eurotunnel and the Emergency Services and is constructing its own tunnel evacuation training simulator.

Summary

- Many traditional management techniques discourage corporate entrepreneurship. These need to be avoided in an entrepreneurial organization. The barriers can be classified into six groups:

    1 Systems;
    2 Structures;
    3 Strategic direction;
    4 Policies and procedures;
    5 People;
    6 Culture.

- Change starts at the top. **Marks & Spencer (M&S)** and **Starbucks** both faced a severe crisis before radical changes in top management were made which resulted in a complete reappraisal of their strategies, policies and procedures. New people were brought in to effect the changes quickly.

- People can resist change even if it is for their own good. To facilitate change 'political and organizational' and 'people-orientated' actions need to be undertaken simultaneously. The change cube demonstrates the complexity of what is required with all aspects of strategy and organization potentially having to change in both the concrete and conceptual dimensions and the formal and informal dimensions.

- In working through change, organizations experience three phases:

    1 Immobilization and denial;
    2 Depression and letting go;
    3 Testing the new reality and putting it together.

- Both **Marks & Spencer (M&S)** and **Starbucks** pushed through change successfully using a range of techniques contained in this chapter.

- In managing autonomy managers must give up control to gain control. Entrepreneurial firms need loose control but tight accountability. Too much control stifles creativity, innovation and entrepreneurship. However, too little control can lead to chaos. Open book management allows autonomy but encourages a focus on the financial performance of the organization.

- Most firms place too many constraints and controls on managers. Some, like **Enron**, do not have enough. What is needed is 'balance':

    ▷ Space or slack – a looseness in resource availability – encourages experimentation and innovation;
    ▷ Direction – the broad strategy and goals – gives innovation a focus;
    ▷ Support – knowledge transfer and training systems – aids innovation;
    ▷ Boundaries – not just rules but underlying morals and ethics – define everything the firm does.

- Risk is an ever-present danger in an entrepreneurial firm. Risk management can be broken down into a five stage process:

    1 Identifying the risks (internal or external) associated with an action;
    2 Evaluating the probability of the risk materializing;
    3 Evaluating the effects of that risk materializing;
    4 Mitigating the risk in whatever way possible;
    5 Monitoring the risk so as to ensure early warning, should the risk materialize.

- The riskiest situation is one which has a high likelihood of occurrence with a high impact – measured by a 'high' composite risk factor – in a situation where you have little control.

- Where risk can be controlled it should be mitigated. **Specsavers** mitigates its financial risks by entering into joint ventures with professional opticians. **Eurostar** has an active business continuity plan that allows it to manage the risks that it faces.

▷ Where risks can be identified it is important to monitor key risk indicators that give early warning signs of the risks materializing. Entrepreneurial firms need to identify the highest risks in the strategies they are following and then monitor the associated key risk indicators.

Essays and discussion topics

1 Discuss why the seven conventional management techniques listed might discourage corporate entrepreneurship. Can you think of other examples that fit with the classifications proposed by Michael Morris?

2 Does your national culture accept failure? Does it encourage success? What are the implications of your views for corporate entrepreneurship?

3 You can never change people. Discuss.

4 Change can be created, but never managed. Discuss.

5 The interrelationships in Mintzberg's change cube are so complicated that no major change is ever likely to be 100% successful. Discuss.

6 Think of a major change you have experienced. What were your emotional reactions to it?

7 Why does tight control stifle creativity, innovation and entrepreneurship?

8 Why is slack or space so important for creativity, innovation and entrepreneurship?

9 How do you achieve 'balance' between freedom and control? Who makes the judgement? How easy is this to manage?

10 How can you have loose control but tight accountability? Give examples.

11 With freedom comes accountability. Discuss.

12 Freedom without accountability leads to anarchy. Discuss.

13 Is open book management practical?

14 Why do so many managers resist open book management?

15 Why are boundaries important?

16 What moral and ethical boundaries would you place on business?

17 If managers focus too much on risk they will ignore opportunities. Discuss.

18 If you cannot measure risk, you cannot manage it. Discuss.

19 If you cannot manage risk, you might as well ignore it. Discuss.

20 Risk is the biggest managerial issue facing corporate entrepreneurship. Discuss.

Exercises and assignments

1 Using an example of a major change of which you have experience, chart how the changes were made, the problems encountered and the solutions put in place. Were the changes successful? Explain.

2 Describe the risks facing an organization of which you have experience (it might be your university). Classify them using the risk cube in Figure 7.5, producing a composite risk factor for each, and indicate the key risk indicators that would need monitoring.

3 Research the reasons for Enron's failure and critically evaluate Birkinshaw's contention that it was at the extremes of boundaries of BP's model for entrepreneurial development. Evaluate BP's own situation.

4 Arthur Andersen was once considered to be the most entrepreneurial of accounting firms. Research the reasons for its failure and apply Birkinshaw's model.

5 Download the Toolkit for Managing Change from www.esdtoolkit.org and use the Worksheets to plan around a change situation.

References

Bennis, W. (2009), *On Becoming a Leader*, New York: Basic Books.

Birkinshaw, J. (2003) 'The Paradox of Corporate Entrepreneurship', *Strategy and Business*, 30.

Case, J. (1997) 'Opening the Books', *Harvard Business Review*, 75, March/April.

Clemmer, J. (1995) *Pathways to Performance: A Guide to Transforming Yourself, Your Team and Your Organization*, Toronto: Macmillan Canada.

Foster, R. and Kaplan, S. (2001) *Creative Destruction: Why Companies that are Built to Last Underperform the Stock Market*, New York: Doubleday/Currency.

Garud, R. and Van de Ven, A. (1992) 'An Empirical Evaluation of the Internal Corporate Venturing Process', *Strategic Management Journal*, 13 (special issue).

Hamel, G. (2000) 'Reinvent your Company', *Fortune*, 12, June.

Jackson, S. and Schuler, R. (2001) 'Turning Knowledge into Business Advantage', in J. Pickford (ed.) *Mastering Management 2.0*, London: Prentice Hall.

Kakabadse, A. (1983) *The Politics of Management*, London: Gower.

Kotter, J.P. (1996), *Leading Change*, Boston, MA: Harvard Business School Press.

Kotter, J.P. and Cohen, D.S. (2002), *The Heart of Change*, Boston, MA: Harvard Business School Press.

Mintzberg, H. (1998) in H. Mintzberg, B. Ahlstrand and J. Lempel, *Strategy Safari*, New York: The Free Press.

Morris, M.H. (1998) *Entrepreneurial Intensity*, Westport: Quorum Books.

Morris, M.H. and Kuratko, D.F. (2002) *Corporate Entrepreneurship*, Fort Worth, TX: Harcourt College Publishers.

Yukl, G. (2002) *Leadership in Organizations*, Upper Saddle River, NJ: Prentice Hall Inc.

Chapter **8**

Encouraging intrapreneurship and corporate venturing

Learning outcomes

By the end of this chapter you should be able to:

▷ Critically analyze the role of internal corporate venturing and intrapreneurship in larger entrepreneurial firms;

▷ Critically analyze the personal characteristics and motivations of intrapreneurs and how they might be encouraged;

▷ Critically analyze the role of venture teams, new venture divisions and R&D departments or divisions in promoting innovation;

▷ Critically analyze the options for dealing with new venture developments and explain which are best in different circumstances;

▷ Critically analyze why large organizations undertake corporate venturing and what is needed to make such a strategy successful.

Corporate venturing, venture teams and intrapreneurship

Internal corporate venturing is concerned with how to encourage and manage new, entrepreneurial businesses whilst aligning them to the larger company's existing activities. They might be managed separately from the mainstream activity and eventually they might be 'spun off'. Internal corporate venturing needs to be distinguished from external corporate venturing which is about acquiring other, usually smaller, companies that have innovations that the acquiring company wishes to own (covered in Chapter 11). Intrapreneurship is one aspect of internal corporate venturing that has gained prominence and, indeed, it is an important strategic tool for the entrepreneurial organization seeking to encourage innovation. It can be practised both individually and in teams.

The term 'intrapreneur' is now generally used to describe the individual charged with pushing through innovations within a larger organization, in an entrepreneurial fashion. They are entrepreneurs in larger organizations. Pinchot (1985) defines them as 'dreamers who do; those who take hands-on responsibility for creating innovation of any kind within an organization; they may be the creators or inventors but are always the dreamers who figure out how to turn an idea into a profitable reality'. Actually they are rarely the inventor of the product, but rather they work with teams to cut through the bureaucracy of the organization to develop it for the market place as quickly as possible.

Intrapreneurship may be an isolated activity, designed to see a new project into the market place, either as part of the existing organization or as a spin-off from it. On the other hand it may be part of a broader strategy to reposition or re-invigorate the whole organization or even re-invent an entire industry. It can be undertaken at many different levels – corporate, divisional, functional or project level. Whilst the intrapreneur is an individual, at some stage it is likely that they will work as part of a larger team – often called a new venture team. The term 'intrapreneurship' may therefore be used to apply to both

'While it is true that every company needs an entrepreneur to get it under way, healthy growth requires a smattering of intrapreneurs who drive new projects and explore new and unexpected directions for business development. Virgin could never have grown into the group of more than 200 companies it is now, were it not for a steady stream of intrapreneurs who looked for and developed opportunities, often leading efforts that went against the grain.'

Richard Branson, www.entrepreneur.com/article/218011, January 2011

'We inadvertently developed this role [of intrapreneur] at Virgin by virtue of the fact that when we've chosen to jump into a business about which we have little or no real knowledge, we've had to enable a few carefully selected people who do know which end is up. When Virgin moved into the mobile phone industry we had no experience, so we looked for our rivals' best managers, hired them away, took off their ties and gave them the freedom to set up on their own ventures within the Virgin Group. Tom Alexander in the UK, Dan Schulman in the US and Andrew Black in Canada have all done this with great success, aggressively taking Virgin companies in new and unexpected directions. Perhaps the greatest thing about this form of enabled intrapreneurship is that often everyone becomes so immersed in what they're doing that they feel like they own their companies. They don't feel like employees working for someone else, they feel much more like ... well, I think the only word to describe it is "belongers".

Richard Branson, www.entrepreneur.com/article/218011, January 2011

intrapreneurs and new venture teams. Intrapreneurship may be happening at a number of different levels within an organization at the same time, centred on different individuals or teams. One advantage of this approach for the organization is that intrapreneurship helps to compartmentalize the change agent(s) and reduce risk, whilst still pursuing commercial opportunities. Levels of intrapreneurship therefore vary and can be adapted to suit different organizations or levels within it. Whilst not dependent upon the size of the organization (Antoncic and Hisrich, 2003), the practice of intrapreneurship does seem to become more difficult to sustain as the firm grows (Ross, 1987).

Some intrapreneurs seem to just emerge, but often they have to be identified, nurtured and developed by the organization. Pinchot (1985) observes that if there are too few intrapreneurs within an organization there are two solutions: attract successful intrapreneurs from other companies or recruit managers with an intrapreneurial character and encourage them to develop. Galloway (2006) stresses the importance of transferring and disseminating intrapreneurial knowledge through appropriate structures and cultures, observing that it is not enough to simply recruit intrapreneurs from outside. Without the appropriate architecture they will not flourish.

Personal characteristics of intrapreneurs

Intrapreneurs share many of the characteristics of entrepreneurs. They need to be able to perceive an opportunity and have a vision for what it might become. They also need to be motivated to proactively take the initiative and run with it. They are action-orientated. Pinchot (1987) says that: 'Vision and imagination make up half of "the dreamers that do". Action is the other half'. Ross and Unwalla (1986) say the best intrapreneurs are result-orientated, ambitious, rational, competitive and questioning. They dislike bureaucracy and are challenged by innovation but have an understanding of their organization and a belief in their colleagues. They are adept at politics and good at resolving conflict – and need to be because they will face a lot of it as they smooth the connections with 'conventional' management. Kanter (2004) found that intrapreneurs were comfortable with change, had clarity of direction, thoroughness, a participative management style and an understanding that they needed to work with others to achieve their goals.

Pinchot (1985) also characterizes them as goal-orientated and self-motivated but, unlike entrepreneurs, he says they are also motivated by corporate reward and recognition – something we shall question in the next section. They are able to delegate but are not afraid to roll their sleeves up and do what needs to be done themselves. Like entrepreneurs, they need to be self-confident and optimistic, but may well be cynical about the bureaucratic systems within which they operate, although they do believe they can circumvent or manipulate them. In that sense they are good at working out problems within the 'system' – or even bypassing the system – rather than leaving the organization. They are often good at sales and marketing and can bring those skills to bear both internally and externally. Like entrepreneurs they are strongly intuitive, but unlike entrepreneurs their corporate background means they are less willing to rely on intuition and more willing to undertake market research into a new project. They are risk-takers and believe that, if they lose their jobs, they will quickly find new ones. However, they are less willing to take personal risks than entrepreneurs. They are also sensitive to the need to disguise risks within the organization so as to minimize the political cost of failure.

Intrapreneurs are adept communicators with strong interpersonal skills that make them good at persuading others to do what they want. In this respect they are similar to entrepreneurs in that they build and rely on relationships. This process of influencing without authority, based upon reciprocity, is at the heart of the skill of intrapreneurs (Cohen and

Could you be an intrapreneur?

Gifford Pinchot proposed the eleven-question test below to see whether people might have what it takes to be an intrapreneur.

1   Does striving to make things work better occupy as much of your time as working on existing systems and duties?
2   Do you get excited about work?
3   Do you think about new business ideas in your spare time?
4   Can you see what needs to be done to actually make new ideas happen?
5   Do you get into trouble sometimes for doing things that exceed your authority?
6   Can you keep your ideas secret until they are tested and more developed?
7   Have you overcome the despondency you feel when a project you are working on looks as if it might fail and pushed on to complete it?
8   Do you have a network of work colleagues you can count on for support?
9   Do you get annoyed and frustrated when others cannot successfully execute your ideas?
10 Can you overcome the desire to do all the work on a project yourself and share responsibility with others?
11 Would you be willing to give up some salary to try out a business idea, provided the final rewards were adequate?

He says that if you answer 'yes' to six or more questions he believes it is likely that you are already behaving like an intrapreneur.

Adapted from Pinchot (1985)

Bradford, 1991). They need to identify potential allies and understand their world and their motivations. They need to be able to use this language and these motivations to their own advantage. Once they understand their language, the intrapreneur can communicate more effectively and on a personal level with potential allies. For example, sport can often act as a bridge in these circumstances. More importantly the intrapreneur can understand what they value and then highlight which of these they might influence or control. They then start establishing a working relationship, in which exchanges of value might take place – a process of give and take. This takes time and they therefore need to be somewhat more patient than entrepreneurs.

In addition, Hornsby et al. (1993) noted the importance of personal characteristics like risk-taking propensity, desire for autonomy, need for achievement, goal orientation, and internal locus of control also having a significant influence on intrapreneurs – all the things you would expect to see in an entrepreneur. Other researchers have noted the importance of external factors that facilitated the development of intrapreneurship such as dynamism, technological opportunities, industry growth and demand for new products (Antoncic and Hisrich, 2004).

Intrapreneurs work within larger organizations and will probably come from within them. They are therefore likely to be hybrids, having to work hard to create entrepreneurial structures and cultures around them, but always having to communicate with more bureaucratic individuals in the organization that employs them. They must be skilled at innovation but also at putting a team together and handling the political constraints of a large organization. And organizations, as in the 3M case in Chapter 3, must support them and put in place an organizational architecture that encourages intrapreneurship.

Motivating intrapreneurs

Knowing what motivates intrapreneurs to do what they do gives us a valuable insight that reinforces the lessons from previous chapters. Whilst Pinchot (1985) and others may believe intrapreneurs are motivated by corporate reward and recognition, there is strong evidence that money does not act as a motivator for individuals undertaking complex or creative jobs that involve even the most rudimentary cognitive tasks. As with entrepreneurs, money is simply a badge of success, recognition of achievement.

Based on the work of Maslow and Herzberg, motivation can be seen as *intrinsic* – derived from personal satisfaction and interest or enjoyment in the task – or *extrinsic* – coming from external factors such as pay, promotion or coercion. Coercion can be the strongest motivator of all, but rarely lasts long. Similarly money can act as a motivator but does not last long. Maslow placed money at the bottom of his motivational hierarchy. However, lack of money can be a disincentive. So, as motivation for simple tasks, money works, and of course if you do not pay people well enough they may be distracted and lack motivation. But if they are paid adequately other intrinsic motivations start to become important. Salary becomes what is called 'a hygiene factor' and increasingly people start looking for personal satisfaction in other things. Recognition gives personal satisfaction – which is the true motivator of entrepreneurs and intrapreneurs rather than money. Personal satisfaction can also be derived from factors such as praise, respect, empowerment and a sense of belonging. Encouraging staff to develop personal satisfaction from the achievements of the organization is at the centre of the approach to leadership and the development of culture outlined in previous chapters. Although not a personal motivator beyond a certain level, remuneration and in particular rewards such as bonuses can help set the organizational culture by signalling what actions the organization values.

Pink (2011) highlights three major factors that contribute to personal satisfaction, particularly for those involved in complex or creative tasks:

1 **Autonomy** If you wish people to be engaged with tasks and proactive, rather than just compliant, self-direction is important. People like autonomy. Whilst Google gives employees 20% 'free time' and 3M 15% both give staff autonomy to pursue innovations within these periods.

2 **Purpose** Increasingly people believe there must be a purpose to work. It should be about more than just making money and profit. This is one reason why so many firms, like retailers Marks & Spencer (M&S) and John Lewis in the UK, and IBM and Timberland in the USA have extensive social responsibility programmes (see Chapter 9). Consider Apple, whose mission is to 'create products and services that change the lives of people around the world'. The mission statement is intended to motivate staff, to encourage them to work long hours, beyond what they are paid for, and certainly staff seem proud of Apple's products. As such, the rewards that motivate them are not simply the potential to earn more money, but the potential to share in the glory of the organization if their ideas succeed.

3 **Mastery** If people feel there is purpose to undertaking a task they naturally want to be good at it. Why else do people want to master a musical instrument and practise in their free time? Why else do people want to contribute to and continuously improve Wikipedia? Why does crowdsourcing (see Chapter 13) work? People are motivated to do these things without payment.

But what motivates an intrapreneur to create wealth for an organization they do not own? The answer may lie in the literature on psychological ownership in organizations (Pierce et al., 2001). Psychological ownership is when an individual 'feels' that they own the organization or part of it, even if they do not. And it is promoted by the three factors outlined above. Pierce et al. (op. cit.) see autonomy or loose control as important because it provides feelings of 'efficacy' and 'effectance'. They argue that it is also promoted by investing time, ideas and energy and acquiring an intimate knowledge of the task – which is all part of mastery. They also argue that psychological ownership creates a sense of responsibility in the individual which can be evidenced as stewardship and a sense of social responsibility – or purpose – for the organization. And as we have already noted, in their study Hornsby et al. (1993) highlighted the importance of the desire for autonomy as a personal motivator in intrapreneurs. So autonomy acts as a motivator because it encourages intrapreneurs to feel they 'own' their project.

One final point is that intrapreneurs seem to care deeply about their organization. They are proud of it and their loyalty to it is a motivator that makes them battle on to try to make it better. It also motivates them not to leave to set up their own business. Perhaps this is just another manifestation of psychological ownership – the intrapreneur feels that the boundaries between them and their organization are porous.

🛄 Case insight Apple's App Store

Involving outsiders in intrapreneurship

Intrapreneurship can involve people not employed by the organization. Apple's highly successful 'App Store' is a good example of this. Apple allows people to develop applications for its iPhone and iPad by selling its own Software Developer Kit for a nominal fee. People can then set their own price and sell their Apps at the App Store. Apple takes a commission for each download. In its first year, the App Store had over 1.5 billion downloads, offered over 65,000 applications, and registered over 100,000 developers in the iPhone developer programme.

Encouraging intrapreneurship

Based on empirical analysis, Kuratko et al. (1990) found that the four most significant enablers of intrapreneurship were: (top) management support; organizational structure; resources (including time); and reward (a motivator discussed in the last section). To these a subsequent study added tolerance of risk-taking (Hornsby et al., 2002). Without these, intrapreneurship would not flourish. Christensen (1985) expanded on what these meant. These are shown in Table 8.1.

Within this framework there also needs to be a clear vision and plan for a longer time horizon that is effectively communicated to employees and highlights the importance of intrapreneurship (Sathe, 2003). And all these factors should be nested in a supportive culture. Hisrich (1990) defines an intrapreneurial culture as one that develops visions, goals, and action

T 8.1 Factors encouraging intrapreneurship

Factor	Basic factors	Intrapreneurial factors
(Top) management support	Sponsors	Commitment
Organizational structure	Hierarchy	Corporate venturing, cross-functional teams, internationalization, external networks
Resources	Finance and materials	Knowledge resources
Reward	Regular pay, job security	Promotion, expanded job responsibility, autonomy, recognition, free time to work on pet projects, bonuses
Risk	Tolerance of lower risks	No penalization

Source: Christensen, K.S. (1985) 'Enabling Intrapreneurship: The Case of a Knowledge-Intensive Industrial Company', *European Journal of Innovation Management*, 8(3).

plans; takes action and rewards action; encourages suggesting, trying and experimenting; encourages creating and developing regardless of the area; and one that encourages the taking of responsibility and ownership.

Because they might lack the authority of a certain level of senior management, intrapreneurs need a high-level sponsor to protect them when times are difficult or vested interests are upset and to help them unblock the blockages to change as they occur. The sponsor will help secure resources, provide advice and contacts. They will need to nurture and encourage the intrapreneur, particularly early on in the life of the project or when things go wrong, and will need to endorse and create visibility for the project at the appropriate time. Underpinning this must be a good relationship between the sponsor and the intrapreneur, based on mutual trust and respect.

Intrapreneurs and new venture teams not only need to feel they have autonomy, they need to have it. However, since they will inevitably end up 'breaking the rules', they need to be kept under a certain amount of control. As we saw in the last chapter, they need a 'light touch' in management but a balance is required between freedom and control. If there is too much freedom there may be a crisis of coordination or even chaos.

However, at the end of the day, intrapreneurs and new venture teams still work within the confines of a large organization and they therefore need to be nurtured and encouraged by supportive entrepreneurial management. Drucker (1985) maintains that entrepreneurial management does not happen by chance in big companies. Just as the intrapreneur needs a high-level sponsor, entrepreneurial management has to have the backing of those at the top of the organization. Firstly, it requires a culture that is receptive to innovation and willing to see change as an opportunity rather than a threat – an entrepreneurial architecture. The company must do the hard work for the intrapreneur and remove, or have mechanisms for removing, as many barriers as possible. It needs to be able to manage

🗂 Case insight Boeing

Encouraging intrapreneurship

Boeing, in the USA, has what it calls its Phantom Works project whose stated mission is: 'To be the catalyst of innovation for the Boeing Enterprise'. Within this there are various programmes designed to encourage intrapreneurship.

The Chairman's Innovation Initiative (CII) was launched in 2000 to encourage employees to develop new business ideas from company-developed technologies and processes. Since then hundreds of new ideas for businesses have been submitted, with some notable successes. The Autonomous Underwater Vehicle (AUV) is now a joint venture involving two other companies that undertake undersea surveying for the gas, oil and telecom industries, IntelliBus Network Systems has developed technology for automotive application and AVChem is a chemical management service provider to the aerospace industry.

Another, larger, programme is called CREATE. This focuses on commercializing military applications, perhaps trying to transform existing technologies that have had disappointing results into money spinners. It brings together intrapreneurial teams made up of both Boeing staff and outside staff – for example from suppliers or universities – to work on each project. These teams come together from far-flung locations to 'brainstorm in meetings punctuated by organic meals and hourly exercise like power walking, yoga and racquetball.' Sometimes projects emerge from the CII programme to be worked on further within the CREATE framework.

change. Secondly, systematic measurement of intrapreneurial and innovatory performance is necessary, so that progress can be monitored. The company must also build in learning from its successes and failures so as to improve its performance. Thirdly, intrapreneurship needs to be structured, supported and rewarded appropriately. Within an entrepreneurial architecture all staff should have the potential to be intrapreneurs.

How intrapreneurs work

An intrapreneur is an entrepreneurial leader of a project. Because they may not have hierarchical authority they tend to use the power of informal influence, and must exhibit a high level of interpersonal skills which requires a high level of emotional intelligence. Pinchot (1985) laid down 'Ten Commandments' for how intrapreneurs should approach their role. They should:

1 Come to work each day willing to be fired.
2 Get round any orders aimed at stopping their dream.
3 Be prepared to do anything needed to make their project work, regardless of their personal job description.

4 Build up a network of good people who are willing to help.

5 Build a highly motivated but flexible team. Choose the best.

6 Work 'underground' for as long as possible. Once they 'go public' barriers will emerge to restrain them.

7 Be loyal and truthful to their corporate sponsor. In this way they build a solid relationship.

8 Remember it is better to ask for forgiveness than permission.

9 Be true to their goals, but realistic in how they can be achieved.

10 Be thoroughly engaged and take ownership of the project – and always persevere, no matter what.

To this list Morris and Kuratko (2002) have added that intrapreneurs should manage expectations and never over-promise. It is better to promise less and deliver more. They also suggest, as with change management, that showing a few early wins with tangible deliverables is good because it creates confidence. What is more, small wins can evolve into significant accomplishments and develop a momentum for the project that becomes difficult to stop. Finally they advise intrapreneurs to try to set the parameters of what they do and how they do it – in other words change the rules of the game – so that they start to control as much of the project and how it is evaluated as they can.

As we have already observed, often intrapreneurs need to build a team around them. Sometimes these teams are informal and often they work outside traditional lines of authority – in the USA it is called 'skunk working'. This eliminates bureaucracy, permits rapid progress and promotes a strong sense of team identity and cohesion – Hofstede's 'in-group'. They subvert the prevailing corporate culture in an attempt to counter the stagnation or inertia often encountered as organizations get larger or older. Often they will 'bootleg' resources – time, materials and so on – because none are formally made available to them. We look at one form these teams might take in the next section.

New venture teams

The importance of team work has been emphasized in previous chapters. Its importance is just as great in pushing through innovative opportunities, although you might expect there to be an intrapreneur or champion at the helm. A single intrapreneur on their own rarely has all the skills required to see a project through to completion. Morris and Kuratko (op. cit.) believe venture teams are a vitally important element in any entrepreneurial organization: 'No matter what particular structures emerge, an important building block for structure should be the concept of the venture team … Venture teams represent a means for achieving a major break-through in terms of innovation productivity in the firm.'

Venture teams can take many forms. Their one characteristic is that they are ad hoc. They form and reform to tackle different projects. They may be led by an intrapreneur. However, they may become a group of intrapreneurs working together. Reich (1987) uses the term 'collective entrepreneurship' where individual skills are integrated into a group and the team's capacity to innovate then becomes greater than the sum of individuals. Whatever form a venture team takes, the 'rules' under which it operates are the same as for the intrapreneur.

To be successful the team as a whole needs to have the core competences required for the project (Stopford and Baden-Fuller, 1994). This is likely to involve managers from a wide range of different disciplines such as engineering, marketing, finance. They will need to balance creativity with project execution. The team also needs to have compatible personal characteristics so that their team roles complement each other's (see Belbin's team roles in Chapter 4). They need to be able to resolve conflicts and to collaborate as the team comes together (Chapter 4). They need to have that strong sense of team identity and cohesion we have already identified as important (Hofstede's 'in-group' in Chapter 5). But, as with all teams, this will take time to build.

Team-working is commonplace now across most businesses and is particularly valuable in pushing through innovations, whether or not they eventually end up as stand-alone new ventures. For example, at Google, all staff are involved in product development work in some form. They work in small teams of three or four people. Larger teams get broken down into smaller sub-teams, each working on specific aspects of the bigger project. Each team has a leader that rotates depending on the changing project requirements and most staff work in more than one team.

Organizing new venture developments

Once the flow of new venture ideas from intrapreneurs and venture teams has started the question will arise as to what to do with them, in particular, whether they are kept 'in-house' or 'spun out' in some way. Bergelman (1984a, 1984b) uses the typology shown in Figure 8.1 which suggests that the answer depends on two factors:

▷ How strategically important the development is for corporate development;
▷ How operationally related it is to the core technology and capabilities of the firm.

Generally, the more important the development and the more operationally related and therefore familiar it is, the more it is likely to be kept 'in-house' and ownership retained. Familiarity is likely to involve innovation that is more incremental and therefore easier to absorb into existing structures. Strategic importance is likely to mean the organization retains control of the development. Using his typologies there are nine organizational options.

		Very important	Uncertain importance	Not important
Operational relatedness	Unrelated	Special business unit	Independent business unit	Complete spin-off
	Partly related	New product business department	New venture divisions	Contracting
	Strongly related	Direct integration	Micro new business department	Nurturing and contracting

Strategic importance

Source: Adapted from Bergelman, 1984a and 1984b.

F 8.1 Organizing new venture developments

Direct integration This is recommended where the development is both strategically important and operationally related, for example, when a new product development is integrated into a product range. Changes in the product or process are likely to have an immediate impact on mainstream operations and staff involved are likely to be those involved in day-to-day operations.

New product or business departments These remain in-house because of their importance but for some operational reason a new department needs to be established to get the product to market. This might be the case with product extension. It is particularly useful where new products are likely to emerge from day-to-day operations fairly frequently but the product needs to be marketed differently in some way. The department therefore needs strong marketing skills, possibly linking with a number of different departments, divisions or subsidiaries dealing with different market segments.

Micro new business departments Where the strategic importance is uncertain the situation needs to be clarified before a final decision is made. This option keeps the development 'in-house' within a department because of the strong operational relatedness, pending that final decision.

Special business unit Where operational relatedness is minimal, new staff with different skills may have to be recruited (or key staff identified and extracted from their day-to-day roles) and the unit given greater independence and operational freedom, whilst the company still retains ownership until decisions are made about its future. Because of its strategic importance it is likely to require strong top-management supervision.

New venture division This should be used to deal with developments that require further investment before their final fate is decided. They could ultimately be spun out or integrated into the mainstream, depending on the final assessment. Because of the uncertainty of its strategic importance, it is also likely to require strong top-management supervision. This very popular organizational form is covered in more detail in the next section.

Spin-offs If there is little or no operational relatedness and the development has little or no strategic importance to the existing business then it should be completely spun off, with no ownership retained. For example, Quaker Oats spun off the toy manufacturer Fisher Price in 1991, realizing the value of the venture whilst allowing it to concentrate on its core grocery business. This was part of its move away from being regarded as a conglomerate, for reasons dealt with in Chapter 11. The most important condition for a spin-off, according to Garvin (1983), is that the core competences are embodied in skilled labour rather than physical assets because the individuals transfer the knowledge to new firms. He argues that when new market segments develop opportunities for industries in the mature stage of their life cycle these industries are most likely to generate spin-offs because of the information advantage of insiders:

> 'An industry whose technology is embodied in skilled human capital is a prime candidate for spin-offs, for techniques, designs, and ideas are readily appropriable by individuals and transferable to new firms … Spin-offs in particular are encouraged by the existence of multiple market segments, information and start-up advantage accruing to members of established firms, readily transferable technologies, and environments in which skilled human capital is the critical factor of production.'

There is some ambiguity in the literature about the ownership of spin-offs (e.g. Ito, 1995). Spin-offs can be partial or complete and ownership (or part of it) can be retained by the parent organization. So, for example, in 2006 McDonald's spun out its Chipotle chain of restaurants by making an initial purchase offering (IPO) whereby investors purchased 20% of the company and Chipotle became a public company. Later that same year McDonald's eliminated its 80% stake by offering to exchange these shares with McDonald's shareholders, leaving Chipotle 100% independent.

Unless the spin-off is a complete sell-off or the result of a management buy-out or buy-in, it is likely that the management will come under some degree of control by the corporate parent. And, as you would expect, the degree of control they exercise is likely to affect the entrepreneurial behaviour of the spin-off. Too much formal control will diminish innovative behavior and stifle creativity (MacMillan et al., 1986). However, most parent companies might like to at least influence and provide direction to that innovation – and herein lies the balancing act that is part of managing the entrepreneurial organization.

There are three 'half-way-houses' under Bergelman's typologies:

Independent business units These have greater independence than other formats. Often they are joint ventures with other strategic partners with different degrees of ownership ranging from subsidiary to minority interest and ultimately the unit be spun off completely as factors become more certain. This format allows the unit to focus exclusively on its own activities rather than those of the larger organization. It is also a convenient legal format for knowledge transfer, facilitating learning from external sources. Finally separation allows associated risks to be mitigated and compartmentalized.

Contracting This is appropriate where the core competences are embodied in some physical assets or processes that are owned by the company but they are of little strategic importance. These can then be offered for use by other firms on a contract or licence basis.

Nurturing and contracting (also called **nurtured divestment**) Where the development has commercial value but is not critical to the mainstream business, it might need to be nurtured prior to being offered to other firms under contract or licence. The development is likely have evolved from mainstream operations.

New venture divisions

The new venture division is a permanent division set up for the purpose of developing innovations when it is not clear whether the development might be integrated into the core business or spun out. Being part of an existing organization, they allow existing competences to be leveraged at the same time as maintaining the potential to learn new ones. New venture divisions may operate at corporate or other levels within the organization. By separating out the development of innovation the organization hopes that the division will be able to establish its own leadership, management, structures and culture that encourage and facilitate innovation as a continuous process. Mainstream activities can continue as 'business-as-usual' in the rest of the organization. Each and any innovation coming out of the division may take the organization in a new strategic direction and therefore how the innovation is integrated into the organization – or indeed sold off or separated out – depends entirely on the nature of the innovation.

Thus, the new venture division may be expected to produce a stream of innovations that include a greater number of bolder breakthroughs than the ad hoc venture team. The scale of each innovation is likely to be greater. Maletz and Nohria (2001) found that placing innovative projects in the organizational 'whitespace' – outside the formal organization with its usual rules and procedures – accelerated natural experimentation. By not imposing the traditional processes of planning, organizing and controlling, projects were nurtured until they were ready for moving over to the regular organization. Managers need to set the boundaries of this whitespace broadly. They need to provide organizational, moral and adequate (but not sufficient) financial support, build enthusiasm among those outside the project and then monitor the project's progress to decide upon the next steps.

This approach is based on the idea of product life cycles (see Chapter 10) and the need for different approaches at different stages in the life cycle. New product/market offerings may need entrepreneurial approaches to management, but those at the mature stage require the secure guiding hand of a strong financial director. The approach recognizes the strength of the *portfolio* of different product/market offerings, each with its different cash-flow profile, but equally the challenge of the very different management approaches. The new venture division is an attempt to institutionalize the continuous flow of innovations within a large and complex organization that has a diverse portfolio to manage. However, having an intrapreneur involved in developing a new venture, rather than a new venture division seems more likely to lead to commercial success (David, 1994). David speculates that this is because the intrapreneur is self-motivated, whereas a new venture manager has their role assigned.

🛄 Case insight Xerox Technology Ventures

New venture divisions

Xerox's Palo Alto Research Center (PARC) is a good example of how innovation might be successfully encouraged but not commercially exploited. PARC was a separate R&D entity, fully funded and resourced by Xerox but kept organizationally separate. In the 1970s PARC became a leader in innovation, developing many of the fundamental computing technologies that were later commercialized by other Silicon Valley companies such as Apple, Adobe and 3M. However, with the one (major) exception of the laser printer (Xerox were in the copier business), Xerox failed to exploit most of the innovations because it could not see their relevance to its existing business.

It was only when it set up a separate company, Xerox Technology Ventures, located almost as far away in the USA as you can get from both Xerox head office and PARC that things began to change. This company was to exploit technologies that did not 'fit' into Xerox's product portfolio. If a product was turned down by head office it could be offered to the new venture group. Once a working model was perfected, the founders, who would be rewarded with a 20% stake in the new business, were moved out of the plush PARC laboratories and into low-cost commercial premises and professional management put in to bring the product to market.

Research and development

New venture divisions are one step beyond the traditional R&D department – staffed by technical staff and focused entirely on technological advancement. The work is research-based and technology-driven. Many R&D departments are better at inventing than innovating – an important distinction explored in Chapter 12.

In a new venture division the activity is technology-enabled but is market-focused and market-driven – where are the opportunities and how can we capitalize on them? Part of the work may be technology-based but the emphasis is on how the product will be delivered to a market and how it will best meet a real market need. This has been one of the real successes of Apple, linking technologies to the needs of customers, particularly in making computers and smartphones easier to use. Whereas R&D departments will undertake most of the technological development work themselves, new venture teams or divisions may outsource, sub-contracting work or even buying in patents and so on where an opportunity related to other organizational core competences is spotted. In this way speed of innovation may be increased.

There are many issues related to R&D management. Because of their fundamental difference from the routine operations of a business, most in-house R&D departments are kept separate. Their productivity depends heavily upon the organizational conditions that encourage creativity (Chapter 13) and the systems that allow their innovations to find their way into the market place. They often face pressure to pursue short-term commercial opportunities. However, the balance between freedom with discipline and integration is a key issue which some firms like Apple and Google are better at achieving than others.

Another issue stems from the fact that there is no predetermined relationship between R&D input and innovation output. Where returns can be identified, they are often long-term. This makes it difficult to decide on the scale of investment in R&D and to evaluate the return received. For example, it has been estimated that it can take 15 years to research and develop a new medicine and cost up to $1.7 billion to get it into production. This has led some organizations to consider outsourcing R&D to smaller firms. A US study (Acs and Audretsch, 1990) found that small firms produce 2.4 times as many innovations per employee as large firms. A UK study (Pavitt et al., 1987) concluded that small firms are more likely to introduce fundamentally new innovations than large firms. However it seems generally accepted that large firms perform better than small firms where resources are important – because of capital intensity or because of scale of spending on R&D, advertising etc. or simply because of barriers to entry. Because of this many companies and whole industries rely heavily on small firms for their R&D activity either by buying or licensing their innovation or buying the company – external corporate venturing, covered in Chapter 11. Pharmaceutical firms have pioneered the outsourcing of innovation. In addition strategic partnerships and alliances are common. For example it has been estimated that 40% of the pharmaceutical giant Astra Zenica's drug pipeline originated outside the company in 2012.

🖰 Case with questions GlaxoSmithKline (GSK)

Organizing R&D

In the 1980s pharmaceutical companies regularly turned in operating margins of 40%. These margins were the norm because the companies were able to extend patents almost at will and charge very high prices for their drugs. A compound could be reformulated with only modest improvements in efficacy but the regulators and courts seemed happy to grant and protect new patents. But things started changing in the 1990s as companies producing generic imitations started to challenge patent extensions and regulators and courts sided with them. By the turn of 2000 over 85% of such patents were being overturned. The result was swift and predictable as generic imitations, often originating from low-cost developing countries, started appearing rapidly in the market. Profits plummeted. At the same time pharmaceutical firms were finding it increasingly difficult to discover pioneering new drugs at anything like the old rate of invention.

GlaxoSmithKline (GSK) may be Britain's biggest drug company, but it was not immune to the winds of change at the turn of the twenty-first century. As profits fell, so too did new drug approvals (two in 2000; one in 2001; three minor ones in 2002). GSK's response was to reorganize how it undertook R&D. It can take 15 years to research and develop a new medicine and cost up to $1.7 billion. The rule of thumb in the industry is that if you spend $1 billion a year on research, you need one new drug approval a year (by the likes of the US Food and Drug Administration) to make an economic return.

GSK reorganized its R&D into groups dedicated to different types of diseases, called Centres of Excellence for Drug Discovery (CEDDs). Areas for research are selected where there are opportunities for new treatments; because there are no medicines, symptoms control can be improved or a disease process is 'ripe' for translation. Early discovery research within CEDDs is conducted in mini-biotechs, called Discovery Performance Units (DPUs). These are small, multi-discipline teams of scientists of between seven and 70, working together and concentrating on one disease mechanism or scientific area. The idea is that each DPU must manage research using commercial criteria and judge its investment decisions by the commercial return they make. Each DPU has to draw up a business plan and bid for funding from a panel called the Discovery Investment Board, made up of senior GSK executives and external specialists with relevant experience in areas such as venture capital and biotech. Funding lasts for up to three years, at which point there is a new bidding round.

Each DPU is responsible for discovering and developing potential new medicines in its particular area and seeing those through to early-stage clinical trials. They are responsible for developing the three-year business plan and managing the agreed budget. They are held accountable for the final deliverables. Late-stage development of potential new medicines is then handed over to Medicines Development Teams (MDTs). Again, these are small units of between six to ten people, responsible for designing and directing potential new medicines through the larger and later stage clinical trials. In 2010 GSK invested almost £4 billion ($2.7 billion) in R&D.

Has this entrepreneurial research environment worked? In 2012 GSK disclosed the results of its last bidding round. Four new DPUs were created and three closed. Of those continuing six received more funding and five suffered a cut. GSK also announced that 15 drugs and vaccines were in the late stages of development, and nine of them had finished clinical trials, three were ready to file with regulators and one had already been filed – Relovair, a replacement for Advair, its former best-selling lung and asthma treatment. More to the point, GSK disclosed that the return on its late-stage pipeline of new drugs rose from 11% to 12% and was projected to rise to 14%.

Alongside its internal research GSK has entered into over 360 research collaborations with universities and academic institutions. Areas of collaboration include research into improving drug discovery, biotechnology, neglected tropical diseases, identifying patient safety issues and rare diseases. GSK also fund basic medical research in academic, charitable and other partner institutions.

Like its competitors, GSK also buys drugs from smaller companies and then uses its marketing power and global distribution network to bring the drugs to a global market place. Indeed GSK employs 42,000 sales and marketing people compared to 15,000 in research and development – a huge investment and a significant competitive advantage. In a critical article about GSKs major rival, Astra Zenica, it was estimated that 40% of Astra's drug pipeline was discovered by scientists outside the company in 2012 (*Sunday Times*, 26 February 2012).

☐ Up-to-date information on GSK can be found on their website: www.gsk.com

QUESTIONS

1 What do you think about GSK's research structures? What are the advantages and disadvantages of this approach?

2 Why is GSK also relying on collaborations and smaller companies to provide it with new medicines?

3 Is its overall strategy sensible?

Successful corporate venturing

Corporate venturing is about regenerating an organization by giving it new competences. Internally, it can manifest itself in various degrees through the structures outlined in this chapter. Not surprisingly, the success of internal corporate venturing does seem to vary from company to company, depending on the conditions encountered. However, it is difficult to assess, not least because of problems of financial measurement. Tidd and Bessant (2009) claim that on average around of half of all new ventures survive to become operating divisions and will typically achieve profitability within two to three years, with almost half profitable within six years. They also suggest that it is a less risky strategy for diversification than the acquisition or merger strategies discussed in Chapter 11. They go on to say that four factors characterize firms that are consistently successful at internal corporate venturing. These firms:

▷ View venturing as a learning process, learning from both success and failure;
▷ Distinguish between bad decisions and bad luck in failed ventures;
▷ Set agreed milestones in advance and check progress regularly, redirecting as necessary;
▷ Are willing to terminate the venture when necessary, rather than making further investments.

They claim that the two main reasons for failure are 'strategic reversal' – when the timescales for the new venture conflict with those of the existing business – and the 'emergency trap' – where internal politicking undermines the venture. To minimize the possibility of both the venture needs to have a clear purpose and a clear time for delivering against agreed milestones, as well as the operational characteristics outlined in this chapter. The failure of the parent company to define and articulate the role of the venture in this way will just lead to conflict. Indeed, without it the appropriate structure for the venture cannot be selected.

Internal corporate venturing is just one of a number of tools managers have to help in the task of corporate renewal. Strategic alliances/partnerships and joint ventures (Chapter 6) and external corporate venturing through acquisitions (Chapter 11) are others. The appropriateness of each of these tools depends on how far the parent company is straying from its core competences, and in particular how far it is straying from its existing products and markets. Figure 8.2 shows how these tools might be best used in connection to new product and market development. Strategic

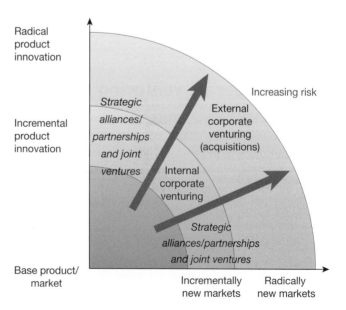

F 8.2 Corporate venturing and other forms of corporate renewal

alliances/partnerships and joint ventures are particularly valuable when the partners have complementary capabilities to each other, facilitating the development of new products or markets. For the partnership to work each partner must have strengths related either to the product or market development being undertaken and be complementary to the other partner. The degree of relatedness of new products or markets will often determine how far a company is able to move into new products and markets on its own through internal corporate venturing, causing it, in some instances, to have to resort to external corporate venturing. In reality these are not alternatives and many companies use all three tools to push the envelope of innovation out as far as possible. We shall return to this concept in Chapter 12 when we consider the risks involved in innovation.

Internal corporate venturing, particularly through intrapreneurship, is almost a day-to-day part of corporate entrepreneurship. It is a vital part of how an entrepreneurial organization needs to function. It is part of how the innovations that it generates need to be managed into the market place. Successfully executed, it helps generate the innovations that, over time, will redefine the core competences and capabilities of the organization, helping it to re-invigorate or reposition, even re-invent itself.

🗁 Case with questions Nokia

Encouraging organizational innovation

Nokia has a number of integrated mechanisms and organizations for encouraging, searching for and commercializing innovation. It has a traditional research centre, *Nokia Research Centre*, and its own venturing organization called *Nokia Ventures Organization* which seeks out internal and external opportunities. Finally it has three corporate venturing arms: *Nokia Venture Partners*, *Nokia Innovent*, and *Nokia Growth Partners*.

Nokia Ventures Organization has as its mission 'the renewal of Nokia'. Nokia's venturing activities have created independent businesses, contributed to the growth and profitability of core business, provided financial returns in their own right and provided intangible assets and insights. It approaches its mission from two directions. Firstly it tries to identify broad opportunities based upon industry analysis and developing new ventures from Nokia employees' ideas as well as those from external sources. Nokia has an annual Venture Challenge ideas campaign for employees. But it also collects ideas from a broad network that extends beyond Nokia and includes external research centres, academics, business partners and entrepreneurs. In collaboration with other Nokia units it systematically scans emerging trends and disruptions from the perspectives of technology, business and users to spot opportunities.

The *Nokia Research Centre* explores new concepts, applications and technologies. On the one hand the Centre develops disruptive technologies that

➞

go beyond the current state of the art and on the other hand it supports the locally-based product development units with technological expertise.

The business units fund the majority of the research undertaken by the Centre. In both cases the Centre helps develop new business/venture ideas. Ideas are collected and evaluated by New Business Development teams across Nokia. New business cases are developed for the most promising ideas and, where appropriate, these are developed further in incubation units of the business unit where the objectives and competences best match the scope of the idea and the resources needed to develop it. Projects where the business case is not yet clear or where there are many opportunities to be explored continue to be incubated in the Research Centre's incubator unit. Later, when the business case is clear, they are transferred to *Nokia Ventures Organization*.

If the technology to support the business idea has not yet been developed, *Nokia Ventures Organization* will commission technology research and development from the Research Centre or outside partners. Nokia uses the same venturing process throughout the organization. The process ensures essential services and tools are available, facilitating the whole venturing process. Support includes personal guidance, dedicated resources, business planning and technology validation. A series of milestone reviews ensure projects move along.

Details of the three corporate venturing arms are:

▷ *Nokia Venture Partners* offers seed finance for early-stage business ideas to both internal and external ventures. It also offers support on legal, communications and human resources issues. Technology experts from the Research Centre also support Venture Partners in evaluating technologies that may become investment opportunities.
▷ *Nokia Innovent* is the early-stage development team focusing only on external opportunities.
▷ *Nokia Growth Partners* invests in mid- to late-stage mobile technology companies. It also provides external funding only and focuses on Nokia's broad vision of 'Life Goes Mobile'.

Examples of Nokia's innovations coming through this integrated network include:

▷ *Nokia One Mobile Connectivity Service* – This offers corporate employees easy and secure access to mobile email, calendar, directory, contacts and mission-critical corporate applications from a mobile phone.
▷ *Nokia Mobile RFID Kit* – This Radio Frequency Identification (RFID) Kit integrates reader technology with the phone and allows mobile phones to be used to access data and initiate familiar mobile phone functions simply by touching a smart object with the phone. It is designed for use by security and maintenance service personnel.
▷ *Nokia Lifeblog* – This is a PC and mobile phone software combination that allows you to keep a real-time multimedia diary – text, photos, videos, text messages – with clear chronology.

☐ Up-to-date information on Nokia can be found on their website: www.nokia.com

QUESTIONS

1 What do you think of this integrated approach to encouraging, searching for and commercializing innovation? What are the advantages and disadvantages of this approach?

2 What category of corporate entrepreneurship does this fall into?

3 Compare and contrast this approach to that of 3M.

📁 Case with questions Nokia and Microsoft

Strategic partnerships

In February 2011, a brutally frank memo from the new CEO of Nokia, Stephen Elop, described a company in crisis – 'The first iPhone shipped in 2007, and we still do not have a product that matches the first iPhone ... Android came on the scene just over two years ago, and this week they took our leadership position in smartphone volumes'. Nokia's market share of the smartphone market actually fell by 10% in 2010. It struggled to compete both at the top end of the market with Apple, Samsung or HTC, but it also failed to compete at the bottom, price-sensitive end with ZTE or Huawei. The perception was that, whilst Nokia were good at producing hardware, they were bad at producing the increasingly sophisticated software that really makes a smartphone desirable. Their Symbian operating system which underpinned their MeeGo phones, was simply not good enough. So what should a company that spent $4 billion on R&D in 2010, and in the past had prided itself on its ability to innovate, do?

The clues might have come from the fact that a new CEO had just been appointed and his previous employer was Microsoft. Within a couple of months of joining he announced that Nokia was to drop its Symbian operating system (although still continuing to offer it as a 'franchise partner') and embark on a 'broad strategic partnership' with Microsoft that would allow it to offer Windows Phone OS smartphone operating system on its top-end smartphones. The two companies would work together on marketing and develop a common road-map to bring their products together. Bing, Microsoft's search engine, would be integrated onto Nokia phones and the Windows Phone 7, launched late in 2010, would be offered by Nokia by 2012. The strategic partnership signalled an enormous strategic shift within Nokia away from its long-standing practice of developing its own software and resulted in cuts to the R&D budget with significant redundancies. The market reaction was overwhelmingly positive, saying the partnership would result in a viable, attractive competitor to the Apple iPhone and Android systems offered by Google.

So why did Nokia and Microsoft decide to become partners? From Nokia's viewpoint it was losing market share rapidly without a smartphone product offering on the horizon, despite its enormous R&D investment. Although swift action was needed, it could have decided to adopt the established Android system, developed by Google. However, this would have made the all-important operating system of Nokia phones identical to that of a number of other producers, commoditizing the product, increasing competition and driving down prices. Also Nokia would have been very much the junior partner in a link-up with Google. By entering into a partnership and adopting the new Windows Phone 7, Nokia grabbed the opportunity to differentiate itself, even if the system offered fewer Apps and needed further development.

There was also value in the partnership for Microsoft, indeed, arguably, prior to the deal both firms were seen as in decline. At 3%, Microsoft had a very low market share of the mobile phone market and were not benefiting from scale economies. The mobile market was broadly seen as the most

→

significant future growth sector. Nokia offered Microsoft the opportunity to gain access to the market with a company that had complementary rather than competing competences. Nokia would contribute expertise on hardware design, language support and help bring Windows Phone 7 to a larger range of price points, market segments and geographical markets. There were other benefits and Nokia Maps became a core part of Microsoft's mapping services and was integrated into Microsoft's Bing search engine and adCentre advertising platform.

We shall never know the role the incoming CEO of Nokia, Stephen Elop, who was previously with Microsoft, really played in brokering the deal. Furthermore, the fight-back is not going to be easy. Smartphone sales continued to fall into 2012, resulting in a second-quarter loss of £1.1 billion. However, by this stage all three major credit rating agencies had cut Nokia bonds to 'junk' status. Despite the fact that sales of the new Lumia smartphone, which uses Microsoft's Windows software, were as forecast, Nokia's reaction to these results was dramatic; it halved the price of its flagship Lumia 900 smartphone in the US. Later in the year it unveiled its new Lumia 920, powered by Microsoft's Windows Phone 8 operating system. This received mixed reviews compared to the iPhone and its Android-based competitors. Only time will tell whether the fight-back started too late.

☐ Visit the company website on: www.nokia.com

QUESTIONS

1 What do Nokia and Microsoft, separately, bring to this partnership? Why is it viable?

2 Under what conditions should a strategic partnership work?

3 Speculate on the role played by Stephen Elop.

Summary

▷ Internal corporate venturing is about generating innovations that, over time, will redefine the core competences and capabilities of the organization, helping it to re-invigorate, reposition, even re-invent itself.

▷ Intrapreneurs push through innovations within larger organizations in an entrepreneurial fashion. Intrapreneurship can also exhibit itself in the form of venture teams. Sometimes entrepreneurial ideas can come from outside the firm, as with **Apple's App Store**.

▷ Intrapreneurs have many of the characteristics of entrepreneurs. They are results-orientated, ambitious, rational, competitive and questioning. They must be adept at handling conflict and the politics of the larger organization in which they operate.

▷ Intrapreneurs are motivated by intrinsic factors, particularly autonomy, purpose and mastery. Autonomy is particularly important because it is the mechanism that allows them to feel they 'own' the project.

▷ The four most significant enablers of intrapreneurship are: senior management support; organizational architecture; resources (including time); and tolerance of risk-taking. Without these, intrapreneurship will not flourish. As at **Boeing**, intrapreneurship can be encouraged in an organization by giving it the facilities it needs to develop.

▷ What to do with new developments depends on how strategically important and how operationally related they are to the business. The more important the development and the more operationally related it is, the more likely it is to be kept in-house. The less important and less operationally important, the more likely it is to be spun out.

▷ New venture divisions like **Xerox Technology Ventures** are designed to deal with projects that require further investment before decisions about their future are taken.

▷ Research and development is one step back from a new venture division. However, R&D departments can be more market-focused by adopting entrepreneurial organizational forms, as at **GSK**. **Nokia** have a range of structures to encourage innovation, but recently has had to enter into a strategic partnership with **Microsoft** to kick-start the process.

▷ Internal corporate venturing, strategic alliances/partnership, joint ventures and external corporate venturing through acquisitions are all tools that allow companies to move into new products and new markets, ultimately extending their core competences.

Essays and discussion topics

1 Is an intrapreneur the same as an entrepreneur? If not, how are they different?

2 Is it easier to be an intrapreneur or an entrepreneur?

3 Under what conditions might intrapreneurship thrive?

4 How are intrapreneurs motivated?

5 How much autonomy or 'space' does an intrapreneur need?

6 What does an organization need to do to encourage intrapreneurship?

7 What are your motivations to do well in your course?

8 Real entrepreneurs leave an organization to set up their own new venture rather than run one belonging to a big company. Discuss.

9 The number of people leaving to set up their own business is a sign of a real entrepreneurial organization. Discuss.

10 Does there always have to be at least one intrapreneur in a venture team?

11 What are the advantages of having a new venture division? What are the risks?

12 How does a new venture division differ from a R&D department?

13 Why are operational relatedness and strategic importance important determinants of what to do with new ventures?

14 Why should new product/service ideas not simply be integrated into an existing business?

15 Why should a large company want to spin out a new venture with good opportunities?

Exercises and assignments

1 Select a large company spin-out. Research and write up its history and describe its success or failure. What lessons are to be learnt from this?

References

Acs, Z.J. and Audretsch, D.B. (1990), *Innovation and Small Firms*, Cambridge, MA: MIT Press.

Antoncic, B. and Hisrich, R.D. (2003), 'Clarifying the Intrapreneurship Concept', *Journal of Small Business and Enterprise Development*, 10(1).

Antoncic, B. and Hisrich, R.D. (2004) 'Corporate Entrepreneurship Contingencies and Organizational Wealth Creation', *Journal of Management Development*, 23(6).

Bergelman, R.A. (1984a) 'Designs for Corporate Entrepreneurship in Established Firms', *California Management Review*, 16(3).

Bergelman, R.A. (1984b) 'Managing the Internal Corporate Venturing Process', *Sloan Management Review*, Winter.

Christensen, K.S. (1985) 'Enabling Intrapreneurship: The Case of a Knowledge-Intensive Industrial Company', *European Journal of Innovation Management*, 8(3).

Cohen, A.R. and Bradford, D. (1991) *Influence without Authority*, New York: Wiley.

David, B.L. (1994) 'How Internal Venture Groups Innovate', *Research Technology Management*, March–April.

Drucker, P. (1985) *Innovation and Entrepreneurship*, London: Heinemann.

Galloway, L. (2006) 'Identifying Intrapreneurship in Organizations: A Human Resources Study', presented at Institute for Small Business and Entrepreneurship conference, Cardiff.

Garvin, D.A. (1983) 'Spin-offs and New Firm Formation Process', *California Management Review*, 25(2).

Hisrich, R.D. (1990) 'Entrepreneurship/ Intrapreneurship', *American Psychologist*, 45(2).

Hornsby, J.S., Kuratko, D.F. and Zahra, S.A. (2002) 'Middle Managers' Perception of the Internal Environment for Corporate Entrepreneurship: Assessing a Measurement Scale', *Journal of Business Venturing*, 17(2).

Hornsby, J.S., Naffziger, D.W., Kuratko, D.F. and Montagno, R.V. (1993) 'An Interactive Model of the Corporate Entrepreneurship Process', *Entrepreneurship, Theory and Practice*, 17(2).

Ito, K. (1995) 'Japanese Spin-offs and New Firm Formation Process', *California Management Review*, 25(2).

Kanter, R.M. (2004) 'The Middle Manager as Innovator', *Harvard Business Review*, 82(7/8).

Kuratko, D.F., Montagno, R.V. and Hornsby, J.S. (1990) 'Developing an Intrapreneurial Assessment Instrument for an Effective Corporate Entrepreneurial Environment', *Strategic Management Journal*, 11(1).

MacMillan, I.C., Block, Z. and Narashima, P.N.S. (1986) 'Corporate Venturing: Alternatives, Obstacles Encountered, and Experience Effects', *Journal of Business Venturing*, 1(2).

Maletz, M.C. and Nohria, N. (2001) 'Managing in the Whitespace', *Harvard Business Review*, 2/01.

Morris, H.M. and Kuratko, D.F. (2002) *Corporate Entrepreneurship*, Fort Worth: Harcourt College Publishers.

Pavitt, K., Robinson, M. and Townsend, J. (1987) 'The Size Distribution of Innovating Firms in the UK: 1945–1983', *Journal of Industrial Economics*, 45.

Pierce, J.L., Kovosta, T. and Dirks, K.T. (2001) 'Towards a Theory of Psychological Ownership in Organizations', *Academy of Management Review*, 26(2).

Pinchot, G.H. (1985) *Intrapreneurship*, New York: Harper & Row.

Pinchot, G.H. (1987) 'Innovation through Intrapreneuring', *Research Management*, 13(2).

Pink, D. (2011) *Drive: The Surprising Truth about what Motivates us*, New York: Riverhead.

Reich, R. (1987) 'Entrepreneurship Reconsidered: The Team As Hero', *Harvard Business Review*, 65(3), May/June.

Ross J. (1987) 'Intrapreneurship and Corporate Culture', *Industrial Management*, 29(1).

Ross, J.E. and Unwalla, D. (1986) 'Who is an Intrapreneur?', *Personnel*, 63(12).

Sathe, V. (2003) *Corporate Entrepreneurship: Top Managers and New Business Creation*, Cambridge: Cambridge University Press.

Stopford, J.M. and Baden-Fuller, C.W.F. (1994) 'Creating Corporate Entrepreneurship', *Strategic Management Journal*, 15(7).

Tidd, J. and Bessant, J. (2009) *Managing Innovation: Integrating Technological, Market and Organizational Change*, Chichester: John Wiley.

Part 4
Strategy

Chapter 9

Developing strategy

Learning outcomes

By the end of this chapter you should be able to:

▷ Critically analyze the nature of strategy development and understand how this should be organized for an entrepreneurial organization;

▷ Develop a vision and mission for an organization, understanding the role of ethics and values, and be able to write a mission statement;

▷ Draw up a SWOT analysis and a SLEPT analysis, and be able to undertake scenario planning and futures thinking;

▷ Be able to develop the strategy for an organization, understanding the importance of strategic options and strategic intent;

▷ Be able to incorporate corporate social responsibility (CSR) and environmental sustainability initiatives into corporate strategy;

▷ Critically analyze the role and importance of the board of directors and the skills they need to undertake their job effectively;

▷ Critically evaluate the effectiveness of the board of directors in their role of providing corporate governance.

Distributed strategizing

In many ways how strategy should be developed is the most distinctive feature of an entrepreneurial organization. In Chapter 2 we characterized this approach as developing a strong *vision* that helps to build a *strategic intent* within the organization so that it is continually *strategizing* at all levels, meaning that strategy will often be seen externally as *emergent*. However, there are always *strategic options* that the organization will have thought through and developed. Decision-making is then based upon opportunistic circumstances at the time, meaning that it will often be seen externally as incremental.

There are a number of views about how strategy is developed. Mintzberg et al. (1998) characterize what they call the 'Entrepreneurial School' of strategy as focused 'exclusively on the single leader' – the entrepreneur: 'Under entrepreneurship, key decisions concerning strategy and operations are centralized in the office of the chief executive. Such centralization can ensure that strategic response reflects full knowledge of the operations. It also encourages flexibility and adaptability: only one person need take the initiative.' For them the entrepreneurial school 'stresses the most innate of mental states and process – intuition, judgement, wisdom, experience, insight. This promotes a view of strategy as *perspective*, associated with image and sense of direction, namely *vision*'. The challenge is to ensure that strategy development, like leadership, is distributed rather than centralized and coordinated rather than controlled. It is also to ensure that 'intuition, judgment, wisdom, experience, insight' – which are all part of a learning organization – are captured as part of the culture of the organization.

The 'Positioning School' treats strategy development as a rational, deductive, more deliberate process that can be depicted as a logical sequence of operations. By way of contrast, academics in what is called the 'Process School' (also associated with Mintzberg) would argue that the strategic process is so inextricably interlinked that in order to understand strategy you should look at how it is *actually* developed, rather than how it *ought* to be developed. For them, the process is all and they pour cold water on the Positioning School saying it neither represents the reality of what happens nor is it effective: 'no one has ever developed a strategy through analytical technique. Fed useful information into the strategy-making process: yes. Extrapolated current strategies or copied those of a competitor: yes. But developed a strategy: never' (Mintzberg et al., op. cit.). In a similar way the proponents of effectual reasoning (see Chapter 2) do not recognize the Positioning School of strategy as an approach taken by successful entrepreneurs in growing their organizations (Read et al., 2011).

A number of academics have observed that formalized strategic planning processes have not served companies well. As Foster and Kaplan (2001) say: 'The conventional strategic planning process has failed most corporations ... New ways of conducting a dialogue and conversation among the leaders of the corporation and their inheritors are needed'. This hints at process being important. Indeed, Grant (2003) observes the spreading use of emergence in the strategic planning practices of large firms in recent years – reduced formality, emphasis on performance goals and a focus on direction rather than content – stating that it has its intellectual roots in complexity theory. Quinn et al. (1988) summed up the dilemma between the 'Positioning' and the 'Process' Schools rather well: 'One cannot decide reliably what should be done in a system as complicated as a contemporary organization without a genuine understanding of how the organization really works. In engineering, no student ever questions having to learn physics; in medicine, having to learn anatomy. Imagine an engineering student's hand shooting up in a physics class. "Listen, prof. It's fine to tell us how the atom does work. But what we want to know is how the atom *should* work"'. Which did come first, the chicken or the egg?

So what do these established schools of thought have to contribute to how our entrepreneurial organization might develop strategy? The debate is essentially a false one. Chapter 2 explained how the development of strategy can be *both* deliberate and emergent but at different times and in different circumstances. However, it must always be underpinned by a strong vision or direction – again one that is deliberate but also adaptable. Chapter 2 went on to highlight the need for continuous strategizing at all levels within an entrepreneurial organization. This process must be underpinned by good information flows which should lead to the development of strategic options for evaluation. We have also highlighted the importance of developing a 'learning organization' culture, facilitating information flows and knowledge acquisition. Continuous strategizing encourages the development of 'consensus strategy'. This evolves from the process of learning but is focused by agreement to a common vision and mission. In that sense entrepreneurial strategy can also be both deliberate in overall vision and emergent in how the details of the vision unfold. What is more, strategy development and action can proceed side-by-side, recognizing that the future is not predictable and planning cannot, therefore, be a simple, linear process. Actions (both successful and unsuccessful) feed into strategy development. Decision-making can be incremental and adaptive to maintain maximum flexibility and adaptability. This is needed to capitalize on change and make the most of any commercial opportunities that appear.

This is the typical strategic and decision-making process in an entrepreneurial organization. It is a distributed, decentralized model that is both emergent and, in part, deliberate. It is non-linear and adaptive, even sometimes opportunistic. It is one that learns from good and bad decisions. As highlighted by complexity theory, it is the capacity to self-organize (through identity, information and relationships) that gives direction to these decisions. However, it is one that still emphasizes the importance of the strategic process and therefore offers advantages highlighted by Mintzberg et al. (op. cit.): 'A successful strategy is one that committed people infuse with energy: they make it good by making it real – and perhaps making it themselves.'

The use of strategic frameworks is important when engaged in distributed strategizing. If you are trying to replicate strategizing across an organization, a set of commonly known and understood techniques and processes can help – not least because they generate a common language and mechanism for communication. Strategic frameworks replicate good practice. They ought to be logical and common-sense. They are not in the nature of a scientific discovery. They are, to quote a colleague, 'a glimpse of the blindingly obvious' – something you knew all along but were never quite able to express in that simple way. As John Kay (1998) explains:

'An organizational framework can never be right, or wrong, only helpful or unhelpful. A good organizational framework is minimalist – it is as simple as is consistent with illuminating the issues under discussion – and is memorable ... The organizational framework provides the link from judgement through experience to learning. A valid framework is one which focuses sharply on what the skilled manager, at least instinctively, already knows. He is constantly alive to strengths, weaknesses, opportunities, threats which confront him ... A successful framework formalizes and extends their existing knowledge. For the less practised, an effective framework is one which organizes and develops what would otherwise be disjointed experience.'

Vision and mission

Developing strategy starts with a vision of what you want an organization to become. Your strategy tells you how you will go about achieving the vision. It is the route map for how you get from where you are now to where you want to be.

Chapter 4 highlighted how a leader might go about developing a shared vision for their organization. For them, vision is an essential tool to help motivate staff in the uncertain environment in which the entrepreneurial firm operates. To summarize from this chapter, a vision is a shared mental image of a desired future state – an idea of what the enterprise can become – a new and better world. It should be inspiring and motivating, transcending logic and contractual relationships. It should be emotional rather than analytical, something that touches the heart so that it engages and energizes people. However, it must also be sufficiently realistic and credible to convince people it is attainable and it must resonate with staff.

Visions, then, are aspirational but they can take many forms. They can be intrinsic, directing the organization to do things better in some way, such as improving customer satisfaction or increasing product innovation.

They can be extrinsic, for example, beating the competition. But then what do you do when you have beaten the competition?

Vision is formally communicated through a vision statement or as part of a mission statement. A mission statement is a formal statement of the purpose of the business. It says what the business aims to achieve and how it will achieve it. It is a way of formalizing the vision, articulating how the vision might be achieved. It encourages this analysis, subjecting the vision to scrutiny as to whether it is realistic and achievable. It usually defines the scope of the business by including reference to the product or service (basis for competitive advantage, quality, innovation and so on), customer groups and the benefits they derive, or competitors. This stops the organization straying into markets where they have no competitive advantage, clarifies strategic options and offers guidance for setting objectives. Often it encompasses the values upheld by the organization.

> *'Entrepreneurs have to make their own decisions and follow their vision. They must motivate their team, get them to ignore shaky markets and a possible war and look positively to the future, to keep exploring uncharted territory. To do that they have to subscribe to the entrepreneur's vision ... but they don't necessarily have to agree with it.'*
>
> **Derrick Collin**, founder and managing director of **Brulines Ltd**
> *The Times* 10 October 2001

> *'Where any three people within an organization will give the same answer to a question on the company's mission statement ... that reflects total coherency and a focused workforce.'*
>
> **Gururaj Deshpande**, serial entrepreneur and founder of **Sycamore Networks**
> *Financial Times* 21 February 2000

Any mission statement should be short, snappy and as memorable as possible. However, this can prove difficult, which is why many have to be explained in greater detail. Examples of four mission statements are given below (easyJet, Starbucks, Dell and Google). One particularly memorable one is that of Skype: 'To be destructive but in the cause of making the world a better place' (presumably because of the absence of phone bills). Mission statements do change over time, for example the original Starbucks mission statement was to 'establish Starbucks as the premier purveyor of the finest coffee in the world while maintaining our uncompromising principles while we grow.' It changed when the founder, Howard Schultz, came back to turn around a struggling Starbucks in 2008.

Mission statements can take many forms but Wickham (2001) suggests a generic format:

> (*The company*) aims to use its (*competitive advantage*) to achieve/ maintain (*aspirations*) in providing (*product scope*) which offers (*benefits*) to satisfy the (*needs*) of (*customer scope*). In doing this the company will at all times strive to uphold (*values*).

As a start-up, articulating a vision may be relatively easy. It may also be somewhat limited to the exploitation of one specific opportunity and restricted by the resources available at start-up. As the business grows and the resource base increases, a vision can become more expansive. But building a shared vision with staff is no easy task – it is not about simply going off and writing a vision or mission statement. It needs to be explained and 'sold' to staff by the leader (see Chapter 4). Often, to really resonate, that vision and mission needs to be underpinned by ethical values.

🗀 Case with questions easyJet, Starbucks, Dell and Google

Mission statements

easyJet

easyJet's mission is to provide our customers with safe, good value, point-to-point air services. To effect and to offer a consistent and reliable product and fares appealing to leisure and business markets on a range of European routes. To achieve this we will develop our people and establish lasting relationships with our suppliers.

Starbucks

Starbucks' mission is to inspire and nurture the human spirit – one person, one cup and one neighborhood at a time.

In doing this Starbucks set out six principles of 'how they live that every day':

Our Coffee – It has always been, and will always be, about quality. We're passionate about ethically sourcing the finest coffee beans, roasting them with great care, and improving the lives of people who grow them. We care deeply about all of this; our work is never done.

Our Partners – We're called partners, because it's not just a job, it's our passion. Together, we embrace diversity to create a place where each of us can be ourselves. We always treat each other with respect and dignity. And we hold each other to that standard.

Our Customers – When we are fully engaged, we connect with, laugh with, and uplift the lives of our customers – even if just for a few moments. Of course, it starts with the promise of a perfectly made beverage, but our work goes far beyond that. It's really about human connection.

Our Stores – When our customers feel this sense of belonging, our stores become a haven, a break from the worries outside, a place where you can meet friends. It's about enjoyment at the speed of life – sometimes slow and savored, sometimes faster. Always full of humanity.

Our Neighborhood – Every store is part of a community, and we take our responsibility to be good neighbors seriously. We want to be invited in wherever we do business. We can be a force for positive action – bringing together our partners, customers, and the community to contribute every day. Now we see that our responsibility – and our potential for good – is even larger. The world is looking to Starbucks to set the new standard. We will lead.

Our Shareholders – We know that as we deliver in each of these areas, we enjoy the kind of success that rewards our shareholders. We are fully accountable to get each of these elements right so that Starbucks – and everyone it touches – can endure and thrive.

→

Dell

Dell's mission is to be the most successful computer company in the world at delivering the best computer experience in markets we serve.

In doing so, Dell says it will meet customer expectations of:

▷ Highest quality;

▷ Leading technology;

▷ Competitive pricing;

▷ Individual and company accountability;

▷ Best-in-class service and support;

▷ Flexible customization capability;

▷ Superior corporate citizenship;

▷ Financial stability.

Google

Google's mission is to organize the world's information and make it universally accessible and useful.

In doing so, Google set out ten core principles that guide their actions:

1 *Focus on the user and all else will follow* – Google's aim is 'providing the best user experience possible';

2 *It's best to do one thing really, really well* – Google 'do search', they solve problems and they hope to 'bring the power of search to previously unexplored areas';

3 *Fast is better than slow* – Google aim to make all their applications work as quickly as possible;

4 *Democracy on the web works* – Google search relies on the links posted on websites by millions of individuals to help decide which other sites offer content of value to users;

5 *You don't need to be at your desk to need an answer* – Google have pioneered new technologies for mobile services, from checking email and calendar events to watching videos, as well as different ways to access Google search on phones;

6 *You can make money without doing evil* – Google have four principles that guide their advertising programmes and practices: that ads must be relevant, cannot be 'flashy', must be identified as 'sponsored links' and that search rankings are never manipulated;

7 *There's always more information out there* – Google continue to look into ways to bring all the world's information to people seeking answers;

8 *The need for information crosses all borders* – Google is available in 130 languages, in more than 60 countries and over 180 domain names;

9 *You can be serious without a suit* – Google continue to believe work can be fun and strive to create a culture that encourages and values creativity;

10 *Great just isn't good enough* – Google 'see being great at something as a starting point, not an endpoint.' They want to continually improve what they do.

QUESTIONS

1 Compare and contrast each of the mission statements. How do they compare with Wickham's generic format?

2 What role do the statements added to the mission statements of Starbucks, Dell and Google play?

Values and ethics

Values are the core beliefs upon which the organization is founded. They underpin the vision and the mission of the organization. They set expectations regarding how the organization operates and how it treats people. Often these values have an ethical dimension, and, as we saw in Chapter 5, ethics have underpinned business for many years. Not only do they help to form a strong bond between all the stakeholders in the business, but also using them to underpin the business can make good commercial sense.

The vision and mission of the organization must be consistent with its values. All three go hand-in-hand, one reinforcing the other. In a start-up they reflect the values of the founder. As the organization grows they often develop to represent a wider community but then face the risk of being diluted to the point where they are not clear. Organizations with strong values tend to recruit staff who are able to identify with those values and thus they become reinforced. They also help to create a bond with customers and suppliers alike that can underpin a strong brand identity.

Values are important because they create a constant framework within which to operate in a turbulent, changing environment. As represented in Figure 9.1, whilst strategies and tactics might change rapidly in an entrepreneurial firm, vision and values are enduring. They form the 'road map' that tells everyone in the organization where it is going and how it might get there, even when one route is blocked. Values form part of the cognitive processes that help shape and develop the culture of the organization. They guide strategy and help delegate authority – telling people the 'right' thing to do. They underpin the dominant logic of the organization. Shared values form a bond that binds the organization together – aligning and motivating people. They help develop a high-trust culture that cements long-term relationships.

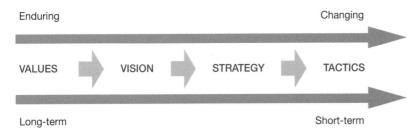

F 9.1 Values, vision, strategies and tactics

Nonaka (1991) recommends the use of language, metaphor and analogy in promoting values, which he sees as promoting the special capabilities of the organization that enable resources to be leveraged internally, thereby creating competitive advantage. But leaders articulate values not only with words but also by 'walking the talk' – practising what they preach. It therefore follows that it is very difficult to pretend to have values that are not real – you'll be caught out when you fail to practise them. Values are not negotiable and need to be reinforced through recognition of staff and reward. They need to be embedded in the systems and procedures of the organization, so that everybody can see clearly that the organization means what it says.

🗁 Case insights Lush and Dell

Corporate values

Lush

Lush is a successful UK high street retailer selling cosmetics from bright, inviting shop fronts that emanate a distinctive, honeyed smell. It is still a privately-owned, family company founded by a husband and wife team, Mark and Mo Constantine, and now has over 600 outlets and sales in excess of £240 million. Like most cosmetic firms, it trades in images and dreams but its founders have some strong ethical beliefs that are reflected in their lifestyle and the values of the company:

▷ We believe in buying ingredients only from companies that do not commission tests on animals and in testing our products on humans.
▷ We invent our own products and fragrances, we make them fresh by hand using little or no preservative or packaging, using only vegetarian ingredients and tell you when they were made.
▷ We believe in happy people making happy soap, putting our faces on our products and making our mums proud.
▷ We believe in long candlelit baths, sharing showers, massage, filling the world with perfume and in the right to make mistakes, lose everything and start again.
▷ We believe our products are good value, that we should make a profit and that the customer is always right.
▷ We also believe words like 'Fresh' and 'Organic' have an honest meaning beyond marketing.

☐ Up to date information on Lush can be found on their website: www.lush.co.uk

Dell

Dell calls its corporate philosophy the 'Soul of Dell'. The core elements are:

▷ *Customers* We believe in creating loyal customers by providing a superior experience at a greater value. We are committed to direct relationships, providing the best products and services based on standards-based technology, and outperforming the competition with value and a superior customer experience.
▷ *The Dell Team* We believe our continued success lies in teamwork and the opportunity each team member has to learn, develop and grow. We are committed to being a meritocracy, and to developing, retaining and attracting the best people, reflective of our worldwide marketplace.

▷ *Direct Relationships* We believe in being direct in all we do. We are committed to behaving ethically: responding to customer needs in a timely and reasonable manner; fostering open communications and building effective relationships with customers, partners, suppliers and each other; and operating without inefficient hierarchy and bureaucracy.

▷ *Global Citizenship* We believe in participating responsibly in the global marketplace. We are committed to understanding and respecting laws, values and cultures wherever we do business; profitably growing in all markets; promoting a healthy business climate globally; and contributing positively in every community we call home, both personally and organizationally.

▷ *Winning* We have a passion for winning in everything we do. We are committed to operational excellence, superior customer experience, leading in the global markets we serve, being known as a great place to work, and providing superior shareholder value over time.

Developing strategic intent

Ohmae (2005) used the Japanese word *kosoryoku* to describe what is needed to develop strategy in the new age of uncertainty. He explained that it meant something that combined 'vision' with the notion of 'concept' and 'imagination'. However, unlike imagination, it has no sense of daydreaming, rather an ability to see what is invisible and shape the future so that the vision succeeds: 'It is the product of imagination based on realistic understanding of what the shape of the oncoming world is and, pragmatically, the areas of business that you can capture successfully because you have the means of realizing the vision.'

However, just sometimes the vision for an organization does not match the resources it commands. This is called a 'strategy misfit' – where there does not appear to be a logical and systematic way that the vision can be realized. Nevertheless we know that many start-ups have managed to realize visions that appeared unrealistic. Hamel and Prahalad (1994) studied firms that had successfully challenged established big companies in a range of industries. They said that to reconcile this lack of fit between aspirations and resources the successful firms used 'strategic intent'. This necessitates developing a common vision about the future, aligning staff behaviour with a common purpose and delegating and decentralizing decision-making – all consistent with what we have called the entrepreneurial architecture.

Hamel and Prahalad (op. cit.) argued that 'the challengers had succeeded in creating entirely new forms of competitive advantage and dramatically rewriting the rules of engagement.' They were daring to be different by challenging market paradigms. Managers in these firms imagined new products, services and even entire industries that did not exist and then went on to create them. They were not just benchmarking and analyzing competition, they were creating new market places that they could dominate because it was a market place of their own making. Some years later, Kim and Mauborgne (2005) looked at this approach to strategy and popularized it with the term 'Blue Ocean strategy', whereby 'creators of blue oceans never used competition as their benchmark. Instead they made it irrelevant by creating a leap in value for both buyers and the company itself … the strategic aim is to create new rules of the game by breaking the existing value/cost trade-off and thereby creating a blue ocean.'

Hamel and Prahalad (op. cit.) claimed that the trick in creating strategic intent is to answer three key questions:

1 What new types of customer benefits should we seek to provide in five, ten, or fifteen years?
2 What new competences will we need to build or acquire in order to offer these benefits?
3 How will we need to reconfigure our customer interface over the next few years?

Whilst these managers may be revolutionaries they must still have their feet firmly on the ground. They must understand very clearly where they start from – the firm's core competences. They must understand the skills and technologies that enable the company to provide these benefits to customers even if they do not (yet) know how they will obtain them. They may also have a view as to how the resources needed can be obtained through partnership with others. They must, however, have a view about the financial losses they are willing to sustain to make the most of these opportunities. Without some grounding in reality, strategic intent is no more than a wish list. Developing strategy is like planning a journey with a road map. It is essentially a three-stage process: deciding where you want to go (vision or strategic intent), understanding where you are, deciding how you can get from where you are to where you want to be. We shall return to strategic intent in the context of introducing disruptive innovation and shifts in market paradigms in Chapter 12.

Developing strategic options

So if strategic intent or vision is important, how might it be developed? A lot of this is down to creative flair and inspiration. However, the strategy toolbox does contain a number of techniques that can help firms to develop their vision of the future.

SLEPT analysis can be a useful aid in thinking about future developments in the wider environment and how they might affect the organization – although not necessarily its position in that environment. The implications of these developments can then be considered and strategic options developed. The analysis looks at the changes that are likely to occur in the areas spelt out by the acronym SLEPT:

Social	Social changes such as an aging population, increasing work participation often from home, 24-hour shopping, increasing crime, increasing participation in higher education, changing employment patterns, increasing number of one-parent families and so on.
Legal	Legal changes such as Health and Safety, changes in employment laws, food hygiene regulations, patent laws and so on.
Economic	Economic changes such as recession, growth, changes in interest rates, inflation, employment, currency fluctuations and so on.
Political	Political changes like local or central government elections, political initiatives, for example on price competitiveness, new or changed taxes, merger and take-over policy and so on.
Technological	Technological developments such as increasing internet bandwidth, the coming together of internet technologies, increasing use of computers and chip technology, increasing use of mobile phones, increasing use of surveillance cameras and so on.

The trick is to brainstorm (see Chapter 13) and think outside the square about how these developments might affect the business. Take the internet as an example. The ability to download films and music has questioned the viability of shops selling DVDs and CDs, but created opportunities for any devices and/or services linked to the internet. The development of internet shopping generally might cause developers to rethink the purpose and structure of our town centres. It might cause individual shops to re-engineer the way they meet customer needs – most shops have websites and many offer internet shopping alongside conventional shopping. The development of cheap teleconferencing via the internet might be seen as a threat to those

'The swift rise of new communication channels such as Facebook and Twitter have caused many executives to reassess how they stay in touch with their customers, employees and, increasingly, with the media itself. People no longer want to be sold to; they want companies to help them find an informed way to buy the right product or service at the right price. They will watch ads, but often online rather than on TV, and they're much more likely to view ads that friends have recommended. When something goes wrong with a product, they want to be able to reach the company instantly and get a quick solution. How companies adapt to this energetic and sometimes chaotic world will define their future success. The website, Facebook page, blog and Twitter feed are no longer add-ons to a business's communication budget. They should be central to its marketing strategy, and used in coordination with other marketing efforts.'

Richard Branson, http://www.entrepreneur.com/article/218098, 8 February 2011

firms providing business travel over long distances, such as airlines. And new social media have enormous implications for how customer communications might be developed in the future.

Grant (2010) lists the 'massive' commercial opportunities coming out of the 'new networked, big-government economy struggling to save the ecosystem' as: 'water supply systems, waste management, high-speed rail systems, alternative energy, next generation wireless services, healthcare and crime prevention'. Schwartz (2003) lists some of the less surprising future shocks such as: the lengthening of the human life span; the changing patterns of migration; the emergence of the military and economic dominance of the USA (or should that now be China and India?); the emergence of unstable nations able to unleash disease, and terror and other forms of disruption. His recipe for companies seeking to cope with this is building better intelligence and information management systems; avoiding denial; and cultivating a sense of timing. He asks the question: 'What processes, practices, and organizations have you actually dismantled in the last year or two? If the answer is none, then perhaps it's time to get some practice in before urgency strikes.'

The key to thinking about the future is not to assume it will necessarily be like the past. Change is now endemic and often discontinuous. As Foster and Kaplan (op. cit.) point out, you cannot even assume that the company will continue to exist, certainly in its present form, let alone customers, competitors and the environment generally. They argue that too many Managing Directors assume the future will be much like the past and what worked before will work again. They cite numerous examples of how this is simply untrue and how failure to recognize this has led to corporate failure. Again this argues for continually questioning the dominant logic of the organization and our own mental models.

Futures thinking is another technique that is often used to think about the future. It follows on easily from a SLEPT analysis. It tries to take a

🗀 Case insight   Monorail Corporation

Company of the future

Monorail Corporation is a virtual organization that could provide a glimpse of the future. Like Dell, it sells computers. Unlike Dell, it owns no factories, warehouses or other assets, operating from a single floor in a leased building in Atlanta, USA. Computers are designed by freelance workers. Customers phone a freephone number connected to the logistics service of Federal Express, which forwards the order to a contract assembler that assembles them from parts supplied by other contract manufacturers. FedEx ships the computer to the customer and sends the invoice to SunTrust Bank, Monorail's agent.

holistic perspective, avoiding a rigid approach to strategic planning that starts from present circumstances. A vision about a desired future state is developed and planning then takes place, backwards from that state to where the organization is at the moment. Current constraints to action are ignored and in this way the barriers to change are identified. Some barriers may indeed prove to be permanent or insurmountable, but many might not be. Objections are therefore outlawed and disbelief suspended at the initial ideas stage. Only later on might options get discarded once the barriers are considered.

One variant to this is to look at a highly undesirable future state and demonstrate how the organization might drift into it unless it takes some radical action. This is a very useful technique for unblocking change in an unresponsive organization. Although its people might not want to change, the state envisaged might be so undesirable and all too easy to drift into, that they are motivated to take the corrective action out of fear.

Scenario planning is a similar tool to futures thinking. It can be valuable for assessing a firm's environment in conditions of high uncertainty over a longer term, say five years or more. With this technique views of possible future situations that might impact on the firm are constructed. The first step is to identify the drivers of change that affect the environment you want to explore and how they interact. Often major trends in the environment are identified from the SLEPT analysis and built into scenarios. Understanding how these drivers interact involves the difficult step of building some sort of model, which in itself aids with understanding the issues. The second step is to develop the scenarios. These situations must be logically consistent possible futures, usually an optimistic, a pessimistic and a 'most likely' future, based around key factors influencing the firm. Optional courses of action or strategies can then be matched to these scenarios. In effect, the scenarios are being used to test the sensitivity of possible strategies. They also allow assumptions about the status quo of the environment in which a firm operates to be challenged. This process involves considerable debate but should create some fundamental insights into assumptions, the interaction of the drivers and their effect on the scenarios. One example of the use of scenario planning would be a company planning overseas expansion. It may be uncertain about factors like exchange-rate fluctuations or tariff barriers and might construct possible futures that help it decide whether to manufacture in the UK and export or to set up a manufacturing base in another country. A real example of the use of scenario planning is given in the case insight into Novo Nordisk.

Scenario planning takes the firm away from the short-term, day-to-day imperatives and helps it think about long-term trends and changes in its environment. Out of these different scenarios strategic options can then be generated as to how the organization will deal with the different possibilities. It allows people to ask the 'what if?' question in a structured way. More and more companies are using this technique as a way of trying to prepare for an increasingly turbulent and unpredictable future. For example, as a result of the economic recession which followed the financial crisis of 2008/9 Lego started using scenario planning as part of its annual budgeting process, allowing it to build contingency plans for each 'crisis' scenario that it identified. In a risky environment scenario planning based upon up-to-date information has a lot to recommend it, and it is a lot cheaper than making mistakes, which is why entrepreneurs intuitively use it to generate their strategic options. The future may be uncertain, which may make it difficult if not impossible to predict, but it cannot be ignored.

The more strategic options that can be identified, the more flexibility the firm has. This lowers the risks it faces. Options are therefore sources of real value to shareholders and ignoring them is a critical flaw in the way the shareholder value model has been applied. So, for example, companies with high financial leverage are likely to have lower cost of capital and higher net profit. But they will also have fewer commercial options in times of economic downturn. Companies and industries that present many options and/or opportunities are more attractive than those with fewer. In the same way, resources that can be used in a number of different ways are more attractive to own, as opposed to rent or buy in, than those with limited use.

📁 Case insight Novo Nordisk – Diabetes and Obesity 2025

Scenario planning

In 2006 Novo Nordisk, the leading provider of diabetes treatments in the world, commissioned the Institute for Alternative Futures to produced four scenarios for what was seen as a looming twin epidemic of diabetes and obesity in the western world. Currently 20.8 million Americans have diabetes. The study estimated that this will more than double to 50 million by 2025 unless action is taken. The scenarios were designed to show the impact of various courses of action: how serious this twin epidemic could become if the West stayed on its current path, to illustrate the range of options available for averting the crisis, and to demonstrate how learning to meet the challenge of diabetes and obesity could play a major role in the evolution of the health-care system. Starting with a scenario that assumed a continuation of the status quo (which would result in 50 million diabetics in the USA by 2025) each of the subsequent scenarios progressively incorporated more diabetes control factors and laid out the consequences of these actions, with the fourth scenario showing the most comprehensive approach to control.

Full details of the scenarios are available on: http://www.altfutures.com/pubs/health/Diabetes_Scenarios_June_1st.pdf, Institute for Alternative Futures, *Diabetes & Obesity 2025: Four Future Scenarios For the Twin Health Epidemics, June 1, 2006.*

And the same applies to capabilities, such as an entrepreneurial architecture, that can be deployed in a number of different ways. These dynamic capabilities are important because they create options and/or opportunities: 'Dynamic capabilities are the organizational and strategic routines by which firms achieve new resource combinations as markets emerge, collide, split, evolve, and die' (Eisenhardt and Martin, 2000). The moral is clear: assume nothing, question everything and think the unthinkable with a view to developing as many strategic options as possible.

Developing strategy

Figure 9.2 sets out a process for how strategy might be developed in a systematic way in an entrepreneurial organization. The strategy literature makes the distinction between business and/or competitive strategy – how the organization competes – and corporate strategy – the scope and structure of the organization. In a multi-business organization, business and/or competitive strategy is determined at the divisional or subsidiary level and corporate strategy at the head office or holding company level.

Vision   Strategy development starts with vision but, at whatever level, strategy should be more than just a wish list driven by a leader's vision. We have already made the point that a vision must be realistic and credible and the leader's job involves developing 'creative tension' by contrasting the vision to the reality of the current situation – so too with strategy. Too little tension produces inertia, too much can create chaos. Even if it is opportunity-driven, to be effective, a strategy must be rooted in the distinctive capabilities of the individual organization at a particular time. However, it should never be constrained by them. Underpinning all of this are the organization's enduring core values and beliefs.

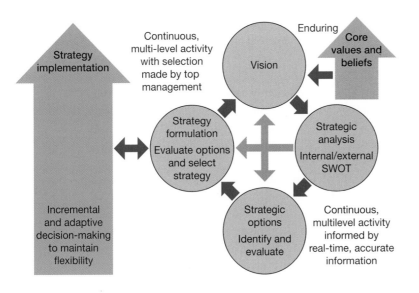

F 9.2 Strategic planning process

Strategic analysis This starts with a thorough understanding of the organization's strengths and weaknesses. It then goes on to contrast this with the opportunities and threats it faces in the environment. This is the classic SWOT analysis (strengths, weaknesses, opportunities and threats) and we shall expand on it in the next section. The process of analysis in an entrepreneurial organization should be a continuous, multilevel activity, informed by real-time, accurate information. It is both emergent and deliberate, combining incremental changes with the occasional radical leap. The vision provides the focus for the analysis of opportunities.

Strategic options The development of strategic options should be a continuous, multilevel activity, informed by real-time, accurate information. Whilst many of these options may come out of the strategic analysis, it is important that they are not constrained by the resources of the organization or the current competitive position in which it finds itself. Often the vision of the organization can generate options that transcend these constraints, but may or may not be realistically attainable. The great entrepreneurs of our time never felt constrained by resources when they set up their businesses.

Strategy formulation A strategy is just a linked pattern of actions and an organization is likely to have a range of strategies linking the development of products/markets with the organization itself. First you identify the strategic options, evaluating each one in terms of fit with the strengths and weaknesses of the organization and finally selecting the most appropriate option. There are some common or generic strategies, particularly in relation to products/markets, that an organization might consider, and there are some strategic frameworks that help identify growth options. We shall return to these in the following chapters. One overarching corporate strategy is likely to be the reinforcement of the organization's entrepreneurial architecture so as to maintain its competitive and innovative edge over rivals. This should ensure that strategy formulation is a continuous process undertaken at many different levels with varying degrees of formality. The 'right' strategies will emerge as part of consultative process but that process should never be sufficiently rigid to inhibit the pursuit of unexpected opportunity. Whilst the vision of the organization informs and influences strategy development, over time it in turn will be influenced by the process it generates.

Strategy implementation Within the overall strategy, day-to-day decision-making will remain incremental and adaptive so as to maintain maximum flexibility in the face of uncertainty. A combination of incremental changes and occasional radical leaps is the best way of achieving a high level of adaptive performance. And remember the entrepreneurial organization has loose control but tight accountability so that managers can make these incremental changes at their discretion. However, strategy implementation also involves leading and managing the process of strategy development, developing the organizational structure and culture to sustain it and planning and allocating resources to make it happen. In fact strategy formulation and implementation are inextricably linked in the hands of a skilled strategist, because the likelihood of the strategy being successfully implemented, given the organizational capabilities, is part of the formulation process. What is more, the process of implementation will feed back on both the analysis and formulation stages, particularly in an entrepreneurial organization. The success or otherwise of implementation will even affect the vision. The whole process is, therefore, an inextricably interlinked and never-ending process – which is where we came into this argument.

Strategic analysis

Strategic tools facilitate strategic analysis, at any level, and are developed throughout this book. They help people to strategize, giving them a framework and the language to approach the task. They might also be used more formally at certain times and less formally at others. They should help us to identify strategic options. In the entrepreneurial firm they should help give direction but should never get in the way of seizing opportunities that present themselves – just so long as they help us towards our ultimate goal. And for the entrepreneurial organization strategy-making is dominated by the active search for new opportunities.

The basic tool of strategic analysis is the SWOT analysis. This seeks to identify an overlap between the business environment and the firm's resources. In other words, a match between the firm's strategic or core competences, capabilities and resources and market opportunities. This match, as such, may not identify *sustainable* competitive advantage. This may be copied by competitors or may change over time. On the other hand, entrepreneurial architecture is likely to produce *sustainable* competitive advantage because this multilevel activity is not easy to copy. Kay (op. cit.) identified three capabilities that he said formed the basis for sustainable competitive advantage, although all three may be viewed as just part of entrepreneurial architecture, as we have defined it:

▷ *Reputation*. This is often encapsulated in brand identity but equally can be communicated through the relationships embedded in the architecture.
▷ *The way the organization innovates*. This is one of the defining characteristics of the organization's entrepreneurial architecture enabling innovation to take place again and again and again.
▷ *The organization's strategic assets*. These are the ones that competitors do not have access to. However, the most valuable is likely to be its entrepreneurial architecture.

The secret to success, therefore, starts with identifying this unique set of competences and capabilities. This portfolio of resources can be combined in various ways to meet opportunities or threats. They could, for example, allow a firm to diversify into new markets by re-applying and reconfiguring what it does best. The whole process of strategic analysis is an art rather than a science. There is no prescriptive approach. To undertake a SWOT analysis brutal honesty is required. That means not pretending that something is a core competence when really it is not. And it means listening to people with different opinions and judging what is the prevailing wisdom in the organization.

The chief proponents of this approach are Prahalad and Hamel (1990). They see core competence as the 'collective learning of the organization, especially how to coordinate diverse production skills and integrate multiple streams of technology ... [through] communication, involvement, and a deep commitment to work across organizational boundaries ... Competences are the glue that binds existing businesses. They are also the engine for new business development.' They suggest that there are three tests which can be applied to identify core competences:

1 They provide potential access to a wide variety of markets rather than generating competitive advantage only in one.
2 They make 'a significant contribution to the perceived customer benefits of the end-product' – they add value.
3 They are difficult for competitors to copy. Products are easier to copy than processes.

The SWOT analysis is also the basis for undertaking customer analysis and deciding on market segmentation. It informs marketing strategy but equally must be interpreted in the context of a particular market, taking into account both customers and competitors. Strengths can be transformed into weaknesses in a different market and vice versa. The market context is crucial. Thus a SWOT analysis on the fast-food chain McDonald's in the context of the US market would yield completely different results from one undertaken in the context of the market in a developing country. In a developing economy it will still be a novel product in high demand. Most opportunities also carry associated threats. Threats may be classified according to their seriousness and probability of occurrence. A view of the overall attractiveness of a market is based upon the opportunities it offers balanced by the threats that it poses. In making this judgement it is often useful to list the factors that are critical to the success of the venture, understanding whether you control or can influence them.

When it comes to existing business, Treacy and Wiersema (1995) pose five questions about the status quo that need to be answered honestly:

1 What are the dimensions of value that customers care about? They claim there are only three value disciplines but each can be described

in more detail through the critical success factors associated with delivering them:

▷ *Operational excellence: a good product/market offering (e.g. McDonald's or Dell)*
▷ *Product leadership: the best quality, most innovative product (e.g. Dyson or Rolls-Royce)*
▷ *Customer intimacy: understanding and developing relationships with customers (e.g. Lush , Dell)*

2 For each dimension, what proportion of customers focus on it as their primary or dominant decision criterion?
3 Which competitors provide the best value in each of these value dimensions?
4 How does your firm compare to the competition on each dimension?
5 Why does your firm fall short of the value leaders in each dimension of value and how can this be remedied?

Figure 9.3 shows a simple pro-forma for capturing this information. The value drivers, which are the critical success factors (CSFs), are listed. Their relative importance is expressed in percentages and their absolute scores are out of 10 (highest). A comparison of simple scores with competitors gives an informative map of different strategies (measured by CSFs) being adopted in the market place. The percentage importance can also be used as a weighting factor to apply to the absolute score for each CSF and these can be added together so as to arrive at an overall, weighted score out of 10.

From the answers to Treacy and Wiersema's questions realistic options can be listed and choices made about existing products/services in relation to both existing and new markets. But, once again, honesty is essential because this means being realistic about the options even if some of them are not very pleasant. For example, if Dell's direct relationship with customers (allowing them to configure their own computers) is of higher value than its product/market offering, why should it not sell other digital consumer electronics and office automation equipment directly rather than just computers? Indeed it has already started doing so. And why should it

Value Drivers: Critical success factors (CSFs)	Importance (%)	Score (1-10)	Wtd. score	Competitor 1 Raw	Competitor 1 Wtd.	Competitor 2 Raw	Competitor 2 Wtd.	Competitor 3 Raw	Competitor 3 Wtd.
1.									
2.									
3.									
4.									
5.									
Total weighted (Wtd.) score									

F 9.3 Competitive performance

not subcontract more of its assembly, focusing rather on the core strength that the customer values – the direct relationship? Again this is something it has started doing. This raises many questions about the scope of Dell's activities and the nature of its business domain. But this is nothing new. Amazon moved from the virtual sale of physical products produced by other people (books, CDs, DVDs etc.) to the virtual sale of virtual items (eBooks and music). It also sells its own brand of eReaders on which to read eBooks and listen to music.

All of this reminds us of Ohmae's (op. cit.) word '*kosoryoku*' and that we need to be quite open-minded about the business domain an organization occupies early in the early stage of strategy development. The SWOT analysis will provide clues about the opportunities emerging for new product/service development on an incremental basis and how they might be pursued. However, it may not provide clues about completely new, disruptive innovations or the shifts in market paradigms, discussed earlier. These 'blue water' opportunities may well require a completely different set of competences, capabilities and resources from those already employed by the organization. But this does not necessarily mean that an organization cannot acquire them. We shall return to this in Chapters 12 and 13.

Ethics and corporate social responsibility (CSR)

Ethics underpin the values and vision for an organization, helping to create its culture and providing the cement that binds it together. Recently this whole area has been formally subsumed within what is called corporate social responsibility (CSR), which includes the whole area of environmental sustainability. Social responsibility is to do with the moral and ethical dimensions of an activity and its effects on society as a whole. Sustainability is broadly to do with our ability to continue into the long term. More and more companies are engaging seriously in CSR, with over 500 in the UK issuing annual CSR reports on their performance and CSR featuring increasingly in the process of strategy development.

It is now widely accepted that many business practices can have negative social and environmental side effects. Growing pressures are leading firms to give careful consideration to CSR and how it might contribute to the sustainability of competitive advantage and growth of the organization. These pressures come from:

▷ *Environmentalists* – who see companies rapidly using up the valuable but limited resources of the planet and at the same time contributing to global warming, which may ultimately cause the destruction of the planet. Green issues and the corporate 'carbon footprint' are rapidly becoming the most important issues facing business today.

▷ *Social reformers* – who see companies behaving in ways that they object to, for example, by 'exploiting' cheap labour in developing countries or providing poor working conditions. Trade unions and consumer groups have both focused on social issues in the past, often with the result that legislation limiting the activity of companies has been enacted (e.g. the minimum wage in Europe).

▷ *Social activists* – who see companies as having a broader social role in the community beyond the boundaries of the working environment. Corporate citizenship programmes, in which employees undertake charitable work in the community, for example, have become fashionable for many companies, whilst others like Lush and Timberland have practised this for years.

▷ *Ethical activists* – who see companies (such as Enron) behaving in ways which are ethically unacceptable, usually by trying to mislead stakeholders. There is, of course, an overlap here with the agendas of the other groups. Nevertheless, business ethics has risen up the agenda of society as a whole and shareholders in particular, and companies are responding.

Much of the CSR literature is highly moralistic in nature, reflecting the idealism of scholars who question the profit maximization objective of companies (Wood, 2000). However there are sound commercial reasons for having a strong CSR policy and organizations can expect three strategic outcomes:

1 Increased sales, brand identity and customer loyalty
Whilst any product must first satisfy the customer's key buying criteria – quality, price and so on – a strong CSR brand can increase sales and customer loyalty by helping to differentiate it (see the Abel & Cole case). Customers are increasingly drawn to brands with a strong CSR profile and CSR has become an element in the continuous process of trying to differentiate one company from another. In 20 developed countries a survey of 20,000 people showed CSR-related factors collectively accounted for 49% of a company's image, compared to 35% for brand image and just 10% for financial management (Environics International, 2001). A strong CSR brand can even create its own market niche for an organization. For example, the Co-operative Bank in the UK has a long history of CSR. It has set itself up as an ethical and ecological investor with an investment policy that is the most frequently cited reason that customers choose the bank. It also has been at the forefront of social auditing practices and, since 1997, has produced an independently audited 'Social Report' that measures the impact and identifies improvements the company could make in social responsibility areas.

On the other hand a bad CSR image can damage sales quite severely. The Environics survey (op. cit.) showed that 42% of consumers in North America would punish companies for being socially irresponsible by not buying their product – a factor BP was very concerned about after the Gulf of Mexico oil spill in 2010. This statistic fell to 25% in Europe but collapsed to 8% in Asia where CSR issues are seen as less important.

🗎 Case insight Jordans

Ethics and market positioning

Specialist cereals producer Jordans is a family company tracing its origins back to 1855 with milling and the supply of animal feed. However, when Bill and David Jordan were travelling through California in the late 1960s they encountered wholegrain food and, when they returned to the family mill in the UK, they decided to create all-natural cereals and champion the nutritious benefits of wholegrains. At this time the company switched from producing white to wholemeal flour in the face of fierce price competition from big conglomerates. It also started producing small quantities of oat-based cereals, which it sold to health food stores.

Jordans Cereals was established in 1972 in Biggleswade, UK. Their first organic wholegrain breakfast cereal, 'Crunchy G', became popular, flying in the face of the trend for highly processed foods. By the 1970s health foods had really caught on and Jordans was selling to the supermarkets. Two keys to their growth since then have been product quality and innovation, although to this day wholegrain oats are still at the heart of all their products. Quality, backed with a respected brand identity, has allowed them not to be drawn too far into the vicious food-price wars. All products are made from cereals sourced from selected local farms and grown to high environmental standards, without the use of artificial colours, flavours, preservatives or genetically modified organisms. Innovation has kept them one step ahead of the big-company competition. They were among the first to introduce 'food on the run' cereal bars. They were also one of the first to add freeze-dried fruits to their breakfast cereals, even innovating in the packaging by introducing cellophane bags. They pioneered the introduction of 'conservation grade' ingredients which are cheaper than organically grown cereals but contain few pesticides.

Jordans has also entered the own-brand market and 20% of its £50 million turnover comes from this source. Even here it trades on its 'brand integrity' – its ability to produce tasty and nutritious cereals in an environmentally-friendly way. But it has had to control costs. It is also entering the adult savoury market with its low-fat cereal-based oven-crisped chips. It now plans a major expansion into Europe.

☐ Up-to-date information on Jordan's can be found on their website: www.jordanscereals.co.uk

2 Reduced operating costs and productivity gains

Sustainability is about measuring and controlling inputs and many environmental initiatives therefore reduce costs (e.g. reducing waste and recycling, having better control of building temperatures or reducing use of agrochemicals). Yahoo saved 60% of its electricity costs simply by opening windows where servers are located so as to let out the hot air. General Electric started a programme of becoming more sustainable ('greener') in 2004. By 2008 this initiative had yielded $100 million in cost savings. Waste-reducing cost savings can come from looking at raw materials usage, the manufacturing process, packaging requirements, transport needs, maintenance and the use of disposal methods.

Actions to improve working conditions, lessen environmental impact or increase employee involvement in decision-making can improve productivity. For example, actions to improve work conditions in the supply chain have been seen to lead to decreases in defect rates in merchandise. Many social initiatives can increase employee motivation and cut absenteeism and staff turnover, and an increasing number of graduates take CSR issues into consideration when making employment decisions. And caring for employees pays dividends. According to one newspaper, Southwest Airlines, the only airline in the USA never ever to lay-off employees was the largest domestic airline in the USA in 2010 with a market capitalization of all its domestic competitors combined (Jeffrey Pfeffer, *Newsweek*, 15 February 2010).

> ### Ten guidelines for reducing waste
>
> 1 Carefully design the product to minimize resources so that it can be re-used in a closed-loop system
> 2 Design products so that they can be disassembled easily
> 3 Reduce the use of hazardous inputs
> 4 Switch to non-hazardous manufacturing methods
> 5 Reduce the amount of energy required in manufacturing and use sustainable energy
> 6 Use newer, cleaner technologies
> 7 Use sustainable re-manufactured, recycled or scrap materials in the manufacture
> 8 Improve quality control and process monitoring
> 9 Find ways to get the product returned for disassembly and harvesting of parts
> 10 Reduce packaging or use recycled materials
>
> *Source*: Scott. J. (2010) 'The Sustainable Business', *Global Focus* vol. 4, EFMD.

3 Improved new product development

Focus on CSR issues can lead to new product opportunities. For example, car manufacturers are striving to find alternatives to fossil fuels, whilst developing conventional engines that are more and more economical (see the Ecotricity case). Innovation linked to sustainability often has major systems-level implications, demanding a holistic and integrated approach to innovation management. The commitment of the UK retailer M&S to be completely carbon-neutral by 2012 has required them to completely re-engineer many of their operations, leading to opportunities for specialist suppliers. General Electric's

🗀 Case insight Rolls-Royce and TotalCare

The environment and business model innovation

Air travel is not seen as environmentally friendly and the jet engines that airplanes use are therefore not something that are usually used as examples of sustainable engineering. But Rolls-Royce demonstrates how sustainability can make good environmental and commercial sense. Rolls-Royce's TotalCare programme offers customers the opportunity to use its jet engines rather than own them – and that delivers the opportunity to re-engineer the complete product so as to make it as environmentally neutral as possible and deliver commercial advantage.

It works like this. Instead of buying a jet engine and a service package, Rolls-Royce enters into a contract with the airline based upon a fee for every hour the engine runs. The company then monitors data beamed directly from these engines to determine the need for intervention – servicing or other operational problems. Rolls-Royce services the engine and repairs or replaces it when it breaks down. The airlines are buying a service rather than a product and it is a service known for its quality that effectively 'locks in' customers and gives Rolls-Royce a competitive advantage over competitors.

However, the other side to this is that the company can look to engineer the product so as to minimize total lifetime costs and that can mean factoring in higher quality so as to minimize service and repair time. Because the engines always belong to Rolls-Royce it also means that they can design them so as to maximize the potential for re-use – when one TotalCare programme comes to an end – and, ultimately, recycling when the engines come to the end of their economic life. Around 80% of Rolls-Royce engines are now 'sold' under TotalCare programmes.

sustainability programme yielded 80 new products and services that generated $17 million in revenues between 2004 and 2008. Berkhout and Green (2003) argue for a systems approach to innovation, linking it with sustainable research, policy and management, and concluding that 'greater awareness and interaction between research and management of innovation, environmental management, corporate social responsibility and innovation and environment will prove fruitful'.

One interesting question arising out of the sustainability debate is the concept of ownership. You do not need to own an asset in order to use it. It has been shown that a 'cradle-to-cradle' (or closed loop) system could eliminate waste because assets would be returned to the manufacturer to be re-used, repaired or re-manufactured. Manufacturers may then decide to build in additional costs at any stage so as to reduce the full life costs of the product. This total-life view is not present in the traditional customer/

supplier model, where disposal costs are hidden and there is little incentive to extend life cycles. However, this can be achieved when the supplier retains ownership and the customer rents or leases the asset (see the Rolls-Royce and TotalCare case). Xerox pioneered the leasing of photocopiers in the 1980s, but these days you can lease anything from jet engines to carpet tiles. Interface, which manufactures 40% of all carpet tiles in the world, uses re-processed carpet waste to manufacture its carpet backing. Not only does this produce a better, cheaper product it also reduces energy usage and environmental pollution, as carpets can take up to 20,000 years to decompose.

Not surprisingly, therefore, strong CSR performance seems to be linked to financial performance. A 2002 study showed that the overall financial performance of the 2001 *Business Ethics* Best Citizen companies in the USA was significantly better than that of the remaining companies in the S&P 500 Index (Verschoor, 2002). There is growing awareness that incorporating CSR into mainstream corporate strategy translates into bottom-line performance. In the short term it at least avoids negative consumer or activist publicity, in the medium term it delivers better performance for investors and the community, and in the long term, by encouraging consideration of abiding social and environmental interests, it can give management a broader, long-term perspective on the sustainability of the company's performance.

📁 Case insight Ecotricity

Environmental sustainability

Dale Vince was once a New Age hippie who toured Britain and the Continent in a peace convoy. These days he is better known as a millionaire entrepreneur who owns the fast-growing company, Ecotricity, which he founded in 1995. Ecotricity generates electricity from its wind turbines around the UK, as far apart as Dundee and Somerset, and sells the 'green' energy to domestic and corporate customers, including Sainsbury's, Tesco and Ford. The idea came to Dale on a hill near Stroud in Gloucestershire where his home – a former army lorry – was powered by a small wind turbine. Why not build a full sized permanent wind turbine in the field, he thought?

These days the company is still based in Stroud but employs some 170 'co-workers'. It is very much a family business. Dale's sons Dane, 25, and Sam, 20, work in the office whilst his brother Simon helps design the turbines and his sister, Sharon, deals with customers' inquiries. Ecotricity made a profit of almost £2 million in 2008 and reinvested most of this in renewable energy sources. It has some 90 turbines and supplies about 12% of the UK's on-shore wind energy.

☐ Up-to-date information on Ecotricity can be found on their website: www.ecotricity.co.uk

Certainly companies like Abel & Cole have used CSR as a major plank in their branding. But CSR pre-dates Abel & Cole by over a century. In the UK Cadbury, Wilkin & Sons (maker of Tiptree Jams) and the Co-op are all early examples of businesses with a CSR dimension. Today many large organizations, like the UK retailers Marks & Spencer (M&S) and John Lewis, and the US company IBM and outdoor wear manufacturer Timberland, have extensive CSR programmes ranging from community involvement (staff working on community projects in company time) through to ethical sourcing (from humans and animals) and into environmental issues (such as M&S' objective to become completely carbon neutral). M&S' 100-point 'Plan A' is generally seen as a model for today's socially responsible large companies.

There is also growing investor pressure to implement CSR. The Environics survey showed that over one-quarter of US share-owners bought or sold shares because of a company's social performance and a similar pattern emerged in Britain, Canada, Italy, Canada and France (Environics International, op. cit.). There are now CSR stock market indices, like the *Dow Jones Sustainability Index* and the *FTSE4Good*. Increasingly mainstream investors see CSR as a strategic business issue and raise it in annual meetings. Activist groups also buy shares in targeted companies to give them access to these annual meetings so that they can raise CSR issues.

📖 Case insight   Richard Branson and Virgin Unite

Philanthropy

'I think every business needs a leader that does not forget the massive impact business can have on the world. All business leaders should be thinking 'how can I be a force for good?'

Richard Branson

Virgin Unite is the working arm of The Virgin Foundation, a charitable foundation set up by Richard Branson and the Virgin Group in 2004. Its aim is to 'unite people to tackle tough social and environmental problems with an entrepreneurial approach'. Its overheads are paid for by Branson and Virgin. In 2006 £1.6 million was pledged – all the profits of the Virgin rail and air interests over 10 years – to help tackle climate change. Virgin Unite focuses its efforts in two main areas:

1 Incubating New Global Leadership Models – creating new models to address conflict, climate change and disease. For example, it supports the 'The Elders' group of 10 visionary leaders such as Archbishop Desmond Tutu, and the Carbon War Room, a project to build a low-carbon economy.

2 Mobilizing Business Action – offering consultancy and practical support to make it simple for businesses to become a force for good. For example,

it supports The Branson Centre of Entrepreneurship, encouraging entrepreneurship in South Africa, and the Bhubezi Community Health Care Centre in South Africa

Virgin Unite encourages Virgin's and associated companies' employees to donate time to partner charities and encourages charitable donations. Staff go into charitable organizations to work on projects – anything from revamping the gym at the children's charity Kids Company in south London, to helping the children's charity Rathbone raise its profile for charitable giving. Branson sees Virgin Unite not just as philanthropy but also as a vehicle for improving staff motivation and cohesion. He believes corporate social responsibility should be embedded in everything an organization does:

> 'What I see is demand from our people to be a business that is good, makes a profit, but also does something for the planet and humanity. I think this is a trend we will see more of ... CSR in my mind is defunct now. Compartmentalizing the social responsibility is not the way to go. I think the model for starting employee engagement activities has to be embedded in everything you do.'
>
> Richard Branson, www.hrmagazine.co.uk 13 July 2010

Building CSR into strategic planning

CSR can be integrated into the strategic planning process outlined in Figure 9.2:

Strategic analysis   Firms need to be aware of legislation and should compare themselves to competitors (Epstein and Roy, 2001) and find out about the expectations of external stakeholders (Smith, 2003). Similarly, companies should find out the expectations of their internal stakeholders (Smith, op. cit.) with a view to assessing the adequacy of their organizational capacity – their resources and processes (de Colle and Gonella, 2002; Epstein and Roy, op. cit.). The firm should then be able to assess the fit between the CSR commitments it might aspire to and its central business objectives (Burke and Logsdon, 1996; Smith, op. cit.), which may or may not result in changing the vision and mission for the business.

Strategy formulation   This is usually demonstrated as a list of commitments. According to Smith (op. cit.), this should reflect 'an understanding of whether (and why) greater attention to CSR is warranted by that particular organization.'

Strategy implementation   This requires concrete actions to be undertaken but also it is important to publicize this to internal and external stakeholders to demonstrate commitment and attainment (Burke and Logsdon, op. cit.). These may have to be audited or evaluated (de Colle and

🛍 Case insight **Starbucks**

Environmental mission statement

Starbucks is committed to a role of environmental leadership in all facets of our business:

▷ Understand environmental issues and share information with our partners.
▷ Develop innovative and flexible solutions to bring about change.
▷ Strive to buy, sell and use environmentally friendly products.
▷ Recognize that fiscal responsibility is essential to our environmental future.
▷ Instill environmental responsibility as a corporate value.
▷ Measure and monitor our progress for each project.
▷ Encourage all partners to share in our mission.

Gonella, op. cit.). For example, Starbucks has a Business Ethics and Compliance programme that 'helps protect our culture and our reputation by providing resources that help partners make ethical decisions at work'. It produces awareness material, facilitates legal compliance and ethics training and investigates ethical issues raised with it by staff.

Sustainability and CSR can therefore be integrated into strategy development and the strategic planning process. Indeed they should be at the heart of any growth strategy. CSR encourages a long-term view and reflects the concerns of the society in which the company is embedded. However, it also makes good business sense, providing market and brand opportunities that translate into bottom-line profits. CSR is set to become more important in the future and is likely to be an essential element of strategy for all companies of every size.

🛍 Case with questions **Abel & Cole**

CSR and competitive advantage

Abel & Cole may be the UK's largest organic food delivery company with sales of more than £30 million in 2008 and over 50,000 regular customers, but it did not start out with any CSR credentials. In 1985 Keith Abel was studying history and economics at Leeds University, and selling potatoes door-to-door to make some money. He was a good salesman and that meant he could charge more for the potatoes than the supermarkets. Keith went on to City University, London, to study law. Unfortunately he failed his bar exams and decided he might as well team up with a friend, Paul Cole, and start doing the same thing to make some money – no notion of organic food, just making money. A Devon-based farmer, Bernard Gauvier, approached them to sell his organic potatoes. They cost more, but after a week of selling them Keith realized that nobody asked the price. He decided to investigate the differences between organic and non-organic products, and went to see what his regular supplier was spraying on his potatoes. Keith was 'pretty appalled' at what he saw. The organic idea slowly started to creep into his consciousness and he started to 'push' the organic side of the business – after all he was good at selling, and he was delivering the produce to the door of the customers. They responded by buying more and asking for other things. Bernard persuaded Keith and Paul to start putting together organic vegetable boxes and by 1991 they converted to selling only organic vegetables, buying them directly from farmers. Sales took off in the 1990s and they started to employ people. Unfortunately, whilst sales increased, the result was mounting losses.

By 1999 Abel & Cole had 1500 regular customers but things came to a head when unpaid debts caused the Inland Revenue to threaten them with bankruptcy. Paul decided to leave and set up his own wholesale company, while Keith decided to retake his bar exams – and passed. Then Keith realized that he could not practise law if he was declared bankrupt. Under threat of losing the family house, Keith's father-in-law, Peter Chipparelli, then chairman of Mobil Oil in South America, decided to bail him out. This may have focused Keith's mind because he started taking advice, first from his father-in-law then from social entrepreneur and author of *The Natural Advantage*, Alan Heeks. He brought with him his 22-year-old daughter, Ella, who stayed to do work experience and went on to become Managing Director three years later. She must take a lot of the credit for the success of Abel & Cole.

In 2007 the private equity firm Phoenix Equity Partners bought a stake in Abel & Cole, valuing it at over £40 million. The success of the company is due to the consistency of its marketing mix. Its ethical, eco-conscious profile is assiduously nurtured. Vegetables are organic, local (never air-freighted), seasonal, and ethically farmed. They are delivered in a recycled cardboard box by a yellow bio-fuel van, together with a newsletter which includes lively vegetable biographies and hints on how to deal with

some of the more obscure vegetables in the box. The company prides itself on employing the formerly long-term unemployed and offers them bonuses for cutting waste. It gives to charity. Customers can deposit keys with the company so that vegetable boxes are left safe and sound indoors. Prices are high, but not outrageously so since the 'middle-man' has been cut out of the distribution chain. Customers are middle class and shopping from Abel & Cole is definitely fashionable. The medium- to long-term question is whether these factors will outweigh the need to economize during the protracted recession which started in 2009.

☐ Up-to-date information on Abel and Cole can be found on their website: www.abelandcole.co.uk

QUESTIONS

1 Why and to whom is the product/market offering of Abel & Cole attractive?

2 Undertake a SLEPT analysis for the company. What are the opportunities and risk it faces?

3 What strategies might you consider in order to roll out the company as quickly as possible but with minimum risk?

📇 Case with questions Marks & Spencer (M&S)

CSR in a public company

M&S has always had an ethical dimension. It started offering staff welfare services that provided pensions, subsidized canteens, health and dental services, hairdressing, rest rooms and camping holidays back in the 1930s. In 1999 it published its own code of practice on Global Sourcing as a minimum standard for all suppliers in an effort to improve conditions for workers overseas. Since 2003 M&S has produced a Corporate Social Responsibility Report. In that year it was ranked top retailer and one of the top UK companies in Business and the Communities First Corporate Social Responsibility Index. Stuart Rose took this even further and started

building it into the M&S brand identity. In 2006 the Look Behind the Label marketing campaign was introduced with the aim of highlighting the M&S range of ethical and environmentally friendly policies.

These included:

▷ Fairtrade products – all coffee and tea sold by M&S is Fairtrade and it also offers clothing lines made from Fairtrade Cotton.

▷ Sustainable fishing – M&S sell only fish from sustainable sources.

▷ Healthy foods – M&S has removed 90% of its foods containing hydrogenated fats and oils and has cut salt across its food range.　　　　　　　➡

▷ Support for charities – M&S supports a number of charities. For example at Christmas 2006 it introduced a range of products to support the housing charity Shelter predominantly in the food-to-go range, including a range of seasonal Christmas sandwiches.

▷ Environment friendly – emphasizing the use of environmentally friendly textile dyes and use of environmentally friendly materials for store fit-outs such as flooring made from natural rubber as well as looking to source electricity from environmentally friendly sources.

However, in 2007 M&S went one very significant step further. It launched its 'Plan A', an ambitious 100-point plan to help combat climate change, reduce waste, safeguard natural resources, trade ethically and promote healthier lifestyles. The business-wide action plan will cost £200 million. By 2012, M&S aimed to:

▷ Become carbon neutral – minimizing energy use, maximizing renewables and using offsets as a last resort.

▷ Send no waste to land fill sites – reducing packaging, recycling and re-using materials.

▷ Extend sustainable sourcing – using recycled materials, extending free range and organic food products, only selling fish from sustainable supplies.

▷ Set new standards in ethical trading – leading in labour standards and extending Fairtrade products.

▷ Help customers and employees live healthier lifestyles – through producing healthier foods and extending health and lifestyle support for employees.

The ambitious plan, which was widely welcomed by environmentalists, has transformed the way M&S operates. M&S have set up a Supplier Exchange to share best practice and innovation. The economics of local and ethical sourcing are less straightforward than they might seem. A surprisingly high proportion of a product's vehicle-miles come from shoppers driving to their local store. However, the move back to UK sourcing, at least for food, and the emphasis on identifiable, free range, often organic and fair trade produce undoubtedly hits a chord with many middle-class shoppers – M&S' target market. And the M&S brand claims influence over 2000 factories, 10,000 farms and 250,000 workers, so if the initiative works its influence will be considerable, albeit tiny on a global scale. Becoming more sustainable is not just about philanthropy, it also make good competitive sense – at least for some businesses. Nevertheless, by mid-2012, the turnaround of M&S was far from complete.

☐ Visit M&S' website www.marksandspencer.com to find out more about their CSR activities.

QUESTIONS

1 How embedded within M&S is CSR?

2 What is the role of CSR in the turnaround of M&S?

3 Visit M&S' website to assess the progress of Plan A. How successful has it been?

Corporate governance and the board of directors

The responsibility for overseeing strategy and ensuring its efficacy legally rests with a company's board of directors. They are responsible for the corporate governance of the organization. Corporate entrepreneurship studies have generally neglected the role of corporate governance and the board of directors (Phan et al., 2009). In particular the fear is that corporate entrepreneurship initiatives might fail if systems of corporate governance do not encourage and incentivize management to put in place the complex architecture and to undertake what might be seen as risky, innovative strategies.

The OECD's *Principles of Corporate Governance* (2004) states that the board of directors is responsible for ensuring 'the strategic guidance of the company, the effective monitoring of management ... and the board's accountability to the company and the shareholders.' A board of directors can be elected or appointed. Its legal duties and responsibilities arise out of common law and statute, varying from country to country, and may also be detailed in the bylaws of an organization. Directors have a fiduciary duty to act honestly and in good faith, exercise skill and care and undertake their statutory duty. They must act in the best interests of the company and its shareholders. The broad functions of the board are summarized in Figure 9.4 using the dimensions of inward/outward looking and past/future orientation.

Arguably the prime function of the board is to be outward looking and future orientated – to review and guide corporate strategy and policy. This might include overall strategic planning, approval of strategies or investments in key areas, changes in the scope or nature of operations, major company decisions and so on. They are also responsible for how these translate into internal policies for the organization such as annual budgets, performance objectives, changes in organizational structure, compensation policy for key objectives, risk policy and so on,

The board then monitors performance against these strategies and policies and the ensuing risks it faces as well as compliance with the law. These responsibilities include ensuring the integrity of the company's accounting and financial reporting systems, monitoring and supervising management performance, planning for management succession, providing proper accountability to other stakeholders in the firm, for example, by appointing auditors and approving the annual financial statements, as well as ensuring that the company complies with all aspects of the law.

Whilst establishing corporate strategy and policy may be the most important job for the board, it is unlikely that it will be given the appropriate weighting in terms of time allocation. Most boards spend too much

	Past and present orientation	Future orientation
Outward looking	Provide accountability	Strategy formulation
Inward looking	Monitoring, supervising and corporate governance	Policy-making

F 9.4 Role of the board of directors

time on the other functions, particularly monitoring management performance and legal compliance. Indeed, in the USA, the Sarbanes-Oxley Act
introduced new standards of accountability on US companies listed on
the stock exchange that made directors directly responsible for internal
control, facing large fines and prison sentences in the case of accounting
crimes.

For an entrepreneurial large organization there are two factors that
can make the role of director particularly difficult. First, by definition, the
organization is going to face greater risks than other organizations and
monitoring risk is a prime task of the directors – in both of the dimensions shown in Figure 9.4. Managing risk is a topic covered in Chapters 7
and 11. Secondly, it is likely that the organization will be more complex, not
least because of the structures and sub-structures it might have to adopt
to encourage entrepreneurial behaviour, particularly in
the multi-business organization. Complexity can mean
that information is masked from or late arriving at the
central board of directors. Indeed there is a tension
between the legal requirements for the board of directors
to take responsibility for the actions of the organization
and the overarching aim of corporate entrepreneurship
to push responsibility for decision-making as far down
the organizational hierarchy as possible so as to make it
more responsive to the needs of the market place.

There are numerous examples of boards failing to exercise their duties properly. In many cases the failure goes
hand-in-hand with the Chief Executive being allowed to
take on too much power, particularly in multi-business,
divisionalized companies; for example, Fred Goodwin at
Royal Bank of Scotland and Ken Lay at Enron. It seems
that the Chief Executive, even if they are based at head
office and separate from the day-to-day business, may
not always place the shareholders' interests first. And the
Chairman of the Board does not always exert sufficient counter-weight.
However, probably the loudest criticism of boards of directors in their
role of oversight has been in relation to executive compensation. These
payments have escalated since the 1990s out of all proportion to inflation
or even corporate performance.

One of the problems, particularly in the UK and USA, is that the board
of directors is probably dominated by executive directors – directors
who are also managers in the organization. What is more, sometimes the
Chief Executive is also Chairman of the Board, particularly in the USA,
and here there can be a conflict of interests. So non-executive directors
are vital and separating the role of Chief Executive and Board Chairman
is highly desirable, indeed it is considered good practice in Europe. Most
of the *Financial Times* Stock Exchange (FTSE) companies comply with the

*'We took out the whole board ... we got rid
of the stores chief, the personnel director
and others. We had an exciting battle with
Philip Green but, after it, we reduced the
board to 12 non-executive directors and
three executive directors ... We sit here and
take decisions very fast. Compared to the old
M&S, we've cut out the jaw-jaw. Everything
goes straight down the line. We're supported
by a strong team of divisional heads, but
it's very different from the old M&S ... It's
not about one person, it's about teams of
people. We've got 85,000 in the organization.
They're responsible for our success.'*

Stuart Rose, former CEO **M&S**,
talking about when he joined M&S in 2004
Management Today December 2006

Strategy: Guiding strategic direction	People: Practising 'human' skills
▷ Strategic thinking ▷ Systems thinking ▷ Awareness of external environment ▷ Entrepreneurial thinking ▷ Developing the vision ▷ Initiating change ▷ Championing causes	▷ Communicating ▷ Creating a personal impact ▷ Giving leadership ▷ Promoting development of others ▷ Networking
Culture: Developing organizational culture	Operations: Exercising executive control
▷ Customer focus ▷ Quality focus ▷ Teamwork focus ▷ People resource focus ▷ Organizational learning focus	▷ Governance ▷ Decision-making ▷ Contributing specialist knowledge ▷ Managing performance ▷ Analyzing situations ▷ Initiating change ▷ Awareness of organizational structure

F 9.5 Institute of Management model of board-level competences

recommendation that they have non-executive directors. However, in small unquoted companies the proportion is much smaller. Often non-executive directors are imposed by financial backers to oversee their investment. However, non-executive directors have a valuable role in bringing different skills, an independent and objective perspective and a new network of contacts that can contribute to organizational knowledge and learning. They can also act as an early warning system for potential future difficulties and can be particularly valuable in helping to resolve conflict in family firms.

To help boards develop and operate more effectively, the Institute of Management has published a useful set of best practice checklists based upon a model of board-level competences (Allday, 1997). Twenty-three board-level skills were identified, grouped together under the four key headings shown in Figure 9.5. These generic competences need to be balanced and tailored to particular circumstances and specific functional board roles.

Summary

▷ The strategic process is more of a distinguishing feature of an entrepreneurial organization than the strategies it adopts.

▷ Strategy development can be both emergent and deliberate but continuous, distributed strategizing at all levels is vital so as to develop strategic options. Accurate and speedy information flow is important. Decision-making can be incremental and adaptive so as to maintain maximum flexibility.

▷ A strong vision is essential in order to give direction to this strategizing. The vision should be underpinned by ethics and enduring values.

▷ A vision is a desired future state. It must be credible – acknowledging the tension created by a realistic appraisal of the current situation.

▷ When there is a misfit between aspirations and resources, strategic intent allows managers to bind the organization together, deal with opportunities and threats as they arise and move forward to change the face of the markets they enter.

▷ A mission statement is a statement of purpose, a way of formalizing the vision (**easyJet**, **Starbucks**, **Dell** and **Google**). This is underpinned by values (**Lush** and **Dell**). Some companies have environmental mission statements (**Starbucks**).

▷ SLEPT analysis, scenario planning and futures thinking are techniques that can help develop strategic options.

▷ A strategic framework is useful but a good framework is minimalist. Effective strategy must be rooted in the distinctive capabilities of the firm. The strategic process involves five stages but is a continuous process:

1 Developing vision.
2 Strategic analysis, which involves undertaking a SWOT analysis and highlighting the core competences of the organization.
3 The development of strategic options.
4 Strategy formulation, which involves: identifying, evaluating and selecting strategic options.
5 Strategy implementation, which involves: leading and managing a change process, putting in place the appropriate organization structure and culture and planning and allocating resources.

▷ Corporate strategy emanates from head office or the holding company and business or competitive strategy from the division or subsidiary.

▷ CSR can be at the heart of any strategy. It encourages taking a long-term view and reflects the concerns of society. Many public companies, like **M&S**, have CSR strategies. Others, like **Richard Branson** and **Virgin Unite**, have developed philanthropic activities.

▷ As **Jordans**, **Ecotricity** and **Abel & Cole** have discovered, environmental and sustainability concerns can also make good economic sense, providing market and brand opportunities that translate into bottom-line profits. Companies like **Rolls-Royce** have adapted CSR concerns to produce new market opportunities.

▷ The most important functions of the board of directors are strategy and policy formulation. They also monitor the performance of management and are accountable to stakeholders for corporate governance. Non-executive directors can provide a different set of skills to executive directors, as well as objectivity and a new network of contacts.

Essays and discussion topics

1 What exactly is strategizing? If it is undertaken at all levels of the organization how is it focused and coordinated?
2 How do you reconcile incremental decision-making with strategizing?
3 What are the differences between the 'Positional' and 'Process' Schools of strategy? Are these differences real and do organizations always fall into one 'School' or another?
4 What is the 'Entrepreneurial School' of strategy? Are there any implications for an organization from the approach to strategy development of this 'School'?
5 Why do the proponents of effectual reasoning believe that the Positional School of strategy is incapable of generating entrepreneurial strategies?
6 'Entrepreneurial strategy is simple. Find out what others are doing and do the opposite.' Discuss.

7 Why are values important? Where do the values of an organization come from?

8 Can you be ethical in business?

9 Can values be fabricated for commercial purposes?

10 How useful are strategic frameworks?

11 Can you really develop strategic intent in a systematic way?

12 If the only thing that links vision with reality is strategic intent, how is credibility maintained?

13 Do you think the values of Lush are 'real'? Why?

14 What values would you like your company to adhere to?

15 'We can only guess what the future might hold, so there is no point in trying to predict it.' Discuss this in the context of futures thinking and scenario planning.

16 'CSR is just a way of gaining competitive advantage by trying to be different.' Discuss.

17 'Sustainability issues have just been hijacked to use as excuses for cost cutting.' Discuss.

18 How important do you believe issues of CSR and sustainability should be for companies?

19 'Boards of directors of public companies have failed in their task of corporate governance.' Discuss. Be sure to give examples.

20 Why has executive pay outstripped the pay of most other people?

21 What is the role of the non-executive director? What do they bring to an organization?

22 How might corporate governance be strengthened?

23 What is the role of government in issues of CSR and corporate governance?

Exercises and assignments

1 Select an organization and undertake a SLEPT analysis. Based upon this, try scenario planning on one major trend that you identify.

2 Select an industry and undertake a SLEPT analysis. Based upon this, try futures thinking about how you might capitalize on these trends and the form your ideal company would therefore take.

3 Select a well known public company and, without checking beforehand, try to develop a mission statement for it. You can normally find the company's mission statement with a Google search. Compare its actual mission statement to the one you have constructed.

References

Allday, D. (1997) *Check-a-Board: Helping Boards and Directors become More Effective*, London: Institute of Management.

Berkhout, F. and Green, K. (2003) *International Journal of Innovation Management*, 6(3), Special issue on Managing Innovation for Sustainability.

Burke, L. and Logsdon, J.M. (1996) 'How Corporate Social Responsibility Pays Off', *Long Range Planning*, 29(4).

de Colle, S. and Gonella, C. (2002) 'The Social and Ethical Alchemy: An Integrative Approach to Social and Ethical Accountability', *Business Ethics: A European Review*, 11(1).

Environics International (2001) *Corporate Social Responsibility Monitor 2001: Global Public Opinion on the Changing Role of Companies*, Toronto, Canada: Environics International (now Globescan).

Epstein, M.J. and Roy, M.J. (2001) 'Sustainability in Action: Identifying and Measuring the Key Performance Drivers', *Long Range Planning*, 34.

Eisenhardt, K.M. and Martin, J.A. (2000) 'Dynamic Capabilities: What are They?', *Strategic Management Journal*, 21.

Foster, R. and Kaplan, S. (2001) *Creative Destruction: Why Companies that are Built to Last Underperform the Stock Market*, New York: Doubleday/Currency.

Hamel, G. and Prahalad, C.K. (1994) *Competing For the Future: Breakthrough Strategies for Seizing Control of your Industry and Creating the Markets of Tomorrow*, Boston, MA: Harvard Business School Press.

Grant, R.M. (2003) 'Strategic Planning In a Turbulent Environment: Evidence from the Oil Majors', *Strategic Management Journal*, 24.

Grant, R.M. (2010) *Contemporary Strategy Analysis*, 7th edn, Chichester: Wiley.

Kay, J. (1998) *Foundations of Corporate Success*, Oxford: Oxford University Press.

Kim, W. and Mauborgne, R. (2005) 'Blue Ocean Strategy: From Theory to Practice', *California Management Review*, 47(3) , Spring.

Mintzberg, H., Ahlstrand, B. and Lampel, J. (1998) *Strategy Safari*, New York: The Free Press.

Mintzberg, H. (1978) 'Patterns in Strategy Formation', *Management Science*, 934–48.

Nonaka, I. (1991) 'The Knowledge-Creating Company', *Harvard Business Review*, November/December.

OECD (2004) *Principles of Corporate Governance*, Paris: OECD.

Ohmae, K. (2005) *The Next Global Stage: Challenges and Opportunities in our Borderless World*, New Jersey: Pearson Education.

Porter, M. (1985) *Competitive Advantage: Creating and Sustaining Superior Performance*. New York: The Free Press.

Phan, P.H., Wright, M., Ucbasaran, D. and Wee, L. (2009) 'Corporate Entrepreneurship: Current Research and Future Decisions', *Journal of Corporate Venturing*, 24.

Prahalad, C.K. and Hamel, G. (1990) 'The Core Competence of the Corporation', *Harvard Business Review*, 68(3), May/June.

Quinn, J.B. Mintzberg, H. and James, R.M. (1988) *The Strategy Process*, Hemel Hempstead: Prentice Hall International.

Read, S., Sarasvathy, S., Dew, N., Wiltbank, R. and Ohlsson, A. (2011) *Effectual Entrepreneurship*, Abingdon/New York: Routledge.

Schwartz, P. (2003) *Inevitable Surprises: Thinking Ahead in a Time of Turbulence*, New York: Gotham Books.

Smith, N.C. (2003) 'Corporate Social Responsibility: Whether or How?', *California Management Review*, 45(4).

Treacy, M. and Wiersema, F. (1995) *The Discipline of Market Leaders*, Reading, MA: Addison-Wesley.

Verschoor, C.C. (2002) 'Best Corporate Citizens have Better Financial Performance', *Strategic Finance*, January.

Wickham, P.A. (2001) *Strategic Entrepreneurship: A Decision-Making Approach to New Venture Creation and Management*, Harlow: Pearson Education.

Wood, D. (2000) 'Theory and Integrity in Business and Society'. *Business and Society*, 39(4).

Chapter **10**

Creating competitive advantage in mature markets

Learning outcomes

By the end of this chapter you should be able to:

▷ Critically analyze the components of competitive advantage in existing product/markets;

▷ Critically evaluate Porter's generic marketing strategies framework and use it to develop strategies that create competitive advantage;

▷ Creatively address how a firm might differentiate itself by understanding value drivers;

▷ Critically evaluate the effects of product life cycles on marketing strategy and how the life cycle can be lengthened through product expansion and extension;

▷ Use the Boston matrix to communicate marketing strategies for a portfolio of products;

▷ Show advance knowledge of the effects of the product portfolio on cash flow and profitability;

▷ Show advance knowledge of how the product portfolio can be managed;

▷ Use Porter's Five Forces analysis to assess the competitiveness of an industry;

▷ Critically analyze the implications of a diverse product portfolio on the strategies related to encouraging corporate entrepreneurship.

Competitive advantage

This chapter looks at competitive advantage at the product/market level. To an economist competitive advantage is a temporary state of disequilibrium between competing firms. It is therefore something that is created either by changes in the market or changes in one of the competing firms. At the corporate level entrepreneurial architecture is valuable because it can both create change internally through innovation and create an ability to react to external change in the market. It is able to create and recreate competitive advantage, thereby making it sustainable and difficult to copy. However, even as an entrepreneurial firm might move from one new product/market configuration to another, it leaves behind it an existing market in which it must compete. For many large firms this involves a multi-business form of organization. And in competing within existing markets the factors underpinning competitive advantage need to be understood, even if they are ultimately copiable, because competitive advantage in existing markets can be extended.

Our economist would say that competitive advantage is found in these existing markets because of imperfections in competition. Their 'ideal' market is called an 'efficient' or 'perfect' market, which involves many buyers and sellers, no barriers to entry or exit, no product differentiation and a free and fast flow of information. When this perfect market is in equilibrium, firms all earn the same rate of profit which is equal to the cost of capital. In the long run it is never possible to beat the perfect market. However, many business academics would observe that most markets do not exhibit these characteristics and much of their literature is concerned with how a perfect market might be disrupted by the individual firm – in other words how they might gain competitive advantage. And, whilst economists might acknowledge that imperfections in markets (particularly trading markets) might be generated by imperfect availability of information or high transaction costs, business academics tend to focus on how the combinations of capabilities and resources in an organization may be combined and recombined uniquely to form some differentiated product/market offering.

If we start with marketing basics, there have really only ever been three ways of selling products or services. You see two of them being used every day in any street market. At one end of the market there is a street trader offering the cheapest goods in the market – fruit, vegetables or whatever. At the other end there is another offering something different – freshest or organically grown fruit, vegetables or whatever. The more different you are, the higher the price you can charge. But there is also a third way to charge a higher price – not to go to the market, but rather to take the product to the customer. This is focusing on customers and their needs.

Michael Porter (1985) gave this piece of common sense the catchy title of 'generic marketing strategies' and the three fundamental ways of achieving sustainable competitive advantage:

▷ **Low price** – based upon cost leadership;
▷ **High differentiation** – based upon some real product/market differences such as quality, but reinforced through marketing and branding;
▷ **Customer focus** – based upon a better understanding of customer needs.

These are quite consistent with Treacy and Wiersema's (1995) three value disciplines outlined in the previous chapter. When combined, they lead to the four market positions, or 'generic marketing strategies' shown in Figure 10.1.

Porter said that the strategies are mutually exclusive and that a firm has to follow one of the four strategies otherwise it would have no clear direction. However, the leading companies in most industries manage to reconcile all three value disciplines in ways that maximize customer appeal. What is more, there are also many examples of leading companies in the same industries successfully offering different configurations because the market is sufficiently large and heterogeneous to accommodate that. For example, the business model of the low-cost airlines easyJet and AirAsia is very different from that of flagship carriers like British Airways and Emirates. Both Dell and Apple exist successfully in the personal computing market but with completely different strategies serving different market segments. There is certainly no golden formula for success. Porter also suggested that firms cannot change their generic strategy successfully. That

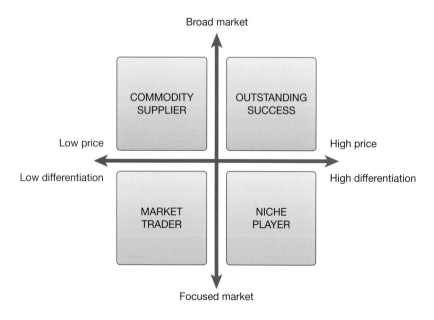

F 10.1 Generic marketing strategies

is generally now held not to be correct either. There are many examples of firms successfully changing strategy, particularly with companies moving from a differentiated product to a product competing on price as it proceeds through its life cycle. This is particularly the case with technology-based products. Nevertheless these generic strategies provide a useful strategic tool that can clarify our thinking about strategic imperatives.

Cost advantage

This is where the firm sets out to be the lowest-priced producer in the industry appealing to a very broad market with a relatively undifferentiated product. To have the lowest price means you must have the lowest costs. This assumes that costs can be reduced, for example through economies of scale, and that this is important and of value to the customer. If a firm sets up in a market where economies of scale are achievable and are important to customers it must grow quickly, just to survive. A firm can find itself in this situation when the market or product is new and economies of scale have yet to be developed. Firms may not yet have grown to their optimal size to achieve these economies and the battle is on to see who can get there first. This is shown in Figure 10.2. Technological changes, particularly those affecting production processes, can cause a step change downward in this curve. Minimum cost is at output A with average cost per unit A1.

Similar to economies of scale are experience curve economies. These are the consequence of the business learning how to generate its outputs more efficiently and effectively. Like economies of scale, experience curve economies are related to output. However, whereas economies of scale depend on output in a particular period, experience curve economies are the result of cumulative output. Another source of low cost might be lower input costs than competitors for things like materials, energy or labour. These might be sustained through special contract arrangements or geographic proximity.

If a firm is a commodity supplier, price is important to its customers and

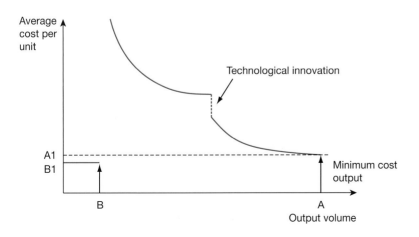

F 10.2 Economies of scale and economies of small scale

it therefore needs to understand how costs can be minimized. Dominance of the market will depend very largely on being the lowest-cost producer in the sector. It is likely that sustainable cost leadership can only be achieved by means of 'substantial relative market share advantage', because this provides the firm with the cost advantages of economies of scale, market power and experience curve effects. Following this strategy means having a focus on new technology, as this is often the best way to reduce costs. It also means fighting competitors hard to sustain any cost advantage through market dominance. Achieving dominance in this sort of market place is risky and the road to high growth will have many casualties along the way. The risks this strategy faces are that cost leadership cannot be sustained: competitors might imitate, technology might change, indeed any basis for that all-important cost leadership to be eroded.

And yet, we do see very small businesses surviving in highly price-competitive markets where economies of scale exist. Just visit your local Saturday market to see some examples. How do they do it? Burns (2011) explains that this can happen in some markets because market traders benefit from economies of small scale, where overheads can be minimal at very low levels of output (see Figure 10.2, where economies of small scale occur at output B and unit cost B1). The problem is that this will only hold true of production levels up to a certain low level and to grow the business beyond this size means that the firm must increase its overheads disproportionately, and then start to move down the cost curve. The firm will need high investment and it will need to grow quickly. The chances of making this dash successfully are therefore relatively low, particularly when there are already larger competitors in the market benefiting from those economies.

The average size of businesses varies from industry to industry. For example, the average size of a chemical firm is very large, whereas the average size of a retail business is relatively small. One of the reasons for this is the extent to which economies of scale affect an industry; that is, how total cost per unit produced changes as more units are produced. Generally this can be expected to decline up to some point, for example, as an expensive piece of machinery is used more fully. However, beyond this point unit costs may start to increase, for example, as economies of scale of production become increasingly offset by rising distribution costs. The potential for economies of scale is often greatest in capital-intensive industries like chemicals. Total costs include production, selling and distri- bution costs and are therefore dependent upon the state of technology, the size of the market and the location of potential customers. The unit cost for one industry may turn up at a relatively low level of output, implying the optimal size of firm is relatively small, in contrast to another industry where there are considerable economies of scale. Porter calls these 'frag- mented' industries where economies of scale just do not exist and large firms cannot, therefore, dominate the industry.

To summarize, a Commodity Supplier must be the most efficient in the market. Therefore, the likely implications for strategy are:

▷ Economies of scale will be important and this has implications for plant investment requirements and access to capital. At the same time, achieving high volume sales and gaining market dominance is vital. It also has implications for capacity utilization and effective pricing policy to encourage take-up of otherwise unused capacity.

▷ Day-to-day control of all costs, but particularly overheads, will be important. This has implications for the design of processes and process R&D and innovation. It also has implications for the location of manufacturing (or outsourcing), where input costs for either labour or raw materials are significant. This has resulted in dramatic shifts in recent years. Similarly transport costs for the finished product, if significant, may influence location. The emphasis on efficiency implies tight job descriptions and management control (quite the opposite of our entrepreneurial firm).

🗂 Case with questions easyJet

Low-price strategy

One firm that has successfully followed the low-price strategy is easyJet. It was founded by Stelios Haji-Ioannou, a graduate of London Business School, in 1995 with £5 million borrowed from his father, a Greek shipping tycoon. Copying similar operations in the USA and Ryanair flying out of Ireland, easyJet was one of the first 'low-cost' airlines in the UK, flying from Luton to Scotland. Stelios then launched similar low-cost, no-frills services to continental Europe. The company has transformed the European air travel market and has beaten off many rival imitators. easyJet was floated on the Stock Market in 2000, making Stelios £280 million profit.

> 'You start the business as a dream, you make it your passion for a while and then you get experienced managers to run it because it's not as much fun as starting. I think there's a lot to be said about starting a business and a lot to be said about running a business when it's mature.'
>
> *Sunday Times*, 29 October 2000

A central strategy of being low-price is being low-cost and that has a number of implications for the way easyJet and its rivals are run. Low costs come from two driving principles – 'sweating' the assets and high operating efficiency. They generally fly 'point-to-point' (average trip length about 1000 kilometres), without the connecting flights and networks that the heritage carriers, like British Airways (BA), have to worry about. easyJet flies its Boeing 737s for 11 hours a day, 4 hours longer than BA. Their pilots fly 900 hours a year, 50% more than BA pilots. In terms of operating efficiency, it means:

▷ Aircraft fly out of low-cost airports. These are normally not the major airport serving any destination and can be some distance from the destination.

▷ Aircraft are tightly scheduled. Rapid turnaround is vital. Low-cost airlines aim to allow only 25 minutes to off-load one set of passengers and load another, less than half the time of heritage rivals.

▷ Aircraft must leave and arrive on time (they will not wait for passengers), and if there are delays they can have horrendous knock-on consequences for the timetable. Nevertheless punctuality

→

is varied, with the low-cost carriers just as good as full-fare airlines on some routes.

▷ There is no 'slack' in the system. easyJet admits to having 'one and a half planes' worth' of spare capacity compared with the dozen planes BA has on stand-by at Gatwick and Heathrow. If something goes wrong with a plane it can lead to cancellations and long delays.

▷ There are fewer cabin crew than full-fare rivals and staff rostering is a major logistical problem.

▷ All operations and processes must be slimmed down and made as simple as possible.

In terms of customer service, it means:

▷ Ticketless flights without seat reservation.

▷ A single class, therefore with more seats on each plane, with no 'frills' such as complimentary drinks, meals or assigned seats. All in-flight services must be paid for.

▷ Lower baggage allowances than heritage carriers and there is no compensation for delays or lost baggage.

▷ Transfers not guaranteed, as the planes could be late.

▷ Aerobridges for boarding and disembarking generally not used, because these add cost.

▷ Concentration on point-to-point flights, whereas the full-fare, heritage airlines tend to concentrate on hub-and-spoke traffic.

easyJet has started to move away from being the lowest-cost carrier. AirAsia is generally regarded to be the lowest-cost carrier in the world with Ryanair, a competitor of easyJet, not far behind. Whilst easyJet claim an average price of £45 per 600 kilometres, Ryanair claim £34. This compares to BA's price of £110. easyJet is focusing more on value-for-money and offering better service. Interestingly Ryanair has so little faith in its timetable that it advises passengers not to book connecting flights.

easyJet is generally regarded as having an excellent branding strategy – originally based on PR around its founder – and having one of the best websites in the sector. easyJet is aggressive in promoting its brand and running advertising promotions to get more 'bums on seats'. It realizes that its planes must have high seat occupancy to be economic. To this end it is particularly inventive with pricing, encouraging real bargain hunters onto the less popular flights during the day and promoting early bookings with cheaper fares. easyJet has been at the forefront of the use of the internet for virtual ticketing, and now sells most of its tickets over the web. This means it does not have to pay commission to travel agents and check-in can be quicker and more efficient. Its website has been held up as a model for the industry and many have copied it. easyJet also try to get more sales from every passenger visiting their website and sell other services such as airport car parking, car hire and hotel bookings. The aim is to try to make travelling easier and simpler.

One of the fears about low-cost airlines has been that they will be tempted to compromise on safety for the sake of cutting costs. The British Airline Pilots Association has claimed that pilots of low-cost airlines have been tempted to cut corners to achieve flight timetables. Stelios himself fuelled the safety debate by expressing doubts about Ryanair's use of 20-year-old planes on some of its routes, pointing out that, although they might improve profits in the short term, they put the future of the whole airline at risk in the event of an accident. Ryanair has phased these planes out and does have an unblemished safety record. But the industry is all too aware that the low-cost US airline, Valuejet, went bankrupt after one of its planes crashed in 1996, killing all 110 people on board. As the *Economist* said (17 August 2002): 'the low cost airline business is not for the faint-hearted'. By partnering with some of the best-known maintenance providers in the industry, easyJet make safety their first priority. In common with other low-cost operators, easyJet operates a single type of aircraft. This offers economies of purchasing, maintenance, pilot training and aircraft utilization.

Only seven years after founding the company and still owning 29% of easyJet, in 2002 Stelios realized that he was not suited to managing an established public company and was better suited to being a serial entrepreneur, so he resigned as Chairman, aged only 35. He was replaced by Sir Colin Chandler, aged 62, who was part of London's financial establishment as chairman of Vickers Defence Systems, deputy chairman of Smiths Group and director of Thales.

> 'Running a company that is listed on the Stock Exchange is different from building up and running a private company. The history of the City is littered with entrepreneurs who hold onto their creations for too long, failing to recognize the changing needs of the company. I am a serial entrepreneur ... It is all part of growing up. I've built something and now it is time to move on.'
>
> *The Times*, 19 April 2002

Shortly after Stelios' departure easyJet took over Go, the low-cost airline set up by BA and sold off to its management. Newspaper comment at the time suggested Stelios had been blocking such a deal and this might have been one reason for his departure. Go had been in fierce price competition with easyJet on certain routes, to the point where tickets were being given away with only airport tax to pay. One of the first things easyJet did was to close the Go flights on these routes and restore prices. As well as eliminating competition, the purchase of Go had other strategic reasoning behind it. easyJet was purchasing market share in a fast-growing market (in 2002 it grew 60%) where there are economies of scale. It was also buying new routes and landing rights, which can be difficult to secure. These days the low-cost airline industry is well-established and far more difficult to enter. AirAsia entered the market in 2002, copying the successful low-cost model but in a new market without competitors.

☐ Up-to-date information on easyJet can be found on their website: www.easyjet.com

Questions

1 Compared to Ryanair and BA, where would you place easyJet in terms of Porter's generic marketing strategies? Is this sustainable?

2 Based upon this information, undertake a SWOT analysis on easyJet.

3 What is the underlying strategy behind all of Stelios' other 'easy' ventures? Can this strategy be replicated in any market? What is required for it to work?

Differentiation advantage

Differentiation means setting out to be unique in the industry along some dimensions that are widely valued by customers. These can be based upon the product or service and can be tangible (observable product/service characteristics such as function, quality, performance or technology etc.) and/or intangible (customer needs such as status, exclusivity etc.). Often differentiation is more sustainable when based not just on tangible factors, which are copiable, but also on intangible factors, which are not. This is often called developing a unique selling proposition (USP). The firm sets out to establish itself as unique and different from its competitors in some ways. It can then charge a premium price. Entrepreneurial firms should be good at this because of their ability to innovate. So, for example, Mercedes Benz cars and Dom Perignon champagne differentiate themselves through product quality and status in their respective sectors. Hi-fi manufacturer Bang & Olufson use aesthetics of design as well as status. In the UK Co-op Bank is about ethical investment, whereas Coutts Bank is about service and status for the wealthy. The UK retailer Lush differentiates itself through its shopping environment, novel products and ethical values. Even companies competing primarily on price attempt to differentiate themselves and not just through brand recognition. Dell may not have differentiated products but attempts to differentiate itself on speed of delivery, uniqueness of personal systems configuration and other elements of service, whilst still maintaining a competitive price. McDonald's has a very recognizable brand associated with value-for-money meals but also tries to differentiate itself, in part, through consistency and quality of service (speed, cleanliness and so on).

Uniqueness can therefore be derived from many things and can be created by 'bundling' these things in different ways – so long as the customer values the 'bundle' and cannot create the 'bundle' easily themselves. Michael Porter (op. cit.) identifies nine drivers of uniqueness commonly used by firms:

▷ Product features and performance;
▷ Technology embodied in product design;
▷ Quality of components used in product;
▷ Related services, such as speed of delivery, credit etc.;
▷ Marketing activity such as advertising spend, promotions etc.;
▷ Skill and expertise of work force;
▷ Location (particularly with retailers);
▷ Procedures associated with all aspects of production, service and marketing;
▷ Degree of vertical integration (which influences the ability to control inputs and intermediate processes).

These drivers may be criticized for being too physical and therefore easily copied. Certainly firms like Apple have made design a key element of differentiation. Good design can not only make a product (or service) more effective in use, it can also appeal to the customers' aesthetic tastes. Apple products are sought after not just for their ease of use but also because of their aesthetics.

Differentiation adds costs and it is essential that the benefits to the customers are seen by them as outweighing the costs. It is also essential that the product or service is clearly identified as being different. This is helped by clear branding. A brand should be the embodiment of the product or service offering to customers. So, for

"When you've got single-digit market share – and you're competing with the big boys – you either differentiate or die ... We put a great deal of emphasis on understanding what drove customer satisfaction, whether it was response times on the telephone, quality of products, valuable features, or ease of experience in using the product. Engaging the entire company – from manufacturing to engineering to sales to support staff – in the process of understanding customer requirements became a constant focus of management energy, training, and employee education.'

Michael Dell

example, the Mercedes Benz, Jaguar and BMW brands all convey quality and status. Virgin is the embodiment of Richard Branson; brash, entrepreneurial, different, anti-establishment – whatever matches the product/service on offer. Effective brands, therefore, are emotional, appealing to the head as much as the heart. They add an extra layer to a differentiated product, as shown in Figure 10.3. The functional qualities of the product or service can be enhanced through the aesthetics of design and reinforced by the emotional values associated with the brand. Apple combine a good, functional product with elegant design, a fashionable, desirable brand and a high price. However, many so-called brands fall far short of this instant recognition of values and virtues, being little more than expensive logos. What do the Barclays, Shell or BT brands convey, other than knowledge of what the firm sells?

In a world where products and services are often all too homogeneous, a good brand is a powerful marketing tool that must be the cornerstone of any strategy of differentiation. Not only can it help turn prospects into customers, if everything else is right it can turn them into regular customers. What is more, it can help turn them into supporters – regular customers who think positively about the brand – or even advocates – who are willing to recommend the product and bring in new customers. In other words it helps to move them up the customer loyalty ladder (Figure 10.4). And here again the entrepreneurial architecture, with its emphasis on long-term relationships, can help. If the architecture is in place it is not just the entrepreneurial leader who will 'walk the talk', but every member of staff. Each of them will be the embodiment of the product or service offering and, because of their sincere belief in it, they will be its best advocates.

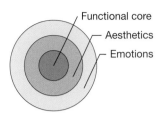

F 10.3 Layers of differentiation

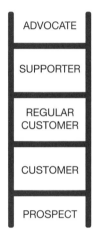

F 10.4 Customer loyalty ladder

🗀 Case insight Quanta Computers

Differential advantage

Born in Shanghai and living much of his early life in Hong Kong, Barry Lam is founder, chairman and chief executive of Quanta Computer Inc., the world's largest maker of notebook computers, with factories in both Taiwan and China. Quanta is now also the world's largest manufacturer of data-storage servers. It has over 30,000 employees, of which some 3500 are engineers. In 2006, *Fortune* magazine recognized Quanta as one of the Fortune Global 500 Companies. And yet few will recognize his name or that of his company because he keeps a low profile. That is because Quanta is a contract manufacturer – a company that designs and manufactures electronic equipment, but leaves the branding and marketing to others – Apple, Dell, HP, Compaq, Sony, Toshiba and many others. Indeed Taiwanese companies now manufacture over half of the world's laptop computers with Quanta being the largest with over 30% of the notebook market.

→

Barry specializes in contract manufacturing. It is what he knows and what he does best. His entrepreneurial career began in the 1970s when he started Kinpo, a company that went on to become the largest contract manufacturer of calculators. Quanta was set up in 1988 and by 2000 had overtaken Toshiba as the world's largest manufacturer of laptops.

Contract manufacturers tend to be either providers of electronic manufacturing services (EMSs) or original design manufacturers (ODMs). EMSs build machines that others design. They look to achieve greater economies of scale with lower risk by amalgamating orders from several companies. However, they sell to fewer and fewer global brand names and have little bargaining power because they do not control design or marketing. Consequently margins are becoming increasingly squeezed. Quanta, however, is an ODM and, because it designs notebooks and tablets, it is able to charge a premium price, which reflects itself in the high profitability of the firm. Quanta's ability to design power and functionality into lightweight computers has been the key to its success. It allows customers to combine different features for each of its products. Once the design is agreed, production moves ahead quickly. These two elements, design capability and outstanding supply-chain management, are the basis of the long-term relationships. Quanta is not just a 'me-too' manufacturer, it invests in research and product innovation through the Quanta Research and Development Center at its headquarters in Taiwan. This is a vital element in the firm's success and it has links with many universities, including MIT.

Where the firm combines differentiation with a focus on a narrow target market segment it is said to be following a strategy of 'focused differentiation', better-known as a 'niche strategy'. Economists call this occupying the 'interstices' of the economy. Clear differentiation often goes with well-aimed segmentation as it is easier to differentiate yourself in a small, clearly identified market. The key to segmentation is the ability to identify the unique benefits that a product or service offers to potential customers. Thus, for example, there may be two electrical engineers producing similar products but, whereas one is a jobbing engineer producing a range of products for many customers with no particular competitive advantage, the other might differentiate itself on the basis of its market – that it sells to a few large companies with whom it has long-term relationships, being integrated into their supply chains.

Establishing a market niche is most effective when aimed at a narrowly defined market segment. One problem of a niche market is its very narrowness. However the environment can change; markets grow or shrink; technology changes and customers move around. As the picture changes, so do opportunities, and what might offer a good niche in one decade may turn into a free-for-all in another. However, an entrepreneurial firm may always successfully develop a portfolio of products or services, each in its own distinct market niche, but thereby mitigating the risks associated with the size of each niche individually.

Sometimes firms that differentiate themselves and their products effectively turn out to have a very broad market appeal. For example Apple started as a niche producer of computers. What may have started as a niche business may then turn out to be an outstanding success that experiences rapid and considerable growth. It is unlikely that many businesses will start life here, except perhaps, like Apple, in areas of real innovation. Many commodity suppliers try desperately to differentiate themselves, with varying degrees of success, and companies try to protect the basis for differentiation in any way possible. It might be that a product can be patented, the design registered or, for written material, copyrighted, but usually branding plays a big part.

To summarize, the likely implications for strategy of a large firm pursuing a policy of differentiation are:

▷ Identifying and reinforcing through marketing and, in particular, branding the elements of differentiation that are important to customers;
▷ Building product service development and innovation upon these differential advantages.

In pursuing a niche strategy it is imperative that the firm has a close and up-to-date knowledge and understanding of the needs of the particular segments of the market that it services and reacts quickly to any changes.

🗁 Case insight Quad Electroaccoustics

Niche strategy

One Huntingdon-based family company that has been very successful in differentiating its products and selling to a small but lucrative market segment is Quad Electroaccoustics. Originally founded in 1936 by Peter Walker as an 'acoustical manufacturing company' to produce 'public address' systems, today its silvery grey, bizarrely sculptured audio equipment looks like no other. It sounds superb as well. When Japanese 'competitors' bring out new models every year, Quad's stay the same and last for ever. Its original electrostatic loudspeaker was in production for 28 years.

Quads are a byword for quality, reliability and design originality – but they are not cheap. Current models sell for over £3000 and still 70% of Quad's sales are exported, especially to Europe, USA and Japan.

☐ Up-to-date information on Quad can be found on their website: www.quad-hifi .co.uk

Value drivers

Real advantages in cost or differentiation need to be found in the chain of activities that a firm performs to deliver value to its customers. Difference needs to be of value to the customer if it is to provide competitive advantage. Michael Porter (op. cit.) says that the value chain, shown in Figure 10.5, should be the start of any strategic analysis. He identified five primary activities:

1 Inbound logistics (receiving storing and disseminating inputs)
2 Operations (transforming inputs into a final product)
3 Outbound logistics (collecting, storing and distributing products to customers)
4 Marketing and sales
5 After-sales service

and four secondary or supporting activities:

1 Procurement (purchasing consumable and capital items)
2 Human resource management
3 Technology development (R&D etc.)
4 Firm infrastructure (general management, accounting etc.).

Porter argues that each generic category can be broken down into discrete activities unique to a particular firm. Although not specifically identified, the important activities of design and branding can be integrated within these activities. The firm can then look at the costs associated with each activity and try to compare it to the value obtained by customers from

PRIMARY ACTIVITIES

Inbound logistics → Operations → Outbound logistics → Marketing and sales → Service

SUPPORT ACTIVITIES

Firm infrastructure

Human resource management

Technology development

Procurement

F 10.5 Value chain

the particular activity. By identifying the cost or value drivers – the factors that determine cost or value for each activity – and the linkages which reduce cost or add value or discourage imitation the firm can develop the strategies that lead to competitive advantage.

This is a way of focusing on the drivers of value in a business that ought to influence the strategy of the firm. For example, the low-cost supply situation may be linked to its proximity to a key supplier and could therefore disappear if the firm decides, as part of its expansion plans, to move to another location. The value chain is also a useful way of thinking about how differentiation might be achieved through activities valued by the customer – and not always by reducing costs. For example, a high-quality product might be let down by low-quality after-sales service – the value to the customer not being matched by sufficient investment. In other words differentiation is likely to be achieved by multiple linkages in the value chain as exemplified by a consistent marketing mix. If multiple, compatible linkages can be established they create additional value and are often more difficult to imitate than single linkages. For example, the introduction of just-in-time deliveries from the manufacturer, with increased delivery reliability and improved distribution time to the retailer, may allow retailers to both decrease their inventory costs and at the same time reduce stock-outs. Similarly, building switch costs into the value chain can also enhance competitive position. However, the advent of the internet and e-commerce has generally made it easier to disaggregate the value chain, establishing markets at different points along it, allowing firms to radically rethink or 're-engineer' the way their product/market offering is put together and focus more on their core strengths.

Entrepreneurial firms can add value to the customer in a number of ways, not least by developing the close relationships they offer to both customers and suppliers. A particularly effective entrepreneurial strategy is to identify a sector in which the relationships are weak and to create value by tightening them up.

⊡ Case insight Hewlett Packard Pavilion 8000 laptop

Global supply chains

Computers provide an excellent example of today's global supply chain. Every element of the value chain can be located so as to provide the best combination of cost and expertise. The value chain for the Hewlett Packard Pavilion 8000 laptop looks like this (adapted from www.hp.com; 'The Laptop Trail', *Wall Street Journal*, 9 June 2005):

Component/Process	Provider and location
Design	HP (USA; and in Taiwan and China in collaboration with third-party manufacturers).
Assembly	Quanta Computers (Taiwan), assembled in China.
Microprocessor	Designed by Intel in USA. Manufactured by Intel in USA and Israel.
Graphics card	Designed by ATI Technologies (Canada). Manufactured by ATI in Taiwan.
Screen	Manufactured by LG Philips – joint venture with LG (South Korea) and Philips (Netherlands) – in South Korea.
Hard disk drive	Designed by Seagate in USA. Manufactured by Seagate in Malaysia.
Lithium ion battery	Manufactured by Sony in Japan.
Logistics	Sub-contracted to 40 third-party providers, some global, some local.
Telephone sales/support	Sub-contracted to third-party providers in Canada, UK, Ireland and India.

However, an important hidden cost of the fragmented supply chain shown above is not just transportation costs but also time involved in delivering computers to customers. For companies emphasizing speed and reliability of delivery, an alternative supply chain may well be more appropriate, even if it increases costs slightly.

Sustainable differential advantage

Which strategies deliver sustainable competitive advantage? Porter (op. cit.) wants you to select cost leadership, differentiation or focus. On the other hand, as we saw in the last chapter, Hamel and Prahalad (1994) want you to focus on core competences and Treacy and Wiersema (1995) want you to select operational excellence, product leadership or customer intimacy. Which theory do you choose? The answer is that all the evidence points to differentiation having a greater potential than low cost for producing sustainable competitive advantage. Differentiation takes more time to copy. For example, just one element of differentiation, quality, has been shown by many studies to be more likely to lead to growth than competing simply on price (Burns, 1994; Harrison and Taylor 1996; Ray and Hutchinson, 1983; Storey et al., 1989). Differentiation can involve physical elements of the product or service but it may also include intangible elements like the aesthetics of design or other elements of marketing like branding as, for example, used very effectively by Apple. Indeed any of the firm's interactions with customers such as service levels can be used to differentiate it from competitors.

Strategy should therefore emphasize something that makes the firm as unique as possible and delivers as much value to the customer as possible today, and more importantly, tomorrow. Speed of execution is also important, particularly in new markets. Whilst first-mover advantage may disappear rapidly if the product/market offering proves too unattractive or too many elements of the market offering prove inappropriate, delay can attract unwelcome competitors. Many surveys show that rapid domination of a market niche is likely to lead to sustainable growth (3i, 1993; Birley and Westhead, 1990; Harrison and Taylor, op. cit.; Macrae, 1991; Siegel et al., 1993; Solem and Steiner, 1989; Storey et al., op. cit.). There is also a strong relationship between market share and financial return (Boston Consulting Group, 1968, 1972; Buzzell et al., 1974; Buzzell and Gale, 1987; Yelle, 1979). Frequent product or service innovation is also seen as important by many researchers, particularly for manufacturing (Dunkelberg et al., 1987; Solem and Steiner, op. cit.; Storey et al., op. cit.; Woo et al., 1989; Wynarczyk et al., 1993).

> 'We learned to identify our core strengths … The idea of building a business solely on cost or price was not a sustainable advantage. There would always be someone with something that was lower in price or cheaper to produce. What was really important was sustaining loyalty among customers and employees, and that could only be derived from having the highest level of service and very high performing products.'
>
> **Michael Dell**

Nohria and Joyce (2003) provide one final note of caution, but also reinforcement. They report the results of a ten-year study of 160 companies and their use of some 200 different management techniques. They conclude what we all know: that it does not really matter so much which technique you apply but it matters very much more that you execute it flawlessly. They claim flawless execution is something too many management theorists have forgotten. Attention to detail is important.

The conclusions, therefore, are obvious. The strategy with the best chance of generating sustainable growth and the highest profits is to differentiate with the aim of dominating the market as quickly as possible, and to continue to innovate around the differential advantage. Gaining rapid market dominance may come from internal growth but may also involve acquisition of competitors. However, this broad strategy does need to be adapted as products go through their life cycle. What is more, at the corporate level, longer-term sustainable competitive advantage in a changing environment is best delivered through an entrepreneurial architecture delivering these principles at the product or service level.

Product/service life cycles

Most organizations sell a range of different products or services into a range of different markets, each with a different strategy. These are called different 'product/market offerings'. The same product can even be sold to different market segments with a slightly different strategy. Slightly different products might also be developed to better meet the needs of different market segments. The permutations are endless. As we have seen, at the extreme this leads to multi-business organizations with separate divisions or even separate subsidiaries, often with different organizational forms, selling quite different products to various markets.

One important influence on strategy is the point the product or service is at in its life cycle. The concept of the product life cycle is based on the idea that all products or services have a finite life cycle and that, to some extent, the appropriate marketing strategy, is dictated by the stage it is at in this life cycle. Life cycles can vary in length from short for fashion products such as clothing and other consumables to long for durable products like cars. Often the life cycle can be extended by a variety of marketing initiatives. Figure 10.6 shows a four-stage product life cycle with the implications for marketing strategy at the different stages. The simplicity of the model has much to recommend it. However, these broad generalizations must be treated with caution as all products are different, as are different market segments and the customers that comprise them.

Introduction   At the introductory phase the objective should be to make potential customers aware of the product and to get them to try it. The benefits need to be explained and the relevance to customer needs to be underlined. Early customers are likely to be 'innovators' – people who think for themselves and try things. Entrepreneurial firms launching innovative new products are particularly interested in this phase as sales can be high and a premium price might be charged. Apple have had customers queuing overnight to purchase many of their new products such as the iPad.

Growth   At the growth phase the objective should be to grab market share as quickly as possible because competitors will be entering the market. This means that prices will have to be more competitive, depending on the uniqueness of the product and how well it can be differentiated. The promotion emphasis should shift to one of promoting the brand and why it is better than that of competitors. 'Early adopters' will now be buying the product. These tend to be people with status in their market segment and opinion leaders. They adopt successful products, making them acceptable and respectable. The product range should start to be developed at this stage so as to give customers more choice and gain advantage over competitors.

Sales

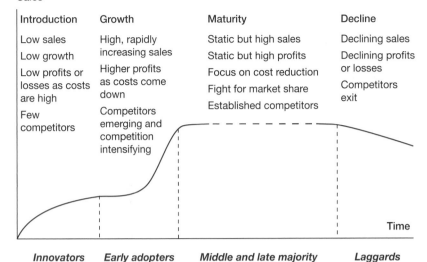

Introduction	Growth	Maturity	Decline
Low sales	High, rapidly increasing sales	Static but high sales	Declining sales
Low growth		Static but high profits	Declining profits or losses
Low profits or losses as costs are high	Higher profits as costs come down	Focus on cost reduction	Competitors exit
Few competitors	Competitors emerging and competition intensifying	Fight for market share	
		Established competitors	

Time

Innovators | *Early adopters* | *Middle and late majority* | *Laggards*

Elements of marketing strategy

Basic product	Develop product extensions and service levels	Wide range in place but expansion slows down or eventually ceases	Range narrows
Price low for repeat purchase products where trial is important	Price competitively to combat competition and penetrate market	Modify and differentiate	Weak products are dropped
Price high where novelty or uniqueness is valued, particularly if purchases are infrequent	Promote actively and aggressively	Develop next generation	Price high if reducing number of competitors means demand still high
Promote actively and aggressively	Build brand	Price defensively – meeting or beating competitors – to ensure maximum return	Price low to dispose of stocks at end of life, in line with declining demand
Explain product benefits	Intensive push on distribution	Emphasize brand	
Build awareness, encourage early adoption	Limited trade discounts	Differentiate	Minimum required to maintain loyalty
Selective distribution		Selective, based around special offers or promotions	Emphasis on low price
		Intensive push on distribution	Distribute selectively
		Trade discounts offered	Phase out weak outlets

F 10.6 Product/service life cycle

Maturity The 'middle and late majority' now start buying the product and take it into the mature phase of its life cycle. The 'middle majority' are more conservative, with slightly higher status and are more deliberate. They only adopt the product after it has become acceptable. The 'late majority' are typically below-average status, are sceptical and adopt the product much later. In this phase competitors are becoming established as some fall by the wayside. In order to maintain market share, pricing tends to be defensive at, or around, the level of competitors. There should be an emphasis on cost reduction so that profits are as high as possible. The accountant's influence should be evident at this stage in the life cycle. It is at this point that products tend to get revamped – by changing designs, colours, packaging etc. – in order to extend their life cycle. Toward the end of this period, price reductions may be hidden by offering extra elements to the product for the same price. Cars, for example, often get this treatment with limited edition models offering many extras for the same price.

Decline 'Laggards' tend to view life through the rear view mirror and will continue buying products because of habit. The interesting thing about the decline phase of the life cycle is that there may still be the opportunity to charge high prices and make good profits, at least in the short term, because competitors may be exiting the market quicker than demand is tailing off. Exactly when to leave a market is therefore a matter of careful judgement.

The consulting firm Arthur D. Little linked the life cycle to competitive position within a product/market sector to produce the resulting implications for strategy based upon Porter's generic strategies. Figure 10.7 summarizes their analysis. In many ways it is an over-simplified version of Figure 10.6, but it does, once more, act as a checklist that allows you to focus on the imperatives for the business. At the two extremes it emphasizes that if you dominate a market at start-up, it pays to grow fast, whilst if you are in a very weak position with a product at the end of its life cycle you might as well cut your losses and get out of the market as quickly as possible.

One problem with the life-cycle concept is trying to establish where a product might actually be at any point in time. Firms plotting their own product sales are not recording the product's life but their ability to manage it. Bad management can lead to an early downturn in sales which is not necessarily the mature phase of the life cycle, and vice versa. What is more, products can be in the mature phase of their life cycle in one market but

Life cycle stage

		Start-up	Growth	Maturity	Decline
Competitive position	**Dominant**	Grow fast	Grow fast Attain cost leadership	Defend position Attain cost leadership Review	Defend position Renew Grow with industry
	Strong	Differentiate Grow fast	Grow fast Catch up Differentiate	Reduce costs Differentiate Grow with industry	Find and hold niche Grow with industry Harvest profit
	Satisfactory	Differentiate Focus Grow fast	Differentiate Focus Grow with industry	Harvest profit Find niche Grow with industry	Consolidate Cut costs
	Weak	Focus Grow with industry	Harvest, catch up Find and hold niche Turn around	Harvest profit Turn around Find niche Consolidate	Divest
	Very weak	Find niche Grow with industry	Turn around Consolidate	Withdraw Divest	Withdraw

F 10.7 Life-cycle and competitive position

at the introductory phase in another. You only have to see the queues and check the prices for McDonald's hamburgers in developing countries to realize that the product has a long way to go in those markets, never mind where it is in mature Western markets. Both the position of a product in its life cycle and the length of the life cycle itself can vary from country to country. Even the duration of each phase seems to vary from country to country. What is more, the duration of each phase in the life cycles also seems to be shrinking throughout the world. Tellis et al. (2003) studied 137 new product launches across 10 consumer categories in 16 European countries and found that the duration of the introductory phase varied considerably from, on average, four years in Scandinavian countries to over seven years in Mediterranean countries. They put this down to cultural rather than economic factors. Not surprisingly given the differences from country to country, multinational firms like Apple phase new product launches across different markets so as to both manage demand and allow them to alter the launch strategy to better meet local needs.

📁 Case with questions Crocs™

Niche product life cycles

The ubiquitous Croc can be found in over 125 countries, having sold more than 150 million pairs by 2011. And that means that about 1 person in every 500 on the entire planet has bought a pair. The Colorado-based company was founded only in 2002 by George Brian Boedecker Jr. and two friends to produce and distribute a plastic clog-like shoe, now available in all the colors of the rainbow, at a relatively cheap price. It was an instant success at the Florida Boat Show, where it was launched. It sold 76,000 pairs in its first year and 649,000 in its second year. The brightly-coloured Crocs are made from Coslite, a durable, soft, lightweight, non-marking and odour-resistant material originally manufactured by Foam Creations, a Canadian company Crocs purchased in 2004. Crocs are now manufactured in Mexico, Italy, Romania and China, having closed their Canadian facility in 2008.

Crocs was a 'fairy-tale' entrepreneurial story, if the press were anything to go by in the early days. *Business 2.0* magazine (3 November 2006) summarized the story: 'Three pals from Boulder, Colorado, go sailing in the Caribbean, where a foam clog one had bought in Canada inspires them to build a business around it. Despite a lack of venture capital funding and the derision of foot fashionistas, the multicolored Crocs with their Swiss-cheese perforations, soft and comfortable soles, and odor-preventing material become a global smash. Celebrities adopt them. Young people adore them. The company goes from $1 million in revenue in 2003 to a projected $322 million this year [2006]. Crocs Inc.'s IPO (Initial Public Offering) in February was the richest in footwear history, and the company has a market cap of more than $1 billion.'

The company went public in 2006 with a hugely successful $200 million stock market float (the biggest float in shoe history). Its initial strategy can be summarized as selling a relatively cheap product to as many people as possible, as quickly as possible. The company used the money to diversify and acquire new businesses, such as Jibbitz, which made charms designed to fit Crocs' ventilating holes, and Fury Hockey, which used Croslite to make sports gear. It built manufacturing plants in Mexico and China, opened distribution centres in the Netherlands and Japan, and expanded into the global market place. A foray into Croslite clothing in 2007 fell flat and was quickly scaled back. The company liquidated Fury Hockey in 2008.

And herein lies the paradox. Popularity breeds contempt in the fashion business. Arguably, the backlash started in 2006, almost as soon as the company went public, with a *Washington Post* article that said: 'Nor is the fashion world enamored of Crocs. Though their maker touts their "ultra-hip Italian styling", lots of folks find them hideous.' A blog named 'I Hate Crocs.com' followed Croc opponents. The shoes and those who wear them – from US ex-President Bush to Michelle Obama and stars such as Al Pacino, Steven Tyler (Aerosmith) and Faith Hill – became objects of satire on US television shows, and, by 2009, over 1.4 million people had joined a Facebook group which had the sole purpose of eliminating the shoes. The site even featured a ritual Croc-burning.

Nevertheless in 2008, Crocs was ranked by the NPD Market Research Group as the number one casual brand in the athletic specialty sporting goods channel for men, women and children. However, having had a bumper year in 2007, the company made a $185 million (£113 million) loss in 2008 and had to cut 2000 jobs. It suddenly began to look very fragile. In late 2008 the company replaced chief executive Ron Snyder, who had been at college with the company's founders, with John Duerden, an industry veteran who ran a consulting firm focused on brand renewal. He believed there was life yet in Crocs and what the company needed was new products to which he could extend the brand.

By 2009 the company was stuck with a surplus of shoes it could not sell and a mountain of expensive debt. The new business lines it had purchased – often at a premium – failed to prosper. As a result the share price plummeted. By this time the company produced a range of different products, mainly plastic clogs and sandals but also a range called 'Bite', aimed at the golf market. The problem was that Crocs were hitting saturation point and the company had failed to successfully diversify. With a nearly indestructible product and about one in every five hundred people owning a pair, how many more can the company sell? And the company had invested enormous amounts into meeting a demand for a product that then seemed endless but now seems ridiculous as the shoe's ubiquity put off even the most ardent Crocophile. In May 2010 *Time* Magazine rated Crocs as one of the world's 50 worst inventions.

But behind the scenes the company brought in Italian designers and started producing a new range of attractive Crocs, albeit at much higher prices than the original clogs, that celebrities such as Brad Pitt,

Ryan Reynolds and Halle Berry once more started wearing. And just to prove that the fashion business can be fickle, in 2011 Crocs sold $1 billion (£630 million) worth of shoes, with one-third of the revenue coming from sales of the original clogs. The 'I Hate Crocs. com' blog gave up and closed in that year. Pondering the turnaround and the ugliness of the original Croc, the *Sunday Times* (22 April 2012) said: 'In the history of retail, has a brand ever thrived so well on adversity? It seems the more the loathers loath[e] them, fans go wild. While for under-10s (a core market) they're a straightforward sell, grown-up clog wearers appear torn between love and hate.' It seems that having an ugly product polarizes opinion and this can give a brand its uniqueness.

☐ Up-to-date information on Crocs can be found on their website: www.crocs.eu

QUESTIONS

1 What went wrong at Crocs and how was it put right?

2 How reliable is the market for the original Croc clogs? Where is the clog in its product life cycle?

3 What do you think of the company's current strategy?

Product portfolios

As already mentioned, if a company has more than one product or service, then it might be following different strategies for each of the different product/market offerings, and one important reason for this is that each of these offerings is at a different stage in its life cycle in the particular market. So, for example, McDonald's may have a different marketing mix for its products in developing countries, where it is at the introductory phase of its life cycle, compared to the USA, where it is a mature product – although the lengths of the phases in the life cycle in developing countries may be shorter than they were in the USA.

This added complexity of having a portfolio of product/market offerings can be handled using a technique adapted from the 'Boston matrix', which derives its name from the Boston Consulting Group that developed it. The original matrix was adapted by McKinsey so as to have more realistic

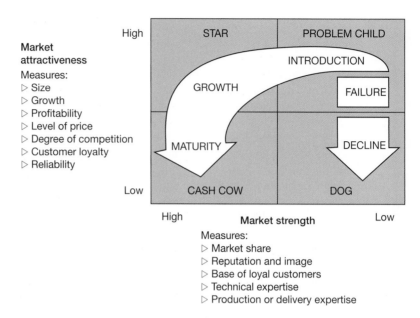

Market attractiveness

Measures:
▷ Size
▷ Growth
▷ Profitability
▷ Level of price
▷ Degree of competition
▷ Customer loyalty
▷ Reliability

Market strength

Measures:
▷ Market share
▷ Reputation and image
▷ Base of loyal customers
▷ Technical expertise
▷ Production or delivery expertise

F 10.8 Boston matrix

multi-dimensional axes. Figure 10.8 shows the adapted matrix. Market attractiveness – the growth and profit potential that relate to the market – is measured on the vertical axis. The strength of product or service offering in the market – sales, relative market share and so on – is measured on the horizontal axis. When a product or service offering is first developed it will be launched into an attractive market (otherwise why do it?), but the firm is unlikely to have a great deal of strength. This is called a Problem Child and is equivalent to the introduction phase of the life cycle. Sometimes the market proves to be unattractive – then the life cycle is very short. This is called a Dog. More often, if the market is attractive, sales will grow and the product or service offering will become more established and will strengthen in the market. This is called a Star. Eventually, however, the market will mature and the product or service will become a Cash Cow. These are market leaders with a lot of stability but little additional growth because they are at the end of their life cycles.

Different business skills are valued at different stages of a product life cycle. Entrepreneurial skills are of most value in the problem child phase of the product/service life cycle. Once the product is in its mature phase it needs to be managed as a cash cow – milked for all the cash flow it can generate. That means high levels of efficiency are needed, probably achieved through a high degree of control and direction. The cash cow is likely to be best managed by an accountant. And, if we are to characterize the management discipline needed to manage the star, it would probably be marketing. In other words, as the product works its way through its life cycle the approach to management needs to change. In a one-product company this presents a challenging but manageable problem. In a multi-product firm the problem is more complex.

There are many problems with the framework at an operational level, centring around measurement of the elements on the two axes; for example, defining the market a firm is in so that you can measure market share or market growth. You can use just one factor on each axis or, indeed, a number of them weighted appropriately using some sort of simple scale. Nevertheless the problem of measurement remains. The Boston matrix is therefore probably best used as a loose conceptual framework that helps clarify complexity. Treated with caution, as we shall see, it can be extremely valuable. In a complex world, anything that simplifies complexity and therefore helps our understanding must be of value.

Marketing strategy and product portfolios

The Boston matrix allows us to make some broad generalizations about marketing strategy for product/service offerings in the different quadrants. These are shown in Figure 10.9. If you can place the product/market offering within its life cycle on the matrix, these would be the elements of marketing strategy you would, a priori, expect to see. But remember that

STAR	PROBLEM CHILD
Objective	**Objective**
Invest for growth	Develop opportunities
▷ Penetrate market	▷ Be critical of prospects
▷ Expand geographically	▷ Invest selectively in products
▷ Sell and promote aggressively	or services
▷ Differentiate	▷ Specialize in strengths
▷ Promote brand, if possible	▷ Shore up weaknesses
▷ Accept moderate short-term profits	
▷ Extend product range	
Objective	**Objective**
Maintain market position	Either kill off or maintain and
and manage for earnings	monitor carefully
▷ Maintain market position with	▷ Minimize expenditure
successful products or services	▷ Improve productivity
▷ Prune less successful ones in range	▷ Maximize cash flow
▷ Differentiate	▷ Live with declining sales until the
▷ Promote brand, if possible	best time to kill off product
▷ Stabilize prices, unless temporary	
aggressive pricing is required in the	
face of competition	
CASH COW	**DOG**

F 10.9 Strategy implications of the Boston matrix

whilst this framework reflects product life cycles, it does not reflect Porter's generic marketing strategies, which need to be superimposed on them. Nevertheless, as a product nears the end of its life cycle, and becomes a cash cow, it is more likely to be on its way to becoming a commodity and therefore having to sell on price.

The Boston matrix also allows us to present complex information more understandably, particularly when linked to forecasting future market positions and strategies involved in getting there. For example, Figure 10.10 represents a hypothetical three-product portfolio for a company. The size of each circle is proportionate to the turnover each achieves. The lighter circles represent the present product positions, the darker circles represent the positions projected in three years time. The portfolio looks balanced and the diagram can be used to explain the strategies that are in place to move the products to where they are planned to be. Again, one essential added complexity is the generic marketing strategies. If products A and B are commodities, selling mainly on price, with low margin under intense pressure, it has implications not only for strategy but also for the cash flow available to invest in product C, particularly if this is a niche market product needing heavy investment.

🗁 Case insight Heineken

International brands and market positioning

Heineken is Europe's largest brewer and is second only to the US brewer Anheuser-Busch world-wide. The brand is recognized around the world. However, its dominant market position, particularly in Europe where 40% of the world's beers are consumed, is maintained by actually having a portfolio of brands that allow it to adjust its marketing mix to suit the tastes and needs of local markets. It also allows the company to create the necessary distribution network and achieve high levels of economies of scale in production. Heineken typically has three core brands in each European country:

▷ A local brand aimed at the largest market segment, offered at a competitive price. In France it has '33', in Spain it has Aguila Pilsner and in Italy it has Dreher.

▷ A brand aimed at the upper end of the market such as Amstel or the locally produced Aguila Master in Spain.

▷ The premium Heineken brand itself where every effort is made to maintain quality and brand integrity. In the UK the product itself has been developed (called product expansion) into Heineken Export Strength, a stronger version more like the usual Heineken found throughout the rest of Europe.

☐   Up-to-date information on Heineken can be found on their website: www.heineken.com

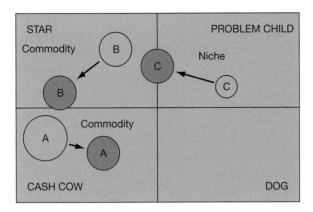

F 10.10 Boston matrix for a hypothetical company

Finance and product portfolios

The structure of the product portfolio has implications for the cash flow of an organization (Guiltinan and Paul, 1982). The problem child consumes cash for development and promotional costs at a rate of knots, without generating much cash by way of revenues. The star might start to generate revenues but will still be facing high costs, particularly in marketing to establish its market position against new entry competitors. It is therefore likely to be cash neutral. Only as a cash cow are revenues likely to outstrip costs and cash flow likely to be positive. There are two kinds of dogs. One is a cash dog that covers its costs and might be worth keeping, for example if it brings in customers for other products or services or it shares overheads. The other is the genuine dog which is losing money – both in cash flow and profit terms – and should be scrapped. It is from this model that phrases like 'shoot the dog', 'invest in stars' and 'milk the cow' came. These implications are shown in Figure 10.11.

STAR			PROBLEM CHILD		
Revenue	+ + +		Revenue	+	
Expenditure	– – –		Expenditure	– – –	
Cash flow	neutral		Cash flow	negative	
Revenue	+ + +		Revenue	+	
Expenditure	–		Expenditure	–	
Cash flow	positive		Cash flow	neutral	
CASH COW			DOG		

F 10.11 Cash flow implications of the Boston matrix

Ideally entrepreneurial companies have a balanced portfolio of product/ service offerings so that the surplus cash from cash cows can be used to invest in the problem children. However, that situation may take many years to achieve. These surplus funds can be used almost as venture capital to invest, selectively, in new products and services. This ideal firm – if it exists – is self-financing. The problem that arises with an unbalanced portfolio is that there is either a surplus of cash (no new products) or a deficit (too many new products). If the entrepreneurial firm has too many problem children and stars in its portfolio (too many good, new ideas) then it will require cash flow injections which will only be forthcoming if it can either borrow the capital – and that largely depends on the strength of the balance sheet – or raise more equity finance. The challenge is to develop and then effectively manage a balanced portfolio using the different structures available.

Remember, however, that cash flow is not the same as profit. Whilst the analysis above refers to cash flow, the following technique uses profitability. The ABC Sales/Contribution analysis measures success in terms of the profitability (or contribution to overheads) of a product in relationship to its sales within the overall product portfolio. High sales and high contribution are the ideal combination. ABC analysis helps identify those products that are of longer-term value to the company – really successful products. An example is shown in Figure 10.12. Sales are measured on the vertical axis and contribution on the horizontal axis. Contribution is the difference between total sales and total variable costs. It represents the profit contribution towards the fixed overheads. The 45° diagonal line from bottom left to top right is the optimum, representing a balance between sales and profit, but of course most products will fall on either side. Class A products are the ideal – they have high sales and make a large contribution to the overheads of the firm. Class B are less attractive and class C least attractive.

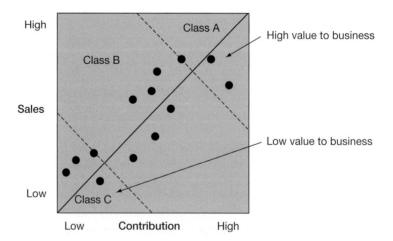

F 10.12 ABC analysis chart

A firm would want to regularly review class C products for viability. They might be an important, albeit small, part of a homogenous product portfolio or because they generate needed cash flow, but there is a danger that they distract from more important products. A firm would want to investigate class B products with high contribution but low sales, to see if sales can be expanded, for example into new markets. And conversely, it would want to investigate class B products with low contribution and high sales to see whether margins can be improved, for example through cost efficiencies. Sales, profitability and cash flow generation are different aspects of performance that all need to be carefully managed. They are unlikely to be perfectly balanced.

Product modification, extension and expansion

Product innovation is not just about entirely new product/market offerings. Product life cycles can be managed in innovative ways so as to expand and extend them and grow the market. Early adopters are the customers characterized as buying products in the growth phase of the life cycle. This is the point when the company can start expanding the product offering and start meeting the needs of selected market segments in order to counter the threat of competition moving in. Expanding the offering means developing product variations. So, for example, a car manufacturer might start offering sports, estate or fuel-efficient variants of a model. A soft drinks manufacturer might start to offer 'light' variants or new flavours for a successful brand. The original product might also be modified in terms of quality, function or style so as to address any weaknesses or omissions in it. In many cases service levels might be improved.

At the same time the company might want to try to find new distribution channels so that more customers gain exposure to the product. Sometimes they move from a selective distribution network to a more intensive network. Associated with this is a more aggressive promotion and pricing strategy that encourages further market penetration ahead of the rapidly emerging competition. Building the brand is important and this will be a vital part of the advertising message.

Further growth may even be possible in the mature phase of the life cycle. In many cases a mature market presents opportunities to start segmenting the market and tailoring the product range that was expanded in the previous phase through product modification, so as to better meet the different needs of the different market segments that purchase them. This might lead to further expansion of the range and further product modification in terms of quality, function or style. Although essentially a defensive strategy to counter competition, product expansion can also be used as a strategy to seek out new markets for similar products. As we shall

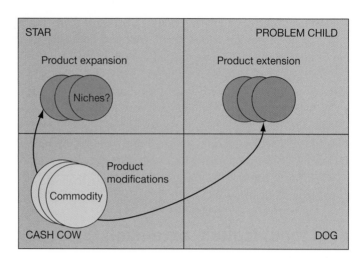

see in the next chapter, Amazon, Apple, Facebook, Google and Microsoft are all doing this as part of a battle to become 'internet utilities'. In this way, using the terminology of the Boston matrix, the cash cow product can be 're-invented' to become a series of smaller star products, all of which are highly profitable.

Another technique is called product extension. In this way a successful brand can be extended to similar but different products that might be purchased by the same customers. For example, a number of chocolate bar manufacturers have successfully extended their brand into ice cream. The key to success here is having a strong brand, one that actually means something to customers, and with values that can be extended onto the other products. Thus Timberland, a company well-known for producing durable outdoor footwear, extended its product range to include durable outdoor clothing. Many so-called new products are in fact line extensions. This strategy is generally a less expensive and lower-risk alternative for firms seeking to increase sales. The cash cow product can therefore also be 're-invented' to become a series of smaller problem children. However, these will face all the challenges of a problem child and may face stiff competition from existing companies in the market. Risk is, however, mitigated compared to a completely new product launch because of customer loyalty to the brand.

Product modification, extension and expansion opportunities can be represented in the Boston matrix. Again this is a useful visual aid to understanding strategy options. An example of this is shown in Figure 10.13.

Finding new markets

An important way of extending the life of a product or service is to find new markets for it, usually overseas – as with McDonald's entry into developing markets. In seeking new overseas markets the lowest-risk option is to seek out segments – or customers – that are similar to the ones to which the firm already sells. Another reason for finding new markets is to achieve economies of scale of production – particularly important if the product is perceived as a commodity and cost leadership is dependent upon achieving those economies. A further reason might also be that a company's key competence lies with the product, for example with capital goods like cars, and therefore the continued exploitation of the product by market development is the preferred route for expansion. Most capital goods companies follow this strategy – opening up new overseas markets as existing markets become saturated because of the high cost of developing new products. By way of contrast, many service businesses such as accounting, insurance, advertising and banking have been pulled into overseas markets because their clients operate there.

Of vital importance in considering whether to enter a new market is its structure – the customers, suppliers, competitors – and the potential substitutes and barriers to entry. These determine the degree of competition and therefore the profitability likely to be achieved. Michael Porter (op. cit.) developed a useful structural analysis of industries which he claims goes some way towards explaining the profitability of firms within it. He claims that five forces determine competitiveness in any industry.

1 *The power of buyers.* This is determined by the relative size of buyers and their concentration. It is also influenced by the volumes they purchase, the information they have about competitors or substitutes, switch costs and their ability to backward integrate. Switch costs are the costs of switching to another product. The extent to which the product they are buying is differentiated in some way also affects relative buying power. The greater the power of the buyers, the weaker the bargaining position of the firm selling to them. So, for example, if buyers are large firms, in concentrated industries, buying large volumes with good price information about a relatively undifferentiated product with low switch costs they will be in a strong position to keep prices low.

Power of buyers
Number/concentration
Extent of differentiation
Switch costs
Margins they earn
Backward integration

2 *The power of suppliers.* This is also determined by the relative size of firms and the other factors mentioned above. So, for example, if suppliers are large firms in concentrated industries, with well-differentiated products that are relatively important to the small firms buying them, then those small firms are in a weak position to keep prices, and therefore their costs, low.

Power of suppliers
Concentration
Extent of substitutes
Importance of supplier
Extent of differentiation
Forward integration

3 *The threat of new entrants.* Barriers to entry keep out new entrants to an industry. These can arise because of legal protection (patents and so on), economies of scale, proprietary product differences, brand identity, access to distribution, government policy, switch costs, capital costs and so forth. For example, a firm whose product is protected by patent or copyright may feel that it is relatively safe from competition. The greater the possible threat of new entry to a market, the lower the bargaining power and control over price of the firm within it.

Barriers to entry
Economies of scale
Product differentiation
Capital requirements
Legal agreements
Switch costs

Threat of substitutes
Changing technology
Changing market
Changing tastes
Switch costs
Extent of differentiation

Competitive rivalry
Number and size of firms
Industry growth
Extent of differentiation
Capacity increments
Exit barriers

4 *The threat of substitutes.* This revolves around their relative price performance, switch costs and the propensity of the customer to switch, for example because of changes in tastes or fashion. The greater the threat of substitutes, the less the ability of the firm to charge a high price. So, for example, a small firm selling a poorly-differentiated product in a price-sensitive, fashion market would find it difficult to charge a high price.

5 *Competitive rivalry in the industry.* The competitive rivalry of an industry will depend on the number and size of firms within it and their concentration, its newness and growth and therefore its attractiveness in terms of profit and value added together with intermittent over-capacity. Crucially important is the extent of product differentiation, brand identity and switch costs. The greater the competitive rivalry, the less the ability of the firm to charge a high price.

Porter claims that these five forces determine the strength of competition in the market – and therefore firm profitability. They are a function of industry structure – the underlying economic and technical characteristics of the industry. They can change over time but the analysis does emphasize the need to select industries carefully in the first place. The forces also provide a framework for predicting, a priori, the success or otherwise of the firm. For example, a small firm competing with many other small firms to sell a relatively undifferentiated product to a few large customers in an industry with few barriers to entry is unlikely to do well without some radical shifts in its marketing strategies.

To Porter's analysis we might add the need for an economic analysis of the environment of the country being considered – domestic demand, local laws and regulations, government policies, exchange rates, related and supporting industries etc. Of course, success in the new market depends upon competitive advantage and, as we have noted, this is achieved when there is a match between a firm's internal strengths in resources and capabilities and the key success factors of the industry – but we would add that this is in the context of the particular national environment.

Two further factors warrant consideration in deciding whether to enter a new market – entry and exit barriers. Entry barriers can arise from geographic constraints, legal requirements or high investment costs. Exit barriers can arise from legal constraints and/or the high costs associated with exit. These factors are represented in Figure 10.14. All things being equal, the most attractive market in terms of profitability is likely to be one with high entry barriers and low exit barriers (quadrant A). This is because few firms can enter the market but poor performers can easily exit. With high entry barriers but high exit barriers (quadrant B), poor performers will be forced to stay on and fight for market share, making the returns more risky. Unfortunately, a firm seeking to enter either of these markets has to overcome the high entry barriers. However, if entry barriers are low, returns are likely to be low. Returns will be stable if exit barriers are

Source: Adapted from Wilson, R.M.S. and Gilligan, C. (1997) *Strategic Marketing Management: Planning, Implementation and Control*, Oxford: Butterworth-Heinemann.

low, since exit is easy and market forces are allowed to operate unimpeded (quadrant C). Returns will be risky if exit barriers are high, since poor performers will be forced to stay on and fight for market share if the market worsens (quadrant D).

Penetrating foreign markets

There are many ways to enter a foreign market. If the firm's competitive advantage is based on resources located in its home country then the form this takes should be exporting. Exporting is also often a low-cost, low-risk way of finding out about the market. It can take the form of spot sales – now much easier to achieve for some firms with the advent of the internet. But to achieve market presence in local distribution channels a local distributor in the selected country may well be needed. The distributor might influence changes in the product or other elements of the marketing mix to suit local needs. The company might be expected to finance advertising and promotion itself and with no certainty of a profitable return. Finding a distributor can be difficult enough but if, for whatever reason, the distributor does not push the firm's products then there is little the firm can do other than change distributors, unless they are willing to take on the job of marketing in the country themselves – and that can be both expensive and risky.

Another approach to penetrating an overseas market is to offer a local firm a licence to produce the product. This allows them to capitalize on their local knowledge and involves them taking on many of the associated risks. For a service business, the equivalent is to appoint a franchisee. Franchisees apply a fairly standard franchise format to the particular market in which they operate. Their local market knowledge and dedication is vital if the market is to be effectively penetrated. If the franchise roll-out is successful they share in the success. To be effective, the firm and their franchisee or distributor must have a symbiotic relationship, one based upon mutual trust and with effective incentives to ensure success. The Body Shop's rapid growth over thirty years owed much to its successful global roll-out using

> ### 📂 Case insight Rolls-Royce Aerospace
>
> **Expanding overseas**
>
> Based in the UK, Rolls-Royce produces about a quarter of all commercial aircraft engines in the world. In 2012 it announced a £355 million ($562 million) investment in Singapore – its first capital investment on this scale outside the UK. Once fully operational, the facility will assemble and test about 250 engines a year – about half of Rolls-Royce's global output. Already almost half of Rolls-Royce's new orders for aircraft engines last year came from airlines in Asia. Rolls-Royce has had a presence in Singapore for 50 years, through joint ventures and servicing for one of its biggest customers, Singapore Airlines. The company was offered tax incentives and training and innovation grants to set up in Singapore. However, the biggest pull was the promise of a steady supply of highly-skilled labour, through partnerships with local universities and polytechnics. It also expects productivity to be higher than in the UK because it will be operating in one building and therefore able to completely reorganize its manufacturing processes. Manufacturing and assembly in the UK is spread across five different facilities.

a franchise format. In most countries a head franchisee was granted exclusive rights as user of the trade mark, distributor and, after an initial trial of running a few shops itself, the right to sub-franchise. In this way the firm built upon local market knowledge and minimized its risks. This model was not always followed because of the quality of the head franchisee. For example, the firm took back control of the franchise in France because the head franchisee was not delivering the volume of sales expected.

The next stage in involvement in a local market might be a strategic alliance/partnership or joint venture, whereby partners bring different resources to the joint venture and share the profits as well as the risks. In some developing economies like China, only joint ventures with Chinese firms are allowed. The final stage in direct investment is the setting up of the wholly-owned subsidiary which may involve simply marketing and distribution or be fully integrated into the operations of the parent company. These different degrees of involvement in foreign markets and the increasing risk associated with them are shown in Figure 10.15. There is no prescriptive 'best' approach and often the degree of involvement in the foreign market increases with the success of the product or service.

F 10.15 Degrees of involvement in foreign markets

| Export | License or franchise | Joint venture | Wholly-owned subsidiary |

Increasing resource commitment

🗁 Case with question B&Q in China

Establishing operations in an overseas market

British retailers have a history of failure in overseas ventures and the experience of B&Q, the UK do-it-yourself (DIY) store chain, in setting up in China is interesting. B&Q opened its first store in China in 1999. Up until 2005, when China joined the World Trade Organization, foreign retailers were prevented from opening more than three stores in any one city and some towns were completely off limits. What is more, they had to work with Chinese partners. B&Q did deals with a number of Chinese organizations, normally giving them a 35% stake in the business, but making it very clear that B&Q intended to buy them out at soon as it could – which it typically did in 2005. Also in 2005, it acquired 13 stores of OBI China for an undisclosed sum, all of which have been converted to the B&Q format.

The stores were a huge success and the Beijing store now boasts the highest average customer spend of any of B&Q's stores in the world (over £50). But it is the cultural similarities and differences and how they affected the retailer that are really interesting. The stores look very similar to those in the UK, although they are usually considerably bigger. At 20,000 sq. ft, the Beijing Golden Four Season store is the largest of its kind in the world. Like their UK counterparts, staff wear orange overalls. The products offered are also very similar, although the space devoted to garden products is considerably smaller and the Chinese B&Q also sells soft furnishings.

But the big difference is that Chinese customers do not want to 'do-it' themselves at all, they prefer to get others to do it for them. The Chinese customers are typically middle class and wealthy. They come to the store to select what they want and get it installed by a professional. The reasons for this are partly cultural and partly economic. Labour is significantly cheaper than in the West but also things like painting would be regarded as a major DIY job in China. What is more, if you buy one of the thousands of apartments being built in Beijing you buy a concrete shell – with no garden – and customers will then purchase everything else they need – plumbing, lighting, kitchens, bathrooms and furnishings – from one store. B&Q therefore started to offer more services to customers – designers and contractors to install its products. The Beijing store has a room full of designers working at computer terminals, ready to design the customer's living room, kitchen or bathroom. Teams of workers then deliver and install the products. Twenty-five per cent of all B&Q sales in China now involve some kind of B&Q service.

In 2008/09 sales at B&Q China fell dramatically. Sales continued to fall into 2012. The ensuing losses resulted in B&Q closing almost one-third of its stores and reducing floor space in others. Local press comments indicated local price competition was also a major factor in ths decline. Time will tell whether B&Q can succeed where other British retailers have failed.

🗆 Up-to-date information on B&Q can be found on their website: www.kingfisher.com

QUESTION

1 What lessons can you learn from the experience of B&Q in China?

Industry life cycles

Just as there is a product/service life cycle, so too there is an industry life cycle – its supply side equivalent – with similar characteristics. An industry, and the firms within it, cannot count on longevity or continuity. Research conducted by McKinsey on more than 1000 companies in 15 industries is cited by Foster and Kaplan (2001) to prove this. They compared the original 1917 *Forbes* magazine list of the top 100 US companies (by size of assets) to a comparable list of companies published in 1987. They found that 61 of the top 100 had ceased to exist and, of the remainder, only 18 remained in the top 100. These included Kodak, DuPont, General Electric, General Motors and Procter & Gamble. However, of these 18, only two – Kodak and General Electric – had outperformed the stock market ... and in 2012 Kodak filed for bankruptcy. The group as a whole made results that were 20% below the market's compound annual growth rate of 7.5% over those 70 years. Foster and Kaplan also looked at Standard & Poor's 500 list in 1957 and compared it to the 1997 list. Only 74 (37%) survived the 40 years and only 12 (6%) outperformed the index over the period.

Deans et al. (2003) claim that an industry has four distinct phases. In the first there is little or no market concentration as start-ups, spin-offs, firms in deregulated industries and smaller companies typically compete in this phase. Concentration, measured by the combined market share of the three biggest companies, is low – less than 20%. This phase typically lasts at least five years. The second phase is the 'scale phase' where size begins to matter. Leading companies start to merge and concentration increases to 30–45%. In the third phase the authors claim that companies extend their core business, eliminating secondary operations or exchanging them with other firms for assets closer to their core business. Concentration in this phase is almost 70%. The final phase sees concentration reaching 90% and witnesses the large companies forming alliances in order to boost growth. This is shown in Figure 10.16. The authors claim that the main factor determining corporate survival and success is the speed with which the company actively moves towards the final phase – 'the endgame curve' – through a series of mergers and acquisitions. We shall deal with each of these strategies in the next chapter. It is by no means clear that they are always successful.

Endurance or longevity, as such, seems to bear no relationship to performance. Foster and Kaplan (op. cit.) concluded: 'Managing for survival, even among the best and most revered corporations, does not guarantee strong, long-term performance. In fact quite the opposite is true ... Unless companies open up their decision-making processes, relax conventional notions of control, and change at the pace and scale of the market, their performances will be drawn into an entropic slide to mediocrity.' They argue that control processes themselves can deaden the company to the vital and constant need for change. They want to abandon outdated,

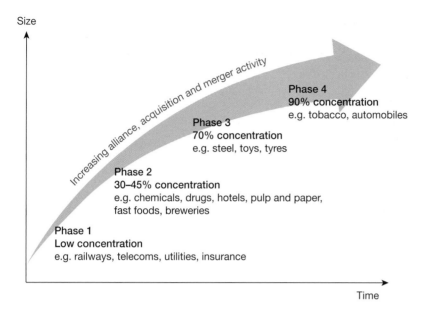

Size

Increasing alliance, acquisition and merger activity

Phase 4
90% concentration
e.g. tobacco, automobiles

Phase 3
70% concentration
e.g. steel, toys, tyres

Phase 2
30–45% concentration
e.g. chemicals, drugs, hotels, pulp and paper,
fast foods, breweries

Phase 1
Low concentration
e.g. railways, telecoms, utilities, insurance

Time

F 10.16 Industry life cycles and acquisitions and mergers

ingrown structures and rules and adopt new decision-making processes, control systems and mental models. The authors' solution to this problem is 'creative destruction' – strategies of discontinuity and transformation – strategies that are outlined throughout this book. However, they argue against incremental change in favour of 'transformational strategies' of continually creating new businesses and selling off or closing down divisions where growth is slowing. This is clearly a radical option and one that risks selling off assets that may be key to future development and not using resources generated by products later in their life cycle. But are these really alternatives? If change is both incremental and radical, is it impossible for one organization to combine both? The answer to this lies in organizational structures.

Organizational structure and product portfolios

This book has put forward an alternative view, saying that a hybrid organic structure can be developed to accommodate divisions or subsidiaries where growth is slowing because of the age profile of their product portfolio. The major reason for the desirability of this is the cash generation potential from a balanced portfolio. This is important to fund innovation. Apple's new products have been funded by existing cash cows like the Mac. Google's Android operating system has been funded by its search advertising. The Virgin Group's start-ups are frequently funded by selling off at least part of existing, more mature, businesses. Indeed, the Virgin Group manages to successfully accommodate very different businesses with different growth prospects, from train services to new media, with very different structures within an overall umbrella organization. We shall discuss this further in the next chapter. But the question remains, should you segregate divisions with products at different stages of their life cycle into different, separate organizations? Perhaps you should group them together to make the most of entrepreneurial expertise? And what happens as they progress through their life cycle? Do you transfer them to different organizations, delineated not by their product specification but by the stage they are at in their life cycle and the managerial style therefore required, and at what point do you make the transfer?

Management is an art not a science, so there are no prescriptive solutions to these problems – and there is often more than one solution to a problem. But there are some clues. As we have seen, size matters and new initiatives or ventures are better off – for all sorts of reasons – starting small. Small organizations can more easily encourage entrepreneurship. Whether they combine at some later stage depends on the synergy that might be obtained from combining them and their operational relatedness. 3M have different divisions into which new ventures are expected to be merged. Divisions might comprise different operating units or companies, each with product/market profiles that are different in significant ways but can be combined in some overriding way. Inevitably practicality involves compromising some of the principles outlined in Chapter 8. New products might spawn new companies or be swallowed up into existing operating units or companies. Xerox has so many completely different new ventures that it is far more relaxed about spinning out completely different companies. The point is that there is unlikely to be any synergy offered through combining them. Indeed, in these circumstances completely spinning off, and even selling off, subsidiaries that are not core to the business may be an appropriate option. There is no prescriptive blueprint. What is more, when these changes take place is an even more complex judgement that depends on individuals as well as products, markets and competitors combined with an array of external factors, many of which will be outside the control of the company.

The real issue, then, is the form of the umbrella organization – head office, parent company, whatever it is called. Unless it is essentially entrepreneurial, this diversity will just not happen. The organizational solution outlined in Chapter 6 is the use of a hybrid organic structure that combines different organizational forms within an overall organic structure (Figure 6.7). The umbrella organization must be able to handle this heterogeneous approach to management with different styles of leadership, structures and cultures in different subsidiaries or divisions. Essentially, it must be willing to delegate day-to-day management, within defined parameters, to these subsidiaries or divisions and it must be able to deal with the apparent inconsistencies this can generate. However, there are different approaches to this, each of which produce a different dominant culture. The BP example in Chapter 8 showed one approach – that of trying to maintain balance within each operating unit belonging to one organization. By way of contrast, as we saw in Chapter 6, the Virgin empire thrives on entirely separate organizations sharing the same culture and brand, but little else.

This sort of organization needs also to be adept at communicating with its shareholders who may be confused and unable to understand what constitutes the core competences of the business. As we shall explain in the next chapter, if they see the organization as a conglomerate of unconnected operations, the share price is likely to be discounted. This was one of the reasons Richard Branson reprivatized the Virgin Group.

🖰 Case with questions Barbie® and Mattel Corporation

Extending the product life cycle

Barbie was born in 1959 but she has never aged because she is a doll. To date over 1 billion Barbies have been sold by the US company that own her – Mattel Corporation. Ruth Handler, who founded the company along with her husband, Elliot, modelled the doll on an 11.5 inch plastic German toy called Lilli sold to adult men. She named the adapted doll after her daughter, Barbara. At its height, it was estimated that the average girl aged between 3 and 11 in the USA owned 10 Barbies, in Britain or Italy she owned 7 and in France or Germany she owned 5. With annual sales of over $1.6 billion, it is little wonder that the Barbie brand is valued at some $2 billion – making it the most valuable toy brand in the world. But how has this plastic doll endured for so long in an industry notorious for its susceptibility to fickleness and fashion? Surely it must have come to the end of its life cycle? The answer lies in innovative marketing and product extension.

When originally introduced into the market Barbie was competing with dolls that were based on babies and designed to be cradled and cared for. By way of contrast, Barbie, with her adult looks, exaggerated female figure normally with blonde hair and pouting lips, was seen as adult and independent – a child of 'liberated' times, one that could become anything or anyone the child wanted. But

Mattel describe Barbie as a 'lifestyle, not just a toy ... a fashion statement, a way of life'. Barbie was not only innovative, it was intended to be more than just a doll.

Every year Mattel devises some 150 different Barbie dolls and 120 new outfits. She has always been trendy and continues to re-invent herself. She was a 'mod' in the 1960s and a hippie in the 1970s. Her hair style has changed from ponytail, bubble-cut, page boy, swirl to side-part flip. She has had various roles in life – from holidaying in Malibu to being an astronaut. Barbie has seen life as a soldier, air force pilot, surgeon, vet, doctor, dentist, engineer, fire-fighter, diplomat, fashion model, Olympic athlete, skier, scuba diver, ball player, TV news reporter, aerobics instructor, rock star, rap musician and even a presidential candidate. Each role has numerous accessories to go with it – from cars to horse and carriage, from jewellery box to lunch box – and including a partner called Ken. Dressing and undressing, grooming and making-up is what Barbie is made for. You can even buy a 'Make-me-pretty talking styling head' play set. And Mattel has worked hard to generate brand extension – more add-ons to the basic Barbie doll. The 2002/03 Rapunzel Barbie came with a handsome prince, not to mention a computer-animated video and 14 product tie-ins. By 2006 the company

→

had produced the sixth Barbie movie, *The 12 Dancing Princesses*, each accompanied by special dolls. By wearing a motion-sensor bracelet and shoe clip, the latest *Let's Dance Barbie!* allows the doll to follow a child's dance steps. A previous video based on Barbie in the *Nutcracker* grossed $150 million in sales, including associated products. In addition, Mattel license production of hundreds of different Barbie products, including make-up, pyjamas, bed clothes, furniture and wallpapers.

Mattel also continue to segment the market – trying to find new markets to sell the doll and its accessories to. The product extensions attempt this. But selling beyond the basic market, for example to older girls, is problematic. The main problem is that 'age compression' – girls getting older sooner – means that it is increasingly hard to hang on to the basic market, let alone trying to extend it. One variation called *My Scene* attempted to sell three Barbie variants, with an older, more 'hip' look, together with perfume, cosmetics and music to this older group. This doll has a movable face feature that allows girls to create expressions on the doll's face like frowns, pouts, smirks and smiles.

Over the years Barbie has become a cult. There are Barbie conventions, fan clubs, magazines, websites and exhibitions. She is seen by many as the ideal vision of an American woman. In 1976 the USA included Barbie in the bicentennial time capsule. There are sociology courses in the USA based upon her, speculating on this image and what it implies. Mattel has cultivated these images. It has also worked hard at defending Barbie's image (or reputation). In 1997 the company prosecuted (unsuccessfully) the pop group Aqua who produced the satirical song 'Barbie Girl'. Nevertheless, Barbie seems now to have become something of a gay icon. Whether gay or not, collectors have been known to pay up to $10,000 for a vintage model. The question is whether, in a changing world, young girls will continue to want the Barbie fantasy world.

The problem remains that Barbie is getting old and must be nearing the end of her product life cycle. Sales peaked at $1.8 million in 1997. Since then they have fallen continuously every year. So the question is how long can innovations sustain Barbie?

☐ Up-to-date information on the Mattel Corporation can be found on their website: www.mattel.com

QUESTIONS

1 Why has Barbie been so successful?

2 Barbie is hardly a high-tech product, but has Mattel been innovative in how it has developed the product and extended its life cycle?

3 What are the lessons for product innovation?

Summary

▷ To an economist competitive advantage exists because of imperfections in the market created by changes in the market or changes in the firm. Business people try to create competitive advantage by combining capabilities and resources of a firm differently so as to offer customers a product or service that they value more than that offered by competitors.

▷ Porter's generic marketing strategies highlight three fundamental ways of gaining competitive advantage:

  ▷ Low price – as we see with **easyJet,** this is based upon an ability to keep costs as low as possible;

  ▷ High differentiation – as we see with **Quanta Computers** and **Crocs**™, this is based upon some real product/market differences that are valued by customers;

▷ Customer focus – based upon a better understanding of customer needs. When combined with a differentiated product this leads to the development of a niche business, as we see with **Quad Electroaccoustics** and the **Morgan Motor Company**.

◁ An understanding of the value chain can lead to a better understanding of how these elements of differentiation may be enhanced. Today supply chains are global (**Hewlett Packard Pavilion**).

◁ High differentiation can be achieved through physical aspects of the product, including design, but also the marketing of the product, particularly branding. Effective branding, for example with **Crocs**™, of a differentiated product can improve customer loyalty.

◁ At the corporate level corporate entrepreneurship generates sustainable competitive advantage because it facilitates change and innovation within the firm.

◁ For existing product/market offerings, marketing strategy should emphasize something that is as unique as possible and delivers as much value to customers as possible today and, more importantly, tomorrow. You should differentiate with the aim of dominating the market and do this effectively and quickly, and then continue to innovate based upon the differential advantage.

◁ Products and services face a predictable life cycle that has implications for marketing strategy at different phases.

◁ Most firms, like **Heineken**, have a range of products and services at different stages of their life cycle, each tailored to the particular needs of their market place. These can be represented in a Boston matrix – a loose conceptual framework that helps clarify the complexity of the portfolio. The two axes of the matrix represent market attractiveness and market strength. Products at different points in the matrix have different strategic imperatives and different marketing strategies.

◁ The product life cycle can be extended through product modification, expansion and extension. By using these strategies, the **Barbie**® doll has managed to remain popular for almost 50 years. **Crocs**™ are now diversifying their range of shoes, based upon the qualities of the original clogs.

◁ The Boston matrix has cash flow implications; problem children use cash, stars are cash-neutral, generating but also using large amounts, and cash cows generate cash. Only when the portfolio is balanced will cash flow be stable.

◁ Cash flow is not the same as profitability. The ABC analysis allows you to analyze product in terms of sales and contribution – those with high levels of both are very attractive (class A products). But equally it can be used to adjust other elements of the marketing mix, such as price, so as to maximize sales.

◁ Problem children are best managed by entrepreneurs – or entrepreneurial firms – cash cows by accountants – or administrative firms. Each requires a different sort of management. The challenge is to find a form of organization that allows both to flourish. There are many different approaches to this and it can be achieved whilst still maintaining an entrepreneurial ethos through a hybrid organic structure.

◁ Finding new, typically foreign, markets for existing products or services is a key part of extending the life cycle of a product. It also allows firms to benefit from economies of scale or to capitalize on their product-knowledge competence.

◁ In deciding which markets to enter, consideration should be given to Porter's Five Forces, coupled with an economic analysis of the national market, as well as entry and exit barriers. Market development of this sort is most successful for companies whose core competences lie in the efficiency of their existing production methods, for example in the capital goods industries, and are seeking economies of scale, or for firms adept at sales, marketing and developing close customer relationships.

▷ There are a number of ways to enter a foreign market, depending upon the degree of commitment the firm is willing to make. These are: to export, to license/franchise, to set up a joint venture (**B&Q**) or to set up a wholly-owned subsidiary. There is no prescriptive approach but often the success of one can lead to increasing commitment.

▷ Companies and industries also have life cycles. Companies do not last forever and they must plan for their own replacement. Similarly industries grow, mature and decline, and by the maturity phase a company should have become a dominant player in the market – perhaps through mergers, acquisitions and alliances – so that it can maximize its returns.

Essays and discussion topics

1 Nobody really knows how to generate competitive advantage. Discuss.

2 How can you differentiate a product or service and then ensure competitors do not copy it?

3 How can you sustain competitive advantage, and over what time span?

4 Value chains are an elegant concept but cannot be operationalized. Discuss.

5 How important is branding? Can a brand be valued?

6 How might you safeguard competitive advantage?

7 Some products – basic necessities such as food and water – do not have a life cycle. Discuss.

8 How useful are the labels of 'innovators', 'early adopters', 'late adopters' and 'laggards' to customers at different stages of the life cycle?

9 In practical terms it is impossible to find out where a product is at in its life cycle. Discuss.

10 What is the relationship between marketing mix and the product life cycle?

11 How useful is the Boston matrix?

12 How would you go about creating a scale for each axis of the Boston matrix that reflects a range of relevant factors? Give a practical example.

13 In what circumstances might you not want to 'shoot a dog'?

14 Give some examples of product expansions and extensions.

15 Can a problem child be profitable? Why and how?

16 Is a star always likely to be a 'class A' product? Explain.

17 In what circumstances might you retain a cash cow that is unprofitable? What would you do with it?

18 If management is an art, there is no point in studying it. Discuss.

19 What is the relationship between life cycles and leadership, culture and structure?

20 How do you go about creating a hybrid organic structure for an organization? How can it be sustained?

21 Even a hybrid organic organizational structure needs a leader. How do they go about leading subsidiaries or divisions that may not be entrepreneurial and have more traditional bureaucratic structures?

22 What is the logic of gradually increasing commitment to a foreign market? Under what circumstances might you wish to establish a wholly-owned subsidiary straight away?

23 How can a company become a dominant market force by the mature stage of its life cycle, other than through mergers and acquisitions?

24 If most firms are destined to fail, we cannot have learned anything about the management of business. Discuss.

Exercises and assignments

1 Select an industry that offers similar products or services, such as the airline or car industry, and position these offerings on the matrix representing Porter's generic strategies (Figure 10.1).

2 Select a well-known product that is now in the mature phase of its life cycle and chart how the marketing strategy has changed over that life cycle.

3 For your university, college or department, analyze the course portfolio using the Boston matrix. What are your conclusions?

4 For a selected company, analyze the product portfolio using the Boston matrix. What are your conclusions?

5 Select a company that has grown rapidly over the last five years. Analyze the strategies it has used to do this.

6 Select an industry and assess its competitiveness using Porter's Five Forces.

7 Select a mature industry. Research the major three companies in this industry and find out how they gained their market dominance.

References

3i European Enterprise Centre (1993) *Britain's Superleague Companies,* Report 9, August.

Birley, S. and Westhead, P. (1990) 'Growth and Performance Contrasts between Types of Small Firms', *Strategic Management Journal,* II.

Boston Consulting Group (1968) *Perspectives on Experience,* Boston, MA: Boston Consulting Group.

Boston Consulting Group (1972) *Perspectives on Experience,* Boston, MA: Boston Consulting Group.

Burns, P. (1994) *Winners and Losers in the 1990s,* 3i European Enterprise Centre, Report 12, April.

Burns, P. (2011) *Entrepreneurship and Small Business,* 3rd edn, Basingstoke: Palgrave Macmillan.

Buzzell, R.D. and Gale, B.T. (1987) *The PIMS Principles – Linking Strategy to Performance,* New York: Free Press.

Buzzell, R.D. Heany, D.F. and Schoeffer, S. (1974) 'Impact of Strategic Planning on Profit Performance', *Harvard Business Review,* 52/2.

Deans, G., Zeisel, S. and Kroeger, F. (2003) *Winning the Merger End Game,* New York: McGraw-Hill.

Dunkelberg, W.G., Cooper, A.C., Woo, C. and Dennis, W.J. (1987) 'New Firm Growth and Performance', in N.C. Churchill, J.A. Hornday, B.A. Kirchhoff, C.J. Krasner and K.H. Vesper (eds) *Frontiers of Entrepreneurship Research,* Babson College, Boston, MA.

Foster, R. and Kaplan, S. (2001) *Creative Destruction: Why Companies that are Built to Last Underperform the Stock Market,* New York: Doubleday/Currency.

Guiltinan, J.P. and Paul, G.W. (1982) *Marketing Management: Strategies and Programs,* New York: McGraw-Hill.

Hamel, G. and Prahalad, C.K. (1994) *Competing For the Future: Breakthrough Strategies for Seizing Control of your Industry and Creating the Markets of Tomorrow,* Boston, MA: Harvard Business School Press.

Harrison, J. and Taylor, B. (1996) *Supergrowth Companies: Entrepreneurs in Action,* Oxford: Butterworth-Heinemann.

Macrae, D.J.R. (1991) 'Characteristics of High and Low Growth Small and Medium Sized Businesses', paper presented at 21st European Small Business Seminar, Barcelona, Spain.

Nohria, N. and Joyce, W. (2003) 'What Really Works', *Harvard Business Review,* July/August.

Porter, M. (1985) *Competitive Advantage: Creating and Sustaining Superior Performance.* New York: The Free Press.

Ray, G.H. and Hutchinson, P.J. (1983) *The Financing and Financial Control of Small Enterprise Development,* London: Gower.

Siegel, R., Siegel, E. and MacMillan, I.C. (1993) 'Characteristics Distinguishing High Growth Ventures, *Journal of Business Venturing,* 8.

Solem, O. and Steiner, M.P. (1989) 'Factors for Success in Small Manufacturing Firms – and with special emphasis on growing firms', paper presented at Conference on SMEs and the Challenges of 1992, Mikkeli, Finland.

Storey, D.J., Watson, R. and Wynarczyk, P. (1989) *Fast Growth Small Business: Case Studies of 40 Small Firms in Northern Ireland,* Department of Employment, Research Paper No 67.

Tellis, G.J., Stremersch, S. and Yin, E. (2003) 'The International Takeoff of New Products: The Role of Economics, Culture, and Country Innovativeness', *Marketing Science*, 22(2).

Treacy, M. and Wiersema, F. (1995) *The Discipline of Market Leaders*, Reading, MA: Addison-Wesley.

Woo, C.Y., Cooper, A.C., Dunkelberg, W.C., Daellenbach, U. and Dennis, W.J. (1989) 'Determinants of Growth for Small and Large Entrepreneurial Start-Ups', paper presented to Babson Entrepreneurship Conference.

Wynarczyk, P., Watson, R., Storey, D.J., Short, H. and Keasey, K. (1993) *The Managerial Labour Market in Small and Medium-Sized Enterprises*, London: Routledge.

Yelle, L.E. (1979) 'The Learning Curve: Historical Review and Comprehensive Survey', *Decision Sciences*, 10.

Chapter **11**

Building value through acquisitions and diversification

Learning outcomes

By the end of this chapter you should be able to:

▷ Critically analyze the role of acquisitions and diversifications in encouraging corporate entrepreneurship;

▷ Critically appraise the reasons for acquiring another business;

▷ Critically analyze the role of external corporate venturing and the factors that might make it a successful strategy;

▷ Critically analyze the risks involved in a strategy of diversification and understand the factors that will create shareholder value, particularly for conglomerates;

▷ Understand how multi-businesses can create shareholder value.

Acquisitions, diversification and conglomerates

This chapter is about two related but different things: acquisitions and diversification. As we shall see, corporate acquisitions or mergers can be undertaken for many reasons. However, sometimes they are undertaken for the purpose of diversification and acquisition is the implementation strategy. Internal corporate venturing can also result in diversification. Diversification involves moving from core areas of activity into completely new and unrelated product/market areas. Diversification, as such, is central to the process of corporate evolution. As products come to the end of their natural life cycles, the longevity of any particular organization will depend on its ability to innovate and in so doing eventually redefine the business it is in, applying existing capabilities to developing new products, perhaps new industries and buying in those capabilities when necessary. It is part of the process of corporate entrepreneurship.

Innovation may involve the development of new products or new markets. Either strategy involves risk, but when it involves both it is at its riskiest. Often, however, these developments can be incremental, thus minimizing risk exposure. Sometimes these innovations can be 'bought in' by acquiring the intellectual property from another company and sometimes the whole company will be purchased. The scale of these company acquisitions is significant. The purchase of a small company is unlikely to change the direction of the acquiring company significantly and can be part of an overall strategy that involves 'corporate venturing'. However, if the acquisition is large it will be more difficult to integrate and may involve shifting the scope of the existing business – redefining the business it is in.

Sometimes, rather than integrating the acquired business, it may be allowed to operate independently. Over time different product/markets will rise and fall in importance, but sometimes a company will make a virtue of maintaining a widely diversified range of product/market offerings without any apparent cohesion or homogeneity. This sort of company is known as a conglomerate. True conglomerates that are public companies tend to be traded at discounts in the stock market for reasons explained in this chapter. Therefore it is important that an entrepreneurial multi-business company, with a hybrid organic structure, is clear about how it creates real value for its shareholders.

Strategic acquisitions

It is important that there is a clear strategic logic to any acquisition. All too often acquisitions have too much corporate ego tied up in the deal and that can lead to a loss of business logic. Apart from sheer opportunism – seeing a business that can be purchased for less than its value and then resold at

	Markets	
Product/Service	**Existing**	**New**
New	Gain market dominance Help with innovation	Diversification
Existing	Gain market dominance Consolidate existing market	Gain market dominance Enter foreign markets

F 11.1 The role of acquisitions in corporate entrepreneurship

Adapted from Ansoff, 1968.

a profit – there are four valid strategic reasons for public companies to acquire another going-concern business. These are shown in the product/market matrix in Figure 11.1.

1 **Existing product and market**

As we saw in the last chapter, research tells us that, at the product/market level, the strategy with the best chance of generating the highest profits is differentiation with the aim of dominating a market niche – and to do this as quickly as possible. Acquisitions may have a role to play in achieving rapid market dominance. It may be attractive to acquire competitors, albeit if the price is right, so as to eliminate them and buy their customer base.

The last chapter also demonstrated the need to consolidate market position at the mature phase of the life cycle as a defensive strategy to maintain market position, possibly involving volume and cost reduction. To achieve this, if the price is attractive, a company might acquire a competitor with the aim of closing the competitor's factories, transferring production to their own factories and achieving better economies of scale. The mobile telecommunications market in Europe saw this happening between 2002 and 2011 as manufacturing moved east.

2 **Existing product into a new market**

Once more, acquisition has a role to play in achieving global dominance quickly by buying competitors in foreign markets. One of the reasons for the early success of Lastminute.com was its aggressive acquisition strategy in European markets after its launch in 1995. It purchased similar online businesses as well as a wide range of related travel and holiday firms such as Lastminute.de in Germany, Dégriftour in France, Destination Holdings Group, Med Hotels, First Option and Gemstone. These acquisitions helped it to gain market dominance as well as scale in both product categories and geographic markets. In this way it consolidated its brand across Europe very quickly.

We also saw in the last chapter that acquisitions can make sense as a way of moving into new, often foreign, markets to sell products as they move through their life cycle. Sometimes, rather than setting up a completely new company or forming a joint venture with one that is established, it makes more sense to purchase a company that is already operating in that market.

3 **New product into an existing market**

Sometimes another company that is selling different but complementary products to the same market may be acquired so that its product range can integrated into that of the acquiring company, thus offering a more comprehensive offering to all customers (which may in itself be attractive) at the same time as gaining access to new customers. This strategy builds on the core competence of customer relations and may offer a cost effective way of increasing the sales to every customer through the consolidated distribution channels. This is why eBay purchased PayPal. The strategy is particularly effective for companies with strong brands.

Acquisitions can also be part of a coherent strategy of corporate venturing, whereby the larger company 'buys in' innovation from smaller companies. We deal with this in greater detail in the next section. Corporate venturing happens frequently where small 'R&D' organizations generate a significant proportion of innovations, for example in the pharmaceutical industry. Of course, it may be possible and cheaper, simply to license the product rather than buy the company. Just sometimes the acquisition is about changing or enhancing the core capabilities of the company – even changing its business scope fundamentally. In this case the acquisition becomes a diversification.

☐ Case insight eBay and PayPal

Acquiring complementary companies

Crucial to success for dot.com firms is the 'business model' – how income will be generated. Arguably the most successful model is that of the online auctioneer eBay. eBay was founded by Pierre Omidyar in 1995. The company now has expanded worldwide, claiming hundreds of millions of registered users, over 15,000 employees and revenues of almost $8 billion. eBay's success comes from being nothing more than an intermediary – software running on a web server. Its customers, both buyers and sellers, do all the work. Sellers pay to set up their own auction, buyers use eBay's software to place their bids, shipping and payment are arranged between the seller and buyer and eBay takes 7–18% of the selling price as commission for letting them use its software. eBay is simply the trading platform. It holds no stocks and its involvement in the trade is minimal. After each transaction the buyer and seller rate each other. Next to each user's identification is a figure in brackets recording the number of positive comments – thus encouraging honesty and trust. It is a truly virtual business which also sells advertising space. ➝

eBay developed a 'virtuous circle' in which more buyers attracted more sellers, who attracted yet more buyers and sellers – called 'network effects'. At the core of eBay's business is software rather than people. The company has bought software companies to gain exclusive use of their technologies and make the auction process more efficient. It therefore faces enormous economies of scale in attracting as many auction transactions as possible and, with that in mind, moved into new areas such as used cars and even plans to host storefronts for small merchants. It has also started to sell private-label versions of its service to companies, for a fee.

In 2002 eBay purchased PayPal, the dominant provider of internet payments in the USA with over 12 million customers, of whom 3.2 million are fee-paying business customers. The two companies are complementary but depend on each other. Indeed, auctions account for two-thirds of PayPal's business. PayPal allows customers to register details of their credit card or bank account with it. Then, when customers buy something on the internet, they just enter their e-mail account and the purchase price. The amount is then taken from their credit card or bank account. The advantage is that these details are not disclosed to the vendor. Like eBay, PayPal is fully automated, relying on software rather than people. Like eBay again, it also relies on 'network effects'. PayPal initially paid users $10 to sign up their friends to enable it to reach its critical mass, but now the firm is signing up 28,000 new users a day without this incentive. The commercial synergy between eBay and PayPal is clear. eBay's basic business model generates revenues from sellers. Driving buyers and sellers to use PayPal means eBay also turns buyers into clients. In addition, it means that for each new PayPal registration it achieves via the eBay site, it also earns off-site revenues when the PayPal account is used for non-eBay transactions.

4 Diversification

Moving into new markets with new products by acquisition may be attractive to management but it is fraught with dangers. We shall look at this in greater detail later in the chapter.

External corporate venturing

External corporate venturing occurs when larger companies 'buy in' innovation by acquiring smaller companies. This may involve a real partnership or a complete take-over of the smaller business. The reasons for corporate venturing rarely involve short-term financial gain but more normally relate to issues of innovation and strategic foresight. Small firms are often good at innovation and larger firms therefore have to buy them out to capitalize on their 'first mover advantage' in a critical area of new technology development. A US study (Acs and Audretsch, 1990) found that small firms produce 2.4 times as many innovations per employee as large firms. Another UK study (Pavitt et al., 1987) concluded that small firms are more likely to introduce fundamentally new innovations than large firms. Deakins and Freel (2006) concluded that they are most likely to play a significant role where technology is still evolving. Generally, the advantages of smaller firms in innovation, particularly their entrepreneurial orientation, mirror the weaknesses of larger firms and therefore collaboration between the two sizes (inside or outside the same company) can create powerful synergistic relationships (Vossen, 1998).

External corporate venturing happens far more in the USA than in the UK with firms like General Electric, Monsanto, Xerox, Apple, IBM, Kyocera, Intel, Dupont, Johnson and Johnson, Dell and Cisco particularly active. It happens in sectors ranging from telecommunications to consumer goods to engineering and is particularly common in the pharmaceutical industry. It has seen booms in the late 1960s, late 1980s and late 1990s and seems to be re-emerging at the time of writing (2012). In 2011 external corporate venturing represented $2.39 billion, or 15%, of total venture capital investment in the USA (www.pwc.com/us/en/press-releases/2012/q4-2011-corp-vc-press-release.jhtml).

The key to success in external corporate venturing is 'strategic fit'. This happens when there is a strong relationship with the core competences of the venturing company or when the venturing company is acquiring skills, technologies or customers and market segments that complement its strategic direction. Ideally there should be strong 'synergy' between the venture company and its smaller 'partner'. We shall explain the word 'synergy' later in the chapter. For the smaller company there can be advantages in gaining resources – money, skills and knowledge – or access to markets that it might not otherwise have. The advantages to the venturing company can be that:

▷ It facilitates innovation and knowledge transfer from external sources, where there are gaps in the venturing company's internal performance;
▷ It can be quick to execute;
▷ External sources of finance may be easier to access for an acquisition than for innovation;
▷ It facilitates the creation of semi-autonomous operating units with their own cultures, incentives and business models and can therefore be part of a strategy of business transformation;
▷ It is often highly motivating to the staff involved.

The disadvantages are that:

▷ It requires investment, normally in the form of equity, which can be risky;
▷ It requires the venture company to invest in mechanisms that set up venture management and networks that search out, evaluate and generate deal flows;
▷ The venture company may not be in complete control of the development of the innovations.

For corporate venturing to work four things need to be in place. Firstly, as with most initiatives, it needs the commitment of senior management. Secondly, it needs to be consistent with corporate strategy, in such a way that an investment 'roadmap' can be produced, listing the areas to be investigated and invested in, the rationale for this and the mechanisms for searching out investments. However, the search mechanism needs to be sufficiently flexible to react to unexpected opportunities. It is important that the strategy is integrated into the overall corporate strategy for growth and innovation. A company can only beat venture capitalists at their own game if it adds value to the process in some way and the venture portfolio is aligned to its overall corporate strategy. It is this ability to share and leverage industry knowledge between portfolio companies and the business units of the investing company that creates true added value. Thirdly, there need to be effective HR policies in place within the venturing company to encourage the retention of talented staff in the acquired company and encourage continuity. There is not much point in acquiring a company only to find that key staff leave shortly after acquisition. Finally, the investing firm needs to have access to sufficient capital to use corporate venturing in this strategic way.

Some large organizations have dedicated teams searching out potential venture acquisitions. For example, within the Intel Corporation, Intel Capital investment professionals work alongside Intel business units to identify venture investments. Existing networks and strategic alliances/partnerships can also help to identify potential acquisitions (Chapter 6). Effective knowledge transfer is at the heart of successful corporate venturing for commercial purposes and many mechanisms can be used to facilitate this. For example, within Motorola, Motorola Ventures has a knowledge transfer team that is tasked with developing relationships between the acquired company and the Motorola parent. In this way engineers can monitor whether the technology acquired meets expectations and identify opportunities between it and existing business units. The same team work with Motorola's own start-ups and spin-outs.

A related activity, falling short of investment or acquisition is the growing number of larger firms that are buying in some form of intellectual capital – in effect 'outsourcing innovation'. This also can take many forms, for example the purchase of patents, copyright and so on or simply acquiring distribution rights. It all depends on what stage the innovative development has reached and how the larger company can best add value. It happens because, as we have already noted, many small firms are often better than larger firms at innovation – they can often do it more cheaply and quickly. The larger firm may be better at the development process or be better able to bring the product to the market quickly because of its extensive distribution network.

The term 'corporate venturing' is also used to explain spin-outs of non-core, but still very profitable, opportunities coming from in-house research, whilst maintaining an equity stake in the new technologies (see Chapter 8). Monsanto, Apple, 3M and Xerox have used independent venture capital conduits for this purpose. Finally, large companies also sometimes run venture funds with social investment criteria, such as creating jobs in areas where the company has made redundancies. Many of these funds have 'not-for-profit' objectives and are part of a larger social or environmental agenda for the company.

🗁 Case insight Pret a Manger

Corporate venturing

Julian Metcalfe and Sinclair Beecham opened their first Pret A Manger sandwich bar in Victoria Street, central London, in 1986. They made sandwiches in the basement from fresh ingredients bought every morning at Covent Garden market. They built Pret on the simple concept of providing gourmet, fresh and organic fast food in modern, clean surroundings in high foot-fall locations. Pret now sells sandwiches, baguettes, soups, salads, coffees and desserts. It still emphasizes its use of fresh, natural ingredients only. Sandwiches are made on the day of purchase in kitchens at the location. Those not sold on the day they are made are given to charity. The business formula has proved successful.

By 2001 Pret had 103 stores in the UK and one in New York, producing a turnover of £100 million and profits of £3.6 million. But Pret does not franchise and finding the funding for expansion was proving challenging. However it came as quite a surprise when McDonald's bought a non-controlling 33% interest in the company for an estimated £26 million. The motives were simple enough. McDonald's could provide not only cash but also the support for Pret's global expansion plans and they were happy not to change the Pret formula in any way. McDonald's, who also owned the Aroma coffee bar chain, saw this as a strategic purchase that would advance their long-term strategy of gaining a greater share of the diverse informal eating-out market and spreading their product portfolio into newer, higher-growth market segments.

In February 2008 Julian and Sinclair sold Pret for £345 million to private equity firm Bridgepoint and US investment bank, Goldman Sachs, retaining 25% of the company for management. McDonald's sold its share in the company as part of the deal. The buy-out firm said it intended to change Pret 'from a domestic to an international business through controlled expansion of its already profitable but small US presence'. There are now some 225 shops worldwide but more than three-quarters of them are in the UK and there are fewer than 30 outlets in the USA.

☐   Up-to-date information on Pret a Manger can be found on their website: www.pret.com

Diversification

Diversification involves moving into new areas of business – new product/market areas. It can come about through internal or external corporate venturing. It is inexorably linked with innovation and often organizations that have a poor innovation track record try to compensate or mask it through an aggressive acquisition strategy. Whilst the rewards for managers successfully diversifying might be high, the risks associated with this strategy are also high. Robert Grant (2010) suggests that it has probably caused more value destruction than any other type of strategic decision. He describes diversification as being 'like sex: its attractions are obvious, often irresistible. Yet the experience is often disappointing. For top management it is a mine field.' The business risks generated by diversification depend upon two things:

▷ *The nature of the diversification.* The literature distinguishes between related and unrelated diversification. As we shall explain, risk is lower in related diversification and it might be said that entrepreneurial firms face a distinct opportunity with this strategy.

▷ *The willingness and ability of the new organization to implement the merger on the ground* and gain the so called 'synergy' associated with it. Also at issue is the ability of management to actually manage the new, larger organization effectively.

🗂 Case insight Royal Bank of Scotland (RBS)

Aggressive acquisition

In 2003 Anik Sen of Goldman Sachs described RBS as 'one of the top three banks in Europe. They are just very good at running businesses, with a high degree of entrepreneurial flair' (*The Times*, 21 July 2003). Five years later RBS was effectively nationalized by the British Government because it nearly failed as a result of the global banking crisis and its exposure to the US sub-prime mortgage market. At the heart of RBS' failure was its undercapitalization which was in turn the result of its quest to become a diversified global provider of financial services and its aggressive acquisition strategy in pursuing this goal.

RBS is one of the oldest banks in the UK. It was founded in 1727 in Edinburgh, by Royal Charter, as the Royal Bank and opened its first branch in Glasgow in 1783. It developed a network of branches across Scotland in the nineteenth century but it was not until 1874 that it opened its first branch office in London. From the 1920s it grew by acquisition, swallowing Drummonds, William Deacon's Bank, Glyn, Mills and Co., and Child & Co., then merging with Edinburgh-based National Commercial Bank of Scotland, which itself comprised the National Bank of Scotland and Commercial Bank of Scotland. At this stage it dominated 40% of Scotland's banking business.

In 1985 RBS merged with Williams & Glyn's to give it a presence in England and ownership of the banker to the Queen, Coutts. RBS diversified into insurance by setting up Direct Line (a direct car insurance company) which quickly went on to become one of the dominant forces in direct insurance. It later purchased Churchill Insurance, a direct competitor to Direct Line.

Realizing it was very dependent on the UK market, RBS acquired Citizens Financial Group of Rhode Island, a small savings bank in the USA. It also started on a round of cost-cutting in its core business of retail banking. It saw that retail banking was becoming a commodity and, to compete on price, it had to achieve economies of scale that were just not available to it in a conventional banking model. Its answer in 1997 was to set up the UK's first online banking service. Not content with this it realized that other organizations were probably better at marketing banking services than the banks themselves and joined forces with a number of well-known brands such as the UK supermarket Tesco, and Virgin One to offer online banking. RBS did the 'back-office' operations, all the time driving down costs because of economies of scale. In 2000 RBS bought its far bigger rival, NatWest (which included Ulster Bank), in what was the biggest take-over in British banking history. Whereas RBS had just 650 branches, NatWest had 1650 and Ulster Bank a further 228 branches. As a result RBS underwent a large round of redundancies to further cut back its cost base – a realization of what the core strategy was for this part of the business.

After 2000 the bank continued its policy of organic growth and opportunistic but tactical acquisitions. It diversified by growing the small wholesale side of its banking operations – corporate lending, derivatives, foreign exchange and leasing – high-risk areas that were not its core business but offered high returns. Its US bank, Citizens, acquired the Mellon Bank's regional retail franchise, Medford Bancorp and Commonwealth Bancorp, increasing its geographical coverage in New England and making it the twentieth largest US bank measured by deposits. It also expanded its wholesale banking operations. RBS expanded into Europe with the acquisition of Santander Direkt, a Frankfurt-based credit card company. But it was the over-priced 2007 acquisition of ABM-AMBRO, the second largest bank in the Netherlands and the eighth largest in Europe with operations in 63 countries, that proved to be a step too far. It was the largest bank take-over in history. However, the timing of the take-over coincided with the global banking crisis, so the large amount of debt created for the purchase left RBS under-capitalized and unable to meet its creditors as its exposure to the sub-prime mortgage market and subsequent bad debts became clear. In order to prevent a run on the bank it was nationalized in 2008.

Was it bad judgement or bad luck? Its strategy of expansion and diversification through acquisition may have led to the creation of a global financial services giant, but instead led directly to the bank's nationalization. Its boss, Fred Goodwin was made to retire, vilified in the press for poor management and lost his knighthood. He was said to be too much of a risk-taker, with inadequate knowledge of and too little information on its newer 'casino-banking' operations. But it was ultimately the Financial Services Agency (FSA) – since disbanded – that allowed it to run its capital levels so low in order to finance the ABM deal and to finance the RBS empire with increasing amounts of short-term debt from international markets. And the FSA, in turn, could say it was following the government policy of 'light-touch' regulation in the banking sector.

What a difference five years can make.

Related diversification   This happens when development extends beyond the present product and market, but within the confines of the 'industry' or 'sector' in which the firm operates. There are three variants:

1 *Backward vertical integration* This is where the firm becomes its own supplier of some basic raw materials or services or provides transport or financing. When Anita Roddick first set up The Body Shop in 1976 it was purely as a retail business. It stayed that way until the 1980s when it started its own warehousing and distribution network and built up a substantial fleet of trucks. It also started manufacturing its cosmetics, mainly in the UK, although many of the ingredients came from overseas under its 'trade-not-aid' policy. These two elements of strategy initially worked well for it and generated substantial sales and profit growth, but these policies was reversed in the late 1990s allowing it to concentrate on its core retailing activity – a business it sold to L'Oréal after the death of its founder.

2 *Forward vertical integration* This is where the firm becomes its own distributor or retailer or perhaps services its own products in some way. For example, Timberland, famous for its sturdy, waterproof boots, opened a number of specialty stores and factory outlets selling its boots and other Timberland-branded outdoor clothes and products whilst continuing to sell predominantly through distributors, franchisees and commissioned agents.

3 *Horizontal integration* This is where there is development into activities which are either directly complementary or competitive with the firm's current activities. For example, Ford diversified into financial services to facilitate car purchase and now earns more from this source than from the manufacture of the vehicles themselves.

The acquisitions that are most likely to succeed are those for which an attractive market presents itself to a company and there is a good 'mesh' between the acquiring company's core competences and those required in the sector it is entering. However, an entrepreneurial firm is likely to be good at internal corporate venturing, allowing it to combine its portfolio of core competences in various ways to meet opportunities, and allowing it to move into new markets with new products without the necessity to acquire other companies.

Unrelated diversification   By way of contrast, unrelated diversification is a high-risk strategy for any firm. It happens where the firm develops beyond its present 'industry' or 'sector' into products/services and markets that, on the face of it, bear little relationship to the one it is in. The risks are high because the firm understands neither the product/service nor the market. The further the company strays from its core competences, the higher the risks because of problems with implementation, particularly when this is coupled with an implementation strategy involving acquisition (Bowman and Faulkner, 1997).

However, the distinction between related and unrelated is not always clear-cut, shading into grey particularly in the areas of rapidly developing new technologies in which new markets are being created where none before existed. Five of the most successful entrepreneurial companies since 2000 – Apple, Amazon, Facebook, Google and Microsoft – have adopted strategies of diversification that are probably starting to redefine their business scope (see Case with questions). This is happening through a combination of organic growth, internal corporate venturing and acquisition. Their moves into new areas have been incremental, bundling additional services to sell to existing customers, finding out about market acceptance of their new products experimentally – a form of market testing. Often they have used acquisition to buy new customers as well as new services. As we shall see in the next chapter, this incremental diversification can offer lower risks to an entrepreneurial organization. It is also a way of mitigating the risks of introducing disruptive innovation by using an incremental approach to test markets and obtain product/service and market information.

🗁 Case with questions Amazon/Apple/Facebook/Google/Microsoft

Cyber-wars: incremental diversification

The boundary between what constitutes incremental moves in products and markets and what constitutes diversification can become very blurred in the fast-moving technology-driven world of the internet. This is particularly the case when the real fight is for a market that, as yet, does not exist. This is the case with the battle currently under way between the five US giants of the digital age: Amazon, Apple, Facebook, Google and Microsoft. In the past these companies have provided hardware, software and various services, each content to 'stick to the knitting' and focus on its core market. However, new hardware such as tablet computers and smartphones linked by wifi and 3G/4G, and new software in the form of apps are breaking down these barriers.

The battle now is to become the sole provider of all our digital requirements, offering a vast range of services tailored to our 'needs', all-day, everyday, anywhere from the best online platform – a kind of digital utility. The reward is not just the profit from the goods or services that may be purchased but also the digital footprint of users (identified by their IP address) – their internet surfing and buying habits, likes and dislikes, including times of day on the internet and even their location. All of this is collected automatically in real time. It is very valuable to advertisers and salespeople alike, allowing them to offer targeted advertising at particular times of day in particular geographic areas. At the moment Google and Facebook own most of this information.

The battle is on to provide the best online platform for the delivery of 'universal internet services'. The more services these companies offer, the more customers they are likely to attract, and the more advertising revenue they are likely to earn. However, each of the Big Five is coming to this new market from different existing markets with new products and services and very different strengths and core competences.

→

Amazon started life selling books online and now sells almost everything. However, with the introduction of the Kindle, which allows the purchase and reading of books online, it entered the hardware market (it subcontracts production). The introduction of the color touch-screen Kindle Fire, usefully preloaded with your Amazon account details, not only makes this easier, it comes with social networking that connects you to others who purchase the same books and films. Amazon also offers a new app shop, online payment system, TV and film streaming and cloud computing facility.

Apple has become an iconic designer brand offering premium-priced electronic gadgets ranging from its computers to the iPod, iPhone and iPad. It recently integrated Twitter into all the Apple devices. Apple redefined how music sold through iTunes and sells books through iBooks. It also offers a range of apps for its devices. It intends to launch a web-enabled Apple TV shortly, selling films and TV programmes through iTunes. It has just launched iCloud, offering to store data and information on Apple servers. Apple is also sitting on $100 billion of cash, more than Amazon, Facebook or Google. (Further background on Apple can be found in the case in Chapter 2.)

Facebook, the ubiquitous social network site, is improving itself and now offers many of the features of Google+. It is about to launch a 'broader, more social' email system that (it says) will make Gmail 'old fashioned'. It is also about to launch its own Facebook phone, from which photos and status updates can be uploaded to your Facebook page at a click. In a strategic alliance with Netflix, the films and TV website, Spotify, the music streamer, and Zynga, the computer gamer, it intends to launch Facebook TV, Facebook movies, Facebook music and Facebook games. It even has Facebook credits, a virtual currency used to play computer games. It is exploring whether to offer its own internal search service based on the data provided by Facebook subscribers, rather than computer algorithms. Facebook's stock market launch in 2012 will help to pay for all these developments (estimated to bring in over $5 billion).

Google has become not only the name of a company but also the name for what we do when we search the internet for information. As well as information searches it offers maps, images and many other services. Google also has Gmail, which is well-established in the market, and Gmail+ is designed to make this more social, in direct competition with Facebook. It has its Chrome internet browser, and, in 2012, its Android operating system had more users than Apple's iPhones and accounted for over half of the worldwide smartphone sales. It already makes mobile phones with HTC and Samsung and in 2012 purchased the consumer division of Motorola, aiming to produce its own Google smartphones and tablet computers shortly thereafter, built by Motorola. It has Google Music offering music downloads and owns YouTube, where you can watch and now rent TV programmes and films, and has plans to launch Google TV. It has its own online payment system called Google Wallet. (For more information on Google see case in Chapter 12.)

Microsoft predates the other four companies, starting as the supplier of the ubiquitous Windows Operating System and then the Microsoft Office suite of software. It also has the internet browser Outlook Express. Many computers come with its software already installed, including the internet browser – which has been the subject of some antitrust actions. It offers server applications and cloud computing services like Azure. It has entertainment systems including the X Box video gaming system, the handheld Zune media player, and the television-based internet appliance MSN TV. Microsoft also markets personal computer hardware including mice, keyboards, and various game controllers such as joysticks and gamepads. Arguably, it missed the internet revolution and since then has been playing catch-up by expanding, often by acquisition, into search engines such as Bing. It recently purchased the video communications company, Skype, and has entered into a strategic alliance with Nokia to produce smartphones with its own operating system – the Windows Phone (see case in Chapter 8). It is also imitating Apple and starting to open its own retail outlets.

All of this leads to the question of where this convergence of competition will lead? Will there be one winner? And where does this leave companies like Microsoft which are starting down this path somewhat late?

QUESTIONS

1 Why are these markets converging? What do you think is the likely outcome?

2 Is this incremental diversification? How do the five companies mitigate the risks they face with this strategy? What role does acquisition play in this?

3 What risks do the companies face as they start to compete directly with each other?

4 Where does this leave Microsoft?

Conglomerates

Diversification through acquisition of other companies was a major feature of post-war western corporate activity until the 1980s. Conglomerates became popular because it was thought that they would reduce risk and increase shareholder value. Often these acquisitions were financed by high levels of borrowing. But the great conglomerate-merger wave did not generally lead to improvements in performance for those firms involved. The trend was reversed by the large-scale selling of unrelated businesses in the 1980s, encouraged by high interest rates. Porter (1987), in his study of 33 major corporations between 1950 and 1986, concluded that more often acquisitions were subsequently sold off rather than retained, and the net result was dissipation of shareholder value rather than an increase.

A focus on core business at corporate level was emphasized in the 1980s by researchers (for example, Abell, 1980). As we saw in the last chapter, the unique elements of a company's differentiation strategy are likely to be based on distinctive capabilities that, applied to a relevant market, become a competitive advantage. This will become its core business, the one in which it has a distinct advantage by adding the greatest value for its customers and shareholders. Many studies showed that more focused firms performed better than diversified ones (for example, Wernerfelt and Montgomery, 1986). This focus on core business was popularized by Peters and Waterman (1982) as 'sticking to the knitting'. Although some studies were subsequently disputed (for example, Luffman and Reed, 1984; Michel and Shaked, 1984; Park, 2002), Peters and Waterman (op. cit.) concluded:

> 'Organizations that do branch out but stick to their knitting outperform the others. The most successful are those that diversified around a single skill ... The second group in descending order, comprise those companies that branch out into related fields ... The least successful are those companies that diversify into a wide variety of fields. Acquisitions especially among this group tend to wither on the vine.'

Developments in financial theory, in particular the Capital Asset Pricing Model (CAPM), also showed that conglomerates did not create shareholder value by reducing risk in stock markets (Levy and Sarnat, 1970; Mason and Goudzwaard, 1976; Weston et al., 1972). Diversification does not reduce systematic risk – i.e. that part of risk associated with how the share price performs compared to the overall market (measured by the company's beta coefficient). Shareholders can simply buy shares in undiversified companies representing the diversified interests of the conglomerate. This spreads their risk, and probably with lower transaction cost. Therefore at the corporate level diversification does not create shareholder value.

Nevertheless diversification seems to remain attractive to managers. In the short term it can demonstrate turnover growth and mask internal growth. What is more, the idea that different products/markets have different cycles of growth and decline and by combining them you can reduce or smooth the effect of these differences, particularly upon the overall cash flow of the organization remains attractive (see Figure 10.11). This form of risk reduction appeals to managers, whose jobs depend on the company continuing to operate, more than shareholders, who can eliminate the risk by holding a diversified portfolio of shares.

Many publicly quoted conglomerate companies have now sold off subsidiaries to focus on their core business. For example, in the USA Philip Morris sold off Kraft Foods, Miller Brewing and 7-Up (purchased by Cadbury Schweppes) to focus on tobacco and became Altria Group. In the UK Cadbury sold off its Schweppes drinks businesses (including 7-Up) to focus on chocolate, ironically only to be taken over by Kraft Foods in 2010.

However acquisitions and the formation of conglomerates remains a powerful driver of strategy for private, unquoted companies, particularly when family wealth is tied up in them. The Virgin Group is a private company. Its scope of business reaches across the world and ranges from transport (airlines, trains and buses) to media (TV, radio, mobile phones and internet), from health and lifestyle (health programmes to gyms) to financial services (credit cards, pension and insurance products and banking). Sometimes these businesses are set up in partnership with another company which is better able to manage operations. Frequently they are bought as going concerns from other companies. In 2011 Virgin purchased the failed building society Northern Rock from the UK government.

Publicly quoted conglomerates continue to exist and prosper, particularly in developing economies, for example, Tata Group and Reliance Industries, the largest publicly traded company in India (by market capitalization). One reason for this may be the higher share transaction costs in these markets. Another might be the high concentration of ownership in family hands. But ultimately the reason probably boils down to inefficiencies in the markets.

🗁 Case insight Reliance Industries

Family-owned conglomerates

Reliance Industries is the largest publicly traded company in India (by market capitalization). It is a family-run conglomerate and was started by Dhirubhai Ambani, the son of a poor Gujarati school teacher who began work at a Shell petrol station in Aden. To make extra money he traded commodities and, at one time, even melted down Yemeni Rial coins so as to sell the silver for more than the currency's face value. He returned to India and started a yarn trading company in 1959 which, by the end of the 1990s, had become an integrated textiles, petrochemicals and oil conglomerate that then diversified into tele-communications and broadband, power, biotechnology, retail business and even financial services. Initially the business grew primarily through exploiting contacts with Indian politicians and bureaucrats but, in the wake of the changes caused by economic liberalization in the early 1990s, it started to do things differently – it built production sites that were competitive in global markets. Dhirubhai also popularized share ownership in India – which is where financial services comes in – and the two holding companies now have over 3.5 million shareholders.

Dhirubhai died in 2002 and the business is now run by his two sons Mukesh and Anil. Both have MBAs from the USA and have been involved with the business for some 20 years, managing the company increasingly since their father had his first stroke in 1986 and having a strong role in forging it into the world-class company that it is today. Although little known outside its native country, Reliance has high brand recognition in India. According to a 2010 survey conducted by Brand Finance and *The Economic Times*, Reliance is the second most valuable brand in India and the 2011 Brand Trust Report ranked it the sixth most trusted brand in India.

Economies of scope and synergy

Synergy is often used as a justification for both related and unrelated diversification, particularly when it involves acquisition or merger. Synergy is concerned with assessing how much extra benefit can be obtained from providing linkages between activities or processes which have been previously unconnected, or where the connection has been of a different type, so that the combined effect is greater than the sum of the parts. It is often described as 'one plus one equals three'. Synergy in related diversification is mainly based upon core product or market characteristics or competences, for example, Mercedes Benz leveraging on its reputation for quality of vehicles. This is often referred to as 'economies of scope' – less of a resource is used when it is spread across multiple activities than would be needed if the activities were separate and independent. They are cost economies arising from the production of multiple products. Economies of scope can come about because:

▷ Tangible assets and their related fixed costs, such as sales and distribution networks or R&D facilities, are spread across more products or services. This is the claim made for large pharmaceutical companies buying innovative small companies in order to sell their products through their extensive distribution networks;

▷ Intangible assets like brands can be profitably extended across more products or services (called brand extension). This is the claim made by Virgin in the UK and Reliance in India for their acquisition strategies;

▷ Organizational capabilities, such as general, sales or technological management, can be extended across more products or services.

Of course, economies of scope can be exploited by simply selling or licensing them. For example, banks have long supplied 'back-office' capabilities for branded store and credit cards such as those of John Lewis, Tesco or Sainsbury. This is one reason why some companies might decide to sell or license their product to another company in a foreign market whilst others decide to establish themselves in the country. The appropriate course of action depends upon cost-benefit analysis of particular circumstances. However, the importance of economies of scope in shared resources and capabilities is likely to be a reason why related diversification is probably more profitable than unrelated diversification.

One of the often-claimed synergies is based on the managerial skills of the head office. However, diversification through merger or acquisition can be time-consuming, expensive and risky. By distracting management it can also damage short-term business performance and there many examples of senior management getting it very wrong. In fact there is no evidence that commercial acquisitions or take-overs – particularly in unrelated areas (other than in a distress sale) – add value to the firm. Many studies show that mergers and acquisitions suffer a higher failure rate than marriages and business history is littered with stories of failed mergers of titanic proportions such as AT&T's purchase of NCR in 1991, the second largest acquisition in the history of the computer industry. This failed largely because of the clash of cultures in the two companies. NCR was conservative, tightly controlled from the top whilst AT&T was 'politically correct', informal and decentralized. Within four years most of NCR's senior managers had left and the new company had become loss-making. In 1997 NCR was made independent again, having lost some 50% of its value.

Reasons why acquisitions fail

The major reason why mergers and acquisitions fail is a failure of implementation. Claimed synergies may not be achieved, perhaps rationalization is insufficiently ruthless. Resources might not be shared and capabilities not transferred more efficiently than before the acquisition or merger. In other words, additional value is not created. It might also be the case that the costs of additional management outweigh the benefits of these linkages. Implementation fails because management fails to push through these changes. This might be because clear management lines and responsibilities are not laid down. This might trigger internal politicking, with managers from the two companies vying for dominance. Underpinning this there could be a clash of organizational cultures. The clash causes conflict and impedes communication. This can arise because of many factors, but it results in the merged organizations being unable to work together effectively. This was certainly the case with NCR and AT&T.

One common outcome of mergers or acquisitions is that many managers in the acquired company will leave within a short space of time – sure evidence of change being resisted. They may, of course, be 'pushed' rather than leave of their own volition, but nevertheless this means that the time scale for proactive management of change can be very short. Management of a merger or acquisition is therefore difficult.

Notwithstanding this, Porter (1991) noted five mistakes that organizations repeatedly make when implementing any strategy:

1 *Misunderstanding industry attractiveness* – Attractiveness has little to do with growth, glamour or new technology but more to do with the Five Forces outlined in the previous chapter.

2 *Not having real competitive advantage* – Organizations need to understand what makes them unique and different, to challenge the status quo and not just copy or incrementally change what competitors do.

3 *Pursuing an unsustainable competitive position* – Organizations need to decide on their core competences and focus their attempts at exploiting them rather than implementing strategies that do not play to these strengths and therefore will be difficult to sustain.

4 *Compromising the strategy for growth with short-term goals* – Short-term growth targets can distract the organization from its long-term competitive strategy as it pursues short-term opportunities that are inconsistent with the core strategy.

5 *Failing to communicate strategy internally* – All employees need to know the organization's strategy and what it means for them. All too often they do not.

📋 **Case with questions** **Cadbury**

Managing a global product portfolio

Cadbury is a very well-known British confectionery company. Originally a family firm started by John Cadbury and grounded in Quaker values and ideals, it started life in 1824 as a shop selling chocolate as a virtuous alternative to alcohol. It went on to become a large-scale manufacturer of chocolate based at the now legendary Bournville factory, built in 1879, and its picturesque workers' village with its red-brick terraces, cottages, duck ponds and wide open parks. Over the next 100 years Cadbury developed the products that have become so familiar: *Dairy Milk* in 1905, *Milk Tray* in 1915, *Flake* in 1920, *Creme Egg* in 1923, *Roses* in 1938 and more.

From 1969 it traded as Cadbury Schweppes, reflecting acquisitions it had made in the beverage industry, but in 2008 it separated out its global confectionery business, retaining the name Cadbury. The newly de-merged Cadbury set as its goal maintaining its market leadership position, and leveraging its scale and advantaged positions so as to maximize growth and returns. Its vision was to become 'the biggest and best confectionery company in the world' and its governing objective was 'to deliver superior shareholder returns'. To this end, Todd Stitzer, Cadbury's Chief Executive, developed the company's 'Vision into Action' plan for 2008 to 2011 which aimed to deliver six financial targets:

▷ Organic revenue growth of 4%–6% every year;
▷ Total confectionery market share gain;
▷ Trading operating margins improvement from around 10% to mid-teens by 2011;
▷ Strong dividend growth;
▷ An efficient balance sheet growth in return on invested capital (ROIC).

By 2009 Cadbury was the second largest confectionery company in the world after Mars-Wrigley. It had a 10% share of the global market and held the number 1 or 2 positions in more than 20 of the top 50 world confectionery markets, with strong brands in the markets for chocolate (Cadbury, Fry, Bournville, Green & Black's and Jaffa), gum (Trebor, Trident and Hollywood Chewing Gum) and candy (Bassett's and Maynards). It also generated 38% of its sales from new 'emerging' markets. Confectionery revenues grew by almost 6%, on average, between 2004 and 2009, despite the fact that most of Cadbury's products were at the mature stage of their life cycle. This growth came from two sources:

▷ Organic growth, mainly through finding new channels of distribution;
▷ Acquisition of new brands.

The company was also very focused on making cost and efficiency savings, as aging products were produced at lower costs and supply-chain savings were made. As a result the business was also hugely cash-generative, giving the company between £300 and £400 million a year. So how did it use this cash surplus to generate continuing growth?

As a starting point, Cadbury was looking for new markets for its products but most of these products already sold around the world. It, therefore, developed a two-pronged growth strategy, with both strands reliant upon the company's strong cash flow. First, because about 70% of its products are bought on impulse, it looked for new channels of distribution so as to encourage sales, or 'indulgence opportunities' as they were called. Chocolate bars are now sold anywhere from petrol stations to off-licences and from restaurants to pubs. Vending machines selling them can be found anywhere from factory floors to train stations.

The second strand was buying into other related high-growth segments where the company could capitalize on its existing distribution chains or use new distribution chains to sell more of its existing products. The company followed an acquisitions strategy for many years, in part to get into the fast-growing chewing gum market. In 2000 Cadbury bought *Hollywood*, the French gum maker, and *Dandy*, the Danish gum maker. In 2002 it purchased the US company, Adams, from Pfizer. Adams' brands include *Halls*, *Trident*, *Dentyne*, *Bubbas*, *Clorets*, *Chiclets* and *Certs*. It also purchased *Intergum* in Turkey and *Kandia-Excelent* in Rumania. By 2008 gum and other 'better for you' products accounted for some 30% of confectionery sales. But there were other confectionery acquisitions, for example *Green & Black's* in 2005. These acquisitions made Cadbury the market leader in non-chocolate confectionery, including gum and 'functional' products such as sore throat remedies, and gave it a foothold in markets such as Japan and Latin America.

The company managed each confectionery category – chocolate, gum and candy – on a global basis, focusing on markets where it saw itself as having a competitive advantage. It concentrated its resources on its top 13 brands, which accounted for around 50% of confectionery revenue in 2008. These brands grew at 10% in 2007 and 8% in 2008. Within this group, five brands were judged to have the strongest potential in existing and new markets on a global basis – Cadbury, Trident, Halls, Green & Black's and The Natural Confectionery Co. The remaining eight brands in the top 13 were: Creme Egg and Flake in chocolate; Hollywood, Dentyne, Stimorol, Clorets and Bubbaloo in gum; and Eclairs in candy.

Cadbury also focused on a limited number of markets in each category, based on their size or their potential for future scale and growth. Six countries – USA, UK, Mexico, Russia, India and China – were judged to have strong growth opportunities across all confectionery categories. Growth opportunities in other countries were more varied: chocolate in South Africa and Australia; gum in Brazil, France, Japan and Turkey; and candy in Brazil, France, South Africa and Australia. The company also focused its efforts on seven leading customers and three

trade channels which, together, accounted for 14% of confectionery revenue in 2008, showing growth of 8%.

Its approach to entry into new markets was to use existing distribution strengths wherever possible. So, for example, the launch of gum in the UK market under the Trident brand complemented an existing strong presence in chocolate and candy. Cadbury's ultimate aim is to have a strong position in all three confectionery categories in all the markets in which it operates.

Cadbury has used different growth strategies to help it grow, particularly in different countries. Together these made up the 'Vision into Action' plan developed by Todd Stitzer, the Chief Executive. Cadbury has consistently extended its existing channels of distribution (market penetration and market development) and also used them to offer more 'indulgence moments' to customers for its full product range – chocolate, gum and candy (product development). In this way it has strived to improve sales and also achieve even greater economies of scale. Cadbury has also bought overseas confectionery firms to gain entry into these new markets simultaneously both increasing its product range and buying established channels of distribution for its existing products in these new markets (acquisitions leading to market and product development).

So has the strategy been successful? The 2009 results showed sales up once more by 5% (11% on actual currency base), with emerging markets showing growth of 9% and developed markets 2%. Chocolate represented 46% of revenues, gum 33% and candy 21%. Emerging markets represented 38% of revenues and developed markets 62%. Cadbury had held or gained market share in markets that generated over 70% of its revenues. Operating margins also improved to 13.5% due to both an improved gross margin and a reduction in sales, general and administrative costs. Recommended dividends were up 10% on 2008.

→

However, we will never know whether the Vision into Action plan would have delivered its 2013 objectives because in 2010, following an acrimonious take-over battle, the US food giant, Kraft Foods, bought Cadbury for £11.5 billion, and de-listed the company from the UK stock exchange. Todd Stitzer, architect of Cadbury's strategy, resigned as Chief Executive following 27 years of service with the company, as did the Cadbury Chairman, Roger Carr.

In a press release on 14 January 2010 Todd Stitzer commented:

> 'Our performance in 2009 was outstanding. We generated good revenue growth despite the weakest economic conditions in 80 years. At the same time, our Vision into Action plan drove a 160 basis point improvement in margin to 13.5%, on an actual currency basis, delivering over 70% of our original target in half the time.'

The merger with Kraft presented an opportunity to gain further synergies, in terms of cost reduction and more effective distribution and market penetration as well as market and product development across the world.

But many cynics saw the take-over simply as a way of Kraft putting some sparkle into its otherwise uninteresting product portfolio and propping up its ailing share price. Did the take-over really add value? Only time will tell.

☐ Investor information on Kraft can be found on: www.kraftfoodscompany.com/investor/index.aspx

☐ Product information can be found on: www.cadbury.co.uk

QUESTIONS

1 Research the Cadbury products that are available in your country and position them on the Boston matrix (Figure 10.9). Give examples of products that might be mature in one market but not in another. Explain how this portfolio is managed.

2 Explain how Cadbury went about achieving its growth targets using the framework shown in Figure 11.1.

3 Explain how Cadbury achieved economies of scope. Explain why it 'focused' its strategic efforts in the ways it did. How did it use its product portfolio to help leverage sales?

4 Research the progress of Cadbury under Kraft ownership.

Multi-businesses and value creation

Mergers and acquisitions are frequently used as a tool for achieving rapid growth and also as a short cut to innovation. The compelling reason for this tactic is the speed with which it allows the firm to enter a new product/market area. This is particularly important in areas of new technology development. It explains the popularity of external corporate venturing. It justifies, at least in part, the acquisitions made by internet and technology companies like Microsoft and Google as they seek to redefine the scope of their activities in a rapidly-changing market where market dominance is the prize. However, to justify the claim of synergy in an acquisition the acquiring company must really be able to create value by operating across multiple businesses and multiple markets. This is particularly the case with diversification. Mere linkages are not enough. The companies must be able to consolidate management and reconcile conflicting cultures. They must be able to share resources and transfer capabilities more effectively than otherwise. Even within our hybrid organic structure there must be scope to demonstrate this and generate claimed synergies.

The justification for the continuing existence of conglomerates relies on them adding real shareholder value in this way. The conglomerate LVMH (Moet Hennessey Louis Vuitton) is the world's largest supplier of branded luxury goods. Its portfolio includes Moet et Chandon champagne (as well as other brands), Hennessey cognac, Louis Vuitton accessories and leather goods, Dior, Givenchy and Guerlain fashion clothes and perfumes, TAG Heuer and Chaumet watches, to name but a few. Its distinctive capability is its ability to manage these luxury brands through market analysis, advertising, promotion, retail management and quality assurance. Economies of scope come from these organizational capabilities. LVMH comprises some 60 subsidiary companies, often independently managed. Interestingly, whilst it is a public company, some 48% of LVMH is owned by Groupe Arnault, the family holding company of Bernard Arnault who brought the company together.

On the other hand, the Virgin Group is a private company comprising a conglomerate of apparently disparate businesses. However, in reality it is a good example of a brand that has been applied to a wide range of diverse products, mainly successfully, linking customers and their lifestyle aspirations. Economies of scope come from brand extension. The core competence of Virgin lies in the brand and associated marketing which often uses Richard Branson to gain press coverage instead of expensive advertising. This is particularly valuable for start-ups. All Virgin companies sell to final customers. Virgin rarely undertakes 'production' in a new venture, relying on partners with developed expertise. Instead it brings the strong Virgin brand and its associations to the partnership. No wonder it now describes itself as a 'branded venture capital company'. Virgin also has a very flexible organization, one that we have described as hybrid organic, and this allows it to operate effectively over multiple businesses with different characteristics.

> '*The approach to running a group of private companies is fundamentally different to that of running public companies. Short-term taxable profits with good dividends are a prerequisite of public life. Avoiding short-term taxable profits and seeking long-term capital growth is the best approach to growing private companies.*'
>
> **Richard Branson**, letter to *The Economist*, 7 March 1998

Multi-businesses must be able to create value by operating effectively across all the operating units – unifying diverse management and sharing resources and capabilities more effectively than might otherwise be the case. And they need to share economies of scope. These are all the qualities created by the architecture of corporate entrepreneurship.

📋 Case with questions BAE Systems

Strategic acquisitions

BAE Systems is Britain's largest manufacturer, with earnings of over £2 billion and staff based in over 100 countries worldwide. It is the largest defence company in Europe, and ranks seventh in the USA. Its size and growth have been largely due to mergers and acquisitions since its very inception.

BAE Systems began life as British Aerospace in 1977, a nationalized (government-owned) corporation formed from the merger of British Aircraft Corporation, Hawker Siddeley Aviation, Hawker Siddeley Dynamics and Scottish Aviation. The company was privatized (sold off) in 1981. The 1980s saw a string of acquisitions, most with little obvious logic: Royal Ordnance in 1987 (munitions), Rover Group in 1988 (cars) and Arlington Securities in 1989 (financial). By 1992 the strategy of unrelated diversification was discredited and the company was on the verge of collapse. The chairman was forced to resign and the company reappraised its strategies, being forced to sell off Rover to BMW in 1993. Throughout the 1990s the company remained reliant upon a single huge weapons contract with Saudi Arabia – a contract that would later prove controversial – but it also started increasingly turning its focus to Europe. This time, rather than acquiring companies, it started forming strategic alliances, doing deals with Dassault, Lagadere, Saab, Daimler Benz Aerospace, Siemens and others. It also took a 20% stake in the restructured Airbus. However, the most important move was its merger with GEC's defence business in 1999, which gave it a far greater presence in the USA, and a greater vertical integration of its activities. The merger heralded a new four-strand strategy:

1 *A focus on the defence industry*
   Acquisitions continued to be important, but this time focused on the international defence industry. It took a 33% stake in Eurofighter, a 37.5% stake in MBDA, the

world's leading missile systems builder, and a 20% stake in Saab AB, the aircraft manufacturer. In 2006 it sold its stake in Airbus, despite the success of the company.

2 *Restructuring, so as to give it greater backward and forward vertical integration, again using acquisitions* In this way BAE became one of the very few fully integrated suppliers of weapons for air, land and naval defence needs. It can supply the platform – for example, the ship or plane – and all the electronics, computers or missiles that go in it, which is where the real profit lies. This positions it with fewer direct competitors and providing the sort of turn-key service governments want. Where acquisitions were not possible, BAE entered into strategic partnerships.

3 *Reduction of market risk by spreading the customer base across the world*
   In particular BAE wanted to move away from an over-reliance on the British market. British defence procurement had become more open to competition than in any other Western country and the widespread use of fixed-price contracts had led to many expensive write-offs.

4 *Using acquisitions to buy its way into the US market* The USA is the largest market for defence procurement in the world. In 2000 BAE sealed its status as defence supplier to the Pentagon by purchasing two electronics businesses from Lockheed Martin. By 2007 it had made 16 acquisitions in the USA, at which point it purchased Armor Holdings – the manufacturer of the famous Humvee armoured vehicles. Armor has 'prime contractor' status, which means it can take overall responsibility for complete weapons systems. This acquisition sealed BAE's status in the US market. Even before the Armor acquisition, the USA accounted for almost 30% of sales, with

joint contracts such as the huge F-35 Joint Strike Fighter project, but by 2012 this had risen to about 50%.

At the beginning of the twenty-first century the focus of defence spending started to shift from hardware to software as cyber security and intelligence became more important. Not to be left behind, in 2008 BAE spent £538 million buying Detica, a company specializing in safeguarding computer networks for government, defence and nuclear facilities.

However, by 2012 BAE's success in the USA had led to an over-dependence on that market. Indeed 70% of sales now came from the USA and UK. At the point it was widely believed that the defence sector was in the early stages of a 10–12 year cyclical downturn. It was estimated that Pentagon defence spending would be cut back from 5% to 3% of GDP by 2016, as wars in Iraq and Afghanistan came to an end. The only buoyant area was cyber security. BAEs share price fell in the face of stagnant earnings. Its response was continued cost-cutting and closures. Despite share buy-backs and increased dividends, it sat on a cash mountain of £3 billion. However, this did not satisfy the stock markets and, in 2012, it was suggested that BAE be split in two, separating its US arm, BAE Inc., from the rest, BAE International, thereby making it easier for investors to value the separate businesses. It has been estimated that this could increase value by 36%. What is more,

it is suggested that BAE Inc. might attract bids from US defence giants such as Boeing and Lockheed Martin. This would leave BAE International as a smaller, more nimble operation with a focus on high technology areas. In response to these pressures, and to the surprise of the markets, BAE announced a proposed merger with EADS, the Franco-German aerospace group behind Airbus. BAE had sold off its shares in this partnership back in 2006, hence the markets' surprise. The deal would give BAE shareholders 40% and EADS shareholders 60% of the new company. And with sales of £57 billion and some 220,000 staff, this new company would be a defence and aerospace giant larger than Boeing or Lockhead in the USA. Importantly, it would insulate BAE from the downturn in the defence sector but give EADS access to it. However, the deal needs the approval of four governments – Britain, France, Germany and the USA – so the outcome is not assured at the time of writing.

☐ Up-to-date information on BAE Systems can be found on their website: www.baesystems.com.

QUESTIONS

1 What do you think of BAE's strategy of using acquisitions, mergers and strategic partnerships to gain market share?

2 What are the dangers of using mergers and acquisitions as such a central part of any strategy?

3 What should BAE do now?

Summary

◁ Acquisitions can be used to help companies:

▷ Gain rapid market dominance, often early in the life of a product but particularly in foreign markets, by buying market share, as have **Cadbury** and **BAE Systems**;

▷ Gain rapid market dominance early in the life of a product by offering a more comprehensive offering to customers, as in the case of **eBay** and **PayPal**;

▷ Consolidate its market position late in the life of a product by taking out capacity and achieving greater economies of scale;

▷ Purchase innovation;

▷ Diversify.

◁ Corporate venturing involves large firms investing in or acquiring smaller businesses in order to capitalize on their innovations. This is the reason McDonald's bought **Pret A Manger.** For corporate venturing to work it needs: the commitment of senior management; consistency and integration with corporate strategy; to add value through effective knowledge transfer, leveraging knowledge from the larger company and the firm it acquires; effective HR policies to encourage the retention of talented staff; and finally to provide access to sufficient capital.

▷ Diversification involves moving from core areas of activity into completely new and unrelated product/market areas. As products come to the end of their natural life cycles, the longevity of any particular organization will depend on its ability to innovate and in so doing eventually redefine the business it is in, applying existing capabilities to developing new products, perhaps new industries and buying in those capabilities when necessary.

▷ Related diversification is lower-risk than unrelated diversification, although the distinction is not clear-cut. Related diversification allowed **BAE Systems** to achieve greater backward and forward integration and become an integrated weapons supplier. However, it was the diversification strategy of **RBS**, based upon an aggressive strategy of acquisition, that sowed the seeds of its failure.

▷ Diversification is central to the process of corporate evolution and part of the process of corporate entrepreneurship. As we saw with **Amazon**, **Apple**, **Facebook**, **Google** and **Microsoft**, this can be done most effectively in increments, constantly bundling new products and services whilst extending the market. In this way these companies hope to develop a new industry for what we might call an 'internet utility'.

▷ The business risk associated with diversification comes from the nature of diversification, the approach adopted and the ability to implement any merger and obtain the planned synergies.

▷ Synergy is often described as 'one plus one equals three'. It comes about through economies of scope – spreading an asset (tangible or intangible) or capability over multiple activities. **Cadbury** has been particularly good at this.

▷ Publicly-quoted conglomerates do not add shareholder value by reducing risk. This is the reason **Cadbury** sold off its beverages business. The consensus is that many conglomerates do not perform as well as their independent parts might otherwise do. Even a company focused on one sector, like **BAE Systems**, can suffer from this.

▷ Multi-businesses, like conglomerates, must be able to create value by operating effectively across all the operating units – unifying diverse management and sharing resources and capabilities more effectively than might otherwise be the case. This explains the success of companies like **Reliance Industries**. And they need to share economies of scope. These are all the qualities created by the architecture of corporate entrepreneurship.

Essays and discussion topics

1 Penetrating the market is just about selling more. Discuss.

2 Penetrating the market is low-risk and therefore always the most attractive option. Discuss.

3 In what circumstances might company acquisitions help you to achieve market dominance?

4 What are the advantages in acquiring an existing company if you want to enter a foreign market?

5 How can the purchase of a company selling different but complementary products help you to achieve market dominance?

6 How important a factor is speed in considering whether to acquire another

company to help achieve market dominance? What needs to be done ahead of purchasing another company?

7 Is corporate venturing any more than an excuse for buying up successful small firms?

8 Explain the importance of effective knowledge transfer for corporate venturing to work best.

9 What is the difference between corporate venturing and venture capital?

10 Why might related diversification work best for entrepreneurial companies?

11 Under what circumstances might diversification be an attractive option?

12 Diversified companies underperform 'focused' companies. Discuss.

13 Why might a firm be looking for another to acquire?

14 Under what circumstances might an acquisition or merger be attractive?

15 What is synergy and how might it be achieved?

16 Why do so many mergers or acquisitions fail? Give examples.

17 What advice would you give to a company taking over another?

18 Why might a strategy of internal growth be less risky than one of acquisition? In what circumstances might it be more attractive?

19 What is needed for a conglomerate to be successful and create shareholder value?

20 Refer back to the Virgin case in Chapter 6. What do you think might happen when Richard Branson retires? If the shareholding is sold to the public, will the company be viewed as a conglomerate and sold at a discount?

Exercises and assignments

1 For your own department in your university or college, use the product/market matrix (Figure 11.1) to list the growth options that it faces for the courses on offer.

2 Select a company that has grown rapidly over the last five years. Analyze the strategies it has followed to secure this growth using the frameworks developed in the last two chapters.

3 Find an example of corporate venturing that has proved unsuccessful and analyze why. What lessons can be learned from this?

References

Abell, D.F. (1980) *Defining the Business*, Hemel Hempstead: Prentice Hall.

Acs, Z.J. and Audretsch, D.B. (1990) *Innovation and Small Firms,* Cambridge, MA: MIT Press.

Ansoff, H.I. (1968) *Corporate Strategy*, London: Penguin.

Bowman, C. and Faulkner, D. (1997) *Competitive and Corporate Strategy*, London: Irwin.

Deakins, D. and Freel, M. (2006) *Entrepreneurship and Small Firms,* 4th edn, London: McGraw Hill.

Grant, R.M. (2010) *Contemporary Strategic Analysis*, 7th edn, Chichester: John Wiley.

Levy, H. and Sarnat, M. (1970) 'Diversification, Portfolio Analysis and the Uneasy Case for Conglomerate Mergers', *Journal of Finance*, 25.

Luffman, G.A. and Reed, R. (1984) *The Strategy and Performance of British Industry*, London: Macmillan.

Mason, R.H. and Goudzwaard, M.B. (1976) 'Performance of Conglomerate Firms: A Portfolio Approach', *Journal of Finance*, 31.

Michel, A. and Shaked, I. (1984) 'Does Business Diversification Affect Performance?', *Financial Management*, 13(4).

Park, C. (2002) 'The Effects of Prior Performance on the Choice between Related and Unrelated Acquisitions', *Journal of Management Studies*, 39.

Pavitt, K., Robinson, M. and Townsend, J. (1987) 'The Size Distribution of Innovating Firms in the UK: 1945–1983', *Journal of Industrial Economics*, 45.

Peters, T.J. and Waterman, R.H. (1982) *In Search of Excellence*, London: Harper & Row.

Porter, M.E. (1987) 'From Competitive Advantage to Competitive Strategy', *Harvard Business Review*, 65(3).

Porter, M.E. (1991) 'Knowing Your Place – How to Assess the Attractiveness of Your Industry and Your Company's Position in It', *Inc.*, 13(9), September.

Vossen, R.W. (1998) 'Relative Strengths and Weaknesses of Small Firms in Innovation', *International Small Business Journal*, 16(3), 88–94.

Wernerfelt, B. and Montgomery, C.A. (1986) 'What is an Attractive Industry?', *Management Science*, 32.

Weston, J.F., Smith, K.V. and Shrieves, R.E. (1972) 'Conglomerate Performance Using the Capital Asset Pricing Model', *Review of Economics and Statistics*, 54.

Part 5
Creativity and innovation

Chapter **12**

Exploiting innovation

Learning outcomes

By the end of this chapter you should be able to:

▷ Critically evaluate the relationships between innovation, creativity and entrepreneurship;

▷ Understand how innovation can be encouraged;

▷ Critically analyze linear and parallel product/service development models;

▷ Understand how disruptive innovation can be encouraged and creatively address how market conventions and paradigms might be challenged;

▷ Critically analyze the relationship between innovation and risk and how risk can be mitigated;

▷ Understand how the risks associated with disruptive innovation can be mitigated;

▷ Assess whether you are an innovative thinker.

Innovation, invention and creativity

Innovation is at the heart of entrepreneurship. Entrepreneurs use it to create change and opportunity. They use it to create competitive advantage. And, occasionally, they use it to create entirely new industries. Firms that grow do so because they innovate in some way. Cannon (1985) points out that 'the ability of the entrepreneurial mold-maker to break free from bureaucratic rigidities, fan the flames of innovation and create new situations has been the basis of the growth of many of today's great corporations'. For all firms, of any size, innovation has become something of a Holy Grail to be sought after and encouraged. And the same applies to nations as they strive to see their economies grow. As Michael Porter said in *The Competitive Advantage of Nations* (1990): 'invention and entrepreneurship are at the heart of national advantage'. But what is the difference between invention and innovation?

Invention is usually associated with a 'mould-breaking' development of a 'new-to-the-world' product or process (the materials used, the process employed or how the firm is organized to deliver them). It is often linked with new technologies, frequently the product of research, for example, the 'invention' of the World Wide Web by Tim Berners-Lee. However, examples abound of inventions that are not commercially successful and even more instances of inventors who did not benefit from their inventions. Thomas Edison, probably the most successful inventor of all time, was so incompetent at introducing his inventions to the market place that his backers had to remove him from every new business he founded. And Tim Berners-Lee did not benefit directly from his invention. Sometimes there are such radical shifts in how products or services are marketed that whole new markets can be created that change the way people think about the product or service and create new customers – called paradigm market shifts. Examples include the emergence of online insurance providers and

🗀 Case insight Charles Babbage

Inventor

Contrary to popular misconception, the computer was not 'invented' by IBM. The principles of the computer were defined by the English scientist Charles Babbage in 1830. He invented a mechanical analytical engine or universal calculator, which was programmed by punch cards, had a store of information (memory) and a calculating engine (processor). But Babbage was forever tinkering with his designs. What is more, he was generally irritable and disagreeable – it is said that he hated humanity. He could not find anyone to pay him to make the machine so he went on to try to devise a foolproof system for betting on horses.

low-cost airlines. Often these paradigm shifts are made possible by developments in technologies, such as the internet, but they might arise through the emergence of new environmental conditions, untapped markets with different value expectations or even changes in legal requirements. Henry Ford did not invent the car but he did revolutionize the way cars were produced and sold, moving from craft-based to production-line and from wealthy customers to an affordable car for everyman. When these ideas are generated by an individual or an organization they can be every bit as valuable as the more traditional invention.

Innovation is more broadly defined. It is the introduction of something new or novel but not necessarily 'mould-breaking.' It includes invention and paradigm shift but these are extreme examples and probably the riskiest form of innovation. Innovation is certainly not necessarily just the product of research. It can be many things, for example:

▷ Product innovation – improvements in the design and/or functional qualities of a product or service;

▷ Process innovation – revisions to how a product or service is produced so that it is better or cheaper, for example substitution of a cheaper material in an existing product;

▷ Marketing innovation – improvements in the marketing of an existing product or service, or even a better way of distributing or supporting an existing product or service. Entrepreneurial firms in particular are often innovative in their approach to marketing, finding more effective, often cheaper, routes to market.

Innovation, therefore, is about doing things differently in some way. Schumpeter (1996) described five types of innovation, emphasizing 'newness':

1 The introduction of a new or improved good or service;
2 The introduction of a new process;
3 The opening up of a new market;
4 The identification of new sources of supply of raw materials;
5 The creation of new types of industrial organization.

To 'newness' Kanter (1983) added 'creative' by defining it as 'the generation, acceptance and implementation of new ideas, processes, products and services … [which] involves creative use as well as original invention.' Mintzberg (1983) defined innovation as 'the means to break away from established patterns.' In other words innovation involves doing things creatively and differently. However, the degree of difference is difficult to define. To an economist, the cross elasticity of demand must be zero for a product to be completely different from another. Simply introducing a new product or service that is similar to others is not innovative, even if it is a replacement for an existing one (the cross elasticity of demand is not zero). New cars are rarely truly innovative, whatever the marketing hype might say. However, the Mini was innovative because it changed the way cars were designed and changed the way people perceived vehicle size. If Schumpeter's description of innovation is inadequate it is because of the myriad forms it can take.

Innovation is therefore difficult to define because it represents a continuum of activity from invention and paradigm shifts to incremental changes in products, processes and marketing. And the sum of many small, incremental innovations – often introduced during the later stages of a product life cycle – can have an enormous impact on competitive advantage (Bessant, 1999). Indeed there is evidence that the majority of commercially significant innovations are indeed incremental rather than radical (Audretsch, 1995). Indeed many incremental innovations carried out at the same time can add up to a revolution. For example, Henry Ford's revolution in the car industry involved extensive incremental changes – to products and processes, component and factory design and in the way labour was organized in his factories.

How frequently innovation is practised is therefore another important dimension to consider alongside the scale of the innovation. This leads to the idea that the impact of innovation on competitive advantage might be measured in these two dimensions – frequency of innovation (number of events) and scale of innovation. Innovative intensity is also measured by these two dimensions, shown in Figure 12.1. The concept of entrepreneurial intensity is very similar (see Figure 3.3). Frequent, small incremental innovations may compensate for the occasional radical innovation or invention. What is more, frequent, small incremental innovations may also be less

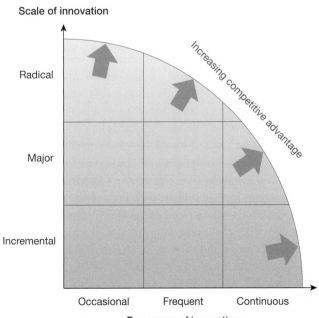

F 12.1 Innovative intensity

risky. However, the two are not mutually exclusive and the entrepreneurial firm gains competitive advantage from both. The aim is to maximize innovative intensity by pushing this envelope of innovation as far as possible, although in doing so the firm may have to compartmentalize and organize itself in different ways so as to handle the different sorts of innovation.

Bolton and Thompson (2000) suggest there are three basic approaches to innovation, none of which are mutually exclusive:

1 *Have a problem and seek a solution.* They cite as an example Edwin Land's invention of the Polaroid camera because his young daughter could not understand why she had to wait to have pictures of herself printed.

2 *Have a solution and seek a problem.* They cite 3M's Post-it notes as an example of a product with loosely-sticking qualities that was applied to the need to mark pages in a manuscript.

3 *Identify a need and develop a solution.* The example they cite is James Dyson's dual cyclone cleaner that he developed because of his frustration with the inadequate suction provided by his existing vacuum cleaner when he was converting an old property.

Creativity underpins both invention and innovation. Whilst Bolton and Thompson (op. cit.) stressed the importance of creativity in the process of invention and innovation, they linked creativity, invention and innovation explicitly with entrepreneurship: 'Creativity is the starting point whether it is associated with invention or opportunity spotting. This creativity is turned to practical reality (a product, for example) through innovation. Entrepreneurship then sets that innovation in the context of an enterprise (the actual business), which is something of recognized value'. In his review of the literature, Van Grundy (1987) said that, whilst creativity contributes to innovation, it may equally be used towards other ends. Mellor (2005) agrees that creativity is only part of the process of invention and innovation. He defined innovation simply as either 'creativity + application' or 'invention + application'. This 'application' is really entrepreneurship.

'Our success is due, in part, to not just an ability but a willingness to look at things differently. I believe opportunity is part instinct and part immersion – in an industry, a subject, or an area of expertise. Dell is proof that people can learn to recognize and take advantage of opportunities that others are convinced don't exist. You don't have to be a genius, or a visionary, or even a college graduate to think unconventionally. You just need a framework and a team ... Seeing and seizing opportunities are skills that can be applied universally, if you have the curiosity and commitment.'

Michael Dell

Entrepreneurship therefore plays a vital role in these processes because it is the mechanism that takes the innovation to the market. Firstly it helps companies to spot the opportunities in the market place that link with the creative inventions/innovations. Secondly it delivers the inventions/innovations into the market place. For example, the early success of the Apple Macintosh was based upon its use of the now ubiquitous mouse and its graphic user interface. However, this technology was invented by

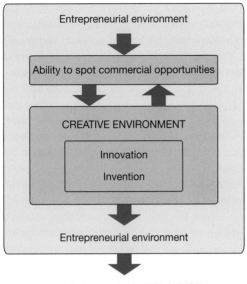

F 12.2 Innovation, creativity and entrepreneurship

scientists at Xerox Palo Alto Research Centre (PARC) and had been tried out unsuccessfully in high-priced computers, such as Xerox Star and Apple Lisa. It was Steve Jobs and Apple who successfully brought the redesigned mouse to the mass market. These links between creativity, invention and innovation, opportunity perception and entrepreneurship are represented in Figure 12.2. Creativity is necessary for both invention and innovation. It is also necessary for spotting commercial opportunities, and the ability to spot opportunities can help with invention and innovation. However, innovations or inventions without apparent commercial application may feed back into the process and lead to new opportunities being identified. Nevertheless, without an entrepreneurial environment created by the appropriate organizational architecture the ability to spot commercial opportunities for the innovation will not exist and the product will not find its way successfully into the market place.

🖿 Case insight James Dyson

Inventor and entrepreneur

James Dyson is the inventor of the revolutionary cyclone vacuum cleaner who challenged established large companies in the market and gained a market share in excess of 50%. He is an habitual inventor, also inventing the 'Ballbarrow', a light plastic wheelbarrow with a ball rather than a wheel. The idea for the vacuum cleaner came to him in 1979 because he was finding that traditional cleaners could not clear all the dust he was creating as he converted an old house. Particles clogged the pores of the dust bags and reduced

→

the suction. He had developed a small version of the large industrial cyclone machines, which separate particles from air by using centrifugal force, in order to collect paint particles from his plastic-spraying operation for Ballbarrow. He believed the technology could be adapted for the home vacuum cleaner, generating greater suction and eliminating the need for bags.

Working from home, investing all his own money and borrowing on the security of his home and drawing just £10,000 a year to support himself, his wife and three children, he produced 5000 different prototypes. However, established manufacturers rejected his ideas and venture capitalists declined to invest in the idea. In 1991 he took the product to Japan and won the 1991 International Design Fair prize. He licensed the manufacture of the product in Japan where it became a status symbol selling at $2000 a time. On the back of this and twelve years after the idea first came to him, he was able to obtain finance from Lloyds Bank to manufacture the machine under his own name in the UK. Today Dyson products can be purchased worldwide and James Dyson is chairman of the Dyson Group and one of the top 50 richest people in the UK.

Encouraging innovation

So, whilst an entrepreneurial environment created by our organizational architecture is necessary to ensure the successful launch of an innovation, we still need to examine in more detail the process by which innovation is encouraged – how ideas are generated and evaluated. Figure 12.3 sets out a simple model for how innovation can be encouraged within our entrepreneurial architecture. Within it, the creative environment is essential to ensure commercial ideas are generated. But how do you generate these ideas? We shall look in detail at this in the next chapter, but at this point it is important to note that the linkages within and across boundaries are important. These provide new ideas and stimuli that can encourage a more questioning approach. They encourage the communication of information

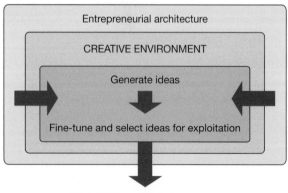

F 12.3 Encouraging innovation

and knowledge. Because of the entrepreneurial architecture the linkages within and outside the organization should be strong – to employees in different parts of the organization and to all the external stakeholders such as customers and suppliers. There will be linkages with other external knowledge resources such as universities and even with potential competitors through strategic alliances. The more linkages and connections the better. This is, after all, a learning organization and generating, transmitting and using information should be a core strength. These linkages are equally important when it comes to fine-tuning and eventually evaluating the commercial potential of an innovation.

For an entrepreneurial firm innovation must be at the core of its strategy, encouraged and facilitated by its entrepreneurial architecture. It must permeate everything it does. This involves commitment:

▷ From top management that innovation is at the core of what the business does;
▷ That innovation is the responsibility of everyone, not just the R&D department;
▷ That innovation happens in everything, from developing new products/services to new processes and new approaches to marketing.

Innovation should not happen by chance or in a haphazard, piecemeal or tactical manner, with innovative projects being seen as burdensome additional work to 'business as usual'. Innovation must be encouraged, facilitated and just part of that 'business as usual'. Strategic innovation involves setting explicit goals and policies for innovation and then following them through, monitoring and evaluating performance and risks and adjusting strategies to reflect shifting realities. This means formulating strategies for the nature of new product/service development. These must reflect the nature of the technology and the realities of the market. They must also reflect an understanding of the needs of customers in different market sectors, so that sub-strategies can be developed to reflect innovation in these different segments.

However, all innovation is not the same. Companies following a marketing strategy of low price and low differentiation are likely to encourage innovations that reduce costs, promoting efficiency but involving capital investment. These are likely to be incremental, process innovations. Companies following a strategy of high differentiation are likely to encourage innovation stimulated by information on user needs and technical inputs. They are likely to implement major innovation frequently, although these will usually be well short of invention or paradigm shift. Encouraging large-scale innovation is not the same as encouraging incremental changes in products, processes and marketing. It requires a different approach throughout all the processes outlined in Figure 12.3. What is more, the risks faced in launching these different types of innovation are also very different. However, the reality in most multi-product businesses is that they will

Ten ways to stifle innovation

1   Regard new ideas with suspicion.
2   Enforce cumbersome approval mechanisms, rules, regulations.
3   Pit departments and individuals against each other.
4   Express criticism without praise.
5   Treat problem identification as a sign of failure.
6   Control everything carefully.
7   Plan reorganization in secret.
8   Keep tight control over information.
9   Delegate unpleasant duties to inferiors.
10 Assume you (the higher-up) know everything important about the business.

Source: Kanter, R.M. (2004) 'The Middle Manager as Innovator', *Harvard Business Review*, 82(7/8)

have to cope with both incremental and large-scale innovations – often on a continuous basis. And then there is the issue of invention and paradigm shift which we call 'disruptive' or 'discontinuous' innovation and requires quite a different mind-set. We shall return to this topic later in this chapter.

New product/service development model

The process of product/service development can be broken down into more detail. Figure 12.4 shows a seven-stage linear model based upon one of the most recognized activity-stage models, developed by the US consultants Booz, Allen and Hamilton (1968, 1982). Of course products are often not developed in a logical, linear and systematic way but rather the path to market is more haphazard, opportunistic even chaotic. Still, the model gives us a framework within which to work and to analyze the processes sequentially. In the real world, with time and resource pressures, some processes may be undertaken concurrently, others ignored completely in the headlong rush to be first to market and gain 'first-mover advantage'. But at each stage the risks of ignoring the systematic, sequential process need to be weighed carefully.

Once beyond the idea-generation stage, addressed in the next chapter, the processes involved are:

Screening: This involves assessing whether the ideas generated match the objectives of the organization, its resources and its core competences. You must decide whether the firm will actually be able to design, produce and market the product idea effectively. At this point the idea may need to be

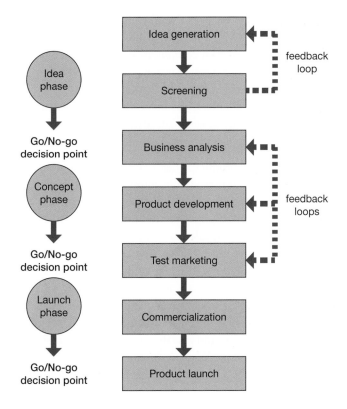

Linear product/
service development

reformulated so as to better match the firm's capabilities or refined so as to enable a more accurate evaluation of its potential.

Business analysis: This is the first major 'go/no-go' point in the decision-making process. More formal analyses of the 'fit' with the company, its core competences and resources will be made. Estimates of sales, costs and profitability need to be made. Does the firm have the cash to invest? Is the investment worthwhile, given the other opportunities the firm faces? How robust is the business model? Can it get the product into the market place in a reasonable period of time? Who are the competitors (if any)? What is the competitive advantage, and can it be sustained? What are the risks involved? Inevitably market research information will be needed – consumer surveys, secondary data and so on – so as to enable an estimate of potential sales to be made. If the business analysis does not produce a robust case for taking the product forward its development may be terminated.

Product development: This stage involves deciding whether it is technically feasible to produce the product at costs that allow adequate profits to be made. Developing a prototype is a process of experimentation, where numerous iterations of an idea are created and tested to see whether it provides the desired results. Prototyping used to be complicated, but now can be done early and inexpensively by using computer simulations.

There are even low-cost tools available like Google's Sketchup. Eventually however a physical prototype will have to be built. For example, cars are now designed and developed on computers and prototype development is left increasingly to the later stages. However, concept cars still represent an important part of product development – an opportunity to test out ideas, not just in terms of mechanical feasibility, but also in terms of market acceptability. And often only by seeing, touching and using the product can the potential consumer make judgements about it.

Test marketing: Often a product is test marketed in a limited geographic area which is chosen to represent the intended target market. The aim is to assess the real response of potential buyers. As such it is not just about trying out a new product, it is a trial product launch. The complete marketing mix needs to be trialled so that weaknesses can be identified and corrected. But market testing takes time and can bring a new product to the attention of competitors. Test marketing may not be economically viable for some products, such as a new car, and it may not be feasible to withdraw some products once introduced. With life cycles becoming increasingly shorter and first-mover advantage very real, many firms like Google decide to launch first and test the market as they go along, making modifications rapidly in response to product or marketing deficiencies. The problem is that failure can be expensive. This is another go/no-go point. If the results of the test marketing are not attractive, the project may again be terminated.

Commercialization: This is the stage where plans for full-scale manufacture and marketing must be refined and finally decided on. Results from the test marketing need to be incorporated in the final product/market offering. Early adopters need to be identified and a promotion campaign agreed on. The company starts to gear up for the full-scale launch and that means finalizing the complete launch strategy. Budgets need to be set and action plans finalized. At the end of this stage is the final go/no-go decision point. Even at this stage a project might be terminated because the firm realizes that, whilst the product is attractive to the market place, it is not best placed to take it there. In that case it may license or sell off the idea.

Parallel development model

In the real world new product/service development does not evolve in such a neat, orderly fashion. It is neither linear nor smooth. Feedback loops result in multiple iteration of the various stages. Sometimes a project will move backwards in the process as the repeat of the stage in the process creates problems that were not previously apparent. There is often an element of chaos as blocks to progress emerge and ways around them are eventually developed. Since different teams might be working on different stages, information-sharing and effective communication are important.

Case insight Levi jeans

Disorderly development processes

The development of Levi jeans was certainly neither linear nor orderly. The tailor Levi Strauss started out making hard-wearing work overalls. These were so popular that he ran out of the brown canvas sailcloth from which they were made so he switched to a sturdy twill fabric that was made in Nîme in France. The material was named 'serge de Nîme', but this soon became shortened to 'denim'. It proved very popular. The next development came when a Nevadan tailor called Jacob David suggested to Strauss that he insert metal rivets at points of stress, typically pocket corners and the base of the fly, to make the trousers even sturdier. The pair patented the idea. The final element was added by a rival tailor, H.D. Lee, who introduced a novelty to replace the button fly, called the Whizit. We know this today as the zip or zipper.

This applies equally to scientific discoveries. William Shockley had to invent a theory of electrons and 'holes' in semiconductors to explain why the transistors that he and his colleagues at Bell Laboratories in the USA had invented in 1948 actually worked. Even then he and his colleagues had to take the transistor idea to Palo Alto in California and start a company that eventually became Intel to get it to see the light of day.

The go/no-go decisions at various points in this model – widely referred to as the stage gate process – have been criticized for being particularly rigid and inflexible and taking far too long. Van De Ven et al. (2000), in their case-study-based research into widely different innovation types, highlighted how in the real world it can be a complex, non-linear and uncertain process involving false starts, recycling between stages, dead ends and jumps out of sequence. Coping with this sort of complexity requires the integration of systems in different functional areas, extensive networking to draw in and sift through information and a flexible, customized response to the situation. The word 'flexible' implies that the response is hard to predict or characterize.

Cooper (1994) proposed that greater creativity within models of product/service development can be achieved by permitting progression to the next stage, even though some issues may remain unresolved. In this way the three stages may be viewed as, potentially, happening in parallel. Takeuchi and Nonaka (1986) proposed that this parallel development process best relies on self-organizing multidisciplinary project teams whose members work together from start to finish such that the process emerges from their constant interaction rather than highly structured stages. Figure 12.5 shows a parallel product/service development process developed by Lambin (2000). The driver for this process is a firm's need to find ways of

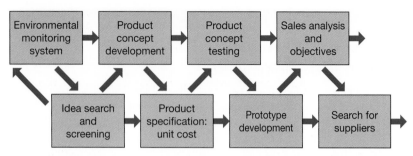

F 12.5 Parallel product/
service development

Source: Lambin, 2000.

cutting back the lead time on new product/service development if they are to gain greater competitive advantage. This saving is achieved by undertaking several activities simultaneously and is also due to the more intensive workload facing team members. Indeed, in this context any activity that takes too much time needs to be reconsidered very carefully – excessive testing, an over-emphasis on accurate cost estimates and so on – in light of its impact on completion time. Other claimed benefits of this approach include facilitation of cross-functional coordination and better control of each activity since it directly determines the subsequent activities.

Disruptive innovation

'Disruptive' or 'discontinuous' innovation are step changes in products, processes or the framing of markets. Generated by major inventions and paradigm shifts, they can have large-scale disruptive effects on markets, industries and even economies. They can generate wealth for the originators and cause bankruptcy and failure for those who cannot adapt quickly. Often their success or failure is difficult to predict and market research – involving asking the views of existing customers – has little to add. Famously Henry Ford once said that if he had asked people what they wanted, they'd have said 'faster horses', rather than 'new-fangled' things called cars. In the same way, despite its technological competences and dominance of the computer market at the time, IBM refused to enter the emerging PC market in the late 1970s because conventional market research could not identify a demand for the product. Potential domestic customers could not understand the portable computer, or more particularly, what it would do for them – how it would add value to their lives. Existing computer applications were commercial. Why would they want a machine to 'do sums', even if it was small? Why was it better than a typewriter? Of course the PC took off when domestic applications such as games and the internet were identified, and now most homes in the Western world have (at least) one. But investment in the early-stage development of PCs was a leap of faith, and one that IBM was unwilling to make, until it was too late.

Established firms have the advantage when it comes to incremental innovation. They have the product experience, established marketing channels and resource capabilities. That advantage can disappear with disruptive innovation – when the game changes in important and fundamental ways so that their product experience, marketing channels and resource capabilities become less important. It is no wonder then that, as we saw in Chapter 11, so many small, entrepreneurial firms can thrive in this environment. Competitive advantage has to be built from scratch and that is where the entrepreneurial DNA becomes important. But there is much to fight over because the returns for successfully managing disruptive innovation can be very high. In a study of 108 company strategies Kim and Mauborgne (2005) found that only 14% of innovations created new markets, whereas 86% were incremental innovations or line extensions. However these innovations that created new markets delivered 38% of new revenues and 61% of profits. How can these opportunities go unnoticed in large organizations?

In Chapter 3 we looked at how the dominant logic (or mental models) within a company or an industry dictates how the world is viewed. It filters the information received, subconsciously interpreting environmental data in a certain way. In fact, managers may only consider information that they believe relevant to the prevailing dominant logic in the organization or industry. This is the main reason why existing, normally large, organizations miss out on disruptive innovation. In his study of a number of industries, Christensen (1997) characterized this as happening in stable markets where companies were geared up to delivering more of what existing customers wanted. He observed that with each generation almost all of the previously successful large firms failed to make the transition effectively and were often squeezed out of the market or into bankruptcy, despite the fact they were often exemplars of good practice – ploughing a high percentage of earnings into R&D; having strong working links with their supply chain; working with lead customers to better understand their needs and develop product innovations; delivering a continuous stream of product and process innovations that were in demand from their existing customers. The problem they had was their inability to identify and capitalize on the emergence of *new markets* with very different needs and expectations – one aspect of the problem of *market disruption*. Essentially these firms were too close to their existing customers, suppliers and technologies. The result was that they failed to see the long-term potential of newly emerging markets. What might have begun as a fringe business – often for something simpler and cheaper – moved into the mainstream and eventually changed the rules under which the mainstream businesses operated so, by the time the mainstream businesses realized this, they had lost their competitive advantage. Often, with the benefit of hindsight, the industry seemed to be driven by technological developments rather than market demand.

For example, Microsoft, arguably missed the internet revolution. It could have dominated the search engine market rather than Google, but new developments that threatened to cannibalize their main source of revenue – the Windows Operating System and the Microsoft Office suite – were not allowed to surface. Instead all the resources were targeted at defending Microsoft's existing dominance of the software market. A good example of ideas that cause paradigm shift is Nintendo and the Wii (see Case with questions), which caused the entire computer games industry to reappraise the technology-driven direction it was taking. As with many radical changes, this idea only came about when Nintendo realized it could no longer compete effectively along the dimension of constantly improving technology and this threatened its very survival.

The challenge for larger companies is whether they can spot the opportunities for disruptive innovation before smaller, more entrepreneurial companies can capitalize on them. Sometimes the spur needed for this is some form of crisis which emphasizes the need for change. Disruptive innovation can come from many sources, some internally derived (as with the Wii), others generated by external factors. Both can be difficult to spot because of dominant logic. Both can be difficult to evaluate because they create new markets. And both can involve high risks.

Sources of disruptive innovation

Tidd et al. (2005) highlight some sources of disruptive or discontinuous innovation:

▷ *New markets* can emerge unpredicted – one instance of disruption that has led to the extinction of many large firms, as highlighted by Christensen (op. cit.), is the dot.com revolution. For example, whereas music was once purchased mainly on records, tapes and/or CDs, it is now mainly purchased online.

▷ *New business models* are established, often by new entrants to a market who dare to question the 'rules of the game' and end up changing them – another example of the market disruption that large firms are not good at dealing with, such as the emergence of the internet shopping popularized by Amazon. We shall return to this in the next section.

▷ *New technologies* can emerge as step changes in product or process technologies (e.g. mobile phones or the internet) or as the result of a single breakthrough (e.g. the LED as a white light source). These can be both in high-technology niches evidenced by pioneering breakthroughs (Utterback and Acee, 2005) or in low-technology niches evidenced by new configurations of existing technologies (Schmidt, 2004), blurring somewhat the distinction between incremental and radical innovation.

▷ *New political rules* can cause markets to change dramatically, such as the fall of communism, which introduced capitalism to countries formerly part of the Soviet bloc and ultimately led to many East European countries joining the European Union.

▷ *Market exhaustion* for firms in mature industries may lead to exit or radical reorientation of the business. For example, the change to digital photography led ultimately to the bankruptcy of Kodak as it failed to reorientate.

▷ *Sea-changes in market sentiment or behaviour.* For example, the growth in the organic foods and growing importance of CSR created new market opportunities.

▷ *Deregulation or shifts in regulatory regimes* can lead to new markets or new market rules. For example, the privatization of much of the public sector in the UK, started in the 1980s, created new businesses such as BAE Systems and HFL Sport Science.

▷ *Fracture along 'fault lines'* that can occur when minority opinions gather momentum and cause systems to 'flip' (e.g. opinions over smoking and the environment have led to changes in legislation).

▷ *Unthinkable events* that cannot be prepared for, like the 9/11 terrorist attacks on the USA, and the consequences for all businesses, not least the airlines.

▷ *Shifts in the 'techno-economic paradigm'* are systems-level changes involving the convergence of technology and market changes that create entirely new markets for new products, for example electricity replacing steam power.

▷ *Architectural innovations* are also systems-level changes for an industry which rewrite the 'rules of the game' as to how things are done, for example, who you might have to talk to in acquiring knowledge to drive innovation.

Arguably the most significant recent disruptive innovation has been the internet, linked to the use of the smartphone. Its impact has been likened to that of the railways in the nineteenth century. It has created significant entrepreneurial business opportunities – both sectors are dominated by 'new' companies – and made many entrepreneurs into millionaires along the way. It gave PCs an important application, changed the way we shop and the way information and knowledge is transmitted. It spawned the 'dot. com boom' and the 'dot.com bust'. It created new social networks and the base for the development of social media. And it helped to change whole political regimes in the Arab spring of 2011.

Another powerful driver of innovation is currently CSR – environmental responsibility, ethical business practices and other issues covered in Chapter 9. Innovation linked to sustainability often has major systems-level implications, demanding a holistic and integrated approach to innovation management. The commitment of the retailer M&S to be totally carbon-neutral requires it to completely re-engineer many of its operations. Berkhout and Green (2003) argue for this systems approach to innovation, linking innovation with sustainable research, policy and management and concluding that 'greater awareness and interaction between research and management of innovation, environmental management, corporate social responsibility and innovation and environment will prove fruitful.'

Paradigm shift

Swatch created a whole new market for cheap watches by daring to be differ-ent. In the 1980s cheaper watches like Citizen and Seiko competed by using quartz technology to improve accuracy and digital displays to make reading the time easier. The industry competed primarily on price and functional performance. People usually owned just one watch. Swatch set out to make fashion accessories that were also accurate time pieces. SMH, the Swiss par-ent, set up a design studio in Italy whose mission was to combine powerful technology with artwork, brilliant colours and flamboyant designs. Swatch changed the reason for buying a watch from the need to tell time to the desire to be fashionable. They differentiated themselves not on the function of the time piece but on its design and also its emotional appeal – what it said to oth-ers about the wearer. In doing this they encouraged repeat purchases because each watch was a different fashion accessory making a different statement offered at an affordable price. Swatch has built up a core of customers who repeat purchase their watches and new Swatch designs come out every year.

Challenging marketing paradigms: Blue Ocean strategy

Kim and Mauborgne (op. cit.) called strategies that delivered these disrup-tive innovations 'Blue Ocean strategies'. Blue Ocean represents all market needs that are currently going unmet and, as yet, are unrecognized. These unmet needs may be represented by individual products or services – in their broadest sense – and may result in the creation of whole new markets and industries. They are created by challenging the boundaries and structures of existing markets and industries and envisioning new ways of doing things. Companies creating Blue Ocean strategies never benchmark against competitors, instead they make this irrelevant by 'creating a leap in value for both the buyers and the company itself'. This echoes the earlier study by Hamel and Prahalad (1994) and underlines the importance of developing strategic intent in implementing this strategy (see Chapter 4). Kim and Mauborgne (op. cit.) contrasted their Blue Ocean strategy to Red Ocean strategy which involves gaining competitive advantage in existing, often mature markets (Chapter 10). They acknowledge that Red Oceans cannot be ignored but criticize conventional marketing strategy as being too focused on building advantage over competition in this way.

Kim and Mauborgne say that, by way of contrast, Blue Ocean strategy creates uncontested market space, making competition irrelevant – there is none. It creates new demand that can be more easily captured because of this. It involves thinking unconventionally, which means going against the dominant logic of the industry, such as the value/cost trade off inherent in Porter's generic marketing strategies, and creating new rules. Indeed Blue Ocean can be created by simultaneously reducing cost and offering something new and different. It therefore involves developing a radically different business model – a new marketing paradigm – as we saw in the case insights of Streetcar (Chapter 3), easyJet (Chapter 9) and Rolls-Royce and TotalCare (Chapter 9). Whilst it can be facilitated by technological or other radical innovations, these do not have to be the driver. Blue Oceans can be created just as easily from within Red Oceans by expanding market or industry boundaries. New marketing configurations – in their broadest sense – can prove equally effective, thus underlining the important point that innovation applies equally to marketing.

> *'We learned the importance of ignoring conventional wisdom … It's fun to do things that people don't think are possible or likely. It's also exciting to achieve the unexpected.'*
>
> **Michael Dell** (1999)

None of this is new. As we noted in Chapter 4, based upon a study of firms that have challenged established big companies in a range of industries, Hamel and Prahalad (op. cit.) claimed that they had succeeded in creating entirely new forms of competitive advantage by asking three key questions:

▷ What new types of customer benefits should we seek to provide in 5, 10 or 15 years?
▷ What new competences will we need to build or acquire in order to offer these benefits?
▷ How will we need to reconfigure our customer interface over the next few years?

Building on this idea in his book *Entrepreneurial Marketing: Competing by Challenging Convention* (2000), Chaston argued that truly entrepreneurial firms have a distinctively different approach to marketing which he defined as 'the philosophy of challenging established market conventions during the process of developing new solutions'. His approach was simple: understand conventional competitors and then challenge the approach they adopt by asking whether a different approach would add customer value or create new customers. As he points out that there are many conventions that can be challenged. He suggests three categories:

1 **Sectoral conventions**: These are the strategic rules that guide the marketing operations of the majority of firms in a sector such as efficiency of plants, economies of scale, methods of distribution and so on. Kim and Mauborgne (op. cit.) talk about reorientating analysis from *competitors* to *alternatives*. So, for example, insurance used to be delivered through insurance brokers until Direct Line came along in the UK, challenged the conventional wisdom, and began to sell direct over the telephone, then on the internet. Now this is the norm.

2 **Performance conventions**: These are set by other firms in the sector such as profit, cost of production, quality and so on. Kim and

Mauborgne (op. cit.) argue that both value enhancement and cost reduction can be achieved by redefining industry problems and looking outside industry boundaries, rather than simply trying to offer better solutions than rivals to existing problems as defined by the industry. In the 1960s Japanese firms ignored Western performance conventions en masse and managed to enter and succeed in these markets.

3 **Customer conventions**: These conventions make certain assumptions about what customers want from their purchases, for example price, size, design and so on. Kim and Mauborgne (op. cit.) talk about reorientating analysis from *customers* to *non-customers.* The Body Shop redefined the cosmetic industry's 'feel-good factor' to include environmental factors. Companies like Ryanair and easyJet pioneered low-price air travel and redefined the airline industry.

In most sectors there are factors that managers believe are critical to the success of their business. Chaston encouraged entrepreneurial organizations to ask 'why?' followed by the questions 'why not?' and 'what if? A technique for asking these questions in a structured way is outlined in Chapter 14. Chaston's book was concerned with start-ups and small firms and he went on to say that opportunities should be matched to capabilities in deciding which to follow. An individual entrepreneur can see opportunities aplenty, but they may not have the resources to exploit them all. He proposed an approach to marketing planning which he called 'mapping the future'. This is the eight-stage process shown in Figure 12.6. Although shown as linear and sequential, the process is interrupted as new market information is discovered and earlier decisions are revisited. The process also includes small-scale market entry and trial in order to gain further information.

The process starts with the development of a detailed understanding of sector/performance/customer conventions. Stage two involves assessing the performance gap between aspirations of future performance and the level of performance currently being delivered. If the size is sufficient to attract an entrepreneurial approach (that is, an incremental approach is not warranted), then the opportunity is investigated using his innovative approach that questions all current assumptions about delivery. Next, the opportunity should be compared to the firm's capabilities to deliver – its core competences and resources. If the firm has the capability then the remaining processes are more straightforward: defining performance objectives, defining strategy, developing a detailed plan and specifying control systems. However, the unanswered question is what to do with commercially attractive opportunities that do not match the capabilities of the firm.

All these approaches to developing disruptive or discontinuous innovation boil down to thinking creatively 'outside the box' – the generation of

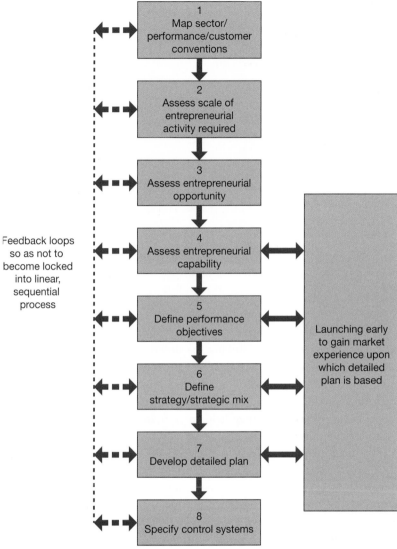

F 12.6 Entrepreneurial marketing planning

Source: Chaston, 2000

new ideas and knowledge, linking market opportunities to key capabilities. They involve challenging conventions, being open to new ideas. They involve dealing with rapidly changing and disparate information in a wide range of new technologies and in diverse, fragmented and often geographically widespread markets. It involves charting a way through often uncertain political and unstable regulatory environments and facing competitors emerging from unexpected directions. In these circumstances knowledge is a powerful source of innovation. Effective knowledge management – picking up and making sense of knowledge signals – is vital. We shall return to this in the next chapter.

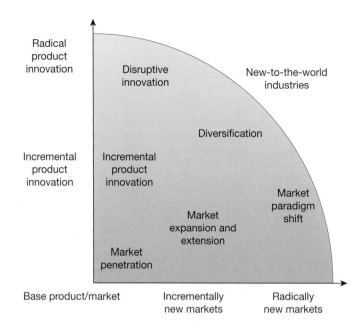

F 12.7 A typography for developing new products and new markets

One way of conceptualizing these different approaches to finding new products and new markets, linking the different terminologies from this and the previous chapter, is shown in Figure 12.7. Simply selling existing products to existing markets is market penetration. Selling them to new markets is market expansion and extension. Incremental innovation can happen continuously and may help to shift the market incrementally – what we have called diversification. But radical innovation is likely to lead at least to an incremental change in markets. Similarly, re-conceptualizing the market in some way – a market paradigm shift – is also likely to involve at least an incremental change in the product. Once the degree of change in product and market becomes radical then we are talking about new-to-the-world industries. The whole process of innovation in products and/or markets is a continuum.

📋 Case with questions Nintendo Wii

Paradigm shift

By the early years of the twenty-first century the computer gaming market had stagnated into one for either young males or old males who had retained their youthful interest in gaming and had time to spend on it. The image of the gamer was that of a solitary male in his bedroom, hunched over a TV screen, grasping a controller with both hands, intensely involved in some game – a lonely, exclusive image. Massive as this market was, sales trends showed there was a limit to how often upgrading the hardware would lead to more sales and it was evident that fewer new gamers were entering the market. Most manufacturers were led by developments in semiconductors and related technologies and what other consumer electronics manufacturers were doing. All this led towards simply adding in more and more computing power to enable games to become quicker and graphics more life-like, and the demand for this seemed to be insatiable. As soon as one upgrade came out, consumers seemed to want more. The whole industry had become technology-driven rather than consumer-led.

Nintendo dared to question whether the gains were now worth the extra investment. Pragmatically Nintendo also doubted whether simply increasing the power of its GameCube (the previous flagship console) would cost-effectively produce anything significantly better. So, if they could not beat the competition in the existing market, what should they do? Faced with this dilemma Nintendo wondered whether there was another, as yet untapped, market for some form of computer game. This was bold thinking but it resulted in the development of the Wii.

The Wii console is wireless-linked to a hand-held device that can detect and accurately digitize motion and rotation in three dimensions and through 360°. The device can become a sword, a tennis racquet, a golf club or a gun, depending on the game you are playing on screen. Up to four people can participate virtually, in real time and using real movement. So how is Wii so different? The first thing is that the wireless controller is held in only one hand – like a mouse, a TV remote or a mobile phone. This changed the posture of gaming, making it more open and inclusive and encouraging a degree of physicality. The second is that, instead of using technology to ramp up output, the designers used it to power the console down, whilst still maintaining gaming specifications. It is a little-known fact that a typical game console running a flight simulator game uses 76% more electricity than a washing machine. So the same technology used in the Wii would use between one-third and one-quarter the electricity of the GameCube. This in turn meant that the Wii could perform other functions. It is designed to be left on continuously as it has several different 'channels' that can, through an integrated web browser, provide a rolling news service with continuous world and local weather reports. It can even be used as a family bulletin board and planner. It can be programmed to switch itself off after a prescribed time and the hard drive features an irreversible memory that catalogues what it has been used for and for how long. Because it is intended for living-room rather than bedroom use, the Wii console is about the size of three DVD cases and is housed in a box that can easily be found a home alongside the AV equipment and TV.

Wii has been described as 'a human-centric, business-technology ecosystem, on a par with the iPod-iTunes-iMac' (Bruce Nussbaum, *Business Week*). It became this icon because, like iPod-iTunes-iMac, its development team dared to think outside the square and to question the status quo. They dared to change the way things were done and the result is a 'low-tech' game that can be more fun, has more functionality and consequently outsells its more powerful rivals. In 2012 Nintendo launched the new and updated Wii U.

☐ For more information on how Wii was developed and for interviews with the development team conducted by Satoru Iwata, President of Nintendo, visit http://www.nintendo.com/wii.

QUESTIONS

1 What was the trigger that led to the Wii being developed? Are there lessons here from managing change (Chapter 7)?

2 What were the key decision points in the development of the Wii that led to it being so different?

3 How easy has it been for competitors to copy Wii?

Innovation and risk

Innovation involves moving into new products and/or new markets and Figure 11.1 can be developed to give a valuable insight into the risks associated with innovation. Bowman and Faulkner (1997) added an extra dimension to the original matrix by considering core competence and method of implementation. Accepting that any move to develop a new product or enter a new market may involve innovation, they pointed out that any move becomes riskier the further the firm strays from its core competences. Figure 12.8 shows the risks associated with different innovation strategies diagrammatically:

▷ The lowest-risk short-term strategy is market penetration, rather than innovation. However, in a growth market, where gaining market share as quickly as possible is important, security might be short-lived and, as the product goes through its life cycle, growth might only be possible through market development. What is more, a long-term strategy of no innovation, or even imitation, is likely to be quite risky.

▷ Innovation through market development is most successful for companies whose core competences lie in the efficiency of their existing production methods, for example in the capital goods industries, and are seeking economies of scale, or for firms adept at sales, marketing and developing close customer relationships. One way of lowering the risks associated with finding new markets is through strategic alliances/partnerships and joint ventures (Chapter 6).

▷ Innovation through product and process development is most successful for those companies whose competences lie in building good customer relationships, often associated with effective branding. However, of equal importance could be the ability to innovate. Again, one way of lowering the risks associated with product innovation is through strategic alliances/partnerships and joint ventures (Chapter 6).

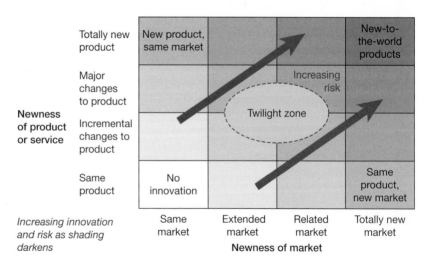

F 12.8 Innovation and risk

▷   As we saw in Chapter 11, the highest-risk strategy of all is diversification, with unrelated diversification being extremely high-risk. This
can be likened to the introduction of new-to-the world products – in
the extreme, disruptive innovation. Related diversification is safest
for companies who are adept at both innovation and developing close
customer relations. Thus it was just as well that the Mini – truly a
mould-breaking innovation in car design – was produced by an established car manufacturer.

Risk increases as you increase the newness of the product/service and
the market to which it is offered. This is shown in Figure 12.8 by the dark-
ening shading, moving from the bottom left to the top right-hand corner.
At the extreme, innovating in both product/service and market dimensions at the same time – disruptive innovation – poses the highest risk.
However, risk is not a linear relationship. In the 'twilight zone' – marked
by the dashed area at the centre of the matrix – risk can be lowered. This
is the zone where continuous, small incremental changes in product and
market can greatly expand the product/service offering and its market
place and risk can be mitigated through knowledge of both customers and
the product/service. As we saw in the cases of Apple, Amazon, Facebook,
Google and Microsoft in Chapter 11, it is the area of incremental diversification, where new products can be bundled into offerings to existing customers. It is also the area where entrepreneurial firms might be expected to
practise internal corporate venturing as part of their day-to-day activity
(Chapter 8). However, new markets can be entered, particularly through
company acquisition, with innovations that can then also be bundled into
existing offerings. This all happens in a rapid process of market entry that
is designed to achieve market dominance. And Apple, Amazon, Facebook,
Google and Microsoft are fighting to dominate an emerging market to
provide an online platform for the delivery of 'universal internet services'
– a sort of internet utility like water, electricity and gas; an emerging 'blue
ocean'.

The twilight zone is where the entrepreneurial firm may have a
competitive advantage – and face lower risks – over other firms through
both internal and external corporate venturing. This is because it has the
entrepreneurial architecture that allows it to better cope with continuous,
market-related changes. In particular, a good understanding of market
needs – linking the innovation to opportunities in the market place –
mitigates this risk. So long as the innovation adds value to the customer,
it is likely to find a market place. And here is where a strong linkage to
customers, an understanding of who they are and their wants and needs,
becomes so important. This is where the entrepreneurial firm should score
over other firms. And, as we shall see in the next chapter, it also applies
to disruptive innovation – 'mould breaking' innovation that creates new
markets.

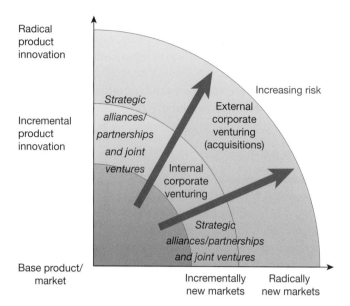

Radical product innovation

Incremental product innovation

Base product/ market

Strategic alliances/ partnerships and joint ventures

Internal corporate venturing

External corporate venturing (acquisitions)

Increasing risk

Strategic alliances/partnerships and joint ventures

Incrementally new markets　　Radically new markets

F 12.9 Corporate venturing and other forms of corporate renewal and risk

The structures and techniques such as intrapreneurship outlined in Chapter 8 can all be used to encourage innovation. And it is worth looking at Figure 8.3 again, where the techniques of strategic alliances/partnerships and joint ventures were considered alongside internal and external corporate venturing. This is reproduced in Figure 12.9 showing the relationship with risk. Strategic alliances/partnerships and joint ventures (Chapter 6) are ways of mitigating risk in unknown markets or with new technologies, and once more an entrepreneurial organization is likely to have a number of these. And where internal corporate venturing (Chapter 8) does not produce the innovations needed, then external corporate venturing through acquisitions (Chapter 11) may provide the answer. What is more, if internal corporate venturing produces innovations that do not have the required synergy with the existing business they may be spun off or sold to companies looking for suitable acquisitions for their own corporate venturing activities. These techniques are not mutually exclusive. An entrepreneurial firm might use them all as part of its growth strategy and it is what the organizational architecture described in previous chapters should encourage and facilitate.

Figure 12.10 shows another way of conceptualizing the risks associated with different approaches to the process of innovation. Dynamic, continuous innovation builds upon existing products/services so that customers understand the nature of the offering, unlike discrete innovation which may address a need but one that has to be explained and accepted by the customer. Continuous innovation is the incremental, step-by-step development of the product/service and market. Finally there is imitation – copying or adapting the innovations of others. Whilst this as an individual activity is low-risk, as an overall strategy, in the long run, it is little better

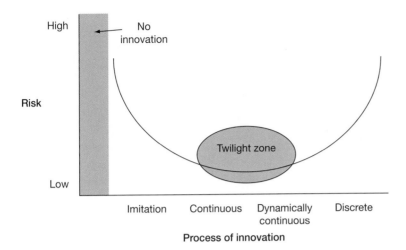

F 12.10 The process of innovation and risk

than no innovation at all. As Morris and Kuratko (2002) point out: 'the imitative company is apt to miss out on entire market opportunities by the time it is able to respond to an innovative new product or service. When the firm does move, it finds its role to be that of niche player in the market place. It also becomes harder and harder to catch up as innovative competitors move from incremental advances in a current technology to a major advance using a new technology. Meanwhile new competitors emerge from other industries to attack the firm's most profitable lines of business with innovative marketing, distribution, and customer services approaches.'

A portfolio approach to innovation risk

A portfolio approach to innovation is essential to the understanding and management of risk. By holding a balanced portfolio of stocks and shares you can eliminate all but market risk. Similarly, although the risk associated with a new-to-the-world project may be high, as part of a balanced portfolio of innovations and activities that business risk is mitigated by the other, less risky, projects. The role of failure is recognized and accepted as part of the cost of achieving winning innovations and a balanced portfolio. Some innovations will be major and other moderate winners, but some will be failures.

The original Figure 12.7 can be used to represent the portfolio of innovations being undertaken by a firm. Figure 12.11 shows an example for a hypothetical company. It is a snapshot at a point of time or for one operating period that changes over time. Each dot represents an innovation project. The company's highest-risk project is project A, a new-to-the-world innovation that will require careful management and risk assessment. There are only two projects (B and C) that are, on the face of it, in the 'twilight zone' where entrepreneurial firms might operate to greatest competitive advantage and we might seek to question why that is the case. More

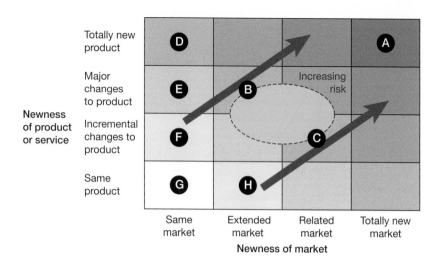

F 12.11 A specimen risk portfolio

worrying is the fact that there are so few new market developments. The reasons for this need to be determined. And why does project G involve no innovation? There might be a good reason, for example that this is a new product and what is required in this period is further market penetration. But the analysis acts as a prompt for the question. For each project a better understanding of the strategic fit with the company's core competences is central to understanding the risks the firm faces overall. However, for this company the risk portfolio does not appear to be balanced. It would appear to be risk averse and focused on its current market. What will happen if that market disappears?

Although innovation will be part of the fabric of the organization, the different forms of innovation may well require different organizational structures to encourage their development. For example, as we have seen, the organizational structure required to facilitate continuous process development of a product in the mature stage of its life cycle is quite different from that required to encourage new-to-the world invention. Strategies need to be developed for sourcing these new ideas. Do they come from internal or external sources, or both? Financing must also be addressed since the needs of different types of innovation, both in volume and nature (internal vs external finance and equity vs loan finance), may be quite different. And again, as we have seen, a balanced portfolio leads to balance in cash flow.

Risk and time taken to innovate

This highlights a further dimension to risk – the time taken to innovate. If the process takes too long you run the risk that the commercial opportunity may be missed. The longer you delay the launch the higher the risk that a competitor may launch first and the greater the risk of losing first-mover advantage. On the other hand if you launch too early you run the risk of the

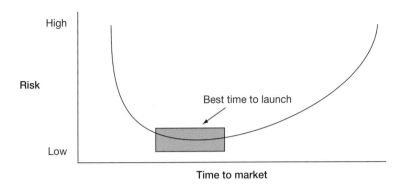

product/service or marketing strategy being ill-prepared or untested and turning customers against it, leaving the market wide open for competitors. Sometimes a product is just 'before its time' and customers need educating about it before it goes into full-scale production – leaving the education costs with the early entrant and an opportunity to launch late with a competitor. Either way, launching too early can often be even more disastrous than launching too late. And every market is different. Often products launched first in the USA will not find a market in other countries until years later. Timing is crucial, which leads us to the link between risk and the time taken to innovate, shown in Figure 12.12. Entrepreneurial firms should have an advantage here, because of their ability to move quickly. Equally, joint ventures and strategic alliances have an important part to play.

🗎 Case insight OnMobile

Timing

Arvindo Rao was working in the financial services sector in New York when he tried to launch a business developing value-added services – ring tones, wallpapers and apps – for mobile phones. Called OnMobile, it was originally incorporated in the USA in 2000, but failed to find a market. Not to be defeated, Arvindo approached telephone operators in India with his ideas and found that his timing was perfect. India's mobile phone market was expanding rapidly. He quickly found one customer, then another and by 2011 OnMobile had become India's largest value-added services provider. Based in Bangalore, it now has offices in London, Paris, the USA and South America.

Managing what is now an international company can be challenging. Arvindo believes in 'walking the talk' and regularly takes day-trips to these offices from his home in Mumbai. But it was when he first moved to India that he had his greatest problem dealing with staff from a different national culture:

'They are more emotional so you have to spend more time ... talking to employees, enquiring about their families, going out having lunch or dinner. It's a personal commitment that is not needed in the US and Europe. It's tough, even today I'm trying to understand the psyche of Indians, how to work with them.'

BBC News Business, 18 April 2011

One reason for getting the timing wrong arises from whether innovations come through technology-push or market-pull. Market-pull starts with customers and the need for the innovation is derived from them. This innovation is more likely to succeed because the timing, by definition, is right. An innovation based upon technology-push may not yet meet a customer need simply because customers cannot visualize how the new product/service might be used. Market research can mislead when it comes to disruptive innovation. This was the case with IBM and its market research into the PC. On the other hand, Steve Jobs at Apple proved incredibly insightful at predicting what the market would value and he was famously disdainful of market research, in particular focus groups. Technology-driven innovations are also more likely to be large, disruptive innovations whereas those driven by the market are more likely to be small, incremental and continuous. Thus technology-driven innovation can be very risky, as indeed can paradigm shift. But once again, entrepreneurial firms should also have an advantage in this because of their market responsiveness and closeness to the customer.

The key to managing risk on a portfolio basis is balance between:

▷ High-risk, high-return innovations and lower-risk, lower-return innovations;
▷ Disruptive, incremental and continuous innovations;
▷ Product/service and market innovations;
▷ Short and long time-to-market innovations;
▷ Innovations that employ new technology and those that employ existing technology.

Mitigating the risks of disruptive innovation

On the face of it, disruptive innovation – introducing new products/services into new markets – presents the greatest risk to an organization. But, as we have seen, the returns can be equally large, and some firms, like Apple and Google, seem to be managing these risk very effectively. Few people, however, would claim the insight into future customer needs that Steve Jobs seemed to have, which may be one reason Google have approached this issue in a different way. The risks associated with disruptive innovation can be mitigated in a number of ways:

Knowledge: Even small amounts of knowledge of new products or markets can mitigate risk, so some degree of relative knowledge is valuable. Put another way, going into totally unknown areas will be high-risk. Whilst Google has expanded well beyond its initial product/market offering, it has not gone into totally unknown areas where it has absolutely no capabilities or competences. I doubt whether it would ever go into the business of manufacturing forms of transport (whatever they might become in the future). This is one reason why the 'twilight zone' of incremental development is so attractive.

Experimentation: One way of building knowledge is through experimentation. This can involve entering new markets with existing products or introducing new products into existing markets with a view to finding out more about the unknown element. The problem with this approach is that it may take time, which itself generates additional risks.

Limited launch: Only one step beyond experimentation is the limited launch of new products into new markets. It involves one further step into that twilight zone. Firms like Google treat this as part of their market research and, rather than going for a 'big-bang' launch every time, they will frequently limit the launch geographically or bundle it into developments of an existing product. In this way they limit their exposure and learn from any failures. It also means that they may achieve first-mover advantage over competitors, assuming the product/market offering is substantially correct. Entrepreneurs instinctively understand the process of experimentation and limited launch. They engage in lots of experiments, test-markets and trial runs. They learn by doing, learning from their failure, and sharpening their response time by constantly progressing the project.

Joint ventures: As we saw in Chapter 6, one way of mitigating these risks is through joint ventures or strategic alliances. Both can be set up relatively quickly. In these circumstances the partner may possess much-needed competences or expertise, such as market knowledge. With such relationships the risks can then be compartmentalized and failure will not endanger either core business. What is more, the strategy avoids high set-up costs. And it relies on what an entrepreneurial firm should be good at – building relationships. On the down side, it does mean that the profits must be shared and control is lost to some extent – which is why firms also consider mergers and acquisitions as a way of diversifying or indeed buying a foothold in a new market. Google has partnered with many organizations to develop its services. Unlike Apple, its Android mobile phone operating system is open access, meaning that other companies can use it on their products.

Compartmentalization: If all else fails, then risk can always be compartmentalized by creating separate legal entities. Companies often do this when entering new geographic markets. It is one of the reasons they spin out new ventures. If they fail they will not endanger the core business.

Hamel and Prahalad (1991) liken firms relying on a 'big-bang' launch strategy to baseball players who concentrate on perfecting their swing and always strive to hit a perfect home run, so returning to base to hit again. As a result they are cautious and hold off until they think they can hit that perfect shot, thus affecting their batting average. The problem is that success is a function of both the ability to bat – your batting average – and the number of times you come to bat. You may need to bat more often. So the team that is not striving for perfection may get more of both and win the game. In the same way, the frequent introduction of incrementally adapted products, continuously learning and improving from them – whilst avoiding total disaster – is better than waiting to get everything right first time. A company relying on a few big projects that it pursues cautiously, always trying to perfect the product/service, resembles the baseball player trying to perfect his swing. If a completely new product can be rolled out into new markets incrementally, learning from mistakes and improving it with each successive launch, it probably stands a better chance of success, so long as it moves quickly enough to eventually dominate the market.

💼 Case with questions Google

Entrepreneurial architecture

The ubiquitous Google, a US multinational, runs over one million servers in data centres around the world and processes over one billion data requests every day. With a turnover in excess of $30 billion, it employs more than 25,000 people worldwide. It has its headquarters in Mountain View, California, in a campus called Googleplex. Google's mission is 'to organize the world's information and make it universally accessible and useful'. Founded in 1996 by Larry Page and Sergey Brin when they were both PhD students at Stanford University, Google has moved beyond being a mere search engine. It now has numerous products and services, including online productivity software such as Gmail, social networking tools such as Orkut and Google Buz, open source web browser Google Chrome, Picasa photo editing and organization software and Google Talk instant messaging. It also led the development of the Android mobile operating system and in 2010 released an Android phone under its own name called Nexus One. Its many subsidiaries include the equally ubiquitous YouTube. Advertising still generates 99% of Google's revenues.

Google is known for the power of its search engine algorithm and the elegance of its business model that matches text ads to searches. It is known for its innovative culture. Google's spectacular growth has come through organic growth combined with new product development (such as Gmail and Streetview), acquisitions (such as Google Maps and YouTube) and partnerships to take it beyond its core search engine business. It exhibits many of the internal architectural features of an entrepreneurial organization as well as following many widely used entrepreneurial growth strategies.

Google has an informal corporate culture and regularly features in *Fortune* magazine's list of best companies to work for. It likes to think of itself as still 'small' despite the fact it is anything but. Phrases used to illustrate the culture include 'you can be serious without a suit', 'work should be challenging and challenge should be fun' and 'you can make money without being evil'. It has a tradition of creating April Fools' Day Jokes. This started in 2000 when it 'launched' MentalPlex – Google's ability to read your mind and visualize the search result you want. It tries to add humour to its services. For example, if you ask the search engine for 'the answer to the ultimate question of life the universe and everything' it will actually give you the answer of '42' (Douglas Adams, *The Hitchhiker's Guide to the Galaxy*). Google supports philanthropy. The not-for-profit Google. org creates awareness about climate change, global public health and poverty. After a two-year search for suitable recipients, in 2010 Google gave some $10 million to various community projects. In 2011 it gave €1 million to the International Mathematics Olympiad.

Google is also a noted supporter of network neutrality.

Google has a flat, decentralized organization structure. It is highly democratic and tightly interconnected – like the internet itself. It has been said that this comes from the founders' own dislike of authority. All of the staff involved in product development – almost half of Google's employees – work in small teams of three or four people. Larger teams are broken down into smaller sub-teams, each working on specific aspects of the bigger project. Each team has a leader who moves round, depending on the changing project requirements. Most staff work in more than one team.

Google encourages creativity in a number of ways. Many companies that work on building successful teams or encouraging creativity are known to facilitate playful environments. The lobby in Googleplex has a piano, lava lamps, old server clusters and a projection of search queries on the wall. The corridors have exercise balls and bicycles. Other playful elements include a slide and a fireman's pole. Recreational facilities – from video games and ping-pong tables to workout rooms – are scattered throughout the campus. It also has functional elements that aid idea-generation and dissemination. For example it has enclosed, noise-free projectors that can be left on at all times and employees can automatically email meeting notes to attendees. As one newspaper commented:

'To visit Google's headquarters in Mountain View, California, is to travel to another planet. The natives wander about in T-shirts and shorts, zipping past volleyball courts and organic-vegetable gardens while holding their open laptops at shoulder height, like waiters' trays. Those laptops are gifts from the company, as is free food, wi-fi-enabled commuter buses, healthcare, dry cleaning, gyms, massages and car washes, all designed to keep its employees happy and on campus.'

Ken Auletta, *Guardian*, 4 March 2010

Marissa Mayer was one of Google's earliest employees. Now President and CEO of Google's arch rival, Facebook, she was promoted to head up Geographic and Local Services, as VP Search Products. She helped launch over 100 products and features including Gmail and Google Instant. She developed Google's 9 Principles of Innovation (20 February 2008, www.fastcompany.com):

1 **Innovation, not instant perfection**: Google has a low-cost, try-it-out, experimental approach to new product development. Because of the mould-breaking nature of many of Google's innovations, it wants its products to be launched early and then developed and perfected as it learns what the market wants: 'The beauty of experimenting in this way is that you never get too far from what the market wants. The market pulls you back'. The problem has been that many of these products have been far from perfect when launched.

2 **Ideas come from everywhere**: The company has several technology-enabled solutions to foster creativity amongst employees. Google Ideas acts as a repository for innovative ideas. It enables employees to share new ideas on products, services and to comment on the ideas of others. The tool also has a feature to rate the ideas submitted on a scale of 0–5, 0 denoting 'Dangerous or harmful if implemented' and 5, 'Great idea! Make it so': 'We have this great internal list where people post new ideas and everyone can go on and see them. It's like a voting pool where you can say how good or bad you think an idea is. Those comments lead to new ideas'.

3 **A licence to pursue your dreams**: Like 3M, Google has built in slack to encourage creativity through its '70/20/10 Rule' – staff spend 70% of their time working on their core projects, 20% on ideas that are closely related to their projects, and 10% on any other ideas they would like to pursue.

→

Half of Google's new product launches have originated from this scheme, including two of Google's best-known products, GMail and Google News. Google News was created by Krishna Bharat. After the 9/11 terrorist attacks, he found himself tracking information from several news sites. This caused him to come up with the idea of creating a tool that could trawl through different news sites to cluster the type of information he wanted to read. Google magnified this idea to form a complete news service on their site. Google also encourage rapid low-cost experimentation early in the life of projects so as to continually check feasibility.

4 **Morph projects, don't kill them**: Google believes every idea that makes it to its Labs must have the kernel of a good idea somewhere, even if the market does not respond to it, and the trick is to see how it can be used. And few innovators are able to succeed every time. Consider the case of Lars and Jens Rasmussen who created Google Maps. The Rasmussen brothers also created Google Wave – billed as a tool that would transform online communication and collaboration – which failed spectacularly to live up to its promise to be a social collaborative platform that would replace email and was closed down in 2009. However Google was positive about learning from such failures, stressing that, whilst there may not be have been the user adoption they would have liked, the knowledge from the technological developments would not be lost. It viewed Wave almost as an experiment. Indeed the first of Google's Principles of Innovation is to launch early then develop the product into what the market really wants – only sometimes the market really does not want the product.

5 **Share as much information as you can**: Google has its own intranet called MOMMA that allows staff to share information. Every week staff write down five or six headings of what they are working on. These are indexed and made into a giant web page allowing anyone to search to find what staff are working on that week. Google also encourages employees to pay attention to what is happening in the outside world – new ideas from many different sources. For example, it hosts regular 'Tech Talks' with speakers including distinguished researchers from around the world and experts in other fields, such as artists, writers, and chefs. Google shows that it values these talks by including the number an employee has hosted in staff performance reviews.

6 **Users, users, users**: Innovations need users. Users generate a market place. With a market place a business model will emerge. This is Google's market focus.

7 **Data is apolitical**: Google believes design is a science, not an art, relying on data: 'Run a 1% test [on 1% of the audience] and whichever design does best against the user happiness metrics over a two-week period is the one we launch'.

8 **Creativity loves constraints**: Google engineers love to be told something cannot be done and then proving you wrong. Google also recognizes the tension between staff freedom and control and the need to have a senior supporter for any project going forward for development. It believes staff need a sponsoring manager to be a 'guardrail' – setting reasonable boundaries within which they can be creative and experiment with ideas. The sponsor and employee must develop an experimentation plan that covers details such as expectations, timelines, and resource commitments. Key milestones for the development of the idea are agreed and regular check-in points scheduled where the employee can update the sponsor on the experiment's progress. Sponsors build 'dashboards' to capture the key metrics of their programmes. They take any opportunity to share these metrics with their peers and superiors so as to remind them about the value of their programme.

9 **You're brilliant? We're hiring**: Google employs only people who it thinks are exceptionally talented. It believes you need to attract the right sort of people to build a successful innovating organization – people with ambition and a high regard for themselves. Then you need to build the team.

Google has pursued an aggressive policy of acquisition, focusing mainly on small venture capital-backed start-up companies. Google Earth came out of the acquisition of Keyhole in 2004, Google Voice out of the acquisition of Grand Central in 2007. It also purchased YouTube in 2006, DoubleClick in 2007 (which developed technology that allows Google to determine user interests and target advertising), video software maker On2 Technologies and social network Aardvark in 2009 and, in 2010, hardware start-up Agnilux and web-based teleconferencing company Global IP Solutions.

Google also has its own venture capital arm, Google Ventures, which invested in some 30 firms between 2008 and 2010 in areas as diverse as educational software and biotechnology. Its annual budget of $100 million is invested in amounts of between $50,000 and $50 million and companies are often sold off (for example, the gaming company, Ngmoco) or floated on the stock market (for example the holiday rentals and bed-and-breakfast portal Home Away). This is separate from Google's in-house projects, which in turn has projects as diverse as driver-less cars and new sources of alternative energy.

Google has also partnered with numerous organizations involved in anything from research to advertising. Examples include Sun Microsystems to share and distribute each other's technologies, AOL to enhance each other's video search services, Fox Interactive Media (part of News Corporation) to provide search and advertising on MySpace, GeoEye to provide satellite images for Google Earth.

Now into its second decade of life Google will need to stay nimble if it is not to come up against barriers to its growth. Its core search business is an enormous revenue generator. However, it has been said that, although it is not obvious from its financial results, Google's diversification policy has simply added costs and done little to boost revenues. There is a lack of coherence in Google's product development strategy and a lack of rigour and urgency in pushing through strategies:

> 'Google's problem has been in focus and execution of strategy. Despite having something like 90% search share in most markets, its fabled search algorithms are being exploited by spammers; despite the huge growth in sales of smartphones using its Android operating software, it hasn't been able to persuade mobile networks or handset makers to give customers the best deals by automatically upgrading their software; and more dangerously it faces an antitrust investigation in Europe over whether it cross-promotes its own services in its search results'.
>
> Charles Arthur, *The Guardian*,
> 21 February 2011

In contrast to Apple, which jealously guards its iPhone operating system, Android is open access and it is interesting to compare the success of these two very different strategies. Google's strategy has been one of open access. Manufacturers could use the operating system free, thereby encouraging the development of a wide range of phones, compared to Apple's limited range. As a result, sales of smartphones increased sevenfold between 2010 and 2011. In the USA some 55% of smartphones use the Android operating system, compared to the 27% market share enjoyed by iPhones (UK 38%, compared to 23% – data from Kantar WorldPanel Comtech, 2011). However, where 90% of users are on the latest version of Apple's operating system, only 58% are on the widely-used 2.2 version of Android and developers are therefore discouraged from developing for it, and the development of apps for the Android has

→

therefore proved problematic. Anyone can write apps for Android, compared to Apple's strict control of its apps store. As a result, quality is variable. Android Market is the main download portal for Android apps. It has been criticized for the way apps are catalogued, promoted and reviewed. In 2010 its sales were only £62 million – lower than those for Blackberry App World (£100 million), Nokia's Ovi store (£64 million) and massively lower than Apple's App Store (£1.1 billion). However, unlike Apple's monopoly, Android's open set-up means any company can set up an app store, which is what Amazon did in 2011. Ironically Amazon's Appstore (named despite the best efforts of Apple) is a closed system, monitored and controlled by Amazon, just like Apple's own App Store. Google expects income to come from advertising, capitalizing on a user's location, and also a mobile music service.

The Android system is one of four main business opportunities facing Google. The second is YouTube, and how to develop a business model for it. The third is the web browser Chrome which has 15% of the market with more than 120 million users. This is being developed into a whole PC operating system that will compete with Microsoft Windows, and Google already has contracts with Acer and Samsung. The fourth opportunity is hosting office services 'in the cloud' – selling computer applications like email and word processing directly to business users.

But the virtual world is changing and Google's lack of success in getting into the social networking market is an area of weakness often commented on in the press. Millions of Facebook users navigate from page to page according to friends' recommendations rather than the complicated algorithms underpinning the Google search engine. As one newspaper commented: 'Google looks positively ancient to the whiz-kids at Facebook and Twitter ... Google is the establishment now, plugged into government and Wall Street' (*Sunday Times*, 3 April 2011). Google Buzz has not taken off and sparked a storm in 2010 when it revealed each Gmail user's list of contacts to others. Similarly Wave, a Twitter-like message platform, has not proved popular.

Just to add to these uncertainties, Eric Schmidt, for 10 years the CEO of Google, resigned in January 2011 to become Executive Chairman, focusing on 'deals, partnerships, customers and broader business relationships.' Replacing him was co-founder Larry Page who, it was said, would be leading product development and technology strategy. Schmidt was seen as providing 'adult supervision' to the 'kids' who founded the company, being a key player in growing the business and presenting the company's public face, something Larry Page was not known for.

In a newspaper article it is claimed that media mogul Barry Diller believes Brin and Page are 'more than most people ... wildly self-possessed'. The same article continues:

> 'Brin, who is more sociable than Page, has his own quirks. He will often get lost in deep thought and forget about meetings. So focused is he on engineering and maths, he sometimes displays a fundamental innocence about how the world works ... Google's engineering culture brings great virtue, but also a vice. The company often lacks an antenna for sensing how governments, companies and people will react to its constant innovations. YouTube, for example, is brilliantly engineered and hosts around 40% of internet videos – yet it makes no money, because advertisers shy away from user-generated content that is unpredictable and might harm their "friendly" ads.'
>
> Ken Auletta, *Guardian*, 4 March 2010

Another of the challenges facing Google is how to continue innovating quickly – beating competitors to the market. Larry Page sees this as a battle against bureaucracy and he aims to speed up decision-making by pushing down responsibility for it. Commentators also observed that the management structure needed to be overhauled: 'The solution to Google's growing size is devolution' (*Sunday Times*, 3 April 2011).

There are a number of videos about Google that can be accessed through the website accompanying this book: www.palgrave.com/business/burns

☐ Find the latest news about Google from its corporate website on: www.google.com/corporate

QUESTIONS

1 In your opinion, has Google lacked focus in the past?

2 Has Google followed the right strategy in getting products to market quickly at the expense of getting them right first time?

3 What aspects of Google's architecture encourage corporate entrepreneurship?

4 Compare and contrast once more the culture at Google with that at Apple (Chapter 5). Why are there differences? Which do you think has greater sustainability?

5 What do you think of Google's four main business opportunities?

6 Do you think Google should decentralize? If so, suggest how this might be done.

Innovative Thinker Test

Innovation is the prime tool entrepreneurs use to create or exploit opportunity and is one of the two most important distinguishing features of their character. The **Innovative Potential Indicator (IPI)** was developed by Dr Fiona Patterson, based upon research on employees in established companies. It is published by Oxford Psychologists Press and claims to be the only psychometric test able to identify those people who have the potential to become innovative thinkers.

Dr Patterson identifies ten types of people:

1 **Change Agent**, who thrives on change and is independent. The change agent conjures up the strangest ways to solve problems and does not stick to what he or she was told. This is the innovative thinker who embodies one of the most essential characteristics that differentiate entrepreneurs from owner-managers.

2 **Consolidator**, whose rigidity and independence militates against innovative thinking but is a safety net because of their preference for the status quo.

3 **Harmoniser**, who likes the challenge but does not disclose good ideas for fear of upsetting people.

4 **Firefighter**, who flits from one idea to another in an imaginative but unpredictable way.

5 **Cooperator**, who likes change but 'goes with the flow'.

6 **Catalyst**, who is good at thinking up ideas but soon loses interest.

7 **Inhibited Innovator**, whose brainwaves could be valuable but lacks the confidence to push them forward.

8 **Incremental Innovator**, who dreams up radical ideas but likes to implement them in a step-by-step way which can appear inflexible.

9 **Spice-of-Life**, whose dominant characteristic is the need to be doing something, anything, new.

10 **Middle-of-the-Road**, who is good at blending ideas but is ambivalent about them.

➡

The IPI questionnaire asks for agreement/disagreement with 36 statements about how you approach change, how adaptable you are and how you stand up to others. Based upon your answers, it scores you on four main areas of behaviour which Dr Patterson's research shows can be used to establish whether a person has innovative potential. Scores can be between 20 and 80 on each dimension. The dimensions are:

▷ Motivation to change (MTC).
▷ Willingness to behave in a challenging way (CB).
▷ Willingness to adapt and use tried-and-tested approaches (AD).
▷ Consistency of working style which indicates efficiency and orderliness (CWS).

Change Agents have high MTC and CB scores, and low AD and CWS scores. For example, according to *The Times* (14 March 2000), Trevor Baylis, the inventor of the clockwork radio, had a high MTC score of 70 and CB score of 60, and a low AD score of 25 and CWS score of 35.

The test can be obtained from Oxford Psychologists Press on www.opp.co.uk

Summary

▷ Innovation is difficult to define. It is about introducing new products, services or processes, opening up new markets, identifying new sources of supply of raw materials or creating new types of industrial organization. At one extreme it includes disruptive innovations – invention and paradigm shifts in marketing that create whole new markets (**Henry Ford**). At the other it includes incremental innovations – changes to products, services or processes and how they are marketed. However, inventors, like **Charles Babbage**, do not necessarily instigate innovation.

▷ Innovative intensity measures innovation on two dimensions; scale and frequency. These dimensions are not mutually exclusive, most firms innovate along both. Whilst the returns from disruptive innovation can be high, many small incremental innovations can also yield high returns with a lower risk.

▷ As demonstrated by **Google**, disruptive innovation is needed to renew the product/service portfolio. Other forms of innovation are needed to compete in existing markets as products progress through their life cycle.

▷ Innovation comes from a creative environment. To be successfully launched into the market it needs to be combined with entrepreneurship, as in the case of **James Dyson**, or developed within an entrepreneurial organization.

▷ Innovation can be managed. Figures 12.4 and 12.5 outline product/service development models. In reality innovation is unlikely to be linear or smooth – as was the case with **Levi** jeans. There is likely to be an element of chaos which results in set-backs when stages have to be repeated.

▷ Disruptive innovation can originate by challenging marketing conventions – sectoral, performance and customer conventions – and reorientating from customers to non-customers and from competitors to alternatives. **Swatch** created a whole new market for watches as cheap fashion accessories. The **Nintendo Wii** challenged the conventions for computer games and created a new market for 'activity' games.

- Innovation is risky. These risks are shown in Figure 12.8. Risk increases with the newness of the product/service and the market to which it is offered. However, firms with an entrepreneurial architecture have an advantage in moving into the twilight zone, because of their close understanding of both product and customer.

- Strategic alliances/partnerships and joint ventures can be used to mitigate the risks of moving into new markets or developing new technologies.

- All the techniques and structures involved in corporate venturing can be used to encourage and exploit innovation. Where internal corporate venturing does not produce the required innovations, external corporate venturing can be tried. These are not mutually exclusive options.

- Innovation risks can also be mitigated by taking a portfolio approach. The key is balance across the portfolio of innovations, balance between:
  - High-risk, high-return innovations and lower-risk, lower-return innovations;
  - Discrete, dynamically continuous and continuous innovations;
  - Product/service and market innovations;
  - Short and long time-to-market innovations;
  - Innovations that employ new technology and those that employ existing technology.

- Risk also increases with the time it takes to get to market because competitors might gain first-mover advantage. As with **OnMobile**, timing is crucial.

- Risks associated with disruptive innovation are mitigated by knowledge, experimentation, limited launches, joint ventures and compartmentalization of risks. **Google** practises many of these techniques of risk mitigation.

- **Google** is an organization that continuously innovates. Some of the innovations are incremental, others are disruptive. It has processes to encourage both. It encourages innovation and manages the associated risks in a systematic way. It is an example of good practice.

Essays and discussion topics

1 Is invention good?

2 Do you agree with Michael Porter that 'invention and entrepreneurship are at the heart of national advantage'?

3 Give some examples of new-to-the-world products that have been successful and some that have not. Why have they been successful or unsuccessful?

4 What do you think constitutes innovation? Give examples.

5 Give examples of innovations for one product/service in each quadrant of Porter's generic strategies (Chapter 10). Explain what the aim of the innovation was.

6 What is the relationship between innovation and change?

7 Why are entrepreneurs interested in innovation?

8 What major commercial opportunities have arisen over the last ten years? How were they exploited? Were they technology-driven or market-led?

9 What major commercial opportunities do you think will arise in the next ten years?

10 What are the problems associated with a structured, systematic product development process? How can they be overcome?

11 What are the advantages and disadvantages of parallel product development processes?

12 How is innovation linked to risk? How can risk be mitigated?

13 If innovation is risky, not exploiting innovation is riskier. Discuss.

14 Why is risk lower in the 'twilight zone' for firms with an entrepreneurial architecture? Why might an entrepreneurial company have competitive advantage by operating here?

15 Why is 'time to market' important?

16 List the advantages and disadvantages small firms have over large firms in introducing innovation.

17 What are the main barriers to innovation in large firms?

18 Why do you need to take a portfolio approach to risk management?

19 The concept of 'balance' in a portfolio of innovation implies such a diverse range of innovative projects that they cannot be managed in the same organization. Discuss.

20 How do discontinuous innovations come about? Why might we see more of them in the future?

21 Give some examples of discontinuous innovations

22 How do you go about challenging marketing conventions?

23 If doing things differently is important, what is the value of conventional marketing frameworks?

24 If you want to make a big return, you need to take big risks – that is what entrepreneurial companies are about. Discuss.

Exercises and assignments

1 Answer the Innovation Potential Indicator questionnaire and assess your innovative potential.

2 List the major social, legal, economic, political and technological changes that you expect to see over the next ten years. List their likely consequences. Finally. note how they might be exploited commercially.

3 Take an existing product/market offering and break down the sectoral, performance and customer conventions that underpin it. Question whether they can be challenged and note any alternatives along with what is required to make them commercially viable.

4 Write up a case study of successful innovation in a small firm and in a large firm. Analyze why they were successful. Compare and contrast the two cases.

References

Audretsch, D.B. (1995), 'Innovation, growth and survival', *International Journal of Industrial Organisation*,13.

Berkhout, F. and Green, K. (2003) *International Journal of Innovation Management*, 6(3), Special issue on Managing Innovation for Sustainability.

Bessant, J. (1999) 'Developing Continuous Improvement Capability', *International Journal of Innovation Management*, 2.

Bolton, B. and Thompson, J. (2000) *Entrepreneurs: Talent, Temperament, Technique*, Oxford: Butterworth-Heinemann.

Bowman, C. and Faulkner, D. (1997) *Competitive and Corporate Strategy*, London: Irwin.

Booz, Allen and Hamilton (1968) *Management of New Products*, New York: Booz, Allen and Hamilton.

Booz, Allen and Hamilton (1982) *New Products Management for the 1980s*, New York: Booz, Allen and Hamilton.

Cannon, T. (1985) 'Innovation, Creativity and Small Firm Organization', *International Small Business Journal*, 4(1).

Chaston, I. (2000) *Entrepreneurial Marketing: Competing by Challenging Convention*, Basingstoke: Palgrave – now Palgrave Macmillan.

Christensen, C. (1997) *The Innovator's Dilemma*, Cambridge, MA: Harvard Business School Press.

Cooper, R.G. (1994) 'Third-Generation New Product Processes', *Journal of Product Innovation Management*, 11.

Hamel, G. and Prahalad, C.K. (1991) 'Corporate Imagination and Expeditionary Marketing', *Harvard Business Review*, 69(4), July/August.

Hamel, G. and Prahalad, C.K. (1994) *Competing For the Future: Breakthrough Strategies for Seizing Control of your Industry and Creating the Markets of Tomorrow*, Boston, MA: Harvard Business School Press.

Kanter, R.M. (1983) *The Change Masters: Innovation and Productivity in American Corporations*, New York: Simon & Schuster.

Kim, W.C. and Mauborgne, R. (2005) 'Blue Ocean Strategy: From Theory to Practice', *California Management Review*, Spring, 47(3).

Lambin, J.J. (2000) *Market-Driven Management: Strategic and Operational Marketing*, Basingstoke: Palgrave – now Palgrave Macmillan.

Mellor, R.B. (2005) *Sources and Spread of Innovation in Small e-Commerce Companies*, Skodsborgvej: Forlaget Globe.

Mintzberg, H. (1983) *Structures in Fives: Designing Effective Organizations*, London: Prentice Hall.

Morris, M.H. and Kuratko, D.F. (2002) *Corporate Entrepreneurship: Entrepreneurial Development within Organizations*, Fort Worth: Harcourt College Publishers.

Porter, M.E. (1990) *The Competitive Advantage of Nations*, New York: Free Press.

Schmidt, G.M. (2004) 'Low-end and High-end Encroachments for New Products', *International Journal of Innovation Management*, 8(2).

Schumpeter, J.A. (1996) *The Theory of Economic Development*, edition copyright 1983, New Jersey: Transaction Publishers.

Takeuchi, H. and Nonaka, I. (1986) 'The New Product Development Game', *Harvard Business Review*, 64(1).

Tidd, J., Bessant, J. and Pavitt, K. (2005) *Managing Innovation: Integrating Technological, Market and Organizational Change*, 3rd edn, Chichester: Wiley.

Utterback, J. and Acee, H.J. (2005) 'Disruptive Technologies: An Expanded View', *International Journal of Innovation Management*, 9(1).

Van De Ven, A., Angle H.L. and Poole, M.S. (2000) *Research in the Management of Innovation: The Minnesota Studies*, New York: Oxford University Press.

Van Grundy, A. (1987) 'Organizational Creativity and Innovation', in S.G. Isaksen, *Frontiers of Creative Research*, New York: Brearly.

Chapter 13

Generating creative ideas

Learning outcomes

By the end of this chapter you should be able to:

▷ Critically analyze the factors that stimulate creativity and innovation both in individuals and across the organization;

▷ Critically analyze the factors that inhibit creativity and innovation both in individuals and across the organization;

▷ Critically analyze the factors that contribute to a creative environment both organizationally and nationally;

▷ Apply creativity and critical thinking.

Discovery skills

Creativity is a key ingredient in the entrepreneurial architecture. It is part of spotting market opportunities and is essential in generating all innovations. It underpins the development of disruptive innovation. It has been estimated that for every eleven ideas that enter the new product development process, only one new product will be successfully launched (Page, 1993). So, new ideas are at a premium and it is a numbers game: the more you generate the more are likely to see the light of day commercially. Entrepreneurial architecture must encourage creativity. But creativity is essentially an individual activity that relies on tacit knowledge (see Chapter 6). Tacit knowledge is embedded in minds and activities so it is difficult to share and primarily an individual activity. The organizational architecture should therefore stimulate individual creativity and learning – tacit knowledge – and facilitate the translation of this into the products and services that the market values (Grant, 1996). This chapter will therefore look at both of these aspects – encouraging individual creativity and the sort of organizational structures and facilities that will enable this. However, we can get some valuable clues about how to nurture creativity by looking at successful entrepreneurs and how they go about generating new ideas.

Dyer et al. (2009) conducted a six-year study of more than 3000 US CEOs, contrasting 25 well-known entrepreneurs (such as Steve Jobs of Apple, Jeff Bezos of Amazon, Pierre Omidyar of eBay, Peter Thiel of PayPal, Niklas Zennström of Skype and Michael Dell) with other CEOs who had no track record for innovation. Whilst these other CEOs saw themselves as 'facilitating innovation', the entrepreneurs did not delegate creativity work and held themselves to be personally responsible for strategic innovations. As a result of this they spent 50% more time on 'discovery activities' than the other CEOs.

The authors highlighted five 'discovery skills' that they believe make people more innovative, but could equally be applied to creativity. The five discovery skills were:

Associating – Innovators connect seemingly unrelated questions, problems or ideas from many different fields. This often comes from mixing with people from diverse backgrounds and disciplines. The minds of the entrepreneur CEOs in the study were able to make connections between seemingly unrelated things, transferring questions, problems or ideas from one discipline to another. They capitalized on apparently divergent associations. What is more this ability to associate seemed to be something that could be encouraged through stimulation: 'The more frequently people in our study attempted to understand, categorize, and store new knowledge, the more easily their brains could naturally and consistently make, store and recombine associations.'

Questioning – Innovators challenge conventional wisdom, asking 'why?', 'why not? and 'what if?' The iconic Apple iPod was developed at a time when MP3 players were well-established. Staff developing Apple's iTunes software for use with MP3 players formed such a low opinion of the ease of use of MP3s that they decided that they could do better. Most of the entrepreneur CEOs were able to remember the specific question they asked that inspired them to set up their business. They were also able to imagine opposites, including some different future state (necessary for strategic intent), and to embrace real-world constraints so that they became opportunities if they could be overcome (see Google case in the last chapter).

Observing – Innovators observe common phenomena and people's behaviour, particularly that of potential customers. They scrutinize these phenomena, noticing fine detail and gaining insight into new ways of doing things. Ratan Tata observed a family of four perched on a moped and asked why they could not afford a car? In 2009, after years of product development which involved new modular production methods, Tata Group launched the lowest-priced car in the world – the Nano. Observing is a prerequisite to associating. It is part of how connections are made. You need to observe detail to be able to associate it across boundaries.

🛆 Case insight Swarfega

Re-using ideas

Not all innovations find a commercial application in the way they were originally envisaged. Swarfega is a green gel which is a dermatologically safe cleaner for the skin. It is widely used to remove grease and oil from hands in factories and households. In 2004 Audley Williamson sold the business he set up to manufacture his innovation for £135 million. But the original product, developed in 1941, was not intended for degreasing hands at all. It was intended as a mild detergent to wash silk stockings. Unfortunately the invention of nylon and its application to stockings rendered the product as obsolete as silk stockings. Watching workmen trying to clean their hands with a mixture of petrol, paraffin and sand which left them cracked and sore led Williamson to realize that there was a completely different commercial opportunity for his product.

Experimenting – Innovators actively try out new ideas, creating prototypes and launching pilots. Where these do not work, they learn from any mistakes and try to use the learning in different projects. Howard Head, the inventor of the steel ski, made some 40 different metal skis before he finally made one that would work consistently. The Apple iPod started life as prototypes made out of foam-core boards, using fishing weights to give it the right feel. All the entrepreneur CEOs engaged in some form of active experimenting ranging from 'intellectual exploration' to 'physical tinkering.' This is really just another example of questioning – why do things work or not work and what if I did it differently? One of their most powerful experiments was visiting, living and/or working in overseas countries. This was all part of being exposed to new ideas and mixing with people from diverse backgrounds. For example Howard Schultz, founder of Starbucks, spent some time in Italy where he visited coffee bars.

📖 Case insight Google

Experimentation

'Google's "just-try-it" philosophy is applied to even the company's most daunting projects, like digitizing the world's libraries. Like every new initiative, Google Book Search began with a makeshift experiment aimed at answering a critical question; in this case: how long does it take to digitize a book? To find out, Page (Larry Page – co-founder) and Mayer (Melissa Mayer – a senior Google executive) rigged up a piece of plywood with a couple of clamps and proceeded to photograph each page of a 300 page book, using a metronome to keep pace. With Mayer flipping pages, and one half of Google's founding team taking digital snapshots, it took 40 minutes to turn the ink into pixels. An optical character recognition program soon turned the digital photos into text, and within five days the pair had ginned up a piece of software that could search the book. That kind of step-wise, learn-as-you-go approach has repeatedly helped Google to test critical assumptions and avoid making bet-the-farm mistakes.'

Hamel G. (2007) *The Future of Management*, Boston, MA: Harvard Business School Press.

Networking – Innovators spent time finding and testing ideas with a network of diverse individuals in different countries. They did not just network with like-minded business people. Networking in this context is just another aspect of observing and is therefore a prerequisite to associating. It is part of the connectivity needed to encourage creativity.

The authors present a convincing analogy:

'Imagine that you have an identical twin, endowed with the same brains and natural talents that you have. You're both given one week to come up with a creative new business venture idea. During that week, you come up with ideas alone in your room. In contrast, your twin (1) talks with 10 people – including an engineer, a musician, a stay-at-home dad, and a designer – about the venture, (2) visits three innovative start-ups to observe what they do, (3) samples five 'new to the market' products, (4) shows a prototype he's built to five people, and (5) asks the questions 'What if I tried this?' and 'Why do you do that?' at least 10 times each day during these networking, observing and experimenting activities, Who do you bet will come up with the more innovative (and doable) idea?'

Creativity and the search for innovation

Dyer's five discovery skills are about applying creativity to the process of innovation. As we have observed, creativity on its own is not necessarily entrepreneurial – it needs to be applied to the process of innovation. Creativity and innovation can be developed and encouraged in a systematic way. Valery (1999) observes that 'innovation has more to do with the pragmatic search for opportunity than the romantic ideas about serendipity or lonely pioneers pursuing their vision against all the odds.' Drucker (1985) takes this further. He believes that innovation can be practised systematically through a creative analysis of change in the environment and the opportunities this generates. It is not the result of 'happenstance' nor, as we saw in the last section, that rare 'eureka moment'. Firms can practise innovation systematically by using their creativity skills to search for change and then evaluate its potential for an economic or social return. Change provides the opportunity for innovation. Skills in creativity help to identify these opportunities.

Drucker (op. cit.) says that innovation is 'capable of being presented as a discipline, capable of being learned and capable of being practiced. Entrepreneurs need to search purposefully for the sources of innovation, the changes and their symptoms that indicate opportunities for successful innovation. And they need to know and to apply the principles of successful innovation.' He lists seven sources of opportunity for firms in search of creative innovation. Four can be found within the firm itself or from the industry of which it is part and are therefore reasonably easy to spot. They are 'basic symptoms' – highly reliable indicators of changes that have already happened or can be made to happen with little effort. They are:

1 **The unexpected** – be it the unexpected success or failure or the unexpected event. Nobody can predict the future but an ability to react quickly to changes is a real commercial advantage, particularly in a rapidly changing environment. Information and knowledge are invaluable.
2 **The incongruity** – between what actually happens and what was supposed to happen. Plans go wrong and unexpected outcomes produce opportunities for firms that are able to spot them.

3 **The inadequacy in underlying processes** – that are taken for granted but can be improved or changed. This is essentially improving process engineering – especially important if the product is competing primarily on price.

4 **The changes in industry or market structure** – that take everyone by surprise. Again, unexpected change, perhaps arising from technology, legislation or other outside events create an opportunity to strategize about how the firm might cope and, as usual, first-mover advantage is usually worth striving for.

These changes produce sources of opportunity that need to be dissected and the underlying causes of change understood. A learning organization of the sort we have described would understand this. The causes give clues about how innovation can be used to increase value added to the customer and economic return to the firm. An entrepreneurial firm should be adept at this.

The other three factors come from the outside world and you might expect them to be anticipated by regular SLEPT analyses (see Chapter 9):

5 **Demographic changes** – population changes caused by changes in birth rates, wars, medical improvements and so on.

6 **Changes in perception, mood and meaning** – that can be brought about by the ups and downs of the economy, culture, fashion etc. In-depth interviews or focus groups can also often give an insight into these changes.

7 **New knowledge** – both scientific and non-scientific.

Drucker (op. cit.) lists the seven factors in increasing order of difficulty, uncertainty and unreliability, which means that he believes that new knowledge, including scientific knowledge, for all its visibility and glamour, is in fact the most difficult, least reliable and least predictable source of innovation. Paradoxically, this is the area to which government, academics and even entrepreneurial firms pay most attention. He argues that innovations arising from the systematic analysis of mundane and unglamorous unexpected successes or failures are far more likely to yield commercial innovations. They have the shortest lead times between start and yielding measurable results and carry fairly low risk and uncertainty.

It is worth remembering Bolton and Thompson's (2000) three basic approaches to innovation, mentioned in the preceding chapter:

1 Have a problem and seek a solution.
2 Have a solution and seek a problem.
3 Identify a need and develop a solution.

Each of these can be applied to the seven sources of innovative opportunity identified by Drucker.

The creative mind

We are now starting to understand how the creative process works on an individual level. Conceptually the brain has two sides that operate in quite different ways. The left side performs rational, logical functions. It tends to be verbal and analytic, operating in a linked, linear sequence (called logical or vertical thinking). The right side operates intuitive and non-rational modes of thought. It is non-verbal, linking images together to get a holistic perspective (called creative or lateral thinking). A person uses both sides, shifting naturally from one to the other. However, the right side is the creative side. Creative innovation is therefore primarily a right-brain activity whilst adaptive innovation is a left-brain activity.

Left-brain thinkers therefore tend to be rational, logical, analytical and sequential in their approach to problem-solving. Right-brain thinkers are more intuitive, value-based and non-linear in their approach. Kirton (1976) characterizes left-brain thinkers as 'adaptors' – convergent thinkers who solve problems with a disciplined, rational approach, and are best at refining current practices. Right-brain thinkers are characterized as 'innovators' – divergent thinkers who discover problems by approaching tasks from unusual angles, and are less concerned with doing things better than with doing things differently. Both are creative, albeit in different ways. The adaptor, however, is better at incremental innovation and the innovator at disruptive innovation. The Kirton Adapter-Innovator (KAI) scale is a psychometric that distinguishes between these two cognitive styles by assessing different dimensions of creativity including originality, attention to detail and following rules. (The test is available on www.kaicentre.com/.)

The cognitive styles are also reflected in the preferred work-styles, with left-brain thinkers preferring to work alone, learn about things rather than experience them and show the ability or preference to make quick decisions. By way of contrast, the right-brain thinker prefers working in groups, experiencing things (e.g. learning by doing) and generating lots of options in preference to focusing on making a speedy decision. People have a preference for one or other approach, but can and do switch between them for different tasks and in different contexts. There are clear parallels here with the approaches to leadership style outlined in Chapter 4 because it is individuals' cognitive processes that shape their preferred style.

> '*There are so few new ideas, so few new things that have not been done. But although the safe place to be is copying what others are doing, I think the people who succeed will be those with the boldness to do something in a totally different way. They take an idea and reinvent it. We have seen that in airlines, where people said, It's just a flying bus, why shouldn't tickets cost £29? And there are still plenty of opportunities.*'
>
> **Rachel Elnaugh**, founder of **Red Letter Days**
> *Sunday Times* 23 May 2004

Normally the two halves of the brain complement each other, but many factors, not least our education, tend to encourage development of left-brain activity – logic. Kirby (2003) speculates that this may well explain why so many successful entrepreneurs appear not to have succeeded in the formal education system. He argues that entrepreneurs are right-brain

Logical		Creative
Seeks answers	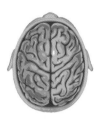	Seeks questions
Converges		Diverges
Asserts best or right view		Explores different views, seeks insights
Uses existing structure		Restructures
Says when an idea will not work		Seeks ways an idea might help
Uses logical steps		Welcomes discontinuous leaps
Concentrates on what is relevant		Welcomes chance intrusions
Closed		Open-ended

F 13.1 Dimensions of creative (lateral) vs logical (vertical) thinking

dominant. But he goes even further by speculating that there may be a link between this and dyslexia, observing that so many entrepreneurs are dyslexic and language skills are left-brain activities. This is an interesting but unproven hypothesis.

However, the point is that most people need to encourage and develop right-brain activity if they wish to be creative. And this is possible, with training. To overcome the habit of logic you need to deliberately set aside this ingrained way of thinking. Creative or lateral thinking is different in a number of dimensions from logical or vertical thinking. It is imaginative, emotional, and often results in more than one solution. Edward de Bono (1971) set out some of the dimensions of difference. Figure 13.1 is based on his work.

One important aspect of high-level creativity is the ability to recognize relationships among objects, processes, cause-and-effect, people and so on that others do not see, searching for different, unorthodox relationships that can be replicated in a different context. These relationships can lead to new ideas, products or services. So, the inconvenience of mixing different drinks to form a cocktail led to the (obvious?) idea of selling them ready-mixed. James Dyson was able to see that a cyclone system for separating paint particles could be used (less obviously?) to develop a better vacuum cleaner. Doctors in the Great Ormond Street Hospital were able to see that the efficiency of Formula 1 pit stops could help them to improve patient care (see Case insight). Most creativity skills can be practised and enhanced, but this particular skill is probably the most difficult to encourage.

Majaro (1992) believes that, while stereotyping is to be avoided, creative types do exhibit some similar characteristics:

▷ *Conceptual fluency* – they are able to produce many ideas.
▷ *Mental flexibility* – they are adept at lateral thinking.
▷ *Originality* – they produce atypical responses to problems.
▷ *Suspension of judgement* – they do not analyze too quickly.
▷ *Impulsive* – they act impulsively to an idea, expressing their 'gut-feel'.
▷ *Anti-authority* – they are always willing to challenge authority.
▷ *Tolerance* – they have a high tolerance threshold towards the ideas of others.

Mintzberg (1976) makes the interesting observation that the very logical activity of planning is essentially a left-brain activity whilst the act of management (implementing the plan) is a right-brain activity that involves elements of emotional intelligence. He bases this claim on the observation that managers split their attention between a number of different tasks, preferring to talk briefly to people rather than to write, reading non-verbal as well as verbal aspects of the interaction and taking a holistic view of the situation. They also rely heavily on intuition. He argues that truly effective managers are those that can harness both sides of the brain.

Generating new ideas

In order to develop the discovery skills identified earlier there are three prerequisites. Staff need:

1 **Exposure to diverse influences, ideas and people.** Knowledge and awareness of diverse practices is a prerequisite to the practice of associating, discussed earlier. This is all part of the connectivity practised by the entrepreneurial CEOs in Dyer et al.'s study. We shall return to connectivity in the next section.

2 **Training and practice in techniques that encourage questioning and experimenting.** lthough it is innate to some, Dyer et al. believe that all of the discovery skills can be developed and strengthened through training and practice. We shall also return to techniques that can encourage creative thinking in individuals in a later section.

3 **Time to think and ponder.** Time is needed to incubate ideas. It is also needed in order to practise associating and experimenting. This is why organizations like Google and 3M build in 'slack' to staff workloads. However, creativity is also encouraged and facilitated within certain physical environments, a topic we shall also return to later in this chapter.

Ideas take time to crystallize. Incubation time happens when people are engaged in other activities and they can let their subconscious mind work on the problem. The best activities to undertake are those instinctive activities that do not require left-brain dominance. In fact the best 'activity' is sleep. Sleep happens when the left-brain gets tired or bored and during this time the right-brain has dominance. The old adage, 'sleep on the problem', has its origins in an understanding of how the brain works. It is little wonder that so many people have creative ideas when they are asleep – the problem is trying to remember them. Creativity therefore takes time and needs 'sleeping on'.

Time is also needed to make the connections – to build the associations – that are needed to be creative. Creativity can therefore help to make connections and the connections can become apparent during or after sleep. There is an element of serendipity here. But the longer the time and the more the potential connections the more likely the ideas are to germinate. Time is also needed to experiment and correct mistakes.

Ideas leading to discontinuous innovation are the most difficult to generate. Most people's mental models are just too tied up in the dominant logic of the organization that they do not notice the connections needed to come up with these ideas. Day and Schoemaker (2006) talk about the need to develop 'peripheral vision', which can be developed by:

▷ Scanning the edges of the business;
▷ Encouraging unfocused, wide-ranging searches of the environment;
▷ Exploring the future and alternative futures, identifying underlying drivers of change;
▷ Talking with all stakeholders in the business;
▷ Finding things out in different ways, taking different perspectives on the same problem;
▷ Experimenting with different approaches and learning from the results;
▷ Developing skills in reframing issues – a problem, the business, even an industry.

⌂ Case insight HFL Sport Science

Stimulating new ideas

As we saw in Chapter 5, HFL's scientific work depends critically on new ideas. To encourage this, HFL's CEO, David Hall, set up a number of structures designed to provide an environment for the free exchange of ideas, to push boundaries, and to harness the creative energies of staff.

Creativity Club David drove the Creativity Club personally, with volunteers from all areas of the company. It met monthly, in groups of 6–8 people, looking at creativity tools and focusing on techniques, not outcomes. He believed that fun and playfulness were important in encouraging creativity. He introduced the groups to creativity exercises such as finger painting for staff to paint what they thought of the organization, then asking them to explain what they had painted. The ideas or problems brought to the Club – both business and non-business – used a wide range of creativity techniques to take the ideas or problems forward, often questioning the definition of the problem so as not to jump to conclusions. Every idea generated by the Club was posted on the company's intranet and staff were invited to comment. The best ideas might be taken forward by project teams. The senior managers also used the Club as a forum to take forward strategic issues that required a 'different way of thinking'.

Innovation Club The Innovation Club focused more on issues of strategic importance and on implementation – corporate innovation. The Club met quarterly at lunch time and all staff were automatically members. David made the distinction that creativity is the generation of novel and useful ideas, whereas innovation is about making money out of creativity.

→

Book Club David established a book club that encouraged the reading of business books. These were discussed and relevant new ideas were then introduced into the organization.

Business Intelligence Group David also established the Business Intelligence Group to trawl the outside world for new ideas and to establish benchmarks for its activities. Everyone who saw or heard interesting things outside the company was debriefed and the ideas were passed on or project teams set up to take the idea further.

Ideas Centre To bring in outside ideas, HFL hosted an Ideas Centre comprising a group of like-minded organizations that have their own Creativity Clubs. It met for a half-day each month. The Centre hosted outside speakers who challenged conventions and tried out new creativity techniques. Members were connected to university-based resources to help them push forward initiatives. The objective was to energize change agents in these organizations.

Connectivity

Connectivity is a prerequisite to creativity. It generates new knowledge and information – reading newspapers, magazines, journals and books and surfing the web are passive forms of connectivity. But essentially it is a social process involving talking with people with different views of the world. Active connectivity involves meeting a diverse range of people. This might mean attending meetings, networks, seminars and conferences. It is likely to involve travel. It is not just about being aware of different approaches or perspectives on a problem, but also about getting the brain to accept that there are different ways of doing things – developing an open and enquiring mind. Many people almost have to give themselves permission to be creative – to think the unthinkable. As Johnson (2010) observes:

> '[Good ideas)] come from crowds, they come from networks. You know we have this clichéd idea of the lone genius having the eureka moment ... But in fact when you go back and you look at the history of innovation it turns out that so often there is this quiet collaborative process that goes on, either in people building on other people's ideas, but also in borrowing ideas, or tools or approaches to problems ... The ultimate idea comes from this remixing of various different components. There still are smart people and there still are people that have moments where they see the world differently in a flash. But for the most part it's a slower and more networked process than we give them credit for.'

He says the key to successful innovation is building upon the achievement of others; taking an object from one context and placing it in another.

The environments that stimulate innovation most are those that encourage this. Organizations need to be receptive to ideas from different contexts, open to different sorts of stimuli. The parallel in nature is the fact that the genomes of plants and animals have been shown to be made up of multiple copies of many genes, some identical but others mutated for quite different purposes.

Connectivity, therefore, extends beyond any industry or market context. Steve Jobs' interest in calligraphy is claimed to be the source for Apple's early development of a wide range of fonts on its computers. Burt (2004) showed that in many business contexts, good ideas do have social origins. He looked at a range of business sectors and measured the number of business ideas that staff came up with. He found that the staff coming up with these ideas spanned 'structural holes' – they looked outwards for their ideas: 'This is not creativity born of genius; it is creativity born out of the import–export business.' Similarly Lakhani (2006) found that it was 'outsiders – those with expertise at the periphery of a problem's field – who were most likely to find answers and do so quickly.' In other words ideas that are commonplace for one group can spark insight for another. It is all about being open to ideas from all and every source and not being inward-looking. Companies like LG and Hallmark have active programmes to encourage staff to be exposed to ideas from a wide, and sometimes unusual, range of sources. And this also adds a dimension to the reasons

📁 Case insight Great Ormond Street Hospital for Children

Connecting ideas

Ideas for innovations can come from unusual sources. The Great Ormond Street Hospital for Children took its inspiration from watching the McLaren and Ferrari Formula 1 racing teams take only six seconds to turn a car around at a pit stop. Doctors at the hospital were concerned by the time they took to move patients from the operating theatre to the intensive care unit where they recovered. Delays in emergency handover could cost lives, so they contacted Ferrari to see how the process might be improved. Ferrari explained that their pit-stop procedure was kept simple, with minimal movements all planned in advance. In fact it was so simple that it could be drawn on a single diagram. From that every member of the Ferrari team knew exactly what they had to do and when to do it in a coordinated fashion. Ferrari then videoed the hospital's handovers. When the doctors watched it they were shocked at the lack of structure. Ferrari concluded that, with an ever-changing team and unpredict- able demand, the hospital's handover teams needed a simple formula they could understand and work to – just like a pit stop. And Ferrari helped the hospital to design it.

why strategic alliances of different organizations are so useful in stimulating innovation. One organization exposes the other to different ways of doing things, different ideas, and from this there is the spark of creativity.

Networking is one form of connectivity and there is considerable evidence of the benefits of networking, in its broadest sense, as a way of stimulating innovation. Chesbrough (2003) calls this process 'open innovation' – sourcing ideas from outside the company, where links and connections become more important than ownership of the knowledge. Procter & Gamble use the phrase 'Connect and Develop' (C&D) and see collaborative networks as crucial in helping them keep in touch with the research that they do not undertake themselves. How you operate an innovation network depends heavily on the type of network and the purpose it is set up to achieve. Tidd et al. (2005) map some of these different networks onto a simple matrix, differentiating between how radical is the innovation outcome and how similar the participating organizations. This is shown in Figure 13.2.

	Similar organizations	Different organizations
Radical innovation	**Zone 2** ▷ Strategic alliances ▷ Sector consortia ▷ New technology development consortia	**Zone 4** ▷ Multi-company innovation networks in complex product systems ▷ New product or process
Incremental innovation	**Zone 1** ▷ Sector fora ▷ Supply chain learning programmes	**Zone 3** ▷ Regional clusters ▷ Best practice clubs ▷ Topic network

F 13.2 Innovation networks   *Source:* Adapted from Tidd et al., 2005.

Zone 1 has similar firms dealing with tactical innovation issues – 'good practice' fora.

Zone 2 has similar firms working together to create new products or processes by challenging existing boundaries, dealing with the issue of knowledge-sharing and risk-taking through the structures of strategic alliances/partnerships and formal joint ventures. We explored the value of these structures in Chapter 6. The danger with these structures is that similar organizations may not question the dominant logic of the sector and therefore would be unlikely to come up with disruptive innovations.

Zone 3 has different firms bringing key pieces of information, perhaps from a wide range of disciplines, to the network. The risks of disclosure can be high so the ground rules for disclosure need to be set well in advance and any intellectual property rights issues resolved.

Zone 4 involves diverse organizations but uses third-party gatekeepers, such as universities, as neutral knowledge-brokers because the stakes involved in unintended disclosure are even higher. The issue with radical and/or disruptive innovation is that networking too closely with existing customers and suppliers can lead you to become blind to external developments. The organization's dominant logic is not questioned. You need to build networks with new and different partners alongside the more traditional partners. These new networks may be different in nature and weaker.

Open innovation and crowdsourcing

Technology has come up with an answer to extending networks beyond organizational boundaries in the form of the internet and techniques called crowdsourcing and open innovation. Crowdsourcing brings a new meaning to connectivity. It is a way of opening up collaboration to people connected on the internet to form a kind of online community. The community or crowd can be self-selecting or can be formed from selected individuals such as customers. In this way the organization can tap a wider range of talent than might be present in its own organization. The crowd might be rewarded or not. There are no rules about crowdsourcing. However, in essence it is about focused problem-solving, often with cross-crowd communication, rather than just a virtual suggestion box. The crowd might be used simply to brainstorm ideas (see later section) or might have a part in sorting through them. Either way, the community comes up with solutions or new perspectives to problems and this can be done a lot quicker and more cheaply in a virtual network than in a real network. Crowdsourcing has been used by many organizations to leverage up creative inputs, giving it a valuable perspective from outside unfettered by any dominant logic (see Starbucks case) It can also have the added advantage of enhancing brand-building by building a community of interest through a feeling of being part of a community that is contributing to its development.

Selected crowdsourcing is the essence of an approach called 'open innovation' (sometimes called 'distributed innovation'). The best known example of this is Wikipedia, launched in 2001. Open innovation links external individuals and organizations with an organization that wishes to solve problems associated with an innovation. It can also help to generate new ideas. Despite the patent or copyright issues, open innovation has been used by a number of companies to develop software in collaboration with outside organizations and sometimes with the help of customers (see Linux and Lego® cases). It has been facilitated by developments in computer and internet technologies. The concept is based upon the paradigm that 'assumes that firms can and should use external ideas as well as internal ideas, and internal and external paths to market, as the firms look to advance their technology' (Chesbrough, op. cit.). This paradigm is part

💼 Case insights Starbucks

Crowdsourcing

When Howard Schultz retook control of Starbucks in 2008 he was keen to innovate. One of the ways he found new ideas was by crowdsourcing. By visiting the Starbucks ideas website anybody can post ideas about products, experience, service, location, community-building and social responsibility, but the site offers more than just a virtual suggestion box. There is a 'question of the day' which Starbuck uses to get market feedback on new ideas. Starbucks' Ideas Partners manage the site, responding to people with questions and ideas. The Partners change over time but are drawn from various teams involved in innovation such as the Research and Development team, developing food and beverages, and the Mobile and Emerging Platforms team, developing new ways of communicating with customers such as in-store digital signage or the development of mobile phone apps.

☐ Visit the Starbucks crowdsourcing website: http://mystarbucksidea.force.com

of an entrepreneurial architecture and is a logical extension to the virtual organization and the principles underlying strategic alliances (Chapter 6) and external corporate venturing (Chapter 11). Open innovation is at its most effective when innovation requires a diverse range of inputs and therefore is best organized by participants who are able to select their own area of contribution. What is more, since physical control is impossible, participants are best left with high levels of autonomy – similar to our entrepreneurial organization.

The most developed example of open innovation is open source software (OSS) communities. OSS was the basis for the successful development of

Six principles of open innovation

1 Smart people are everywhere – they don't just work for you.
2 To be successful you need to get ideas from everywhere, inside and outside the organization.
3 It's better to get the business model right than to get to market first.
4 External ideas help create value but internal R&D helps you own some of that value.
5 R&D should include knowledge brokerage as well as knowledge generation.
6 Don't be afraid of buying intellectual property when it advances your business model.

Source: Chesbrough (op. cit.)

the Linux operating system. In OSS all contributed software is available to all users both within and outside the community. Some of the largest holders of intellectual property such as Apple, IBM, Oracle and Sun have encouraged staff to participate and donated software and patents to OSS communities. OSS software has also been integrated into the product/service offerings.

Open or distributed innovation systems only operate within a receptive organizational architecture. As Lakhani and Panetta (2007) conclude: 'Traditional organizations should not, however, seize on distributed innovation systems as some silver bullet that will solve their internal innovation problems. Rather, these systems are an important addition to an organization's portfolio of innovation strategies. Those who would adopt or create a distributed innovation system, however, must be prepared to acknowledge the locus of innovation to be outside the boundaries of the focal organization. And this will require a fundamental reorientation of views about incentives, task structure, management, and intellectual property.'

🗁 Case insights Linux

Open innovation

Linus Torvald first suggested setting up a free operating system to compete with the DOS/Windows monopoly in 1991. It was out of the programming 'cooperative' set up to achieve this goal that Linux grew. It provided free source codes to all potential developers, thus encouraging incremental development. The link with various user groups encouraged concurrent development and debugging. The growth of the internet and later web forms of collaborative working, such as Web 2.0, facilitated the growth of Linux. It is now the best example of a successful Open Source Software (OSS) system. It has also spawned many commercial opportunities and is now seen on servers, desktops and packaged software. Linux has been the platform of choice in the film industry for many years and it has become one of the leading operating systems with over 90% of the top 500 supercomputers running some variant of it.

☐ Source: Lyons, D. 'Linux rules supercomputers'. *Forbes*, 2005. http://www.forbes.com/home/enterprisetech/2005/03/15/cz_dl_0315linux.html.

Creative environments

Encouraging the creative process is not just about the organizational architecture, it is also about the physical environment, which reinforces the creative ethos of the organization. Encouraging connectivity is vital and most organizations now realize that social spaces such as coffee bars, restaurants and so on can be more important than formal systems.

Essentially creativity is a social process. Perhaps the best-known example of this is the headquarters of Google – Googleplex – where connectivity and experimentation are designed into the campus. Because of the extensive social facilities from free restaurants to launderettes, staff are encouraged to spend time on the campus and interact with others. The 'playful' environment is designed to stimulate right-brain activity.

However, other organizations have taken a different approach, maintaining more traditional office designs for day-to-day work but establishing separate facilities where staff can go when they want to be more creative – where they are almost 'given permission' to think outside the box. For example, the UK Royal Mail Group has its own 'Creativity Laboratory'. This is made up of a number of open areas – facilitating groups forming, breaking out and coming together again – all with very informal seating arrangements. Standing and walking are encouraged. There is background music as well as toys and drinks and other distractions for the left brain. All the walls are 'white walls' which can be written on with felt-tip pens when

⌂ Case insight   Googleplex

Creative environments

As we saw in the previous chapter, many companies that work on building successful teams or encouraging creativity are known to facilitate playful environments. Google's headquarters in Mountain View, California – Googleplex – is probably the best known example of this. In the lobby you will find a piano, lava lamps, old server clusters and a projection of search queries on the wall. The corridors have exercise balls and bicycles. Other playful elements include a slide and a fireman's pole. Recreational facilities – from video games and ping-pong tables to workout rooms – are scattered throughout the campus. It also has functional elements that aid idea generation and dissemination. For example it has enclosed, noise-free projectors that can be left on at all times and employees can automatically email meeting notes to attendees. As we noted in the last chapter, one newspaper commented:

'To visit Google's headquarters in Mountain View, California, is to travel to another planet. The natives wander about in T-shirts and shorts, zipping past volleyball courts and organic-vegetable gardens while holding their open laptops at shoulder height, like waiters' trays. Those laptops are gifts from the company, as is free food, wi-fi-enabled commuter buses, healthcare, dry cleaning, gyms, massages and car washes, all designed to keep its employees happy and on campus.'

Ken Auletta, *Guardian*, 4 March 2010

☐ Pictures and videos of the campus can be seen on Google's website: www.google.com/corporate. For an alternative view go to: http://www.youtube.com/watch?v=43wZNGzXjFg

ideas are in free flow. Pens are everywhere. There are computer systems that allow ideas to be posted and voted on anonymously. And records are kept of the whole process – even the white walls are photographed – so agreed actions and outcomes can be followed up back in the work place.

National creativity

Just as creative environments can be developed in an organization, many people believe they can be developed at a national level. Creativity leading to innovation has become a driving force for economic growth and countries are increasingly interested in how it might be encouraged. They see economic growth coming from sectors where value can be added through the creation and application of knowledge. Florida (2002) argued that, rather than people moving to where investment and technology are concentrated, as much of the competitiveness literature assumes, firms increasingly follow the talented, creative people he calls 'the new creative class'. He claims that the ability to compete and prosper in the new global economy 'increasingly turns on the ability of nations to attract, retain and develop creative people.' And his insights at a national level have implications for organizations seeking to attract creative people. Florida (op. cit.) argues that this new 'creative class' is drawn to a particular sort of place; 'open, diverse communities where differences are welcome and cultural creativity is easily accessed.' He argues that it is *tolerance* that attracts the creative class and they have the *talent* to develop new *technologies*. New knowledge-based economies thrive in locations and countries that combine these three elements – technology, talent and tolerance – to provide economic growth in the way shown in Figure 13.3.

Florida's work is controversial. The implication of its conclusion is that, as part of the process of encouraging creativity, countries need to foster a culture of openness and tolerance. He claims to have found a strong relationship between openness to gays, Bohemians and immigrants and the ability of regions to innovate, generate high-technology industry and secure

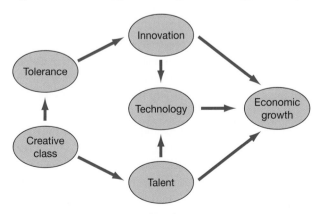

Source: Adapted from Florida and Tinagli (2004).

F 13.3 Technology, talent, tolerance and economic growth high value-added economic growth (Florida, op. cit.). It is not that these groups create the economic growth, rather that their existence is a proxy that indicates something about the culture of a community that encourages growth – one that is open to new people and new ideas. The work also has implications for city planners as they try to mirror the sort of environment these people like – with space for interaction like parks, cafes and small shops and with streets that are safe for these activities to take place.

If this sort of community attracts creative people there is also evidence that this community also helps generate some of those creative ideas – this connectivity develops a virtuous circle of creativity. Johnson (op. cit.) uses the coral reef as the analogy for the perfect creative environment, be it work place or city – one that encourages connectivity. The coral reef is a huge diverse eco-system where, despite competition for resources, existence is dependent on cooperation and everything is recycled on a matrix of calcium carbonate built up by the coral. A creative environment is one where ideas come in contact with each other and stimulation is continuous. To Johnson innovation is not something you do, say, once a year. It is something you do continuously but one that needs the right environment for it to take place. Johnson goes on to make the point that invention is time- and environment-dependent. It depends on the right circumstances that give it the possibilities. So the internet depends on computers, microwave ovens on electricity and people depend on their environment.

In a subsequent work Florida and Tinagli (2004) produced indices to measure these three variables – technology, talent and tolerance – for different European countries and looked at the trend over time. The tolerance variable in this study measured attitudes and values rather than concentrations of immigrants, gays, Bohemians and minority groups. The talent index combined data on the proportion of the workforce employed in the creative industries and its trend, with data on the percentage of the population aged 25–64 with a bachelor degree or above and the number of scientists and engineers per thousand workers. The technology index was based on R&D as a percentage of GDP, the number of patent applications per million population and the number of high-technology patents for certain key areas per million population. These indices were combined to produce a creativity index and a creativity trend index. The resulting ranking of countries, with the USA for comparison, is shown in Table 13.1.

Florida and Tinagli went on to classify countries under four headings, using a combination of their creativity index and creativity trend results. As can be seen in Figure 13.4, the *leaders* were the countries of Finland, Sweden, Denmark, the Netherlands and the USA. All have considerable technological capabilities, continue to invest in developing creative talent and have the values and attributes associated with attracting creative, talented people from anywhere in the world – although, compared to the USA, the European countries still have some way to go on this measure. Sweden outperformed the USA on the creativity index. Those countries

T 13.1 Comparison of creativity indices

Creativity index	Creativity trend
Sweden	Ireland
USA	Finland
Finland	Portugal
Netherlands	Denmark
Denmark	Spain
Germany	Greece
Belgium	Sweden
UK	Belgium
France	Austria
Austria	USA
Ireland	Netherlands
Spain	Germany
Italy	Italy
Greece	UK
Portugal	France

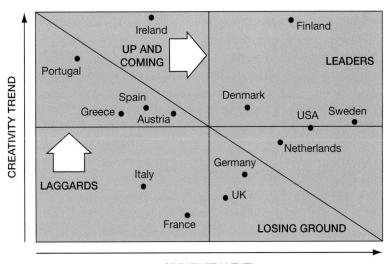

Source: Adapted from Florida and Tinagli, 2004.

F 13.4 The creativity matrix

losing ground, albeit from a high creativity base, were France, the UK and Germany. *Up and coming* was Ireland. *Laggards* were those countries combining a low creativity index with a worsening trend like Italy. However, Spain, Austria, Portugal and Greece appear to be in a difficult position and France borders on coming into this classification. A decade on, and in a worldwide recession, these results make interesting reading

An interesting observation on Florida's work is that, if true, the template for stimulating creativity by attracting creative people to 'open, diverse communities' should apply equally to organizations as well as whole nations. However, that does beg the question of the conflict between the cultures in the different communities that individuals inhabit. Florida's work underlines the fact that creativity and innovation are at their heart social processes. People need to spark off other people. At a physical level, we have already noted how certain environments can stimulate creativity and how some organizations have set up Creativity Laboratories. But, equally, at a more general level this realization has implications for the design of the workplace. Being shut away in an office all day does not stimulate creativity. People need to interact in social spaces – at coffee, at water coolers, at the photocopier – and these social spaces can be just as important as the space they inhabit to undertake specific tasks. As Gladwell (2000) puts it: 'Innovation is fundamentally social. Ideas arise as much out of casual conversations as they do out of formal meetings … Innovation comes from the interactions of people at a comfortable distance from each other.'

Knowledge and learning

If connectivity is important in generating information, how that information is disseminated and used within the organization is vital. To be useful information needs to be turned into knowledge. This only happens through learning (see the wheel of learning, Figure 3.1). Rowley (2000) used the simple model shown in Figure 13.5 to demonstrate the process. Information comes into the organization from a range of sources. It is conceptualized through the wheel of learning in a way that is consistent with the organization's norms, cognitive frameworks, context and culture. This is learning, which in turn leads either to tacit knowledge (embedded in minds and activities) or explicit knowledge (stated in verbal communications or documents). This knowledge informs decisions, actions and behaviours and feeds back into the processes creating this knowledge. The many feedback loops represent the continuous process implicit in the wheel of learning. This brings us back to that aspect of the entrepreneurial architecture that mirrors a learning organization discussed in Chapter 3 – the emphasis on organizational learning; the ability of the organization to understand the

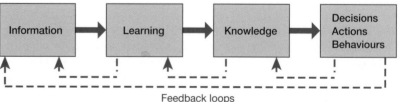

F 13.5 Creating organizational knowledge

Source: Adapted from Rowley, 2000.

causes of a problem and question 'why'; its emphasis on tacit knowledge. Knowledge-creating companies constantly encourage the process whereby personal knowledge is made available to others to use to extend their own tacit knowledge base. A learning organization should therefore facilitate this whole process and the cross-fertilization of tacit and organizational knowledge. So, for example, both HFL Sport Science and Google have processes to encourage this.

Rowley (op. cit.) argues for greater integration of the learning processes emphasized in the learning organization literature with the systems focus of the knowledge management literature. He coins the phrase 'knowledge entrepreneur' for organizations that can do this. These organizations build bridges between people (tacit knowledge) and systems which transmit organizational knowledge. This is vital in large organizations or multinationals where systems are the only practical way to transmit some information and create knowledge. It is also vital in tackling the challenge of organizational sustainability.

⌂ Cases with questions LG and Hallmark

Encouraging creativity and innovation

LG

The Korean electronics firm LG aims to integrate technological developments with design. Design is a key part of LG's culture. The company's design philosophy for mobile phones is to 'appeal to customers' emotions' a concept originally called 'haptic', meaning the feeling of touch but broadened to include all five senses – 'touch, smell, the glowing lights, all the emotional things'. LG's products must be technologically advanced and functionally effective, but then most electronic products are. The reasons why people buy one product rather than another are to do with the intangible elements – and design and brand image have a crucial part to play in this. And whilst the functional elements of any product are usually easy to copy, these less tangible elements are more difficult. LG believes that good design enhances its brand image and this allows it to position its products at the premium end of the market.

Designers are encouraged to do 'town-watching' – visiting the chic streets of Hongdae or Cheongdam-dong to spot new design trends. It was on one of these trips that the trend towards more natural shapes was identified. Eventually, this was incorporated into the KG800 mobile phone – the 'Chocolate Phone' – which won a Red Dot award. The phone has nothing to do with chocolate, LG just thought that the name was memorable. This was the first mobile phone in the world to have a touch sensitive key pad. Seventeen months after its launch it had sold 10 million units and spawned a limited edition 'White Chocolate' phone with a lavender-scented keypad which was sold on Valentine's Day 2006. The phone model for 2007 was the sophisticated Prada phone.

☐ More information on LG can be found on their website: www.lge.com ➔

Hallmark

The well-known US greeting cards company Hallmark was founded in 1910 when Joyce Clyde Hall started selling from two shoeboxes of postcards in Kansas City. Hallmark now design about 19,000 new greeting cards every year. Each card costs about £40,000 to produce and is expected to generate some £85,000 in sales. Hallmark takes creativity and innovation seriously. Their philosophy, work environment and development programmes are designed to encourage creative thinking. Their global headquarters is still in Kansas and their 800 in-house creative staff are based there. They have access to the world's biggest creative library with some 20,000 volumes and 175 current periodicals. They also have a programme of visiting speakers, including writers, photographers and artists. Their staff development programme is diverse, with courses on working with Hallmark's colour management process but also classes on sculpting and even doll-making. They have a 'creative renewal program' for staff who feel they are losing their edge which is based at their own 'creativity retreat', Kearney Farm, an old farmhouse set in a 172-acre estate. It boasts its own art studio and regular creative brainstorming sessions are held there. Hallmark also organizes research visits to overseas countries so that staff keep in touch with 'emotions' in different countries. However there is a hard edge and slogans on some office walls remind staff how much a card that does not sell will cost.

The company takes trend-spotting seriously and employs staff to constantly scan the environment to monitor new developments. Innovations include e-cards that can be sent via Hallmark's own website. You can even create your own card. The site also has a hugely popular 'Say-it-with-music' line where you can send a CD-quality sound card with a choice of more than 100 music artists as well as dialogue and themes from popular movies and TV shows. With over 250 'designs', they feature the original artists and songs and link to the captions and sentiment of the card. The cards even appear on websites such as YouTube, with people lip-synching along to the cards' 45-second music clips.

☐   More information on Hallmark can be found on their website: www.hallmark.com

QUESTIONS

1 Why is innovation important to each of these companies?

2 How does each company encourage the generation of new ideas?

3 How do they link creativity and innovation with market opportunities?

Techniques for generating new ideas

There are many techniques to help generate new ideas. We covered three in Chapter 9 when we looked at how to develop strategic options – SLEPT analysis, scenario planning and futures thinking. Generating ideas is a numbers game – the more ideas you come up with the more likely you are to find one that is viable. So it is worth distinguishing between those techniques designed to generate volume and those designed to improve quality. As you might expect, people with different thinking styles will respond differently to each of them. Here are just a few of the more widely used idea generation techniques.

Brainstorming

This is one of the most widely used techniques, designed to generate volume. It is practised in a group. In the session you do not question or criticize ideas. You suspend disbelief. The aim is to encourage the free flow of ideas – divergent thinking – and as many ideas as possible. Everyone has thousands of good ideas within them just waiting to come out. But people inherently fear making mistakes or looking foolish in front of others. Here making 'mistakes' and putting forward ideas which don't work is not only acceptable, it is encouraged.

You might start with a problem to be solved or an opportunity to be exploited. You encourage and write ideas down as they come by facilitating all the dimensions of creative thinking in Figure 13.1. There are no 'bad' ideas. All ideas are, at the very least, springboards for other ideas. You allow the right side of the brain full rein and only engage the left brain to analyze the ideas you come up with at a later date. Brainstorming is often best undertaken with a multidisciplinary team so that the issue can be approached from many different perspectives, encouraging the cross-fertilization of ideas.

How to run a brainstorming session

1 Describe the outcome you are trying to achieve – the problem or opportunity – BUT NOT THE SOLUTION. This could be a broad area of investigation – new ideas and new markets can be discovered if you don't follow conventional paths.

2 Decide how you will run the session and who will take part. You need an impartial facilitator who will introduce things, keep to the rules and watch the time. This person will restate the creative process if it slows down. The group can be anything from 4 to 30. The larger the number the more diverse the inputs but the slower (and more frustrating) the process – so something around 12 is probably ideal.

3 Set out the room in a participative (i.e. circular) and informal style. Comfortable chairs are important. Refreshments should be available continuously. Make certain there are flip charts, coloured pens and so on or, if you want to be high tech, you can use some of the specialist software that is available (e.g. Brainstorming Toolbox). Each person should also have a note pad so they can write down ideas.

4 Relax participants as much as possible. The style is informal. The rules of engagement should be posted clearly for all to see and run through so that everybody understands:

  ▷ Quantity counts, not quality – postpone judgement on all ideas;
  ▷ Encourage wild, exaggerated ideas – all ideas are of equal value;
  ▷ Build on ideas rather than demolish them.

→

5 Open the session by asking for as many ideas as possible. Get people to shout out. Write every one down on the flip chart and post the sheets on the wall. Encourage and engage with people. Close down criticism. Try to create group engagement.

6 When the ideas have dried up – it might take a little time for it finally to do so – close the session, thanking participants and keeping the door open for them should they have any ideas later.

7 Analyze the ideas posted. Brainstorming helps to generate ideas, not analyze them. What happens from here is up to you. Sometimes the people who generated the ideas can also help to sort them, but remember to separate out the sessions clearly. Perhaps excellent ideas can be implemented immediately, but do not forget to investigate the interesting ones – no matter how 'off-the-wall'.

☐ For more information on the technique visit www.brainstorming.co.uk.

Negative brainstorming – thinking about the negative aspects of a problem or situation – can often be used initially to unblock more creative and positive brainstorming. It is particularly useful in getting people to think about what might happen if they do not think more creatively and can be used to help change motivations and behaviour.

A variant on this is called *brainwriting*, whereby ideas are written down anonymously and then communicated to the group (computer technologies can help with this), thus avoiding the influence of dominant individuals. Brainstorming can obviously be used in conjunction with *scenario planning* and *futures thinking* (Chapter 9).

Why? Why? exercise

Chapter 12 encouraged the challenging of market conventions by asking the questions 'why?', 'why not?' and 'what if?' The Why? Why? exercise is a technique for doing this systematically using a diagram. Figure 13.6 is an example of how the reasons for a fall in sales might be explored using the diagram. Although all trails have not been followed to their conclusion, the root cause will lie at the end of one (or more) of the 'why?' trails. Outcomes from asking Why? might be eliminated if they do not reflect reality. Remaining options continue to be explored in this way until there are a number of final possibilities. At this point we might start asking the questions 'why not?' or 'what if?' So, for example, if one of the reasons for the fall in sales is unreliable deliveries due to transport problems you might ask the question 'why not close the transport department?' and 'what if we subcontract deliveries?' Of course, other questions can also be asked.

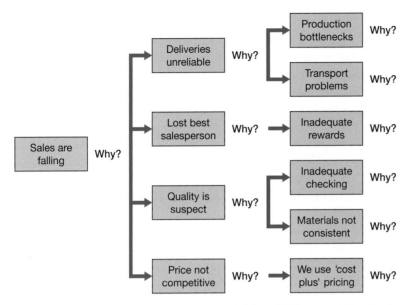

Source: Adapted from Vyakarnham, S. and Leppard, J. (1999) *A Marketing Action Plan for the Growing Business*, 2nd edn., London: Kogan Page.

F 13.6 Why? Why? diagram

Analogy

This is a product-centred technique that attempts to join together apparently unconnected or unrelated combinations of features of a product or service and benefits to the customer to come up with innovative solutions to problems. It is therefore designed to provide more focused ideas. Analogies are proposed once the initial problem is stated. The analogies are then related to opportunities in the market place. Operated in a similar way to brainstorming, it is probably best explained with an example. Georges de Mestral noticed that burdock seed heads stuck to his clothing. On closer examination he discovered the seed heads contained tiny hooks. His analogy was to apply this principle to the problem of sticking and unsticking things and to develop what we recognize today as Velcro.

In this way, the first steps to building an analogy are to ask some basic questions:

▷ What does the situation or problem remind you of?
▷ What other areas of life or work experience similar situations?
▷ Who does these similar things and can the principles be adapted?

Often the analogy contains the words '... *is like* ...', so you might ask why something 'is like' another? For example, why is advertising like cooking? The answer is because there is so much preamble to eating. Anticipation from presentation and smell, even the ambience of the restaurant you eat it in, are just as important as the taste and nutritional value of the food itself.

Attribute analysis

This is another more focused product-centred technique designed to evolve product improvements and line extensions – used as the product reaches the mature phase of its life cycle. It employs the basic marketing technique of looking at the features of a product or service which perform a series of functions but, most importantly, deliver benefits to the customers. An existing product or service is stripped down to its component parts and the group explores how these features might be altered but then focuses on whether those changes might bring valuable benefits to the customer. The 'Why? Why?' technique can be used to question why the existing product or service is designed in a particular way. Nothing must be taken for granted.

So, for example, you might focus on a domestic lock. This secures a door from being opened by an unwelcome intruder. The benefit is security and reduction/elimination of theft from the house. But you can lose keys or forget to lock doors and some locks are difficult or inconvenient to open from the inside. A potential solution is to have doors that sense people approaching from the outside and lock themselves. You could have a reverse sensor on the inside – a device that unlocks the door when someone approaches (which could be activated or deactivated centrally). The exterior sensor could recognize 'friendly' people approaching the door because of sensors they carry in the form of 'credit cards' or it could be over-ridden by a combination lock. This technology already exists for cars.

The 'Why? Why?' technique can also be used to question why an existing product or service is designed in a particular way. For example the technique could have been used to question why the domestic lock was designed in a particular way, taking nothing for granted. In this way the technique should uncover the prime attributes that users are seeking. An alternative solution to the problem can then be constructed.

Gap analysis

This is a market-based approach that attempts to produce a 'map' of product/market attributes based on dimensions that are perceived as important to customers, analyzing where competing products might lie and then spotting gaps where there is little or no competition. Because of the complexity involved, the attributes are normally shown in only two dimensions. There are a number of approaches to this task:

Perceptual mapping maps the attributes of a product within specific categories. So, for example, the dessert market might be characterized as hot vs cold and sophisticated vs unsophisticated. Various desserts would then be mapped onto these two dimensions. This could be shown graphically (see opposite). The issue is whether the 'gap' identified is one that customers would value being filled – and means understanding whether they value the dimensions being measured. That is a question for market research to attempt to answer.

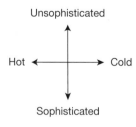

Non-metric mapping maps products in groups that customers find similar and then tries to explain why these groupings exist. A classic example would be in the soft drinks market where products might be clustered and then described simply in terms of still vs carbonated and flavoured vs non-flavoured. The key here is also finding the appropriate dimensions that create opportunities for differentiating the product and creating competitive advantage. The mapping of soft drinks on the two dimensions above is unlikely to reveal any gaps in the market.

Repertory grid is a more systematic extension of this technique. Customers are asked to group similar and dissimilar products within a market, normally again in pairs. They are then asked to explain the similarities and dissimilarities. The sequence is repeated for all groups of similar and dissimilar products. The explanations are then used to derive 'constructs' which describe the way in which people relate and evaluate the products. These constructs form a grid that can be used to map the products, quoting the words used by the customers themselves.

Personal Construct Theory and the Repertory Grid

George Kelly was an American engineer who became a highly respected clinical psychologist, best known for the development in 1955 of his own theory of personality, known as Personal Construct Theory, and a tool to explore people's personalities in terms of the theory, called the Repertory Grid. Kelly believed that the personality theories of the day suffered from three things: an inherent observer bias, a lack of precision and prediction and an over-reliance on the expert.

Kelly believed that we all have our own 'constructs' – views of the world or biases – that help us navigate our way around the world quickly. Certain words will trigger certain preconceptions, be they logical or otherwise. When you walk through a door you do so without consciously thinking what you are doing but you are preconditioned to act in a way that has opened a similar door before. The fact that it is locked can often come as quite a sharp surprise. Construct systems influence our expectations and perceptions subconsciously – and introduce bias. This means that one person's constructs are not those of another – and sometimes they can even be internally inconsistent because we never question them.

The Repertory Grid attempts to get rid of this bias. The technique identifies a small set of *elements* (objects, entities) and the user is asked to define some *constructs* (attributes, slots) which characterize those elements. All these terms are identified in terms of the user's own language. So, for example, 'good' can only exist in contrast to the concept of 'bad'. Any construct can reasonably be measured by answering the question 'compared to what?'. Construct values are given for each element on a limited scale between extreme polar points. The process of taking three elements and asking for two of them to be paired in contrast with the third is the most effective way in which the poles of the construct can be discovered and articulated.

It is beyond this book to explain, in detail, how this technique should be deployed. However, one of the most accessible and short books on the topic is by Devi Jankowicz (2003), *The Easy Guide to Repertory Grids*. It really lives up to its title.

Delphi method

This method is useful when expert opinion is needed on aspects of developments in the future. It is often used to try to identify new technologies that might trigger discontinuities or disruption. First, relevant experts need to be identified. These might include experts in non-technological fields so that the economic, social and environmental impact of the changes are not overlooked. The experts are then asked to complete a carefully constructed questionnaire survey of their opinion on what the key future issues might be and their likelihood of occurrence. Having been analyzed, the questionnaire is then refined into a second more focused version and the experts resurveyed. The process is repeated until there is some convergence of opinion that yields a Delphi forecast of the probability and time scale of certain events. The process can be costly and time-consuming and depends upon the quality and appropriateness of experts and the questionnaires used.

Blocks to creativity

People are inherently creative, but most of us stifle it because we find change threatening. We all create rituals and routines that we feel comfortable with and these normally mitigate against questioning the status quo. These routines help us through the day. Being creative often takes people outside their 'comfort-zone'. They are uneasy with it. In that sense, encouraging creativity within an organization has many similarities with managing change (Chapter 7). The same skills and approaches are needed. But first blocks and barriers need to be attacked. Some blocks originate with individuals but others can be institutional. Roger von Oech (1998) focuses on the individual blocks and argues that there are ten which are critical to creativity:

1 The fallacy that there is only one correct solution to a problem.
2 The fallacy that logic is important in creativity.
3 The tendency to be practical.
4 The tendency to follow established rules unquestioningly.
5 The tendency to avoid ambiguity in viewing a situation.
6 The tendency to assign blame for failure.
7 The unwillingness to recognize the creative power of play.
8 The tendency to think too narrowly and with too much focus.
9 The unwillingness to think unconventionally because of the fear of appearing foolish.
10 The lack of belief that you can be creative.

Realizing these blocks may exist in yourself can be the first step to dismantling them. It is never easy to change an inherent tendency, but it can be done and the techniques in the next section can help. However, just as individuals have blocks to their creativity, so organizations can block creativity. Sloane (2003), Majaro (op. cit.) and Klein (1990) identified a number of organizational blocks to creativity, many of which will be familiar from previous chapters:

▷ *Lack of organizational slack*. As we have seen, creativity takes time. A lean and fit organization that is constantly going from crisis to crisis is unlikely to have this.

▷ *Too much bureaucracy*. Where systems and procedures are designed to ensure a high degree of control, particularly for the purpose of efficiency or productivity, creativity is unlikely to flourish.

▷ *Tight financial control*. Just like bureaucracy, overly tight financial control is likely to stifle creativity because it stresses efficiency and effectiveness.

▷ *Poor communication*. Ideas need to be discussed, worked out and made visible.

▷ *Not invented here*. Organizations that resist external influences are unlikely to be creative ones, indeed they are likely to resist change of any sort.

▷ *Too much criticism and punishment of mistakes*. Blame cultures inhibit creativity and discourage anybody from even attempting to do something differently. The only people who will never make mistakes are those who do not take the initiative or try out creative ideas. The important thing is to learn from mistakes and never repeat them.

▷ *Over-tight planning*. Like tight financial control, this can stifle initiative and opportunity-seeking. Entrepreneurial organizations need to plan.

▷ *Promoting too many like-minded people from within*. To be creative an organization needs to take on board ideas from outside and one way to do this is to recruit outsiders.

▷ *Hoarding of problems*. People in blame cultures tend to hoard problems because they know that if they share them they will be criticized. Ideally problems need to be shared and decision-making and problem-solving pushed down to the lowest level.

▷ *Insufficient training*. Training can be used as a strategic tool to encourage creativity and innovation.

▷ *Banning of brainstorming*. We saw just how useful these sessions can be. Using tools like these regularly institutionalizes the process of creativity.

Encouraging creativity and innovation

Firms with a good track record for innovation practise it systematically. It does not happen by chance. They look for both incremental and disruptive innovation. Drucker (op. cit.) advocates a five-stage approach to the purposeful, systematic search for innovation:

1 **Start with the analysis of opportunities, inside the firm and its industry and in the external environment.** Information and knowledge are invaluable – from as many sources as possible. Do not innovate for the future, innovate for now. Timing is everything. The right idea at the wrong time is worth nothing.

2 **Innovation is both conceptual and perceptual.** Therefore look at the financial implications but also talk to people, particularly customers, and analyze how to meet the opportunity. Use creativity tools such as scenario planning and futures thinking (see Chapter 9). Information and knowledge – connectivity – help to generate ideas as well as minimizing risk in an otherwise risky endeavour and continual strategizing is the key to success.

3 **To be effective, an innovation must be simple and has to be 'focused'.** Keep it as simple as possible. Don't try to be too clever. Don't try to do too many things at once. The slightly-wrong-but-can-be-improved idea can always be improved and still earn a fortune.

4 **To be effective, start small.** Don't be grandiose. Take an incremental approach. Minimize the commitment of resources for as long as possible using trial launches, thus maximizing information and knowledge and minimizing risk. Think 'skunk-works'. Clearly, for certain types of innovation this can be problematic.

5 **In the longer term, aim at market leadership and dominate the competition in the particular area of innovation as soon as possible.** Opportunities for this come from disruptive innovation. Remember the marketing strategies for products at the start of their life cycle. As we have seen, niche domination is the key to financial success as the product moves through its life cycle, but the investment necessary can drain cash flow.

Creativity and innovation need to be encouraged within any organization. That means valuing and rewarding them. They are most likely to flourish with a trusting management that does not over-control and has open internal and external channels of communication. Encouraging creativity and innovation means tolerating the unconventional and encouraging people to challenge the conventional way things are done. It means encouraging curiosity and seeing problems as challenges. It means providing support for creativity – opportunities to connect inside and outside the organization, training, resources and time. It means expecting and tolerating mistakes. It means developing an organizational culture where dreaming is encouraged and being creative is fun. But unfettered creativity can be dangerous. This sort of exciting place to work may all too easily turn out to be anarchic. It may be unprofitable and even fail if the creativity is not anchored in the quest for entrepreneurial opportunity and commercial reality. And that involves not only a disciplined approach to creativity but also a disciplined approach to exploiting the opportunities it generates. The ultimate issue is the degree of freedom or autonomy given to individuals (Sinetar, 1985). Creative people need autonomy in the way they work, and slack in the resources they control – and this applies at whatever level they operate.

One important message for the management of an entrepreneurial organization is that it needs to recognize that different people have different thinking styles that need to be respected and encouraged. Indeed if these different styles are encouraged so that they generate different ideas, assumptions, approaches, frames of references and even solutions to problems, they will inevitably lead to conflict that has to be managed and resolved (see Chapter 4). What needs to be encouraged, ultimately, is for a whole-brain solution to a problem (or opportunity) to be formulated eventually, perhaps using left and right sides more dominantly at different stages in the process.

Within this process there will, inevitably, be periods of divergence – breaking from the familiar ways of doing things – and convergence when there is some agreement about pursuing a certain course of action (Leonard and Swap, 1999). Without convergence there is anarchy, but equally, without divergence there are few new ideas. Both need to be carefully balanced, but the process inevitably, again, leads to conflict. Friction and conflict are inevitable by-products of a creative environment that needs to be channelled in a constructive rather than a destructive way. Different approaches and ideas need to be aired but teams need to be able to air their differences in such a way that they can continue to work together.

Hischberg (1998) talks about developing 'creative abrasion' that facilitates divergence of thinking, supplemented by a leadership style and organizational structures that then seek closure and convergence. This calls for the development of leadership styles 'that focus on first identifying and then incorporating polarized viewpoints. In doing so, the probabilities for unexpected juxtapositions are sharply increased, as are the levels of mutual understanding. The irony is that out of a process keyed on abrasiveness, a corporate culture of heightened sensitivity and harmony is achieved.' This is clearly a delicate task that takes time and patience. It is not about fostering clashes that are personal or built on ego, but rather realizing that there is diversity of viewpoints, ideas and approaches and making the airing of these something that is routine and cannot be avoided.

Creativity is the ability to develop new ideas, concepts and processes. In the business context it is the ability to develop creative, imaginative and original solutions to problems or opportunities that customers face and results in a wide range of product and marketing innovations. Encouraging creativity and innovation in an organization involves utilizing all the tools we have to encourage entrepreneurship: leadership, structure, culture and strategy. It is about developing an entrepreneurial architecture and is at the heart of corporate entrepreneurship.

🗄 Case with questions **LEGO®**

Driving corporate transformation

LEGO – the well-known children's building system – has been around for a long time and, in an age when new toys come and go with astonishing rapidity and technology-based toys like computer games are reaching astonishing heights of sophistication, it might be difficult to understand the enduring market appeal of these basic building blocks. Approximately 20 billion LEGO bricks and other components are made every year: if all the Lego bricks ever produced were divided among the world population each person would have 62 bricks. The name 'LEGO' is an abbreviation of two Danish words 'leg godt', meaning 'play well'. The company was founded by Ole Kirk Christiansen in 1932. It is now one of the world's largest manufacturers of toys, with its head office in Billund, Denmark, branches throughout the world and some 5000 employees. Its products are sold in more than 130 countries. The traditional interlocking LEGO brick has twice been named toy of the century by *Fortune* magazine, then by the British Association of Toy Retailers, although it was only launched in its present form in 1958.

The product range is now far wider than the basic brick with 'classic' products like LEGO DUPLO, LEGO CITY, LEGO TECHNIC being constantly upgraded and augmented with concepts like LEGO MINDSTORMS (robot building sets). There are theme-based products like LEGO Harry Potter, Spiderman 2, Bob the Builder and Star Wars, introduced under licence, and there are brand new products like CLIKITS and BIONICLES. BIONICLES allows children to construct action figures like knights and to develop a detailed online world into which they can be placed to play through a story. LEGO has also moved into different market segments. LEGO BELVILLE is aimed at young girls, allowing them to construct scenes from everyday life and, more recently, moving into the world of fairy tale with princesses, fairies and butterflies. These developments have evolved through four 'eras': the first was developing construction and building as the central elements in play; in the second the LEGO products gained motion through wheels, small motors and gears; role play formed the third era, when LEGO figures were born; and the fourth era introduced intelligence and behaviour. Alongside this, LEGO has developed numerous 'play themes' for all their products such as fire stations, police, airport, knights, castles and racing cars. There are also four LEGOLAND theme parks around the world in Denmark, England, Germany and California, and a LEGOLAND Discovery Centre opened in Berlin in 2007.

But the journey has been far from smooth and in 2003 the company reported a record loss of $240 million, spawning rumors that it might be taken over. Kjeld Kirk Christiansen, grandson of the founder, CEO and owner of LEGO, decided to stand down, appointing Jorgen Vig Knudstrop in his place. The family injected additional funding of $178 million, which gave the company space for a remarkable turnaround. The turnaround involved a number of parallel initiatives. The most important was the need to cut the company's cost base. Competition from lower-priced, similar products was starting to eat into sales. Based in the high-cost country of Denmark, LEGO's supply chains were long and expensive, geared to supplying small retailers rather than the big-box stores. To address this, the company had to eliminate inefficiencies and re-gear to compete in the big-box retail world.

So how did Jorgen Vig Knudstrop go about turning around LEGO when he took over in 2004? Knudstrop, a one-time management consultant who had joined the company as director of strategic development in 2001, was given a clear mandate for radical change by the Kristiansen family. Although Kjeld Kirk

Christiansen stood down as CEO, he worked closely with Knudstrop and other members of the board and the leadership team to pinpoint the company's problems.

Of immediate urgency was the need to improve efficiency and focus on the changes needed in the supply line to be competitive. The team decided to approach this issue holistically, analyzing the entire process from product development, sourcing, manufacturing and finally distribution. Whilst the team believed the company was good at innovating, it quickly discovered that each successive generation of innovation in established product lines seemed to deliver slimmer margins as product complexity increased. Designers were simply not factoring in the price of materials or costs of manufacture when they developed new products. For example, a pirate kit included eight pirates with 10 different legs, developed without a thought of the cost of manufacture or stock holding. The management team's first action was to reduce the number of unique pieces manufactured from over 12,000 to some 6,000 and to establish new manufacturing bases in the lower-cost countries of Hungary and Mexico. Individual products were cut as a review revealed that just 30% of products generated 80% of sales. Indeed two-thirds of the company's stock turned out to be items that were no longer manufactured. With more than 11,000 suppliers, growing all the time as designers sought new materials to develop new products, there was plenty of scope to rationalize sourcing and leverage the buying power of the company. With over 800 machines, the Danish factory was one of the largest injection-moulding operations in the world. And yet it operated a fragmented, batch-production system, responding to frequent changes in production demands, giving yield capacity utilization of only 70%. Although the 200 largest toy chains generated over two-thirds of sales, LEGO devoted as much effort to supplying the thousands of smaller shops that generated the balance, often supplying them with small orders at short notice.

Knudstrop adopted a twin-track approach to driving the transformation, each involving different multidisciplinary teams. A leadership team developed the strategies and a management team, consisting of managers from sales, IT, logistics and manufacturing, drove the changes at an operational level. The management team met daily in a 'war room' to prioritize and coordinate the changes, assigning responsibility for specific initiatives to individual managers. They tracked progress, anticipating resistance and dealing with obstacles as they arose. The room itself had white boards and often these were covered in action lists and schedules. Knudstrop himself would visit the war room regularly, checking on the status of various initiatives, always pushing to get the changes through as quickly as possible. The teams worked in a very open way, debating how to change in the first place but, once agreed, only deviating from it should the approach prove ineffective.

The leadership team also operated in an open way, taking time for consensus-building, between themselves and the management team. The work force was also involved and the need for the changes – including redundancies – made clear. The policy was one of transparency, including debate around the realities of the situation. The work force was involved in how redundancies would be implemented. The belief was that, although this process took time, the changes would be more effectively implemented and the benefits more lasting if they were understood and, as far as possible, staff 'bought into them'.

The team piloting changes to sourcing was headed by LEGO's Chief Financial Officer, Jesper Ovesen, with the intention of signalling the importance of this initiative. The first task it tackled was the cost of the different coloured resins that went into the production of the bricks – the largest material cost the company faced. The team included the head of product innovation and the manager of the company's supply chain. The team cut the

→

number of colours used in bricks by almost half, cut back on slow-moving lines and slashed the number of different suppliers by 80%. By leveraging LEGO's buying power, resin costs were cut by a massive 50%. The speedy success of this initiative and its effect on the finances of the company led to an early sense of optimism – a 'quick win' for the change initiative that increased confidence that they would succeed.

One management team took on the task of encouraging designers to consider costs in their new product decisions. They developed a cost matrix that allowed them to see the costs associated with making changes to established bricks. In this way designers were encouraged to think about designing to price points, using existing bricks as far as possible and generally reducing complexity.

Cutting the number of resins and bricks made the task of simplifying the production cycles easier. Specific moulds were assigned to specific machines and set production cycles established based upon monthly sales schedules. The leadership team assigned decision rights and protocols for changing production schedules so that account-ability for changes was clear. Manufacturing of some of LEGO's simpler products was outsourced. At the same time manufactur-ing was also moved to lower-cost countries. However, by selecting countries close to its main markets rather than in Asia, it cut its delivery lead times, resulting in a further net saving. Logistics was also rationalized, with providers reduced from 26 to 4, reducing costs by a further 10%.

Finally the marketing team started work-ing more closely with the large retailers LEGO had previously ignored to improve sales forecasts and stock management at the same time as offering customized, big-box products for which the company would provide marketing support. Working closely with these larger chains yielded the added advantage of providing LEGO with greater in-sight into buyer behaviour and market trends at the same time as helping with product development.

These efficiency gains were forecast to yield savings of over $200 million and since 2005 LEGO has returned to profitability. Getting the core business right – product development, sourcing, manufacturing and distribution – allowed them to focus once more on creativity and innovation (see LEGO Case with questions on focused open innovation).

☐ Visit the company website on www.lego.com.

QUESTIONS

1 How important was it for LEGO to think holistically about innovation in the supply chain?

2 How did LEGO go about transforming itself?

3 How important was the commitment of top management? How did this show itself?

🛆 Case with questions LEGO®

Focused open innovation

One of the reasons for LEGO's continuing popularity is that it has changed with the market. The company continues to invest large sums around the world to understand changes in children's tastes and to explore new product developments based around its mission 'to inspire children to explore and challenge their own creative potential'. As we saw in the previous LEGO® case, the com-pany's turnaround in the mid-2000s involved a number of parallel initiatives. And whilst the most important was the need to cut the company's cost base, perhaps the most interesting change was the company's more focused approach to innovation – despite the fact that it was thought to be an inherent strength. LEGO has, over the decades, proved to be good at innovation – it was deep in the corporate culture – including extending the boundaries of the LEGO product. LEGO's experience in theme parks, video games, retail stores and clothing had taught it the potential value of different types of innovation.

Concept and product development take place primarily in the Concept Lab at the company's headquarters in Billund, Denmark. This creative core is made up of 120 designers representing about 15 nationalities, most having trained at art school. But the company also sets great store on learning from the creativity of its customers – children – in how LEGO can be used to play games. It has what it calls 'listening posts' in Munich, Barcelona, Los Angeles and Tokyo. These are Creativity Labs at which children from four very different countries are encouraged to try out different combinations with the same LEGO pieces and create worlds of their own, which the company can incorporate into its 'play themes' – often later developed on their website. The Lab tries to spot trends in children's play, understand the motivations behind them and translate them into what it means for the company and new product development – effectively trying to systematically understand children's' creativity by observing them at play. It also draws on inputs from customer communities, supported by Community, Education and Direction (CED). The Lab also takes an active role in the product concept and early development phase of any new product.

However by 2004, customers and retailers felt it had wandered too far away from its original concept of a 'creative building experience' and some of these innovations had resulted in substantial losses. It had to get back to basics but continue innovating. As a result it developed its Innovation Matrix to help identify, staff and coordinate the different types of innovation needed to develop a new product. It acted as a guide for restructuring the company and clarifying the specific innovation responsibilities of each department. The matrix listed four key areas of the firm: the functional groups (such as sales or manufacturing), the Concept Lab,

Product and Marketing Development (PMD) and Community, Education and Direction (CED). These areas could enjoy eight areas for innovation, split into three groups.

The first group of innovations comprised:

1 Core processes – sales, operations and financial planning, performance management.
2 Enabling processes – forecasting, marketing planning.

These are controlled by the functional groups. They create core and enabling business processes and the degree of innovation from these sources can range widely.

The second group comprised:

3 Messaging – advertising campaigns, websites.
4 Offerings – products and packaging.
5 Platforms – toys' technology elements.

These are controlled by the Concept Lab, which develops fundamentally new products and play experiences, and PMD, which develops the next generation of existing products and innovates on existing play themes such as 'pirates', packaging and marketing campaigns. The degree of innovation from the Concept Lab is likely to be high and that from PMD is likely to be medium to low.

The final group comprised:

6 Customer interaction – communities, customer services, including the Creativity Labs.
7 Sales channels – retailers, direct to customers.
8 Business models – revenue, pricing.

These are controlled by CED which supports customer communities and taps them for product ideas, manages the LEGO retail chain, the online store and educational-market offerings and creates online play experiences. Again, the degree of innovation from this source can range widely

LEGO also introduced a cross-functional Executive Innovation Governance Group to strategically coordinate the process of innovation. It decides on the portfolio of innovation projects LEGO undertakes, delegates authority for each new development across the four, allocates resources and monitors development. LEGO takes a broad view of innovation that includes pricing plans, community building, business processes and distribution channels as well as new products

The story of LEGO MINDSTORMS shows how LEGO's policies to encourage innovation have evolved. Strategic partnerships have played an important part in LEGO innovations over the years but recently the company has also relied on customer involvement to leverage innovation – stage 6 in the innovation matrix – and has turned to policies of open innovation and crowdsourcing. The story of MINDSTORMS starts in 1984, before digital development really took off, when LEGO entered into a partnership with Media Laboratory at Massachusetts Institute of Technology. By blending physical and virtual worlds into an integrated play universe, the company came up with new products. LEGO TECHNIC Computer Control was the first tangible product of the partnership, launched in 1986. These programmable bricks paved the way for the introduction in 1998 of MINDSTORMS, integrating robot technology, electric motors and sensors with LEGO bricks and LEGO TECHNIC pieces such as gears, axles and beams. It enabled children to create and program intelligent LEGO models and rapidly became one of the company's best-selling lines.

The programmable brick at the heart of MINDSTORMS has undergone several updates. MINDSTORM NXT, launched in 2006, includes sensors that detect touch, light, sound and ultrasonic waves. It allows children to build and program their own robot so that it can see, hear, speak, feel and move – in as little as just half an hour. The original brick was programmed using proprietary, copyrighted software that ran only on PCs, but in the early 1990s Chris Rogers, a professor at Tufts University in the USA who was using MINDSTORMS for teaching purposes, adapted it to run on Macs using a program produced by a company called National Instruments, later licensing this development back to LEGO. The complexity of these original programs was a key limitation which, curiously, probably explained why over 70% of users were in fact adults. Simplification was a key objective for NXT. Early in its development, LEGO had decided to use an open innovation approach involving customers. It discovered early in the life of MINDSTORMS that adults like Chris Rogers were illegally hacking into their original software and changing it but, rather than trying to control or restrict this, LEGO decided to facilitate it by making source codes available and allowing hacking as part of the software licence. They realized that it would be impossible to predict how customers might use MINDSTORMS and decided instead to encourage experimentation and innovation. LEGO also facilitated the development of online communities and organized robot competitions. For example, in partnership with a US non-profit organization called FIRST (For Inspiration and Recognition of Science and Technology), LEGO established FIRST LEGO League, a worldwide tournament in which children compete by designing their own robots and participate in a series of scientific and mathematical or technical projects. These vibrant user communities comprised not just customers but also suppliers and partners who earn a living from the product, as well as professors, teachers, consultants and others who used MINDSTORMS as part of their day-to-day job. They acted as promoters and champions of MINDSTORMS. LEGO identified this group as vital to the development of NXT and had a development team member whose sole responsibility was to manage this community and ensure that the company listened and responded to them. But LEGO went further. It identified 'lead customers' and then involved them – without payment – in the development of NXT. Lead customers were among the most advanced users of MINDSTORMS – each inventing new ways to extend the functionality of the original product – and reflected the large customer base of adults. Chris Rogers was designated a lead customer and he reintroduced LEGO to National Instruments, the company that eventually developed the software platform for NXT. Lead customers also helped to develop complementary products like sensors, software, books and educational programs. NXT has become the best ever selling LEGO product. As a result of the success of this open innovation approach, LEGO now has some 40 'LEGO Ambassadors' in over 20 countries representing user communities. They are responsible for transmitting information and are integrated into the design of new products.

Despite the greater involvement of customers, LEGO has also slashed new product development time to an average of 12 months. The first stage in this is the identification of market trends and developments – a continuous process. The second stage is the design of the new product. Since 2008 this has been done using 3D modelling software to generate CAD drawings from initial sketches. Designs are then prototyped and tested with focus groups of parents and children. Virtual models of completed LEGO products are built at the same time as the writing of user instructions. CAD systems are in turn linked to computer-aided manufacturing, helping to reduce overall time and cost in manufacturing.

It is interesting to look at the company's website, LEGO.com. This is more than just a showcase for the company's products; it allows children to play games, enjoy stories and undertake activities, stimulating ideas and creativity. This is important because stories spur children to play games – and the website encourages those games to include LEGO. Over 25% of all toy sales are now related to movies or TV series and, since none to date have featured LEGO parts, it is important for the company to be able to inspire children through its own communication medium. In 2006 the website was one of the top 25 'Lifestyles and children's websites' in the USA, achieving its objective of building a virtual community of LEGO enthusiasts.

☐ Visit the company website on www.lego.com to see some of the features described in this case.

QUESTIONS

1 How does LEGO use customers to develop new products and markets?

2 What role does the company's website play in innovation and stimulating sales?

3 Why has MINDSTORMS been so successful?

4 How important is the collection of new ideas and development of innovation for LEGO? How systematically does it go about it?

CREAX creativity resources and creativity test

To find what must be the world's largest resource of creativity and innovation resources go to www.creax.com/. The website contains hyperlinks to around 1000 other sites around the world. These include: authors, articles, books, basic research, creative environments, creative thinking pioneers, design, e-learning and creativity, education, creativity tools, ideas factory, ideas markets, imagination tools, innovation tools, internet-assisted creativity, mind mapping, online techniques, ideas management, tests and puzzles and many, many more. All the techniques discussed here – and more – are covered in more detail somewhere on this website. There are also tools and resources to help you try them.   →

Find out how creative you are by taking the creativity test on www.creax.com/csa/. It is free and the analysis assesses you on eight dimensions against answers from others with similar backgrounds. The dimensions are:

▷ **Abstraction** – the ability to apply abstract concepts/ideas.
▷ **Connection** – the ability to make connections between things that do not appear to be connected.
▷ **Perspective** – the ability to shift one's perspective on a situation in terms of space, time and other people.
▷ **Curiosity** – the desire to change or improve things that others see as normal.
▷ **Boldness** – the confidence to push boundaries beyond accepted conventions. Also the ability to eliminate the fear of what others might think of you.
▷ **Paradox** – the ability to simultaneously accept and work with statements that are contradictory.
▷ **Complexity** – the ability to carry large quantities of information and be able to manipulate and manage the relationships between such information.
▷ **Persistence** – the ability to force oneself to keep trying to find more and stronger solutions even when good ones have already been generated.

Summary

◁ Creativity, focused on spotting market opportunities and generating innovation, is a key ingredient of entrepreneurial architecture.

◁ Innovative entrepreneurs have five discovery skills: associating, questioning, observing, experimenting and networking. Products like **Swarfega** have emerged out of this process, despite initial setbacks.

◁ Drucker (op. cit.) lists seven sources of opportunity: the unexpected, incongruity, inadequacy of underlying processes, changes in industry or market structure, demographic changes, changes in perceptions, mood and meaning and new knowledge.

◁ Creativity is a right-brain activity that involves lateral as opposed to vertical thinking. It is intuitive, imaginative and rule-breaking. It requires interpersonal and emotional skills and is people-focused. Creative types do exhibit certain common characteristics and there are tests that purport to detect them.

◁ The ability to generate new ideas is influenced by three things: connectivity, training and time. Organizations like **HFL Sport Science** organize to provide staff with all these elements.

◁ Connectivity is a prerequisite to creativity. It involves being open to diverse influences from people and written sources and connecting problems or opportunities from one source to another – the ability to spot relationships and then replicate them in a different context. It showed itself in how ideas from Formula 1 racing were used to speed processes at **Great Ormond Street Hospital**.

◁ Crowdsourcing uses the internet to generate new ideas and address problems, for example at **Starbucks**. Open innovation involves organizing groups to generate new ideas or address problems systematically. The best-known example is the development of open source software (OSS) and the **Linux** operating system. **Lego**® continues to use open innovation very successfully to develop its product range.

▷ Creativity is influenced by its environment. Right-brain activity is stimulated by a 'playful' environment like the one at **Googleplex**. Richard Florida argues that firms increasingly follow talented, creative people and these people are drawn to communities which are open and diverse, where differences are welcome and cultural creativity is easily accessed.

▷ It is important that individual connectivity that generates knowledge and learning is disseminated and retained in the organization. Companies like **LG** and **Hallmark** have processes to ensure this happens.

▷ There are techniques, such as brainstorming, analogy, attribute analysis and gap analysis that can help in the creative process. Appropriate facilities and environments can help with this.

▷ Creativity is encouraged by giving individuals freedom and some slack in the resources they control. They need stimulation and encouragement to 'think outside the box' but this can generate 'creative abrasion' – conflict that will need to be resolved. There will be periods of divergence and convergence as different ideas and approaches are analyzed, adopted and discarded. This whole process needs to be managed carefully so that the team stays together.

▷ As we saw with **Lego**®, creativity and innovation can be used as an impetus to mobilize change in an organization.

Essays and discussion topics

1 Assess your creative potential using the CREAX test. Provide evidence to support (or otherwise) the conclusions. Does this agree with the results from the GET test (Chapter 2)?

2 'Creativity favours the connected mind.' Discuss.

3 What are the advantages and disadvantages of crowdsourcing?

4 What are the advantages and disadvantages of open innovation?

5 What constitutes a creative organizational environment? Why?

6 What constitutes a creative national environment? Why? What lessons are there for an organization?

7 Can you be creative on your own?

8 Compare and contrast creative vs logical thinking.

9 Try using a SLEPT analysis to identify trends where there are new product or service opportunities.

10 Are you a left- or right-brain person? How does this show itself? Are you comfortable being creative?

11 'Creativity is a more difficult skill than entrepreneurship to develop.' Discuss.

12 'Systematic is not a word you associate with creativity and innovation.' Discuss.

13 Do you believe people can be trained to be more creative?

14 Is creativity the same as opportunity perception? What is the link?

15 Looking back to Chapter 4, what might be needed to build a creative team?

16 How might creativity be both discouraged and encouraged?

17 Reflect on the need for freedom and slack to encourage creativity. How does the issue of balance, introduced in Chapter 7, affect this? Is more or less freedom needed to encourage creativity rather than entrepreneurship?

18 Is creativity good in all organizations? Give examples to support your case.

Exercises and assignments

1 Assess your creative potential using an online test. Provide evidence to support (or otherwise) the conclusions. You can find

many tests by undertaking an internet search on 'creativity', for example on:

▷ www.creax.com/csa
▷ www.angelfire.com/wi/2brains

2 List the barriers that you feel inhibit you from being creative at home and at your college or university. How might they be removed or circumvented?

3 List the sources for awareness and new ideas you have at your disposal. What do you need to do to capitalize on them in a systematic way?

4 Try brainstorming in a group to generate new ideas. Try thinking of a new product/service application. Define an area for review, for example by looking at a problem you face in your everyday life and trying to find a solution to it. If you have problems with the technique, go to www.brainstorming.co.uk for further explanation.

5 Trying to use analogy in a group to come up with innovative solutions to problems can be more difficult than brainstorming – even with a group of friends. Start with a problem to be solved and find the way similar problems might be solved in a different context. Alternatively find a natural solution to a problem and consider whether it can be applied to a different circumstance.

6 Try using attribute analysis in a group. Again, this can be difficult. Focus the group on an everyday product or service. Select one feature or aspect and ask 'Why does it have to be that way – what benefit does it bring to the customer?' Try it a few times with different product/service features.

7 Try using gap analysis. Select an everyday product or service. Characterize it in two dimensions and use perceptual mapping to plot where competing products lie on these dimensions. Is there a gap in the market? Repeat the exercise for another product/service.

8 Try applying some of the creativity techniques to generate new ideas. Try thinking of a new product/service application. Define an area for review, for example by looking at a problem you face in your everyday life and trying to find a solution to it.

9 Try using a SLEPT analysis to identify trends where there are new product or service opportunities.

References

Bolton, B. and Thompson, J. (2000) *Entrepreneurs: Talent, Temperament, Technique*, Oxford: Butterworth-Heinemann.

Burt, S.B. (2004) 'Structural Holes and Good Ideas', *American Journal of Sociology*, 110(2), September.

Chesbrough, H. (2003) *Open Innovation: The New Imperative for Creating and Profiting from Technology*, Boston: Harvard Business School Press.

Day, G. and Schoemaker, P. (2006) *Peripheral Vision*, Boston: Harvard Business School Press.

de Bono, E. (1971) *Lateral Thinking for Management*, Harmondsworth: Penguin.

Drucker, P. (1985) *Innovation and Entrepreneurship*, London: Heinemann.

Dyer, J.H., Gregersen, H.D. and Christensen, C.M. (2009) 'The Innovator's DNA', *Harvard Business Review*, December.

Florida, R. (2002) *The Rise of the Creative Classes: And How It's Transforming Work, Leisure, Community and Everyday Life*, New York: Basic Books.

Florida, R. and Tinagli, I. (2004) *Europe in the Creative Age*, Demos.

Gladwell, M. (2000) 'Designs for Working', *The New Yorker*, December 11.

Grant, R.M. (1996) 'Towards a Knowledge-based Theory of the Firm', *Strategic Management Journal*, 17 (Winter Special Issue).

Hischberg, J. (1998) *The Creative Priority*, New York: Harper Books.

Jankowicz, D. (2003) *The Easy Guide to Repertory Grids*, New York: John Wiley & Sons.

Johnson S. (2010) *Where Good Ideas Come From: The Natural History of Innovation*, London: Allen Lane.

Kirby, D. (2003) *Entrepreneurship*, London: McGraw-Hill.

Kirton, M. (1976) 'Adaptors and Innovators: A Description and Measure', *Journal of Applied Psychology*, October.

Klein, A.R. (1990) 'Organizational Barriers to Creativity … and How to Knock them Down', *Journal of Consumer Marketing*, 7(1).

Lakhani, K. (2006) 'Open Space Science: A New Model for Innovation', *Working Knowledge: Harvard Business School Newsletter*, November 20.

Lakhani, K.R. and Panetta, J.A. (2007) 'The Principles of Distributed Innovation', *Innovations*, Summer 2007.

Leonard, D. and Swap, W. (1999) *When Sparks Fly*, Boston: Harvard Business School.

Majaro, S. (1992) 'Managing Ideas for Profit', *Journal of Marketing Management*, 8.

Mintzberg, H. (1976) 'Planning on the Left Side and Managing on the Right', *Harvard Business Review*, 54, July/August.

Page, A.L. (1993) 'Assessing New Product Development Practices and Performance: Establishing Crucial Norms', *Journal of Product Innovation Management*, 10.

Rowley, J. (2000) 'From Learning Organization to Knowledge Entrepreneur', *Journal of Knowledge Management*, 4(1).

Sinetar, M. (1985) 'Entrepreneurs, Chaos and Creativity: Can Creative People Really Survive Large Company Structure?', *Sloan Management Review*, 65(5).

Sloane, P. (2003) *The Leader's Guide to Lateral Thinking Skills: Powerful Problem-Solving Techniques to Ignite Team's Potential*, London: Kogan Page.

Tidd, J. Bessant, J. and Pavitt, K. (2005) *Managing Innovation: Integrating Technological, Market and Organizational Change*, 3rd edn, Chichester: Wiley.

Valery, N. (1999) 'Innovation in Industry', *Economist*, 5(28).

von Oech, R. (1998) *A Whack on the Side of the Head*, New York: Warner Books.

Vyakarnham, S. and Leppard, J. (1999) *A Marketing Action Plan for the Growing Business*, 2nd edn., London: Kogan Page.

Chapter **14**

The architecture of corporate entrepreneurship

▷ **Context**
▷ **Leadership**
▷ **Culture**
▷ **Structure**
▷ **Strategies**
▷ **Environment**
▷ **Corporate Entrepreneurship Audit (CEA)**
▷ **Strategic direction**

Case reviews
▷ 3M, Apple, Dell Corporation, HFL
  Sport Sciences, Google and Virgin

Learning outcomes

By the end of this chapter you should be able to:

▷ Synthesize and therefore better understand the interrelationships in the elements of the organizational architecture of corporate entrepreneurship;

▷ Undertake an audit on the architecture of an organization so as to be able to judge whether it encourages and facilitates entrepreneurship.

Context

So just what does an entrepreneurial organization look like? Whilst there is no one-size-fits-all blueprint, there are some elements that mean you really will know one when you see one. To start with, it will be creative and innovative, priding itself on its ability to thrive in a competitive, changing environment. Indeed it will see itself as helping to shape that environment. And it will be successful. But there will be other internal characteristics reflecting an organizational architecture that encourages entrepreneurial, innovative activity at all levels. Remember, however, that not all parts of a multi-business organization may exhibit these characteristics because of differences in their operational needs (for example, the stage in the life cycle of products) and/or their contextual situations (for example, they do not operate in an entrepreneurial environment). We have characterized the entrepreneurial environment as one of rapid change and uncertainty where speed of response and innovation are vital and knowledge and learning are of paramount importance. Where a multi-business has different organizational needs in its various operating divisions or subsidiaries, what is important for it to be entrepreneurial is that the overarching structure linking the operating divisions or subsidiaries has an entrepreneurial architecture.

Leadership

We know that effective leadership depends upon a range of contextual factors including group, task and situation. Whilst there is therefore no blueprint for successful leadership, we have characterized good leadership in an entrepreneurial environment as visionary, transformational but distributed (team-based). The high-level leadership team ideally comprises just half a dozen executives who trust each other, share information and cover for each other. That model is replicated across the entire organization. To be effective, leaders need to have good emotional intelligence – self and social awareness and social skills. The ten characteristics of a good leader in an entrepreneurial organization are set out below:

1   **Visionary**   The leader of this organization should be driven by a strong vision, underpinned by equally strong values. However, this vision should be grounded in sufficient reality to make the vision appear achievable, albeit causing some tension.

2   **Good communicator/motivator**   The leader should be able to communicate this vision effectively, through many mechanisms, but particularly informal influence. They should lead by example – 'walking the talk'. They should, somehow, embody the vision and values that they have for the organization. Staff motivation should be underpinned by loyalty to both the leader and the organization.

3 **Strategic thinker and learner** The leader should be a strategic thinker, able to rise above day-to-day crises and see the bigger picture, perpetually scanning the environment both for opportunities and risks. They should be a strategic learner, trying to find patterns in the environment over time and looking for complex interactions so as to understand the underlying causes that give clues about the opportunities and risks. They should be continually strategizing and developing strategic options for the organization.

4 **Emotionally intelligent with strong interpersonal skills** The leader should be able to listen, to influence others rather than to direct, and therefore be able to manage 'with a light touch'. They should be adept at reconciling conflict and dealing with ambiguity and uncertainty. To be emotionally intelligent they should be self-aware and reflective. They also need to exercise a degree of self-management. And again, they should 'walk the talk', modelling the behaviour they expect from others.

5 **Relationship builder** Using their emotional intelligence and interpersonal skills, the leader should be good at building strong personal relationships with all the stakeholders in the organization. This will have been built up by acting consistently over time based upon a dominant set of values so as to generate trust. The leader should be firm but fair with staff and care and respect them.

6 **Team player** The leader should value team-working and be a team player, willing to share information and delegate to the team. They should have built a cohesive, open and trusting top management team although that might comprise just three or four individuals who share knowledge and, although having specialized roles, are able to cover for one another. This team structure should be replicated throughout the organization

7 **Builder of confidence** The leader should be able to encourage organizational self-confidence and self-efficacy in the face of uncertainty and risk-taking. They should be able to inspire others to share their visions and dreams through their emotional intelligence and ability to build relationships.

8 **Builder of an open organization that shares information** The leader should encourage the sharing of knowledge, information and ideas. They should encourage staff to develop the discovery skills of associating, questioning, observing, experimenting and networking. Staff will require a degree of space or slack to be able to do this. The leader should encourage staff to question their own mental models through continual learning and also the dominant logic of the organization. Staff should be involved in networks both inside and outside the organization and there should be organizational initiatives that bring outsiders with different ideas and perspectives into

the organization. Experimentation should be encouraged and failure learned from rather than penalized.

9 **Clarifier of ambiguity and uncertainty** The leader should be able to give a clear focus on the key issues and concerns facing the organization in the face of rapid change. This comes from their ability to be a strategic thinker and an effective communicator.

10 **Builder of empowering opportunities** Finally, the leader should be able to make staff want to do 'the right thing' for the organization without necessarily being asked. Staff should feel empowered to do this, having the knowledge, skills, and motivation, without fearing that they will be countermanded or penalized for using their initiative or making an unintended mistake.

Culture

Establishing an appropriate corporate culture is vital if you want to develop an entrepreneurial organization. Based on values, norms and beliefs, it influences individual and social behavioural norms. The culture should see change as the norm, certainly not something to be feared. Above all it should value strong relationships, creativity and innovation, empowerment, measured risk-taking through experimentation and continual learning. It should value relationships sufficiently to generate a strong sense of group identity. It should have confidence in its future. It should be egalitarian but slightly anti-authoritarian – always daring to be different. It will tolerate mistakes, but should encourage learning from them. Individuals should feel empowered and motivated to make decisions for the good of the organization. Indeed decision-making will be delegated down as far as possible, and information will be shared rather than hoarded. There will be a 'can-do' attitude around that values achievement.

A strong organizational culture is particularly needed because of the informal organization structure and loose management control. The culture needs to build a strong identity (Hofstede's 'in-group'). This can be built around the vision for the organization as well as its recognizable values, norms and beliefs. It needs to be consistent with the leadership style within the organization.

In Hofstede's dimensions the organizational culture should exhibit:

▷ Balance between individualism and collectivism, implying that, whilst individual initiative is valued, so too are cooperative relationships and networks with a strong sense of 'in-group', and a clear identity and a feeling of competition against 'out-groups';

▷ Low power distance, implying an egalitarian organization with flat structures and open and informal relationships and open, unrestricted information flows;

F 14.1 An entrepreneurial cultural web

▷ Low uncertainty avoidance, implying a tolerance of risk and ambiguity, a preference for flexibility and an empowered culture that rewards personal and team initiative;

▷ Balance between masculine and feminine dimensions, implying encouragement to build a culture of achievement against 'out-groups' through cooperation, networks and relationships within the 'in-group'.

A cultural web of recognizable values, norms, beliefs and behaviours of the entrepreneurial organization is shown in Figure 14.1.

Structure

Structures create order in an organization but there is no single 'best' solution. The most appropriate structure depends on the nature of the organization, the strategies it employs, the tasks it undertakes, the culture it wishes to encourage, the environment it operates in and its size. Entrepreneurial organizations typically face a high degree of environmental turbulence. If the tasks they need to undertake are complex, they are best served by an organic organizational structure that may well change and evolve in different situations.

An organic structure is like a spider's web made up of smaller spider's webs – teams working with other teams – with membership based upon expertise, not role, and each with considerable autonomy. Such organizations have limited hierarchy and are highly flexible, decentralized with a minimum of levels within the structures. They are flexible and respond to different situations. Spans of control are likely to be broad and controls should be loose, with an emphasis on getting things done. Authority for decision-making should be delegated so that individuals are empowered to make decisions. Accountability should therefore be tight. Structures, behaviours, even controls are likely to be more informal than formal, based on strong relationships. It certainly will not be bureaucratic in any way. There should be an emphasis on flexible team-working and open communication, with team-based, project-based and process-based structures.

Organic structures are not appropriate for all organizations and it is probable that a multi-business will need to have different operating divisions or subsidiaries with more traditional structures, reflecting their different capabilities. What will emerge is a hybrid-organic structure. Operating divisions or subsidiaries will be relatively autonomous but linked to head office through an organic structure with entrepreneurial architecture. Control should be loose, or at least balanced, but there needs to be tight accountability. The idea is to give people autonomy but hold them accountable for the outcomes of their actions.

In response to an increasingly competitive environment all large organizations are likely to:

▷ Downsize and deconstruct, outsourcing non-core activities and downscoping;
▷ Delayer and flatten organizational structures and invest in information technology so as to improve communications.

Entrepreneurial organizations are likely to exhibit a number of organizational characteristics and/or forms:

▷ Structures to encourage and facilitate intrapreneurship, including project and new venture teams;
▷ Facilities that can be used to encourage creative thinking;
▷ Structures to encourage and facilitate internal and external corporate venturing;
▷ Participation in numerous formal and informal, real and virtual networks, including crowdsourcing and open innovation;
▷ Strategic alliances/partnerships and joint ventures with other organizations, including licensing of technologies and so on;
▷ Spin-offs.

Strategies

The strategies that an organization pursues are particular to its situation and difficult to generalize. However, an entrepreneurial organization faces a complex and inherently unpredictable environment and is likely to develop strategy in a certain way and to pursue a number of typical strategies. These are the common themes:

1 Strategy development might be either emergent or deliberate, but characterized by continuous strategizing at all levels in the organization, underpinned by a strong vision and sense of direction. This vision should be ambitious but rooted in reality, creating a tension sufficient to motivate the organization to change. The organization will be good at scanning the environment for opportunities and threats. Strategic options will be available and there may be a strong strategic intent if the vision is particularly challenging. Strategy will come from both the top and the bottom of the organization with a strong involvement of all levels of management.

2 Decision-making will tend to be decentralized, incremental and adaptive, so as to maintain maximum flexibility, but underpinned by the strong vision and an understanding of the strategies being adopted to achieve the vision. There may be some simple rules that provide guidance, but staff will know enough about the organization and be motivated to do the best they can. Mistakes will be tolerated and learned from. In this way the organization will be able to respond speedily to opportunities or threats.

3 The organization will understand its strengths and its core competences at both corporate and business levels. At the corporate level a major strategic imperative will be the continuing development of its entrepreneurial architecture and all that entails. If it is pursuing a policy of acquisition this should be part of a coherent strategy (for example, as part of buying into new markets, product developments or developing industries). If it is a multi-business, it will create value by operating effectively across all the operating units – unifying diverse management and sharing resources and capabilities more effectively than might otherwise be the case.

4 At the business level this will display itself as an inherent understanding of the basis of its competitive advantage and an understanding of how customer value can be enhanced. There will be an understanding of marketing issues such as differentiation, branding, pricing, customer focus and product life cycles. Customer needs and competitors will be monitored continuously. If there is a portfolio of products/services, these will be managed strategically as a portfolio.

5 The organization should have strategies to encourage internal growth through innovation, new products or services developments and entry into new markets. These developments should be continuous and incremental with some discontinuous or radical innovations. Both types of innovation are required, often simultaneously. This requires facilitating structures. There should also be an emphasis on continual

improvement. The organization should be willing to experiment and take measured risks, but should identify and monitor them, learning from any mistakes. Revenue and profit growth is likely to come mainly from these internal developments and then used for the more radical innovations.

6 There should be a strategy to encourage creativity with a commercial focus. Strategies to encourage creativity are likely to encourage development of the discovery skills of associating, questioning, observing, experimenting and networking, in particular bringing diverse outside influences into the organization. They should encourage the questioning of existing marketing paradigms, questioning sectoral, performance and customer conventions.

7 There should be a strategy to encourage innovation. Strategies to encourage innovation are likely to include internal and external corporate venturing, networking, strategic alliances/partnerships and joint ventures. There should be a strategy for mitigating the risks associated with innovation, particularly disruptive innovation, such as experimentation, limited launches, joint ventures and compartmentalization. The organization should take a portfolio approach to its innovative activities.

It is one thing to describe this 'mythical beast', but quite another to create one. And the most difficult task of all is to turn around an existing organization so as to become one – a really challenging exercise in change management. This sort of turnaround is often only possible when the organization itself faces an imminent crisis, such as one of survival. If entrepreneurs are the super-heroes of the business world, what does that make those who practise corporate entrepreneurship?

Environment

The exact form of an effective entrepreneurial architecture depends on the environment. It can be sectorally and geographically dependent. It can vary with the nature of the entrepreneurial intensity. The point is that there can be no prescriptive blueprint. This means structuring the organization so that each operating unit can be organized in such a way as to best deal with the environment it faces, possibly with structures within structures, sub-cultures within cultures and different approaches to leadership within an overall approach.

Entrepreneurial firms thrive in environments of change, chaos, complexity, competition, uncertainty and even contradiction. The interconnections in these markets tend to amplify the effect of small initial changes. This rapid, continuous interconnected change makes for instability and unpredictability and it means that traditional forms of strategic planning no longer work. These sorts of environments are likely to be characterized by rapid technological change in markets where this is important and valued by customers – for example because of their need for knowledge and information. Such markets offer considerable 'first-mover advantage' and reinforce the importance of a rapid response to developments. Markets might be highly price-sensitive, with low barriers to entry and high economies of scale. New competitors might be emerging all the time and these new competitors might be very price-competitive and/or good at innovating. New markets could be emerging and the whole structure of the market might be changing, with many mergers or take-overs. In these circumstances customers might be seen as promiscuous as their 'needs' change rapidly and, as a result, the industry spends increasing amounts on advertising in order to get their attention. As product life cycles shorten, all this can lead to an unbalanced product/service portfolio. Adding to all these problems might be rapid economic and social change, pressures for greater corporate social responsibility and problems in attracting suitable staff. This is the sort of environment that an entrepreneurial architecture is designed to deal with.

Corporate Entrepreneurship Audit (CEA)

The Corporate Entrepreneurship Audit (CEA) offers a structured approach to assessing the entrepreneurial orientation of organizational architecture. An interactive version of this diagnostic tool is available on the website accompanying this book: www.palgrave.com/business/burns. It allows an organization's architecture to be measured against 'best practice' in the industry (if available) as well as the appropriateness of the organization's footprint, measured in terms of the environment. Part 1 catalogues the observed characteristics of an entrepreneurial organization in the four dimensions of architecture – leadership, culture, structure and strategies. Table 14.1 on pp. 478–9 shows 100 questions about the organization that are contained in the diagnostic tool. Respondents are asked simply to score each statement on a scale from 0 (= not true at all) to 6 (= very true). Part 2 lists 25 questions concerning the environment the organization faces. These are shown in Table 14.2 on p. 480. They assess whether the organization operates within an environment that requires an entrepreneurial response – one best suited to an organization with an entrepreneurial architecture. Again, respondents are asked simply to score each statement on the above scale.

The interactive tool is easy to use. It automatically maps the results for the organization onto a CEA grid, measured as percentages (100% being highly entrepreneurial) and compares this to the environment within which it operates (100% requiring an entrepreneurial response, best achieved with an entrepreneurial architecture). An example of this is shown in Figure 14.2. The higher the percentage architecture scores, the more entrepreneurial the organizational profile. Ideally the profile should be balanced. The example in Figure 14.2 shows an organization with a high entrepreneurial

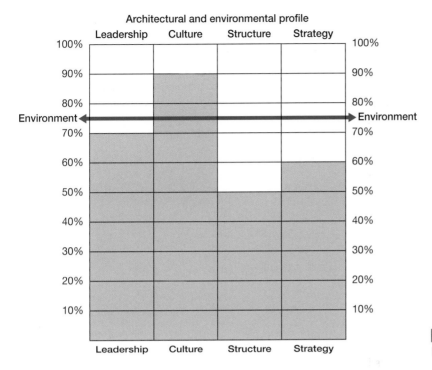

Architectural and environmental profile

F 14.2 An example of a CEA profile

profile of: Leadership 70%, Culture 90%, Structure 50% and Strategy 60%. By going back over the questions for structure, the reasons for the lower score should become clear.

The example shows an environmental score of 75% – an environment that does require an entrepreneurial response. The organizational profile can be compared to the environmental assessment and differences investigated. A low environmental score indicates that the organization operates in an environment in which an entrepreneurial architecture may be inappropriate.

This simple diagnostic tool can be applied to any level of organization – the organization overall, division, department and so on. It provides a means of analyzing potential areas for improvement based upon issues flagged in this book, rather than a crude pass/fail test. This involves making informed judgments about certain criteria and, as such, is subjective rather than objective. It does not answer the question as to why things are the way they are. Where benchmark comparisons are required, they should be made against competitor organizations. However, there is no such thing as an absolute score. The audit should really be used as a basis for a more detailed discussion about the architecture of the organization – understanding what are those underlying causes that are so important and why. In looking at this detail, never forget to also look at the results generated by the organization – whether or not it is performing well in its industry. But that, in many ways, just brings out another set of issues about how success is measured.

T 14.1 Leadership, culture, structure and strategy questions in the CEA

Leadership	Culture	Structure	Strategy
1 There is a clear vision for the organization	1 The organization encourages entrepreneurial risk-taking	1 The senior management team is organized organically	1 There is a clear vision for the organization that is realistic and achievable but stretching
2 Senior managers model the vision and values of the organization – they 'walk the talk'	2 The organization is an empowering one	2 The organization is broken down into small sub-structures	2 There are clear values underpinning everything the organization does
3 The vision for the organization is clearly communicated	3 The organization sees change as normal	3 The organization is not hierarchical	3 There is a clear strategy for achieving the vision
4 There are clear values underpinning everything the organization does	4 The organization encourages staff to build relationships at all levels	4 The organization is not bureaucratic	4 There is continuous innovation to improve the product/service offering and/or reduce costs
5 There is a clear strategy for achieving the vision	5 The organization encourages creativity and innovation	5 The organization structure is flexible	5 There are clear strategic objectives
6 The vision is realistic and achievable but stretching	6 The organization encourages continuous innovation	6 Spans of control are broad	6 Staff are encouraged to strategize
7 There is an understanding of the opportunities and threats that the organization faces	7 The organization is egalitarian	7 There is loose organizational control but tight accountability	7 Staff are encourage to spot commercial opportunities for the organization
8 The organization has strategic options for the future	8 The organization is tolerant of mistakes	8 Team-working is encouraged and facilitated	8 Strategy development is both top-down and bottom up, involving everyone
9 Senior managers work as a team	9 The organization encourages and facilitates delegated decision-making	9 The organization participates in strategic alliances/partnerships or joint ventures	9 There is an understanding of the opportunities and threats that the organization faces
10 Senior managers are accessible and approachable	10 The organization encourages team-working	10 The organization has developed and participates in a number of professional networks	10 There are strategic options for the future
11 Senior managers listen	11 The organization encourages internal information- and knowledge-sharing	11 There is a new venture division/department	11 Decision-making is decentralized, incremental and adaptive
12 Senior managers influence rather than direct; they manage with a 'light touch'	12 The organization encourages building networks of relationships with external people and organizations	12 Intrapreneurs and/or new cross-functional venture teams are used to take new business ideas forward	12 There is an understanding of the organization's core competences

13 Senior managers are good at reconciling conflict	13 The organization encourages continual learning from both inside and outside	13 Structures encourage and facilitate intrapreneurship	13 Encouraging entrepreneurship is central to the organization's strategy
14 Senior managers are good at clarifying uncertainties going forward, focusing effort on important things	14 The organization encourages experimentation	14 Structures encourage delegated decision-making	14 There is an understanding of the basis for competitive advantage in the organization's different markets
15 Senior managers are reflective and self-aware	15 The organization celebrates success	15 Operating divisions or subsidiaries are relatively autonomous	15 There are strategies to encourage and facilitate innovation
16 Senior managers have good relationships with staff	16 The organization is informal	16 There are facilities and resources that encourage creative thinking	16 There are strategies to encourage and facilitate commercially-orientated creativity
17 Senior managers show care and respect for staff	17 The organization is achievement-orientated	17 There are facilities that encourage and facilitate internal and external corporate venturing	17 There are strategies and structures to get customer feedback
18 Senior managers are trustworthy	18 There is time for learning and innovation	18 Crowdsourcing and open innovation are encouraged and facilitated	18 Strategies are aimed at achieving year-on-year growth
19 Senior managers are consistent in their behaviour with staff	19 The organization encourages strategizing	19 There have been spin-offs from new venture activities	19 Resources and capabilities are shared across the organization
20 Senior managers think and act strategically	20 People are valued in the organization	20 There are structures to provide resources for new venture activities	20 Benchmarking against competitors is regular and continuous
21 Team-working is encouraged in the organization	21 Staff feel responsible for the future of the organization	21 There are structures to facilitate continuous innovation	21 The risks associated with strategic options are identified
22 Cross-functional team-working is commonplace in the organization	22 Staff feel they 'belong' to the organization	22 There are structures to encourage and facilitate training and development	22 The organization identifies and implements risk-mitigation strategies
23 Information and knowledge is shared in the organization	23 The voice of the customer is important	23 There is an R&D department and/or budget	23 The product/market portfolio is managed strategically
24 Senior managers empower people to deal with problems and opportunities	24 The voice of the supplier is important	24 Entrepreneurship and innovation are recognized and rewarded	24 Environmental developments in the future are reviewed regularly
25 Decision-making is delegated	25 The organization encourages open communication, top-down, bottom-up and across the organization	25 There are structures to monitor and manage risk	25 Strategy can be implemented quickly

T 14.2 Environmental questions in the CEA

1   The commercial environment is highly competitive

2   The commercial environment is unstable and unpredictable

3   The commercial environment changes rapidly and continuously

4   Technological change is rapid and strongly influences the market

5   The structure of the market is changing

6   There are no barriers to entry in the market

7   New competitors are emerging all the time

8   The future is highly uncertain

9   Predicted economic and societal changes will greatly impact the industry

10   There are continual innovations in the industry

11   Innovation is valued by customers

12   There is considerable 'first-mover advantage' with innovation

13   The market is highly price-sensitive

14   There are large, achievable economies of scale

15   Customers are not loyal

16   Customer needs are changing all the time

17   Competitors innovate continuously

18   Competitors are very price-competitive

19   There is heavy expenditure on marketing within the industry

20   There are many mergers and take-overs in the industry

21   New markets are continually emerging

22   The product/service portfolio is unbalanced

23   Suppliers exert a great deal of power

24   Good managers and staff are difficult to attract

25   Developments in the industry depend very much on knowledge and information

Strategic direction

Just because an organization has an appropriate entrepreneurial architecture does not guarantee that it will be successful. Survival might be a badge of success in some circumstances. And bad luck, in particular completely unpredictable events, always plays a part. There is no certainty in life, no matter how thorough an organization might be in trying to predict and prepare for the future. All we can ever do in business is play the odds. In order to better understand the architecture it is quite probable that we will need to delve deeper into the organization.

A good starting point is always to better understand the degree of innovative intensity within the organization, measured in terms of scale

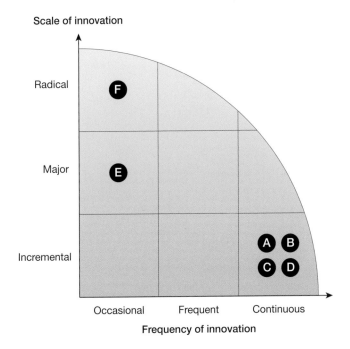

Scale of innovation

F 14.3 A specimen innovation portfolio

and frequency of innovation (Figure 12.1). Figure 14.3 shows a map of all the incidents of innovation over the last year for a hypothetical company. This tells you about the nature and extent of innovative activity taking place in the organization. Figure 14.3 shows that our hypothetical company had four small-scale innovations in addition to one major and one radical innovation. You can then investigate these innovations in further detail and arrive at an assessment. For example, numerous incremental innovations may not have been a sufficient response in an industry facing disruptive innovation. However, if they relate to products at the end of their life cycle it may be the appropriate product strategy. The innovation strategy needs to be placed in the context of the company's product portfolio and the market challenges it faces.

The next step is to better understand the organization's growth strategy and in particular the nature of its shifts in developing new products and new markets (Figure 12.7, reproduced as 14.4) and the strategies it has pursued to develop these (Figure 12.9, reproduced as 14.5). As well as looking at the past (the last year) we need to look to the future and the planned outcomes of the existing strategies represented in Figure 14.4. This should be built upon an understanding of the organization's existing product/service portfolio and how it might be developed. You can then critically evaluate these strategies, the risks associated with them and the safeguards to provide early warning signs and deal with them. Are the strategies coherent and consistent with the firm's vision/mission and its core strengths or competences? Is there a coherent strategic rationale for any acquisitions? Does the organization have the resources to undertake these strategies?

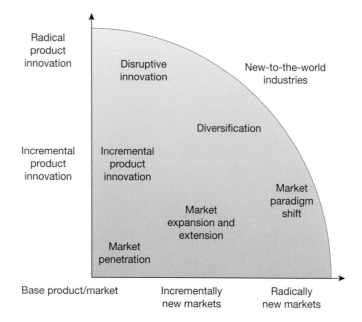

A typography for developing new products and new markets

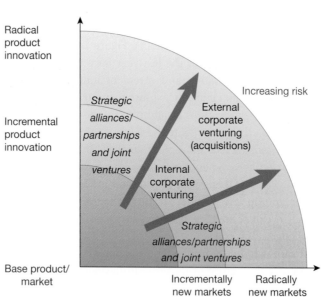

Corporate venturing and other forms of corporate renewal and risk

The CEA is a snapshot at a point of time based upon your judgements, and possibly those of others within the organization. Combining it with an understanding of the strategic direction the organization is taking and the context of its portfolio of operations, gives you the opportunity to really understand, not only the entrepreneurial orientation of the organization, but also how this might be improved. Organizations need to be more entrepreneurial. This framework and the CEA give you a roadmap as to how this can be achieved.

🗂 Case reviews

This book has reviewed the activities of a number of entrepreneurial firms, albeit not always in terms of their complete architecture. Apply the CEA to assess the architecture of the organizations listed below. Where there is insufficient information to evaluate any statement, score zero, noting the question you are unable to answer. Identify the heading(s) under which these questions fall from Table 14.1 and adjust the score(s) for the heading(s) accordingly. You will then need to adjust the percentage score for each element of architecture to reflect the fact that you have responses to fewer than 25 statements. For example, if 20 out of 25 statements were scored, multiply by 1.25 (25 ÷ 20). Compare your conclusions here to your original analysis. What have you learnt?

Organizations to review

3M (Chapter 3), Apple (Chapter 4), Dell Corporation (Chapter 5), HFL Sport Science (Chapter 4), Google (Chapter 12), Virgin (Chapter 6)

Assignment

Select a company and, using the CEA, undertake an audit of its architecture and the environment in which it operates. Assess its strategic direction in more detail using the framework outlined in this chapter. Write a report on your findings.

Further reading and journals

Selected further reading

Corporate entrepreneurship

DeSouza, K.C. (2011) *Intrapreneurship*, Toronto: University of Toronto Press.

Hirsh, R. and Kearney, C. (2011) *Corporate Entrepreneurship: How to Create a Thriving Entrepreneurial Spirit Throughout Your Company*, Maidenhead: McGraw-Hill.

Morris, M.H., Kuratko, D.F. and Covin J.G. (2010) *Corporate Entrepreneurship and Innovation*, Fort Worth: Harcourt College Publishers.

Sathe, V. (2003) *Corporate Entrepreneurship: Top Managers and New Business Creation*, Cambridge: Cambridge University Press.

Selected topics in alphabetic order

Entrepreneurship

Blundel, R. and Lockett, N. (2010) *Exploring Entrepreneurship: Practice and Perspectives*, Oxford: Oxford University Press.

Burns, P. (2011) *Entrepreneurship and Small Business: Start-up, Growth and Maturity*, 3rd edn, Basingstoke: Palgrave.

Hisrich, R.D., Peters, M.P. and Shepherd, D.A. (2012) *Entrepreneurship*, 9th edn, Maidenhead: McGraw Hill.

Stokes, D. Wilson, N. and Mador, M. (2010) *Entrepreneurship*, Mason: South Western Cengage Learning.

Westhead, P. Wright, M. and McElwee, G. (2011) *Entrepreneurship: Perspectives and Case*, Harlow: FT Prentice Hall.

Innovation

Drucker, P.F. (1985) *Innovation and Entrepreneurship: Practice and Principles*, London: Heinemann.

Tidd, J., Bessant, J. and Pavitt, K. (2009) *Managing Innovation: Integrating Technological,Market and Organizational Change*, 4th edn, New York: Wiley.

Leadership and culture

Guirdham, M. (2011) *Communicating across Cultures at Work*, 2nd edn, Basingstoke: Palgrave Macmillan.

Hofstede, G., Hofstede, G. J. and Minkov, M. (2010) *Culture and Organizations: Software of the Mind*, 3rd edn., Maidenhead: McGraw Hill.

Northouse, P.G. (2010) *Leadership: Theory and Practice*, 5th edn, London: Sage.

Samovar, L. A., Porter, R. E. and McDaniel, E. R. (2009) *Communicating between Cultures*, Boston: Wadsworth Cengage Learning.

Strategy

Grant, R.M. (2010) *Contemporary Strategy Analysis*, 7th edn, Chichester: John Wiley

Grant, R.M. and Jordan, J. (2012) *Foundations of Strategy*, Chichester: John Wiley.

Johnson, G., Whittington, R. and Scholes, K. (2011) *Exploring Strategy: Text and Cases*, 9th edn, Harlow: FT Prentice Hall.

Kay, J. (1998) *Foundations of Corporate Success*, Oxford: Oxford University Press.

Mintzberg, H., Ahlstrand, B. and Lampel, J. (2008) *Strategy Safari: The Complete Guide Through the Wilds of Management*, 2nd edn, Harlow: FT Prentice Hall.

Selected journals

There is no one journal dedicated to corporate entrepreneurship. Articles on the topic can appear in journals in the areas of entrepreneurship, general management, organization studies and strategic management as well as innovation. The UK Association of Business Schools produces a grading of journal quality (4 = high to 1 = low). The list below shows the leading journals (graded 4, 3 and 2) in these fields:

Entrepreneurship

4   *Entrepreneurship, Theory and Practice*
    Journal of Business Venturing
3   *Entrepreneurship and Regional Development*
    International Small Business Journal
    Journal of Small Business Management
    Small Business Economics
    Strategic Entrepreneurship Journal
2   *Family Business Review*
    International Journal of Entrepreneurial Behaviour and Research
    International Journal of Entrepreneurship and Innovation
    Journal of Small Business and Enterprise Development
    Venture Capital: An International Journal of Entrepreneurial Finance

General management

4 *Academy of Management Review*
Academy of Management Journal
Administrative Science Quarterly
Journal of Management
Journal of Management Studies
Harvard Business Review
British Journal of Management
3 *California Management Review*
MIT Sloan Management Review
International Journal of Management Reviews
Academy of Management Perspectives
Journal of Management Inquiry
2 *International Review of Administrative Sciences*
Canadian Journal of Administrative Sciences
European Management Journal
European Business Review
International Studies of Management and Organization
Competition and Change
Journal of General Management
Scandinavian Journal of Management
Asia Pacific Journal of Management

Organization studies

4 *Organization Science*
Organization Studies
Leadership Quarterly
Human Relations
3 *Research in Organizational Behavior*
Organizational Research Methods
Group and Organization Management
Organization
Organizational Dynamics
2 *Journal of Organizational Behaviour Management*
Group Processes and Intergroup Relations
Organization and Environment
Group Dynamics: Theory, Research and Practice
Journal of Organizational Change Management
Systemic Practice and Action Research
Negotiation Journal
Culture and Organization
Journal of Knowledge Management
Management Communication Quarterly

Strategic management

4   *Strategic Management Journal*
3   *Journal of Economics and Management Strategy*
     Advances in Strategic Management
     Long Range Planning
2   *Technology Analysis and Strategic Management*
     Strategic Change
     Business Strategy and the Environment
     Strategic Organization

Innovation

4   *Journal of Product Innovation Management*
3   *R&D Management*
     Technovation
2   *International Journal of Innovation Management*
     Industry and Innovation

Subject index

Author index

Quotes index